The Power of Words

 ————————————

Documents in American History

VOLUME II: FROM 1865

T. H. Breen, Editor

 HarperCollinsCollegePublishers

Executive Editor: Bruce D. Borland
Developmental Editor: Jeffrey W. Brown
Project Coordination and Text Design: Ruttle, Shaw & Wetherill, Inc.
Cover Designer: Paul Lacy
Cover Photograph: The Bettmann Archive
Photo Researcher: Leslie Coopersmith
Electronic Production Manager: Angel Gonzalez, Jr.
Manufacturing Manager: Willie Lane
Electronic Page Makeup: Ruttle, Shaw & Wetherill, Inc.
Printer and Binder: R.R. Donnelley & Sons Company
Cover Printer: The Lehigh Press, Inc.

For permission to use copyrighted material, grateful acknowledgment is made to the copyright holders on pp. 348–350, which are hereby made part of this copyright page.

The Power of Words: Documents in American History, **Volume II: From 1865**

Copyright © 1996 by HarperCollins College Publishers

HarperCollins® and 🏛® are registered trademarks of HarperCollins Publishers Inc.

All rights reserved. Printed in the United States of America. No part of this book may be used or reproduced in any manner whatsoever without written permission, except in the case of brief quotations embodied in critical articles and reviews. For information address HarperCollins College Publishers, 10 East 53rd Street, New York, NY 10022. *For information about any HarperCollins title, product, or resource, please visit our World Wide Web site at* **http://www.harpercollins.com/college**.

Library of Congress Cataloging-in-Publication Data

The power of words: documents in American history / T. H. Breen, editor.
    p.   cm.
    ISBN 0-06-501112-0 (v. 1). — ISBN 0-06-501113-9 (v. 2)
    1. United States—History—Sources. I. Breen, T. H.
E173.P83   1996   95-18487
973—dc20   CIP

95 96 97 98 9 8 7 6 5 4 3 2 1

Contents

Preface   x

General Introduction: Interrogating the Past   xii

CHAPTER 1
Reconstruction   1

DOCUMENT 1 • Carl Schurz, Report on the Condition of the South (1865)   2

DOCUMENT 2 • Clinton B. Fisk, *Plain Counsels for Freedmen* (1865)   6

DOCUMENT 3 • James C. Beecher, Report on Land Reform in the South Carolina Islands (1865, 1866)   7

DOCUMENT 4 • "Address from the Colored Citizens of Norfolk, Virginia, to the People of the United States" (1865)   9

DOCUMENT 5 • The Fourteenth Amendment to the United States Constitution (1868)   12

DOCUMENT 6 • *The Nation*, "The State of the South" (1872)   13

DOCUMENT 7 • Albion W. Tourgee, Letter on Ku Klux Klan Activities (1870)   16

DOCUMENT 8 • James T. Rapier, Testimony Before U.S. Senate Regarding the Agricultural Labor Force in the South (1880)   20

Study Questions   23

CHAPTER 2
The West   24

DOCUMENT 1 • Horace Greeley, *An Overland Journey* (1860)   25

DOCUMENT 2 • Lydia Allen Rudd, Diary of Westward Travel (1852)   28

DOCUMENT 3 • Edward Gould Buffum, *Six Months in the Gold Mines* (1850)   31

DOCUMENT 4 • Joseph G. McCoy, *Historic Sketches of the Cattle Trade of the West and Southwest* (1874)   33

DOCUMENT 5 • Memorial of the Chinese Six Companies to U.S. Grant, President of the United States (1876)   35

DOCUMENT 6 • Congressional Report on Indian Affairs (1887)   37

DOCUMENT 7 • Tragedy at Wounded Knee (1890)   39

DOCUMENT 8 • Frederick Jackson Turner, "The Significance of the Frontier in American History" (1893)   41

Study Questions   43

CHAPTER 3
Labor and Capital   44

DOCUMENT 1 • Andrew Carnegie, "Wealth" (1889)   45

DOCUMENT 2 • Proceedings of the Thirteenth Session of the National Grange of the Patrons of Husbandry (1879)   48

DOCUMENT 3 • Interstate Commerce Act (1887)   50

DOCUMENT 4 • Suit by the United States Against the Workingmen's Amalgamated Council of New Orleans (1893)   52

DOCUMENT 5 • Frederick Winslow Taylor, "A Piece-Rate System" (1896)   54

DOCUMENT 6 • Address by George Engel, Condemned Haymarket Anarchist (1886)   56

DOCUMENT 7 • Edward Bellamy, *Looking Backward* (1888)   60

Study Questions   62

CHAPTER 4
Urban Society   63

DOCUMENT 1 • Adna Weber, *The Growth of Cities in the Nineteenth Century* (1899)   64

DOCUMENT 2 • Upton Sinclair, *The Jungle* (1905)   67

DOCUMENT 3 • Caroline Manning, *The Immigrant Woman and Her Job* (1930)   69

DOCUMENT 4 • Mary Antin, *The Promised Land* (1912)   72

DOCUMENT 5 • William Riordan, *Plunkitt of Tammany Hall* (1905)   74

DOCUMENT 6 • Charlotte Perkins Gilman, "If I Were a Man" (1914)   77

DOCUMENT 7 • Proposal to Buffalo, New York, Park Commission (1888)   80

DOCUMENT 8 • The *New York Times*, Review of Opening Night at Coney Island (1904)   82

Study Questions   84

CHAPTER 5
Imperial Power and Domestic Unrest   85

DOCUMENT 1 • Josiah Strong, *Our Country* (1885)   87

DOCUMENT 2 • Eugene V. Debs, "The Outlook for Socialism in the United States" (1900)   89

DOCUMENT 3 • Ida B. Wells, "Lynch Law in America" (1900)   91

DOCUMENT 4 • Henry Cabot Lodge, "The Business World vs. the Politicians" (1895)   93

DOCUMENT 5 • Theodore Roosevelt, Third Annual Message to Congress (1903)   95

DOCUMENT 6 • William Graham Sumner, *What the Social Classes Owe to Each Other* (1883)   98

DOCUMENT 7 • The People's Party Platform (1892)   100

DOCUMENT 8 • William Jennings Bryan, Cross of Gold Speech (1896)   102

Study Questions   104

CHAPTER 6
Progressivism   105

DOCUMENT 1 • Herbert Croly, *Progressive Democracy* (1914)   107

DOCUMENT 2 • Louis Brandeis, *Other People's Money and How the Bankers Use It* (1913)   109

DOCUMENT 3 • Walker Percy, "Birmingham under the Commission Plan" (1911)   111

DOCUMENT 4 • Report of the Vice Commission, Louisville, Kentucky (1915)   114

DOCUMENT 5 • Jane Addams, *Twenty Years at Hull House* (1910)   116

DOCUMENT 6 • James H. Patten, Chairman of the National Legislative Committee of the American Purity Federation, Testimony Before Congress (1910)   118

DOCUMENT 7 • Platform Adopted by the National Negro Committee (1909)   120

DOCUMENT 8 • Helen M. Todd, "Getting Out the Vote" (1911)   122

Study Questions   125

CHAPTER 7
Corporate Society   126

DOCUMENT 1 • Warren G. Harding, Campaign Speech at Boston (1920)   128

DOCUMENT 2 • Edward Earle Purinton, "Big Ideas from Big Business" (1921)   129
DOCUMENT 3 • Sinclair Lewis, *Babbitt* (1922)   132
DOCUMENT 4 • Robert and Helen Lynd, *Middletown* (1929)   134
DOCUMENT 5 • Jane Littell, "Meditations of a Wage-Earning Wife" (1924)   136
DOCUMENT 6 • Letters from the Great Migration (1917)   139
DOCUMENT 7 • Langston Hughes, "The Negro Artist and the Racial Mountain" (1926)   140
DOCUMENT 8 • Mary Heaton Vorse, "Gastonia" (1929)   142
Study Questions   145

CHAPTER 8
The Great Depression and the Rise of the Welfare State   146

DOCUMENT 1 • *Fortune*, Editorial on Economic Conditions (1932)   148
DOCUMENT 2 • Franklin Delano Roosevelt, Speech at San Francisco (1932)   150
DOCUMENT 3 • Herbert Hoover, Speech at New York City (1932)   152
DOCUMENT 4 • J. Frederick Essary, "The New Deal for Nearly Four Months" (1933)   154
DOCUMENT 5 • Lorena Hickok, Report on Federal Relief Efforts (1933)   156
DOCUMENT 6 • Huey P. Long, *My First Days in the White House* (1935)   158
DOCUMENT 7 • Charlie Storms, "Memories of the Depression" (1939)   161
DOCUMENT 8 • Letters to F. D. R. (1934, 1937)   163
Study Questions   166

CHAPTER 9
World War II   167

DOCUMENT 1 • Franklin Delano Roosevelt, Annual Message to Congress (1941)   169
DOCUMENT 2 • Charles Lindbergh, Radio Address (1941)   172
DOCUMENT 3 • The Atlantic Charter (1941)   174
DOCUMENT 4 • I. F. Stone, "For the Jews—Life or Death?" (1944)   176
DOCUMENT 5 • Yoshiko Uchida, *Desert Exile* (1942)   178
DOCUMENT 6 • A. Philip Randolph, "Why Should We March?" (1942)   181
DOCUMENT 7 • Sterling A. Brown, "Out of Their Mouths" (1942)   183

DOCUMENT 8 • Juanita Loveless, from *Rosie the Riveter Revisited* (1942–1945)   185
Study Questions   189

CHAPTER 10
The Culture of Prosperity   190

DOCUMENT 1 • Kenneth MacFarland, "The Unfinished Work" (1946)   191
DOCUMENT 2 • George F. Kennan, "Long Telegram" (1946)   194
DOCUMENT 3 • National Security Council Memorandum Number 68 (1950)   196
DOCUMENT 4 • Richard Gerstell, "How You Can Survive an Atomic Bomb Blast" (1950)   199
DOCUMENT 5 • Norman Vincent Peale, *The Power of Positive Thinking* (1952)   202
DOCUMENT 6 • David Riesman, "The National Style" (1957)   204
DOCUMENT 7 • *Ladies Home Journal*, "Young Mother" (1956)   206
DOCUMENT 8 • *Life*, Essay on Teen-age Consumption (1959)   209
DOCUMENT 9 • Michael Harrington, *The Other America* (1962)   210
Study Questions   213

CHAPTER 11
Demand for Civil Justice   214

DOCUMENT 1 • Dr. Martin Luther King, Jr., "Letter from Birmingham Jail" (1963)   216
DOCUMENT 2 • Malcolm X, "The Ballot or the Bullet" (1964)   219
DOCUMENT 3 • Students for a Democratic Society, The Port Huron Statement (1962)   221
DOCUMENT 4 • Charles Sherrod, Student Nonviolent Coordinating Committee Memorandum (1961)   225
DOCUMENT 5 • Lyndon B. Johnson, Commencement Address at Howard University (1965)   228
DOCUMENT 6 • Shirley Chisholm, "I'd Rather Be Black than Female" (1970)   231
DOCUMENT 7 • Richard M. Nixon, "What Has Happened to America?" (1967)   233
DOCUMENT 8 • Donald Wheeldin, "The Situation in Watts Today" (1967)   236
Study Questions   238

CHAPTER 12
The Vietnam War 240

DOCUMENT 1 • Dwight D. Eisenhower, Press Conference (1954) 241
DOCUMENT 2 • The Gulf of Tonkin Resolution (1964) 242
DOCUMENT 3 • Dr. Martin Luther King, Jr., "A Time to Break the Silence" (1967) 245
DOCUMENT 4 • Charlotte Keyes, "Suppose They Gave a War and No One Came" (1966) 248
DOCUMENT 5 • Columbia Strike Coordinating Committee, "Columbia Liberated" (1968) 251
DOCUMENT 6 • Richard Hofstadter, Columbia University Commencement Address (1968) 253
DOCUMENT 7 • Richard Boyle, *The Flower of the Dragon* (1972) 256
DOCUMENT 8 • George Swiers, " 'Demented Vets and Other Myths' " (1983) 259
Study Questions 263

CHAPTER 13
Multicultural America 264

DOCUMENT 1 • Nathan Glazer, "The Peoples of America" (1965) 265
DOCUMENT 2 • Lyndon B. Johnson, Remarks upon Signing the Immigration Bill (1965) 267
DOCUMENT 3 • Mrs. Robert H. V. Duncan, Testimony Before Congress on Immigration Reform (1964) 269
DOCUMENT 4 • *Los Angeles Times*, "Asian Influx Alters Life in Suburbia" (1987) 271
DOCUMENT 5 • Ione Malloy, *Southie Won't Go* (1975) 275
DOCUMENT 6 • Cesar Chavez, "God Is Beside You on the Picket Line" (1966) 278
DOCUMENT 7 • The Gay Liberation Front, *Come Out* (1970) 279
Study Questions 282

CHAPTER 14
Republican Hegemony 283

DOCUMENT 1 • Ronald Reagan, First Inaugural Address (1981) 284
DOCUMENT 2 • Paul Craig Roberts, *The Supply-Side Revolution* (1984) 286
DOCUMENT 3 • T. Boone Pickens, "My Case for Reagan" (1984) 288

DOCUMENT 4 • Patricia Morrisroe, "The New Class" (1985)   290
DOCUMENT 5 • Leah Rosch, "Modern-Day Mentors" (1987)   294
DOCUMENT 6 • Jerry Falwell, *Listen America!* (1981)   296
DOCUMENT 7 • Sidney Blumenthal, "The G.O.P. 'Me Decade'" (1984)   299
DOCUMENT 8 • Diana Hembree, "Dead End in Silicon Valley" (1985)   302
Study Questions   307

CHAPTER 15
The End of the Cold War   308

DOCUMENT 1 • Ronald Reagan, Address to the National Association of Evangelicals (1983)   309
DOCUMENT 2 • Bill Chappell, Speech to the American Security Council Foundation (1985)   312
DOCUMENT 3 • Stephen Sestanovich, "Did the West Undo the East?" (1993)   314
DOCUMENT 4 • Wade Huntley, "The United States Was the Loser in the Cold War" (1993)   318
DOCUMENT 5 • Cynthia Enloe, "The Morning After" (1993)   321
DOCUMENT 6 • The *New York Times*, "The Workplace, After the Deluge" (1993)   324
Study Questions   327

CHAPTER 16
Toward Postindustrial Society   328

DOCUMENT 1 • Robert Reich, *The Work of Nations* (1991)   329
DOCUMENT 2 • Paul Hawken, "A Declaration of Sustainability" (1993)   334
DOCUMENT 3 • Doug Bandow, "Social Responsibility: A Conservative View" (1992)   337
DOCUMENT 4 • Myron Magnet, "Rebels with a Cause" (1993)   338
DOCUMENT 5 • Camilo José Vergara, "A Guide to the Ghettos" (1993)   341
DOCUMENT 6 • Roger Swardson, "Greetings from the Electronic Plantation" (1992)   344
Study Questions   347

Acknowledgments   348

Preface

The *Power of Words* is a collection of documents arranged in roughly chronological order from the Conquest of the Americas to the present. The work was designed to supplement major survey texts in American history, but could also stand alone. It invites students and teachers to employ a wide range of primary materials in developing their own interpretations of the past. The selection of documents attempts to strike a balance between social and political history. Each of the thirty units follows a clear pedagogical plan, which moves from the general to the specific, from the political to the personal, and from the public sphere to the private. The presentation of distinct, often conflicting perspectives allows readers to reconstruct the variety of ways that ordinary men and women explained to themselves, their families, and local communities events, movements, and policies over which they had no effective control.

Sections open with an overview of a period. The first document might be a traveler's journal or a major presidential address. These statements set an agenda; they raise issues of broad significance. The reader is then asked to consider the implementation of government or corporate policies. And here the student sees how institutional decisions affect ordinary men and women. The general policies do not work as planned: They create new problems; they spark resistance. The collection captures different voices as they attempt to carve out interpretive space. The various units include the declarations of powerful leaders—the captains of industry or the heads of government agencies, for example. These may explain, justify, or rationalize decisions in which they had a direct interest. The collection also includes the critics—men and women often classified as intellectuals who asked hard questions about subjects such as civil rights, Indian removals, industrial working conditions, and military adventures. The goal is to show the student that the American past is not a story of consensus. Even events that mobilized huge popular support—the American Revolution and World War II, for instance—generated doubts and expectations, opened doors for some, and frustrated others.

The Power of Words presents more than elite explanations of change over time. It also gives ordinary men and women a chance to speak. Each unit shows such people accommodating themselves to changing external conditions, making sense of threats and opportunities, interpreting institutional demands, and resisting what they perceived as unwarranted intrusions into their lives. In the end, the editor wanted to provide the student reader with full appreciation of conflict as well as cooperation and of the pervasive articulation, however subtle, of class, race, and gender as these categories helped mediate larger shaping forces. The collection reconstructs a long, often-disturbing conversation that Americans have had with themselves about the character of the good society. It is a story with winners and losers who, whatever their experiences, all understood—as we must—the power of words.

Many generous and thoughtful people have shaped my understanding of this project. My debt to my colleague and friend James Oakes is great. So too is my obligation to four splendid students who have helped me at every stage of the enterprise. Without David Gellman, Andrew Podolsky, Steven Reich, and Bradley Schrager, the book would have been something less than it is. I thank Bruce Borland for his continuing faith in this work. Betty Slack, Jeffrey Brown, Gloria Klaiman and Jessica Bayne offered creative suggestions, and, as usual, Susan Breen was my most demanding critic. The volumes are dedicated to Russell Maylone, head of Special Collections at the Northwestern University Library. He not only preserves historical documents but also shares his love and excitement for rare manuscripts with students, who are transformed by the experience.

T. H. Breen

General Introduction: Interrogating the Past

However dramatically technology has transformed the character of modern society, we still derive pleasure and satisfaction from studying the past. College students continue to attend history courses in large numbers. And well they should. Learning about the past helps us to understand how we got to be the way we are. Yet even enthusiastic students face a problem, of which they may only be dimly aware. They seldom have a chance actually to "do history." They usually read books and articles produced by historians who have researched an event and who have brought order to an unruly assemblage of facts. Such people interpret the past for us; they tell us what the past means. If they write clearly and smoothly, we enjoy their narratives, rarely pausing to consider the implications of having an historian stand between us and the past.

As Alice explained to the White Rabbit, the problems gets curiouser and curiouser. Consider, for example, how we acquire a rudimentary knowledge of other academic subjects. Chemistry? Mathematics? Biology? We might think it odd if a college-level course in chemistry assigned only books describing great chemists at work. After a while, someone might inquire about labs, about opportunities to conduct experiments on one's own. We would expect to "do" chemistry, discovering for ourselves why materials react in certain ways. Much the same thing could be said for other academic fields. Mathematicians teach us to solve real problems. Economists show us how to interpret statistical data or manipulate models.

This is not how history is usually taught. College lecturers tell us stories about the past or assign books that interpret the flow of events. The facts have already been organized, the meanings highlighted. What is missing is a full appreciation of the research behind these accounts. In this sense, students find themselves studying history without ever learning how to do history. Such an approach puts them at a disadvantage. How do they know whether a narrative that sounds reasonable has, in fact, real merit? They would like to know a little more about the process of "doing history," about interpreting documents, and about the character of the records themselves. Indeed, they might inquire what it means for an historian to interpret the past.

The process starts with words. Ordinary people have always generated accounts of their lives. Government and corporate leaders recorded decisions—often in formal bureaucratic language—and then, if the decisions did not work out quite as they planned, they put forth justifications, defenses, and rationalizations. Over the centuries, foreign visitors have provided insights into the assumptions of American culture. We encounter these words in archives or in collections of printed documents. These are the primary sources of history, the foundation of interpretation. And when we confront the voices of the past, we generally pay close attention to the stories that they have to tell. Depending on the character of the materials, we find the tales from the archives bizarre, interesting, or unsettling. Documents beguile us with claims that their makers have borne witness to a world that we have lost. They seem to provide a direct link between us and a distant past.

What is so easy to forget is that documents themselves—even the most poignant accounts—have a history. Like other artifacts, they are human constructions. Writers prepared them for a purpose, often with a specific audience in mind. Although they may purport to tell a complete story, they offer only perspectives, points of view, and pieces of a larger past. Even their preservation raises troubling questions, for not all documents have had an equal chance of surviving. It is more likely that archives contain the records of powerful institutions and privileged families than of marginal men and women.

The history of one early American document helps us better to understand these complex interpretive issues. It comes from the earliest period of contact between Native American peoples and European colonists. During the summer of 1642, a Narragansett leader addressed a body of Montauks, living on the eastern end of Long Island. Miantonomi, the Narragansett sachem, wanted the Montauks to join him in resisting whites who had settled Connecticut and Massachusetts Bay.

> . . . for so we are all Indians as the English are, and say brother to one another; so we must be one [people] as they are, otherwise we shall be gone shortly, for you know our fathers had plenty of deer and skins, our plains were full of deer, as also our woods, and of turkies [sic], and our coves full of fish and fowl. But these English having gotten our land, they with scythes cut down the grass, and with axes fell the trees; their cows and horses eat the grass, and their hogs spoil our clam banks, and we shall be all starved; therefore it is best for you to do as we, for we are all the Sachems from east to west . . . and we are all resolved to fall upon them all, at one appointed day; and therefore I come to you privately first, because you can persuade the Indians and the Sachem to what you will . . . and when you see the three fires that will be made forty days hence, in a clear night, then do as we, and the next day fall on and kill men, women, and children, but no cows, for they will serve to eat till our deer be increased again.

What do we make of Miantonomi's fervent appeal to the Indians of southern New England? It certainly rings true. We know from other sources that the settler economy transformed the ecology and, in the process, pushed the Native Americans aside. The Narragansetts seem fully justified in their fears. The speech records a critical moment in the history of the Indians of this region. The future appears bleak, but if the Montauks fail to respond to the "three fires," these desperate peoples will have no future at all.

Before accepting this moving document at face value, we should ask some hard questions. As historians, we begin the process of interrogating the past. First, we might inquire how this information came to be recorded. The Native Americans of seventeenth-century New England had no written language. The printed account of a general Indian uprising against the settlers must owe its existence to a literate European colonist who somehow gained knowledge of the plan. But common sense tells us that the writer probably did not witness the events. Considering the inflammatory content of Miantonomi's speech, the Narragansett sachem would never have allowed a colonist quietly to record the details of conspiracy.

In fact, the story of a planned insurrection—really a warning—can be traced to one of the Montauks who attended the meeting. This man passed the intelligence to Wyandanch, the most powerful Montauk sachem, and it was he who carried the news to Lieutenant Lion Gardiner, an English soldier possessing only primitive knowledge of the local Indian language. Even if Wyandanch had acquired a small English vocabulary, the conversation between the Montauk sachem and Gardiner represented quite a feat of communication. As Gardiner writes, "So he [Wyandanch] came over to me and acquainted me with the manner of the Narragansetts being there with his men, and asked me what I thought of it; and I told him that the Narragansett Sachem was naught to talk with his men secretly in his absence, and I bid him go home, and told him a way he might know all, and then he should come and tell me; and so he did."

We find ourselves trying to unravel a conspiracy within a conspiracy. Since Wyandanch is apparently Gardiner's only source for the Narragansett story, we might inquire whether he was a credible witness. Would he have had any motive for stirring up animosity between Gardiner and the Narragansetts? Might he have had reason to embellish the translation of Miantonomi's oration?

On that matter, there seems no doubt. The Montauk leader had already thrown his lot in with the English colonists. The Long Island Indians were eager to establish regular trade with the Europeans. In an earlier exchange between Gardiner and Wyandanch, the New England soldier noted that the sachem had asked "if we were angry with *all* Indians. I answered No, but only with such as had killed Englishmen. He asked me whether they that lived upon Long-Island might come to trade." Gardiner sensed immediately that he held the upper hand. He observed the Montauks could demonstrate their trustworthiness by capturing and killing Indians currently at war with the whites. "If you have any Indians that have killed English," Gardiner explained, "you must bring their heads also . . . So he [Wyandanch] went away and did as I had said, and sent me five heads."

Wyandanch's manipulation of this affair does not necessarily mean that he fabricated the evidence. Miantonomi may well have appealed to Native American unity. Or perhaps Wyandanch played on Gardiner's deepest fears, a covenant among *all* Indians to drive the white settlers from the continent. By raising the possibility of a general Indian confederation, Wyandanch might have bargained on improving the standing of the Montauks in future negotiations. Or so he may have thought. Although the general insurrection did not take place, the Narragansetts got a measure of revenge, sending a huge armada against the Long Island Indians and killing most of the Montauk warriors.

This reconstruction of Miantonomi's impassioned speech tells us how Gardiner first learned of the threat of Indian alliance. But what of the document itself? How did the story of the destruction of preconquest abundance—the deer, turkeys, and clams—come to be recorded? Gardiner did not write his account until 1660, a full eighteen years after the conversation with Wyandanch. By that time Gardiner was an old man. Two aging veterans of the early wars against the Indians asked him to record his memories of these events. The request took Gardiner by surprise. Before answering his "Loving Friends," he "rummaged and found some old papers then written" [i.e., in the 1640s]. Gardiner confessed that these materials were "a great help to my memory." Whatever materials he employed in preparing his narrative seem to have been lost.

Memory, of course, is a notoriously unreliable source. It is a matter of no little interest, therefore, what Gardiner's frame of mind was at the time of putting pen to paper. Age does not seem to have mellowed the man, at least, not when it came to describing the Native Americans. In 1660 he still believed that they were plotting to kill the whites, and the old soldier thought the New Englanders were too complacent in defending themselves against the Indians. As he declared, "And now I am old, I would fain a natural death, or like a soldier in the field, with honor, and not to have a sharp stake set in the ground, and thrust into my fundament, and to have my skin flayed off by piece-meal, and cut in pieces and bits, and my flesh roasted and thrust down my throat." Gardiner's vitriolic language does not necessarily mean that we cannot trust his account of the Narragansett sachem's speech, but it does suggest that extreme bias affected anything he had to say about Indians.

Gardiner's "Relation"—a twelve-page, almost illegible document—found its way into the possession of several prominent New England families. The Winthrops of Connecticut apparently held the account for almost a century, and then, probably in the 1750s, it passed into the hands of the Trumbulls, a dynasty that produced several governors, revolutionary officers, and local historians. When Governor Jonathan Trumbull died in 1809, his nephew William T. Williams discovered the Gardiner manuscript among Trumbull's private papers. The governor had made a copy of the original document. We have no way of knowing why he went to the trouble of transcribing Gardiner's words, but whatever Trumbull's purpose may have been, Williams dispatched the two manuscripts to the Massachusetts Historical Society.

The organization's publication committee found these materials fascinating. However, there was a problem. The printer contracted to set Gardiner's "Relation" in type could not decipher the soldier's seventeenth-century handwriting. The members of the committee did not do much better, and, finally, in the interest of completing the 1833 volume of the Society's collections, they relied on Trumbull's copy. An editorial explanation appended to Gardiner's narrative states, "The Committee, on account of the difficulty the printer would find in deciphering the original, have followed the orthography of the copy, excepting proper names, where they thought it of more importance to adhere to the ancient orthography."

We have come a long way from the putative meeting between Narragansetts and Montauks in 1642. The path from that gathering to the short document printed in this introduction began with an account supplied to Wyandanch by a loyal supporter who betrayed the conspiracy. A scheming Wyandanch, eager to gain favor with the white settlers, tells Lion Gardiner. The aging Indian fighter does not get around to recording the speech until much later, and, then, only to please two old friends who seem no more sympathetic to the Native Americans than does Gardiner. After a century or more, someone copies the manuscript, and since

Gardiner's handwriting defies easy reading, the copy rather than the original becomes the source of the final printed document. In other words, the history of the "Relation" involves oral history, translation from an Indian tongue into English, the fabrication of memory, long preservation under conditions that might have damaged the text, transcription by someone with no direct knowledge of these events, and, finally, publication. Our grasp of a distant reality suddenly seems tenuous. One can almost feel Miantonomi's powerful story of a ravaged physical environment slipping away.

This exercise in detection was not designed to create despair. The reader should know that most documents that they will encounter have not gone through such a tortured history. They seldom involve so many people standing between us and distant events. Rather, the point of interrogating Gardiner's narrative was to encourage skepticism. It is probably the historian's most important mental tool. Before accepting an account as a direct window to the past, the historian must ask hard questions. This is especially true in cases where the sources tell us what we want to hear. At such moments, we must be particularly careful, since it is all too easy to persuade ourselves that agreeable accounts are closer to the "truth" than are stories that we find objectionable. We want to know: Who actually produced the document? What was the man or woman's motive? Who did they think they were addressing? Was the audience a few personal friends or members of a family or did the author intend the words to reach a broader public?

The word *truth* appears above in quotation marks as a warning. We may talk of a past reality as if we were really there, as if we had listened to the words of a Narragansett sachem, or an antebellum president, or a slave at the moment of freedom, or an unemployed worker during the Great Depression. But, of course, we were not present. Our only knowledge of these happenings comes through the documents that have somehow survived, and, as the Gardiner story reveals, such sources offer perceptions, partial truths, and self-serving explanations. In this sense, the documents of American history are interpretations of events—stories people in the past have told themselves about life experiences. The search for an objective account is doomed to failure. No one can strip away the biases and assumptions of everyday life. They are unquestioned aspects of human existence.

This apparent limitation on "objectivity" does not deter the skeptical historian. For if the documents, in fact, do record contesting perceptions, different opinions, and interpretations, the historian can weigh the merits of the various accounts. To be sure, most of the time we do not have as much information about the construction of a document as we do for the Gardiner "Relation." But that is not a serious problem. The people who produced interpretations of the past—diaries, letters, newspaper articles, and traveler's reports, for example—adopted rhetorical strategies. They wanted someone to find their stories credible; their goal was persuasion.

And it is precisely here that we must be most suspicious. Throughout American history, certain authors have claimed to "speak for" a group or a people or the members of a certain race. To enhance the credibility of their arguments, they have often drawn on the authority of science, tradition, or public opinion. Thus, a generally liberal figure such as Thomas Jefferson informs us in his *Notes on the State of Virginia* that African Americans are not fully human, at least, not in the way that whites are human, and to lend greater authenticity to the racial argument, he cites the findings of contemporary science. The language of science is employed to trump opposing positions or to cut off debate.

Other American writers—many of them represented in this collection of documents—have claimed authority on the basis of Christian scripture, Western civilization, or simple common sense. In the context of the times in which the author lived such rhetorical devices added greatly to the power of the word. It took courage for ordinary men and women to challenge those who assumed an "objective" voice. The unlettered person is usually reluctant to question the alleged findings of science. During the height of the Cold War, scientists working for the government assured the public that people could survive a nuclear bomb. The dangers of radioactivity, they announced, had been greatly exaggerated. Who could doubt that these experts knew what they were talking about? They spoke for science. With such examples in mind, the skeptical historian should always ask who empowered a particular writer to "speak for" the entire community, especially if that collectivity was the American people.

Wary interpreters of documents quickly develop an ear for silences. Like the famous British detective Sherlock Holmes, they must listen carefully for the dog that did *not* bark in the night. American writers who have presumed to "speak for" the people often left out entire groups. Sometimes it was the Native Americans. On other occasions, it was the African Americans, or women, or industrial workers, or members of new ethnic minorities. Documents of this type do not overtly slander women or blacks or Indians; they just leave them out of the story. They relegate them to silence. Modern readers must restore the missing voices. When national leaders speak of general prosperity, for example, the skeptical historian immediately asks whether the good times were shared by all. When writers celebrate the growth of American democracy, the skeptical historian asks whether anyone has been silenced. Does the concept include the poor? Women? African Americans? Others? And if not, why not? The goal is not to belittle prosperity or democracy—we need a lot more of both—but to understand more fully how these familiar terms evolved over the course of American history.

The reader will encounter another type of document in this collection. These statements might be best characterized as "speaking to" some imagined audience. During Reconstruction, for example, federal officers employed by the Freemen's Bureau lectured the newly liberated slaves about the benefits of wage labor. The captains of late nineteenth-century industry—among them, Andrew Carnegie—informed the members of the working classes about blessings of diligence and responsibility. These performances were designed to persuade the members of other groups of the justice and superiority of the speaker's values. They assume that any reasonable, well-intentioned person would agree with the argument being advanced. Slaves should appreciate the advantages of free labor, even if that system means that African Americans work for their former masters at low wages. The factory workers should see the virtues of hard work and honest ambition, even if most of them spend their days in dangerous, low-paying jobs. The skeptical historian learns to spot self-interested rhetoric and to strip away assumptions about gender and race that usually pass without comment.

In our discussion of the interrogation of documents, we have stressed one aspect of the "power of words." Throughout recorded history, people have employed words to gain dominance, to justify policies, to rationalize decisions that represent the interests of a minority, and to persuade others to accept a specific set of values and to behave in certain ways. But even as we study the texts for such rhetorical practices, we should remember that words possess other powers. They announce freedom. They can call forth nobility and self-sacrifice. They invite scattered strangers to unite in common cause. To classify such performances as "speaking against" makes them seem too defensive—the stuff of resistance rather than liberation. They were both, and sometimes more. Words often simply helped ordinary men and women to make sense out of their lives, to accommodate economic and social change, and to assure themselves that there was more to existence than material reward.

Each chapter in *The Power of Words* brings together different voices. Sometimes the documents address common issues; sometimes they speak at cross-purposes. They challenge the skeptical historian to make sense out of contesting claims and conflicting assumptions. The process of interrogating the past dramatically opens up the story of American history. Skepticism about the claims of professional authority and insistence on having a meaningful voice in the interpretation of the nation's past are important to all Americans at the end of the twentieth century.

* * * * * *

A word of advice is necessary for students unfamiliar with historical documents, especially texts dating from before the American Revolution. I have not attempted to modernize these sources. Unless the meaning is unclear, I have reproduced the words exactly as they were written. This decision means that I have preserved the texture of words; I remind readers of how hard it was for poorer or semi-literate people in the past to express themselves effectively on paper. Sometimes the spelling will seem odd, and the voices contained in this collection sometimes speak of *howses* rather than *houses*, *cattell* rather than *cattle*, *publique* rather than *public*. Because the standardization of spelling is a relatively modern phenomenon, writers in the early period often spelled the same word several different ways in the same document. The goal here is not to force these men and women to conform to our rules, but to listen carefully to what they had to say about worlds—or more precisely—words we have lost.

1

Reconstruction

The North's victory in the Civil War established the indivisibility of federal union and ensured the abolition of slavery. Yet the unconditional surrender of the rebellious southern states on the battlefield raised numerous questions for the nation's political leaders. Primary among these were how to reintegrate former Confederate states into the federal system and what position the millions of newly freed African Americans should occupy in society now that they were no longer slaves. Thus "Reconstruction," while focusing largely on the South, provoked national discussion of unprecedented scope (Document 1).

Abraham Lincoln, who successfully guided the Union through the war, only lived to implement the first tentative steps of reconstruction. Lincoln's assassination just a few days after the Confederacy surrendered at Appomattox elevated Vice President Andrew Johnson. Lincoln had selected Johnson, a Democratic senator from Tennessee—who at the time of his state's secession proclaimed staunch pro-Union sentiments—as his running mate in order to balance the 1864 presidential ticket. The rough-edged Johnson matched his contempt for wealthy white planters with his loathing of blacks. His temperament and his views on Reconstruction soon clashed with a Republican-dominated Congress wary of both the loyalty of southern whites and their intentions toward free blacks.

The Freedmen's Bureau oversaw Reconstruction in the South. A temporary and underfunded office of the War Department, the bureau nonetheless sought to reconcile the clashing needs of former slaves and former masters amid the physical devastation and social upheaval of the postwar landscape. Anticipating the transition to a free-wage economy, bureau agents and other northerners sought to introduce the values and customs of the market economy to the freed people (Document 2). Yet without a mandate to upset the traditional economic hierarchy, the bureau disappointed African American hopes of land reform, sparking protests of Bureau policies (Document 3). In an age of limited government and awkward race relations, condescending moral pronouncements and contradictory policies often substituted for effective action.

Yet African American ambitions and congressional concerns temporarily dove-tailed to construct a scaffolding for a more integrated political future. Blacks throughout the South participated in organizations demanding equal rights and drawing attention to the obstacles that whites placed in their way (Document 4).

The U.S. Congress, now thoroughly estranged from President Johnson, passed a series of civil rights laws and constitutional amendments (Document 5) to ensure the full citizenship and voting rights of the freed people. Congress predicted the readmission of southern states to the Union on the ratification of these amendments.

For a time, a coalition of whites, consisting of former unionists as well as notorious "carpetbaggers" who had moved from the North to the South after the war, and blacks governed the southern states. Only in one state, South Carolina, did African Americans ever gain a majority of state legislative offices, but for the first time in American history, blacks held office at all levels of government. Republican rule, however, depended on the symbolic presence of the small number of federal troops stationed in the South, the goodwill of national public opinion, and the enforcement of federal laws to keep reactionary forces at bay.

Over time, the impact of each of these factors diminished. The foremost sources of northern opinion, increasingly appalled by political malfeasance in their own midst, seized on corruption and fiscal crises in southern Republican governments as evidence that the entire enterprise of Reconstruction and racial equality had been illegitimate (Document 6). Meanwhile, the Ku Klux Klan mounted a brutally effective campaign of terror against blacks, as well as Republican whites, making political participation in the South increasingly hazardous (Document 7). White "redeemer" governments regained power throughout the South, rewriting recently revised state constitutions and passing laws to deny African Americans access to power and deprive them of social services, such as education, essential to their economic advancement (Document 8). The last federal troops withdrew from the South in 1877 as a part of a compromise in which the Congress ratified Republican Rutherford B. Hayes's election as president with several electoral votes of disputable validity in his column. When redeemers reclaimed the remaining Reconstruction governments, prospects for African Americans fell into eclipse.

DOCUMENT 1

Carl Schurz, Report on the Condition of the South (1865)

The unprecedented emancipation of millions of slaves gave the federal government little time to savor the fruits of victory. In December 1865, President Andrew Johnson reluctantly presented Congress with Senator Carl Schurz's report on conditions in five southern states. Schurz, a German immigrant and high-minded Republican representing Missouri, stressed that a successful Reconstruction policy must ensure the smooth transition to a free-labor economy.

[W]e ought to keep in view, above all, the nature of the problem which is to be solved. As to what is commonly termed "reconstruction," it is not only the political machinery of the States and their constitutional relations to the general government, but the whole organism of southern society that must be reconstructed, or rather constructed anew, so as to bring it in harmony with the rest of American society. The difficulties of this task are not to be considered overcome when the people of the south take the oath of allegiance and elect governors and legislatures and members of Congress, and militia captains. That this would be done had become certain as soon as the surrenders of the southern armies had made further resistance impossible, and nothing in the world was left, even to the most uncompromising rebel, but to submit or to emigrate. It was also natural that they should avail themselves of every chance offered them to resume control of their home affairs and to regain their influence in the Union. But this can hardly be called the first step towards the solution of the true problem, and it is a fair question to ask, whether the hasty gratification of their desire to resume such control would not create new embarrassments.

The true nature of the difficulties of the situation is this: The general government of the republic has, by proclaiming the emancipation of the slaves, commenced a great social revolution in the south, but has, as yet, not completed it. Only the negative part of it is accomplished. The slaves are emancipated in point of form, but free labor has not yet been put in the place of slavery in point of fact. And now, in the midst of this critical period of transition, the power which originated the revolution is expected to turn over its whole future development to another power which from the beginning was hostile to it and has never yet entered into its spirit, leaving the class in whose favor it was made completely without power to protect itself and to take an influential part in that development. The history of the world will be searched in vain for a proceeding similar to this which did not lead either to a rapid and violent reaction, or to the most serious trouble and civil disorder. It cannot be said that the conduct of the southern people since the close of the war has exhibited such extraordinary wisdom and self-abnegation as to make them an exception to the rule.

In my despatches from the south I repeatedly expressed the opinion that the people were not yet in a frame of mind to legislate calmly and understandingly upon the subject of free negro labor. And this I reported to be the opinion of some of our most prominent military commanders and other observing men. It is, indeed, difficult to imagine circumstances more unfavorable for the development of a calm and unprejudiced public opinion than those under which the southern people are at present laboring. The war has not only defeated their political aspirations, but it has broken up their whole social organization. When the rebellion was put down they found themselves not only conquered in a political and military sense, but economically ruined. The planters, who represented the wealth of the southern country, are partly laboring under the severest embarrassments, partly reduced to absolute poverty. Many who are stripped of all available means, and have nothing but their land, cross their arms in gloomy despondency, incapable of rising to a manly resolution. Others, who still possess means, are at a loss how to use them, as their old way of doing things is, by the abolition of slavery, rendered impracticable, at least where the military arm of the government has enforced emancipation. Others are still trying to go on in the old way, and that old way is in fact the only one they understand, and in which they have any confidence. Only a minority is trying to adopt the new order of things. A large number of the plantations, probably a considerable majority of the more valuable estates, is under heavy mortgages, and the owners know that, unless they retrieve their fortunes in a comparatively short space of time, their property will pass out of their hands. Almost all are, to some extent, embarrassed. The nervous anxiety which such a state of things produces extends also to those classes of society which, although not composed of planters, were always in close business connexion with the planting interest, and there was hardly a branch of commerce or industry in the south which was not directly or indirectly so connected. Besides, the southern soldiers, when returning from the war, did not, like the northern soldiers, find a prosperous community which merely waited for their arrival to give them remunerative employment. They found, many of them, their homesteads destroyed, their farms devastated, their families in distress; and those that were less unfortunate found, at all events, an impoverished and exhausted community which had but little to offer them. Thus a great many have been thrown upon the world to shift as best they can. They must do something honest or dishonest, and must do it soon, to make a living, and their prospects are, at present, not very bright. Thus that nervous anxiety to hastily repair broken fortunes, and to prevent still greater ruin and distress, embraces nearly all classes, and imprints upon all the movements of the social body a morbid character.

In which direction will these people be most apt to turn their eyes? Leaving the prejudice of race out of the question, from early youth they have been acquainted with but one system of labor, and with that one system they have been in the habit of identifying all their interests. They know of no way to help themselves but the one they are accustomed to. Another system of labor is presented to them, which, however, owing to circumstances which they do not appreciate, appears at first in an unpromising light. To try it they consider an experiment which they cannot afford to make while their wants are urgent. They have not reasoned calmly enough to convince themselves that the trial must be made. It is, indeed, not wonderful that, under such circumstances, they should study, not how to introduce and develop free labor, but how to avoid its introduction, and how to return as much and as quickly as possible to something like the old order of things. Nor is it wonderful that such studies should find an expression in their attempts at legislation. But the circumstance that this tendency is natural does not render it less dangerous and objectionable. The practical question presents itself: Is the immediate restoration of the late rebel States to absolute self-control so necessary that it must be done even at the risk of endangering one of the great results of the war, and of

This sketch, "Electioneering in the South," by W. L. Sheppard, displays the newfound freedom for African Americans to participate in politics after the passage of the Fifteenth Amendment in 1869. Though African Americans represented a majority in many former slave states, only a small number were elected to Congress.

bringing on in those States insurrection or anarchy, or would it not be better to postpone that restoration until such dangers are passed? If, as long as the change from slavery to free labor is known to the southern people only by its destructive results, these people must be expected to throw obstacles in its way, would it not seem necessary that the movement of social "reconstruction" be kept in the right channel by the hand of the power which originated the change, until that change can have disclosed some of its beneficial effects?

It is certain that every success of free negro labor will augment the number of its friends, and disarm some of the prejudices and assumptions of its opponents. I am convinced one good harvest made by unadulterated free labor in the south would have a far better effect than all the oaths that have been taken, and all the ordinances that have as yet been passed by southern conventions. But how can such a result be attained? The facts enumerated in this report, as well as the news we receive from the south from day to day, must make it evident to every unbiased observer that unadulterated free labor cannot be had at present, unless the national government holds its protective and controlling hand over it. It appears, also, that the more efficient this protection of free labor against all disturbing and reactionary influences, the sooner may such a satisfactory result be looked for. One reason why the southern people are so slow in accommodating themselves to the new order of things is, that they confidently expect soon to be permitted to regulate matters according to their own notions. Every concession made to them by the government has been taken as an encouragement to persevere in this hope, and, unfortunately for them, this hope is nourished by influences from other parts of the country. Hence their anxiety to have their State governments restored *at once*, to have the troops withdrawn, and the Freedmen's Bureau abolished, although a good many discerning men know well that, in view of the lawless spirit still prevailing, it would be far better for them to have the general order of society firmly maintained by the federal power until things have arrived at a final settlement. Had, from the beginning, the conviction been forced upon them that the adulteration of the new order of things by the admixture of elements belonging to the system of slavery would under no circumstances be permitted, a much larger number would have launched their energies into the new channel, and, seeing that they could do "no better," faithfully co-operated with the government. It is hope which fixes them in their perverse notions. That hope nourished or fully gratified, they will persevere in the same direction. That hope destroyed, a great many will, by the force of necessity, at once accommodate themselves to the logic of the change. If, therefore, the national government firmly and unequivocally announces its policy not to give up the control of the free-labor reform until it is finally accomplished, the progress of that reform will undoubtedly be far more rapid and far less difficult than it will be if the attitude of the government is such as to permit contrary hopes to be indulged in.

The machinery by which the government has so far exercised its protection of the negro and of free labor in the south—the Freedmen's Bureau—is very unpopular in that part of the country, as every institution placed there as a barrier to reactionary aspirations would be. That abuses were committed with the management of freedmen's affairs; that some of the officers of the bureau were men of more enthusiasm than discretion, and in many cases went beyond their authority: all this is certainly true. But, while the southern people are always ready to expatiate upon the shortcomings of the Freedmen's Bureau, they are not so ready to recognize the services it has rendered. I feel warranted in saying that not half of the labor that has been done in the south this year, or will be done there next year, would have been or would be done but for the exertions of the Freedmen's Bureau. The confusion and disorder of the transition period would have been infinitely greater had not an agency interfered which possessed the confidence of the emancipated slaves; which could disabuse them of any extravagant notions and expectations and be trusted; which could administer to them good advice and be voluntarily obeyed. No other agency, except one placed there by the national government, could have wielded that moral power whose interposition was so necessary to prevent southern society from falling at once into the chaos of a general collision between its different elements. That the success achieved by the Freedmen's Bureau is as yet very incomplete cannot be disputed. A more perfect organization and a more carefully selected personnel may be desirable; but it is doubtful whether a more suitable machinery can be devised to secure to free labor in the south that protection against disturbing influences which the nature of the situation still imperatively demands.

DOCUMENT 2

Clinton B. Fisk, Plain Counsels for Freedmen (1865)

Fisk, chief of the Tennessee Freedman's Bureau, published a series of lectures advising emancipated African Americans on life after slavery. Fisk's lectures warned freed people not to entertain extravagant hopes about freedom. He condescendingly offered instead the eventual rewards of thrift and hard work, and urged the importance of knowing one's place.

I come to speak to you this evening about work; yes, work, good, honest, hard work. Do not turn away, and say you will not hear me,—that you know all about it, and that it is not a good subject for a lecture.

Listen! The very first verse of the Holy Bible tells us that God is a worker,—that in six days he made all this great world on which we dwell, and the sun and moon and stars.

All the holy angels in heaven are very busy. They go forth to do the will of the Great Being, and find their greatest bliss in action.

Good and great men are all hard workers. And do you know what it is that makes a free state so rich and strong? It is, above all things save God's blessing, *patient, honest work.*

There is nothing degrading in *free* labor,—nay, it is most honorable. Why, when God placed Adam and Eve in the garden of Eden, before either of them had ever done any wrong thing, and while they were as pure as the angels, he made gardeners of them. He required them to dress the garden and keep it nice and in good condition.

The blessed Saviour himself worked at the bench, at the carpenter's trade, until he was about thirty years of age.

And yet, some very silly people are above work,—are ashamed to have hard hands,—and do their best to get through the world without honest toil.

But this was not the case with Abraham Lincoln, the man who wrote the Proclamation of Emancipation. He used the hoe, the ax, and the maul, cleared ground, and fenced it with the rails he had split, and was ready to turn his hands to any honest work.

I know that it is quite natural that you should associate work with slavery, and freedom with idleness, because you have seen slaves working all their lives, and free people doing little or nothing. And I should not blame you if you should ask, "What have we gained by freedom, if we are to work, work, work!"

Now, let me explain. A slave works all his life for others. A free man works for himself,—that is, he gets pay for his labor; and if he saves what he earns and manages well, he can get on so well that he may spend the afternoon of his life in his own pleasant home, and never want for any thing. . . .

If you earn twelve dollars in a month, and spend thirteen, you are on the road to misery, for you will get into debt, deeper and deeper, until after awhile it will be a load you can not carry.

You should make it a rule, therefore, to spend less each month and each year than you make. If you do this, you will become well to do in the world.

A free man should always consider before he buys an article, whether he can afford it. He would like a new hat,—price five dollars,—but if he needs the five for other and more pressing uses, to make a payment, for example, for something he has bought, then he should deny himself the pleasure of the new hat, and brush up the old one. A new coat might be very desirable, but if its purchase would create a debt, better keep the old one in good repair as possible, and stick to it another season. It is much pleasanter to wear the old clothes than to have the constable chasing you in the new ones.

Many a poor man has been driven almost out of his wits by constables, who were pursuing him for the payment of debts made to gratify the vanity of his wife. She wanted a handsome breastpin, and begged him to buy it. He could not resist, and bought it with the proceeds of a week's hard toil, and, as a consequence, was obliged to go in debt for meat and bread. Then she wanted a fine dress; then this, and then that; and so he sank into debt, step by step, until he was ruined.

A wife can soon destroy her husband's good name, by urging him to buy her things she could do without, and for which he is unable to pay.

It is a good plan for a man and woman who are just setting out as you are to make a living, to balance their accounts—that is count up what they earn and what they spend, and see how they compare—a great many times in the year. It will not take them long to do it, and the task will be both pleasant and useful.

Resolve that you will, by the blessing of God, live within your means. This is one of the most important secrets of success. It may cost you a struggle, but stick to it resolutely, and the day will come when you will be able to purchase not only the necessaries, but the luxuries of life.

I am not counseling you to be mean and stingy,—by no means; but no man has a right to be liberal with another man's money and at another man's expense.

For the sake of your good name, do not make a splurge in society with jewelry and fine clothes which have not been paid for, and for which you will never be able to pay. That is almost as mean as theft.

"The borrower," says the Bible, "is servant to the lender," and, let me assure you, a creditor is a very hard master. Do not put your necks in his iron yoke.

I am acquainted with many white persons who commenced married life twenty-five years ago with as little as you have now, and who worked with their hands for less than is given to you, who are now owners of handsome houses and farms, and are in very easy circumstances. They made it a rule to spend less than they earned.

DOCUMENT 3

James C. Beecher, Report on Land Reform in the South Carolina Islands (1865, 1866)

Freed blacks, southern whites, and the federal government often harbored conflicting interpretations of the practical effects of emancipation. Former masters sought to regain plantations seized by slaves or distributed by Union officers and to gain access to the labor of their former slaves. The War Department cooperated in this land reclamation project, creating awkward confrontations. In this selection, Freedmen's Bureau officer James C. Beecher reports on black opposition to the return to white ownership of islands off the South Carolina coast promised to the ex-slaves by the Union's General Sherman.

8 ◆ Chapter 1   Reconstruction

The controversial Reconstruction of the South after the Civil War was a difficult time for African Americans. Though given the right to voice political opinions for the first time, their voices often went unheeded. As southern whites slowly regained control of political offices after Reconstruction, African Americans slowly lost much of their newfound political freedom.

November 29, 1865

Maj. Gen. R. Saxton
General:

I am to leave for Edisto Island in the morning. It seems that some of the planters whose lands have been restored were driven off by the freed people. Gen. Sickles immediately ordered that a company of white troops be sent there. Gen. Devens agreed with me that my troops were the ones to send if any and so I take a company with me.

I have apprehended trouble ever since the Govt determined to rescind the authority to occupy those lands. It is true that the War Dept. did not, in so many words, approve Gen. Sherman's order, but it certainly did *act* upon it, and there is an apparent bad faith in the matter which I am sure the freed people will feel. I cannot refrain from expressing grave fears of collisions on the island. The same difficulty is affecting the Combahee plantations. I hope to visit that section by Monday next.

James C. Beecher
National Archives

January 9, 1866

I . . . called the people together and carefully instructed them in their rights and duties. They said they had been assured by certain parties that Mr. Heyward [a local white planter] would be obliged to lease his land to them, and that they would not work for him at any price. They were perfectly good natured about it but firm. I then announced Mr. Heyward's offer:

That they were to retain their houses and gardens, with the privilege of raising hogs, poultry, etc. That he would pay for full hands, men $12, women $8 per month. They to find themselves—or he would pay $10 per month to men, $4 to women and ration them.

I am satisfied that no higher wages will be offered this year. Therefore I told the people that they could take it or leave it, and that if they declined to work the plantation the houses must be vacated. I proceeded to call the roll of all the able bodied men and women, each of whom responded "no." I then notified them that every house must be vacated on or before the 18th inst. I propose to remain and see everyone outside the plantation lines on that date.

Today I have pursued the same course on another large plantation, with the same results. Of course I anticipated this. It could not be otherwise considering the instructions which these people have received. I do not blame them in the slightest degree, and so long as they show no violence, shall treat them with all possible kindness. But it is better to stop the error they are laboring under, at once.

January 31, 1866

I am informed that on or about 12th inst a meeting was called on Wadmalaw Island to take measures to prevent white persons from visiting the island—that the Captain Commanding (very properly) forbade the proceeding, and notified the actors that in future no meetings could be held until notice of the same should be given him.

I am further informed that certain parties immediately proceeded to Charleston and returned with a document signed "By order Maj. Gen. Saxton" stating that the military authorities had nothing to do with them and they were at liberty to hold meetings when and where they pleased. This document was brought by three colored men calling themselves Commissioners from Edisto Island, attended by an escort of forty or fifty freedmen, and exhibited to the Officer. They then proceeded to Rockville, and held the meeting.

It is to be regretted that the Bureau should seem to bring the freed people in collision with the Military Police of the islands. Already in two instances the freed people have committed themselves seriously by acts of stupid violence and I have record of hurtful advice given by speakers at the meeting in question. I shall be exceedingly grieved to find myself in collision with the [Bureau] but being responsible for the military police of these islands cannot do otherwise than prevent disorder by any means in my power.

I respectfully request that instruction be sent to the same "Commissioners" to the effect that the order in question must be respected on Wadmalaw and Johns Island. Such instructions will prevent collision between the [freedmen] and the U.S. forces.

DOCUMENT 4

"Address from the Colored Citizens of Norfolk, Virginia, to the People of the United States" (1865)

African Americans quickly grasped the great divide separating formal emancipation from social and political equality. Organization and communication provided southern blacks with vehicles for advancing their cause. In this document "The Colored Citizens of Norfolk" assert the need for black activism and urge the "People of the United States" to defeat the opponents of freedom.

[We] believe our present position is by no means so well understood among the loyal masses of the country, otherwise there would be no dely in granting us the express relief which the nature of the case demands. It must not be forgotten that it is the general assumption, in the South, that the effects of the immortal Emancipation Proclamation of President Lincoln go no further than the emancipation of the Negroes then in slavery, and that it is only constructively even, that that Proclamation can be said, in any legal sense, to have abolished slavery, and even the late constitutional amendment, if duly ratified, can go no further; neither touch, nor can touch, the slave codes of the various southern States, and the laws respecting free people of color consequent therefrom, which, having been passed before the act of secession, are presumed to have lost none of their vitality, but exist, as a convenient engine for our oppression, until repealed by special acts of the State legislature. By these laws, in many of the southern

States, it is still a crime for colored men to learn or be taught to read, and their children are doomed to ignorance; there is no provision for insuring the legality of our marriages; we have no right to hold real estate; the public streets and the exercise of our ordinary occupations are forbidden us unless we can produce passes from our employers, or licenses from certain officials; in some States the whole free Negro population is legally liable to exile from the place of its birth, for no crime but that of color; we have no means of legally making or enforcing contracts of any description; we have no right to testify before the courts in any case in which a white man is one of the parties to the suit, we are taxed without representation, and, in short, so far as legal safeguards of our rights are concerned, we are defenceless before our enemies. While this is our position as regards our legal status, before the State laws, we are still more unfortunately situated as regards our late masters. The people of the North, owing to the greater interest excited by war, have heard little or nothing, for the past four years, of the blasphemous and horrible theories formerly propounded for the defence and glorification of human slavery, in the press, the pulpit and legislatures of the southern States; but, though they may have forgotten them, let them be assured that these doctrines have by no means faded from the minds of the people of the South; they cling to these delusions still, and only hug them closer for their recent defeat. Worse than all, they have returned to their homes, with all their old pride and contempt for the Negro transformed into bitter hate for the new-made freeman, who aspires for the suppression of their rebellion. That this charge is not unfounded, the manner in which it has been recently attempted to enforce the laws above referred to proves. In Richmond, during the three days sway of the rebel Mayor Mayo, over 800 colored people were arrested, simply for walking the streets without a pass; in the neighboring city of Portsmouth, a Mayor has just been elected, on the avowed platform that this is a white man's government, and our enemies have been heard to boast openly, that soon not a colored man shall be left in the city; in the greater number of counties in this State, county meetings have been held, at which resolutions have been adopted *deploring*, while accepting, the abolition of slavery, but going on to pledge the planters composing the meeting, to employ no Negroes save such as were formerly owned by themselves, without a written recommendation from their late employers, and threatening violence towards those who should do so, thereby keeping us in a state of serfdom, and preventing our free selection of our employers; they have also pledged themselves, in no event, to pay their late adult slaves more than $60 per year for their labor. In the future, out of which, with characteristic generosity, they have decided that we are to find clothes for ourselves and families, and pay our taxes and doctors' bills; in many of the more remote districts individual planters are to be found who still refuse to recognize their Negroes as free, forcibly retaining the wives and children of their late escaped slaves; cases have occurred, not far from Richmond itself, in which an attempt to leave the plantation has been punished by shooting to death; and finally, there are numbers of cases, known to ourselves, in the immediate vicinity of this city, in which a faithful performance, by colored men, of the duties or labor contracted for, has been met by a contemptuous and violent refusal of the stipulated compensation. These are facts, and yet the men doing these things are, in many cases, loud in their professions of attachment to the restored Union, while committing these outrages on the most faithful friends that Union can ever have. Even well known Union men have often been found among our oppressors; witness the action of the Tennessee legislature in imposing unheard of disabilities upon us, taking away from us, and giving to the County Courts, the right of disposing of our children, by apprenticing them to such occupations as the court, not their parents, may see fit to adopt for them, and in this very city, and under the protection of military law, some of our white friends who have nobly distinguished themselves by their efforts in our behalf, have been threatened with arrest by a Union Mayor of this city, for their advocacy of the cause of freedom.

Fellow citizens, the performance of a simple act

of justice on your part will reverse all this; we ask for no expensive aid from military forces, stationed throughout the South, overbearing State action, and rendering our government republican only in name; give us the suffrage, and you may rely upon us to secure justice for ourselves, and all Union men, and to keep the State forever in the Union.

While we urge you to this act of simple justice to ourselves, there are many reasons why you should concede us this right in your own interest. It cannot be that you contemplate with satisfaction a prolonged military occupation of the southern States, and yet, without the existence of a larger loyal constituency than, at present, exists in these States, a military occupation will be absolutely necessary, to protect the white Union men of the South, as well as ourselves, and if not absolutely to keep the States in the Union, it will be necessary to prevent treasonable legislation. . . .

You have not unreasonably complained of the operation of that clause of the Constitution which has hitherto permitted the slaveocracy of the South to wield the political influence which would be represented by a white population equal to three-fifths of the whole Negro population; but slavery is now abolished, and henceforth the representation will be in proportion to the enumeration of the whole population of the South, *including people of color,* and it is worth your consideration if it is desirable or politic that the fomentors of this rebellion against the Union, which has been crushed at the expense of so much blood and treasure, should find themselves, after defeat, more powerful than ever, their political influence enhanced by the additional voting power of the other two-fifths of the colored population, by which means four Southern votes will balance in the Congressional and Presidential elections at least seven Northern ones. The honor of your country should be dear to you, as it is, but is that honor advanced, in the eyes of the Christian world, when America alone, of all Christian nations, sustains an unjust distinction against four millions and a half of her most loyal people, on the senseless ground of a difference in color? You are anxious that the attention of every man, of every State legislature, and of Congress, should be exclusively directed to redressing the injuries sustained by the country in the late contest; are these objects more likely to be effected amid the political distractions of an embarrassing Negro agitation? You are, above all, desirous that no future intestine wars should mar the prosperity and destroy the happiness of the country; will your perfect security from such evils be promoted by the existence of a colored population of four millions and a half, placed, by your enactments, outside the pale of the Constitution, discontented by oppression, with an army of 200,000 colored soldiers, whom you have drilled, disciplined, and armed, but whose attachment to the State you have failed to secure by refusing them citizenship? You are further anxious that your government should be an example to the world of true Republican institutions; but how can you avoid the charge of inconsistency if you leave one eighth of the population of the whole country without any political rights, while bestowing these rights on every immigrant who comes to these shores, perhaps from a despotism, under which he could never exercise the least political right, and had no means of forming any conception of their proper use? . . .

It is hardly necessary here to refute any of the slanders with which our enemies seek to prove our unfitness for the exercise of the right of suffrage. It is true, that many of our people are ignorant, but for *that* these very men are responsible, and decency should prevent *their* use of such an argument. But if our people are ignorant, no people were ever more orderly and obedient to the laws; and no people ever displayed greater earnestness in the acquisition of knowledge. Among no other people could such a revolution have taken place without scenes of license and bloodshed; but in this case, and we say it advisedly, full information of the facts will show that no single disturbance, however slight, has occurred which has not resulted from the unprovoked aggression of white people, and, if any one doubts how fast the ignorance, which has hitherto cursed our people, is disappearing, 'mid the light of freedom, let him visit the colored schools of this city and neighborhood, in which between two and three thousand pupils are being taught, while, in the evening, in colored schools may be seen, after the labors of the day, hundreds of our adult population from budding manhood to hoary age, toiling, with intensest eagerness, to acquire the invaluable arts of reading and writing, and the rudimentary branches of knowledge. One other objection only will we notice; it is that our people are lazy and idle; and, in support of this allegation, the objectors refer to the crowds of colored people subsisting on Government rations, and flocking into the towns. To the first statement we reply that we are poor, and that thousands of our young and able-bodied men, having been enlisted in the army to fight the battles of their country, it is but reasonable that that country should contribute something to the support of those whose natural protectors that country has taken away. With reference to the crowds collected round the military posts and in the cities, we say that though some may have come there under misapprehensions as to the nature of the freedom they have just received, yet this is not the case with the majority; the colored man knows that freedom means freedom to labor, and to enjoy its fruits, and in that respect evinces at least an equal appreciation of his new position with his late owners; if he is not to be found laboring for these late owners, it is because he cannot trust them, and feels safe, in his new-found freedom, nowhere out of the immediate presence of the national forces; if the planters want his labor (and they do) fair wages and fair treatment will not fail to secure it.

In conclusion, we wish to advise our colored brethren of the State and nation, that the settlement of this question is to a great extent dependent on them, and that supineness on their part will do as much to dely if not defeat the full recognition of their rights as the open opposition of avowed enemies. Then be up and active, and everywhere let associations be formed having for their object the agitation, discussion and enforcement of your claims to equality before the law, and equal rights of suffrage. Your opponents are active; be prepared, and organize to resist their efforts. We would further advise that all political associations of colored men, formed within the limits of the State of Virginia, should communicate the fact of their existence, with the names and post office addresses of their officers, to Joseph T. Wilson, Norfolk, Va., in order that communication and friendly cooperation may be kept up between the different organizations, and facilities afforded for common and united State action, should occasion require it.

DOCUMENT 5

The Fourteenth Amendment to the United States Constitution (1868)

The Fourteenth Amendment attempted to fortify the position of the former slaves against challenges to their full rights as citizens. As a condition of readmittance to the Union, Congress required southern states to ratify the amendment. Supreme Court decisions interpreting the amendment narrowly and the North's failure to oversee forcefully the implementation of its principles diluted the provision's impact, as well as the effect of other federal legislation.

Amendment XIV

Section 1

All persons born or naturalized in the United States, and subject to the jurisdiction thereof, are citizens of the United States and of the State wherein they reside. No State shall make or enforce any law which shall abridge the privileges or immunities of citizens of the United States; nor shall any State deprive any person of life, liberty, or property, without due process of law; nor deny to any person within its jurisdiction the equal protection of the laws.

Section 2

Representatives shall be apportioned among the several States according to their respective numbers, counting the whole number of persons in each State, excluding Indians not taxed. But when the right to vote at any election for the choice of electors for President and Vice President of the United States, Representatives in Congress, the Executive and Judicial officers of a State, or the members of the Legislature thereof, is denied to any of the male inhabitants of such State, being twenty-one years of age, and citizens of the United States, or in any way abridged, except for participation in rebellion, or other crime, the basis of representation therein shall be reduced in the proportion which the number of such male citizens shall bear to the whole number of male citizens twenty-one years of age in such State.

Section 3

No person shall be a Senator or Representative in Congress, or elector of President and Vice President, or hold any office, civil or military, under the United States, or under any State, who, having previously taken an oath, as a member of Congress, or as an officer of the United States, or as a member of any State legislature, or as an executive or judicial officer of any State, to support the Constitution of the United States, shall have engaged in insurrection or rebellion against the same, or given aid or comfort to the enemies thereof. But Congress may by a vote of two-thirds of each House, remove such disability.

Section 4

The validity of the public debt of the United States, authorized by law, including debts incurred for payment for pensions and bounties for services in suppressing insurrection or rebellion, shall not be questioned. But neither the United States nor any State shall assume or pay any debt or obligation incurred in aid of insurrection or rebellion against the United States, or any claim for the loss or emancipation of any slave; but all such debts, obligations and claims shall be held illegal and void.

Section 5

The Congress shall have power to enforce, by appropriate legislation, the provisions of this article.

DOCUMENT 6

The Nation, "The State of the South" (1872)

Northern leaders grew increasingly uncertain about Reconstruction. Particularly alarming to some northerners was the fraud and graft perpetuated by various, mostly white, Reconstruction politicians. Singled out for particular criticism was a group known as carpetbaggers, whites who had moved south to capitalize on a devastated postwar economy. *The Nation,* a weekly political magazine founded in 1865 to voice reform-minded views on politics both North and South, captured the northern sense of frustration with the alleged course of events.

The indolent excuse for our failure to understand the condition of the South is that nobody can very accurately comprehend it who has not been there to see for himself. With regard to troubles of a social character, this excuse is valid; but there are some plain statistical facts recently brought to light and published which it is our duty to recognize and confront. We must acknowledge that the condition of the South from almost every point of view is extremely wretched. The property of the eleven States in 1860, exclusive of slaves, was valued at $2,728,825,006. At the end of the war their increased liabilities and loss, exclusive of slaves, was $1,272,900,390, nearly one-half the assessed value of their property at the beginning of the war. This, however, was only the State loss. Secretary Belknap fixes the rebel debt, on the 1st of April, 1865, at $2,345,297,823. This estimate would make the total loss of the rebellious States by the war $5,262,303,554. This sum, it will be seen, is about twice the assessed value of all Southern property in 1860, exclusive of slaves. Five-eighths of Southern property is gone, and the taxes upon the remainder are four times that upon the original property before the war. How much of the money wrung from this impoverished country is expended upon public improvements, it is difficult to tell; but it is likely that most of it, and certain that much of it, goes to feed the vulgar and rapacious rogues who rob and rule a people helpless and utterly exhausted.

With the exception of Virginia and Tennessee, the debts of all the States have been increased since the end of the war. The near neighborhood of those communities to the Ohio may have had some influence in driving rogues further south. The real reason, however, is the comparative fewness of the negroes. The debt of Alabama in 1866 was $5,000,000; under the rule of the enlightened and disinterested economists who have undertaken to repair her finances, that debt has been increased to $24,000,000. In North Carolina the new government was established in 1868. In 1860, the State debt was $14,000,000; in 1865, $20,000,000; in 1868, $24,000,000; and in 1871, $34,000,000. Thus the increase of debt since the war has been more than twice the increase during the war—which looks as if war were a cheaper and more prosperous condition than peace. At any rate, reconstruction seems to be morally a more disastrous process than rebellion. Guile is the strength of the weak, and the carpet-baggers have taught the Southern people to meet rogues with trickery. The Ku-klux Committee, commenting upon their dreadful poverty at the close of the war, says that manifestly they must have at once succumbed under their loss of $5,000,000,000 had it not been for the benefactions of the North. It states that the Freedmen's Bureau has spent $13,000,000 upon Southern sufferers of both colors. This does not seem a considerable sum when we think that the increased debt since the war in North Carolina has been $14,000,000. Certainly, our charities have done less good than our carpet-baggers have done damage. The theory, of course, is that something remains from the enormous sums raised by taxation, that they have been expended upon needed public improvements. In North Carolina, it was alleged, the large subsidies given to railroads would encourage immigration. There has been no immigration, however; the bonds have been sold at a disadvantage; some of the money has been stolen, and a few of the rogues have been indicted. It is impossible to say how much of the sums raised remain to the States. The carpet-baggers have had it pretty much their own way. If they chose to rob, there was nothing to prevent them. Give men a chance to be tyrants or scamps, and there is no fear that some will not be found who will avail themselves of it. Here in New York, where we have all the rascals and all the plunderers within a radius of five miles, we know how long we have been in bringing the Ring to bay. The carpet-baggers have an immense extent of country to rifle; they do not buy the legislatures, they constitute them; they enact their own registration acts and vote their supplies. The persons they rob are not of that apathetic and well-to-do class too indifferent to go to the polls, but people who could not go if they would.

All accounts agree as to the widespread misery and penury. In Mississippi, a large planter testified that it took all his cotton for the year 1871 to pay his taxes. It is South Carolina, however, that enjoys the unenviable eminence of being the worst-robbed State of the whole eleven. In the single county of Kershaw, possessing a population of only 11,000, there were 3,600 tax-executions issued. The taxation during 1870, $2,365,047, was more than the whole taxation on double the property for five years before the war. In order to change the fiscal year, they proposed to double this, and, in 1871, to levy a tax of $4,730,094; whether this law was executed we do not know, but the fact remains that it was enacted. Peculation and corruption are as universal as poverty and distress. In 1860, South Carolina paid for offices and salaries, $123,800; in 1871, the State expended on these $581,640. In two years, $1,208,577 67 have been paid out, for which no vouchers are to be found in the Treasury. According to the minority report of the Ku-klux Committee, the disbursements exceed the appropriations by $170,683. This report, though spoiled by some rather low allusions to "ebony legislators," "men and brothers," etc., brings to light some amusing facts. Money voted with which to fit up committee-rooms has been expended on the private apartments of the colored members of the legislatures. Their rooms were furnished with Brussels carpets, sofas, mirrors, etc. About seventy-five imported porcelain spittoons, bought for the South Carolina State-House, likewise adorned their private apartments. This fact seemed to affect the democratic minority of the committee even more profoundly than the vast robberies and excessive taxations. They remark, with rugged, Spartan simplicity, that they themselves, in "the splendid capital of the nation," had never had anything but "an article of common, plain brown earthenware, of domestic manufacture." This striking disparity between fortune and desert does not excite in us any feeling of indignation against the negroes. Emerging from a long night of slavery and cruel bondage, who can grudge them their fantastic lease of liberty and luxury? Did not graver considerations check us, our humor would be to vote them State barbers and the most delightful of oriental baths. We suspect the truth to be that in the distribution of spoils the poor African gets the gilt and plush, the porcelain spittoons, the barbaric upholstery, while the astuter Caucasian clings to the soldier and more durable advantages. The negroes by themselves would be but little to be feared; yet, in the hands of the carpet-baggers, they have been the unwitting instruments of most of the harm that has been done. The swindlers could not have so got the control of things without the help of the negroes. They have made numerically the largest part of the conventions and legislatures in South Carolina. The Convention of 1868, which drew up a State constitution, was composed of 72 negroes and 49 white men. This convention made provision for a levy of $2,230,950 upon the State, which would necessitate taxation at the rate of 6 per cent; yet but 13 of the 72 negroes paid taxes. In the Legislature of 1869, there were twelve black and twenty white senators; eight of the twelve black senators paid no taxes. In the House, there were 86 black and 37 white members; 68 of the 86 black members paid no taxes. As things are at present, there seems to be no limit to the power of the carpet-baggers to plunder the South as they choose. The only ray of hope is in the passage of an act of universal amnesty. We have given the negro the ballot to protect him against his old master; we need now to give the white citizen the vote to protect him against the carpet-bagger.

Seven years have gone over us since the close of the war, and, instead of occupying this precious season with endeavors to re-establish prosperity and to sow the seeds of a peace which, in another generation, would ripen into good-will and forgetfulness, we have averted our eyes from the whole problem, refused to listen to the complaints of men whose hands we have tied, and have fallen back upon the lazy belief that in some way this great country is bound to go through. The unconscious syllogism working in the indolent Northern mind seems to be: "Things are no doubt very bad—how bad, we haven't the time or the inclination to ascertain. Examination of such unpleasant matters, if a duty at all, is a disagreeable one. After all, the rebels have made their own bed, and they must lie in it." Perhaps their sufferings are only the just punishment of their crimes; but at any rate, there can be no reason for giving over the criminals into the hands of the carpet-baggers. What services have these persons rendered the country that we should grant them the monopoly of robbing rebels? It would be better to levy tribute-money, and get some national advantage from the merciless exactions inflicted upon the Southern people. Let us make up our minds one way or the other—do we or do we not propose further to punish the rebel States for their rebellion? If we do, let us at once proceed to devise some intelligent means for that purpose. If we do not, let us make haste to protect society from the ravages of ignorance and rapacity, or give society the means to protect itself. We thought it worth four years of war to retain the Southern States in the Union, now we hardly deem it worth an act of Congress to preserve them.

DOCUMENT 7

Albion W. Tourgee, Letter on Ku Klux Klan Activities (1870)

Violence proved an effective weapon for whites seeking to curb black participation in politics and to unseat Republican rule in the South. The Ku Klux Klan, a secret organization with a diverse white membership, perpetrated brutal attacks throughout the South, intimidating blacks and whites alike from publicly voicing their opinions and asserting their rights. Albion Tourgee, a so-called carpetbagger who settled in North Carolina and served as a judge during Reconstruction, vividly describes the Klan's tactics in a letter to the *New York Tribune* in May 1870.

Some of the Outrages—Letter from Judge Tourgee to Senator Abbott

Greensboro, N.C. May 24, 1870.

Gen. Jos. C. Abbott—*My Dear General:* It is my mournful duty to inform you that our friend John W. Stephens, State Senator from Caswell, is dead. He was foully murdered by the Ku-Klux in the Grand Jury room of the Court House on Saturday or Saturday night last. The circumstances attending his murder have not yet fully come to light there. So far as I can learn, I judge these to have been the circumstances: He was one of the Justices of the Peace in that township, and was accustomed to hold court in that room on Saturdays. It is evident that he was set upon by some one while holding this court, or immediately after its close, and disabled by a sudden attack, otherwise there would have been a very sharp resistance, as he was a man, and always went armed to the teeth. He was stabbed five or six times, and then hanged on a hook in the Grand Jury room, where he was found on Sunday morning. Another brave, honest Republican citizen has met his fate at the hands of these fiends. Warned of his danger, and fully cognizant of the terrible risk which surrounded him, he still manfully refused to quit the field. Against the advice of his friends, against the entreaties of his family, he constantly refused to leave those who had stood by him in the day of his disgrace and peril. He was accustomed to say that 3,000 poor, ignorant, colored Republican voters in that county had stood by him and elected him, at the risk of persecution and starvation, and that he had no idea of abandoning them to the Ku-Klux. He was determined to stay with them, and either put an end to these outrages, or die with the other victims of Rebel hate and national apathy: Nearly six months ago I declared my belief that before the election in August next the Ku-Klux would have killed more men in the State than there would be members to be elected to the Legislature. A good beginning has been made toward the fulfillment of this prophecy.

The following counties have already filled, or nearly so, their respective "quotas:" Jones County, quota full, excess 1; Orange County quota full; excess, 1. Caswell County quota full; excess, 2; Alamance County quota full; excess, 1. Chatham County quota nearly full. Or, to state the matter differently, there have been twelve murders in five counties of the district during the past eighteen months, by bands of disguised villains. In addition to this, from the best information I can derive, I am of the opinion that in this district alone there have been 1,000 outrages of a less serious nature perpetrated by the same masked fiends. Of course this estimate is not made from any absolute record, nor is it possible to ascertain with accuracy the entire number of beatings and other outrages which have been perpetrated. The uselessness, the utter futility of complaint from the lack of ability in the laws to punish is fully known to all. The danger of making such complaint is also well understood. It is therefore not unfrequently by accident that the outrage is found out, and unquestionably it is frequently absolutely concealed. Thus, a respectable, hard working white carpenter was working for a neighbor, when accidentally his shirt was torn, and disclosed his back scarred and beaten. The poor fellow begged for the sake of his wife and children that nothing might be said about it, as the Ku-Klux had threatened to kill him if he disclosed how he had been outraged. Hundreds of cases have come to my notice and that of my solicitor....

Men and women come scarred, mangled, and bruised, and say: "The Ku-Klux came to my house last night and beat me almost to death, and my old woman right smart, and shot into the house, 'bust' the door down, and told me they would kill me if I made complaint;" and the bloody mangled forms attest the truth of their declarations. On being asked if any one knew any of the party it will be ascertained that there was no recognition, or only the most uncertain and doubtful one. In such cases as these nothing can be done by the court. We have not been accustomed to enter them on record. A man of the best standing in Chatham told me that

Members of the white supremacist Ku Klux Klan in typical regalia. The Klan was most active during elections, when members terrorized African Americans in an effort to keep them from voting.

he could count up 200 and upward in that county. In Alamance County, a citizen in conversation one evening enumerated upward of 50 cases which had occurred within his own knowledge, and in one section of the county. He gave it as his opinion that there had been 200 cases in that county. I have no idea that he exceeded the proper estimate. That was six months ago, and I am satisfied that another hundred would not cover the work done in that time.

These crimes have been of every character imaginable. Perhaps the most usual has been the dragging of men and women from their beds, and beating their naked bodies with hickory switches, or as witnesses in an examination the other day said, "sticks" between a "switch" and a "club." From 50 to 100 blows is the usual allowance, sometimes 200 and 300 blows are administered. Occasionally an instrument of torture is owned. Thus in one case two women, one 74 years old, were taken out, stripped naked, and beaten with a paddle, with several holes bored through it. The paddle was about 30 inches long, 3 or 4 inches wide, and $1/4$ of an inch thick, of oak. Their bodies were so bruised and beaten that they were sickening to behold. They were white women and of good character until the younger was seduced, and swore her child to its father. Previous to that and so far as others were concerned her character was good.

Again, there is sometimes a fiendish malignity and cunning displayed in the form and character of the outrages. For instance, a colored man was placed astride of a log, and an iron staple driven through his person into the log. In another case, after a band of them had in turn violated a young negro girl, she was forced into bed with a colored man, their bodies were bound together face to face, and the fire from the hearth piled upon them. The K. K. K. rode off and left them, with shouts of laughter. Of course the bed was soon in flames, and somehow they managed to crawl out, though terribly burned and scarred. The house was burned.

I could give other incidents of cruelty, such as hanging up a boy of nine years old until he was nearly dead, to make him tell where his father was hidden, and beating an old negress of 103 years old with garden pallings because she would not own that she was afraid of the Ku-Klux. But it is unnecessary to go into further detail. In this district I estimate their offenses as follows, in the past ten months: Twelve murders, 9 rapes, 11 arsons, 7 mutilations, ascertained and most of them on record. In some no identification could be made.

Four thousand or 5,000 houses have been broken open, and property or persons taken out. In all cases all arms are taken and destroyed. Seven hundred or

800 persons have been beaten or otherwise maltreated. These of course are partly persons living in the houses which were broken into.

And yet the Government sleeps. The poor disarmed nurses of the Republican party—those men by whose ballots the Republican party holds power—who took their lives in their hands when they cast their ballots for U.S. Grant and other officials—all of us who happen to be beyond the pale of the Governmental regard—must be sacrificed, murdered, scourged, mangled, because some contemptible party scheme might be foiled by doing us justice. I could stand it very well to fight for Uncle Sam, and was never known to refuse an invitation on such an occasion; but this lying down, tied hand and foot with the shackles of the law, to be killed by the very dregs of the rebellion, the scum of the earth, and not allowed either the consolation of fighting or the satisfaction that our "fall" will be noted by the Government, and protection given to others thereby, is somewhat too hard. I am ashamed of the nation that will let its citizens be slain by scores, and scourged by thousands, and offer no remedy or protection. I am ashamed of a State which has not sufficient strength to protect its own officers in the discharge of their duties, nor guarantee the safety of any man's domicile throughout its length and breadth. I am ashamed of a party which, with the reins of power in its hands, has not nerve or decision enough to arm its own adherents, or to protect them from assassinations at the hands of their opponents. A General who in time of war would permit 2,000 or 3,000 of his men to be bushwhacked and destroyed by private treachery even in an enemy's country without any one being punished for it would be worthy of universal execration, and would get it, too. How much more worthy of detestation is a Government which in time of peace will permit such wholesale slaughter of its citizens? It is simple cowardice, inertness, and wholesale demoralization. The wholesale slaughter of the war has dulled our Nation's sense of horror at the shedding of blood, and the habit of regarding the South as simply a laboratory, where every demagogue may carry on his reconstructionary experiments at will, and not as an integral party of the Nation itself, has led our our Government to shut its eyes to the atrocities of these times. Unless these evils are speedily remedied, I tell you, General, the Republican party has signed its death warrant. It is a party of cowards or idiots—I don't care which alternative is chosen. The remedy is in our hands, and we are afraid or too dull to bestir ourselves and use it.

But you will tell me that Congress is ready and willing to act if it only knew what to do. Like the old Irish woman it wrings its hands and cries, "O Lawk, O Lawk; if I only knew which way." And yet this same Congress has the control of the militia and can organize its own force in every county in the United States, and arm more or less of it. This same Congress has the undoubted right to guarantee and provide a republican government, and protect every citizen in "life, liberty, and the pursuit of happiness," as well as the power conferred by the XVth Amendment. And yet we suffer and die in peace and murderers walk abroad with the blood yet fresh upon their garments, unharmed, unquestioned and unchecked. Fifty thousand dollars given to good detectives would secure, if well used, a complete knowledge of all this gigantic organization of murderers. In connection with an organized and armed militia, it would result in the apprehension of any number of these Thugs *en masque* and with blood on their hands. What then is the remedy? *First:* Let Congress give to the U. S. Courts, or to Courts of the States under its own laws, cognizance of this class of crimes, as crimes against the nation, and let it provide that this legislation be enforced. Why not, for instance, make going armed and masked or disguised, or masked or disguised in the night time, an act of insurrection or sedition? *Second:* Organize militia, National—State militia is a nuisance—and arm as many as may be necessary in each county to enforce its laws. *Third:* Put detectives at work to get hold of this whole organization. Its ultimate aim is unquestionably to revolutionize the Government. If we have not pluck enough for this, why then let us just offer our throats to the knife, emasculate ourselves, and be a nation of self-subjugated slaves at once.

And now, Abbott, I have but one thing to say to you. I have very little doubt that I shall be one of the next victims. My steps have been dogged for months, and only a good opportunity has been wanting to secure to me the fate which Stephens has just met, and I speak earnestly upon this matter. I feel that I have a right to do so, and a right to be heard as well, and with this conviction I say to you plainly that any member of Congress who, especially if from the South, does not support, advocate, and urge immediate, active, and thorough measures to put an end to these outrages, and make citizenship a privilege, is a coward, a traitor, or a fool. The time for action has come, and the man who has now only speeches to make over some Constitutional scarecrow, deserves to be damned.

DOCUMENT 8

James T. Rapier, Testimony Before U.S. Senate Regarding the Agricultural Labor Force in the South (1880)

As white southern Democrats reclaimed control in state after state, they enacted laws and constitutional provisions that attempted to ensure that blacks could never again compete for political power. State governments severely curtailed their ability to provide the social and educational services necessary for black upward mobility. "Redeemer" governments instead placed emphasis on creating a compliant agricultural labor force that would pose no threat to the wealthy whites who had regained their positions. In testimony given to a U.S. Senate Committee in 1880, James T. Rapier, an African American political leader and one-term congressman from Alabama during Reconstruction, described the results of this process among southern blacks.

A. Well, sir, there are several reasons why the colored people desire to emigrate from Alabama; one among them is the poverty of the South. On a large part of it a man cannot make a decent living. Another is their want of school privileges in the State: and there is a majority of the people who believe that they cannot any longer get justice in the courts; and another and the greatest reason is found in the local laws that we have, and which are very oppressive to that class of people in the black belt.

Q. State what some of them are.—A. First, we have only schools about three months in the year, and I suppose I need not say anything more on that head. In reference to the poverty of the soil, 33 to 40 per cent of the lands in Alabama is about all on which a man can make a living.

Q. Do you mean the parts that are subdued?—A. Yes, sir; the arable land. The average is one-third of a bale of cotton to the acre, not making three bales to the hand; and a hundred bushels of corn to the hand, on an average. Then take the price of cotton for the last two years; it has not netted more than $45 to $47.50 to the bale; and I suppose it would not be amiss for me to state something of the plans of working the land in Alabama.

Mr. Vance. It will be very proper.

The Witness. The general plan is that the landlord furnishes the land and the teams and feed for the teams and the implements, for which he draws one half of the crop. I remarked that the three bales of cotton and a hundred bushels of corn is about all that you can make to a hand. We allow in Alabama that much, for that is as much as a man can get out of it, and that is not enough to support his family, including himself and the feed of his family; $95 to $100 is as much as a hand can make, and that is not enough to feed any man in a Christian country. . . .

A. . . . Now, it is very clear that a man cannot live on such terms, and hence the conclusion of many of these people, that there is not a decent living for them in that State. They are like the white people, and their living no better. Numbers of them, probably not less than 20,000 whites, have left Alabama since the war and gone to Texas to better their condition, and the blacks are doing the same thing, and that is the whole there is of it. So far as the negroes are concerned now they have a high desire to submit their fate to their own keeping in another country. Now here is one of the laws which also affects us, to which I will call attention. It is found in the acts of Alabama for 1878–'79, page 63, act No. 57, section 1.

Section 1. *Be it enacted by the general assembly of Alabama,* That section 4369 of the Code be, and the same is hereby, amended so as to read as follows: Any person who shall buy, sell, receive, barter, or dispose of any cotton, corn, wheat, oats, pease, or potatoes after the hour of sunset and before the hour of sunrise of the next succeeding day, and any person who shall in any manner move, carry, convey, or transport, except within the limits of the farm or plantation on which it is raised or grown, any seed cotton between the hours of sunset and sunrise of the next succeeding day, shall be guilty of a misdemeanor, and, on conviction, shall be fined not less than ten nor more five hundred dollars, and may also be imprisoned in the county jail, or put to hard labor for the county, for not more than twelve months. But this section shall not effect the right of municipal corporations to establish and regulate under their charters public markets within their limits for the sale of commodities for culinary purposes, nor the right of any proprietor or owner of any plantation or premises to sell on such plantation or premises the necessary grain and provisions for the subsistence of man and beast for the night to traveling or transient persons, or for the use of agricultural laborers in his own employment on such plantation or premises: *Provided,* That the provisions of such section shall not apply to any person carrying seed cotton to a gin for the purpose of having the same ginned.

Now, the effect of this upon the labor of the South is this: A great many laborers work by the month, but all of them are under contract. If I live three miles from a store, and I must work from sunup to sundown, I cannot go where I can do my trading to the best advantage. A man is prevented, no matter whether his family is sick from sundown to sunrise, from going and selling anything that he has, as the landlord will not give them time between sunrise and sundown.

Q. What was the purpose of this law?—A. It was, as appears from the debates, to keep the negroes from going to stores and taking off seed cotton from the plantation. Certainly it was to have that effect, but it goes further and prevents a man from selling what he has raised and has a right to sell. If a man commits a crime he ought to be punished, but every man ought to have a right to dispose of his own property.

Q. Is there any particular limitation of time to which this law applies?—A. No, sir.

Q. It runs all the year round?—A. Yes, sir.

Q. After the division of the crops as well as before?—A. Yes, sir; it operates so that a man cannot sell his crop at all in many cases.

Q. Do you say that the landlord will not let him sell his crop or that he can prevent it?—A. I say he will not let him do it, because the landlord will not let him take two or three hours out of the time due him in the day to sell it, and the law prevents him from selling at night.

Q. You say the effect of it is not to let him sell his crop at all?—A. I do; for if a man agrees to work from sunup to sundown he is made to do it. I work them that way myself, and I believe all the rest do....

Q. It shall not be lawful to buy or sell seed cotton?—A. Yes, sir.

Q. At any time?—A. Yes, sir; night or day.

Q. From nobody?—A. From nobody.

Q. White or black?—A. White or black; but you see it applies wholly to black counties.

Q. But there are some white people there, are there not?—A. Yes, sir; but I do not know many who raise seed cotton.

Q. I thought something, may be, was left out of that act?—A. No, sir; that is to say, the gist of the matter is this: I may raise as much cotton as I please in the seed, but I am prohibited by law from selling it to anybody but the landlord, who can buy it because he has advanced to me on the crop. One of the rules is this: I have people working for me to day, but I give them an outside patch. If a man makes outside 1,200 pounds of seed cotton, which is worth $2.50 per 100 pounds, he cannot sell it unless to me. I may say I will give him $1.50 per 100 pounds for it, and he will be forced to take it; but I cannot sell it again unless I have a merchantable bale, which is 500 pounds, or 450 pounds by the cotton congress.

Q. Then the effect of that law is to place all the seed cotton into the hands of the landlord?—A. Yes, sir.

Q. He is the only purchaser who is allowed by law to buy it?—A. Yes, sir; nobody else can buy it....

Q. I thought the law said that grand larceny should consist of as much as $235 worth?—A. No, sir; you have not got it right yet. Two ears or a stalk of corn is a part of an outstanding crop, and any man who sells any part of an outstanding crop can be prosecuted and convicted of grand larceny....

The Witness. The point is this: Under the laws of Alabama the probate judge, the clerk, and the sheriff have had the drawing of jurors, and have had since Alabama was admitted as a State; but this bill comes in and covers those counties where the Republicans are likely to have a majority, and where they would draw the jurors. The proper heading of the law might have been, "An act to keep negroes off the juries." I want to state that it is the general opinion of the colored people in Alabama, and I will say of some of the judges, that it is a difficult matter for a colored man to get justice when there is a case between him and a white man. I will cite one of those cases: There was a case in Montgomery in which Judge J. Q. Smith presided. It was a civil suit. A white man had a black man's crop attached, and he had lost it. The colored man sued him on the attachment bond, and employed Judge Gardiner to defend or prosecute it for him. Soon after the case was given to the jury they brought in a verdict for the defendant. Judge Gardiner moved for a new trial, on the ground that the verdict was not in accordance with the facts; and the judge said, "I have observed that where an issue is between a white and a black man before a jury the verdict is almost invariably against the black man. The grounds on which the judge said he would not grant a new trial would be because he thinks the next verdict would not be different from that rendered, and as I do not think there would be a different verdict, I decline to give the new trial."

Study Questions

1. Did various actors in Reconstruction address one another's concerns, or did they merely advance separate agendas?

2. How did competing perspectives and assumptions divide freed blacks from their presumed allies in the Freedman's Bureau?

3. What assumptions led northerners to believe first that Reconstruction might work and then that it could not succeed?

4. Why did blacks believe that northerners might endorse their efforts to assert their equality?

5. From whose perspective was Reconstruction a failure? From whose perspective could it be seen as a success? Did northern officials adequately comprehend the concerns of either blacks or whites in the South?

2

The West

Through sectional crises, Civil War, and Reconstruction, the vast territories west of the Mississippi River inspired both awe and greed. The annexation of Texas, the expulsion of Mexico from the southwest and California, and negotiations with Great Britain over the Oregon country in the northwest added huge new tracts to the federal domain. But gaining title to these lands was not the same thing as actually settling them or, from the Native American perspective, fully conquering them. The Gold Rush of 1849 lured thousands of eastern immigrants to California, some who thought they would get rich quickly, others to start new lives in a rapidly growing state. That the nation had become a continental empire was not lost on eastern politicians and railroad investors who urgently argued for a fast, dependable overland route connecting East and West (Document 1).

    The aspirations and sacrifices of ordinary people played a central role in westward expansion long before railroads bridged the continent. The difficult overland journey severely taxed the travelers' physical and emotional stamina. To be sure, a few adventurers achieved fame and fortune, but, for many, the great western trek brought crushing disappointment, often a lonely death on the trail itself (Document 2). Moreover, the legendary "frontier justice" of the West did not necessarily produce equitable results and bespoke as much of mob psychology as judicial due process (Document 3).

    The great expanse lying between the Mississippi River and the Pacific coast seemed at first a mere obstacle on a longer journey. Gradually, however, white settlers came to appreciate this territory in its own right as a region affording rich resources for grazing, farming, and mining. Whatever motivated people to remain in this area—the cowboys who roamed the plains, the immigrant workers who built the railroads, and the sod farmers who struggled to make a living—all found themselves subject to market forces beyond their control. The cowboy heroically battling the elements on a cattle drive depended ultimately for his income on processing and sales in the industrial cities of the Northeast and Midwest (Document 4). For their part, Chinese workers who came to America largely in response to a booming demand for railroad laborers combated a hostility born of anti-Asian stereotypes and jealousy of whites who perceived them as an economic threat (Document 5).

    For the Indians of the Far West and Great Plains, white settlement represented disaster. For several decades white expansion westward had led to the killing off of the bison herds central to the economy and culture of many Native Americans. Through a combination of war and treaty, the federal government and Indian groups pursued their conflicting visions of the future of the West. Occasional Indian victories, including the defeat of General George Custer at Little Big Horn in 1876, and negotiations preserving pieces of Indian territory, did not reverse the larger trend of military defeat and additional seizure of land. Desire for gold in the sacred Black Hills of the Dakota territory, like white contempt for the Indian way of life in general, proved stronger than any white promises.

Indeed, whites rationalized their policy to settle the Indians on small tracts of land—known as reservations—as part of the benign and inevitable extension of civilization to the West. Federal officials saw their victory in cultural terms, believing that the Indians' only hope lay in abandoning traditional values in exchange for white ways (Document 6). The Indians themselves defined neither their past nor their future in these terms. To them federal policies betokened broken promises, poverty, and humiliation. Resistance led only to bloody defeat and confirmation of what many already believed: the Indians now occupied native lands at the white man's pleasure (Document 7).

Reflecting on the preceding decades of westward expansion from the vantage point of the 1890s, Americans recognized that they had experienced an extraordinary, perhaps even unique, period of history. The acquisition of huge territories in the name of the United States and the economic development of physical resources in the name of progress came to be regarded as the defining character of American culture, providing essential elements in a story that Americans told themselves about the rise of pioneer democracy. With the final conquest of the frontier, a seemingly triumphant American civilization had to reinvent the sources of its own mythic greatness, a challenge that proved more difficult than anyone then imagined (Document 8).

DOCUMENT 1

Horace Greeley, An Overland Journey (1860)

Horace Greeley, editor of the New York *Tribune* and passionate advocate of westward expansion, toured the West and published his observations in *An Overland Journey, from New York to San Francisco, in the Summer of 1859*. He concluded his book with a passionate argument for a transcontinental railroad to bind the country together. Shortly after this plea, the nation dissolved into Civil War. Nonetheless, congressmen sympathetic to Greeley's view passed legislation during the war such as the Homestead Act to stimulate further migration. Moreover, east and west officially intersected in 1869 when the Union Pacific and Central Pacific rail lines met in Promontory, Utah.

The social, moral, and intellectual blessings of a Pacific railroad can hardly be glanced at within the limits of an article. Suffice it for the present that I merely suggest them.

1. Our mails are now carried to and from California by steamships, via Panama, in twenty to thirty days, starting once a fortnight. The average time of transit from writers throughout the Atlantic states to their correspondents on the Pacific exceeds thirty days. With a Pacific railroad, this would be reduced to ten; for the letters written in Illinois or Michigan would reach their destinations in the mining counties of California quicker than letters sent from New York or Philadelphia would reach San Francisco. With a daily mail by railroad from each of our Atlantic cities to and from California, it is hardly possible that the amount of both letters and printed matter transmitted, and consequently of postage, should not be speedily quadrupled.

2. The first need of California to-day is a large influx of intelligent, capable, virtuous women. With a railroad to the Pacific, avoiding the miseries and perils of six thousand miles of ocean transportation, and making the transit a pleasant and interesting overland journey of ten days, at a reduced cost, the migration of this class would be immensely accelerated and increased. With wages for all kinds of women's work at least thrice as high on the Pacific as in this quarter, and with larger opportunities for honorable and fit settlement in life, I cannot doubt

The race to link the Atlantic and Pacific oceans via railroad ended on May 10, 1869, when the last spike was hammered at Promontory, Utah. Here, workers are shown unloading materials to be carried by freight wagons to Union Pacific track crews.

that tens of thousands would annually cross the Plains, to the signal benefit of California and of the whole country, as well as the improvement of their own fortunes and the profit of the railroad.

3. Thousands now staying in California, expecting to "go home" so soon as they shall have somewhat improved their circumstances, would send or come for their families and settle on the Pacific for life, if a railroad were opened. Tens of thousands who have been to California and come back, unwilling either to live away from their families or to expose them to the present hardships of migration thither, would return with all they have, prepared to spend their remaining days in the land of gold, if there were a Pacific railroad.

4. Education is the vital want of California, second to its need of true women. School-books, and all the material of education, are now scarce and dear there. Almost all books sell there twice as high as here, and many of the best are scarcely attainable at any rate. With the Pacific railroad, all this would be changed for the better. The proportion of school-houses to grogshops would rapidly increase. All the elements of moral and religious melioration would be multiplied. Tens of thousands of our best citizens would visit the Pacific coast, receiving novel ideas and impressions, to their own profit and that of the people thus visited. Civilization, intelligence, refinement, on both sides of the mountain—still more, in the Great Basin inclosed by them—would receive a new and immense impulse, and the Union would acquire a greater accession of strength, power, endurance, and true glory, than it would from the acquisition of the whole continent down to Cape Horn.

The only points of view in which a railroad from the Missouri to the Pacific remains to be considered are those of its practicability, cost, location, and the ways and means. Let us look at them:

I. As to practicability, there is no room for hesitation or doubt. The Massachusetts Western, the Erie, the Pennsylvania, and the Baltimore and Ohio, have each encountered difficulties as formidable as any to be overcome by a Pacific railroad this side of the Sierra Nevada. Were the railroad simply to follow the principal emigrant trail up the Platte and down the Snake and Columbia to Oregon, or south-westwardly from the South Pass to the foot of the Sierra, it would encounter no serious obstacle. . . .

But let that government simply resolve that the Pacific road shall be built—let Congress enact that sealed proposals for its construction shall be invited, and that whichever responsible company or corporation shall offer adequate security for that construction, to be completed within ten years, on the lowest terms, shall have public aid, provided the amount required do not exceed fifty millions of dollars, and the work will be done, certainly for fifty millions' bonus, probably for much less. The government on its part should concede to the company a mile in width, according to the section lines, of the public lands on either side of the road as built, with the right to take timber, stone and earth from any public lands without charge; and should require of said company that it carry a daily through-mail each way at the price paid other roads for conveying mails on first-class routes; and should moreover stipulate for the conveyance at all times of troops, arms, munitions, provisions, etc., for the public service, at the lowest rates, with a right to the exclusive possession and use of the road whenever a national exigency shall seem to require it. The government should leave the choice of route entirely to the company, only stipulating that it shall connect the navigable waters of the Mississippi with those of the Pacific Ocean, and that it shall be constructed wholly through our own territory. . . .

By adopting this plan, the rivalries of routes will be made to work for, instead of working against, the construction of the road. Strenuous efforts will be made by the friends of each to put themselves in position to bid low enough to secure the location; and the lowest rate at which the work can safely be undertaken will unquestionably be bid. The road will be the property of the company constructing it, subject only to the rights of use, stipulated and paid for by the government. And, even were it to cost the latter a bonus of fully fifty millions, I feel certain that every farthing of that large sum will have been reimbursed to the treasury within five years after the completion of the work in the proceeds of land sales, in increased postages, and in duties on goods imported, sold, and consumed because of this railroad—not to speak of the annual saving of millions in the cost of transporting and supplying troops.

Men and brethen! let us resolve to have a railroad to the Pacific—to have it soon. It will add more to the strength and wealth of our country than would the acquisition of a dozen Cubas. It will prove a bond of union not easily broken, and a new spring to our national industry, prosperity and wealth. It will call new manufactures into existence, and increase the demand for the products of those already existing. It will open new vistas to national and to individual aspiration, and crush out filibusterism by giving a new and wholesome direction to the public mind. My long, fatiguing journey was undertaken in the hope that I might do something toward the early construction of the Pacific Railroad; and I trust that it has not been made wholly in vain.

DOCUMENT 2

Lydia Allen Rudd, Diary of Westward Travel (1852)

Aspirations for a better life in the West often met with the harsh realities of both the journey and the ultimate destination. In the following passages excerpted from her diary, Lydia Allen Rudd records six months of travel by wagon to Oregon.

May 6 1852 Left the Missouri river for our long journey across the wild uncultivated plains and unhabitated except by the red man. As we left the river bottom and ascended the bluffs the view from them was handsome! In front of us as far as vision could reach extended the green hills covered with fine grass. . . . Behind us lay the Missouri with its muddy water hurrying past as if in great haste to reach some destined point ahead all unheeding the impatient emigrants on the opposite shore at the ferrying which arrived faster than they could be conveyed over. About half a miles down the river lay a steamboat stuck fast on a sandbar. Still farther down lay the busy village of St. Joseph looking us a good bye and reminding us that we were leaving all signs of civilised life for the present. But with good courage and not one sigh of regret I mounted my pony (whose name by the way is Samy) and rode slowly on. In going some two miles, the scene changed from bright sunshine to drenching showers of rain this was not quite agreeable for in spite of our good blankets and intentions otherwise we got some wet. The rain detained us so that we have not made but ten miles today. . . .

May 7 I found myself this morning with a severe headache from the effects of yesterday's rain. . . .

There is a toll bridge across this stream kept by the Indians. The toll for our team in total was six bits. We have had some calls this evening from the Indians. We gave them something to eat and they left. Some of them [had] on no shirt only a blanket, whiles others were ornamented in Indian style with their faces painted in spots and stripes feathers and fur on their heads beeds on their neck brass rings on their wrists and arms and in their ears armed with rifles and spears.

May 8 . . . We have come about 12 miles and were obliged to camp in the open prairie without any wood. Mary and myself collected some dry weeds and grass and made a little fire and cooked some meat and the last of our supply of eggs with these and some hard bread with water we made our supper.

May 9 . . . We passed a new made grave today . . . a man from Ohio We also met a man that was going back: he had buried his Wife this morning She died from the effects of measels we have come ten miles today encamped on a small stream called Vermillion creek Wood and water plenty Their are as many as fifty waggons on this stream and some thousand head of stock It looks like a village the tents and waggons extend as much as a mile. . . .

Some are singing some talking and some laughing and the cattle are adding their mite by shaking their bells and grunt[ing]. Mosquitoes are intruding their unwelcome presence. Harry says that I must not sit here any longer writing but go to bed for I will not want to get up early in the morning to get breakfast.

Moving West was a grueling and perilous journey, but the promise of the West outweighed the risks for many people. The Homestead Act, passed by Congress in 1862, granted 160 acres of public land in the West to anyone willing to pay a small filing fee and cultivate the land for five years.

May 10 I got up this morning and got breakfast and before sunrise we had eat in spite of Harry's prophecies to the contrary. . . .

May 11 We had a very heavy fog this morning which cleared up about noon. Our men are not any of them very well this morning. We passed another grave to day which was made this morning. The board stated that he died of cholera. He was from Indiana. We met several that had taken the back track for the states homesick I presume let them go. We have passed through a handsome country and have encamped on the Nimehaw river, the most beautiful spot that ever I saw in my life. I would like to live here. As far as the eye can reach either way lay handsome rolling prairies, not a stone a tree nor a bush even nothing but grass and flowers meets the eye until you reach the valley of the river which is as level as the house floor and about half a mile wide, where on the bank of the stream for two or three rods wide is one of the heaviest belts of timber I ever saw covered with thick foliage so thick that you could not get a glimpse of the stream through it. You can see this belt of timber for three or four miles from the hills on both sides winding through the prairie like some huge snake. We have traveled twelve miles. . . .

May 12 . . . Our men not much better.

May 13 . . . Henry has been no better to day. Soon after we stopped to night a man came along with a wheel barrow going to California: he is a dutchmann. He wheels his provisions and clothing all day and then stops where night overtakes him sleeps on the ground in the open air. He eats raw meat and bread for his supper. I think that he will get tired wheeling his way through the world by the time he gets to California.

May 14 Just after we started this morning we passed four men dig[g]ing a grave. They were packers. The man that had died was taken sick yesterday noon and died last night. They called it cholera morbus. The corpse lay on the ground a few feet from where they were dig[g]ing. The grave it was a sad sight. . . .

On the bank of the stream waiting to cross, stood a dray with five men harnessed to it bound for California. They must be some of the persevering kind I think. Wanting to go to California more than I do. . . . We passed three more graves this afternoon. . . .

Sept. 5 Traveled eighteen miles today encamped on a slough of powder river poor camp not much grass water nor wood. I am almost dead tonight. I have been sick two or three days with the bowel complaint and am much worse tonight.

Sept. 6 We have not been able to leave this miserable place today. I am not as well as yesterday and no physician to be had. We got a little medicine from a train tonight that has checked the disease some, the first thing that has done me any good.

Sept. 7 . . . I am some better today so much so that they ventured to move me this for the sake of a better camp. Mrs. Girtman is also sick with the same disease. Our cattle are most all of them ailing—there are two more that we expect will die every day. . . .

Oct. 8 started early this morning without any breakfast for the very good reason that we had nothing to eat   still three miles from the falls safely landed about eight o'clock tired hungry and with a severe cold from last nights exposure something like civilization here in the shape of three or four houses there is an excuse here for a railroad of a mile and half on which to convey bag[g]age below the falls where they can again take water for the steamboat landing. Harry packed our bag[g]age down the railroad and the rest of us walked   the car is drawn across the railroad by a mule and they will car[r]y no persons but sick. We again hired an Indian with his canoe to take us from the falls to the steamboat landing   ar[r]ived about sundown a great many emigrants waiting for a chance to leave the steamboat and several flat boats lying ready to start out in the morning encamped on the shore for the night.

October 9–October 13 . . .

October 14 . . . I am so anxious to get some place to stop and settle that my patience is not worth much.

October 15–18 . . .

October 19 . . . We have had a very bad day today for traveling   it has rained nearly all the time and it has rained very hard some of the time and we have had a miserable road the rain has made the hills very slippery and had to get up and down we have made but eleven miles of travel encamped on the prairie no water for our stock and not much for ourselves.

October 21 . . .

October 22 . . . Traveled three miles this morning and reached the village of Salem it is quite a pretty town a much handsomer place than Oregon City and larger. . . .

I am afraid that we shall be obliged to pack from here the rest of our journey and it will be a wet job another wet rainy day I am afraid that the rain will make us all sick. I am already begin to feel the affects of it by a bad cold.

October 23 . . . We cannot get any wagon to take us on our journey and are obliged to pack the rest of the way Mr. Clark and wife have found a house to live in and employment for the winter and they will stop here in Salem It took us until nearly noon to get our packs fixed for packing went about two miles and it rained so fast that we were obliged to stop got our dinner and supper in one meal cooked in a small cabin ignorant people but kind started again just

October 24–25 . . .

October 26 . . . we reached Burlington about two o'clock. There is one store one blacksmith shop and three or four dwelling houses. We encamped close by found Mr. Donals in his store an old acquaintance of my husband's. I do not know what we shall yet conclude on doing for the winter. There is no house in town that we can get to winter in. We shall probably stay here tomorrow and by the time know what we are to do for a while at least.

October 27 . . . Our men have been looking around for a house and employment and have been successful for which I feel very thankful. Harry has gone into copartnership with Mr. Donals in the mercantile business and we are to live in the back part of the store for this winter. Henry and Mary are going into Mr. D———house on his farm for the winter one mile from here. Mr. D———will also find him employment if he wants. I expect that we shall not make a claim after all our trouble in getting here on purpose for one. I shall have to be poor and dependent on a man my life time.

DOCUMENT 3

Edward Gould Buffum, Six Months in the Gold Mines *(1850)*

Edward Gould Buffum, originally from New York, published an account of life in and around the gold mines after spending three years in California. He commented with dismay on the manner in which three accused robbers—two from France, the other from Chile—met their death after a disgruntled throng rendered its verdict.

A scene occurred about this time that exhibits in a striking light, the summary manner in which "justice" is dispensed in a community where there are no legal tribunals. We received a report on the afternoon of January 20th, that five men had been arrested at the dry diggings, and were under trial for a robbery. The circumstances were these:—A Mexican gambler, named Lopez, having in his possession a large amount of money, retired to his room at night, and was surprised about midnight by five men rushing into his apartment, one of whom applied a pistol to his head, while the others barred the door and proceeded to rifle his trunk. An alarm being given, some of the citizens rushed in, and arrested the whole party. Next day they were tried by a jury chosen from among the citizens, and sentenced to receive thirty-nine lashes each, on the following morning. Never having witnessed a punishment inflicted by Lynch-law, I went over to the dry diggings on a clear Sunday morning, and on my arrival, found a large crowd collected around an oak tree, to which was lashed a man with a bared back, while another was applying a raw cowhide to his already gored flesh. A guard of a dozen men, with loaded rifles pointed at the prisoners, stood ready to fire in case of an attempt being made to escape. After the whole had been flogged, some fresh charges were preferred against three of the men—two Frenchmen, named Garcia and Bissi, and a Chileno, named Manuel. These were charged with a robbery and attempt to murder, on the Stanislaus River, during the previous fall. The unhappy men were removed to a neighbouring house, and being so weak from their punishment as to be unable to stand, were laid stretched upon the floor. As it was not possible for them to attend, they were tried in the open air, in their absence, by a crowd of some two hundred men, who had organized themselves into a jury, and appointed a *pro tempore* judge. The charges against them were well substantiated, but amounted to nothing more than an attempt at robbery and murder; no overt act being even alleged. They were known to be bad men, however, and a general sentiment seemed to prevail in the crowd that they ought to be got rid of. At the close of the trial, which lasted some thirty minutes, the Judge put to vote the question whether they had been proved guilty. A universal affirmative was the response; and then the question "What punishment shall be inflicted?" was asked. A brutal-looking fellow in the crowd, cried out, "Hang them." The proposition was seconded, and met with almost universal approbation. I mounted a stump, and in the name of God, humanity, and law, protested against such a course of proceeding; but the crowd, by this time excited by frequent and deep potations of liquor from a neighbouring groggery, would listen to nothing contrary to their brutal desires, and even threatened to hang me if I did not immediately desist from any further remarks. Somewhat fearful that such might be my fate, and seeing the utter uselessness of further argument with them, I ceased, and prepared to witness the horrible tragedy. Thirty minutes only were allowed the unhappy victims to prepare themselves to enter on the scenes of eternity. Three ropes were procured, and attached to the limb of a tree. The prisoners were marched out, placed upon a wagon, and the ropes put round their necks. No time was given them for explanation. They vainly tried to speak, but none of them understanding English, there were obliged to employ their native tongues, which but few of those assembled understood. Vainly they called for an interpreter, for their cries were drowned by the yells of a now infuriated mob. A black handkerchief was bound around the eyes of each; their arms were pinioned, and at a given signal, without priest or prayer-book, the wagon was drawn from under them, and they were launched into eternity. Their graves were dug ready to receive them, and when life was entirely extinct, they were cut down and buried in their blankets. This was the first execution I ever witnessed.—God grant that it may be the last!

DOCUMENT 4

Joseph G. McCoy, Historic Sketches of the Cattle Trade of the West and Southwest (1874)

One of the most enduring images of the West is of the cowboys riding herds of cattle across the plains. The ultimate destination of the stock was often the slaughterhouses of cities such as Chicago or Kansas City, which in turn processed the meat for consumption in towns across the nation. Joseph G. McCoy, one of the first entrepreneurs to appreciate the potential of the long-distance cattle drive, described aspects of the cowboy experience in the following selection from an 1874 publication.

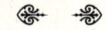

We left the herd fairly started upon the trail for the northern market. Of these trails there are several: one leading to Baxter Springs and Chetopa; another called the "Old Shawnee trail," leaving Red river and running eastward, crossing the Arkansas not far above Fort Gibson, thence bending westward up the Arkansas river. But the principal trail now traveled is more direct and is known as "Chisholm trail," so named from a semicivilized Indian who is said to have traveled it first. It is more direct, has more prairie, less timber, more small streams and less large ones, and altogether better grass and fewer flies (no civilized Indian tax or wild Indian disturbances) than any other route yet driven over, and is also much shorter in distance because direct from Red river to Kansas. Twenty-five to thirty-five days is the usual time required to bring a drove from Red river to the southern line of Kansas, a distance of between two hundred and fifty and three hundred miles, and an excellent country to drive over. So many cattle have been driven over the trail in the last few years that a broad highway is tread out, looking much like a national highway; so plain, a fool could not fail to keep in it. . . .

Few occupations are more cheerful, lively, and pleasant than that of the cowboy on a fine day or night; but when the storm comes, then is his manhood and often his skill and bravery put to test. When the night is inky dark and the lurid lightning flashes its zigzag course athwart the heavens, and the coarse thunder jars the earth, the winds moan fresh and lively over the prairie, the electric balls dance from tip to tip of the cattle's horns—then the position of the cowboy on duty is trying, far more than romantic. When the storm breaks over his head, the least occurrence unusual, such as the breaking of a dry weed or stick, or a sudden and near flash of lightning, will start the herd as if by magic, all at an instant, upon a wild rush, and woe to the horse or man or camp that may be in their path. The only possible show for safety is to mount and ride with them until you can get outside the stampeding column. It is customary to train cattle to listen to the noise of the herder, who sings in a voice more sonorous than musical a lullaby consisting of a few short monosyllables. A stranger to the business of stock driving will scarce credit the statement that the wildest herd will not run, so long as they can hear distinctly the voice of the herder above the din of the storm.

But if by any mishap the herd gets off on a real stampede, it is by bold, dashing, reckless riding in the darkest of nights, and by adroit, skillful management that it is checked and brought under control.

The moment the herd is off, the cowboy turns his horse at full speed down the retreating column and seeks to get up beside the leaders, which he does not attempt to stop suddenly, for such an effort would be futile, but turns them to the left or right hand and gradually curves them into a circle, the circumference of which is narrowed down as fast as possible until the whole herd is rushing wildly round and round on as small a piece of ground as possible for them to occupy. Then the cowboy begins his lullaby note in a loud voice, which has a great effect in quieting the herd. When all is still and the herd well over its scare, they are returned to their bed ground, or held where stopped until daylight. . . .

After a drive of twenty-five to one hundred days the herd arrives in western Kansas, whither, in advance, its owner has come, and decided what point at which he will make his headquarters. Straightway a good herding place is sought out, and the herd, upon its arrival, placed thereon, to remain until a buyer is found, who is dilligently sought after; but if not found as soon as the cattle are fat, they are shipped to market. But the drover has a decided preference for selling on the prairie, for there he feels at home and self-possessed; but when he goes on the cars he is out of his element and doing something he doesn't understand much about and doesn't wish to learn, especially at the price it has cost many cattle shippers. . . .

We have in a former paper said that Texan drovers, as a class, were clannish, and easily gulled by promises of high prices for their stock. As an illustration of these statements we cite a certain secret meeting of the drovers held at one of the camps in 1867, whereat they all, after talking the matter over, pledged themselves to hold their cattle for 3 cents per pound gross and to sell none for less. One of the principal arguments used was that their cattle must be worth that price or those Illinoisans would not be expending so much money and labor in preparing facilities for shipping them. To this resolution they adhered persistently, refusing $2.75 per 100 pounds for fully 10,000 head; and afterwards, failing to get their 3 cents on the prairie for their cattle, shipped them to Chicago on their own account and sold them there at $2.25 to $2.50 per 100 pounds; and out of that paid a freight of $150 per car, realizing from $10 to $15 per head less than they had haughtily refused upon the prairie. Some of them refused to accept these prices and packed their cattle upon their own account. Their disappointment and chagrin at their failure to force a buyer to pay 3 cents per pound for their cattle was great and bitter, but their refusal to accept the offer of $2^3/4$ cents per pound was great good fortune to the would-be buyers, for at that price $100,000 would have been lost on 10,000 head of cattle. An attempt was made the following year to form a combination to put up prices; but a burnt child dreads the fire, and the attempted combination failed, and every drover looked out sharply for himself.

Now one instance touching their susceptibility to being gulled by fine promises. In the fall of 1867, when Texan cattle were selling at from $24 to $28 per head in Chicago, a well-dressed, smooth-tongued individual put in an appearance at Abilene and claimed to be the representative of a certain (bogus) packing company of Chicago, and was desirous of purchasing several thousand head of cattle. He would pay Chicago prices at Abilene or, rather than be particular, $5 or $10 per head more than the same cattle would sell for in Chicago. It was astonishing to see how eagerly certain drovers fell into his trap and bargained their cattle off to him at $35 per head at Abilene, fully $15 more than they would pay out. But, mark you, the buyer, so "childlike and bland," could only pay the little sum of $25 down on 400 to 800 head, but would pay the balance when he got to Leavenworth with the cattle, he being afraid to bring his wealth up in that wild country. In the meantime they would load the cattle on the cars, bill them in the name of the buyer, and of course everything would be all right. Strange as it may appear, several of the hitherto most suspicious drovers of 1867 fell in with this swindler's scheme; and were actually about to let him ship their herds off on a mere verbal promise, when the parties in charge of the yards, seeing that the drovers were about to be defrauded out of their stock, posted them to have the cattle billed in their own name, and then, if the pay was not forthcoming, they would have possession of their own stock without troublesome litigation, as every man of sense anticipated they would have. When the swindler, after various excuses for his failures to pay at Leavenworth, Quincy, and Chicago (all the while trying to get the cattle into his own hands) found that he must come down with the cash, he very plainly told the Texan to go to Hades with his cattle. Instead of obeying this warm parting injunction of his newfound, high-priced buyer, he turned his cattle over to a regular commission man and received about $26 per head at Chicago less freight charges, or almost $18 per head at Abilene instead of $35 per head.

DOCUMENT 5

Memorial of the Chinese Six Companies to U.S. Grant, President of the United States (1876)

Thousands of Chinese came to the United States to satisfy the demand for railroad laborers and mineworkers. They became the focus of hatred by nativists and white workers fearing competition. Leaders of the San Francisco Chinese community protested racist propaganda and riots in a letter to President Ulysses Grant. Hostility toward these Asian immigrants led to the Federal Chinese Exclusion Act of 1882, which cut off any further immigration for a decade.

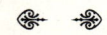

To His Excellency U. S. Grant, President of the United States of America

Sir: In the absence of any Consular representative, we, the undersigned, in the name and in behalf of the Chinese people now in America, would most respectfully present for your consideration the following statements regarding the subject of Chinese emigration to this country:

We understand that it has always been the settled policy of your honorable Government to welcome emigration to your shores from all countries, without let or hindrance. The Chinese are not the only people who have crossed the ocean to seek a residence in this land. . . .

American steamers, subsidized by your honorable Government, have visited the ports of China, and invited our people to come to this country to find employment and improve their condition. Our people have been coming to this country for the last twenty-five years, but up to the present time there are only 150,000 Chinese in all these United States. 60,000 of whom are in California, and 30,000 in the city of San Francisco.

Our people in this country, for the most part, have been peaceable, law-abiding, and industrious. They performed the largest part of the unskilled labor in the construction of the Central Pacific Railroad, and also of all other railroads on this coast. They have found useful and remunerative employment in all the manufacturing establishments of this coast, in agricultural pursuits, and in family service. While benefiting themselves with the honest reward of their daily toil, they have given satisfaction to their employers and have left all the results of their industry to enrich the State. They have not displaced white laborers from these positions, but have simply multiplied the industrial enterprises of the country.

The Chinese have neither attempted nor desired to interfere with the established order of things in this country, either of politics or religion. They have opened no whiskey saloons for the purpose of dealing out poison and degrading their fellow-men. They have promptly paid their duties, their taxes, their rents, and their debts.

It has often occurred, about the time of the State and general elections, that political agitators have stirred up the minds of the people in hostility to the Chinese, but formerly the hostility has usually subsided after the elections were over.

At the present time an intense excitement and bitter hostility against the Chinese in this land, and against further Chinese emigration, has been created in the minds of the people, led on by His Honor the Mayor of San Francisco and his associates in office, and approved by His Excellency the Governor, and other great men of the State. These great men gathered some 20,000 of the people of this city together on the evening of April 5, and adopted an address and resolutions against Chinese emigration. They have since appointed three men (one of whom we understand to be the author of the address and resolutions) to carry that address and those resolutions to your Excellency, and to present further objections, if possible, against the emigration of the Chinese to this country.

It is charged against us that not one virtuous Chinawoman has been brought to this country, and that here we have no wives nor children. The fact is, that already a few hundred Chinese families have been brought here. These are all chaste, pure, keepers-at-home, not known on the public street. There are also among us a few hundred, perhaps a thousand, Chinese children born in America. The reason why so few of our families are brought to this country is because it is contrary to the custom and against the inclination of virtuous Chinese women to go so far from home, and because the frequent outbursts of popular indignation against our people have not encouraged us to bring our families with us against their will. . . .

It is charged against us that we have purchased no real estate. The general tone of public sentiment has not been such as to encourage us to invest in real estate, and yet our people have purchased and now own over $800,000 worth of real estate in San Francisco alone.

It is charged against us that we eat rice, fish, and vegetables. It is true that our diet is slightly different from the people of this honorable country; our tastes in these matters are not exactly alike, and cannot be forced. But is that a sin on our part of sufficient gravity to be brought before the President and Congress of the United States?

It is charged that the Chinese are no benefit to this country. Are the railroads built by Chinese labor no benefit to the country? Are the manufacturing establishments, largely worked by Chinese, no benefit to this country? Do not the results of the daily toil of a hundred thousand men increase the riches of this country? Is it no benefit to this country that the Chinese annually pay over $2,000,000 duties at the Custom house of San Francisco? Is not the $200,000 annual poll-tax paid by the Chinese any benefit? And are not the hundreds of thousands of dollars taxes on personal property, and the foreign miners' tax, annually paid to the revenues of this country, any benefit? . . .

It is charged that all Chinese laboring men are slaves. This is not true in a single instance. Chinamen labor for bread. They pursue all kinds of industries for a livelihood. Is it so then that every man laboring for his livelihood is a slave? If these men are slaves, then all men laboring for wages are slaves.

It is charged that the Chinese commerce brings no benefit to American bankers and importers. But the fact is that an immense trade is carried on between China and the United States by American merchants, and all the carrying business of both countries, whether by steamers, sailing vessels or railroads, is done by Americans. No China ships are engaged in the carrying traffic between the two countries. Is it a sin to be charged against us that the Chinese merchants are able to conduct their mercantile business on their own capital? And is not the exchange of millions of dollars annually by the Chinese with the banks of this city any benefit to the banks?

We respectfully ask a careful consideration of all the foregoing statements. The Chinese are not the only people, nor do they bring the only evils that now afflict this country.

DOCUMENT 6

Congressional Report on Indian Affairs (1887)

The federal government sought to force Indians into a sedentary way of life on limited parcels of land known as reservations. The stated goal of such a policy was to compel the Indians to assimilate to the culture and politics of the United States. As the secretary of the interior's 1887 report to Congress made clear, requiring the Indians to forsake tribal languages for English was a key ingredient in the government's strategy.

Longer and closer consideration of the subject has only deepened my conviction that it is a matter not only of importance, but of necessity that the Indians acquire the English language as rapidly as possible. The Government has entered upon the great work of educating and citizenizing the Indians and establishing them upon homesteads. The adults are expected to assume the role of citizens, and of course the rising generation will be expected and required more nearly to fill the measure of citizenship, and the main purpose of educating them is to enable them to read, write, and speak the English language and to transact business with English-speaking people. When they take upon themselves the responsibilities and privileges of citizenship their vernacular will be of no advantage. Only through the medium of the English tongue can they acquire a knowledge of the Constitution of the country and their rights and duties thereunder.

Every nation is jealous of its own language, and no nation ought to be more so than ours, which approaches nearer than any other nationality to the perfect protection of its people. True Americans all feel that the Constitution, laws, and institutions of the United States, in their adaptation to the wants and requirements of man, are superior to those of any other country; and they should understand that by the spread of the English language will these laws and institutions be more firmly established and widely disseminated. Nothing so surely and perfectly stamps upon an individual a national characteristic as language. So manifest and important is this that nations the world over, in both ancient and modern times, have ever imposed the strictest requirements upon their public schools as to the teaching of the national tongue. Only English has been allowed to be taught in the public schools in the territory acquired by this country from Spain, Mexico, and Russia, although the native populations spoke another tongue. All are familiar with the recent prohibitory order of the German Empire forbidding the teaching of the French language in either public or private schools in Alsace and Lorraine. Although the population is almost universally opposed to German rule, they are firmly held to German political allegiance by the military hand of the Iron Chancellor. If the Indians were in Germany or France or any other civilized country, they should be instructed in the language there used. As they are in an English-speaking country, they must be taught the language which they must use in transacting business with the people of this country. No unity or community of feeling can be established among different people unless they are brought to speak the same language, and thus become imbued with the like ideas of duty.

Deeming it for the very best interest of the Indian, both as an individual and as an embryo citizen, to have this policy strictly enforced among the various schools on Indian reservations, orders have been issued accordingly to Indian agents. . . .

It is believed that if any Indian vernacular is allowed to be taught by the missionaries in schools on Indian reservations, it will prejudice the youthful pupil as well as his untutored and uncivilized or semicivilized parent against the English language, and, to some extent at least, against Government schools in which the English language exclusively has always been taught. To teach Indian school children their native tongue is practically to ex-

There were more than five million Native Americans in the United States in 1492, but by 1900 those numbers had been reduced to 250,000. One of the most devastating blows for Native Americans was the destruction of the buffalo upon which they were dependent. Buffalo had numbered perhaps fifteen million in 1865 and were almost entirely gone by 1883.

clude English, and to prevent them from acquiring it. This language, which is good enough for a white man and a black man, ought to be good enough for the red man. It is also believed that teaching an Indian youth in his own barbarous dialect is a positive detriment to him. The first step to be taken toward civilization, toward teaching the Indians the mischief and folly of continuing in their barbarous practices, is to teach them the English language. The impracticability, if not impossibility, of civilizing the Indians of this country in any other tongue than our own would seem to be obvious, especially in view of the fact that the number of Indian vernaculars is even greater than the number of tribes. Bands of the same tribes inhabiting different localities have different dialects, and sometimes can not communicate with each other except by the sign language. If we expect to infuse into the rising generation the leaven of American citizenship, we must remove the stumbling blocks of hereditary customs and manners, and of these language is one of the most important elements. . . .

But it has been suggested that this order, being mandatory, gives a cruel blow to the sacred rights of the Indians. Is it cruelty to the Indian to force him to give up his scalping-knife and tomahawk? Is it cruelty to force him to abandon the vicious and barbarous sun dance, where he lacerates his flesh, and dances and tortures himself even unto death? Is it cruelty to the Indian to force him to have his daughters educated and married under the laws of the land, instead of selling them at a tender age for a stipulated price into concubinage to gratify the brutal lusts of ignorance and barbarism?

Having been governed in my action solely by what I believed to be the real interests of the Indians, I have been gratified to receive from eminent educators and missionaries the strongest assurance of their hearty and full concurrence in the propriety and necessity of the order.

DOCUMENT 7

Tragedy at Wounded Knee (1890)

Some Indian leaders resisted the federal government's policies attempting to transform their peoples into self-sufficient farmers. Spurred by desperate hopes of reversing their prospects, a group of Sioux left their reservation. When federal soldiers attempted to take away the weapons of an Indian group at Wounded Knee Creek, South Dakota, bloody tragedy ensued. M. I. McCreight published a speech by Red Cloud and recollections of Flying Hawk in 1936, describing the events surrounding the massacre.

Red Cloud's Speech

I will tell you the reason for the trouble. When we first made treaties with the Government, our old life and our old customs were about to end; the game on which we lived was disappearing; the whites were closing around us, and nothing remained for us but to adopt their ways,—the Government promised us all the means necessary to make our living out of the land, and to instruct us how to do it, and with abundant food to support us until we could take care of ourselves. We looked forward with hope to the time we could be as independent as the whites, and have a voice in the Government.

The army officers could have helped better than anyone else but we were not left to them. An Indian Department was made with a large number of agents and other officials drawing large salaries—then came the beginning of trouble; these men took care of themselves but not of us. It was very hard to deal with the government through them—they could make more for themselves by keeping us back than by helping us forward.

We did not get the means for working our lands; the few things they gave us did little good.

Our rations began to be reduced; they said we were lazy. That is false. How does any man of sense suppose that so great a number of people could get work at once unless they were at once supplied with the means to work and instructors enough to teach them?

Our ponies were taken away from us under the promise that they would be replaced by oxen and large horses; it was long before we saw any, and then we got very few. We tried with the means we had, but on one pretext or another, we were shifted from one place to another, or were told that such a transfer was coming. Great efforts were made to break up our customs, but nothing was done to introduce us to customs of the whites. Everything was done to break up the power of the real chiefs.

Those old men really wished their people to improve, but little men, so-called chiefs, were made to act as disturbers and agitators. Spotted Tail wanted the ways of the whites, but an assassin was found to remove him. This was charged to the Indians because an Indian did it, but who set on the Indian? I was abused and slandered, to weaken my influence for good. This was done by men paid by the government to teach us the ways of the whites. I have visited many other tribes and found that the same things were done amongst them; all was done to discourage us and nothing to encourage us. I saw men paid by the government to help us, all very busy making money for themselves, but doing nothing for us. . . .

The men who counted (census) told all around that we were feasting and wasting food. Where did he see it? How could we waste what we did not have? We felt we were mocked in our misery; we had no newspaper and no one to speak for us. Our rations were again reduced.

You who eat three times a day and see your children well and happy around you cannot understand what a starving Indian feels! We were faint with hunger and maddened by despair. We held our dying children and felt their little bodies tremble as their soul went out and left only a dead weight in our hands. They were not very heavy but we were faint and the dead weighed us down. There was no hope on earth. God seemed to have forgotten.

Some one had been talking of the Son of God and said He had come. The people did not know; they did not care; they snatched at hope; they screamed like crazy people to Him for mercy they caught at the promise they heard He had made.

The white men were frightened and called for soldiers. We begged for life and the white men thought we wanted theirs; we heard the soldiers were coming. We did not fear. We hoped we could tell them our suffering and could get help. The white men told us the soldiers meant to kill us; we did not believe it but some were frightened and ran away to the Bad Lands. The soldiers came. They said: "don't be afraid—we come to make peace, not war." It was true; they brought us food. But the hunger-crazed who had taken fright at the soldiers' coming and went to the Bad Lands could not be induced to return to the horrors of reservation life. They were called Hostiles and the Government sent the army to force them back to their reservation prison.

Flying Hawk's Recollections of Wounded Knee (1936)

This was the last big trouble with the Indians and soldiers and was in the winter in 1890. When the Indians would not come in from the Bad Lands, they got a big army together with plenty of clothing and supplies and camp-and-wagon equipment for a big campaign; they had enough soldiers to make a round-up of all the Indians they called hostiles.

The Government army, after many fights and loss of lives, succeeded in driving these starving Indians, with their families of women and gaunt-faced children, into a trap, where they could be forced to surrender their arms. This was on Wounded Knee creek, northeast of Pine Ridge, and here the Indians were surrounded by the soldiers, who had Hotchkiss machine guns along with them. There were about four thousand Indians in this big camp, and the soldiers had the machine guns pointed at them from all around the village as the soldiers formed a ring about the tepees so that Indians could not escape.

The Indians were hungry and weak and they suffered from lack of clothing and furs because the whites had driven away all the game. When the soldiers had them all surrounded and they had their tepees set up, the officers sent troopers to each of them to search for guns and take them from the owners. If the Indians in the tepees did not at once hand over a gun, the soldier tore open their parfleech trunks and bundles and bags of robes or clothes,—looking for pistols and knives and ammunition. It was an ugly business, and brutal; they treated the Indians like they would torment a wolf with one foot in a strong trap; they could do this because the Indians were now in the white man's trap,—and they were helpless.

Then a shot was heard from among the Indian tepees. An Indian was blamed; the excitement began; soldiers ran to their stations; officers gave orders to open fire with the machine guns into the crowds of innocent men, women and children, and in a few minutes more than two hundred and twenty of them lay in the snow dead and dying. A terrible blizzard raged for two days covering the bodies with Nature's great white blanket; some lay in piles of four or five; others in twos or threes or singly, where they fell until the storm subsided. When a trench had been dug of sufficient length and depth to contain the frozen corpses, they were collected and piled, like cord-wood, in one vast icy tomb. While separating several stiffened forms which had fallen in a heap, two of them proved to be women, and hugged closely to their breasts were infant babes still alive after lying in the storm for two days in 20° below zero weather.

I was there and saw the trouble,—but after the shooting was over; it was all bad.

DOCUMENT 8

Frederick Jackson Turner, "The Significance of the Frontier in American History" (1893)

Professor Frederick Jackson Turner delivered what may have been the most important address ever given by an academic historian. The federal census of 1890 indicated to Turner that after almost three hundred years of European settlement, the American frontier had finally closed. It was a critical moment in the national culture for, as Turner argued so persuasively, Americans had come to view the frontier as a source of democracy. Turner's frontier was as much a mythic concept as an actual space, and its closing represented a major challenge to how Americans perceived themselves and their institutions.

Up to our own day American history has been in a large degree the history of the colonization of the Great West. The existence of an area of free land, continuous recession, and the advance of American settlements westward, explain American development.

Behind institutions, behind constitutional forms and modifications, lie the vital forces that call these organs into life and shape them to meet changing conditions. The peculiarity of American institutions is, the fact that they have been compelled to adapt themselves to the changes of an expanding people—to the changes involved in crossing a continent, this winning a wilderness, and in developing at each area of this progress out of the primitive economic and political conditions of the frontier into the complexity of city life. . . .

Thus American development has exhibited not merely advance along a single line, but a return to primitive conditions on a continually advancing frontier line, and a new development for that area. American social development has been continually beginning over again on the frontier. This perennial rebirth, this fluidity of American life, this expansion westward with its new opportunities, its continuous touch with the simplicity of primitive society, furnish the forces dominating American character. The true point of view in the history of this nation is not the Atlantic coast, it is the great West. . . .

The frontier is the line of most rapid and effective Americanization. The wilderness masters the colonist. It finds him a European in dress, industries, tools, modes of travel, and thought. It takes him from the railroad car and puts him in the birch canoe. It strips off the garments of civilization and arrays him in the hunting shirt and the moccasin. It puts him in the log cabin of the Cherokee and Iroquois and runs an Indian palisade around him. Before long he has gone to planting Indian corn and plowing with a sharp stick; he shouts the war cry and takes the scalp in orthodox Indian fashion. In short, at the frontier the environment is at first too strong for the man. He must accept the conditions which it furnishes, or perish, and so he fits himself into the Indian clearings and follows the Indian trails. Little by little he transforms the wilderness, but the outcome is not the old Europe, not simply the development of Germanic germs, any more than the first phenomenon was a case of reversion to the Germanic mark. The fact is, that here is a new product that is American. At first, the frontier was the Atlantic coast. It was the frontier of Europe in a very real sense. Moving westward, the frontier became more and more American. As successive terminal moraines result from successive glaciations, so each frontier leaves its traces behind it, and when it becomes a settled area the region still partakes of the frontier characteristics. Thus the advance of the frontier has meant a steady movement away from the influence of Europe, a steady growth of independence on American lines. And to study this advance, the men who grew up under these conditions, and the political, economic, and social results of it, is to study the really American part of our history. . . .

Since the days when the fleet of Columbus sailed into the waters of the New World, America has been another name for opportunity, and the people of the United States have taken their tone from the incessant expansion which has not only been open but has even been forced upon them. He would be a rash prophet who should assert that the expansive character of American life has now entirely ceased. Movement has been its dominant fact, and, unless this training has no effect upon a people, the American energy will continually demand a wider field for its exercise. But never again will such gifts of free land offer themselves. For a moment, at the frontier, the bonds of custom are broken and unrestraint is triumphant. There is not *tabula rasa*. The stubborn American environment is there with its imperious summons to accept its conditions; the inherited ways of doing things are also there; and yet, in spite of environment, and in spite of custom, each frontier did indeed furnish a new field of opportunity, a gate of escape from the bondage of the past; and freshness, and confidence, and scorn of older society, impatience of its restraints and its ideas, and indifference to its lessons, have accompanied the frontier. What the Mediterranean Sea was to the

Greeks, breaking the bond of custom, offering new experiences, calling out new institutions and activities, that, and more, the ever retreating frontier has been to the United States directly, and to the nations of Europe more remotely. And now, four centuries from the discovery of America, at the end of a hundred years of life under the Constitution, the frontier has gone, and with its going has closed the first period of American history.

Study Questions

1. Why does the West enjoy such importance in the interpretation of American history?

2. Assess the motivations of the various individuals and groups who flocked to the West between 1850 and 1890. What values did cowboys, railroad men, immigrant laborers, and women migrants share?

3. Is the westward expansion of the United States best viewed in political, economic, or cultural terms?

4. Do the other documents you have read support Turner's explanation of American history and westward expansion? How might Red Cloud or Flying Hawk have responded to Turner's thesis?

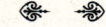

3

Labor and Capital

During the years between the conclusion of the Civil War and the end of the nineteenth century, the United States developed into a mature industrial economy. In this phase of American capitalism, steam replaced waterpower as the driving force of industrialization. People demanded steel instead of iron. With each passing decade, more and more American workers accepted employment in the factories. These laborers did not have much say in the organization of the industrial workplace, however, for key decisions about productivity were made by a new generation of professional managers. Moreover, changes in the structure of capitalism dramatically concentrated wealth in the hands of a few captains of industry, men who owned the factories and who used their personal resources to finance ever larger commercial projects.

While the majority of Americans could still be found in agricultural areas, men and women increasingly defined their lives in relationship to manufacturing. And for this group of people, dependence on factory work presented serious problems. Late nineteenth-century industrialists and bankers did not fully understand the powerful economic forces that they had unleashed, and, for most of this period, the national economy fluctuated wildly between boom and bust. Whatever insecurity they brought to ordinary American workers, the captains of industry generally enjoyed a good reputation. The new class of multimillionaires came to symbolize national progress, especially in the areas of steel and oil (Document 1). But not for everyone. Even in the age of Rockefeller and Carnegie, a few articulate voices encouraged smaller, fairer forms of capitalism (Document 2).

Although the federal government could not possibly have resolved the tensions of industrial capitalism—a contest pitting the interests of the factory owners against those of workers and consumers—it tried. Heeding complaints that industries like the railroads not only fixed prices but also rigged contracts in favor of other large businesses, Congress passed legislation such as the Sherman Antitrust Act (1890) and the interstate commerce regulations (Document 3). These statutes—at least in theory—limited the formation of huge holding companies designed to control entire industries. But, in fact, federal regulators seldom enforced economic reform with much enthusiasm. The courts also obstructed efforts to create a more equitable national economy, interpreting regulatory legislation in ways that limited the worker's right to organize rather than checking the concentration of industrial power (Document 4).

Industrial capitalism sparked conflict between the owners of the nation's factories and the working classes who actually labored for wages. Leading industrialists charged engineers and managers not only with inventing new products and manufacturing processes but also with increasing worker efficiency on the factory floor. The innovators argued that simplifying tasks and creating wage incentives would generate greater profits (Document 5). Not surprisingly, many employees resisted the new managerial class. They resented interventions that discouraged workers from exercising their own judgment. They also suspected that efficiency meant little more than exploiting the American labor force.

Industrial conflict soon spilled beyond the factory walls. Resentment over chronic economic instability, hostility to labor unions among the upper classes, and routine indignities associated with urban poverty, dangerously long hours, and unsafe working conditions exploded in massive, occasionally violent confrontation. Workers and capital fought each other in the city streets and in the mine pits. The most common weapon available to labor was the strike. In 1894, President Grover Cleveland called out soldiers to break the American Railway Union's strike against the Pullman railroad company. Workers and strikebreakers engaged in bloody battle, such as the Chicago Haymarket Square demonstrations of 1886 (Document 6). Whenever labor relations turned violent, public opinion condemned the workers, many of whom were recent European immigrants.

Thoughtful Americans agreed that industrial capitalism had to be tamed. They longed to benefit from technological invention and industrial organization without having to endure social unrest. Many people of this persuasion responded enthusiastically to proposals put forward by imaginative thinkers like Edward Bellamy. He insisted that mass production and economic centralization were fully compatible with social harmony (Document 7). Bellamy's industrial utopia—presented in the form of a novel—existed a hundred years in the future. What Americans needed were practical and immediate solutions to problems that seemed endemic to industrial capitalism.

DOCUMENT 1

Andrew Carnegie, "Wealth" (1889)

Few Americans championed modern industrialism with as much enthusiasm as Andrew Carnegie (1835–1919). Born in Scotland, the young Carnegie obtained a position as a bobbin boy in a Pennsylvania cotton factory and rose to become the owner of a huge steel company. Like Benjamin Franklin, Carnegie congratulated himself on achieving the American Dream. In this article he discusses what came to be known as the Gospel of Wealth. According to Carnegie, hard work promoted "civilization" and "progress." He also insisted that the truly wealthy had a responsibility to give something back to society.

❦ ❦

The problem of our age is the proper administration of wealth, so that the ties of brotherhood may still bind together the rich and poor in harmonious relationship. The conditions of human life have not only been changed, but revolutionized, within the past few hundred years. In former days there was little difference between the dwelling, dress, food, and environment of the chief and those of his retainers. The Indians are to-day where civilized man then was. When visiting the Sioux, I was led to the wigwam of the chief. It was just like the others in external appearance, and even within the difference was trifling between it and those of the poorest of his braves. The contrast between the palace of the millionaire and the cottage of the laborer with us to-day measures the change which has come with civilization.

This change, however, is not to be deplored, but welcomed as highly beneficial. It is well, nay, essential for the progress of the race, that the houses of some should be homes for all that is highest and best in literature and the arts, and for all the refinements of civilization, rather than that none should be so. Much better this great irregularity than universal squalor. . . . The "good old times" were not good old times. Neither master nor servant was as well situated then as to-day. A relapse to old conditions would be disastrous to both—not the least so to him who serves—and would sweep away civilization with it. But whether the change be for good or ill, it is upon us, beyond our power to alter, and therefore to be accepted and made the best of. It is a waste of time to criticise the inevitable.

It is easy to see how the change has come. One illustration will serve for almost every phase of the cause. In the manufacture of products we have the whole story. It applies to all combinations of human industry, as stimulated and enlarged by the inventions of this scientific age. Formerly articles were manufactured at the domestic hearth or in small shops which formed part of the household. The master and his apprentices worked side by side, the latter living with the master, and therefore subject to the same conditions. When these apprentices rose to be masters, there was little or no change in their mode of life, and they, in turn, educated in the same routine succeeding apprentices. There was, substantially, social equality, and even political equality, for those engaged in industrial pursuits had then little or no political voice in the State.

But the inevitable result of such a mode of manufacture was crude articles at high prices. To-day the world obtains commodities of excellent quality at prices which even the generation preceding this would have deemed incredible. In the commercial world similar causes have produced similar results, and the race is benefited thereby. The poor enjoy what the rich could not before afford. What were the luxuries have become the necessaries of life. The laborer has now more comforts than the farmer had a few generations ago. The farmer has more luxuries than the landlord had, and is more richly clad and better housed. The landlord has books and pictures rarer, and appointments more artistic, than the King could then obtain.

The price we pay for this salutary change is, no doubt, great. We assemble thousands of operatives in the factory, in the mine, and in the counting-house, of whom the employer can know little or nothing, and to whom the employer is little better than a myth. All intercourse between them is at an end. Rigid Castes are formed, and, as usual, mutual

An 1880s photo of workers in the rail mill of the Carnegie Steel plant in Homestead, Pennsylvania. Growing labor disputes would lead to a bitter strike at the Homestead plant in 1892, one of the first large-scale disputes between organized labor and big business.

ignorance breeds mutual distrust. Each Caste is without sympathy for the other, and ready to credit anything disparaging in regard to it. Under the law of competition, the employer of thousands is forced into the strictest economies, among which the rates paid to labor figure prominently, and often there is friction between the employer and the employed, between capital and labor, between rich and poor. Human society loses homogeneity.

The price which society pays for the law of competition, like the price it pays for cheap comforts and luxuries, is also great; but the advantages of this law are also greater still, for it is to this law that we owe our wonderful material development, which brings improved conditions in its train. But, whether the law be benign or not, we must say of it, as we say of the change in the conditions of men to which we have referred: It is here; we cannot evade it; no substitutes for it have been found; and while the law may be sometimes hard for the individual, it is best for the race, because it insures the survival of the fittest in every department. We accept and welcome, therefore, as conditions to which we must accommodate ourselves, great inequality of environment, the concentration of business, industrial and commercial, in the hands of a few, and the law of competition between these, as being not only beneficial, but essential for the future progress of the race. Having accepted these, it follows that there must be great scope for the exercise of special ability in the merchant and in the manufacturer who has to conduct affairs upon a great scale. That this talent for organization and management is rare among men is proved by the fact that it invariably secures for its possessor enormous rewards, no matter where or under what laws or conditions. The experienced in affairs always rate the MAN whose services can be obtained as a partner as not only the first consideration, but such as to render the question of his capital scarcely worth considering, for such men soon create capital; while, without the special talent required, capital soon takes wings. Such men become interested in firms or corporations using millions; and estimating only simple interest to be made upon the capital invested, it is inevitable that their income must exceed their expenditures, and that they must accumulate wealth. Nor is there any middle ground which such men can occupy, because the great manufacturing or commercial concern which does not earn at least interest upon its capital soon becomes bankrupt. It must either go forward or fall behind: to stand still is impossible. It is a condition essential for its successful operation that it should be thus far profitable, and even that, in addition to interest on capital, it should make profit. It is a law, as certain as any of the others named, that men possessed of this peculiar talent for affairs, under the free play of economic forces, must, of necessity, soon be in receipt of more revenue than can be judiciously expended upon themselves; and this law is as beneficial for the race as the others.

Objections to the foundations upon which society is based are not in order, because the condition of the race is better with these than it has been with any others which have been tried. Of the effect of any new substitutes proposed we cannot be sure. The Socialist or Anarchist who seeks to overturn present conditions is to be regarded as attacking the foundation upon which civilization itself rests, for civilization took its start from the day that the capable, industrious workman said to his incompetent and lazy fellow, "If thou dost not sow, thou shalt not reap."

DOCUMENT 2

Proceedings of the Thirteenth Session of the National Grange of the Patrons of Husbandry (1879)

Many American farmers—themselves participants in a worldwide market—voiced growing concern about the concentration of economic power in the hands of a few corporate giants. The farmers were particularly worried about railroad monopolies and price fixing. Organizing themselves into groups such as the National Grange of the Patrons of Husbandry, they advocated a fairer distribution of wealth and called on the federal government to guarantee that ordinary working men would not lose out in competition with huge companies.

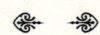

Your Special Committee, raised "to take into consideration the state and condition of American agriculture, and to report such measures and policies as in their judgment will tend to afford relief from the weights, hindrances and difficulties that may beset it, and to suggest such methods as will restore to American farmers greater prosperity and promote their political and material welfare," have given the subject such consideration as opportunity and circumstances allowed, and present the following report.... American farming is growing less profitable and less encouraging.

In a country possessing so many facilities of cheap production this discouraging aspect of agriculture must be and is the result of other than natural causes. The annual additions of wealth under the enlightened system of agriculture are enormous, but from the unequal divisions of the profits of labor and the unjust discriminations made against it, the enlistments of property show that the farmers of the

United States are not prospering. While it is rapidly extinguishing all debts and restoring an equilibrium to the currency of the country, its votaries are deprived of a just share of the rewards of their toil. Capital concentrates to make corners and form rings to fix prices. Transportation companies are allowed to make and unmake prices at will by their unjust and discriminating tariffs and freights. Subsidies and tariffs are created to protect other industries to the prejudice of agriculture. Commerce is shackled. American productions are denied the markets of the world through partial and restrictive laws. Agricultural property is made to bear an unequal and undue proportion of taxation to afford exemptions and privileges to other industries. Monopolies are permitted to assume power and control and exercise perogatives and privileges justly belonging to sovereignty. Encouraged by legislation and stimulated by power, they have grown dictatorial and imperious in their demands, unrelenting in their exactions, and cruel and unmerciful in their impositions. Society has become extravagant and is now a heedless spendthrift of the painful earnings of labor. Government has become proud and autocratic, while her toiling laborers are humiliated in their poverty. States are lavish and prodigal with the people's money. Cities and towns grow rich at the expense and impoverishment of the country. Laws are ingeniously formulated to make justice tardy and thus tend to encourage crime and disorder. In view of the well-established fact that the productive industries must bear the burdens of society, chief among which is agriculture, the national nursing mother of all the occupations, trades, and professions of our people, it is found that it is over-taxed and over-burdened with unnecessary, unjust, unequal, and flagrant impositions, that a just sense of right would transfer to where they justly belong. The farmers of America have on all occasions shown themselves to be a patient and enduring people, and further submission to wrong and injustice will be a sacrifice of manhood and exhibition of cowardice. Stirred with a just sense of right and supported by the integrity of our purpose, the National Grange of the Patrons of Husbandry, in the name and interests of the farmers of the United States, sternly demand—

1st. That the Department of Agriculture shall be made an Executive Department, and the Commissioner a Cabinet officer.

2d. That the Agricultural Department shall be sustained and supported by annual appropriations commensurate with the importance of the great and permanent industry it represents.

3d. That commercial treaties shall be made with all foreign countries, giving to American products equal and unrestricted intercourse with the markets of the world.

4th. That governments be administered in a cheaper and simpler manner, consonant with the conditions of the people.

5th. That a more rigid economy in the expenditures of public moneys be re-established.

6th. That the laws shall be plain and simple, to the end that justice shall be speedy, crime punished, and good government maintained.

7th. That the creation or allowing of monopolies to exist is in violation of the spirit and genius of free republican government.

8th. That the tariffs of freight and fare over railroads and all transportation companies shall be regulated, and all unjust discriminations inhibited by law.

9th. That taxation shall be equal and uniform, and all values made to contribute their just proportion to the support of the government.

10th. That the revenue laws of the United States shall be so adjusted as to bear equally upon all classes of property, to the end that agriculture shall be relieved of the disproportion of burdens it bears.

11th. That the patent laws of the United States be so revised that innocent purchasers of patent rights shall be protected, and fraudulent venders alone held responsible for infringements of rights and violations of law.

12th. That a system of elementary agricultural education shall be adopted in the common schools of the country.

13th. That we are entitled to and should have a

fair representation in the legislative halls of the country, chosen from the ranks of the farmers.

Emphatically asserting our unalterable determination to support and maintain these principles, we demand that they shall be incorporated in the laws of the country for the protection of American agriculture, and invoke the aid of the farmers of the United States in their support, regardless of party affiliations and party mandates. To follow the dictation of partizan influences whilst our earnings are spirited away, and our families beggared, is a degradation and sacrifice that cannot longer be endured.

With manly dignity we boldly declare our rights and interests, and with unwavering devotion will maintain and defend them on all occasions, and this warning is defiantly thrown to the world.

DOCUMENT 3

Interstate Commerce Act (1887)

In an effort to achieve competitive advantage, the nation's railroads engaged in what a Senate committee called "reckless strife." Farmers in particular complained of discriminatory rate schedules. Since the railroads held virtual monopolies over the transportation of freight to market, they demanded whatever rates they pleased, sometimes refusing even to publish their charges. When the situation became intolerable, Congress finally acted, creating the Interstate Commerce Commission (ICC). Authorized to establish "reasonable and just" rates, the commission found it hard to bring the powerful railroads under effective government control.

Be it enacted by the Senate and House of Representatives of the United States of America in Congress assembled, That the provisions of this act shall apply to any common carrier or carriers engaged in the transportation of passengers or property wholly by railroad, or partly by railroad and partly by water when both are used, under a common control, management, or arrangement, for a continuous carriage or shipment, from one State or Territory of the United States or the District of Columbia, to any other State or Territory of the United States. . . .

All charges made for any service rendered or to be rendered in the transportation of passengers or property as aforesaid, or in connection therewith, or for the receiving, delivering, storage, or handling of such property, shall be reasonable and just; and every unjust and unreasonable charge for such service is prohibited and declared to be unlawful.

SEC. 2. That if any common carrier subject to the provisions of this act shall, directly or indirectly, by any special rate, rebate, drawback, or other device, charge, demand, collect, or receive from any person or persons a greater or less compensation for any service rendered, or to be rendered, in the transportation of passengers or property, subject to the provisions of this act, than it charges, demands, collects, or receives from any other person or persons for doing for him or them a like and contemporaneous service in the transportation of a like kind of traffic under substantially similar circumstances and conditions, such common carrier shall be deemed guilty of unjust discrimination, which is hereby prohibited and declared to be unlawful.

SEC. 3. That it shall be unlawful for any common carrier subject to the provisions of this act to make or give any undue or unreasonable preference or advantage to any particular person, company, firm, corporation, or locality, or any particular description of traffic, in any respect whatsoever, or to subject any particular person, company, firm, corporation, or locality, or any particular description of traffic, to any undue or unreasonable prejudice or disadvantage in any respect whatsoever.

Every common carrier subject to the provisions of this act shall, according to their respective powers, afford all reasonable, proper, and equal facilities for the interchange of traffic between their respective lines, and for the receiving, forwarding, and delivering of passengers and property to and from their several lines and those connecting there with, and shall not discriminate in their rates and charges between such connecting lines; but this shall not be construed as requiring any such common carrier to give the use of its tracks or terminal facilities to another carrier engaged in like business. . . .

SEC. 6. That every common carrier subject to the provisions of this act shall print and keep for public inspection schedules showing the rates and fares and charges for the transportation of passengers and property which any such common carrier has established and which are in force at the time upon its railroad, as defined by the first section of this act. The schedules printed as aforesaid by any such common carrier shall plainly state the places upon its railroad between which property and passengers will be carried, and shall contain the classification of freight in force upon such railroad, and shall also state separately the terminal charges and any rules or regulations which in any wise change, affect, or determine any part or the aggregate of such aforesaid rates and fares and charges. Such schedules shall be plainly printed in large type, of at least the size of ordinary pica, and copies for the use of the public shall be kept in every depot or station upon any such railroad, in such places and in such form that they can be conveniently inspected. . . .

And when any such common carrier shall have established and published its rates, fares, and charges in compliance with the provisions of this section, it shall be unlawful for such common carrier to charge, demand, collect, or receive from any person or persons a greater or less compensation for the transportation of passengers or property, or for any services in connection therewith, than is specified in such published schedule of rates, fares, and charges as may at the time be in force.

Every common carrier subject to the provisions of this act shall file with the Commission hereinafter provided for copies of its schedules of rates, fares, and charges which have been established and published in compliance with the requirements of this section, and shall promptly notify said Commission of all changes made in the same. Every such common carrier shall also file with said Commission copies of all contracts, agreements, or arrangements with other common carriers in relation to any traffic affected by the provisions of this act to which it may be a party. . . .

SEC. 9. That any person or persons claiming to be damaged by any common carrier subject to the provisions of this act may either make complaint to the Commission as hereinafter provided for, or may bring suit in his or their own behalf for the recovery of the damages for which such common carrier may be liable under the provisions of this act, in any district or circuit court of the United States of competent jurisdiction; but such person or persons shall not have the right to pursue both of said remedies, and must in each case elect which one of the two methods of procedure herein provided for he or they will adopt. In any such action brought for the recovery of damages the court before which the same shall be pending may compel any director, officer, receiver, trustee, or agent of the corporation or company defendant in such suit to attend, appear, and testify in such case, and may compel the production of the books and papers of such corporation or company party to any such suit; the claim that any such testimony or evidence may tend to criminate the person giving such evidence shall not excuse such witness from testifying, but such evidence or testimony shall not be used against such person on the trial of any criminal proceeding. . . .

SEC. 12. That the Commission hereby created shall have authority to inquire into the management of the business of all common carriers subject to the provisions of this act, and shall keep itself informed as to the manner and method in which the same is conducted, and shall have the right to obtain from such common carriers full and complete information necessary to enable the Commission to perform the duties and carry out the objects for which it was created; and for the purposes of this act the Commission shall have power to require the attendance and testimony of witnesses and the production of all books, papers, tariffs, contracts, agreements, and documents relating to any matter under investigation, and to that end may invoke the aid of any court of the United States in requiring the attendance and testimony of witnesses and the production of books, papers, and documents under the provisions of this section. . . .

SEC. 15. That if in any case in which an investigation shall be made by said Commission it shall be made to appear to the satisfaction of the Commission, either by the testimony of witnesses or other evidence that anything has been done or omitted to be done in violation of the provisions of this act, or of any law cognizable by said Commission, or any common carrier, or that any injury or damage has been sustained by the party or parties complaining, or by other parties aggrieved by consequence of any such violation, it shall be the duty of the Commission to forthwith cause a copy of its report in respect thereto to be delivered to such common carrier, together with a notice to said common carrier to cease and desist from such violation, or to make reparation for the injury so found to have been done, or both, within a reasonable time, to be specified by the Commission.

DOCUMENT 4

Suit by the United States Against the Workingmen's Amalgamated Council of New Orleans (1893)

American workers responded to the growing concentration of corporate power by establishing unions. They made slow progress, however, for during this period labor organizers faced severe handicaps. Middle-class Americans suspected unions of promoting radical foreign ideologies. Moreover, the courts viewed unions as a threat to free labor and the prosperity of the nation's industries. As the following decision handed down by a federal court in New Orleans indicates, judges applied statutes designed to regulate the growth of industrial combinations to prevent ordinary workers from using their most potent weapon, the strike.

The bill of complaint in this case is filed by the United States under the act of congress entitled "An act to protect trade and commerce against unlawful restraint and monopolies." The substance of the bill is that there is a gigantic and widespread combination of the members of a multitude of separate organizations for the purpose of restraining the commerce among the several states and with foreign countries. It avers that a disagreement between the warehousemen and their employes and the principal draymen and their subordinates had been adopted by all the organizations named in the bill, until, by this vast combination of men and of organizations, it was threatened that, unless there was an acquiescence in the demands of the subordinate workmen and draymen, all the men in all of the defendant organizations would leave work, and would allow no work in any department of business; that violence was threatened and used in support of this demand; and that this demand included the interstate and foreign commerce which flows through the city of New Orleans. The bill further states that the proceedings on the part of the defendants had taken such a vast and ramified proportion that, in consequence of the threats of the defendants, the whole business of the city of New Orleans was paralyzed, and the transit of goods and merchandise which was being conveyed through it from state to state, and to and from foreign countries, was totally interrupted. The elaborate argument and brief of the solicitors for the defendants parents six objections. . . .

The theory of the defense is that this case does not fall within the purview of the statute; that the statute prohibited monopolies and combinations which, using words in a general sense, were of capitalists, and not of laborers. I think the congressional debates show that the statute had its origin in the evils of massed capital; but, when the congress came to formulating the prohibition which is the yardstick for measuring the complainant's right to the injunction, it expressed it in these words: "Every contract or combination in the form of trust, or otherwise in restraint of trade or commerce among the several states or with foreign nations, is hereby declared to be illegal." The subject had so broadened in the minds of the legislators that the source of the evil was not regarded as material, and the evil in its entirety is dealt with. They made the interdiction include combinations of labor, as well as of capital; in fact, all combinations in restraint of commerce, without reference to the character of the persons who entered into them. It is true this statute has not been much expounded by judges, but, as it seems to me, its meaning, as far as relates to the sort of combinations to which it is to apply, is manifest, and that it includes combinations which are composed of laborers acting in the interest of laborers. . . .

The defendants urge . . . that the corporations of the various labor associations made defendants are in their origin and purposes innocent and lawful. I believe this to be true. But associations of men, like individuals, no matter how worthy their general character may be, when charged with unlawful combinations, and when the charge is fully established, cannot escape liability on the ground of their commendable general character. In determining the question of sufficiency of proof of an accusation of unlawful intent, worth in the accused is to be weighed; but when the proof of the charge is sufficient,—overwhelmingly sufficient,—the original purpose of an association has ceased to be available as a ground of defense.

The defendants urge . . . that the combination to secure or compel the employment of none but union men is not in the restraint of commerce. To determine whether the proposition urged as a defense can apply to this case, the case must first be stated as it is made out by the established facts. The case is this: The combination setting out to secure and compel the employment of none but union men in a given business, as a means to effect this compulsion, finally enforced a discontinuance of labor in all kinds of business, including the business of transportation of goods and merchandise which were in transit through the city of New Orleans, from state to state, and to and from foreign countries. When the case is thus stated,—and it must be so stated to embody the facts here proven,—I do not think there can be any question but that the combination of the defendants was in restraint of commerce....

It was . . . brought about by the employed that all the union men—that is, all the members of the various labor associations—were made by their officers, clothed with authority under the various charters, to discontinue business, and one of these kinds of business was transporting goods which were being conveyed from state to state, and to and from foreign countries. In some branches of business the effort was made to replace the union men by other workmen. This was resisted by the intimidation springing from vast throngs of the union men assembling in the streets, and in some instances by violence; so that the result was that, by the intended effects of the doings of these defendants, not a bale of goods constituting the commerce of the country could be moved. The question simply is, do these facts establish a case within the statute? It seems to me this question is tantamount to the question, could there be a case under the statute? It is conceded that the labor organizations were at the outset lawful. But, when lawful forces are put into unlawful channels,—i.e. when lawful associations adopt and further unlawful purposes and do unlawful acts,—the associations themselves become unlawful. The evil, as well as the unlawfulness, of the act of the defendants, consists in this: that, until certain demands of theirs were complied with, they endeavored to prevent, and did prevent, everybody from moving the commerce of the country.

It is the successful effort of the combination of the defendants to intimidate and overawe others who were at work in conducting or carrying on the commerce of the country, in which the court finds their error and their violation of the statute. One of the intended results of their combined action was the forced stagnation of all the commerce which flowed through New Orleans. This intent and combined action are none the less unlawful because they included in their scope the paralysis of all other business within the city as well.

DOCUMENT 5

Frederick Winslow Taylor, "A Piece-Rate System" (1896)

Frederick Taylor's (1856–1915) name became synonymous with efforts to maximize profit on the factory floor. His time and motion studies helped determine how fast workers could perform particular tasks. Such data allowed Taylor and others to redesign manufacturing processes to achieve greater managerial control at lower costs. He reported his theories in the following article published by the American Economic Association.

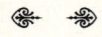

The ordinary piece-work system involves a permanent antagonism between employers and men, and a certainty of punishment for each workman who reaches a high rate of efficiency. The demoralizing effect of this system is most serious. Under it, even the best workmen are forced continually to act the part of hypocrites, to hold their own in the struggle against the encroachments of their employers.

The system introduced by the writer, however, is directly the opposite, both in theory and in its results. It takes each workman's interests the same as that of his employer, pays a premium for high efficiency, and soon convinces each man that it is for his permanent advantage to turn out each day the best quality and maximum quantity of work....

Elementary rate-fixing differs from other methods of making piece-work prices in that a careful study is made of the time required to do each of the many elementary operations into which the manufacturing of an establishment may be analyzed or divided. These elementary operations are then classified, recorded, and indexed and when a piece-work price is wanted for work the job is first divided into its elementary operations, the time required to do each elementary operation is found from the records, and the total time for the job is summed up from these data. While this method seems complicated at the first glance, it is, in fact, far simpler and more effective than the old method of recording the time required to do whole jobs of work, and then, after looking over the records of similar jobs, guessing at the time required for any new piece of work.

The differential rate system of piece-work consists briefly, in offering two different rates for the same job, a high price per piece in case the work is finished in the shortest possible time and in perfect condition, and a low price if it takes a longer time to do the job, of if there are any imperfections in the work. (The high rate should be such that the workman can earn more per day than is usually paid in similar establishments.) This is directly the opposite of the ordinary plan of piece-work in which the wages of the workmen are reduced when they increase their productivity.

The system by which the writer proposes managing the men who are on day-work consists in paying men and not *positions*. Each man's wages, as far as possible, are fixed according to the skill and energy with which he performs his work, and not according to the position which he fills. Every endeavor is made to stimulate each man's personal ambition. This involves keeping systematic and careful records of the performance of each man, as to his punctuality, attendance, integrity, rapidity, skill, and accuracy, and a readjustment from time to time of the wages paid him, in accordance with this record.

The advantages of this system of management are:

First. That the manufactures are produced cheaper under it, while at the same time the workmen earn higher wages than are usually paid.

Second. Since the rate-fixing is done from accurate knowledge instead of more or less by guess-work, the motive for holding back on work, or "soldiering," and endeavoring to deceive the employers as to the time required to do work, is entirely removed, and with it the greatest cause for hard feelings and war between the management and the men.

Third. Since the basis from which piece-work as well as day rates are fixed is that of exact observation, instead of being founded upon accident or deception, as is too frequently the case under ordinary systems, the men are treated with greater uniformity and justice, and respond by doing more and better work.

Fourth. It is for the common interest of both the management and the men to coöperate in every way, so as to turn out each day the maximum quantity and best quality of work.

Fifth. The system is rapid, while other systems are slow, in attaining the maximum productivity of each machine and man; and when this maximum is once reached, it is automatically maintained by the differential rate.

Sixth. It automatically selects and attracts the best men for each class of work, and it develops many first class men who would otherwise remain slow or inaccurate, while at the same time it discourages and sifts out men who are incurably lazy or inferior.

Finally. One of the chief advantages derived from the above effects of the system is, that it promotes a most friendly feeling between the men and their employers and so renders labor unions and strikes unnecessary....

It is not unusual for the manager of a manufacturing business to go most minutely into every detail of the buying and selling and financiering, and arrange every element of these branches in the most systematic manner and according to principles that have been carefully planned to insure the business against almost any contingency which may arise, while the manufacturing is turned over to a superintendent or foreman, with little or no restrictions as to the principles and methods which he is to pursue, either in the management of his men or the care of the company's plant....

Such managers belong distinctly to the old school of manufacturers; and among them are to be found, in spite of their lack of system, many of the best and most successful men of the country. They believe in men, not in methods, in the management of their shops; and what they would call system in the office and sales departments, would be called red tape by them in the factory. Through their keen insight and knowledge of character they are able to select and train good superintendents, who in turn secure good workmen; and frequently the business prospers under this system (or rather, lack of system) for a term of years.

The modern manufacturer, however, seeks not only to secure the best superintendents and workmen, but to surround each department of his manufacture with the most carefully woven net-work of system and method, which should render the business, for a considerable period at least, independent of the loss of any one man, and frequently of any combination of men.

It is the lack of this system and method which, in the judgment of the writer, constitutes the greatest risk to manufacturing; placing, as it frequently does, the success of the business at the hazard of the health of whims of a few employees.

DOCUMENT 6

Address by George Engel, Condemned Haymarket Anarchist (1886)

A workers' demonstration at Haymarket Square in Chicago turned into a riot when a bomb blast killed seven police officers and wounded sixty-six. Labor activists had called the rally after police shot two striking workers the previous day. Eight anarchists stood trial for the bombing and, although prosecutors failed to produce any evidence that could link them to the crime, the suspects were convicted. Four were hanged. Supporters published the speeches that the accused made on their own behalf before the court. Anarchist George Engel, a German immigrant, explained his hostility to the reigning economic and political system in his defiant remarks.

When, in the year 1872, I left Germany because it had become impossible for me to gain there, by the labor of my hands, a livelihood such as man is worthy to enjoy—the introduction of machinery having ruined the smaller craftsmen and made the outlook for the future appear very dark to them—I concluded to fare with my family to the land of America, the land that had been praised to me by so many as the land of liberty.

On the occasion of my arrival at Philadelphia, on the 8th of January, 1873, my heart swelled with joy in the hope and in the belief that in the future I would live among free men and in a free country. I made up my mind to become a good citizen of this country, and congratulated myself on having left Germany, and landed in this glorious republic. And I believe my past history will bear witness that I have ever striven to be a good citizen of this country. This is the first occasion of my standing before an American court, and on this occasion it is murder of which I am accused. And for what reasons do I stand here? For what reasons am I accused of murder? The same that caused me to leave Germany—the poverty—the misery of the working classes.

And here, too, in this "free republic," in the richest country of the world, there are numerous proletarians for whom no table is set; who, as outcasts of society, stray joylessly through life. I have seen human beings gather their daily food from the garbage heaps of the streets, to quiet therewith their knawing hunger. . . .

When in 1878, I came here from Philadelphia, I strove to better my condition, believing it would be less difficult to establish a means of livelihood here than in Philadelphia, where I had tried in vain to make a living. But here, too, I found myself disappointed. I began to understand that it made no difference to the proletarian, whether he lived in New York, Philadelphia, or Chicago. In the factory in which I worked, I became acquainted with a man who pointed out to me the causes that brought about the difficult and fruitless battles of the workingmen for the means of existence. He explained to me, by the logic of scientific Socialism, how mistaken I was in believing that I could make an independent living by the toil of my hands, so long as machinery, raw material, etc., were guaranteed to the capitalists as private property by the State. . . .

I took part in politics with the earnestness of a good citizen; but I was soon to find that the teachings of a "free ballot box" are a myth and that I had again been duped. I came to the opinion that as long as workingmen are economically enslaved they cannot be politically free. It became clear to me that the working classes would never bring about a form of society guaranteeing work, bread, and a happy life by means of the ballot. . . .

I . . . joined the International Working People's Association, that was just being organized. The members of that body have the firm conviction, that the workingman can free himself from the tyranny of capitalism only through force; just as all advances of which history speaks, have been brought about through force alone. We see from the history of this country that the first colonists won their liberty only through force that through force slavery was abolished, and just as the man who agitated against slavery in this country, had to ascend the gallows, so also must we. He who speaks for the workingman today must hang. And why? Because this Republic is not governed by people who have obtained their office honestly.

Who are the leaders at Washington that are to guard the interests of this nation? Have they been elected by the people, or by the aid of their money? They have no right to make laws for us, because they were not elected by the people. These are the reasons why I have lost all respect for American laws.

The fact that through the improvement of machinery so many men are thrown out of employment, or at best, working but half the time, brings them to reflection. They have leisure, and they consider how their conditions can be changed. Reading matter that has been written in their interest gets into their hands, and, faulty though their education may be, they can nevertheless cull the truths contained in those writings. This, of course, is not pleasant for the capitalistic class, but they cannot prevent it. And it is my firm conviction that in a comparatively short time the great mass of proletarians will understand that they can be freed from their bonds only through Socialism. One must consider what Carl Schurs said scarcely eight years ago: That, "in this country there is no space for Socialism;" and yet today Socialism stands before the bars of the court. For this reason it is my firm conviction that if these few years sufficed to make Socialism one of the burning questions of the day, it will require but a short time more to put it in practical operation.

All that I have to say in regard to my conviction is, that I was not at all surprised; for it has ever been

The Haymarket Bombing in Chicago on May 4, 1886, where an otherwise peaceful demonstration turned violent when a bomb went off, killing seven policemen. Police responded by killing four demonstrators and charging eight anarchists with inciting a riot and murder. The Haymarket bombing weakened public perception of the national labor movement by associating organized labor with anarchism.

that the men who have endeavored to enlighten their fellow man have been thrown into prison or put to death, as was the case with John Brown. I have found, long ago, that the workingman has no more rights here than any where else in the world. The State's Attorney has stated that we were not citizens. I have been a citizen this long time; but it does not occur to me to appeal for my rights as a citizen, knowing as well as I do that this does not make a particle of difference. Citizen or not—as a workingman I am without rights, and therefore I respect neither your rights nor your laws, which are made and directed by one class against the other; the working class.

Of what does my crime consist?

That I have labored to bring about a system of society by which it is impossible for one to hoard millions, through the improvements in machinery, while the great masses sink to degradation and misery. As water and air are free to all, so should the inventions of scientific men be applied for the benefit of all. The statute laws we have are in opposition to the laws of nature, in that they rob the great masses of their rights "to life, liberty, and the pursuit of happiness."

I am too much a man of feeling not to battle against the societary conditions of today. Every considerate person must combat a system which makes it possible for the individual to rake and hoard millions in a few years, while, on the other side, thousands become tramps and beggars.

Is it to be wondered at that under such circumstances men arise, who strive and struggle to create other conditions, where the humane humanity shall take precedence of all other considerations. This is the aim of Socialism, and to this I joyfully subscribe.

The States Attorney said here that "Anarchy" was "on trial."

Anarchism and Socialism are as much alike, in my opinion, as one egg is to another. They differ only in their tactics. The Anarchists have abandoned the way of liberating humanity which Socialists would take to accomplish this. I say: Believe no more in the ballot, and use all other means at your command. Because we have done so we stand arraigned here today—because we have pointed out to the people the proper way. The Anarchists are being hunted and persecuted for this in every clime, but in the face of it all Anarchism is gaining more and more adherents, and if you cut off our opportunities of open agitation, then will the work be done secretly. If the State's Attorney thinks he can root out Socialism by hanging seven of our men and condemning the other to fifteen years servitude, he is laboring under a very wrong impression. The tactics simply will be changed—that is all. No power on earth can rob the workingman of his knowledge of how to make bombs—and that knowledge he possesses. . . .

If Anarchism could be rooted out, it would have been accomplished long ago in other countries. On the night on which the first bomb in this country was thrown, I was in my apartments at home. I knew nothing of the conspiracy which the States Attorney pretends to have discovered.

It is true I am acquainted with several of my fellow-defendants with most of them, however, but slightly, through seeing them at meetings, and hearing them speak. Nor do I deny, that I too, have spoken at meetings, saying that, if every workingman had a bomb in his pocket, capitalistic rule would soon come to an end.

That is my opinion, and my wish; it became my conviction, when I mentioned the wickedness of the capitalistic conditions of the day.

When hundreds of workingmen have been destroyed in mines in consequence of faulty preparations, for the repairing of which the owners were too stingy, the capitalistic papers have scarcely noticed it. As with what satisfaction and cruelty they make their report, when here and there workingmen have been fired upon, while striking for a few cents increase in their wages, that they might earn only a scanty subsistance.

Can any one feel any respect for a government that accords rights only to the privileged classes, and none to the workers? We have seen but recently how the coal barons combined to form a conspiracy to raise the price of coal, while at the same time reducing the already low wages of their men. Are they accused of conspiracy on that account? But when working men dare ask an increase in their wages, the militia and the police are sent out to shoot them down.

For such a government as this I can feel no respect, and will combat them, despite their power, despite their police, despite their spies.

I hate and combat, not the individual capitalist, but the system that gives him those privileges. My greatest wish is that workingmen may recognize who are their friends and who are their enemies.

As to my conviction, brought about as it was, through capitalistic influence, I have not one word to say.

DOCUMENT 7

Edward Bellamy, Looking Backward (1888)

Author Edward Bellamy (1850–1898) captured the frustrations and tapped the hopes of many Americans in his futuristic novel *Looking Backward, 2000–1887*. The story revolved around a man accidentally sealed in a Boston vault only to be unearthed alive more than a hundred years later. He discovers that the social catastrophes seemingly imminent in 1887 have not occurred. Instead, Americans have organized their productive energies under a centralized, egalitarian government capable of satisfying everyone's wants. The vision expressed in passages like this one inspired the formation of Bellamy Clubs across the nation to further the cause of reform.

"What should you name as the most prominent feature of the labor troubles of your day?"

"Why, the strikes, of course," I replied.

"Exactly; but what made the strikes so formidable?"

"The great labor organizations."

"And what was the motive of these great organizations?"

"The workmen claimed they had to organize to get their rights from the big corporations," I replied.

"That is just it," said Dr. Leete, "the organization of labor and the strikes were an effect, merely, of the concentration of capital in greater masses than had ever been known before. Before this concentration began, while as yet commerce and industry were conducted by innumerable petty concerns with small capital, instead of a small number of great concerns with vast capital, the individual workman was relatively important and independent in his relations to the employer. Moreover, when a little capital or a new idea was enough to start a man in business for himself, workingmen were constantly becoming employers and there was no hard and fast line between the two classes. Labor unions were needless then, and general strikes out of the question. But when the era of small concerns with small capital was succeeded by that of the great aggregations of capital, all this was changed. The individual laborer, who had been relatively important to the small employer, was reduced to insignificance and powerlessness over against the great corporation, while at the same time the way upward to the grade of employer was closed to him. Self-defense drove him to union with his fellows.

"The records of the period show that the outcry against the concentration of capital was furious. Men believed that it threatened society with a form of tyranny more abhorrent than it had ever endured. They believed that the great corporations were preparing for them the yoke of a baser servitude than had ever been imposed on the race, servitude not to men but to soulless machines incapable of any motive but insatiable greed. Looking back, we cannot wonder at their desperation, for certainly humanity was never confronted with a fate more sordid and hideous than would have been the era of corporate tyranny which they anticipated. . . .

"The fact that the desperate popular opposition to the consolidation of business in a few powerful hands had no effect to check it proves that there must have been a strong economical reason for it. The small capitalists, with their innumerable petty concerns, had in fact yielded the field to the great aggregations of capital, because they belonged to a

The 1893 World's Colombian Exposition in Chicago coincided with the 400th anniversary of Columbus's arrival in America. The fair's 150 white plaster building facades, which became known as the White City," would influence future urban planning by providing an efficient and visually pleasing example of city planning.

day of small things and were totally incompetent to the demands of an age of steam and telegraphs and the gigantic scale of its enterprises. To restore the former order of things, even if possible, would have involved returning to the day of stage-coaches. Oppressive and intolerable as was the régime of the great consolidations of capital, even its victims, while they cursed it, were forced to admit the prodigious increase of efficiency which had been imparted to the national industries, the vast economies effected by concentration of management and unity of organization, and to confess that since the new system had taken the place of the old the wealth of the world had increased at a rate before undreamed of. To be sure this vast increase had gone chiefly to make the rich richer, increasing the gap between them and the poor. . . .

"The movement toward the conduct of business by larger and larger aggregations of capital, the tendency toward monopolies, which had been so desperately and vainly resisted, was recognized at last, in its true significance, as a process which only needed to complete its logical evolution to open a golden future to humanity.

"Early in the last century the evolution was completed by the final consolidation of the entire capital of the nation. The industry and commerce of the country, ceasing to be conducted by a set of irresponsible corporations and syndicates of private persons at their caprice and for their profit, were intrusted to a single syndicate representing the people, to be conducted in the common interest for the common profit. The nation, that is to say, organized as the one great business corporation in which all other corporations were absorbed; it became the one capitalist in the place of all other capitalists, the sole employer, the final monopoly in which all previous and lesser monopolies were swallowed up, a monopoly in the profits and economies of which all citizens shared. The epoch of trusts had ended in The Great Trust. In a word, the people of the United States concluded to assume the conduct of their own business, just as one hundred odd years before they had assumed the conduct of their own government, organizing now for industrial purposes on precisely the same grounds that they had then organized for political purposes. At last, strangely late in the world's history, the obvious fact was perceived that no business is so essentially the public business as the industry and commerce on which the people's livelihood depends, and that to entrust it to private persons to be managed for private profit is a folly similar in kind, though vastly greater in magnitude, to that of surrendering the functions of political government to kings and nobles to be conducted for their personal glorification."

"Such a stupendous change as you describe," said I, "did not, of course, take place without great bloodshed and terrible convulsions."

"On the contrary," replied Dr. Leete, "there was absolutely no violence. The change had been long foreseen. Public opinion had become fully ripe for it, and the whole mass of the people was behind it. There was no more possibility of opposing it by force than by argument. On the other hand the popular sentiment toward the great corporations and those identified with them had ceased to be one of bitterness, as they came to realize their necessity as a link, a transition phase, in the evolution of the true industrial system. The most violent foes of the great private monopolies were now forced to recognize how invaluable and indispensable had been their office in educating the people up to the point of assuming control of their own business. Fifty years before, the consolidation of the industries of the country under national control would have seemed a very daring experiment to the most sanguine. But by a series of object lessons, seen and studied by all men, the great corporations had taught the people an entirely new set of ideas on this subject. They had seen for many years syndicates handling revenues greater than those of states, and directing the labors of hundreds of thousands of men with an efficiency and economy unattainable in smaller operations. It had come to be recognized as an axiom that the larger the business the simpler the principles that can be applied to it; that, as the machine is truer than the hand, so the system, which in a great concern does the work of the master's eye in a small business, turns out more accurate results. Thus it came about that, thanks to the corporations themselves, when it was proposed that the nation should assume their functions, the suggestion implied nothing which seemed impracticable even to the timid. To be sure it was a step beyond any yet taken, a broader generalization, but the very fact that the nation would be the sole corporation in the field would, it was seen, relieve the undertaking of many difficulties with which the partial monopolies had contended."

Study Questions

1. With which aspects of Carnegie's defense of industrial society would other people represented in this chapter have agreed? What objections would they have raised?

2. Did farmers and workers share the same attitudes toward industrial society?

3. Why were the government and the courts so reluctant to regulate the industrial economy?

4. Why might workers object to Taylorism? What criticisms would Carnegie or Bellamy level at Taylor's theories?

5. Why did so many Americans respond positively to Bellamy's *Looking Backward?*

4

Urban Society

Throughout the nineteenth century, new "mushroom cities" (fast-growing plains cities) such as Chicago and St. Louis burst on the American landscape. This explosive process occurred while older cities such as New York, Philadelphia, and Boston experienced spectacular growth. As the centers of commerce, cities often owed their existence to advantageous locations on rivers, lakes, and oceans. When compared to the vast agricultural hinterlands, cities exhibited a fast-paced, diverse culture—the result of large numbers of people from a variety of ethnic and racial backgrounds seeking the good life in a single area. Industrialization accelerated these trends, making American cities even more unique and variegated than ever before.

Migrants from the countryside and immigrants from around the globe converged on America's cities and towns because mechanized farming required fewer laborers, and industrial centers offered jobs (Document 1). For the first time in U.S. history large numbers of immigrants were arriving from Central and Southern Europe. Italians, Poles, Hungarians, Slovaks, Romanians, Russians, Greeks, and others were generally Catholic, Eastern Orthodox, or Jewish rather than Protestant. The concentrated communities they established—more often than not reflecting some degree of poverty—placed stress on the urban infrastructure and introduced the nation to new customs related to family, worship, and politics.

No single description captures the experience of even one ethnic group, let alone the new immigrants as a whole. Certainly many women and men labored under oppressive conditions, whether in the factory, the streets, or in crowded tenement buildings. Disease and injury seemed an inevitable byproduct of such a life (Document 2). Hard work by no means guaranteed economic security (Document 3). But life in America allowed some immigrants to return to their native lands with hard-earned cash and others to bring their relatives to America. At least some immigrants benefited from the wealth generated by the massive American economy (Document 4). Politics in the burgeoning immigrant neighborhoods had a distinct flavor, as politicians, often successful immigrants or the children of immigrants themselves, competed for the favor of local communities by delivering needed services in creative, albeit irregular means (Document 5).

The urban economy also required an ever-growing number of clerks, accountants, secretaries, and salespeople to staff banks, insurance companies, corporate offices, and, just as important, the stores that distributed the products of industry and agriculture. The train systems built in America's largest cities carried both blue-collar and white-collar commuters across the expanding urban landscape each day. While middle- and upper-class husbands enjoyed an expanded range of employment options, many of their wives saw their lives confined narrowly to raising children and keeping comfortable homes. Nonetheless some women questioned whether the distinctions made between the sexes were natural or necessary (Document 6).

City life changed the manner in which urbanites of all classes regarded time, space, and money. Despite, or perhaps because of, its rigors, city dwellers sought the relaxation and amusement that factory, office, or home failed to provide. Entrepreneurs and urban planners recognized the demand for recreation in the crowded city. Thus plans were made to build parks to give people whose lives had become confined a chance to enjoy the outdoors (Document 7). Perhaps more characteristic of the age, however, was the rise of entertainment such as for-profit amusement parks designed to draw thousands of visitors to spend portions of their hard-earned wages on novel rides and exhibitions (Document 8).

The urban culture of the late nineteenth and early twentieth centuries thus provided ordinary men and women with innovative ways not only to survive life but also, when possible, to enjoy it. Whether judged a success or failure, the rise of the industrial metropolis permanently altered American culture. New types of people worked in novel enterprises on a scale that defied the comprehension of many of the cities' own inhabitants. The experience changed the lives of not only the city dwellers but also the millions of rural people, still a majority of Americans, who increasingly fell within the economic orbit of urban America.

DOCUMENT 1

Adna Weber, The Growth of Cities in the Nineteenth Century (1899)

Nineteenth-century Americans—like social scientists of our own time—sought to comprehend the massive expansion of the nation's cities. In his 1899 scholarly monograph, Adna Weber offered a thoughtful explanation for the rise of American urban centers that placed the amazing process in broad historical context.

In a new country the rapid growth of cities is both natural and necessary, for no efficient industrial organization of a new settlement is possible without industrial centres to carry on the necessary work of assembling and distributing goods. A Mississippi Valley empire rising suddenly into being without its Chicago and its smaller centres of distribution is almost inconceivable to the nineteenth century economist. That America is the "land of mushroom cities" is therefore not at all surprising.

But, on the other hand, it is astonishing that the development of the cities in a new country should outstrip that of the rural districts which they serve. The natural presumption would be that so long as land remains open to settlement, the superfluous population of the older States or of Europe would seek the fundamental, or food-producing, industry of agriculture, and build up cities only in a corresponding degree. Yet in the great cereal regions of the West, the cities have grown entirely out of proportion to the rural parts, resulting there, as in the East and in Europe, in an increasing concentration of the population....

It is now clear that the growth of cities must be studied as a part of the question of distribution of population, which is always dependent upon the economic organization of society—upon the constant striving to maintain as many people as possible upon a given area. The ever-present problem is so to distribute and organize the masses of men that they can render such services as favor the maintenance of the nation and thereby accomplish their own preservation. Population follows the line of least resistance in its distribution, and will consequently be affected by changes in the methods of production. When the industrial organization demands the presence of laborers in particular localities in order to increase its efficiency, laborers will be found there; the means of attraction will have been "better living"—in other words, an appeal to the motive of self-interest. Economic forces are therefore the principal cause of concentration of population in cities....

Now, without stretching the analogy, we may liken industrial society of to-day—embracing all countries within the circle of exchange of products—to a great organism composed of heterogeneous parts. This organism, however, is the product of ages of slow growth. Originally, in place of the one all-embracing social organism, there were myriads of small social units, each complete in itself and independent of the others, if not positively hostile to them. The history of civilization is simply the narrative description of the breaking down of the barriers that separated the primitive social units—the original family group, clan, patriarchal family, the enlarged village community or the manorial group. And the most conspicuous and influential role in the process was played by the trader, working upon men's desires for what they did not possess or produce. Neither war (conquest) nor religion has been of so vital and far-reaching influence in the integration and amalgamation of isolated social groups as trade and commerce.

When, therefore, it is pointed out that towns owe their origin to trade, that the commercial metropolis of to-day is the successor of the primitive market-place established beside the boundary stone between hostile but avaricious tribal groups, that the extension of the market means the enlargement of the market-centre—then one will readily perceive the connection of the growth of industrial society to its present world-wide dimensions with our problem of the concentration of population....

If men were like other animals and had no further wants than bodily appetites and passions, there would be no large aggregations of people; for in order to produce food, men must live either in scattered habitations like American farmers, or in hamlets like the ancient family or tribal group, the village community, the Russian *mir,* and the modern agricultural village of Continental Europe. Even with a comparatively high grade of wants, men may live in these small groups, each of which is economically autonomous and self-sufficing, producing for itself and buying and selling little if anything. It is the period of the *Naturalwirthschaft,* in which all payments are in kind. The principle of division of labor finally led to the disruption of the village community, but its triumph was long delayed. The principle was of course grasped only imperfectly by primitive man. At first the only division was that based on sex, age, muscular power, or relation to the governing head of the group; in other respects there was no assignment of special tasks to particular individuals. Very gradually men discovered among themselves differences of natural aptitude. The members of a community at length realized that it was more economical to have their flour made in a village mill by one member who should give all his time to that particular work, than to have it made by bits in a score of individual mills. One by one other industries have followed the mill—have departed from the separate households and taken up their abode in a central establishment. Clothing ceased to be made at home; there arose a village weaver and a village shoemaker. To this process of development there is almost no conceivable end. Only a few years ago the American farmer not only raised his own food, but furnished his own fuel and sometimes made his own clothing. Now, however, he is a specialist, and thinks nothing of going to the market even for table supplies. Formerly, the farmer made his own tools; now he buys implements made in factories. But yesterday, and the men who reaped the fields of ripe grain were bound to the soil and compelled to dwell in isolated homes or small communities; to-day these men live in cities and make machinery to reap the grin.

Thus, it appears that agriculture, the industry that disperses men, has ever narrowed its scope. Formerly, when men's wants were few and simple, agriculture was the all-embracing occupation. The agriculturist produced the necessary sustenance, and in his idle moments made whatever else he needed. But human wants have greatly multiplied and can no longer be satiated with food-products alone. Moreover, the business of providing for the new wants has been separated from agriculture. The total result is that the proportion of people who must devote themselves to the satisfaction of the elementary wants of society has vastly diminished and is still diminishing.

And this result is attained not only by the diminishing importance of bread and butter in the realm of human wants, but also by the increased per capita product which a specialized body of workers can win from the soil. By the use of fertilizers, by highly scientific methods of cultivation, by labor-saving machinery, and by the construction of transportation systems to open up distant and virgin fields, the present century has immensely reduced the relative number of workers who must remain attached to the soil to provide society's food-supply.

These facts are of fundamental importance in seeking the causes of urban growth. For cities are made up of persons who do not cultivate the soil; their existence presupposes a surplus food-supply, which in turn premises either great fertility of the soil or an advanced stage of the agricultural arts, and in either case convenient means of transportation.

DOCUMENT 2
Upton Sinclair, The Jungle (1905)

Upton Sinclair, a crusading reformer and respected author, attempted to bring home the horrors of the urban experience in his novel *The Jungle*. Although in the novel he presents a fictionalized account of a Lithuanian immigrant family, Sinclair employed a realistic style to expose how the lack of health standards in American industry exposed both workers and consumers to risk. His exposé of the meatpacking industry led to federal legislation. In the following passage, he highlights the inequity of city life in both home and factory.

During this time that Jurgis was looking for work occurred the death of little Kristoforas, one of the children of Teta Elzbieta. Both Kristoforas and his brother, Juozapas, were cripples, the latter having lost one leg by having it run over, and Krstoforas having congenital dislocation of the hip, which made it impossible for him ever to walk. He was the last of Teta Elzbieta's children, and perhaps he had been intended by nature to let her know that she had had enough. At any rate he was wretchedly sick and undersized; he had the rickets, and though he was over three years old, he was no bigger than an ordinary child of one. All day long he would crawl around the floor in a filthy little dress, whining and fretting; because the floor was full of drafts he was always catching cold, and snuffling because his nose ran. This made him a nuisance, and a source of endless trouble in the family. For his mother, with unnatural perversity, loved him best of all her children, and made a perpetual fuss over him—would let him do anything undisturbed, and would burst into tears when his fretting drove Jurgis wild.

And now he died. Perhaps it was the smoked sausage he had eaten that morning—which may have been made out of some of the tubercular pork that was condemned as unfit for export. At any rate, an hour after eating it, the child had begun to cry with pain, and in another hour he was rolling about on the floor in convulsions. Little Kotrina, who was all alone with him, ran out screaming for help, and after a while a doctor came, but not until Kristoforas had howled his last howl. No one was really sorry about this except poor Elzbieta, who was inconsolable. Jurgis announced that so far as he was concerned the child would have to be buried by the city, since they had no money for a funeral; and at this the poor woman almost went out of her senses, wringing her hands and screaming with grief and despair. Her child to be buried in a pauper's grave! And her stepdaughter to stand by and hear it said without protesting! It was enough to make Ona's father rise up out of his grave to rebuke her. If it had come to this, they might as well give up at once, and be buried all of them together! . . . In the end Marija said that she would help with ten dollars; and Jurgis being still obdurate, Elzbieta went in tears and begged the money from the neighbors, and so little Kristoforas had a mass and a hearse with white plumes on it, and a tiny plot in a graveyard with a wooden cross to mark the place. The poor mother was not the same for months after that; the mere sight of the floor where little Kristoforas had crawled about would make her weep. He had never had a fair chance, poor little fellow, she would say. He had been handicapped from his birth. If only she had heard about it in time, so that she might have had the great doctor to cure him of his lameness! . . . Some time ago, Elzbieta was told, a Chicago billionaire had paid a fortune to bring a great European surgeon over to cure his little daughter of the same disease from which Kristoforas had suffered. And because this surgeon had to have bodies to demonstrate upon, he announced that he would treat the children of the poor, a piece of magnanimity over which the papers became quite eloquent. Elzbieta, alas, did not read the papers, and no one had told her; but perhaps it was as well, for just then they would not have had the carfare to spare to go every day to wait upon the surgeon, nor for that matter anybody with the time to take the child.

All this while that he was seeking for work, there was a dark shadow hanging over Jurgis; as if a savage beast were lurking somewhere in the pathway of his life, and he knew it, and yet could not help approaching the place. There are all stages of being out of work in Packingtown, and he faced in dread the prospect of reaching the lowest. There is a place that waits for the lowest man—the fertilizer plant!

The men would talk about it in awe-striken whispers. Not more than one in ten had ever really tried it; the other nine had contented themselves with hearsay evidence and a peep through the door. There were some things worse than even starving to death. They would ask Jurgis if he had worked there yet, and if he meant to; and Jurgis would debate the matter with himself. As poor as they were, and making all the sacrifices that they were, would he dare to refuse any sort of work that was offered to him, be it as horrible as ever it could? Would he dare to go home and eat bread that had been earned by Ona, weak and complaining as she was, knowing that he had been given a chance, and had not had the nerve to take it?—And yet he might argue that way with himself all day, and one glimpse into the fertilizer works would send him away again shuddering. He was a man, and he would do his duty; he went and made application—bur surely he was not also required to hope for success!

The fertilizer works of Durham's lay away from the rest of the plant. Few visitors ever saw them, and the few who did would come out looking like Dante, of whom the peasants declared that he had been into hell. To this part of the yards came all the "tankage" and the waste products of all sorts; here they dried out the bones,—and in suffocating cellars where the daylight never came you might see men and women and children bending over whirling machines and sawing bits of bone into all sorts of shapes, breathing their lungs full of the fine dust, and doomed to die, every one of them, within a certain definite time. Here they made the blood into albumen, and made other foul-smelling things into things still more foul-smelling. In the corridors and caverns where it was done you might lose yourself as in the great caves of Kentucky. In the dust and the steam the electric lights would shine like far-off twinkling stars—red and blue-green and purple stars, according to the color of the mist and the brew from which it came. For the odors in these ghastly charnel houses there may be words in Lithuanian, but there are none in English. The person entering would have to summon his courage as for a cold-water plunge. He would go on like a man swimming under water; he would put his handkerchief over his face, and begin to cough and choke; and then, if he were still obstinate, he would find his head beginning to ring, and the veins in his forehead to throb, until finally he would be assailed by an overpowering blast of ammonia fumes, and would turn and run for his life, and come out half-dazed.

On top of this were the rooms where they dried the "tankage," the mass of brown stringy stuff that was left after the waste portions of the carcasses had had the lard and tallow tried out of them. This dried material they would then grind to a fine powder, and after they had mixed it up well with a mysterious but inoffensive brown rock which they brought in and ground up by the hundreds of carloads for that purpose, the substance was ready to be put into bags and sent out to the world as any one of a hundred different brands of standard bone phosphate. And then the farmer in Maine or California or Texas would buy this, at say twenty-five dollars a ton, and plant it with his corn; and for several days after the operation the fields would have a strong odor, and the farmer and his wagon and the very horses that had hauled it would all have it too. In Packingtown the fertilizer is pure, instead of being a flavoring, and instead of a ton or so spread out on several acres under the open sky, there are hundreds and thousands of tons of it in one building, heaped here and there in haystack piles, covering the floor several inches deep, and filling the air with a choking dust that becomes a blinding sandstorm when the wind stirs.

It was to this building that Jurgis came daily, as if dragged by an unseen hand. The month of May was an exceptionally cool one, and his secret prayers were granted; but early in June there came a record-breaking hot spell, and after that there were men wanted in the fertilizer mill.

DOCUMENT 3

Caroline Manning, The Immigrant Woman and Her Job (1930)

In 1930, the Women's Bureau of the U.S. Department of Labor published several case studies of the working lives of immigrant women. These Americans endured many hardships over the years to help support themselves and their families.

An early marriage did not give Anna T. the leisure and economic security she expected. Instead her burdens increased, and now she is glad if she has food and clothing for her family. In 1912, shortly after her father died in Hungary, Anna at the age of 16 came alone to the United States. With neither friends nor relatives to help her find work she followed women on their way to work and on her own initiative found a job in a cigar factory, where she began as a bunch maker and earned $2.50 the first week. Within a year she married a laborer, but he was often ill, his job was too heavy, and he lost much time, so they could not count on a full week's pay. In the 10 years of her married life she had given birth to six children, four of whom where living at the time of the interview. But childbirth never interfered long with her status as a wage earner; she worked within a week or so of confinement and always returned when the babies were very little. Sometimes her baby was brought to the factory for her to nurse during working hours.

Since 1912 Anna has worked 9 hours, 10 hours, day after day, and now one week's pay barely covers the monthly rental of $15. She lives in a dingy house with no gas and no sewer connection but she is thankful that, having lived in communities where bunch makers are in demand, she has always been able to find work. Realizing how close they are to the poverty dead line, she added: "So much baby; if I no work. I no eat." . . .

In 1905 Agnes D., aged 17, accompanied by a friend, left her farm home in Galicia bound for America, thinking she would make more money and have an easier time in the land of opportunity. Her sister, who had come to Philadelphia some time before, secured the first job for Agnes as a domestic

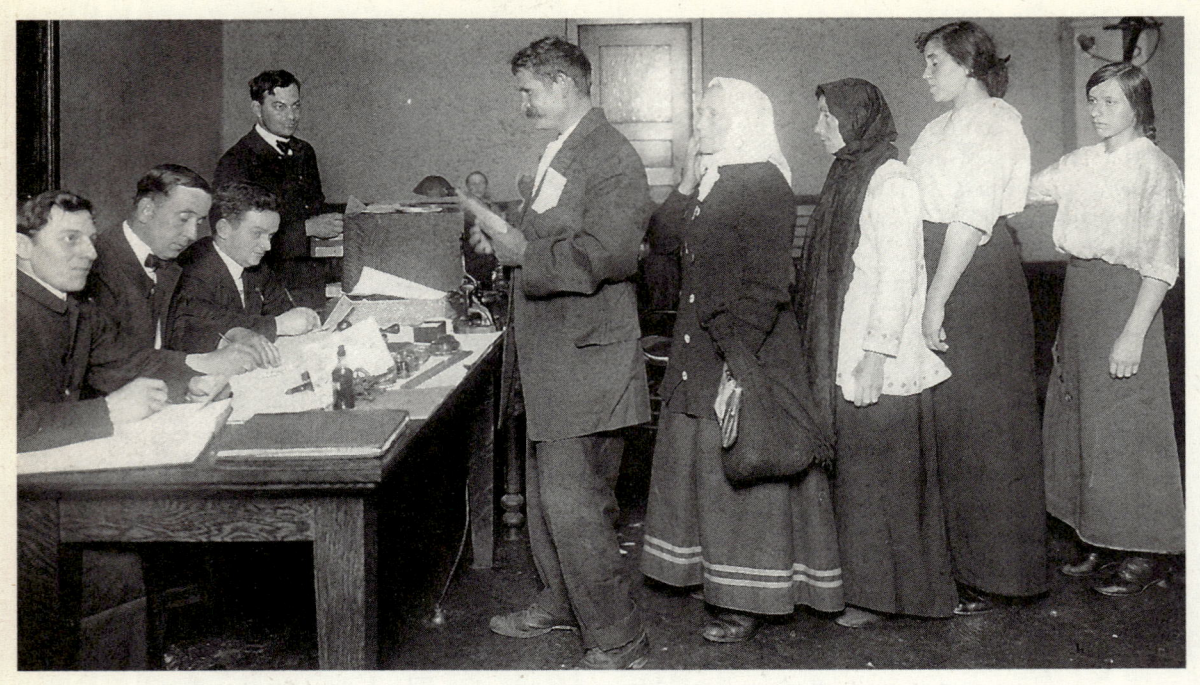

The growth of the cities between 1877 and 1890 attracted many immigrants to the United States with the promise of jobs, plentiful food supplies, and the chance to start a new life. Here, aliens are shown at Ellis Island, where some twelve million immigrants were processed between 1895 and 1924.

worker at $4 a week, but she found it so hard that after two months she left it. Her sister then took Agnes to an agency and for a fee of $1 Agnes was placed as a kitchen maid in a restaurant. Here her working day was from 5 A.M. to 11 P.M. Much of the time her hands were in hot water and the continuous standing made her feet tired and sore, but she hesitated to give up the job, since her sister had paid a fee to secure it for her, and she kept hoping that she would mind it less if she gave it a good trial. In about a year, having secured another job through the help of a friend, she quit the restaurant and began work "painting leather" (seasoning) in a tannery, for $6 a week. She continued at this place for almost eight years, until she married in 1914. Her husband proved to be no good and worked very irregularly and in 1921, when the eldest boy was 7 years old and the children could shift for themselves, she returned to her old job in the tannery, where she is still employed. When she has a full week she can earn as much as $17, but lately the business has been too bad and she has forgotten what a full pay envelope looks like. She takes pride in her work and regrets that she can never do "measuring," as she does not know her "numbers." Measuring is one of the most desirable jobs in a leather plant as the skins are measured automatically by a machine, which records their surface in square inches. The operator merely feeds the hides into the machine and copies the measurement, but Agnes can neither read nor write the numbers, for she has never attended school.

For three years this worker has been the chief support of the family, although the husband helps intermittently. She is concentrating all her energy to make ends meet, working by day in the tannery and by night at home, where in addition to the housework for her own family, she washes for a lodger . . .

Mrs. E. told a most unusual story of a long life spent as a cigar maker. She is still rolling cigars, with a background of about 40 years of cigar making in the United States and years of work in the same trade in Germany. Mrs. E.'s brother in this country kept writing to her, and "something did drive me like to come. I don't know if it was lucky or not, but anyway in 1885 had we come to America." Since her husband was a slow worker, it was necessary for Mrs. E. to go to work in the new country, and she has worked ever since except for interruptions due to slack times, strikes, an occasional change of job when shop conditions did not suit her, always sharing the support of the family with her husband.

Widowed, and 81 years old, she still cares for her little home and works in a shop daily from 9 to 5—shorter hours than formerly. "If I can't make a living from 9 to 5, some one else can do it." She earns only $8 or $9 a week but feels quite independent though her children see to it that she does not need anything. . . .

Thirteen years ago Angelina, then a girl of only 16, anxious to see the world, came with some neighbors to her cousin's in New York. She thought she knew what life in America would be like and only in a vague sort of way did she expect to work, but she supposed her money would buy beautiful clothes and that her life would be like that of the women in restaurant scenes in the movies. When, the day after she arrived, her cousin spoke quite emphatically about her going to work, she was surprised, but it was an even greater surprise when she found that she could not get the kind of work she wanted. She had started to learn dressmaking in Italy, but her cousin told her it was altogether different here, where each person makes but one special part of the dress and work is so scarce one has to take whatever can be found. So her cousin took her that day—her second in the United States—to an underwear shop and she was given pressing of corset covers, at 3 cents a dozen. Her full pay was $3.15. Adjustment to her work and her new life was difficult and she did not always succeed in keeping back the tears. She, who had come to this country to make and wear pretty clothes, never had a shirt waist that cost over $1 in the five years before she was married. "Why, if I had a dollar dress on, I thought I was somebody." She went on to say that she wore three or four fresh waists a week and succeeded at least in her desire to keep clean, but the family of cousins laughed at her because she was always washing and ironing. . . .

—Although Teresa M. was only 12 years old when she came to America, she can not read English; however, she speaks it better than do most of her neighbors. In Hungary there were cigar factories near her home and she was glad to find them here and eager to get to work; so her father helped her to find a job as a roller in a cigar factory and there, except for the interruptions of childbearing, she has been during the last 20 years. Altogether, she estimates that she has lost about 4 years from work during her 14 years of married life. "My man made me stay home for babies," and there had been five, although only three are living.

In spite of the 20 years, most of which had been spent in only two shops, she still was keen about working and was contented with her job. "I can always have my place. If I do not feel so good and stay home a day, I phone the boss and he says, 'All right, I'll get another roller in your place to-day but be sure you come back.' If we work, then the boss he likes."

Her husband also is thrifty and has one of the few steady jobs in a wire mill. There is an air of prosperity about their home and garden. Her husband could support the family, Teresa says, but they couldn't have things "nice" unless she worked; and she took the visitor to see the cellar, that had been cemented recently and paid for with her earnings—$200. There is electricity in the house, a washing machine, and modern plumbing.

The fact that her husband helps her with the housework, with the washings, and "sometimes he cook" makes it possible for Teresa to do two jobs. She says she could not do it "without my man, in everything he help," nor could the husband have such an attractive home if Teresa had not helped as a wage earner also.

She intends to continue working, hoping to be ready to meet adversity when it comes, for "everybody sick or old some day." She also hopes some day "to sit and rock on the porch like other ladies. I'll be old lady then."

DOCUMENT 4

Mary Antin, The Promised Land (1912)

The writer Mary Antin described her childhood immigrant experiences in her autobiography. She and her family traveled from Russia to join her father in Massachusetts during the late 1890s.

In our flat we did not think of such a thing as storing the coal in the bathtub. There was no bathtub. So in the evening of the first day my father conducted us to the public baths. As we moved along in a little procession, I was delighted with the illumination of the streets. So many lamps, and they burned until morning, my father said, and so people did not need to carry lanterns. In America, then, everything was free, as we had heard in Russia. Light was free; the streets were as bright as a synagogue on a holy day. Music was free; we had been serenaded, to our gaping delight, by a brass band of many pieces, soon after our installation on Union Place.

Education was free. That subject my father had written about repeatedly, as comprising his chief hope for us children, the essence of American opportunity, the treasure that no thief could touch, not even misfortune or poverty. It was the one thing that he was able to promise us when he sent for us; surer, safer than bread or shelter. On our second day I was thrilled with the realization of what this freedom of education meant. A little girl from across the alley came and offered to conduct us to school. My father was out, but we five between us had a few words of English by this time. We knew the word school. We understood. This child, who had never seen us till yesterday, who could not pronounce our names, who was not much better dressed than we, was able to offer us the freedom of the schools of Boston! No application made, no questions asked, no examinations, rulings, exclusions; no machinations, no fees. The doors stood open for every one of us. The smallest child could show us the way.

This incident impressed me more than anything I had heard in advance of the freedom of education in America. It was a concrete proof—almost the thing itself. One had to experience it to understand it. . . .

The kind of people who assisted us in these important matters form a group by themselves in the gallery of my friends. If I had never seen them from those early days till now, I should still have remembered them with gratitude. When I enumerate the long list of my American teachers, I must begin with those who came to us on Wall Street and taught us our first steps. To my mother, in her perplexity over the cookstove, the woman who showed her how to make the fire was an angel of deliverance. A fairy godmother to us children was she who led us to a wonderful country called "uptown," where, in a dazzlingly beautiful palace called a "department store," we exchanged our hateful homemade European costumes, which pointed us out as "greenhorns" to the children on the street, for real American machine-made garments, and issued forth glorified in each other's eyes.

With our despised immigrant clothing we shed also our impossible Hebrew names. A committee of our friends, several years ahead of us in American experience, put their heads together and concocted American names for us all. Those of our real names that had no pleasing American equivalents they ruthlessly discarded, content if they retained the initials. My mother, possessing a name that was not easily translatable, was punished with the undignified nickname of Annie. Fetchke, Joseph, and Deborah issued as Frieda, Joseph, and Dora, respectively. As for poor me, I was simply cheated. The name they gave me was hardly new. My Hebrew name being Maryashe in full, Mashke for short, Russianized into Marya (*Mar-ya*), my friends said that it would hold good in English as *Mary*; which was very disappointing, as I longed to possess a strange-sounding American name like the others....

In Chelsea, as in Boston, we made our stand in the wrong end of the town. Arlington Street was inhabited by poor Jews, poor Negroes, and a sprinkling of poor Irish. The side streets leading from it were occupied by more poor Jews and Negroes. It was a proper locality for a man without capital to do business. My father rented a tenement with a store in the basement. He put in a few barrels of flour and of sugar, a few boxes of crackers, a few gallons of kerosene, an assortment of soap of the "save the coupon" brands; in the cellar, a few barrels of potatoes, and a pyramid of kindling-wood; in the showcase, an alluring display of penny candy. He put out his sign, with a gilt-lettered warning of "Strictly Cash," and proceeded to give credit indiscriminately. That was the regular way to do business on Arlington Street. My father, in this three years' apprenticeship, had learned the trick of many trades. He knew when and how to "bluff." The legend of "Strictly Cash" was a protection against notoriously irresponsible customers; while none of the "good" customers, who had a record for paying regularly on Saturday, hesitated to enter the store with empty purses.

If my father knew the tricks of the trade, my mother could be counted on to throw all her talent and tact into the business. Of course she had no English yet, but as she could perform the acts of weighing, measuring, and mental computation of fractions mechanically, she was able to give her whole attention to the dark mysteries of the language, as intercourse with her customers gave her opportunity. In this she made such rapid progress that she soon lost all sense of disadvantage, and conducted herself behind the counter very much as if she were back in her old store in Polotzk. It was far more cosey than Polotzk—at least, so it seemed to me; for behind the store was the kitchen, where, in the intervals of slack trade, she did her cooking and washing. Arlington Street customers were used to waiting while the storekeeper salted the soup or rescued a loaf from the oven.

Once more Fortune favored my family with a thin little smile, and my father, in reply to a friendly inquiry, would say, "One makes a living," with a shrug of the shoulders that added "but nothing to boast of." It was characteristic of my attitude toward bread-and-butter matters that this contented me, and I felt free to devote myself to the conquest of my new world. Looking back to those critical first years, I see myself always behaving like a child let loose in a garden to play and dig and chase the butterflies. Occasionally, indeed, I was stung by the wasp of family trouble; but I knew a healing ointment—my faith in America. My father had come to America to make a living. America, which was free and fair and kind, must presently yield him what he sought. I had come to America to see a new world, and I followed my own ends with the utmost assiduity; only, as I ran out to explore, I would look back to see if my house were in order behind me—if my family still kept its head above water.

In after years, when I passed as an American among Americans, if I was suddenly made aware of the past that lay forgotten,—if a letter from Russia, or a paragraph in the newspaper, or a conversation overheard in the street-car, suddenly reminded me of what I might have been,—I thought it miracle enough that I, Mashke, the granddaughter of Raphael the Russian, born to a humble destiny, should be at home in an American metropolis, be free to fashion my own life, and should dream my dreams in English phrases. But in the beginning my admiration was spent on more concrete embodiments of the splendors of America; such as fine houses, gay shops, electric engines and apparatus, public buildings, illuminations, and parades. My early letters to my Russian friends were filled with boastful descriptions of these glories of my new country. No native citizen of Chelsea took such pride and delight in its institutions as I did. It required no fife and drum corps, no Fourth of July procession, to set me tingling with patriotism. Even the common agents and instruments of municipal life, such as the letter carrier and the fire engine, I regarded with a measure of respect. I know what I thought of people who said that Chelsea was a very small, dull, unaspiring town, with no discernible excuse for a separate name or existence.

DOCUMENT 5

William Riordan, Plunkitt of Tammany Hall (1905)

Politics in many American cities became synonymous with "bosses" and "machines." Men such as George Washington Plunkitt, son of Irish immigrants, served as intermediaries between various ethnic communities and municipal government. They spoke for influential political organizations like the New York City Democratic Party's Tammany Hall. Such machines blended community service with blatant corruption. Journalist William Riordan chronicled Plunkitt's career as a local political boss.

If he holds his district and Tammany is in power, he is amply rewarded by a good office and the opportunities that go with it. What these opportunities are has been shown by the quick rise to wealth of so many Tammany district leaders. With the examples before him of Richard Croker, once leader of the Twentieth District; John F. Carroll, formerly leader of the Twenty-ninth; Timothy ("Dry Dollar") Sullivan, late leader of the Sixth, and many others, he can always look forward to riches and ease while he is going through the drudgery of his daily routine.

This is a record of a day's work by Plunkitt:

2 A.M.: Aroused from sleep by the ringing of his doorbell; went to the door and found a bartender, who asked him to go to the police station and bail out a saloonkeeper who had been arrested for violating the excise law. Furnished bail and returned to bed at three o'clock.

6 A.M.: Awakened by fire engines passing his house. Hastened to the scene of the fire, according to the custom of the Tammany district leaders, to give assistance to the fire sufferers, if needed. Met several of his election district captains who are always under orders to look out for fires, which are considered great vote-getters. Found several tenants

who had been burned out, took them to a hotel, supplied them with clothes, fed them, and arranged temporary quarters for them until they could rent and furnish new apartments.

8:30 A.M.: Went to the police court to look after his constituents. Found six "drunks." Secured the discharge of four by a timely word with the judge, and paid the fines of two.

9 A.M.: Appeared in the Municipal District Court. Directed one of his district captains to act as counsel for a widow against whom dispossess proceedings had been instituted and obtained an extension of time. Paid the rent of a poor family about to be dispossessed and gave them a dollar for food.

11 A.M.: At home again. Found four men waiting for him. One had been discharged by the Metropolitan Railway Company for neglect of duty, and wanted the district leader to fix things. Another wanted a job on the road. The third sought a place on the Subway and the fourth, a plumber, was looking for work with the Consolidated Gas Company. The district leader spent nearly three hours fixing things for the four men, and succeeded in each case.

3 P.M.: Attended the funeral of an Italian as far as the ferry. Hurried back to make his appearance at the funeral of a Hebrew constituent. Went conspicuously to the front both in the Catholic church and the synagogue, and later attended the Hebrew confirmation ceremonies in the synagogue.

7 P.M.: Went to district headquarters and presided over a meeting of election district captains. Each captain submitted a list of all the voters in his district, reported on their attitude toward Tammany, suggested who might be won over and how they could be won, told who were in need, and who were in trouble of any kind and the best way to reach them. District leader took notes and gave orders.

8 P.M.: Went to a church fair. Took chances on everything, bought ice cream for the young girls and the children. Kissed the little ones, flattered their mothers and took their fathers out for something down at the corner.

9 P.M.: At the clubhouse again. Spent $10 on tickets for a church excursion and promised a sub-

American cities once consisted of a mass of small structures. With the introduction of the skyscraper, cities were able to expand upward as well as outward.

scription for a new church bell. Bought tickets for a baseball game to be played by two nines from his district. Listened to the complaints of a dozen push-cart peddlers who said they were persecuted by the police and assured them he would go to Police Headquarters in the morning and see about it.

10:30 P.M.: Attended a Hebrew wedding reception and dance. Had previously sent a handsome wedding present to the bride.

12 P.M.: In bed.

That is the actual record of one day in the life of Plunkitt. He does some of the same things every day, but his life is not so monotonous as to be wearisome.

Sometimes the work of a district leader is exciting, especially if he happens to have a rival who intends to make a contest for the leadership at the primaries. In that case, he is even more alert, tries to reach the fires before his rival, sends out runners to look for "drunks and disorderlies" at the police stations, and keeps a very close watch on the obituary columns of the newspapers.

A few years ago there was a bitter contest for the Tammany leadership of the Ninth District between John C. Sheehan and Frank J. Goodwin. Both had had long experience in Tammany politics and both understood every move of the game.

Every morning their agents went to their respective headquarters before seven o'clock and read through the death notices in all the morning papers. If they found that anybody in the district had died, they rushed to the homes of their principals with the information and then there was a race to the house of the deceased to offer condolences, and, if the family were poor, something more substantial.

On the day of the funeral there was another contest. Each faction tried to surpass the other in the number and appearance of the carriages it sent to the funeral, and more than once they almost came to blows at the church or in the cemetery.

On one occasion the Goodwinites played a trick on their adversaries which has since been imitated in other districts. A well-known liquor dealer who had a considerable following died, and both Sheehan and Goodwin were eager to become his political heir by making a big showing at the funeral.

Goodwin managed to catch the enemy napping. He went to all the livery stables in the district, hired all the carriages for the day, and gave orders to two hundred of his men to be on hand as mourners.

Sheehan had never had any trouble about getting all the carriages that he wanted, so he let the matter go until the night before the funeral. Then he found that he could not hire a carriage in the district.

He called his district committee together in a hurry and explained the situation to them. He could get all the vehicles he needed in the adjoining district, he said, but if he did that, Goodwin would rouse the voters of the Ninth by declaring that he (Sheehan) had patronized foreign industries.

Finally, it was decided that there was nothing to do but to go over to Sixth Avenue and Broadway for carriages. Sheehan made a fine turnout at the funeral, but the deceased was hardly in his grave before Goodwin raised the cry of "Protection to home industries," and denounced his rival for patronizing livery-stable keepers outside of his district. The cry had its effect in the primary campaign. At all events, Goodwin was elected leader.

A recent contest for the leadership of the Second District illustrated further the strenuous work of the Tammany district leaders. The contestants were Patrick Divver, who had managed the district for years, and Thomas F. Foley.

Both were particularly anxious to secure the large Italian vote. They not only attended all the Italian christenings and funerals, but also kept a close lookout for the marriages in order to be on hand with wedding presents.

At first, each had his own reporter in the Italian quarter to keep track of the marriages. Later, Foley conceived a better plan. He hired a man to stay all day at the City Hall marriage bureau, where most Italian couples go through the civil ceremony, and telephone to him at his saloon when anything was doing at the bureau.

Foley had a number of presents ready for use and, whenever he received a telephone message from his man, he hastened to the City Hall with a ring or a watch or a piece of silver and handed it to the bride with his congratulations. As a consequence, when Divver got the news and went to the home of the couple with his present, he always found that Foley had been ahead of him. Toward the end of the campaign, Divver also stationed a man at the marriage bureau and then there were daily foot races and fights between the two heelers.

DOCUMENT 6

Charlotte Perkins Gilman, "If I Were a Man" (1914)

The middle class expanded with the growth of cities, and as it did so the distance between a woman's life in the home and a man's in the business world became more evident. In her short story "If I Were a Man," Charlotte Perkins Gilman, a pioneering feminist and social critic, imagined what a woman might discover about the division between the sexes if she could spend a day as her husband.

   Mollie was "true to type." She was a beautiful instance of what is reverentially called "a true woman." Little, of course—no true woman may be big. Pretty, of course—no true woman could possibly be plain. Whimsical, capricious, charming changeable, devoted to pretty clothes and always "wearing them well," as the esoteric phrase has it. (This does not refer to the clothes—they do not wear well in the least—but to some special grace of putting them on and carrying them about, granted to but few, it appears.)

   She was also a loving wife and a devoted mother possessed of "the social gift" and the love of "society" that goes with it, and with all these was fond and proud of her home and managed it as capably as—well, as most women do.

   If ever there was a true woman it was Mollie Mathewson, yet she was wishing heart and soul she was a man.

   And all of a sudden she was!

   She was Gerald, walking down the path so erect and square-shouldered, in a hurry for his morning train, as usual, and, it must be confessed, in something of a temper....

   A man! Really a man—with only enough subconscious memory of herself remaining to make her recognize the differences.

   At first there was a funny sense of size and weight and extra thickness, the feet and hands seemed strangely large, and her long, straight, free legs swung forward at a gait that made her feel as if on stilts.

   This presently passed, and in its place, growing all day, wherever she went, came a new and delightful feeling of being *the right size*.

   Everything fitted now. Her back snugly against the seat-back, her feet comfortably on the floor. Her feet?... His feet! She studied them carefully. Never before, since her early school days, had she felt such freedom and comfort as to feet—they were firm and solid on the ground when she walked; quick, springy, safe—as when, moved by an unrecognizable impulse, she had run after, caught, and swung aboard the car.

   Another impulse fished in a convenient pocket for change—instantly, automatically, bringing forth a nickel for the conductor and a penny for the newsboy.

   These pockets came as a revelation. Of course she had known they were there, had counted them, made fun of them, mended them, even envied them; but she never had dreamed of how it felt to have pockets.

   Behind her newspaper she let her consciousness, that odd mingled consciousness, rove from pocket to pocket, realizing the armored assurance of having all those things at hand, instantly get-at-able, ready to meet emergencies. The cigar case gave her a warm feeling of comfort—it was full; the firmly held fountain pen, safe unless she stood on her head; the keys, pencils, letters, documents, notebook, checkbook, bill folder—all at once, with a deep rushing sense of power and pride, she felt what she had never felt before in all her life—the possession of money, of her own earned money—hers to give or to withhold, not to beg for, tease for, wheedle for—hers. . . .

When he took his train, his seat in the smoking car, she had a new surprise. All about him were the other men, commuters too, and many of them friends of his.

To her, they would have been distinguished as "Mary Wade's husband," "the man Belle Grant is engaged to," "that rich Mr. Shopworth," or "that pleasant Mr. Beale." And they would all have lifted their hats to her, bowed, made polite conversation if near enough—especially Mr. Beale.

Now came the feeling of open-eyed acquaintance, of knowing men—as they were. The mere amount of this knowledge was a surprise to her—the whole background of talk from boyhood up, the gossip of barber-shop and club, the conversation of morning and evening hours on trains, the knowledge of political affiliation, of business standing and prospects, of character—in a light she had never known before.

They came and talked to Gerald, one and another. He seemed quite popular. And as they talked, with this new memory and new understanding, an understanding which seemed to include all these men's minds, there poured in on the submerged consciousness beneath a new, a startling knowledge—what men really think of women.

Good, average, American men were there; married men for the most part, and happy—as happiness goes in general. In the minds of each and all there seemed to be a two-story department, quite apart from the rest of their ideas, a separate place where they kept their thoughts and feelings about women.

In the upper half were the tenderest emotions, the most exquisite ideals, the sweetest memories, all lovely sentiments as to "home" and "mother," all delicate admiring adjectives, a sort of sanctuary, where a veiled statue, blindly adored, shared place with beloved yet commonplace experiences.

In the lower half—here that buried consciousness woke to keen distress—they kept quite another assortment of ideas. Here, even in this clean-minded husband of hers, was the memory of stories told at men's dinners, of worse ones overheard in street or car, of base traditions, coarse epithets, gross experiences—known, though not shared.

And all these in the department "woman," while in the rest of the mind—here was new knowledge indeed.

The world opened before her. Not the world she had been reared in—where Home had covered all the map, almost, and the rest had been "foreign," or "unexplored country," but the world as it was—man's world, as made, lived in, and seen, by men.

It was dizzying. To see the houses that fled so fast across the car window, in terms of builders' bills, or of some technical insight into materials and methods; to see a passing village with lamentable knowledge of who "owned it" and of how its Boss was rapidly aspiring in state power, or of how that kind of paving was a failure; to see shops, not as mere exhibitions of desirable objects, but as business ventures, many were sinking ships, some promising a profitable voyage—this new world bewildered her.

She—as Gerald—had already forgotten about that bill, over which she—as Mollie—was still crying at home. Gerald was "talking business" with this man, "talking politics" with that, and now sympathizing with the carefully withheld troubles of a neighbor.

Mollie had always sympathized with the neighbor's wife before.

She began to struggle violently with this large dominant masculine consciousness. She remembered with sudden clearness things she had read, lectures she had heard, and resented with increasing intensity this serene masculine preoccupation with the male point of view.

Mr. Miles, the little fussy man who lived on the other side of the street, was talking now. He had a large complacent wife; Mollie had never liked her much, but had always thought him rather nice—he was so punctilious in small courtesies.

And here he was talking to Gerald—such talk!

"Had to come in here," he said. "Gave my seat to a dame who was bound to have it. There's nothing they won't get when they make up their minds to it—eh?"

"No fear!" said the big man in the next seat. "They haven't much mind to make up, you know—and if they do, they'll change it."

"The real danger," began the Rev. Alfred Smythe, the new Episcopal clergyman, a thin, nervous, tall man with a face several centuries behind the times, "is that they will overstep the limits of their God-appointed sphere."

"Their natural limits ought to hold 'em, I think," said cheerful Dr. Jones. "You can't get around physiology, I tell you."

"I've never seen any limits, myself, not to what they want, anyhow," said Mr. Miles. "Merely a rich husband and a fine house and no end of bonnets and dresses, and the latest thing in motors, and a few diamonds—and so on. Keeps us pretty busy."

There was a tired gray man across the aisle. He had a very nice wife, always beautifully dressed, and three unmarried daughters, also beautifully dressed—Mollie knew them. She knew he worked hard, too, and she looked at him now a little anxiously.

But she smiled cheerfully.

"Do you good, Miles," he said. "What else would a man work for? A good woman is about the best thing on earth."

"And a bad one's the worse, that's sure," responded Miles.

"She's a pretty weak sister, viewed professionally," Dr. Jones averred with solemnity, and the Rev. Alfred Smythe added, "She brought evil into the world."

Gerald Mathewson sat up straight. Something was stirring in him which he did not recognize—yet could not resist.

"Seems to me we all talk like Noah," he suggested drily. "or the ancient Hindu scriptures. Women have their limitations, but so do we, God knows. Haven't we known girls in school and college just as smart as we were?"

"They cannot play our games," coldly replied the clergyman.

Gerald measured his meager proportions with a practiced eye.

"I never was particularly good at football myself," he modestly admitted, "but I've known women who could outlast a man in all-round endurance. Besides—life isn't spent in athletics!"

This was sadly true. They all looked down the aisle where a heavy ill-dressed man with a bad complexion sat alone. He had held the top of the columns once, with headlines and photographs. Now he earned less than any of them. . . .

"Yes, we blame them for grafting on us, but are we willing to let our wives work? We are not. It hurts our pride, that's all. We are always criticizing them for making mercenary marriages, but what do we call a girl who marries a chump with no money? Just a poor fool, that's all. And they know it.

"As for Mother Eve—I wasn't there and can't deny the story, but I will say this. If she brought evil into the world, we men have had the lion's share of keeping it going ever since—how about that?"

They drew into the city, and all day long in his business, Gerald was vaguely conscious of new views, strange feelings, and the submerged Mollie learned and learned.

DOCUMENT 7

Proposal to Buffalo, New York, Park Commission (1888)

The growth of the city could be unpredictable and uncontrollable. City leaders did attempt—albeit with limited success—to anticipate the need for open spaces that would evoke the pleasures of rural life for harried urban residents. The landscape architecture firm Olmstead, Vaux & Company offered the following plan to the City of Buffalo, New York, Park Commission to ensure suitable recreational spaces for an industrial city.

To the Park Commissioners:

Sirs,—We have the honor to submit drawings showing a plan for a park adapted to a site on the shore of Lake Erie, south of the city, as contemplated in a resolution of the Common Council of February, 1887, and in subsequent action of your Commission, recorded in its last Annual Report. For distinction's sake, we shall refer to the proposed park as the South Park, and to your present park as the North Park.

It is believed that many citizens of Buffalo are of the opinion that discussion of the subject of this report might better be deferred until it has been more maturely considered whether the city just now wants to engage in another park enterprise, and whether if it does so, the required park had better be in a place naturally so unattractive within itself as that which you have had in view. Mature consideration can be given to neither of these questions, without a much more definite statement of the project than has hitherto been possible, and a better knowledge than has hitherto been had by the public, of what could be made of the conditions of the locality. What is thus wanting to open a profitable discussion, it is hoped that this report may supply....

Twenty years hence Buffalo will be not only a city of much larger trade, much larger wealth and much larger population, but it will be a city of much more metropolitan character, than, notwithstanding its recent rapid advance in this respect, it has yet come to be. The currents of civilization, which in all metropolitan centres have, in modern times, been increasingly manifest, will have been growing correspondingly stronger. The drift of these currents in relation to parks is indicated by the fact that eleven cities of Europe and America have, during the last thirty years, added twenty thousand acres of land to their park properties, and that towns which a few years ago were thought to be particularly well provided, have been recently adding largely to what they had; as London, 6000 acres, New York, 3000, Boston, 700.

The drift being as thus indicated, the question upon which this report bears, is not whether the people of Buffalo require just now more and other park provisions than they have, but whether the people of Buffalo twenty years hence will have required no more and no other? It is wholly probable that in less time than that a considerable additional park will have been required and will have been provided for. If so, it is not to be questioned that going about the business now in a deliberate way, pursuing the same steady, methodical, frugal but efficient methods that have distinguished the proceedings of your Commission from its origin, such additional park provision as will be required may be obtained of a much more valuable character and at much less outlay than it will be, if all effective action toward the result is now staved off indefinitely. This consideration, rather than a conviction of any immediate urgent necessity for an additional park, accounts for such favor as the project has hitherto received from conservative citizens. . . .

Your present North Park is rarely well adapted to certain quiet forms of recreation, favoring a contemplative or musing turn of mind and restful refreshment. It is not in the least larger than it should be for a park designed to that end, and in a single park of its size, provision for no other end is more desirable for a city. But it is not always that merely soothing, out-of-door refreshment is wanted. Occasionally by all, but oftenest by those who pass most of their time in monotonous occupations and amid sombre surroundings, tranquilizing natural scenes are less demanded than those by which gayety, liveliness, and a slight spirit of adventure are stimulated. This being the case, it is inevitable that an inclination will arise, and year by year increase, to have better provision made for the purpose on the North Park. It will follow that unless comprehensive provision for it is soon undertaken elsewhere, you will be constrained to meet the requirement by a succession of small, feeble, imperfect and desultory interpolations upon the design of the North Park. An unconsciously indulged tendency in that direction has, we think, already been manifest in the minds of some of your number. If it should continue and spread, the North Park will come in time to lose the character in which otherwise it will, year after year, be gaining, and by which it would take a more and more distinguished position among the parks of the world, while, because not having been broadly designed for anything else, it can be made respectable in no other character. Thus the question now to be decided may be this:

Twenty years hence shall Buffalo have one park, of a poor, confused character, or two, each of a good, distinct character?

Assuming that it is wise that the City should enter upon proceedings looking to the acquisition, in good time, of another park, and of a park which shall have a character essentially different from that of the park which it set about obtaining twenty years ago, argument will hardly be needed to make the following conclusions acceptable:

1st. Buffalo owes its importance as a city to its position on Lake Erie. It has in Lake Erie really great natural scenery. It has no other, and can have no other to be compared with it in value. It has no work of art and can have no work of art that will compare with it in value. Having made no use of its good fortune in this particular for the aggrandizement of its first large park, it ought not, except for absolutely conclusive reasons, to fail of making use of it in its second. The new park should be in a position to annex to itself the grandeur of Lake Erie.

2d. The situation of the first park having secured much greater advantages of access and use to those who would visit it in carriages upon common roads, than those who could come to it only by other means of transit, it will be better, in fixing the place and determining the plan of the second park, that special regard should be given to the point of providing inexpensive, convenient and agreeable means of access to it and conveyance within it, independently of ordinary road vehicles.

The site which we were specially invited by your Board to consider, has the following obvious advantages:

1st. It looks upon the Lake.

2d. There is navigable water and there are four lines of railway already in operation, and others contemplated, between the place and the heart of the City.

3d. To acquire the site, nothing of importance would have to be paid for buildings or other improvements. The land as a whole has little productive value, and probably none as near the heart of the city has had as little commercial or speculative value.

DOCUMENT 8

The New York Times, *Review of Opening Night at Coney Island (1904)*

Urban living gave rise to new forms of large-scale public entertainment. Businessmen discovered exciting ways to accommodate the desire of citydwellers to maximize pleasure during leisure hours. Amusement parks attracted millions of Americans to human-made mechanical thrills and exotic pageantry. A front-page story in the May 15, 1904, *New York Times* reviews the season's opening night at Coney Island, home of the era's most celebrated amusement park.

They took the lid off Coney Island last night, and a quarter of a million men and women got a glimpse of a swaying, rocking, glittering magic city by the sea. It was Coney Island's opening day, but Coney Island never before experienced such a bewildering opening. First of all, there were more people there than had ever been at Coney Island at one time before. Then there were more dazzling, wriggling, spectacular amusements offered than had ever before been collected together at any one place at any time.

Picturesque Luna Park, with its added acres of new attractions, and the much-talked-about Dreamland presented a bewildering mixture of men, animals, and things that words can scarcely describe. They had been gathered from every corner of the globe, and represented about everything that nature and science have ever produced. Coney Island is regenerated, and almost every trace of Old Coney has been wiped out. Frankfurters, peanuts, and popcorn were among the few things left to represent the place as it was in the old days.

With the new order of things came herds of elephants, genuine Nautch girls, Indian rajahs, snake charmers, Eskimos, Indians, Japs, Russians, Chinamen, acrobats, jugglers, performing camels, pugilistic horses, and bears that could ride a horse as well as some of the jockies of the race track.

Sixteen of the newly acquired acres of land in Luna Park were set aside for the reproduction of the glittering Durbar of Delhi. There was the Vice Royal palace in the city that had been reproduced in miniature, and a pageant of Oriental splendor was presented. There were gilded chariots and prancing horses, and trained elephants and dancing girls, regiments of soldiers, and an astonishing number of real Eastern people and animals in gay and stately trappings. The magnificence of the scene was such as to make those who witnessed it imagine they were in a genuine Oriental city. In fact, there was a charm about the streets of Delhi that kept the people spellbound until the exhibition ended. Five thousand people at a time saw this remarkable show, and then went back to see it a second time.

Outside in Luna Park proper, 20,000 or more men, women, and children gazed in wonderment at the daring feats of the acrobats, tight-rope walkers, and horsemen who appeared in connection with the three-ring circus. They saw two wonderful horses with gloves strapped on their forefeet rear up and box in a manner that would have done credit to old-time pugilists. The pugilistic horses boxed in rounds and clinched now and then with their legs about each other's neck just as prizefighters clinch.

Then came the bears that rode in jockey fashion, much to the amusement of the thousands of children who were there.

The Trip to the Moon, Twenty Thousand Leagues Under the Sea, the chutes, the scenic railway, and the other features of Luna Park were all well patronized. A new feature, known as whirl-the-whirl, proved to be a money coiner. In that boats are arranged to sail through the air in circular fashion at a height of almost a hundred feet. The newly arranged dancing platforms and the new theatres in Luna Park were as well patronized as they possibly could be, for they were crowded from the time the gates opened until closing time at midnight.

On the way out the crowd found a complete printing plant and newspaper office in operation, turning out a newspaper—The Evening Star—which will be published daily in Luna Park. The first issue contained an interview with Police Commissioner McAdoo, in which the Commissioner was quoted as saying that the new Coney Island was clean, moral, and magnificent.

There were many city and country officials among the visitors at Luna Park yesterday. Messrs. Thompson & Dundy, the proprietors of the park, entertaining them, together with a thousand other guests, after the banquet in the big dining hall over the dancing pavilion.

Dreamland, the site of which extends from Henry's Bathing Pavilion to the Iron Steamboat Company's pier, takes in the old pier and reaches from Surf Avenue far into the ocean. Dreamland opened its gates for the first time yesterday, and scarcely at any time were there less than 20,000 persons visiting its wonderful features. Illuminated at night, it resembled a city in itself. But the visitor who went there yesterday found that after getting in it contained many miniature cities. It proved to be a veritable fairyland, with its mystic palaces and Aladdin-like shows. In addition to these there was a circus in three rings, high divers, jugglers, aerial performances, and other things that are difficult to describe.

Probably one of its most interesting features is

Coney Island provided a retreat from the pressures of city living that was in stark contrast to the rural escape offered by Central Park. By 1900, nearly 500,000 people would frequent Coney Island on a typical summer weekend.

the Dwarf City, with its thousand tiny inhabitants. Storekeepers, policemen, firemen, musicians, wagon drivers, and others who live there are all dwarfs. They have a Liliputian Fire Department, with little fire engines, a miniature livery stable, a midget theatre, midget circus, diminutive horses, bantam chickens, and everything else that would go to make up a midget city, even to its midget Chinese laundrymen. Although everything there is on the smallest possible scale, it is perhaps one of the biggest features of the regenerated Coney Island.

The Incubator Building in Dreamland is designed in farmhouse style, the first story being of brick and the upper part in half timber. The tiled roof has a gable with a large storck overlooking a nest of cherubs. It is a scientific demonstration of how the lives of babies can be saved. It cost $36,000, and the building is full of babies.

The Scenic Railway Building in Dreamland has a front that expresses very successfully "l'art nouveau." The Dog and Monkey Building contains Wormwood's Dog and Monkey Show. The front of the structure symbolizes its purpose and is decorated with cocoanut trees, in which monkeys spring from branch to branch.

One of the principal attractions of Dreamland is the famous Bostock animal show.

The attraction called the "Destruction of Pompeii" is lodged in the Pompeiian Building. A painting back of the columns was executed by Charles S. Shean, a gold medalist of the Paris Salon. The subject of the work is the Bay of Naples and the surrounding neighborhood before the destruction of Pompeii.

The ballroom in Dreamland is of generous proportions, and of the style of the French Renaissance. It is reached by passing through the restaurant, the latter being 240 feet long by 100 feet wide. A movable stairway with a capacity of 7,000 persons an hour takes the visitors to the restaurant and grand ballroom, illuminated with 20,000 electric lights....

Chilkoot Pass consists of a huge proscenium arch in classic style. In ascending and descending this arch the visitors are transported by a movable stairway in a reproduction of the game of bagatelle on an enormous scale. After the visitors have ascended to the high platform, they slide down an inclined plane and roll over and strike against various obstructions which take the place of pegs, and finally reach the bottom and land in holes which are numbered, prizes being given according to the numbers entered.

Dreamland was the conception of ex-Senator William H. Reynolds of Brooklyn, and cost more than $3,000,000 to construct. Mr. Reynolds and a number of prominent New Yorkers were present last night when it formally opened with the Fire Show. Four thousand persons were employed in producing this spectacle. Upon the ringing of the fire alarm firemen leaped from their beds in real engine houses, and slid down brass poles as they do in the New York Department. Their machines and horses were hitched in the regular way, and then they attended a real fire, which was certainly startling. A hotel appeared to burn, with scores of guests apparently trying to escape, and altogether this show proved a great success.

Study Questions

1. From the standpoint of the urban dwellers themselves, what advantages did city life offer? What tradeoffs did urban residents have to make to gain such advantages?

2. To what degree did immigrants assimilate to urban American culture? What institutions or experiences assisted them in their adjustment?

3. Did women and men comprehend urban culture in different ways? Did immigrant women and native-born women have similar experiences?

4. Why did urban planners worry about parks? How did Coney Island reflect the new urban culture?

5

Imperial Power and Domestic Unrest

Events at the turn of the century transformed the United States into a world power. They also destabilized domestic politics. America's industrial might and its success at incorporating territory from the Atlantic to the Pacific stimulated national interest in global competition with European powers. Some imperialists even speculated—in racist fashion—that north European culture was destined to rule the world's allegedly inferior peoples (Document 1). Dreams of empire dazzled the public at the same time that working-class Americans—farmers as well as factory workers—became fearful of subjugation by almighty capitalists. Despite military triumphs abroad, dramatic confrontations at home exposed the deep divisions and inequalities of American life (Document 2).

The pseudo-scientific racism of the era threatened further to debase the nation's African Americans. Their political and social rights had eroded with the end of Reconstruction, but during the 1890s blacks suffered increasingly severe enforcement of racial separation. Indeed, in the 1896 case *Plessy* v. *Ferguson*, the U.S. Supreme Court endorsed segregation in public places and private businesses alike. White violence against blacks across the South accompanied inequitable legal treatment (Document 3).

Discrimination against marginalized inhabitants flared at roughly the same time that many national leaders enthusiastically advocated American intervention throughout the world. U.S. interest in territories beyond its continental shores had a long history, especially with regard to the Caribbean islands. Spain maintained colonial control of Cuba and Puerto Rico, whose rich plantations were highly attractive to American eyes. Similarly, North Americans and Europeans, who coveted Central America, hoped to control a future canal linking the Atlantic and the Pacific. Meanwhile, after solidifying its hold on the Pacific Coast of North America, the United States sought to extend its influence over Samoa and the Hawaiian Islands in order to facilitate commercial contact with Asia (Document 4).

The nation realized the full extent of its imperial ambitions during the 1890s. In 1893 Americans deposed Hawaii's Queen Liliuokalani and in 1898 formally annexed the islands. Cuban rebellion against Spanish rule in 1895 seized the imagination of American citizens and politicians, as newspapers covered in gruesome detail Spain's fierce response to the Cuban insurgency. Such jingoism, sparking hyperbolic

"Well, I Hardly Know Which to Take First." The American appetite for land at the end of the nineteenth century was for naval bases and strategic commercial centers on major trade routes—a sharp contrast from early U.S. expansion, which focused on the search for new territories to populate.

reaction when the U.S. battleship *Maine* exploded in the port of Havana, helped persuade President William McKinley and Congress to declare war on Spain. After hostilities commenced, it took less than four months for U.S. forces to seize not only Cuba and Puerto Rico but also the Philippine Islands. Over the vociferous objections of some Americans, the Philippines and Puerto Rico were made U.S. possessions. Perhaps the icing on the imperial cake came five years later, when President Theodore Roosevelt, a hero of the Spanish-American war, sponsored a revolution of Panamanian patriots against Colombia in order to establish American jurisdiction over a future Panama canal (Document 5).

The drive for cultural and commercial dominance abroad had parallels at home. Social theorists who perverted Darwinian science speculated that nature demanded the sorting of winners and losers without interference from the government or moral reformers (Document 6). For those Americans who, despite hard work and great personal sacrifice, felt themselves falling farther behind, another answer suggested itself. The structure of the economy was unfair. Farmers of a conspiratorial turn of mind wondered why their earnings were down, why railroad rates were up, and why no credit was available. The Republican and Democratic Parties seemed unconcerned with the workers' plight. In time, various regional Farmers' Alliances united to form a third party, the People's Party (Document 7). Their candidate for president in 1892 received more than a million votes running on a platform of economic reform. After a national depression struck in 1893, the Populist crusade appeared to enjoy a bright future.

One of the more divisive issues of the day was whether or not the federal government should increase the circulation of money and thus alleviate the squeeze on many cash-poor farmers and workers by coining silver instead of relying on the gold supply. Populists fought for the unrestricted coinage of silver. When the Democratic convention nominated William Jennings Bryan, a passionate spokesman for silver, to run against the Republican McKinley for president, the People's Party made common cause with the Democrats (Document 8). McKinley's victory in every northern state was more than enough to defeat Bryan, who swept the South and the West. The Populist movement crumbled in the face of the Democratic alliance and suffered a devastating defeat.

DOCUMENT 1

Josiah Strong, Our Country (1885)

Some Americans viewed expansion overseas as both cultural destiny and religious duty. Mixing racist belief in the superiority of Anglo-Saxons, the evolutionary theories of Charles Darwin, and Christian commitment to missionary work, the Reverend Josiah Strong (1847–1916) helped stimulate the nation's interest in expansion in his best-seller *Our Country*.

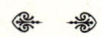

It seems to me that God, with infinite wisdom and skill, is training the Anglo-Saxon race for an hour sure to come in the world's future. Heretofore there has always been in the history of the world a comparatively unoccupied land westward, into which the crowded countries of the East have poured their surplus populations. But the widening waves of migration, which millenniums ago rolled east and west from the valley of the Euphrates, meet to-day on our Pacific coast. There are no more new worlds. The unoccupied arable lands of the earth are limited, and will soon be taken. The time is coming when the pressure of population on the means of subsistence will be felt here as it is now felt in Europe and Asia. Then will the world enter upon a new stage of its history—*the final competition of races, for which the Anglo-Saxon is being schooled.* Long before the thousand millions are here, the mighty *centrifugal* tendency, inherent in this stock and strengthened in the United States, will assert itself. Then this race of unequaled energy, with all the majesty of numbers and the might of wealth behind it—the representative, let us hope, of the largest liberty, the purest Christianity, the highest civilization—having developed peculiarly aggressive traits calculated to impress its institutions upon mankind, will spread itself over the earth. If I read not amiss, this powerful race will move down upon Mexico, down upon Central and South America, out upon the islands of the sea, over upon Africa and beyond. And can any one doubt that the result of this competition of races will be the "survival of the fittest?" "Any people," says Dr. Bushnell, "that is physiologically advanced in culture, though it be only in a degree beyond another which is mingled with it on strictly equal terms, is sure to live down and finally live out its inferior. Nothing can save the inferior race but a ready and pliant assimilation. Whether the feebler and more abject races are going to be regenerated and raised up, is already very much of a question. What if it should be God's plan to people the world with better and finer material?

"Certain it is, whatever expectations we may indulge, that there is a tremendous overbearing surge of power in the Christian nations, which, if the others are not speedily raised to some vastly higher capacity, will inevitably submerge and bury them forever. These great populations of Christendom—what are they doing, but throwing out their colonies on every side, and populating themselves, if I may so speak, into the possession of all countries and climes?" To this result no war of extermination is needful; the contest is not one of arms, but of vitality and of civilization. "At the present day," says Mr. Darwin, "civilized nations are everywhere supplanting barbarous nations, excepting where the climate opposes a deadly barrier; and they succeed mainly, though not exclusively, through their arts, which are the products of the intellect." Thus the Finns were supplanted by the Aryan races in Europe and Asia, the Tartars by the Russians, and thus the aborigines of North America, Australia and New Zealand are now disappearing before the all-conquering Anglo-Saxons. It seems as if these inferior tribes were only precursors of a superior race, . . .

Every civilization has its destructive and preservative elements. The Anglo-Saxon race would speedily decay but for the salt of Christianity. Bring savages into contact with our civilization, and its destructive forces become operative at once, while years are necessary to render effective the saving influences of Christian instruction. Moreover, the pioneer wave of our civilization carries with it more scum than salt. Where there is one missionary, there are hundreds of miners or traders or adventurers ready to debauch the native.

Whether the extinction of inferior races before the advancing Anglo-Saxon seems to the reader sad or otherwise, it certainly appears probable. I know of nothing except climatic conditions to prevent this race from populating Africa as it has peopled North America. And those portions of Africa which are unfavorable to Anglo-Saxon life are less extensive than was once supposed. The Dutch Boers, after two centuries of life there, are as hardy as any race on earth. The Anglo-Saxon has established himself in climates totally diverse—Canada, South Africa, and India—and, through several generations, has preserved his essential race characteristics. He is not, of course, superior to climatic influences; but even in warm climates, he is likely to retain his aggressive vigor long enough to supplant races already enfeebled. Thus, in what Dr. Bushnell calls "the out-populating power of the Christian stock," may be found God's final and complete solution of the dark problem of heathenism among many inferior peoples. . . .

Thus, while on this continent God is training the Anglo-Saxon race for its mission, a complemental work has been in progress in the great world beyond. God has two hands. Not only is he preparing in our civilization the die with which to stamp the nations, but, by what Southey called the "timing of Providence," he is preparing mankind to receive our impress.

DOCUMENT 2

Eugene V. Debs, "The Outlook for Socialism in the United States" (1900)

Eugene V. Debs (1855–1926), railroad union organizer and Socialist Party candidate for president on several occasions, surveyed the political struggles of the previous decade as he prepared for his 1900 presidential campaign.

The sun of the passing century is setting upon scenes of extraordinary activity in almost every part of our capitalistic old planet. Wars and rumors of wars are of universal prevalence. In the Philippines our soldiers are civilizing and Christianizing the natives in the latest and most approved styles of the art, and at prices ($13 per month) which commend the blessing to the prayerful consideration of the lowly and oppressed everywhere....

The picture, lurid as a chamber of horrors, becomes complete in its gruesome ghastliness when robed ministers of Christ solemnly declare that it is all for the glory of God and the advancement of Christian civilization....

The campaign this year will be unusually spectacular. The Republican Party "points with pride" to the "prosperity" of the country, the beneficent results of the "gold standard" and the "war record" of the administration. The Democratic Party declares that "imperialism" is the "paramount" issue, and that the country is certain to go to the "demnition bow-wows" if Democratic officeholders are not elected instead of the Republicans. The Democratic slogan is "The Republic vs. the Empire," accompanied in a very minor key by 16 to 1 and "direct legislation where practical."

Both these capitalist parties are fiercely opposed to trusts, though what they propose to do with them is not of sufficient importance to require even a hint in their platforms.

Needless is it for me to say to the thinking workingman that he has no choice between these two capitalist parties, that they are both pledged to the same system and that whether the one or the other succeeds, he will still remain the wage-working slave he is today.

What but meaningless phrases are "imperialism," "expansion," "free silver," "gold standard," etc., to the wage worker? The large capitalists represented by Mr. McKinley and the small capitalists represented by Mr. Bryan are interested in these "issues," but they do not concern the working class.

What the workingmen of the country are profoundly interested in is the private ownership of the means of production and distribution, the enslaving and degrading wage system in which they toil for a pittance at the pleasure of their masters and are bludgeoned, jailed or shot when they protest—this is the central, controlling, vital issue of the hour, and neither of the old party platforms has a word or even a hint about it.

As a rule, large capitalists are Republicans and small capitalists are Democrats, but workingmen must remember that they are all capitalists, and that the many small ones, like the fewer large ones, are all politically supporting their class interests, and this is always and everywhere the capitalist class.

Whether the means of production—that is to say, the land, mines, factories, machinery, etc.—are owned by a few large Republican capitalists, who organize a trust, or whether they be owned by a lot of small Democratic capitalists, who are opposed to the trust, is all the same to the working class. Let

Eugene Debs addressing a crowd. Debs's slogan "I am for socialism because I am for humanity," and his pro-socialist philosophy helped him earn 920,000 votes in the 1920 presidential election even though he was in jail for violating the Espionage Act.

the capitalists, large and small, fight this out among themselves.

The working class must get rid of the whole brood of masters and exploiters, and put themselves in possession and control of the means of production, that they may have steady employment without consulting a capitalist employer, large or small, and that they may get the wealth their labor produces, all of it, and enjoy with their families the fruits of their industry in comfortable and happy homes, abundant and wholesome food, proper clothing and all other things necessary to "life, liberty and the pursuit of happiness." It is therefore a question not of "reform," the mask of fraud, but of revolution. The capitalist system must be overthrown, class rule abolished and wage slavery supplanted by cooperative industry.

We hear it frequently urged that the Democratic Party is the "poor man's party," "the friend of labor." There is but one way to relieve poverty and to free labor, and that is by making common property of the tools of labor. . . .

What has the Democratic Party to say about the "property and educational qualifications" in North Carolina and Louisiana, and the proposed general disfranchisement of the Negro race in the Southern states?

The differences between the Republican and Democratic parties involve no issue, no principle in which the working class has any interest. . . .

Between these parties socialists have no choice, no preference. They are one in their opposition to socialism, that is to say, the emancipation of the working class from wage slavery, and every workingman who has intelligence enough to understand the interest of his class and the nature of the struggle in which it is involved will once and for all time sever his relations with them both; and recognizing the class struggle which is being waged between producing workers and nonproducing capitalists, cast his lot with the class-conscious, revolutionary Socialist Party, which is pledged to abolish the capitalist system, class rule and wage slavery—a party which does not compromise or fuse, but, preserving inviolate the principles which quickened it into life and now give it vitality and force, moves forward with dauntless determination to the goal of economic freedom.

The political trend is steadily toward socialism. The old parties are held together only by the cohesive power of spoils, and in spite of this they are steadily disintegrating. Again and again they have been tried with the same results, and thousands upon thousands, awake to their duplicity, are deserting them and turning toward socialism as the only refuge and security. Republicans, Democrats, Populists, Prohibitionists, Single Taxers are having their eyes opened to the true nature of the struggle and they are beginning to

> Come as the winds come, when
> Forests are rended;
> Come as the waves come, when
> Navies are stranded.

For a time the Populist Party had a mission, but it is practically ended. The Democratic Party has "fused" it out of existence. The "middle-of-the-road" element will be sorely disappointed when the votes are counted, and they will probably never figure in another national campaign. Not many of them will go back to the old parties. Many of them have already come to socialism, and the rest are sure to follow.

There is no longer any room for a Populist Party, and progressive Populists realize it, and hence the "strongholds" of Populism are becoming the "hotbeds" of Socialism.

It is simply a question of capitalism or socialism, of despotism or democracy, and they who are not wholly with us are wholly against us.

DOCUMENT 3

Ida B. Wells, "Lynch Law in America" (1900)

Some Americans detected a relationship between overseas expansion and domestic racial oppression. In a forum published in *The Arena* magazine entitled "The White Man's Problem," Ida B. Wells (1862–1931) contributed a piece chronicling the public lynching of blacks in America. Violence, she argued, was a political tool to subordinate African Americans. Wells, born a slave, organized a national campaign against lynching as part of her rich career as journalist, social activist, and civil rights advocate.

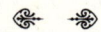

Our country's national crime is *lynching*. It is not the creature of an hour, the sudden outburst of uncontrolled fury, or the unspeakable brutality of an insane mob. It represents the cool, calculating deliberation of intelligent people who openly avow that there is an "unwritten law" that justifies them in putting human beings to death without complaint under oath, without trial by jury, without opportunity to make defense, and without right of appeal....

The alleged menace of universal suffrage having been avoided by the absolute suppression of the negro vote, the spirit of mob murder should have been satisfied and the butchery of negroes should have ceased. But men, women, and children were the victims of murder by individuals and murder by mobs, just as they had been when killed at the demands of the "unwritten law" to prevent "negro domination." Negroes were killed for disputing over terms of contracts with their employers. If a few barns were burned some colored man was killed to stop it. If a colored man resented the imposition of a white man and the two came to blows, the colored man had to die, either at the hands of the white man then and there or later at the hands of a mob that speedily gathered. If he showed a spirit of courageous manhood he was hanged for his pains, and the killing was justified by the declaration that he was a "saucy nigger." Colored women have been murdered because they refused to tell the mobs where relatives could be found for "lynching bees." Boys of fourteen years have been lynched by white representatives of

American civilization. In fact, for all kinds of offenses—and for no offenses—from murders to misdemeanors, men and women are put to death without judge or jury; so that, although the political excuse was no longer necessary, the wholesale murder of human beings went on just the same. A new name was given to the killings and a new excuse was invented for so doing.

Again the aid of the "unwritten law" is invoked, and again it comes to the rescue. During the last ten years a new statute has been added to the "unwritten law." This statute proclaims that for certain crimes or alleged crimes no negro shall be allowed a trial; that no white woman shall be compelled to charge an assault under oath or to submit any such charge to the investigation of a court of law. The result is that many men have been put to death whose innocence was afterward established; and to-day, under this reign of the "unwritten law," no colored man, no matter what his reputation, is safe from lynching if a white woman, no matter what her standing or motive, cares to charge him with insult or assault.

It is considered a sufficient excuse and reasonable justification to put a prisoner to death under this "unwritten law" for the frequently repeated charge that these lynching horrors are necessary to prevent crimes against women. The sentiment of the country has been appealed to, in describing the isolated condition of white families in thickly populated negro districts; and the charge is made that these homes are in as great danger as if they were surrounded by wild beasts. And the world has accepted this theory without let or hindrance. In many cases there has been open expression that the fate meted out to the victim was only what he deserved. In many other instances there has been a silence that says more forcibly than words can proclaim it that it is right and proper that a human being should be seized by a mob and burned to death upon the unsworn and the uncorroborated charge of his accuser. No matter that our laws presume every man innocent until he is proved guilty; no matter that it leaves a certain class of individuals completely at the mercy of another class; no matter that it encourages those criminally disposed to blacken their faces and commit any crime in the calendar so long as they can throw suspicion on some negro, as is frequently done, and then lead a mob to take his life; no matter that mobs make a farce of the law and a mockery of justice; no matter that hundreds of boys are being hardened in crime and schooled in vice by the repetition of such scenes before their eyes—if a white woman declares herself insulted or assaulted, some life must pay the penalty, with all the horrors of the Spanish Inquisition and all the barbarism of the Middle Ages. The world looks on and says it is well.

Not only are two hundred men and women put to death annually, on the average, in this country by mobs, but these lives are taken with the greatest publicity. In many instances the leading citizens aid and abet by their presence when they do not participate, and the leading journals inflame the public mind to the lynching point with scare-head articles and offers of rewards. Whenever a burning is advertised to take place, the railroads run excursions, photographs are taken, and the same jubilee is indulged in that characterized the public hangings of one hundred years ago. There is, however, this difference: in those old days the multitude that stood by was permitted only to guy or jeer. The nineteenth century lynching mob cuts off ears, toes, and fingers, strips off flesh, and distributes portions of the body as souvenirs among the crowd. If the leaders of the mob are so minded, coal-oil is poured over the body and the victim is then roasted to death. This has been done in Texarkana and Paris, Tex., in Bardswell, Ky., and in Newman, Ga. In Paris the officers of the law delivered the prisoner to the mob. The mayor gave the school children a holiday and the railroads ran excursion trains so that the people might see a human being burned to death. In Texarkana, the year before, men and boys amused themselves by cutting off strips of flesh and thrusting knives into their helpless victim. At Newman, Ga., of the present year, the mob tried every conceivable torture to compel the victim to cry out and confess, before they set fire to the faggots that burned him. But their trouble was all in vain—he never uttered a cry, and they could not make him confess. . . .

Quite a number of the one-third alleged cases of assault that have been personally investigated by the writer have shown that there was no foundation in fact for the charges; yet the claim is not made that there were no real culprits among them. The negro has been too long associated with the white man not to have copied his vices as well as his virtues. But the negro resents and utterly repudiates the effort to blacken his good name by asserting that assaults upon women are peculiar to his race. The negro has suffered far more from the commission of this crime against the women of his race by white men than the white race has ever suffered through *his* crimes. Very scant notice is taken of the matter when this is the condition of affairs. What becomes a crime deserving capital punishment when the tables are turned is a matter of small moment when the negro woman is the accusing party....

No scoffer at our boasted American civilization could say anything more harsh of it than does the American white man himself who says he is unable to protect the honor of his women without resort to such brutal, inhuman, and degrading exhibitions as characterize "lynching bees." The cannibals of the South Sea Islands roast human beings alive to satisfy hunger. The red Indian of the Western plains tied his prisoner to the stake, tortured him, and danced in fiendish glee while his victim writhed in the flames. His savage, untutored mind suggested no better way than that of wreaking vengeance upon those who had wronged him. These people knew nothing about Christianity and did not profess to follow its teachings; but such primary laws as they had they lived up to. No nation, savage or civilized, save only the United States of America, has confessed its inability to protect its women save by hanging, shooting, and burning alleged offenders.

DOCUMENT 4

Henry Cabot Lodge, "The Business World vs. the Politicians" (1895)

Massachusetts Republican Senator Henry Cabot Lodge derided Democratic President Grover Cleveland for not pursuing a sufficiently expansionist foreign policy. According to Lodge's article in the March 1895 issue of *The Forum*, a national journal, assertiveness in both the Caribbean and the Pacific Ocean not only would fulfill vital commercial needs but would be the logical extension of past American policy and experience.

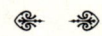

If the Democratic party has had one cardinal principle beyond all others, it has been that of pushing forward the boundaries of the United States. Under this Administration, governed as it is by free-trade influences, this great principle of the Democratic party during nearly a century of existence has been utterly abandoned. Thomas Jefferson, admitting that he violated the Constitution while he did it, effected the Louisiana purchase, but Mr. Cleveland has labored to overthrow American interests and American control in Hawaii. Andrew Jackson fought for Florida, but Mr. Cleveland is eager to abandon Samoa.... It is the melancholy outcome of the doctrine that there is no higher aim or purpose for men or for nations than to buy and sell, to trade jack-knives and make everything cheap. No one underrates the importance of the tariffs or the still greater importance of a sound currency. But of late years we have been so absorbed in these economic questions that we have grown unmindful of others. We have had something too much of these disciples of the Manchester school, who think the price of calico more important than a nation's honor, the duties on pig iron of more moment than the advance of a race.

It is time to recall what we have been tending to forget: that we have always had and that we have now a foreign policy which is of great importance to our national well-being. The foundation of that policy was Washington's doctrine of neutrality. To him and to Hamilton we owe the principle that it was not the business of the United States to meddle in the affairs of Europe. When this policy was declared, it fell with a shock upon the Americans of that day, for we were still colonists in habits of thought and could not realize that the struggles of Europe did not concern us. Yet the establishment of the neutrality policy was one of the greatest services which Washington and Hamilton rendered to the cause of American nationality. The corollary of Washington's policy was the Monroe doctrine, the work of John Quincy Adams, a much greater man than the President whose name it bears. Washington declared that it was not the business of the United States to meddle in the affairs of Europe, and John Quincy Adams added that Europe must not meddle in the Western hemisphere. As I have seen it solemnly stated recently that the annexation of Hawaii would be a violation of the Monroe doctrine, it is perhaps not out of place to say that the Monroe doctrine has no bearing on the extension of the United States, but simply holds that no European power shall establish itself in the Americas or interfere with American governments.

The neutrality policy and the Monroe doctrine are the two great principles established at the outset by far-seeing statesmen in regard to the foreign relations of the United States. But it would be a fatal mistake to suppose that our foreign policy stopped there, or that these fundamental propositions in any way fettered the march of the American people. Washington withdrew us from the affairs of Europe, but at the same time he pointed out that our true line of advance was to the West. He never for an instant thought that we were to remain stationary and cease to move forward. He saw, with prophetic vision, as did no other man of his time, the true course for the American people. He could not himself enter into the promised land, but he showed it to his people, stretching from the Blue Ridge to the Pacific Ocean. We have followed the teachings of Washington. We have taken the great valley of the Mississippi and pressed on beyond the Sierras. We have a record of conquest, colonization, and territorial expansion unequalled by any people in the nineteenth century. We are not to be curbed now by the doctrines of the Manchester school which have never been observed in England, and which as an importation are even more absurdly out of place here than in their native land. It is not the policy of the United States to enter, as England has done, upon the general acquisition of distant possession in all parts of the world. Our government is not adapted to such a policy, and we have no need of it, for we have an ample field at home; but at the same time it must be remembered that while in the United States themselves we hold the citadel of our power and greatness as a nation, there are outworks essential to the defence of that citadel which must neither be neglected nor abandoned.

There is a very definite policy for American statesmen to pursue in this respect if they would prove themselves worthy inheritors of the principles of Washington and Adams. We desire no extension to the south, for neither the population nor the lands of Central or South America would be desirable additions to the United States. But from the Rio Grande to the Arctic Ocean there should be but one flag and one country. Neither race nor climate forbids this extension, and every consideration of national growth and national welfare demands it. In the interests of our commerce and of our fullest development we should build the Nicaragua canal, and for the protection of that canal and for the sake of our commercial supremacy in the Pacific we should control the Hawaiian Islands and maintain our influence in Samoa. England has studded the West Indies with strong places which are a standing menace to our Atlantic seaboard. We should have among those islands at least one strong naval station, and when the Nicaragua canal is built, the island of Cuba, still sparsely settled and of almost unbounded fertility, will become to us a necessity. Commerce follows the flag, and we should build up a navy strong enough to give protection to Americans in every quarter of the globe and sufficiently powerful to put our coasts beyond the possibility of successful attack.

The tendency of modern times is toward consolidation. It is apparent in capital and labor alike, and it is also true of nations. Small States are of the past and have no future. The modern movement is all toward the concentration of people and territory into great nations and large dominions. The great nations are rapidly absorbing for their future expansion and their present defence all the waste places of the earth. It is a movement which makes for civilization and the advancement of the race. As one of the great nations of the world, the United States must not fall out of the line of march.

For more than thirty years we have been so much absorbed with grave domestic questions that we have lost sight of these vast interests which lie just outside our borders. They ought to be neglected no longer. They are not only of material importance, but they are matters which concern our greatness as a nation and our future as a great people. They appeal to our national honor and dignity and to the pride of country and of race. If the humiliating foreign policy of the present Administration has served to call attention to these questions and to remind us that they are quite as important at least as tariffs or currency, it will perhaps prove to have been a blessing in disguise. When we face a question of foreign relations it should never be forgotten that we meet something above and beyond party politics, something that rouses and appeals to the patriotism and the Americanism of which we never can have too much, and of which during the last two years our Government has shown altogether too little.

DOCUMENT 5

Theodore Roosevelt, Third Annual Message to Congress (1903)

One of the nation's leading proponents of an aggressive foreign policy, Theodore Roosevelt made the most of his opportunity when he was elevated to the presidency after William McKinley's assassination in 1901. In his third annual message he assessed America's foreign affairs and recounted his version of how the United States came into possession of the territory needed to construct the Panama Canal.

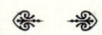

I heartily congratulate the Congress upon the steady progress in building up the American Navy. We can not afford a let-up in this great work. To stand still means to go back. There should be no cessation in adding to the effective units of the fighting strength of the fleet. Meanwhile the Navy Department and the officers of the Navy are doing well their part by providing constant service at sea under conditions akin to those of actual warfare. Our officers and enlisted men are learning to handle the battleships, cruisers, and torpedo boats with high efficiency in fleet and squadron formations, and the standard of marksmanship is being steadily raised. The best work ashore is indispensable, but the highest duty of a naval officer is to exercise command at sea.

The establishment of a naval base in the Philippines ought not to be longer postponed. Such a base is desirable in time of peace; in time of war it would be indispensable, and its lack would be ruinous. Without it our fleet would be helpless. Our naval experts are agreed that Subig [Subic] Bay is the proper place for the purpose. The national interests require that the work of fortification and development of a naval station at Subig Bay be begun at an early date; for under the best conditions it is a work which will consume much time. . . .

By the act of June 28, 1902, the Congress authorized the President to enter into treaty with Colombia for the building of the canal across the Isthmus of Panama; it being provided that in the event of failure to secure such treaty after the lapse of a reasonable time, recourse should be had to building a canal through Nicaragua. It has not been necessary to consider this alternative, as I am enabled to lay before the Senate a treaty providing for the building of the canal across the Isthmus of Panama. This was the route which commended itself to the deliberate judgment of the Congress, and we can now acquire by treaty the right to construct the canal over this route. The question now, therefore, is not by which route the isthmian canal shall be built, for that question has been definitely and irrevocably decided. The question is simply whether or not we shall have an isthmian canal. . . .

A new Republic, that of Panama, which was at one time a sovereign state, and at another time a mere department of the successive confederations known as New Granada and Columbia, has now succeeded to the rights which first one and then the other formerly exercised over the Isthmus. But as long as the Isthmus endures, the mere geographical fact of its existence, and the peculiar interest therein which is required by our position, perpetuate the solemn contract which binds the holders of the territory to respect our right to freedom of transit across it, and binds us in return to safeguard for the Isthmus and the world the exercise of that inestimable privilege. . . .

The above recital of facts [not included here] establishes beyond question: First, that the United States has for over half a century patiently and in good faith carried out its obligations under the treaty of 1846; second, that when for the first time it became possible for Colombia to do anything in requital of the services thus repeatedly rendered to it for fifty-seven years by the United States, the Colombian Government preemptorily and offensively refused thus to do its part, even though to do so would have been to its advantage and immeasurably to the advantage of the State of Panama, at that time under its jurisdiction; third, that throughout this period revolutions, riots, and factional disturbances of every kind have occurred one after the other in almost uninterrupted succession, some of them lasting for months and even for years, while the central government was unable to put them down or to make peace with the rebels; fourth, that these disturbances instead of showing any sign of abating have tended to grow more numerous and more serious in the immediate past; fifth, that the control of Colombia over the Isthmus of Panama could not be maintained without the armed intervention and assistance of the United States. In other words, the Government of Colombia, though wholly unable to maintain order on the Isthmus, has nevertheless declined to ratify a treaty the conclusion of which opened the only chance to secure its own stability and to guarantee permanent peace on, and the construction of a canal across, the Isthmus.

Under such circumstances the Government of the United States would have been guilty of folly and weakness, amounting in their sum to a crime against the Nation, had it acted otherwise than it did when the revolution of November 3 last took place in Panama. This great enterprise of building the interoceanic canal can not be held up to gratify the whims, or out of respect to the governmental impotence, or to the even more sinister and evil political peculiarities, of people who, though they dwell afar off, yet, against the wish of the actual dwellers on the Isthmus, assert an unreal supremacy over the territory. The possession of a territory fraught with such peculiar capacities as the Isthmus in question carries with it obligations to mankind. The course of events has shown that this canal can not be built by private enterprise, or by any other nation than our own; therefore it must be built by the United States.

Every effort has been made by the Government of the United States to persuade Colombia to follow a course which was essentially not only to our interests and to the interests of the world, but to the interests of Colombia itself. These efforts have failed; and Colombia, by her persistence in repulsing the advances that have been made, has forced us, for the sake of our own honor, and of the interest and well-being, not merely of our own people, but of the people of the Isthmus of Panama and the people of the civilized countries of the world, to take decisive steps to bring to an end a condition of affairs which had become intolerable. The new Republic of Panama immediately offered to negotiate a treaty with us. This treaty I herewith submit. By it our interests are better safeguarded than in the treaty with Colombia which was ratified by the Senate at its last session. It is better in its terms than the treaties offered to us by the Republics of Nicaragua and Costa Rica. At last the right to begin this great undertaking is made available. Panama has done her part. All that remains is for the American Congress to do its part, and forthwith this Republic will enter upon the execution of a project colossal in its size and of well-nigh incalculable possibilities for the good of this country and the nations of mankind.

By the provisions of the treaty the United States guarantees and will maintain the independence of the Republic of Panama. There is granted to the United States in perpetuity the use, occupation, and control of a strip ten miles wide and extending three nautical miles into the sea at either terminal, with all lands lying outside of the zone necessary for the construction of the canal or for its auxiliary works, and with the islands in the Bay of Panama. The cities of Panama and Colon are not embraced in the canal zone, but the United States assumes their sanitation and, in case of need, the maintenance of order therein; the United States enjoys within the granted limits all the rights, power, and authority which it would possess were it the sovereign of the territory to the exclusion of the exercise of sovereign rights by the Republic. All railway and canal property rights belonging to Panama and needed for the canal pass to the United States, including any property of the respective companies in the cities of Panama and Colon; the works, property, and personnel of the canal and railways are exempted from taxation as well in the cities of Panama and Colon as in the canal zone and its dependencies. Free immigration of the personnel and importation of supplies for the construction and operation of the canal are granted. Provision is made for the use of military force and the building of fortifications by the United States for the protection of the transit.

DOCUMENT 6

William Graham Sumner, What the Social Classes Owe to Each Other (1883)

William Graham Sumner (1840–1910), Yale professor and leading sociologist, became an outspoken critic of social reform. His works, including the following selection, championed the doctrine of *laissez-faire*. Sumner insisted that the natural laws of society required individuals and classes to fend for themselves. Government, he thought, had no business regulating the economy.

❦ ❧

The amateur social doctors are like the amateur physicians—they always begin with the question of *remedies*, and they go at this without any diagnosis or any knowledge of the anatomy or physiology of society. They never have any doubt of the efficacy of their remedies. They never take account of any ulterior effects which may be apprehended from the remedy itself. It generally troubles them not a whit that their remedy implies a complete reconstruction of society, or even a reconstitution of human nature. Against all such social quackery the obvious injunction to the quacks is, to mind their own business.

The social doctors enjoy the satisfaction of feeling themselves to be more moral or more enlightened than their fellow-men. They are able to see what other men ought to do when the other men do not see it. An examination of the work of the social doctors, however, shows that they are only more ignorant and more presumptuous than other people. We have a great many social difficulties and hardships to contend with. Poverty, pain, disease, and misfortune surround our existence. We fight against them all the time. The individual is a centre of hopes, affections, desires, and sufferings. When he dies, life changes its form, but does not cease. That means that the person—the centre of all the hopes, affections, etc.—after struggling as long as he can, is sure to succumb at last. We would, therefore, as far as the hardships of the human lot are concerned, go on struggling to the best of our ability against them but for the social doctors, and we would endure what we could not cure. But we have inherited a vast number of social ills which never came from Nature. They are the complicated products of all the tinkering, muddling, and blundering of social doctors in the past. These products of social quackery are now buttressed by habit, fashion, prejudice, platitudinarian thinking, and new quackery in political economy and social science. It is a fact worth noticing, just when there seems to be a revival of faith in legislative agencies, that our States are generally providing against the experienced evils of over-legislation by ordering that the Legislature shall sit only every other year. During the hard times, when Congress had a real chance to make or mar the public welfare, the final adjournment of that body was hailed year after year with cries of relief from a great anxiety. The greatest reforms which could now be accomplished would consist in undoing the work of statesmen in the past, and the greatest difficulty in the way of reform is to find out how to undo their work without injury to what is natural and sound. All this mischief has been done by men who sat down to consider the problem (as I heard an apprentice of theirs once express it), What kind of a society do we want to make? When they had settled this question *a priori* to their satisfaction, they set to work to make their ideal society, and to-day we suffer the consequences. Human society tries hard to adapt itself to any conditions in which it finds itself, and we have been warped and distorted until we have got used to it, as the foot adapts itself to an ill-made boot. Next, we have come to think that that is the right way for things to be; and it is true that a change to a sound and normal condition would for a time hurt us, as a man whose foot has been distorted would suffer if he tried to wear a well-shaped boot. Finally, we have produced a lot of economists and social philosophers who have invented sophisms for fitting our thinking to the distorted facts.

Society, therefore, does not need any care or supervision. If we can acquire a science of society, based on observation of phenomena and study of forces, we may hope to gain some ground slowly toward the elimination of old errors and the re-establishment of a sound and natural social order. Whatever we gain that way will be by growth, never in the world by any reconstruction of society on the plan of some enthusiastic social architect. The latter is only repeating the old error over again, and postponing all our chances of real improvement. Society needs first of all to be freed from these meddlers—that is, to be let alone. Here we are, then, once more back at the old doctrine—*Laissez faire*. Let us translate it into blunt English, and it will read, Mind your own business. It is nothing but the doctrine of liberty. Let every man be happy in his own way. If his sphere of action and interest impinges on that of any other man, there will have to be compromise and adjustment. Wait for the occasion. Do not attempt to generalize those interferences or to plan for them *a priori*. We have a body of laws and institutions which have grown up as occasion has occurred for adjusting rights. Let the same process go on. Practise the utmost reserve possible in your interferences even of this kind, and by no means seize occasion for interfering with natural adjustments. Try first long and patiently whether the natural adjustment will not come about through the play of interests and the voluntary concessions of the parties.

I have said that we have an empirical political economy and social science to fit the distortions of our society. The test of empiricism in this matter is the attitude which one takes up toward *laissez faire*. It no doubt wounds the vanity of a philosopher who is just ready with a new solution of the universe to be told to mind his own business. So he goes on to tell us that if we think that we shall, by being let alone, attain to perfect happiness on earth, we are mistaken. The half-way men—the professorial socialists—join him. They solemnly shake their heads, and tell us that he is right—that letting us alone will never secure us perfect happiness. Under all this lies the familiar logical fallacy, never expressed, but really the point of the whole, that we *shall* get perfect happiness if we put ourselves in the hands of the world-reformer. We never supposed that *laissez faire* would give us perfect happiness. We have left perfect happiness entirely out of our account. If the social doctors will mind their own business, we shall have no troubles but what belong to Nature. Those we will endure or combat as we can. What we desire is that the friends of humanity should cease to add to them. Our disposition toward the ills which our fellow-man inflicts on us through malice or meddling is quite different from our disposition toward the ills which are inherent in the conditions of human life.

To mind one's own business is a purely negative and unproductive injunction, but, taking social matters as they are just now, it is a sociological principle of the first importance. There might be developed a grand philosophy on the basis of minding one's own business.

DOCUMENT 7

The People's Party Platform (1892)

The People's Party held its first convention in Omaha, Nebraska, in July 1892. The platform adopted at that meeting catalogued Populist demands for the redistribution of political power and economic opportunity.

We have witnessed for more than a quarter of a century the struggles of the two great political parties for power and plunder, while grievous wrongs have been inflicted upon the suffering people. We charge that the controlling influences dominating both these parties have permitted the existing dreadful conditions to develop without serious effort to prevent or restrain them. Neither do they now promise us any substantial reform. They have agreed together to ignore in the coming campaign every issue but one. They propose to drown the outcries of a plundered people with the uproar of a sham battle over the tariff, so that capitalists, corporations, national banks, rings, trusts, watered stock, the demonetization of silver, and the oppressions of the usurers may all be lost sight of. They propose to sacrifice our homes, lives and children on the altar of mammon; to destroy the multitude in order to secure corruption funds from the millionaires....

We declare, therefore,—

First. That the union of the labor forces of the United States this day consummated shall be permanent and perpetual; may its spirit enter all hearts for the salvation of the republic and the uplifting of mankind!

Second. Wealth belongs to him who creates it, and every dollar taken from industry without an equivalent is robbery. "If any will not work, neither shall he eat." The interests of rural and civic labor are the same; their enemies are identical.

Third. We believe that the time has come when the railroad corporations will either own the people or the people must own the railroads; and, should the government enter upon the work of owning and managing all railroads, we should favor an amendment to the Constitution by which all persons engaged in the government service shall be placed under a civil service regulation of the most rigid character, so as to prevent the increase of the power of the national administration by the use of such additional government employees.

First, *Money.* We demand a national currency, safe, sound, and flexible, issued by the general government only, a full legal tender for all debts, public and private, and that, without the use of banking corporations, a just, equitable, and efficient means of distribution direct to the people, at a tax not to exceed two per cent per annum, to be provided as set forth in the sub-treasury plan of the Farmers' Alliance, or a better system; also, by payments in discharge of its obligations for public improvements.

(a) We demand free and unlimited coinage of silver and gold at the present legal ratio of sixteen to one.

(b) We demand that the amount of circulating medium be speedily increased to not less than fifty dollars per capita.

(c) We demand a graduated income tax.

(d) We believe that the money of the country shall be kept as much as possible in the hands of the people, and hence we demand that all state and national revenues shall be limited to the necessary expenses of the government economically and honestly administered.

(e) We demand that postal savings banks be established by the government for the safe deposit of the earnings of the people and to facilitate exchange.

Second, *Transportation*. Transportation being a means of exchange and a public necessity, the government should own and operate the railroads in the interest of the people.

(a) The telegraph and telephone, like the post-office system, being a necessity for the transmission of news, should be owned and operated by the government in the interest of the people.

Third, *Land*. The land, including all the natural sources of wealth, is the heritage of the people, and should not be monopolized for speculative purposes, and alien ownership of land should be prohibited. All land now held by railroads and other corporations in excess of their actual needs, and all lands now owned by aliens, should be reclaimed by the government and held for actual settlers only.

Resolutions

Whereas, Other questions have been presented for our consideration, we hereby submit the following, not as a part of the platform of the People's party, but as resolutions expressive of the sentiment of this convention.

1. *Resolved*, That we demand a free ballot and a fair count in all elections, and pledge ourselves to secure it to every legal voter without federal intervention, through the adoption by the States of the unperverted Australian or secret ballot system.

2. *Resolved*, That the revenue derived from a graduated income tax should be applied to the reduction of the burden of taxation now resting upon the domestic industries of this country.

3. *Resolved*, That we pledge our support to fair and liberal pensions to ex-Union soldiers and sailors.

4. *Resolved*, That we condemn the fallacy of protecting American labor under the present system, which opens our ports to the pauper and criminal classes of the world, and crowds out our wage-earners; and we denounce the present ineffective laws against contract labor, and demand the further restriction of undesirable immigration.

5. *Resolved*, That we cordially sympathize with the efforts of organized workingmen to shorten the hours of labor, and demand a rigid enforcement of the existing eight-hour law on government work, and ask that a penalty clause be added to the said law.

6. *Resolved*, That we regard the maintenance of a large standing army of mercenaries, known as the Pinkerton system, as a menace to our liberties, and we demand its abolition; and we condemn the recent invasion of the Territory of Wyoming by the hired assassins of plutocracy, assisted by federal officials.

7. *Resolved*, That we commend to the favorable consideration of the people and the reform press the legislative system known as the initiative and referendum.

8. *Resolved*, That we favor a constitutional provision limiting the office of President and Vice-President to one term, and providing for the election of senators of the United States by a direct vote of the people.

9. *Resolved*, That we oppose any subsidy or national aid to any private corporation for any purpose.

10. *Resolved*, That this convention sympathizes with the Knights of Labor and their righteous contest with the tyrannical combine of clothing manufacturers of Rochester, and declares it to be the duty of all who hate tyranny and oppression to refuse to purchase the goods made by said manufacturers, or to patronize any merchants who sell such goods.

DOCUMENT 8

William Jennings Bryan, Cross of Gold Speech (1896)

William Jennings Bryan delivered to the 1896 Democratic Convention what has become one of the most famous speeches in American political history. His evocative denunciation of the gold standard won him the presidential nomination and ultimately the support of the People's Party as well.

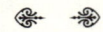

Mr. Chairman and Gentlemen of the Convention: I would be presumptuous, indeed, to present myself against the distinguished gentlemen to whom you have listened if this were a mere measuring of abilities; but this is not a contest between persons.

William Jennings Bryan's formidable public speaking skills won him a seat in the House of Representatives from 1891 to 1895. A force in politics for almost three decades, he served as secretary of state under Woodrow Wilson from 1913 to 1915, when he resigned to protest America's involvement in World War I. Though nominated for president by the Democratic Party on three separate occasions, Bryan failed to ever win the presidency.

The humblest citizen in all the land, when clad in the armor of a righteous cause, is stronger than all the hosts of error. I come to speak to you in defense of a cause as holy as the cause of liberty—the cause of humanity. . . .

We say to you that you have made the definition of a business man too limited in its application. The man who is employed for wages is as much a business man as his employer; the attorney in a country town is as much a business man as the corporation counsel in a great metropolis; the merchant at the cross-roads store is as much a business man as the merchant of New York; the farmer who goes forth in the morning and toils all day—who begins in the spring and toils all summer—and who by the application of brain and muscle to the natural resources of the country creates wealth, is as much a business man as the man who goes upon the board of trade and bets upon the price of grain; the miners who go down a thousand feet into the earth, or climb two thousand feet upon the cliffs, and bring forth from their hiding places the precious metals to be poured into the channels of trade are as much business men as the few financial magnates who, in a back room, corner the money of the world. We come to speak for this broader class of business men.

Ah, my friends, we say not one word against those who live upon the Atlantic coast, but the hardy pioneers who have braved all the dangers of the wilderness, who have made the desert to blossom as the rose—the pioneers away out there [pointing to the West], who rear their children near to Nature's heart, where they can mingle their voices with the voices of the birds—out there where they have erected schoolhouses for the education of their young, churches where they praise their Creator, and cemeteries where rest the ashes of their dead—these people, we say, are as deserving of the consideration of our party as any people in this country. It is for these that we speak. We do not come as aggressors. Our war is not a war of conquest; we are fighting in the defense of our homes, our families, and posterity. We have petitioned, and our petitions have been scorned; we have entreated, and our entreaties have been disregarded; we have begged, and they have mocked when our calamity came. We beg no longer; we entreat no more; we petition no more. We defy them. . . .

We say in our platform that we believe that the right to coin and issue money is a function of government. We believe it. We believe that it is a part of sovereignty, and can no more with safety be delegated to private individuals than we could afford to delegate to private individuals the power to make penal statutes or levy taxes. Mr. Jefferson, who was once regarded as good Democratic authority, seems to have differed in opinion from the gentleman who has addressed us on the part of the minority. Those who are opposed to this proposition tell us that the issue of paper money is a function of the bank, and that the Government ought to go out of the banking business. I stand with Jefferson rather than with them, and tell them, as he did, that the issue of money is a function of government, and that the banks ought to go out of the governing business. . . .

We go forth confident that we shall win. Why? Because upon the paramount issue of this campaign there is not a spot of ground upon which the enemy will dare to challenge battle. If they tell us that the gold standard is a good thing, we shall point to their platform and tell them that their platform pledges the party to get rid of the gold standard and substitute bimetalism. If the gold standard is a good thing, why try to get rid of it? I call your attention to the fact that some of the very people who are in this convention today and who tell us that we ought to declare in favor of international bimetallism—thereby declaring that the gold standard is wrong and that the principle of bimetallism is better—these very people four months ago were open and avowed advocates of the gold standard, and were then telling us that we could not legislate two metals together, even with the aid of all the world. If the gold standard is a good thing, we ought to declare in favor of its retention and not in favor of abandoning it; and if the gold standard is a bad thing why should we wait until other nations are willing to help us to let go? Here is the line of battle, and we care not upon which issue they force the fight; we are prepared to meet them on either issue or on both. If they tell us that the gold standard is the standard of civilization, we reply to them that this, the most enlightened of all the nations of the earth, has never declared for a gold standard and that both the great parties this year are declaring against it. If the gold standard is the standard of civilization, why, my friends, should we not have it? If they come to meet us on that issue we can present the history of our nation. More than that; we can tell them that they will search the pages of history in vain to find a single instance where the common people of any land have ever declared themselves in favor of the gold standard. They can find where the holders of fixed investments have declared for a gold standard, but not where the masses have. . . .

Upon which side will the Democratic party fight; upon the side of "the idle holders of idle capital" or upon the side of "the struggling masses?" That is the question which the party must answer first, and then it must be answered by each individual hereafter. The sympathies of the Democratic party, as shown by the platform, are on the side of the struggling masses who have ever been the foundation of the Democratic party. There are two ideas of government. There are those who believe that, if you will only legislate to make the well-to-do prosperous, their prosperity will leak through on those below. The Democratic idea, however, has been that if you legislate to make the masses prosperous, their prosperity will find its way up through every class which rests upon them.

You come to us and tell us that the great cities

are in favor of the gold standard; we reply that the great cities rest upon our broad and fertile prairies. Burn down your cities and leave our farms, and your cities will spring up again as if by magic; but destroy our farms and the grass will grow in the streets of every city in the country.

My friends, we declare that this nation is able to legislate for its own people on every question, without waiting for the aid or consent of any other nation on earth; and upon that issue we expect to carry every State in the Union. I shall not slander the inhabitants of the fair State of Massachusetts nor the inhabitants of the State of New York by saying that, when they are confronted with the proposition, they will declare that this nation is not able to attend to its own business. It is the issue of 1776 over again. Our ancestors, when but three millions in number, had the courage to declare their political independence of every other nation; shall we, their descendants, when we have grown to seventy millions, declare that we are less independent than our forefathers? No, my friends, that will never be the verdict of our people. Therefore, we care not upon what lines the battle is fought. If they say bimetallism is good, but that we cannot have it until other nations help us, we reply that, instead of having a gold standard because England has, we will restore bimetallism, and then let England have bimetallism because the United States has it. If they dare to come out in the open field and defend the gold standard as a good thing, we will fight them to the uttermost. Having behind us the producing masses of this nation and the world, supported by the commercial interests, the laboring interests, and the toilers everywhere, we will answer their demand for a gold standard by saying to them: You shall not press down upon the brow of labor this crown of thorns, you shall not crucify mankind upon a cross of gold.

Study Questions

1. In what ways did imperial power and domestic unrest appear to stem from similar causes?
2. What were some arguments in favor of American imperialism?
3. Was imperialism inevitable? For whom?
4. How might Sumner have responded to Wells's article?
5. Do the Socialist and Populist analyses of society help us to understand the racial problems confronting America?
6. Were the Populists a "radical" party?

6

Progressivism

The defeat of Populism, the hardening of racism, and the rise of adventurism might have inhibited serious discussion of social reform. But that did not happen. However tumultuous the nation's recent history may have been, turn-of-the-century Americans addressed hard problems: the distribution of political and economic power, the maintenance of public morality, and the position of outsiders, such as immigrants, in society.

During the Progressive Era, which roughly coincided with the first two decades of the twentieth century, reformers offered new solutions and brought renewed vigor to familiar causes—everything from women's rights to reorganization of the nation's banking system (Document 1). They discovered widespread support for change among a growing professionally trained middle class and businessmen.

Of paramount concern to leading progressive politicians like Presidents Theodore Roosevelt (1901–1909) and Woodrow Wilson (1913–1921) was the issue of industrial concentration. Many Americans expressed hostility at business trusts that controlled multiple companies or all aspects of a particular industry. They wondered whether bankers had too much power and whether monopolistic practices hindered healthy economic competition (Document 2). Despite Roosevelt's reputation as a "trust-buster" and the passage early in the Wilson administration of a new antitrust law, the progressives never succeeded in slowing corporate growth. Meanwhile, in the name of regulated economic effectiveness Wilson reorganized the nation's banking system in the Federal Reserve Act of 1913.

Another major progressive cause was political reform. The crusade to clean up politics and make government more efficient took place primarily at state and local levels. Many Americans, particularly in the growing middle class, objected to the deal-making, parochialism, and public pandering that they feared had corrupted politics. They regarded the urban political machines, which dominated many cities and frequently parlayed the votes of recent immigrants into power, as undermining the cost-effective delivery of public services. Thus states and municipalities adopted such measures as commission government, city managers, public referenda, and voter registration—steps that often decreased voter turnout and placed power in the hands of educated, middle-class professionals (Document 3). In the South, progressive reform

Reforms for African Americans came slowly, and lynchings were still common during the Progressive Era. One of the biggest steps in reform came with the creation of the National Association for the Advancement of Colored People (NAACP), which was formed to fight racial inequality and discrimination for all Americans.

ensured the exclusion of both blacks and poor whites from the polls.

Reformers of all stripes recognized that combating the social problems facing the country required more than fine-tuning the electoral process. Indeed, they often saw themselves as the guardians of moral order and the more civilized aspects of American life. Thus the vice commissions that sprang up in various cities aimed to shame politicians, police, and citizens into combating social problems such as prostitution (Document 4). A new breed of well-educated social workers descended on the poorer neighborhoods to inculcate "good" values and habits, as well as to deliver the services regarded as necessary to nurture members of society (Document 5). Many native-born Americans sought not to integrate newcomers to the lower classes but, rather, to prevent further immigration, fearing that the traditional American way of life could not withstand future European influx (Document 6).

The paradoxical tendencies of the Progressive Era toward both exclusionary moralism and humanistic empathy, toward fear of politics and devotion to democratic ideals, can be seen in the continuous struggle by African Americans and women for civil rights. A group of black and white leaders responded to the retrenchment of blacks' rights by founding a new organization—the National Association for the Advancement of Colored People (NAACP)—in 1910, a step designed to keep in the public eye an issue most Americans preferred to ignore (Document 7). Enjoying more immediate success, women's rights advocates secured a new constitutional amendment permitting women to vote in nationwide elections. They argued that expanding the franchise to include women would protect the women and children of America from dangers inherent to contemporary industrial society (Document 8).

DOCUMENT 1

Herbert Croly, Progressive Democracy (1914)

Herbert Croly reviewed the historical background of progressivism in the introduction to his 1914 book *Progressive Democracy*. Croly, a leading intellectual exponent of reform and a founder of the progressive journal *The New Republic*, hoped that a principled movement would signal a break from the conservatism and piecemeal reforms that had traditionally characterized American politics.

[W]hile fully admitting that the transition may not be as abrupt as it seems, we have apparently been witnessing during the past year or two the end of one epoch and the beginning of another. A movement of public opinion, which believes itself to be and calls itself essentially progressive, has become the dominant formative influence in American political life.

The best evidence of the power of progressivism is the effect which its advent has had upon the prestige and the fortunes of political leaders of both parties. For the first time attractions and repulsions born of the progressive idea, are determining lines of political association. Until recently a man who wished actively and effectively to participate in political life had to be either a Democrat or a Republican; but now, although Republicanism and Democracy are still powerful political forces, the standing of a politician is determined quite as much by his relation to the progressive movement. The line of cleavage between progressives and non-progressives is fully as important as that between Democrats and Republicans. Political leaders, who have deserved well of their own party but who have offended the progressives, are retiring or are being retired from public life. Precisely what the outcome will be, no one can predict with any confidence; but one result seems tolerably certain. If the classification of the great majority of American voters into Democrats and Republicans is to endure, the significance of both Democracy and Republicanism is bound to be profoundly modified by the new loyalties and the new enmities created by the aggressive progressive intruder....

[T]he complexion, and to a certain extent even the features, of the American political countenance have profoundly altered. Political leaders still pride themselves upon their conservatism, but candid conservatives, in case they come from any other part of the country but the South, often pay for their candor by their early retirement. Conservatism has come to imply reaction. Its substantial utility is almost as much undervalued as that of radicalism formerly was. The whole group of prevailing political values has changed. Proposals for the regulation of public utility companies, which would then have been condemned as examples of administrative autocracy, are now accepted without serious public controversy. Plans of social legislation, which formerly would have been considered culpably "paternal," and, if passed at the solicitation of the labor unions, would have been declared unconstitutional by the courts, are now considered to be a normal and necessary exercise of the police power. Proposed alterations in our political mechanism, which would then have been appraised as utterly extravagant and extremely dangerous, are now being placed on the headlines of political programs and are being incorporated in state constitutions. In certain important respects the radicals of 1904 do not differ in their practical proposals from the conservatives of 1914....

Thus by almost imperceptible degrees reform became insurgent and insurgency progressive. For the first time in four generations American conservatism was confronted by a pervasive progressivism, which began by being dangerously indignant and ended by being far more dangerously inquisitive. Just resentment is useful and indispensable while it lasts; but it cannot last long. If it is to persist, it must be transformed into a thoroughgoing curiosity which will not rest until it has discovered what the abuses mean, how they best can be remedied, and how intimately they are associated with temples and doctrines of the traditional political creed. The conservatives themselves have provoked this curiosity, and they must abide by its results.

Just here lies the difference between modern progressivism and the old reform. The former is coming to be remorselessly inquisitive and unscrupulously thorough. The latter never knew any need of being either inquisitive or thorough. The early political reformers confined their attention to local or to special abuses. Civil service reform furnishes a good example of their methods and their purposes. The spoils system was a very grave evil, which was a fair object of assault; but it could not be successfully attacked and really uprooted merely by placing subordinate public officials under the protection of civil service laws and boards. Such laws and boards might do something to prevent politicians from appropriating the minor offices; but as long as the major offices were the gifts of the political machines, and as long as no attempt was made to perfect expert administrative organization as a necessary instrument of democracy, the agitation for civil service reform remained fundamentally sterile. It was sterile, because it was negative and timid, and because its supporters were content with their early successes and did not grow with the growing needs of their own agitation. In an analogous way the movement towards municipal reform attained a sufficient following in certain places to be embarrassing to local political bosses; but as long as it was a non-partisan movement for "good government" its successes were fugitive and sterile. It did not become really effective until it became frankly partisan, and associated good municipal government with all sorts of changes in economic and political organization which might well be obnoxious to many excellent citizens. In these and other cases the early political reformers were not sufficiently thorough. They failed to carry their analysis of the prevailing evils far or deep enough, and in their choice of remedies they never got beyond the illusions that moral exhortation, legal prohibitions and independent voting constituted a sufficient cure for American political abuses....

All this disconnected political and economic agitation had, however, a value of which the agitators themselves were not wholly conscious. Not only was the attitude of national self-satisfaction being broken down in spots, but the ineffectiveness of these local, spasmodic and restricted agitations had its effect on public opinion and prepared the way for a synthesis of the various phases of reform. When the wave of political "muck-raking" broke over the country, it provided a common bond, which tied reformers together. This bond consisted at first of the indignation which was aroused by the process of exposure; but it did not remain for long merely a feeling. As soon as public opinion began to realize that business exploitation had been allied with political corruption, and that the reformers were confronted, not by disconnected abuses, but by a perverted system, the inevitable and salutary inference began to be drawn. Just as business exploitation was allied with political corruption, so business reorganization must be allied with political reorganization. The old system must be confronted and superseded by a new system—the result of an alert social intelligence as well as an aroused individual conscience.

DOCUMENT 2

Louis Brandeis, Other People's Money and How the Bankers Use It *(1913)*

Louis Brandeis, a successful lawyer, advocate of labor and business reform, and adviser to President Woodrow Wilson, captured the concern of many progressives that large banks and trusts exercised too much control over the American economy. He provided a detailed evaluation of the problem in his 1913 book *Other People's Money and How the Bankers Use It*. Brandeis later served as a justice on the U.S. Supreme Court.

The dominant element in our financial oligarchy is the investment banker. Associated banks, trust companies and life insurance companies are his tools. Controlled railroads, public service and industrial corporations are his subjects. Though properly but middlemen, these bankers bestride as masters of America's business world, so that practically no large enterprise can be undertaken successfully without their participation or approval. These bankers are, of course, able men possessed of large fortunes; but the most potent factor in their control of business is not the possession of extraordinary ability or huge wealth. The key to their power is Combination—concentration intensive and comprehensive—advancing on three distinct lines:

First: There is the obvious consolidation of banks and trust companies; the less obvious affiliations—through stockholdings, voting trusts and interlocking directorates—of banking institutions which are not legally connected; and the joint transactions, gentlemen's agreements, and "banking ethics" which eliminate competition among the investment bankers.

Second: There is the consolidation of railroads into huge systems, the large combinations of public service corporations and the formation of industrial trusts, which, by making businesses so "big" that local, independent banking concerns cannot alone supply the necessary funds, has created dependence upon the associated New York bankers.

But combination, however intensive, along these lines only, could not have produced the Money Trust—another and more potent factor of combination was added.

Third: Investment bankers, like J. P. Morgan & Co., dealers in bonds, stocks and notes, encroached upon the functions of the three other classes of corporations with which their business brought them into contact. They became the directing power in railroads, public service and industrial companies through which our great business operations are conducted—the makers of bonds and stocks. They became the directing power in the life insurance companies, and other corporate reservoirs of the people's savings—the buyers of bonds and stocks. They became the directing power also in banks and trust companies—the depositaries of the quick capital of the country—the life blood of business, with which they and others carried on their operations. Thus four distinct functions, each essential to business, and each exercised, originally, by a distinct set of men, became united in the investment banker. It is to this union of business functions that the existence of the Money Trust is mainly due.

The development of our financial oligarchy followed, in this respect, lines with which the history of political despotism has familiarized us: — usurpation, proceeding by gradual encroachment rather than by violent acts; subtle and often long-concealed concentration of distinct functions, which are beneficent when separately administered, and dangerous only when combined in the same persons. It was by processes such as these that Caesar Augustus became master of Rome. The makers of our own Constitution had in mind like dangers to our political liberty when they provided so carefully for the separation of governmental powers. . . .

The goose that lays golden eggs has been considered a most valuable possession. But even more profitable is the privilege of taking the golden eggs laid by somebody else's goose. The investment bankers and their associates now enjoy that privilege. They control the people through the people's own money. If the bankers' power were commensurate only with their wealth, they would have relatively little influence on American business. Vast fortunes like those of the Astors are no doubt regrettable. They are inconsistent with democracy. They are unsocial. And they seem peculiarly unjust when they represent largely unearned increment. But the wealth of the Astors does not endanger political or industrial liberty. It is insignificant in amount as compared with the aggregate wealth of America, or even of New York City. It lacks significance largely because its owners have only the income from their own wealth. The Astor wealth is static. The wealth of the Morgan associates is dynamic. The power and the growth of power of our financial oligarchs comes from wielding the savings and quick capital of others. In two of the three great life insurance companies the influence of J. P. Morgan & Co. and their associates is exerted without any individual investment by them whatsoever. Even in the Equitable, where Mr. Morgan bought an actual majority of all the outstanding stock, his investment amounts to little more than one-half of one per cent of the assets of the company. The fetters which bind the people are forged from the people's own gold. . . .

The fact that industrial monopolies arrest development is more serious even than the direct burden imposed through extortionate prices. But the most harm-bearing incident of the trusts is their promotion of financial concentration. Industrial trusts feed the money trust. Practically every trust created has destroyed the financial independence of some communities and of many properties; for it has centered the financing of a large part of whole lines of business in New York, and this usually with one of a few banking houses. This is well illustrated by the Steel Trust, which is a trust of trusts; that is, the Steel Trust combines in one huge holding company the trusts previously formed in the different branches of the steel business. Thus the Tube Trust combined 17 tube mills, located in 16 different cities, scattered over 5 states and owned by 13 different companies. The wire trust combined 19 mills; the sheet steel trust 26; the bridge and structural trust 27; and the tin plate trust 36; all scattered similarly over many states. Finally these and other companies were formed into the United States Steel Corporation, combining 228 companies in all, located in 127 cities and towns, scattered over 18 states. Before the combinations were effected, nearly every one of these companies was owned largely by those who managed it, and had been financed, to a large extent, in the place, or in the state, in which it was located.

DOCUMENT 3

Walker Percy, "Birmingham under the Commission Plan" (1911)

One measure instituted to ensure the primacy of business values and to curb democratic deal-making in urban politics was the commission form of government. After it was first implemented in Galveston, Texas, many cities followed the example. The American Academy of Political and Social Science reported on progressive innovation around the country in the November 1911 edition of its *Annals*, which included the following report by Walker Percy, designer of Birmingham's commission statute.

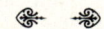

Commission government for the city of Birmingham became effective April 10, 1911. Prior to that time the city government was vested in the mayor and thirty-two aldermen. These aldermen were chosen from different wards in the city and served without legal compensation. For several years prior to the adoption of commission government, the thoughtful, patriotic citizens of Birmingham had regarded, with growing distrust and apprehension the operations of the unpaid ward aldermanic system. Birmingham has always been fortunate in having some honest, intelligent, public-spirited men upon its board of aldermen, but the system, inherently bad, bore in Birmingham its usual fruit of incapacity, unwieldiness, clique, domination, individual greed and graft and the taint of corruption. The leaders in city politics, and the bosses, in and out of office, feeling sure of their position, daily became bolder, more brazen and more contemptuous of decent public opinion.

Believing that with the increasing wealth and importance of the community and the resulting increase in the importance of public contracts handled by the board of aldermen corruption would increase and efficiency diminish; realizing that with the increase in the duties and responsibilities resting upon the board of aldermen it would become more and more difficult to secure good men to fill the positions; and believing that no permanent improvement could be had except by a change in the system of government, I appeared before the state legislature with the avowed intention of procuring the en-

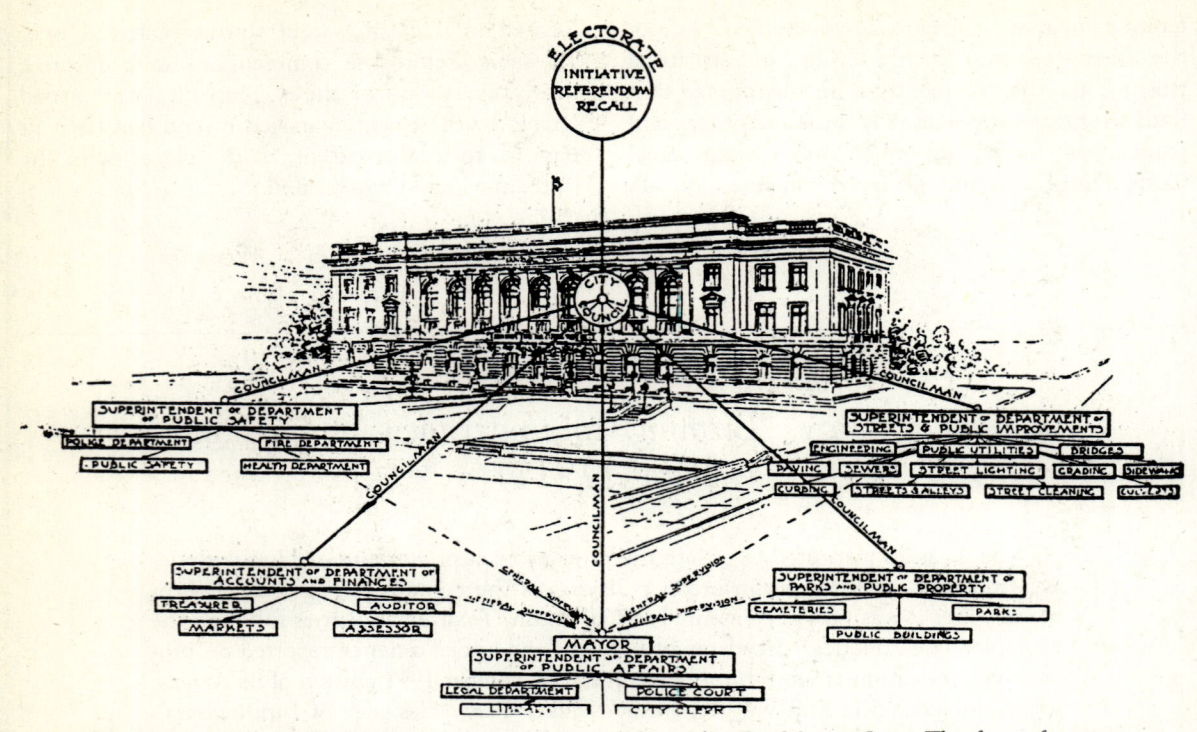

A diagram of the commission form of city government as implemented in Des Moines, Iowa. This form of government adapted a business model to manage city affairs, investing political power in a mayor and four commissioners who were elected by the city populace but who had no party designation.

actment of commission government for the City of Birmingham. In a city primary, shortly preceding the convening of the legislature, the democratic voters of Birmingham declared in favor of commission government by a vote of about ten to one.

Popular sentiment in Birmingham had crystallized so strongly and had been manifested so plainly for commission government, and the interest in this new form of city government had so developed over the state, that there was no open, organized opposition to the passage of legislation on this subject, and the commission bill applying to cities of the size of Birmingham was approved by the governor on the thirty-first of March, 1911.

In drafting the Birmingham bill, I derived more benefit from the Des Moines charter than from any other legislation; and yet, in a few important respects, our commission plan differs from any other. Manifestly, commission government has its fundamentals in the concentration of power and responsibility, coupled with the payment of reasonably adequate compensation. Birmingham has three commissioners. I believe the small number preferable, because of the increased honor and responsibility, and because the smaller number permits, with due regard to economy, the payment of better salaries. Our commissioners, receiving seven thousand dollars each, are the best paid commissioners I know of. . . .

In the election of commissioners, every safeguard that I could devise is thrown around the election to prevent the use of money or, what might be more dangerous, the building up of a machine by the large power of patronage. All city employees are prohibited by law from endeavoring to influence any voter in favor of or against any candidate for commissioner. The Birmingham bill does not permit voters to initiate legislation. I doubt the wisdom or practicability of the initiative in either city or state government. Our law authorizes a referendum to the voters on nothing but the granting of franchises to public utility corporations. Activities in procuring such franchises have been one of the frequent causes of municipal corruption. No referendum is provided on the refusal of such franchises, because the possibilities of corruption and evil on this account are manifestly insignificant. The law contains a provision for elections for the recall of commissioners on petitions signed by three thousand voters. The great power concentrated in the hands of a few men made the recall seem to me most valuable as a check. I want to say frankly, and with regret, that there has always been serious doubt in my mind as to the constitutionality of the recall provision under our state constitution. . . .

Commission government in Birmingham has been an unqualified business success. With the appointment of our commissioners there dawned a new day in our civic progress. We are realizing the fruition of long cherished hopes. The same sort of fidelity, honesty, energy, loyalty and intelligence is being displayed by these public employees that we have been accustomed to expect from private employees. A dollar of city money in Birmingham can buy as much in labor, service, and material as a dollar of individual money. When the commissioners entered upon their duties, Birmingham's floating debt under aldermanic government had been piling up with alarming rapidity. A favored bank had selfishly dominated the city's finances, and the other banking institutions of the city had felt that it was useless for them to consider, or endeavor to aid in, the city's financial problems. Practically all of the Birmingham bankers were enthusiastic believers in commission government, and have rallied in loyal support of the new administration. . . .

The Birmingham commissioners issue monthly a compact summary of their proceedings for the previous month, showing in the simplest and plainest terms all receipts and disbursements of the city and all transactions of the least importance. The first aim of the commissioners was to reduce the current expenses of the city to fit its income. All sinecures were abolished. Operating expenses were cut to the bone, and the regular operating expenses of the city, in the first twenty days the commission was in existence, were reduced in the annual sum of ninety-four thousand five hundred and thirty-four dollars, without decreasing the efficiency of the city government. While the Birmingham commission has resorted to every intelligent economy, it has not hesitated to spend money so as to secure better results and increased efficiency.

The commission has abandoned the use of horses in its fire department and purchased at one time sixteen motor-driven engines for its fire department at a cost of sixty-nine thousand three hundred and twenty-eight dollars. With its large industrial population, one of the most pressing needs of Birmingham is adequate parks and playgrounds; and at the request of the commissioners, some of the most capable and public-spirited men in the community have agreed to serve without compensation as park commissioners for the purpose of devising plans for a park system for the city. There is no "red tape" in the conduct of Birmingham's city affairs. The commissioners devote all of their time to the public business, and a crippled negro mendicant can secure an audience with the commission as easily as a street car magnate.

The work of city government is divided by the commissioners into departments headed by the respective commissioners. Under the law the division into departments can be made and rearranged by the commissioners to suit themselves. But all important questions are passed upon by the entire commission and the recommendations of a commissioner as to his department are in no sense binding upon the board.

The continued success of the Birmingham commission will, of course, depend upon the character of its commissioners, but I confidently predict that in place of the scornful apathy and indifference which formerly characterized the selection of our aldermen, intelligent, public-spirited, enthusiastic and organized interest will be displayed by the best people of Birmingham in maintaining the personnel of the Birmingham commission at its present high standard.

DOCUMENT 4

Report of the Vice Commission, Louisville, Kentucky (1915)

Progressive reformers also battled what they saw as moral depravity in urban society. Louisville, Kentucky, appointed a vice commission composed of two ministers, a lawyer, a bank executive, and the chief of police to combat prostitution and related threats to the community.

Conspiracy of Silence

In our judgment, the evil of prostitution, particularly commercialized prostitution, is the most abhorrent of all evils with which modern generations have to deal. It is subversive of every moral sense of decency, and its nature is such that for years there has existed a terrible "conspiracy of silence," which has thrown a shroud of secrecy around it, thus enabling the evil to grow with appalling magnitude in all parts of the world.

Your commission joins in the universal protest against this "conspiracy of silence." The time for secrecy and whisperings has passed. Every phase of prostitution, in all of its bare and hideous manifestations, must be revealed to all the community. The only way to combat evil is to know what the evil is. Wisdom in a campaign against prostitution of a public nature can be obtained only by revealing the facts of such prostitution and wisely lending unified efforts toward such regulation or suppression as within the power of a community, through its officials, may lie.

Why Evil Should be Combated

Commercialized prostitution should be combated, not only because it constitutes the most cancerous growth on a community, but because of its direful results; because it stalks broadcast through the land, reaping its harvest of guilty and innocent alike, leaving in its serpentine trail thousands upon thousands of cases of paralysis, blindness, idiocy, insanity and unspeakable physical and moral degeneracy. Couple with all this, the degradation of womanhood, the greed and passion of men arising therefrom, and you have a duty presented to you as plain and clear as the noonday sun.

We are convinced that prostitution cannot be obliterated. We are convinced that prostitution in all of its phases cannot be completely suppressed. Generations of education and better thought will be required to even apparently obtain its total abolition. In our judgment, only slow, determined repression, together with moral and physical education, can furnish for the present the remedy which now appears most practical.

Commercialized Aspect

We are convinced, however, that an end can be put, within a reasonable time, to the most malignant manifestations of prostitution. We are convinced that by a slow, progressive, determined, earnest campaign the power lies within the officials of the city to greatly reduce the commercialized aspect of prostitution. We believe there are in Louisville sufficient open-minded, forward-thinking people to champion a campaign to arouse a public conscience, to give to the community an unvarnished statement of existing facts and to create such attitude as will incite rebellion toward the evil, and control to the greatest possible degree.

Everybody's Problem

Officials of the city can act, and we believe they will. Regulations can be made, and will be made. The police can be made to do their full duty, and we believe they will do their full duty. But all of this is of little lasting avail unless the intelligent, public-spirited portion of the community assumes an active and progressive attitude toward the evil. People in all branches of life—the doctor, the lawyer, the clergyman, the tradesman, the laborer, the public official, the social worker, men and women in every phase, either of public or private activity—should learn to consider the question of commercialized vice as a problem and responsibility which is their own. There must be uniformity and solidity of opinion on the part of all thinking people. There must find root in the mind of the public an attitude different from that which has heretofore prevailed. There must be engendered a spirit of hope, an idea of belief in the possibility of achieving the cherished end. . . .

Every Woman Would be Decent

We have been pleased to start with the assumption, and, regardless of inquiry which may have persuaded us to the contrary, we continue to assume, that every woman seeks to lead a decent, respectable life, and shuns unnatural sexual immorality. It is simple to cast aside and avoid a fallen woman, but we have been unable to trace a single case, either in the city of Louisville or in other places, where that poor, unfortunate creature has not been brought to the position in which she finds herself through the misuse, abuse or dissipation of some man even lower than herself. It is well for men to talk of economic pressure upon women, of their isolation or loneliness, of the lure of the streets, leading to bad company and unwholesome companionship, but in the end it will be found that the lonesomeness has been impressed upon her by some degraded man; that the lure of the street has been painted lurid by some degraded man; that economic pressure would not have brought home to her mind so forcibly had it not been for some degraded man.

The Need for Women

The great need, to our notion, is the establishing of such institutions and such means of gratifying social and economic needs of young girls as will be conducive to their leading a wholesome and respectable life. We should throw around the girl those protective influences which will enable her to reinforce the natural instincts which every woman has to be respectable. Even in cases where the woman has fallen, this community, like all other communities, all too frequently, through the attitude of its public mind, makes hard the road back to moral strength. In another section of this report recommendation is made for the establishment of an institution for the training, direction and education of such girls who, at a tender age, are made the victims of immorality, thereby furnishing an opportunity long neglected to start them upon the right road by teaching a means of decent livelihood through trade or otherwise. . . .

The Business of Life

[W]ith development of twentieth century invention; with the commercialization of almost every phase of human interest; with means of quick transportation at hand; with the invention of the telephone and the telegraph, the moving picture, the phonograph, modern drama and a thousand other things of convenience and amusement, the old order of things has changed. The hours of labor are shorter. Opportunity for recreation is greater;

and the commercialization of human interest has brought people to the condition where the *main business of life is the seeking of pleasure*. This condition has been productive in an increase of immorality among women. The modern-day craze for pleasure has made easy and has accentuated the opportunity for women to be exploited. However, the pendulum never swings in one direction that it does not swing back again. Just as the search for pleasure has risen high, just as the ease of entering and practicing a life of immorality has risen to a dangerous pitch of profit and ease, just so there will be a recession; just so public sentiment expressed against such practices will swing back and down, suppressing and controlling that which the toleration of years, that which thoughtlessness on the part of the community had caused to be recognized as a concomitant necessary ailment of modern-day life.

DOCUMENT 5

Jane Addams, Twenty Years at Hull House (1910)

One of the most celebrated methods of urban reform was the settlement house movement. Jane Addams, founder of a Chicago settlement house, reported on her experience working with the poor in her 1910 book *Twenty Years at Hull House*. In that volume, she published the following passages, originally presented to fellow settlement advocates in 1892 as a paper entitled "The Subjective Necessity for Social Settlements."

This paper is an attempt to analyze the motives which underlie a movement based, not only upon conviction, but upon genuine emotion, wherever educated young people are seeking an outlet for that sentiment of universal brotherhood, which the best spirit of our times is forcing from an emotion into a motive. These young people accomplish little toward the solution of this social problem, and bear the brunt of being cultivated into unnourished, oversensitive lives. They have been shut off from the common labor by which they live which is a great source of moral and physical health. They feel a fatal want of harmony between their theory and their lives, a lack of coördination between thought and action. I think it is hard for us to realize how seriously many of them are taking to the notion of human brotherhood, how eagerly they long to give tangible expression to the democratic ideal. These young men and women, longing to socialize their democracy, are animated by certain hopes which may be thus loosely formulated: that if in a democratic country nothing can be permanently achieved save through the masses of people, it will be impossible to establish a higher political life than the people themselves crave; that it is difficult to see how the notion of a higher civic life can be fostered save through common intercourse; that the blessings which we associate with a life of refinement and cultivation can be made universal and must be made universal if they are to be permanent; that the good we secure for ourselves is precarious and uncertain, is floating in mid-air, until it is secured for all of us and incorporated into our common life. It is easier to state these hopes than to formulate the line of motives, which I believe to constitute the trend of the subjective pressure toward the Settlement. There is something primordial about these motives, but I am perhaps overbold in designating them as a great desire to share the race life. . . .

We have in America a fast-growing number of cultivated young people who have no recognized outlet for their active faculties. They hear constantly of the great social maladjustment, but no way is provided for them to change it, and their uselessness hangs about them heavily. . . . These young people have had advantages of college, of European travel, and of economic study, but they are sustaining this shock of inaction. They have pet phrases, and they tell you that the things that make us all alike are stronger than the things that make us different. They say that all men are united by needs and sympathies far more permanent and radical than anything that temporarily divides them and sets them in opposition to each other. If they affect art, they say that the decay in artistic expression is due to the decay in ethics, that art when shut away from the human interests and from the great mass of humanity is self-destructive. They tell their elders with all the bitterness of youth that if they expect success from them in business or politics or in whatever lines their ambition for them has run, they must let them consult all of humanity; that they must let them find out what the people want and how they want it. It is only the stronger young people, however, who formulate this. Many of them dissipate their energies in so-called enjoyment. Others not content with that, go on studying and go back to college for their second degrees; not that they are especially fond of study, but because they want something definite to do, and their powers have been trained in the direction of mental accumulation. Many are buried beneath this mental accumulation with lowered vitality and discontent. . . .

The Settlement . . . is an experimental effort to aid the solution of the social and industrial problems which are engendered by the modern conditions of life in a great city. It insists that these problems are not confined to any one portion of a city. It is an attempt to relieve, at the same time, the overaccumulation at one end of society and the destitution at the other, but it assumes that this overaccumulation and destitution is most sorely felt in the things that pertain to social and educational advantages. From its very nature it can stand for no political or social propaganda. It must, in a sense, give the warm welcome of an inn to all such propaganda, if perchance one of them be found an angel. The one thing to be dreaded in the Settlement is that it lose its flexibility, its power of quick adaptation, its readiness to change its methods as its environment may demand. It must be open to conviction and must have a deep and abiding sense of tolerance. It must be hospitable and ready for experiment. It should demand from its residents a scientific patience in the accumulation of facts and the steady holding of their sympathies as one of the best instruments for that accumulation. It must be grounded in a philosophy whose foundation is on the solidarity of the human race, a philosophy which will not waver when the race happens to be represented by a drunken woman or an idiot boy. Its residents must be emptied of all conceit of opinion and all self-assertion, and ready to arouse and interpret the public opinion of their neighborhood. They must be content to live quietly side by side with their neighbors, until they grow into a sense of relationship and mutual interests. Their neighbors are held apart by differences of race and language which the residents can more easily overcome. They are bound to see the needs of their neighborhood as a whole, to furnish data for legislation, and to use their influence to secure it. In short, residents are pledged to devote themselves to the duties of good citizenship and to the arousing of the social energies which too largely lie dormant in every neighborhood given over to industrialism. They are bound to regard the entire life of their city as organic, to make an effort to unify it, and to protest against its over-differentiation.

It is always easy to make all philosophy point one particular moral and all history adorn one particular tale, but I may be forgiven the reminder that the best speculative philosophy sets forth the solidarity of the human race; that the highest moralists have taught that without the advance and improvement of the whole, no man can hope for any lasting improvement in his own moral or material individual condition; and that the subjective necessity for Social Settlements is therefore identical with that necessity, which urges us on toward social and individual salvation.

DOCUMENT 6

James H. Patten, Chairman of the National Legislative Committee of the American Purity Federation, Testimony Before Congress (1910)

Many native-born Americans grew increasingly hostile to the immigrants from southern and central Europe who had poured into the country for a generation, worrying that immigrants undermined the Anglo-Saxon character of America. James H. Patten testified at a congressional hearing on the perceived dangers of unrestricted immigration. Congress did not impose immigration quotas until the 1920s.

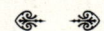

❦ ❦

MR. PATTEN: I am positive that the census figures of 1890 show that over one-fifth of our foreign-born criminals are illiterate. As I said a moment ago, the illiteracy test is not proposed as a means of excluding criminals, it is not offered as a substitute for existing laws debarring criminals, but as an additional selective and restrictive measure, and on the ground that, for an enlightened democracy such as we have, on the average, the man who can read and write is more likely to be better fitted for American citizenship than the one who can not. If the steamships can not bring illiterates they will bring literates. Of course an elementary—even a high school—education is no absolute guaranty against rascality. The test is proposed merely as another means of sifting out the more unassimilative aliens. It would seem, as Commissioner-General Sargent argued, that the man who can read, write, and figure must necessarily be better equipped for the struggle for existence—better prepared for American citizenship, and more likely to take up with our standards and ideals, else our whole public-school system is wrong. There are of course individual cases of illiterate persons making excellent citizens, but statistics show, as one would expect, that it is the illiterate who generally has criminal propensities, is averse to country life, settles down in the crowded quarters, takes no permanent interest in the country, lacks a knowledge of a trade, has lower standards of life, a less ambition to seek a better——

MR. KÜSTERMANN. He may not have had any chance to learn.

MR. PATTEN. That is true, but the public-school system, forms of government, and other institutions are reflections of capacities, characteristics, etc., of people——

MR. KÜSTERMANN. A good many countries do not offer the opportunities that we offer.

MR. SABATH. How many of those that are employed, we will say, in building the railroads and in the mines can read and write? It is not absolutely necessary that a man should be a scholar, is it, to develop our country, to develop our farms, and to build our railroads? . . .

MR. KÜSTERMANN. You, as the paid agent of the Immigration Restriction League, seem to be very anxious to have immigrants have proper accommodations and quarters, while the purpose of your league is to exclude them as much as possible and to make it unnecessary to have any immigrant stations?

MR. PATTEN. I beg pardon, but the object of the Immigration Restriction League and of the American Purity Federation is not exclusion, except as to undesirables. Each stands for certain exclusions and restrictions, but neither is opposed to immigration per se. I do not believe an increase in the "head tax," or rather steamship per capita tax, to $10 would increase the steerage rates, and consequently as I do not believe there is a bit of restriction even in it. I think as Mr. Gardner, of this committee, has ably argued in the House, that it would have to be put up to $25 or $50 in order to compel the steamship companies to charge as much or more to this country than they charge to other countries to which they are running and thus materially affect the number coming here. The present rates are from $5 to $65 less than to South America and South Australia. I have considerable data from the steamship companies on that point, and feel quite certain of my conclusions. Now, in order to restrict you would have to make the steamship tax $40 or $50, in my opinion, before the transportation companies which are now charging "all the traffic will bear," would raise their rates sufficiently to deter any number of immigrants from coming.

MR. KÜSTERMANN. You want to go step by step and eventually reach that point?

MR. PATTEN. That is not the controlling idea or motive with me or the public-spirited organizations I represent, I am sure; and if I could show you the minutes of the meetings of the executive committees, you would find that they have never advocated this increased tax for that purpose whatever the members may think individually or the organizations may do after the illiteracy test becomes a law. The most selective and restrictive measure which the Immigration Restriction League of Boston and the Purity Federation have advocated has been the illiteracy test. I do not believe you can find in their private records or public utterances or in their pamphlets anything to the contrary———

MR. KÜSTERMANN. I should like to refer to one of the pamphlets issued by the League wherein it is stated that the reason so few children were found in American families was simply because they did not want those poor children, if born, exposed to the children of the immigrants, that they do not want them to come together. That is the spirit of your League?

MR. PATTEN. I beg pardon, Mr. Küstermann, I think if you will look at that pamphlet you will find that that is an article or quotation from an author of international reputation, the late Gen. Francis A. Walker, president of the Massachusetts Institute of Technology and the chief of two United States censuses, who made a very close and thorough statistical study of the question.

MR. KÜSTERMANN. They were very anxious to quote it. I do not care who said it, they had it in their own pamphlet.

MR. PATTEN. You will remember that the investigations of the industrial commission bore out General Walker's conclusions; for it concluded: "It is a hasty assumption which holds that immigration during the nineteenth century has increased the total population" of the United States. The point being that recent foreign immigration has been a substitution for rather than an addition to our population, in the manner in which your statement indicated. Census statistics show that the population of the South has increased faster out of its own loins alone than has the population of the North out of its loins and from foreign immigration, both together.

MR. SABATH. You are referring to the colored population of the South?

MR. PATTEN. I am referring to the population of the South, either or both, colored and uncolored.

MR. SABATH. Just put in the word "colored."

MR. PATTEN. You can take it either white or black, or both. I think the census will show that the average increase in the native birth rate in the South has been about 30 per cent per decade, whereas in the North it has fallen off to almost nothing, as Walker and the industrial commission point out exclusively in the very States, counties, and localities where recent foreign immigration has competed. There is, for instance, no place in this country where you will find so many old maids, bachelors, late marriages, small families, and so much "race suicide" as you will find in the very towns and communities of the Northeast to which is destined fully 90 per cent of the present influx. I am speaking of the masses, and not of the so-called "flower of society" which is small and dies off everywhere.

There are a number of factors, but the cause of causes, for many reasons, is the enormous inflow and efflux of aliens with lower standards and different ideals. It is the character of the present immigration, the fact that about three-fourths are unmarried male adults, that the bulk comes without any visible means of support, ignorant of our conditions, lacking a knowledge of our language, illiterate, and unused to self-government and self-care; for instance, last year one-fourth of those coming did not have money enough to prepay their passage to this country, and almost one-third of the adults could not read and write. They were unable to speak our language. Less than 10 per cent of them had ever been here before. They were unacquainted with our conditions, and had to find some kind of work at almost any wage, and thus in certain northeast labor centers subjected workers to a cutthroat, ruinous competition, which seems to need protection. They come as birds of passage, about half of those who came have gone back during the last ten years, and have gone back with large savings—"Grasshopper immigrants," Editor John Temple Graves calls them.

DOCUMENT 7

Platform Adopted by the National Negro Committee (1909)

Although some leading white progressives like Jane Addams supported African American civil rights, the era confirmed the racially exclusionary trends established at the end of the nineteenth century. The National Negro Committee, composed of prominent blacks and whites, outlined its goals for a new organization, the National Association for the Advancement of Colored People, in the following platform composed in 1909.

We denounce the ever-growing oppression of our 10,000,000 colored fellow citizens as the greatest menace that threatens the country. Often plundered of their just share of the public funds, robbed of nearly all part in the government, segregated by common carriers, some murdered with impunity, and all treated with open contempt by officials, they are held in some States in practical slavery to the white community. The systematic persecution of law-abiding citizens and their disfranchisement on account of their race alone is a crime that will ultimately drag down to an infamous end any nation that allows it to be practiced, and it bears most heavily on those poor white farmers and laborers whose economic position is most similar to that of the persecuted race.

The nearest hope lies in the immediate and patiently continued enlightenment of the people who have been inveigled into a campaign of oppression. The spoils of persecution should not go to enrich any class or classes of the population. Indeed persecution of organized workers, peonage, enslavement of prisoners, and even disfranchisement already threaten large bodies of whites in many Southern States.

We agree fully with the prevailing opinion that the transformation of the unskilled colored laborers in industry and agriculture into skilled workers is of vital importance to that race and to the nation, but we demand for the Negroes, as for all others, a free and complete education, whether by city, State or nation, a grammar school and industrial training for all and technical, professional, and academic education for the most gifted.

But the public schools assigned to the Negro of whatever kind or grade will never receive a fair and equal treatment until he is given equal treatment in the Legislature and before the law. Nor will the practically educated Negro, no matter how valuable to the community he may prove, be given a fair return for his labor or encouraged to put forth his best efforts or given the chance to develop that efficiency that comes only outside the school until he is respected in his legal rights as a man and a citizen.

We regard with grave concern the attempt manifest South and North to deny black men the right to work and to enforce this demand by violence and bloodshed. Such a question is too fundamental and clear even to be submitted to arbitration. The late strike in Georgia is not simply a demand that Negroes be displaced, but that proven and efficient men be made to surrender their long-followed means of livelihood to white competitors.

As first and immediate steps toward remedying these national wrongs, so full of peril for the whites as well as the blacks of all sections, we demand of Congress and the Executive:

(1) That the Constitution be strictly enforced and the civil rights guaranteed under the Fourteenth Amendment be secured impartially to all.

(2) That there be equal educational opportunities for all and in all the States, and that public school expenditure be the same for the Negro and white child.

(3) That in accordance with the Fifteenth Amendment the right of the Negro to the ballot on the same terms as other citizens be recognized in every part of the country.

DOCUMENT 8

Helen M. Todd, "Getting Out the Vote" (1911)

Women campaigned for a constitutional amendment guaranteeing women the right to vote as part of a general trend during the Progressive Era toward a more prominent female presence in public life. Helen M. Todd of Illinois, a state factory inspector by profession, recounted her experience in an article for *The American Magazine* entitled "Getting Out the Vote: An Account of a Week's Automobile Campaign by Women Suffragists."

On a June day last year, six or eight insurgent women met in the library of the Chicago Women's Club and decided to add the Sixteenth Amendment to the Constitution of the United States. . . .

It would be untrue to leave the impression that we found this fraternal feeling toward woman suffrage ready made. It was only achieved in many instances by effort and experience.

The men were sometimes obviously thankful their women folks were incapable of going gallivanting through the country making speeches. Often, as our automobile, covered with banners, stopped in front of the blacksmith shop or on the street corner where we were scheduled to speak, we realized that the temper of the audience was not one of unmixed approval; but they were interested, and above all they were there. The rest was for us to do. Every type of man was represented in these down-State audiences, and every kind of vehicle. The stores were left in charge of whoever was unfortunate enough to have to stay, generally the errand boy, and the rest of the village turned out to "hear the women talk."

We opened our plea for women by showing our audience that the mother and wife could not long protect herself and her children unless she had a vote. That the milk the city mother gave her baby; the school her children were educated in; the purity of the water they drank; the prices she paid for meat and clothes; the very wages her husband received; the sanitary and moral condition of the streets her children passed through were all matters of politics. When once we had clearly established the fact that women wanted to vote to protect their homes we had won a large part of our audience. . . .

When we reached Warren the place was decorated with flags and yellow banners. The big street meeting had already gathered. "Let me take up all the time," Mrs. McCulloch said, "because we have only a thirty minutes' stop here." "With all your banners and welcome," she said, getting energetically upon the seat of the automobile, "the man that you have sent to represent you in the Legislature has knifed our Suffrage bill every time it came up. I am just going to tell you your Representative's history and ask you to keep him at home," and she did.

Mixed with the arraignment of Representative Gray was the pathos and wit of the story of the struggles of the women of Illinois in the Legislature to protect its children. When she had finally finished the story of Mr. Gray's part in this struggle you could feel the audience with her. They came crowding about the machine. "All right, we will get somebody else; we never knew about all this. We cannot do much for you ladies because he has got another year to serve," was suggested. This seemed final, and just as the automobile was beginning to move, a crowd of men and women pushing forward a central

The Fifteenth Amendment, ratified in 1870, prohibited discrimination against voters on account of race, color, or previous conditions of servitude. Fifty years later in 1920, the Nineteenth Amendment outlawed "discrimination against voters on account of sex," thus finally extending the franchise to women.

figure that was half laughing and half resisting bore down upon us and called for the chauffeur to stop. "Here he is!" they shouted. "We went to his house and got him. You just ask him whether he is going to stand for that Suffrage bill this fall and we'll stand back and see what he says. This is Representative Gray." Mrs. McCulloch who had become acquainted with him in the Legislature looked coldly at him. The Rev. Kate Hughes, who had also had the pleasure of meeting him in the same place, sniffed, I might almost say snorted, audibly and looked absently over his head. Dr. Blount greeted him with friendly interest as one would a sinner in whom there were possibilities of repentance. And I, being nearest on the outside, hastily assumed my most ingratiating and feminine air and held out my hand. "Well, Mr. Gray," I said, "will you promise us to stand for our Woman's Suffrage bill this time?" "It looks as if I would have to," he said, disengaging himself with difficulty from the press of the crowd in order to take off his hat. "I have always thought women were about the best things there were in the world, but I never thought you were so in earnest about this voting. If you have really set your hearts on it why there is nothing for me to do but give in. I can't fight against a woman's campaign. I'm for you," he shouted as we drove off amid the laughter and cheers of the crowd.

On the Fourth of July we spoke in the city square. Truths, familiar to city men through a prevalence of speakers, are sometimes new to a down-State audience. We told them that in a country that boasted of its representative government half the population of women were not represented at all, that they were classed with the criminal and insane even though they had given their sons to make a Fourth of July possible. When we had finished, an old man pushed his way to the automobile and gave us some money. He had an old, weather-beaten face and instead of week-day overalls wore a stiff suit of "store" clothes in honor of the Fourth; his trousers guiltless of any crease looked like two sections of stovepipe. So serious and almost forbidding was the expression that we waited for him to speak before making any overtures of friendship. Accustomed as we were to the more mobile city face, we often could not tell from the faces of our audience what they were feeling. This old man might have been going to say, "I hate what you are saying; I wish you would go away," but he handed us a two-dollar bill and leaning over the machine squeezed each of our hands with a grip that brought tears to our eyes. "I would just give anything in the hull world if my wife had been well enough to come along, but she's been poorly all this winter and couldn't stand the long drive. I'm giving you this two dollars for her. The idea," he continued, gazing angrily at us, "of a woman like my wife bein' put along with imbeciles and criminals. Why, she came out with me from New York in the pioneer days when Illinois was nothing but woods and bears and swamps and we drove the hull way in a mover's wagon and took our three children too." . . .

Power and confidence are as valuable assets to a woman as a man; and as one of our party remarked, it is not only the people we have reached on this trip that matters, but we have learned how to do it.

After all, with women, isn't it largely a question of learning how?

There is a comradeship which only comes from working together for a common cause. Although most men know the pleasure of this, comparatively few women have experienced it, and although we were as tired as any pioneer women who had crossed the country in a mover's wagon after this last meeting and our week's campaign, yet our party was loath to break up.

It had been inspiring to depend upon the honesty, personal kindness, the spirit of fair play and neighborliness, the quick response to anyone in sorrow or need, which were characteristics of our country audiences. And we lingered taking to each other and to members of the crowd who were seeing us home until it was very late when I entered the farmhouse where I was to spend my last night down State.

Late as it was, the old bed-ridden mother was awake and called softly for me to come in and tell her about the meetin'. "I knew it would be a fine meetin'," she said. "I had my bed turned 'round to the window. I seen the wagons coming in from out of town since morning. I knew you'd be leaving for Chicago early, and I just thought I would wait up for you so's I could hear all about it and tell Lucy. You see," she explained, "Daughter Lucy and the hired girl couldn't both go and leave me alone, since I have had my stroke. Lucy, she was born and brought up to woman's rights, bein' my daughter; but our hired girl's new in our family and she's real ignorant about it. So Lucy she felt it was her duty to send our girl to get converted, and stay to home herself. I'm a believer," she said, "and Maggie ain't. But Lucy she felt terrible put out about it though she didn't let on to me of course, and I made up my mind I'd ask you to just say over what you said so's I could tell it to her. I had hoped," she added, "that I'd last to see the day when women would vote in Illinois, but if Susan B. Anthony can die without seein' it, I guess I can. It's a comfort to see you young women back keepin' up the same fight that we started back East when we was young and spry. It makes us feel as if we hadn't educated you for nothing, for we did educate you. 'What, educate shes!' the men said when we wanted the girls to go to school. 'What's the use spendin' money on educatin' shes?' Well I guess we've showed them what the use was. I've seen that done anyhow." . . .

No words can better express the soul of the woman's movement, lying back of the practical cry of "Votes for Women," better than this sentence which had captured the attention of both Mother Jones and the hired girl, "Bread for all, and Roses too." Not at once; but woman is the mothering element in the world and her vote will go toward helping forward the time when life's Bread, which is home, shelter and security, and the Roses of life, music, education, nature and books, shall be the heritage of every child that is born in the country, in the government of which she has a voice.

There will be no prisons, no scaffolds, no children in factories, no girls driven on the street to earn their bread, in the day when there shall be "Bread for all, and Roses too."

To help to make such a civilization possible is the meaning of "Votes for Women." It was the power of this idea which sent the women of Illinois "down State" on their automobile campaign.

Study Questions

1. Are there any unifying themes among reformers during the Progressive Era?
2. Did the Progressive Era advance or retard the spread of democracy?
3. What motivated Progressive Era reformers?
4. What methods did Progressive Era reformers share to achieve their goals?
5. Why did issues affecting women become prominent during the Progressive Era? Explain the phrase "Bread for all, and roses too."

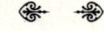

7

Corporate Society

By 1920 Americans had become disillusioned with intervention in Europe and with progressive reform at home. The glorious crusade to "make the world safe for democracy" now seemed an unnecessary sacrifice and senseless loss of life. Many people regarded the League of Nations as overly idealistic, and fearing that it would overextend U.S. commitments abroad, they welcomed its defeat in the Senate.

Civil unrest at home in the immediate aftermath of the war also alarmed the nation. Strikes, race riots, and the "Red menace" dominated headlines throughout 1919 and 1920. Longing for stability, voters embraced the conservatism of the Republican presidential candidate, Warren G. Harding. This self-proclaimed spokesman for small-town, middle-class values distanced himself from the activist administrations of Theodore Roosevelt and Woodrow Wilson. During his campaign he declared that America needed "not heroism, but healing, not nostrums, but normalcy," and he promised to "set our own house in order" (Document 1). Voters agreed, sending him to the White House by the largest margin of victory since before the Civil War.

To set America's house in order, Harding, and his Republican successors Calvin Coolidge and Herbert Hoover, initiated an economic program intended to create a friendly relationship between government and business. Although some policies, such as tax cuts for the wealthy and high tariffs, suggested a return to *laissez faire*, the government's role in the economy actually expanded in the 1920s. Republicans doubled the number of federal employees and organized new bureaus to promote industrial cooperation. The policy seemed to work. Between 1922 and 1929 the American economy soared.

To the nation's corporate leaders, the economic boom of the 1920s, or New Era as some called it, vindicated the values of big business. America, they insisted, had much to learn from corporate capitalism. Employment in a top industrial firm, they maintained, promoted thrift, discipline, and efficiency while offering boundless opportunity for upward mobility—essentials for a healthy, moral, and prosperous nation. Considering themselves benefactors, not robber barons, corporate elites argued that their enlightened style of management dissuaded workers from joining unions and fostered a true harmony of interests between labor and capital (Document 2).

Not all accepted these benign assertions. Critics, such as novelist Sinclair Lewis, ridiculed the typical American businessman as a smug, vulgar, self-satisfied

The United States suffered some 112,000 casualties in World War I, with an estimated eight to ten million total war casualties worldwide. When the war was over, many Americans felt that the loss of life had been senseless and that little good had come from the conflict.

conformist. To Lewis, the values revered in Rotary Clubs across the country promoted mediocrity rather than excellence (Document 3). Sociologists Robert and Helen Lynd claimed that the new economy of mass production and mass consumption devalued work. They concluded that the urge to consume, rather than any intrinsic value to work itself or the promise of upward mobility, now compelled men and women to work hard and remain loyal to employers (Document 4).

Other groups seized opportunities opened by the new industrial boom. Women entered the professions in unprecedented numbers, challenging prevailing assumptions about the proper roles of men and women in the household economy and in society at large (Document 5). African Americans fled the South in droves. They took advantage of employment in war industries and in other northern manufacturing concerns (Document 6). This southern exodus, or Great Migration, fueled an important black cultural and artistic movement. New York City's Harlem district—"the Negro Capital of the World"—became the center of this cultural ferment. There, writers such as Langston Hughes sought to create an artistic expression that captured the complexities of the black experience in America (Document 7).

Not everyone enjoyed the benefits of New Era prosperity. While productivity expanded by 32 percent between 1922 and 1929, average wage rates rose by only 8 percent. Thus the capacity to produce far outpaced the potential to consume. Part of the problem lay in the production process. To boost productivity, manufacturers pioneered new technologies designed to maximize output. These changes had enormous consequences for workers, especially in the southern textile industry, where mill owners expected employees to produce more at reduced wages. In 1929 southern textile workers resisted in a series of strikes that were crushed through police force and mob violence. Strike reports revealed in graphic detail that beneath the prosperity of the New Era all was not well (Document 8). Labor and capital were in conflict, not harmony. America's house was far from in order.

DOCUMENT 1

Warren G. Harding, Campaign Speech at Boston (1920)

Harding was a dark-horse contender for the presidency in 1920. Formerly the editor of a Marion, Ohio, newspaper, Harding had served only one term in the U.S. Senate when he was nominated as the Republican candidate for president. He conducted a stay-at-home, front-porch campaign in which he identified himself with the common man and the virtues of small-town life. In the following speech, delivered before business leaders in May 1920, Harding articulated the growing reaction against progressive legislation and intervention in foreign affairs. In the course of the address, he misread "normality," pronouncing it "normalcy," and thus coined the slogan for the Republican administrations of the 1920s.

There isn't anything the matter with world civilization, except that humanity is viewing it through a vision impaired in a cataclysmal war. Poise has been disturbed and nerves have been racked, and fever has rendered men irrational; sometimes there have been draughts upon the dangerous cup of barbarity and men have wandered far from safe paths, but the human procession still marches in the right direction.

Here in the United States, we feel the reflex, rather than the hurting wound, but we still think straight, and we mean to act straight, and mean to hold firmly to all that was ours when war involved us, and seek the higher attainments which are the only compensations that so supreme a tragedy may give mankind.

America's present need is not heroics, but healing; not nostrums but normalcy; not revolution, but restoration; not agitation, but adjustment; not surgery but serenity; not the dramatic, but the dispassionate; not experiment but equipoise; not submergence in internationality, but sustainment in triumphant nationality.

It is one thing to battle successfully against world domination by a military autocracy, because the infinite God never intended such a program, but it is quite another thing to revise human nature and suspend the fundamental laws of life and all of life's acquirements.

The world called for peace, and has its precarious variety. America demands peace, formal as well as actual, and means to have it, regardless of political exigencies and campaign issues. If it must be a campaign issue, we shall have peace and discuss it afterwards, because the actuality is imperative, and the theory is only illusive. Then we may set our own house in order. We challenged the proposal that an armed autocrat should dominate the world, it ill becomes us to assume that a rhetorical autocrat shall direct all humanity.

This republic has its ample tasks. If we put an end to false economics which lure humanity to utter chaos, ours will be the commanding example of world leadership today. If we can prove a representative popular government under which a citizenship seeks what it may do for the government rather than what the government may do for individuals, we shall do more to make democracy safe for the world than all armed conflict ever recorded. The world needs to be reminded that all human ills are not curable by legislation, and that quantity of statutory enactment and excess of government offer no substitute for quality of citizenship. . . .

My best judgment of America's needs is to steady down, to get squarely on our feet, to make sure of the right path. Let's get out of the fevered delirium of war, with the hallucination that all the money in the world is to be made in the madness of war and the wildness of its aftermath. Let us stop to consider that tranquility at home is more precious than peace abroad, and that both our good fortune and our eminence are dependent on the normal forward stride of all the American people.

DOCUMENT 2

Edward Earle Purinton, "Big Ideas from Big Business" (1921)

"What we want in America," declared Warren Harding in 1920, "is less government in business and more business in government." His successor, Calvin Coolidge, quipped that the "business of America is business." Such statements reflected a growing faith in the values, wisdom, and judgment of America's successful business leaders. Edward Earle Purinton, an efficiency analyst and dean of the American Efficiency Foundation, was one of the leading spokespersons for the promise of business enterprise. He authored books such as *Efficient Living* (1915), *The Triumph of the Man Who Acts* (1916), and *Practical Course to Personal Efficiency* (1917). In the following article, written for *The Independent* in 1921, Purinton explains why business will lead to the salvation of America.

Among the nations of the earth today America stands for one idea: *Business*. National opprobrium? National opportunity. For in this fact is, potentially, the salvation of the world.

Thru business, properly conceived, managed and conducted, the human race is finally to be redeemed. How and why a man works foretells what he will do, think, have, love and be. And real salvation is in doing, thinking, having, giving and being—not in sermonizing and theorizing. I shall base the facts of this article on the personal tours and minute examinations I have recently made of twelve of the world's largest business plants: U.S. Steel Corporation, International Harvester Company, Swift & Company, E. I. du Pont de Nemours & Company, National County Bank, National Cash Register Company, Western Electric Company, Sears, Roebuck & Company, H. J. Heinz Company, Peabody Coal Company, Statler Hotels, Wanamaker Stores.

These organizations are typical, foremost representatives of the commercial group of interests loosely termed "Big Business." A close view of these corporations would reveal to any trained, unprejudiced observer a new conception of modern business activities. Let me draw a few general conclusions regarding the best type of business house and business man.

What is the finest game? Business. The soundest science? Business. The truest art? Business. The fullest education? Business. The fairest opportunity? Business. The cleanest philanthropy? Business. The sanest religion? Business.

You may not agree. That is because you judge business by the crude, mean, stupid, false imitation of business that happens to be located near you.

The finest game is business. The rewards are for everybody, and all can win. There are no favorites—Providence always crowns the career of the man who is worthy. And in this game there is no "luck"—you have the fun of taking chances but the sobriety of guaranteeing certainties. The speed and size of your winnings are for you alone to determine; you needn't wait for the other fellow in the game—it is always your move. And your slogan is not "Down the Other Fellow!" but rather "Beat Your Own Record!" or "Do It Better Today!" or "Make Every Job a Masterpiece!" The great sportsmen of the world are the great business men.

The soundest science is business. All investigation is reduced to action, and by action proved or disproved. The idealistic motive animates the materialistic method. Hearts as well as minds are open to the truth. Capital is furnished for the researches of "pure science"; yet pure science is not regarded pure until practical. Competent scientists are suitably rewarded—as they are not in the scientific schools.

The truest art is business. The art is so fine, so exquisite, that you do not think of it as art. Language, color, form, line, music, drama, discovery, adventure—all the components of art must be used in business to make it of superior character.

The fullest education is business. A proper blend of study, work and life is essential to advancement. The whole man is educated. Human nature itself is the open book that all business men study; and the mastery of a page of this educates you more than the memorizing of a dusty tome from a library shelf. In the school of business, moreover, you teach yourself and learn most from your own mistakes. What you learn here you live out, the only real test.

The fairest opportunity is business. You can find more, better, quicker chances to get ahead in a large business house than anywhere else on earth. The biographies of champion business men show how they climbed, and how you can climb. Recognition of better work, of keener and quicker thought, of deeper and finer feeling, is gladly offered by the men higher up, with early promotion the rule for the man who justifies it. There is, and can be, no such thing as buried talent in a modern business organization.

The cleanest philanthropy is business. By "clean" philanthropy I mean that devoid of graft, inefficiency and professionalism, also of condolence, hysterics and paternalism. Nearly everything that goes by the name of Charity was born a triplet, the other two members of the trio being Frailty and Cruelty. Not so in the welfare departments of leading corporations. Savings and loan funds; pension and insurance provisions; health precautions, instructions and safeguards; medical attention and hospital care; libraries, lectures and classes; musical, athletic and social features of all kinds; recreational facilities and financial opportunities—these types of "charitable institutions" for employees add to the worker's self-respect, self-knowledge and self-improvement, by making him an active partner in the welfare program, a producer of benefits for his employer and associates quite as much as a recipient of bounty from the company. I wish every "charity" organization would send its officials to school to the heads of the welfare departments of the big corporations; the charity would mostly be transformed into capability, and the minimum of irreducible charity left would not be called by that name.

The sanest religion is business. Any relationship that forces a man to follow the Golden Rule rightfully belongs amid the ceremonials of the church. A great business enterprise includes and presupposes this relationship. I have seen more Christianity to the square inch as a regular part of the office equipment of famous corporation presidents than may ordinarily be found on Sunday in a verbalized but not vitalized church congregation. A man is not wholly religious until he is better on week-days than he is on Sunday. The only ripened fruits of creeds are deeds. You can fool your preacher with a sickly sprout or a wormy semblance of character, but you can't fool your employer. I would make every business house a consultation bureau for the guidance of the church whose members were employees of the house.

I am aware that some of the preceding statements will be challenged by many readers. I should not myself have made them, or believed them, twenty years ago, when I was a pitiful specimen of a callow youth and cocksure professional man combined. A thoro knowledge of business has implanted a deep respect for business and real business men.

The future work of the business man is to teach the teacher, preach to the preacher, admonish the parent, advise the doctor, justify the lawyer, superintend the statesman, fructify the farmer, stabilize the banker, harness the dreamer, and reform the reformer. Do all these needy persons wish to have these many kind things done to them by the business man? Alas, no. They rather look down upon him, or askance at him, regarding him as a mental and social inferior—unless he has money or fame enough to tilt their glance upward.

A large variety of everyday lessons of popular interest may be gleaned from a tour of the world's greatest business plants and a study of the lives of their founders. We suggest a few. . . .

Only common experiences will unite the laborer and the capitalist. Each must get the viewpoint of the other by sharing the work, duties and responsibilities of the other. The sons of the families of Swift, McCormick, Wanamaker, Heinz, du Pont, have learned the business from the ground up; they know the trials, difficulties and needs of workers because they *are* workers; and they don't have to settle agitations and strikes because there aren't any.

Further, by councils and committees of employees, management courses for department heads and foremen, plans of referendum and appeal, offers of stock and voting power to workers, employee representation on the board of directors, and other means of sharing authority and responsibility, owners of a business now give the manual workers a chance to think and feel in unison with themselves. All enmity is between strangers. Those who really know each other cannot fight.

DOCUMENT 3

Sinclair Lewis, Babbitt (1922)

Sinclair Lewis produced some of the most highly acclaimed literary works of the 1920s. In novels such as *Main Street* (1920) and *Babbitt* (1922), Lewis portrayed Midwestern society as ruled by an unenlightened bourgeoisie that ignored the democratic promise of American life. In *Babbitt* he sketched his classic satirical portrait of the petty American businessman. To Lewis, George F. Babbitt, the title character, represented the source of America's crass materialism, its self-righteousness, and its bigotry, hypocrisy, and complacency. In the following passage from the novel, Babbitt lends his support to Lucas Prout, a candidate for mayor of Zenith, a fictitious midwestern city.

※ ※

This autumn a Mr. W. G. Harding, of Marion, Ohio, was appointed President of the United States, but Zenith was less interested in the national campaign than in the local election. Seneca Doane, though he was a lawyer and a graduate of the State University, was candidate for mayor of Zenith on an alarming labor ticket. To oppose him the Democrats and Republicans united on Lucas Prout, a mattress-manufacturer with a perfect record for sanity. Mr. Prout was supported by the banks, the Chamber of Commerce, all the decent newspapers, and George F. Babbitt.

Babbitt was precinct-leader on Floral Heights, but his district was safe and he longed for stouter battling. His convention paper had given him the beginning of a reputation for oratory, so the Republican-Democratic Central Committee sent him to the Seventh Ward and South Zenith, to address small audiences of workmen and clerks, and wives uneasy with their new votes. He acquired a fame enduring for weeks. Now and then a reporter was present at one of his meetings, and the headlines (though they were not very large) indicated that George F. Babbitt had addressed Cheering Throng, and Distinguished Man of Affairs had pointed out the Fallacies of Doane. Once, in the rotogravure section of the Sunday *Advocate-Times*, there was a photograph of Babbitt and a dozen other business men, with the caption "Leaders of Zenith Finance and Commerce Who Back Prout."

He deserved his glory. He was an excellent campaigner. He had faith; he was certain that if Lincoln were alive, he would be electioneering for Mr. W. G. Harding—unless he came to Zenith and electioneered for Lucas Prout. He did not confuse audiences by silly subtleties; Prout represented honest industry, Seneca Doane represented whining laziness, and you could take your choice. With his broad shoulders and vigorous voice, he was obviously a Good Fellow; and, rarest of all, he really liked people. He almost liked common workmen. He wanted them to be well paid, and able to afford high rents—though, naturally, they must not interfere with the reasonable profits of stockholders. Thus nobly endowed, and keyed high by the discovery that he was a natural orator, he was popular with audiences, and he raged through the campaign, renowned not only in the Seventh and Eighth Wards but even in parts of the Sixteenth.

Crowded in his car, they came driving up to Turnverein Hall, South Zenith—Babbitt, his wife,

Verona, Ted, and Paul and Zilla Riesling. The hall was over a delicatessen shop, in a street banging with trolleys and smelling of onions and gasoline and fried fish. A new appreciation of Babbitt filled all of them, including Babbitt.

"Don't know how you keep it up, talking to three bunches in one evening. Wish I had your strength," said Paul; and Ted exclaimed to Verona, "The old man certainly does know how to kid these roughnecks along!"

Men in black sateen shirts, their faces new-washed but with a hint of grime under their eyes, were loitering on the broad stairs up to the hall. Babbitt's party politely edged through them and into the whitewashed room, at the front of which was a dais with a red-plush throne and a pine altar painted watery blue, as used nightly by the Grand Masters and Supreme Potentates of innumerable lodges. The hall was full. As Babbitt pushed through the fringe standing at the back, he heard the precious tribute, "That's him!" The chairman whistled down the center aisle with an impressive, "The speaker? All ready, sir! Uh—let's see—what was the name, sir?"

Then Babbitt slid into a sea of eloquence:

"Ladies and gentlemen of the Sixteenth Ward, there is one who cannot be with us here to-night, a man than whom there is no more stalwart Trojan in all the political arena—I refer to our leader, the Honorable Lucas Prout, standard-bearer of the city and county of Zenith. Since he is not here, I trust that you will bear with me if, as a friend and neighbor, as one who is proud to share with you the common blessing of being a resident of the great city of Zenith, I tell you in all candor, honesty, and sincerity how the issues of this critical campaign appear to one plain man of business—to one who, brought up to the blessings of poverty and of manual labor, has, even when Fate condemned him to sit at a desk, yet never forgotten how it feels, by heck, to be up at five-thirty and at the factory with the ole dinner-pail in his hardened mitt when the whistle blew at seven, unless the owner sneaked in ten minutes on us and blew it early! (Laughter.) To come down to the basic and fundamental issues of this campaign, the great error, insincerely promulgated by Seneca Doane—"

There were workmen who jeered—young cynical workmen, for the most part foreigners, Jews, Swedes, Irishmen, Italians—but the older men, the patient, bleached, stooped carpenters and mechanics, cheered him; and when he worked up to his anecdote of Lincoln their eyes were wet.

Modestly, busily, he hurried out of the hall on delicious applause, and sped off to his third audience of the evening. "Ted, you better drive," he said. "Kind of all in after that spiel. Well, Paul, how'd it go? Did I get 'em?"

"Bully! Corking! You had a lot of pep."

Mrs. Babbitt worshiped, "Oh, it was fine! So clear and interesting, and such nice ideas. When I hear you orating I realize I don't appreciate how profoundly you think and what a splendid brain and vocabulary you have. Just—splendid."

But Verona was irritating. "Dad," she worried, "how do you know that public ownership of utilities and so on and so forth will always be a failure?"

Mrs. Babbitt reproved, "Rone, I should think you could see and realize that when your father's all worn out with orating, it's no time to expect him to explain these complicated subjects. I'm sure when he's rested he'll be glad to explain it to you. Now let's all be quiet and give Papa a chance to get ready for his next speech. Just think! Right now they're gathering in Maccabee Temple, and *waiting* for us!"

DOCUMENT 4
Robert and Helen Lynd, Middletown (1929)

In 1924 sociologists Robert and Helen Lynd began an extensive study of life in Muncie, Indiana. The Lynds were particularly interested in ascertaining the changes affecting the lives of working people in the thirty years since 1890. The results of their research, published in 1929 as *Middletown: A Study in Contemporary American Culture*, has remained one of the most influential sociological studies of the 1920s. In the following selection, the Lynds describe the transformative effects of consumerism on American life in the 1920s.

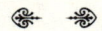

One emerges from the offices, stores, and factories of Middletown [Muncie, Indiana] asking in some bewilderment why all the able-bodied men and many of the women devote their best energies for long hours day after day to this driving activity seemingly so foreign to many of the most powerful impulses of human beings. Is all this expenditure of energy necessary to secure food, clothing, shelter, and other things essential to existence? If not, precisely what over and beyond these subsistence necessaries is Middletown getting out of its work?

For very many of those who get the living for Middletown the amount of robust satisfaction they derive from the actual performance of their specific jobs seems, at best, to be slight. Among the business men the kudos accruing to the eminent in getting a living and to some of their minor associates yields a kind of incidental satisfaction; the successful manufacturer even tends today to supplant in local prestige and authority the judge, preacher, and "professor" of thirty-five to forty years ago. But for the working class both any satisfactions inherent in the actual daily doing of the job and the prestige and kudos of the able worker among his associates would appear to be declining....

The shift from a system in which length of service, craftsmanship, and authority in the shop and social prestige among one's peers tended to go together to one which, in the main, demands little of a worker's personality save rapid, habitual reactions and an ability to submerge himself in the performance of a few routinized easily learned movements seems to have wiped out many of the satisfactions that formerly accompanied the job. Middletown's shops are full of men of whom it may be said that "there isn't 25 per cent. of them paying attention to the job." And as they leave the shop in the evening, "The work of a modern machine-tender leaves nothing tangible at the end of the day's work to which he can point with pride and say, 'I did that—it is the result of my own skill and my own effort.'"

The intangible income accruing to many of the business group derives in part from such new devices as membership in Rotary and other civic clubs, the Chamber of Commerce, Business and Professional Women's Club, and the various professional clubs. But among the working class not only have no such new groups arisen to reward and bolster their work, but the once powerful trade unions have for the most part either disappeared or persist in attenuated form....

This decrease in the psychological satisfactions formerly derived from the sense of craftsmanship and in group solidarity, ... serves to strengthen the impression gained from talk with families of the working class that, however it may be with their better-educated children, for most of the present generation of workers "there is no break through on their industrial sector." It is important for the consideration of other life-activities to bear in mind this fact, that the heavy majority of the numerically dominant working class group live in a world in which neither present nor future appears to hold as much prospect of dominance on the job or of the breaking through to further expansion of personal powers by the head of the family as among the business group.

Frustrated in this sector of their lives, many workers seek compensations elsewhere. The president of the Middletown Trades Council, an alert and energetic molder of thirty and until now the most active figure in the local labor movement, has left the working class to become one of the minor officeholders in the dominant political machine. Others who do not leave are finding outlets, if no longer in the saloon, in such compensatory devices as hooking up the radio or driving the "old bus." The great pressure toward education on the part of the working class is, of course, another phase of this desire to escape to better things.

For both working and business class no other accompaniment of getting a living approaches in importance the money received for their work. It is more this future, instrumental aspect of work, rather than the intrinsic satisfactions involved, that keeps Middletown working so hard as more and more of the activities of living are coming to be strained through the bars of the dollar sign. Among the business group, such things as one's circle of friends, the kind of car one drives, playing golf, joining Rotary, the church to which one belongs, one's political principles, the social position of one's wife apparently tend to be scrutinized somewhat more than formerly in Middletown for their instrumental bearing upon the main business of getting a living, while, conversely, one's status in these various other activities tends to be much influenced by one's financial position. As vicinage has decreased in its influence upon the ordinary social contacts of this group, there appears to be a constantly closer relation between the solitary factor of financial status and one's social status. A leading citizen presented this matter in a nutshell to a member of the research staff in discussing the almost universal local custom of "placing" newcomers in terms of where they live, how they live, the kind of car they drive, and similar externals: "It's perfectly natural. You see, they know money, and they don't know you."

This dominance of the dollar appears in the apparently growing tendency among younger working class men to swap a problematic future for immediate "big money." Foremen complain that Middletown boys entering the shops today are increasingly less interested in being moved from job to job until they have become all-round skilled workers, but want to stay on one machine and run up their production so that they may quickly reach a maximum wage scale.

The rise of large-scale advertising, popular magazines, movies, radio, and other channels of increased cultural diffusion from without are rapidly changing habits of thought as to what things are essential to living and multiplying optional occasions for spending money. Installment buying, which turns wishes into horses overnight, and the heavy increase in the number of children receiving higher education, with its occasions for breaking with home traditions, are facilitating this rise to new standards of living. In 1890 Middletown appears to have lived on a series of plateaus as regards standard of living; old citizens say there was more contentment with relative arrival; it was a common thing to hear a remark that so and so "is pretty good for people in our circumstances." Today the edges of the plateaus have been shaved off, and every one lives on a slope from any point of which desirable things belonging to people all the way to the top are in view. . . .

Although neither business men nor working men like the recurring "hard times," members of both groups urge the maintenance of the present industrial system. The former laud the group leaders who urge "normalcy" and "more business in government and less government in business," while the following sentences from an address by a leading worker, the president of the Trades Council, during the 1924 political campaign, sets forth the same faith in "free competition" on the part of the working class: "The important issue is the economic issue. We can all unite on that. We want a return to active free competition, so that prices will be lower and a man can buy enough for himself and his family with the money he makes." Both groups, as they order a layoff, cut wages to meet outside competition, or, on the other hand, vote for La Follette in the hope of his being able to "do something to help the working man," appear to be fumbling earnestly to make their appropriate moves in the situation according to the rules of the game as far as they see them; but both appear to be bound on the wheel of this modern game of corner-clipping production. The puzzled observer may wonder how far any of them realizes the relation of his particular move to the whole function of getting a living. He might even be reminded of a picture appearing in a periodical circulated in Middletown during the course of the study: A mother leans over her two absorbed infants playing at cards on the floor and asks, "What are you playing, children?"

"We're playing 'Putcher,' Mamma. Bobby, putcher card down."

In the midst of such a partially understood but earnestly followed scheme of getting a living, the rest of living goes on in Middletown.

DOCUMENT 5

Jane Littell, "Meditations of a Wage-Earning Wife" (1924)

During the 1920s, increasing numbers of married women sought gainful employment outside the home. This trend sparked a national debate. Nearly every major magazine periodically published forums on "woman's place," posing questions like "Can a Woman Run a Home and Job, Too?" Yet by 1930, only 12 percent of married women earned wages outside the home, and only 4 percent were balancing a career and a marriage. Nevertheless, the intense public scrutiny devoted to the issue revealed that many believed that women's pursuit of economic independence had far more radical implications than the attainment of female suffrage. In the following article, written in 1924, Jane Littell, a free-lance publicity writer and advertiser, meditates on the obstacles confronting a wage-earning wife in the 1920s.

It seems a bit strange that the mere dropping of a letter into the post box should at the same moment drop on to my shoulders such a feeling of weight—especially since the letter had been written and lying on the desk for a month. The deliberate severing of connections with the monthly pay-check, unless of course there is another pay-check in the offing, is always a serious thing, for, plebeian as it sounds, one must eat.

The letter was my husband's resignation—his deliberate abandonment of a position he has held unhappily for about twelve years. We have been talking about his resignation for two years. He finally wrote the letter a month ago, and then left it on the desk where we could read it occasionally until we were sure we knew what it meant.

It really means that I, the wife, am to be the breadwinner for some time to come. A reversal of the usual domestic situation, true, but one that, under the circumstances, I am happy to be able to be a party to. . . .

To-day there are too many wage-earning wives to make our ten years together seem unusual. Even so, the wage-earning wife has problems all her own. We are still too much in the minority to have had anyone work out rules to fit our cases. Each wage-earning wife has to work out her own rules. She has to find ways and means of holding down two jobs at once—three if she is a mother—and doing such work creditably.

We have some advantages, though, we working wives. We have passed that dissatisfied period that comes to every woman, whether she be married or single. Most of us have been told by doctors and friends, if we voiced our dissatisfaction, that we ought to have children—or, having some, then more children. Almost never do doctors or family or friends realize that a woman, as much as a man, needs an interest completely divorced from herself and her family and household. We working wives have that interest.

In the usual course of events, one of the most terrible moments in a woman's life comes when she discovers that her husband has limitations. It is akin to the moment when the small child discovers that his father is not the strongest and the most powerful man in the world—a man who can somehow bring all the desired things to pass. Tragedy, such a moment is—the sheerest tragedy!

What this discovery does to a wife depends upon the sort of woman she is. The wage-earning wife is quite likely to love her husband the more because of his limitations. If his limitation extends to his earning capacity she is not helpless before it, for she appreciates her own capacity to earn. The maternal element is likely to enter into her love for him at this point and that will bind her more closely to him than any amount of conjugal affection.

The first problem the married woman has to solve, usually, arises from her husband's objection to her working for pay. That was one I missed. I had always worked, therefore I kept right on working.

The second problem for the working wife lies in so managing her ménage that her husband is not made unhappy by an untidy home and by delicatessen meals. Any woman who wants to work can earn money enough to pay a competent maid—and have some money left over. Meantime, if her work makes her happy, she need not worry about the outlay for the maid's wages.

Another problem for the working wife is to find the sort of work in which she can continue for years without having to compete with the new crop of eighteen-year-old girls that each year brings into the business market. For the reason that many employers prefer youth, the wife must find or make for herself a job in which age does not count adversely, and where the quality of the service rendered is the main thing. Social-service work, charity work, politics, selling, free-lance work of any sort, and a business of her own, are the things that appeal most to the wise working wife. She looks ahead toward the time when her experience and years are assets and not the liabilities they become in the general business office.

When the married business woman becomes a success, especially if she earns as much money as her husband, she has new problems. A man may be perfectly willing to have his wife work for money if her happiness lies in that direction, but he hates to have her earn as much money as he does. It touches his pride. He feels his crown as master of the household slipping. He acquires an inferiority complex that sometimes causes him to do all sorts of queer things. It takes a steady hand to keep a marriage off the rocks at this period. The husband wants to be the strong one of the family. He wants his wife to look up to him, to admire his superior ability, and to come to him with a coaxing manner when she wants something, so that he may feel very magnanimous when he gives her what she wants. Really he wants her to keep her place as the minor part of the family. The wise wife learns, if necessary, to hide the facts of her progress, and always to give her husband the admiration he needs. If she fails as an admirer she can look for another woman in her husband's life—and the chances are the interloper will be an inferior sort of woman, one whose main hold on the husband is that of flattery.

The difference between the way a successful business woman and a stay-at-home wife will handle the problems of 'a woman in the case' is vast and typical of the difference in their lives. The business woman says in effect, 'You can't give me anything but companionship anyway. If you don't want to give me that there is nothing left between us. We might as well be divorced.' The stay-at-home wife sees her very bread and butter threatened by the other woman, and what a fuss she makes about it! The queer part of it is that there are fewer successful business women dragged through the divorce courts than there are so-called parasite wives.

When the married business woman comes to the place where she earns as much as her husband the sea of matrimony becomes strewn with rocks. There are plenty of women who become so ego-ridden over their small successes that they are a trial to everyone. Such a woman does little to keep her marriage intact. Her income intoxicates her—and so does the deference shown her by business associates. She loses her perspective. Her conversations bristle with the pronoun—first person singular. She spends most of the time she is at home carefully balancing a chip on her shoulder. If her husband inadvertently brushes it off, there is another case for the divorce mills.

Business is too new to women for anyone to expect us to take it calmly. And when business success comes to a woman she needs a level head to keep cool about it. I was one of a group of business and professional women the other day when the talk turned to just this subject. Most of them admitted laughingly that they had gone through the 'Look-at-me-see-what-I've-done!' stage, which one of them attributed to growing-pains.

One of the good things that come to a home from which both the husband and the wife go forth to business every day is a new comradeship—a new sort of partnership. A working wife has a better chance of being friends with her husband than the stay-at-home wife. And being friends with someone to whom the law binds one is not so easy as it sounds. The wage-earning wife meets her husband on an equality basis. She is no longer a dependent. She is an equal partner. The chances for domestic happiness seem greater than in the old-fashioned marriage where a woman could be nothing but what her husband made her.

There are many more problems that the wage-earning wife must face. The biggest thing that worries all of us is what our husbands think about it all and how they are affected by our independence.

In my own case, I am beset by doubts. Am I making it too easy for my husband to do what he wants to do? Certainly if I were not a wage-earning wife he would be unable to leave his position and gamble with his future. Will he be happy in the day-after-day grind at a desk? Will he be too much discouraged when his manuscripts come back from editors? Can he stand the gaff and be happy?

It takes a brave man and a man not bound by conventions to accept such an arrangement as ours. My husband is both. He is free for the first time in his thirty-five years—free to follow the path of ambition, inclination, and ability. I glory in being one of the factors of that new freedom, but still I wonder where that path will lead.

DOCUMENT 6

Letters from the Great Migration (1917)

Between 1916 and 1920 some 500,000 black southerners migrated north, and nearly a million followed in the 1920s. During World War I, as European immigration slowed and the war emergency intensified, labor agents traveled South offering African Americans jobs, high wages, and free transportation North. Blacks also took their own initiative in seeking new opportunities. They responded to employment advertisements in the Chicago *Defender*, one of the most widely circulated black newspapers in America. They also established migration networks, corresponding and transmitting information to family and friends. The first two letters reveal the energy and determination of southern blacks to improve their lives. In the third letter, a migrant describes to a friend back home the differences between life in the North and in the South.

Houston, Texas, 4–29–17.

Dear Sir: I am a constant reader of the "Chicago Defender" and in your last issue I saw a want ad that appealed to me. I am a Negro, age 37, and am an all round foundry man. I am a cone maker by trade having had about 10 years experience at the business, and hold good references from several shops, in which I have been employed. I have worked at various shops and I have always been able to make good. It is hard for a black man to hold a job here, as prejudice is very strong. I have never been discharged on account of dissatisfaction with my work, but I have been "let out" on account of my color. I am a good brassmelter but i prefer core making as it is my trade. I have a family and am anxious to leave here, but have not the means, and as wages are not much here, it is very hard to save enough to get away with. If you know of any firms that are in need of a core maker and whom you think would send me transportation, I would be pleased to be put in touch with them and I assure you that effort would be appreciated. I am a core maker but I am willing to do any honest work. All I want is to get away from here. I am writing you and I believe you can and will help me. If any one will send transportation, I will arrange or agree to have it taken out of my salary untill full amount of fare is paid. I also know of several good fdry. men here who would leave in a minute, if there only was a way arranged for them to leave, and they are men whom I know personally to be experienced men. I hope that you will give this your immediate attention as I am anxious to get busy and be on my way. I am ready to start at any time, and would be pleased to hear something favorable.

New Orleans, La., June 10, 1917.

Kind Sir: I read and hear daly of the great chance that a colored parson has in Chicago of making a living with all the priveleg that the whites have and it mak me the most ankious to want to go where I may be able to make a liveing for my self. When you read this you will think it bery strange that being only my self to support that it is so hard, but it is so. everything is gone up but the poor colerd peple wages. I have made sevle afford to leave and come to Chicago where I hear that times is good for us but owing to femail wekness has made it a perfect failure. I am a widow for 9 years. I have very pore learning altho it would not make much diffrent if I would be throughly edacated for I could not get any better work to do, such as house work, washing and ironing and all such work that are injering to a woman with femail wekness and they pay so little for so hard work that it is just enough to pay room rent and a little some thing to eat. I have found a very good remady that I really feeling to belive would cure me if I only could make enough money to keep up my madison and I dont think that I will ever be able to do that down hear for the time is getting worse evry day. I am going to ask if you peple hear could aid me in geting over her in Chicago and seeking out a position of some kind. I can also do plain sewing. Please good peple dont refuse to help me out in my trouble for I am in gret need of help God will bless you. I am going to do my very best after I get over here if God spair me to get work I will pay the expance back. Do try to do the best you can for me, with many thanks for so doing I will remain as ever,

Yours truly.

Philadelphia, Pa., Oct. 7, 1917.

Dear Sir: I take this method of thanking you for yours early responding and the glorious effect of the treatment. Oh. I do feel so fine. Dr. the treatment reach me almost ready to move   I am now housekeeping again I like it so much better than rooming. Well Dr. with the aid of God I am making very good I make $75 per month. I am carrying enough insurance to pay me $20 per week if I am not able to be on duty. I don't have to work hard. dont have to mister every little white boy comes along   I havent heard a white man call a colored a nigger you no now—since I been in the state of Pa. I can ride in the electric street and steam cars any where I get a seat. I dont care to mix with white what I mean I am not crazy about being with white folks, but if I have to pay the same fare I have learn to want the same acomidation. and if you are first in a place here shoping you dont have to wait until the white folks get thro tradeing yet amid all this I shall ever love the good old South and I am praying that God may give every well wisher a chance to be a man regardless of his color, and if my going to the front would bring about such conditions I am ready any day—well Dr. I dont want to worry you but read between lines; and maybe you can see a little sense in my weak statement the kids are in school every day I have only two and I guess that all. Dr. when you find time I would be delighted to have a word from the good old home state. Wife join me in sending love you and yours.

I am your friend and patient.

DOCUMENT 7

Langston Hughes, "The Negro Artist and the Racial Mountain" (1926)

During the 1920s New York City's African American population more than doubled, rising from 150,000 to more than 325,000, with the majority living in Harlem. These southern migrants provided the social base for the Harlem Renaissance, a blossoming of black social thought and literary expression. Writers such as Claude McKay, Zora Neal Hurston, and Alain Locke challenged the status quo in race relations. Jazz artists like Louis Armstrong, Duke Ellington, and Bessie Smith developed their own musical styles and earned the acclaim of white critics. Harlem, headquarters of the National Association for the Advancement of Colored People (NAACP) as well as Marcus Garvey's Universal Negro Improvement Association, was also the scene of inventiveness in black political organization. In the following article, black author Langston Hughes discusses the obstacles confronting aspiring black artists. Like Sinclair Lewis and other writers of the era, Hughes detested the tendency toward conformity in American society.

One of the most promising of the young Negro poets said to me once, "I want to be a poet—not a Negro poet," meaning, "I want to write like a white poet"; meaning subconsciously, "I would like to be a white poet"; meaning behind that, "I would like to be white." And I was sorry the young man said that, for no great poet has ever been afraid of being himself. And I doubted then that, with his desire to run away spiritually from his race, this boy would ever be a great poet. But this is the mountain standing in the way of true Negro art in America—this urge within the race toward whiteness, the desire to pour racial individuality into the mold of American standardization, and to be as little Negro and as much American as possible.

But let us look at the immediate background of this young poet. His family is of what I suppose one would call the Negro middle class: people who are by no means rich yet never very uncomfortable nor hungry—smug, contented, respectable folk, members of the Baptist church. The father goes to work every morning. He is a chief steward at a large white club. The mother sometimes does fancy sewing or supervises parties for the rich families of the town. The children go to a mixed school. In the home they read white papers and magazines. And the mother often says, "Don't be like niggers" when the children are bad. A frequent phrase from the father is, "Look how well a white man does things." And so the word white comes to be unconsciously a symbol of all virtues. It holds for the children beauty, morality, money. The whisper of "I want to be white" runs silently through their minds. This young poet's home is, I believe, fairly typical of the colored middle class. One sees immediately how difficult it would be for an artist born in such a home to interest himself in interpreting the beauty of his own people. He is never taught to see that beauty. He is taught rather not to see it, or if he does, to be ashamed of it when it is not according to Caucasian patterns.

For the racial culture the home of a self-styled "high-class" Negro has nothing better to offer. Instead there will perhaps be more aping of things white than in a less cultured or less wealthy home. The father is perhaps a doctor, a lawyer, landowner, or politician. The mother may be a social worker, or a teacher, or she may do nothing and have a maid. Father is often dark, but he has married the lightest woman he could find. The family attend a fashionable church where few really colored faces are to be found. And they themselves draw the color line. In the North they go to white theatres and white movies. And in the South they have at least two cars and a house, "just like white folks." Nordic manners, Nordic faces, Nordic hair, Nordic art (if any), and an Episcopal heaven. A very high mountain indeed for the would-be racial artist to climb in order to discover himself and his people....

Certainly there is, for the American Negro artist who can escape the restrictions the more advanced among his own group would put upon him, a great field of unused material for his art. Without going outside his race, and even among the better classes with their "white" culture and conscious American manners, but still Negro enough to be different, there is sufficient matter to furnish a black artist with a lifetime of creative work. And when he chooses to touch on the relations between Negroes and whites in this country with their innumerable overtones and undertones, surely, and especially for literature and the drama, there is an inexhaustible supply of themes at hand. To these the Negro artist can give his racial individuality, his heritage . . . and his incongruous humor that so often, as in the Blues, becomes ironic laughter mixed with tears. . . .

Most of my own poems are racial in theme and treatment, derived from the life I know. In many of them, I try to grasp and hold some of the meanings and rhythms of jazz. I am sincere as I know how to be in these poems, and yet after every reading I answer questions like these from my own people: Do you think Negroes should always write about Negroes? I wish you wouldn't read some of your poems to white folks. How do you find anything interesting in a place like a cabaret? Why do you write about black people? You aren't black. What makes you do so many jazz poems?

But jazz to me is one of the inherent expressions of Negro life in America: the eternal tom-tom beating in the Negro soul—the tom-tom of revolt against weariness in a white world, a world of subway trains, and work, work, work; the tom-tom of joy and laughter, and pain swallowed in a smile. Yet the Philadelphia clubwoman is ashamed to say that her race created it and she does not like me to write about it. The old subconscious "white is best" runs through her mind. Years of study under white teachers, a lifetime of white books, pictures and papers, and white manners, morals, and Puritan standards made her dislike the spirituals. And now she turns up her nose at jazz and all its manifestations—likewise anything else distinctly racial. She doesn't care for the Winold Reiss portraits of Negroes because they are "too Negro." She does not want a true picture of herself from anybody. She wants the artist to flatter her, to make the white world believe that all Negroes are as smug and near-white in soul as she wants to be. But, to my mind, it is the duty of the younger Negro artist, if he accepts any duties at all from outsiders, to change through the force of his art that old whispering "I want to be white," hidden in the aspirations of his people, to "Why should I want to be white? I am a Negro—and beautiful!"

DOCUMENT 8

Mary Heaton Vorse, "Gastonia" (1929)

In 1929 a wave of spontaneous strikes swept the southern textile industry. Millhands from Tennessee to Georgia, driven by desperation, revolted. Strikers protested the accelerating trend toward efficiency in the textile mills. Throughout the 1920s, mill owners introduced labor-saving machinery, initiated methods of scientific management designed to standardize and routinize the labor process, and switched to a multiple-loom system, which put thousands of weavers out of work. Workers called the new system the "stretch-out," which forced them to produce more at reduced wages. In the following article, journalist and labor activist Mary Heaton Vorse describes what she witnessed on her strike-sightseeing tour of Gastonia, North Carolina. The incidents she recounts contrasts with the mill owners' own image of their work force as docile and content.

LOST - 9 Men
But They'll Never Be Missed!

Thanks to Alemite and [...]co-Lowell, 4 Men Replace the 13 Who Were Formerly Needed to Keep the Pickers Humming

This 1927 advertisement portrays the growing pressure for businesses to become more efficient and to produce more with fewer people. The ad also suggests the growing problem of factory and worker relations.

There are many mill owners throughout the South whose paternalism is infused with an ardent desire to do all that they can for the workers. There are few mills within corporate limits to-day which have not some form of welfare work. There are often women nurses and welfare workers attached to the factory. Some mills have ball fields, recreation grounds, community houses. Frequently day nurseries and rooms are provided where women may nurse their babies, the time they are absent being taken, of course, from their pay. The workers buy their food at the company store. They buy their coal, oil, and wood from the company. If they are ill a company doctor attends them. All this, of course, will be deducted from their pay.

Conscientious mill owners frankly consider their "hands" as children, incapable of taking care of themselves. But whether their conditions are good or bad does not depend upon the workers' joint effort to control hours, wages, and factory conditions. All depends upon the policy of the owners.

Company houses covered with roses still remain company houses. The workers cannot own them. Community activities do not raise the wage scale, which is so low that almost without exception children of fourteen go to the mill as a matter of course. Mothers of young children must work at night.

I heard of these things in terms of human lives. The strikers wanted to talk about themselves. Every day yielded stories like that of Mary Morris, who passed all the young years of her marriage in want because "when I was goin' to have a baby and got so I couldn't work, they'd fire my husband. Lots of mills won't have you unless there's two hands in the family working." Or of Daisy McDonald, who told me she has to support a husband and family of seven children on $12.90 a week.

"My husband lost his leg and has a tubercular bone. What do you think's left to feed my people on when I pay my weekly expenses? My home rent is $1.50, light 50 cents to 85 cents, furniture $1.00, insurance $1.25. What do you think was left the week I paid $2.20 for wood?"

"I used to work in the Myers Mill in South Gastonia, and they wouldn't take my husband unless I worked too, and I had a little baby."

James Ballentyne added another detail. It was a story of police brutality which recurred often in different forms. "I was leading the picket line and I was trying to get through a mob of deputies. They said, 'What do you think you're doing?' I said 'Leading a picket line if I can get through,' and I walked through. They jumped on me and hit me with clubs over the head and in the belly so I was spitting blood and hemorrhaging all night. It was two weeks ago, and I ain't well yet. I was all mashed up inside."

When I had seen some of the sights of Gastonia I went strike-sightseeing with a minister from Greensboro. We were going about strike headquarters getting the addresses of some of the people who had been chased with bayonets by the police, in order to verify to our satisfaction some of the well-nigh incredible stories poured into our ears by strikers and organizers, when Amy Schechter, the relief director, came up saying, "They're evicting people over in the ravine!" We drove to the place, a striker guiding us.

A woman I had noticed at headquarters, a Mrs. Winebarger, was standing in front of a lamentable little heap of household furnishings. Pots, pans, bedding, bureaus were piled helter-skelter. What had been a home of a sort had in a moment become rubbish.

Three yellow-haired children sat solemnly on the heaped-up wreckage. The baby was asleep at a neighbor's. It waked up presently, and the little girl lugged it around. We went into the house, which like most houses in the neighborhood was built without a cellar and stood on little brick pillars. The lumber was of the cheapest. There were knot-holes in the floor through which the wind poured. (This was not a company house but was owned by a private landlord.)

Mrs. Winebarger told us, "It rained in like a sieve. When it rained we had to keep moving our beds around to keep them dry." She had never had the electric lights turned on. "Where'd I get my five dollars for the deposit?" she asked angrily, for she was angry at her house, at the circumstances of her life, and she wanted to go back to the mountains whence she had come. "But it would cost an awful lot to get us back—fifteen dollars." Her husband had pellagra, and she was supporting him and her four children on what she made. She had a venomous feeling toward the house which had finally spewed her forth.

"Look at that chimney! It always smoked! We couldn't have no fire here! We couldn't keep warm. Once, I was buyin' a coal stove for my kitchen and I had $19 paid on it. Then I had to buy medicine for him and I couldn't make my payments and they tuk my stove away."

The furniture of the mill workers is almost inevitably bought on the installment plan. Mrs. Winebarger made $12.50 a week. She paid $1.50 a week for house rent, between fifty cents and a dollar for fuel and light, and more than a dollar a week for medicine. The house was a bungalow of four rooms. It had a fairly wide hall and small shallow fireplaces. Except for its flimsiness it was much better than the tenements of Passaic, New Jersey, or the overcrowded houses of Lawrence, Massachusetts, with their four courtyards.

We went next to the house of Mrs. Ada Howell, an old woman who had been beaten up on Monday, April 22, after the withdrawal of the militia.

Mrs. Howell sat in a rocking chair, her two eyes blackened, her face discolored. It gave one a sense of embarrassment and impotent anger to look at her. She told her story in a detached way. She was curiously without passion as she described something as unbelievable as a nightmare. She had been going to the store for supper on Monday, April 22nd. Policemen came down the street "chasing the strikers before them like rats." A policeman rushed at her with a bayonet.

"He cut my dress and he cut me too. Lawyer Jimison told me I should keep that dress without washing it so I could show it, but I didn't have enough dresses to lay those clothes away." Her idea was that the policeman had gone crazy.

"They acted like crazy men. They was drunk crazed," her son said.

"They had been a-drinkin'," she admitted, "an' they must 'a been a-drinkin' to chase women and little kids with baynits. They chased 'em in and out the relief store like dogs huntin' rats.

"An' they hadn't no call to go in that relief store—the laws hadn't. You can't go in any place if you ain't any warrent.

"An' then the policeman came up an' hit me between the eyes with his fist. He hit me more'n twenty times, I reckon. I was all swelled up an' black an' blue."

I had seen photographs of her mutilated face. We didn't say anything. There didn't seem to be anything to say. I suppose when comfortable people read such stories they think, "This can't be true. Why, that just couldn't happen in our town. Such things *don't* happen." No wonder they feel this way.

We went on. Strike-sightseeing is a rather awful thing. There is obscenity in the fact that old women can be beaten for no reason when they are peacefully proceeding on their business; there is equal obscenity in the fact that a mother with four children to support has to work all night for $12.50 a week, and then be evicted because she cannot pay her rent. It does not seem reasonable that such things should happen here in this country, in 1929.

Study Questions

1. Why did national leaders like Harding and Coolidge place so much faith in big business?

2. Do you think Edward Purinton's assertion that business owners differ little from manual workers is fair? What might have motivated his claim?

3. What does Sinclair Lewis find abhorrent about American businessmen? How might working people have responded to the campaign rhetoric of George Babbitt?

4. To what extent did the New Era create new possibilities for women? How might the women of Gastonia have reacted to the meditations of Jane Littell?

5. What inspiration do you think Langston Hughes would have found in the letters of African Americans participating in the Great Migration?

8

The Great Depression and the Rise of the Welfare State

In 1929 Republican Herbert Hoover assumed the presidency, having defeated Democrat Alfred E. Smith in a landslide. Hoover insisted that New Era prosperity would continue unabated. "The questions before our country are problems of progress to higher standards," he proclaimed in his inaugural address, praising the United States as a nation "filled with millions of happy homes" and "blessed with comfort and opportunity." But by year's end, a concatenation of factors—overproduction, underconsumption, deflation in farm prices, reckless speculation, underinvestment—precipitated a severe economic crisis. Hoover, who had expected to govern a nation of plenty, faced the challenge of managing the Great Depression.

To guide the nation back to recovery, Hoover relied on policies combining tenets of managerial liberalism with faith in self-reliance and voluntarism. Far from being the idle president of popular memory, Hoover actually initiated state intervention in the economy through such agencies as the Federal Farm Board, which purchased surplus crops, and the Reconstruction Finance Corporation, which lent federal money to insolvent financial institutions. Hoover tempered such measures, however, with an insistence on self-reliance. Thus, instead of providing assistance to homeless families, the Home Loan Bank Board lent money to building and mortgage companies. Instead or providing direct relief to the poor, Hoover relied on private charities and local governments. Such measures proved woefully inadequate, as the ranks of the unemployed swelled to more than 12 million by 1932. Hoover tried to boost Americans' confidence with bold forecasts of an impending recovery and with assurances that the situation was not so bad as it seemed. Such rhetoric only angered Americans and fueled their frustration with the Republican administration, especially when it contradicted reports of the poor and unemployed (Document 1).

The federal government's role in administering the economy became the central issue of the 1932 presidential election. Democratic nominee Franklin Delano Roosevelt pledged "a new deal for the American people." He spoke of the government's responsibility to ensure economic justice, regulate the economy when necessary, and protect Americans from the excesses of the corporate oligarchy (Document

2). Hoover warned that Roosevelt's "new deal" amounted to nothing more than an extension of the federal bureaucracy that would threaten economic and political freedom (Document 3). With the crisis deepening and popular discontent mounting, Americans repudiated the Republicans, electing Roosevelt easily.

In his first hundred days in office, Roosevelt initiated fifteen pieces of legislation, aimed principally at recovery and relief. The National Recovery Administration attempted to revive industry by establishing codes of fair competition, firm guidelines on prices, and standards of minimum wages as well as guaranteeing workers the right to collective bargaining through unions. In a stark break from the preceding administration, New Dealers launched a massive program of federal spending on direct relief and on public works projects designed to provide temporary jobs for the unemployed. Although these measures looked decisive, even revolutionary (Document 4), many of the programs became mired in red tape and thus failed to reach those most in need of their services (Document 5).

As the Depression and unemployment continued, Americans began to press for more radical changes. In 1934 Upton Sinclair nearly won the California gubernatorial campaign on the slogan "End Poverty in California" (EPIC). Wisconsin voters sent progressive Robert LaFollette, Jr., to the Senate, and other midwesterners elected members of the Minnesota Farmer-Labor Party to office. Senator Huey Long of Louisiana advocated one of the most sweeping plans for redistribution of wealth. His Share Our Wealth campaign, which promised to confiscate all private fortunes in excess of $5 million and distribute $5,000 to every American household, attracted millions of followers until a political foe assassinated Long in 1935 (Document 6).

Others turned to organized labor. Under protection of the National Labor Relations Act of 1935, which outlawed a host of unfair labor practices, millions of industrial workers joined unions. Through the American Federation of Labor (AFL) and the Congress of Industrial Organizations (CIO), workers succeeded in improving wages and work conditions (Document 7). By 1940 nearly a third of the American labor force belonged to a union.

Perhaps most of all, the New Deal changed how Americans related to the federal government. Roosevelt's weekly radio addresses, or fireside chats, created an aura of familiarity and confidence between the people and the president that inspired millions to confide in their leader. Through an average of 5,000 to 8,000 letters per day, ordinary Americans communicated their fears and worries, explained their situations, and advised the president on what they thought the government ought to do (Document 8).

DOCUMENT 1

Fortune, *Editorial on Economic Conditions (1932)*

To counter charges that he had mishandled the economic crisis, President Herbert Hoover repeatedly assured the nation that prosperity would soon return and that the situation was not so critical as it appeared. He even boasted that "no one has starved." Outraged by his callous comments, the editors of *Fortune* magazine, mouthpiece of the conservative corporate establishment, mocked the president, presenting uncontrovertible evidence that men and women across the country were indeed starving, many of them reduced to digging for scraps in garbage heaps. The article, which appeared two months before the presidential election of 1932, likely persuaded many conservative readers to abandon the Republican Party and support Franklin D. Roosevelt.

              ❦ ❧

It should be remarked at this point that nothing the federal government has yet done or is likely to do in the near future constitutes a policy of *constructive* action. Unemployment basically is not a social disease but an industrial phenomenon. The natural and inevitable consequence of a machine civilization is a lessened demand for human labor. (An almost total elimination of human labor in plowing, for example, is now foreseeable.) And the natural and inevitable consequence of a lessened demand for human labor is an increase of idleness. Indeed the prophets of the machine age have always promised an increase of idleness, under the name of leisure, as one of the goals of industry. A constructive solution of unemployment therefore means an industrial solution—a restatement of industrialism which will treat technological displacement not as an illness to be cured but as a goal to be achieved—and achieved with the widest dispensation of benefits and the least incidental misery.

But the present relief problem as focused by the federal Act is not a problem of ultimate solutions but of immediate palliatives. One does not talk architecture while the house is on fire and the tenants are still inside. The question at this moment is the pure question of fact. Having decided at last to face reality and do something about it, what is reality? How many men are unemployed in the U.S.? How many are in want? *What are the facts?*

Twenty-five millions

The following minimal statements may be accepted as true—with the certainty that they underestimate the real situation:

(1) Unemployment has steadily increased in the U.S. since the beginning of the depression and the rate of increase during the first part of 1932 was more rapid than in any other depression year.

(2) The number of persons totally unemployed is now at least 10,000,000.

(3) The number of persons totally unemployed next winter will, at the present rate of increase, be 11,000,000.

(4) Eleven millions unemployed means better than one man out of every four employable workers.

(5) This percentage is higher than the percentage of unemployed British workers registered under the compulsory insurance laws (17.1 per cent in May, 1932, as against 17.3 per cent in April and

18.4 per cent in January) and higher than the French, the Italian, and the Canadian percentages, but lower than the German (43.9 per cent of trade unionists in April, 1932) and the Norwegian.

(6) Eleven millions unemployed means 27,500,000 whose regular source of livelihood has been cut off.

(7) Twenty-seven and a half millions without regular income includes the families of totally unemployed workers alone. Taking account of the numbers of workers on part time, the total of those without adequate income becomes 34,000,000 or better than a quarter of the entire population of the country.

(8) Thirty-four million persons without adequate income does not mean 34,000,000 in present want. Many families have savings. But savings are eventually dissipated and the number in actual want tends to approximate the number without adequate income. How nearly it approximates it now or will next winter no man can say. But it is conservative to estimate that the problem of next winter's relief is a problem of caring for approximately 25,000,000 souls. . . .

But it is impossible to think or to act in units of 25,000,000 human beings. Like the casualty lists of the British War Office during the Battle of the Somme, they mean nothing. They are at once too large and too small. A handful of men and women and children digging for their rotten food in the St. Louis dumps are more numerous, humanly speaking, than all the millions that ever found themselves in an actuary's column. The 25,000,000 only become human in their cities and their mill towns and their mining villages. And their situation only becomes comprehensible in terms of the relief they have already received.

That is to say that the general situation can only be judged by the situation in the particular localities. But certain generalizations are possible. Of which the chief is the broad conclusion that few if any of the industrial areas have been able to maintain a minimum decency level of life for their unemployed. Budgetary standards as set up by welfare organizations, public and private, after years of experiment have been discarded. Food only, in most cases, is provided and little enough of that. Rents are seldom paid. Shoes and clothing are given in rare instances only. Money for doctors and dentists is not to be had. And free clinics are filled to overflowing. Weekly allowances per family have fallen as low as $2.39 in New York with $3 and $4 the rule in most cities and $5 a high figure. And even on these terms funds budgeted for a twelve-month period have been exhausted in three or four. While city after city has been compelled to abandon a part of its dependent population. "We are merely trying to prevent hunger and exposure," reported a St. Paul welfare head last May. And the same sentence would be echoed by workers in other cities with such additions as were reported at the same time from Pittsburgh where a cut of 50 per cent was regarded as "inevitable," from Dallas where Mexicans and Negroes were not given relief, from Alabama where discontinuance of relief in mining and agricultural sections was foreseen, from New Orleans where no new applicants were being received and 2,500 families in need of relief were receiving none, from Omaha where two-thirds of the cases receiving relief were to be discontinued, from Colorado where the counties had suspended relief for lack of funds . . . from Scranton . . . from Cleveland . . . from Syracuse . . .

DOCUMENT 2

Franklin Delano Roosevelt, Speech at San Francisco (1932)

In his famous campaign address before the Commonwealth Club in San Francisco, Democratic presidential nominee Franklin Delano Roosevelt insisted that additional capitalist expansion would not solve the nation's economic crisis. He declared that America had to address the business "of meeting the problem of underconsumption, of adjusting production to consumption, of distributing wealth and products more equitably, of adapting existing economic organizations to the service of the people." To meet these tasks, Roosevelt envisioned an active role for the federal government and hinted that he would support the creation of a welfare state.

As I see it, the task of Government in its relation to business is to assist the development of an economic declaration of rights, an economic constitutional order. This is the common task of statesman and business man. It is the minimum requirement of a more permanently safe order of things....

The Declaration of Independence discusses the problem of Government in terms of a contract. Government is a relation of give and take, a contract, perforce, if we would follow the thinking out of which it grew. Under such a contract rulers were accorded power, and the people consented to that power on consideration that they be accorded certain rights. The task of statesmanship has always been the re-definition of these rights in terms of a changing and growing social order. New conditions impose new requirements upon Government and those who conduct Government....

I feel that we are coming to a view through the drift of our legislation and our public thinking in the past quarter century that private economic power is, to enlarge an old phrase, a public trust as well. I hold that continued enjoyment of that power by any individual or group must depend upon the fulfillment of that trust. The men who have reached the summit of American business life know this best; happily, many of these urge the binding quality of this greater social contract.

The terms of that contract are as old as the Republic, and as new as the new economic order.

Every man has a right to life; and this means that he has also a right to make a comfortable living. He may by sloth or crime decline to exercise that right; but it may not be denied him. We have no actual famine or dearth; our industrial and agricultural mechanism can produce enough and to spare. Our Government formal and informal, political and economic, owes to everyone an avenue to possess himself of a portion of that plenty sufficient for his needs, through his own work.

Every man has a right to his own property; which means a right to be assured, to the fullest extent attainable, in the safety of his savings. By no other means can men carry the burdens of those parts of life which, in the nature of things, afford no chance of labor; childhood, sickness, old age. In all thought of property, this right is paramount; all other property rights must yield to it. If, in accord with this principle, we must restrict the operations of the speculator, the manipulator, even the financier, I believe we must accept the restriction as needful, not to hamper individualism but to protect it.

These two requirements must be satisfied, in the main, by the individuals who claim and hold con-

Franklin Delano Roosevelt promised America a "New Deal," which was meant to alleviate the problems of the Depression. While partially successful in its ambitious goals, the New Deal fell under great criticism. In the end, it was World War II, not the New Deal, that brought America out of economic Depression.

trol of the great industrial and financial combinations which dominate so large a part of our industrial life. They have undertaken to be, not business men, but princes of property. I am not prepared to say that the system which produces them is wrong. I am very clear that they must fearlessly and competently assume the responsibility which goes with the power. So many enlightened business men know this that the statement would be little more than a platitude, were it not for an added implication.

This implication is, briefly, that the responsible heads of finance and industry instead of acting each for himself, must work together to achieve the common end. They must, where necessary, sacrifice this or that private advantage; and in reciprocal self-denial must seek a general advantage. It is here that formal Government—political Government, if you chose—comes in. Whenever in the pursuit of this objective the lone wolf, the unethical competitor, the reckless promoter, the Ishmael or Insull whose hand is against every man's, declines to join in achieving an end recognized as being for the public welfare, and threatens to drag the industry back to a state of anarchy, the Government may properly be asked to apply restraint. Likewise, should the group ever use its collective power contrary to the public welfare, the Government must be swift to enter and protect the public interest.

The Government should assume the function of economic regulation only as a last resort, to be tried only when private initiative, inspired by high responsibility, with such assistance and balance as Government can give, has finally failed. As yet there has been no final failure, because there has been no attempt; and I decline to assume that this Nation is unable to meet the situation.

The final term of the high contract was for liberty and the pursuit of happiness. We have learned a great deal of both in the past century. We know that individual liberty and individual happiness mean nothing unless both are ordered in the sense that one man's meat is not another man's poison. We know that the old "rights of personal competency," the right to read, to think, to speak, to choose and live a mode of life, must be respected at all hazards. We know that liberty to do anything which deprives others of those elemental rights is outside the protection of any compact; and that Government in this regard is the maintenance of a balance, within which every individual may have a place if he will take it; in which every individual may find safety if he wishes it; in which every individual may attain such power as his ability permits, consistent with his assuming the accompanying responsibility.

All this is a long, slow talk. Nothing is more striking than the simple innocence of the men who insist, whenever an objective is present, on the prompt production of a patent scheme guaranteed to produce a result. Human endeavor is not so simple as that. Government includes the art of formulating a policy, and using the political technique to attain so much of that policy as will receive general support; persuading, leading, sacrificing, teaching always, because the greatest duty of a statesman is to educate. But in the matters of which I have spoken, we are learning rapidly, in a severe school. The lessons so learned must not be forgotten, even in the mental lethargy of a speculative upturn. We must build toward the time when a major depression cannot occur again; and if this means sacrificing the easy profits of inflationist booms, then let them go; and good riddance.

DOCUMENT 3

Herbert Hoover, Speech at New York City (1932)

Throughout the campaign Herbert Hoover continually rebuked charges that he was responsible for prolonging what many now called the "Hoover Depression" and that he had not dedicated himself to relieving the suffering and misery of the American people. In the following speech, delivered at Madison Square Garden in New York just days before the election, Hoover attacked Roosevelt's "new deal," warning that an expansion of government could not promote economic recovery and that it would only undermine American liberties.

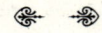

I may say at once that the changes proposed from all these Democratic principals and allies are of the most profound and penetrating character. If they are brought about this will not be the America which we have known in the past.

Let us pause for a moment and examine the American system of government, of social and economic life, which it is now proposed that we should alter. Our system is the product of our race and of our experience in building a nation to heights unparalleled in the whole history of the world. It is a system peculiar to the American people. It differs essentially from all others in the world. It is an American system.

It is founded on the conception that only through ordered liberty, through freedom to the individual, and equal opportunity to the individual will his initiative and enterprise be summoned to spur the march of national progress.

It is by the maintenance of equality of opportunity and therefore of a society absolutely fluid in the movement of its human particles that our individualism departs from the individualism of Europe. We resent class distinction because there can be no rise for the individual through the frozen strata of classes, and no stratification of classes can take place in a mass livened by the free rise of its particles. Thus in our ideals the able and ambitious are able to rise constantly from the bottom to leadership in the community. And we denounce any intent to stir class feeling and class antagonisms in the United States.

This freedom of the individual creates of itself the necessity and the cheerful willingness of men to act cooperatively in a thousand ways and for every purpose as the occasion requires; and it permits such voluntary cooperations to be dissolved as soon as they have served their purpose, and to be replaced by new voluntary associations for new purposes.

There has thus grown within us, to gigantic im-

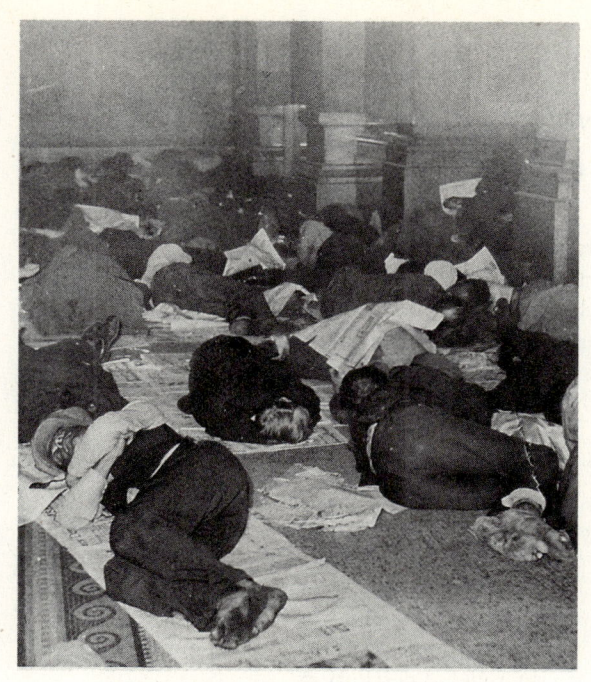

Hoover maintained that government intervention was not necessary to help the United States' collapsing economy and that "prosperity was right around the corner." In the period from 1929 to 1933 more than 15 million people were unemployed, industrial stocks lost 80 percent of their values, almost 11,000 banks failed, farm prices fell by 53 percent, and almost $2 billion in bank deposits evaporated.

portance, a new conception. And that is, this voluntary cooperation within the community. Cooperation to perfect the social organization; cooperation for the care of those in distress; cooperation for the advancement of knowledge, of scientific research, of education; cooperative action in a thousand directions for the advancement of economic life. This is self-government by the people outside of government; it is the most powerful development of individual freedom and equal opportunity that has taken place in the century and a half since our fundamental institutions were founded. . . .

We have heard a great deal in this campaign about reactionaries, conservatives, progressives, liberals and radicals. I think I belong to every group. I have not yet heard an attempt by any one of the orators who mouth these phrases to define the principles upon which they base these classifications. There is one thing I can say without any question of doubt—that is, that the spirit of liberalism is to create free men; it is not the regimentation of men under government. It is not the extension of bureaucracy. I have said in this city before now that you cannot extend the mastery of government over the daily life of a people without somewhere making it master of people's souls and thoughts. Expansion of government in business means that the government in order to protect itself from the political consequences of its errors or even its successes is driven irresistibly without peace to greater and greater control of the nation's press and platform. Free speech does not live many hours after free industry and free commerce die. It is a false liberalism that interprets itself into government operation of business. Every step in that direction poisons the very roots of liberalism. It poisons political equality, free speech, free press and equality of opportunity. It is the road not to liberty, but to less liberty. True liberalism is found not in striving to spread bureaucracy, but in striving to set bounds to it. It is found in an endeavor to extend cooperation between free men. True liberalism seeks all legitimate freedom first in the confident belief that without such freedom the pursuit of other blessings is in vain. Liberalism is a force truly of the spirit proceeding from the deep realization that economic freedom cannot be sacrificed if political freedom is to be preserved.

Even if the government conduct of business could give us the maximum of efficiency instead of least efficiency, it would be purchased at the cost of freedom. It would increase rather than decrease abuse and corruption, stifle initiative and invention, undermine development of leadership, cripple mental and spiritual energies of our people, extinguish equality of opportunity, and dry up the spirit of liberty and progress. Men who are going about this country announcing that they are liberals because of their promises to extend the government in business are not liberals; they are reactionaries of the United States.

DOCUMENT 4

J. Frederick Essary, "The New Deal for Nearly Four Months" (1933)

At the outset of his administration, President Franklin Roosevelt enjoyed the overwhelming support of the Washington press corps. Many journalists praised the president's decisive action and marveled at his ability to convince Congress to pass his legislative agenda. In the following essay, J. Frederick Essary, Washington correspondent for the *Baltimore Sun*, reflects on the New Deal's first few months.

❧ ❧

This is Chapter 1—in epitome—of the Roosevelt régime. And what a chapter! What a régime!

Fifteen weeks have elapsed since the New Dealers began dealing. Fifteen weeks of high-pressure activity. Fifteen weeks of whirlwind changes in the old order, of experimental panaceas, of legislative novelties and of practically unchallenged Executive domination of the colossal organism which we call the Federal Government.

More history has been made during these fifteen weeks than in any comparable peacetime period since Americans went into business for themselves on this continent. The legislation that has now been written into law, under the Roosevelt leadership, touches practically every interest in our national life. It touches some of them lightly and by indirection only. It touches others heavily and will leave a mark on them not to be erased for a generation, if at all.

Powers have been reposed in the Presidency that have made that office a virtual dictatorship. It may be looked upon both as a benevolent and a necessary dictatorship. Undoubtedly it is so looked upon in most quarters. It may not be irrevocable. But soften the phrasing as much as one may, the fact remains that the present governmental set-up amounts to temporary Executive absolutism.

These new Presidential powers, let it be recalled, extend not only to the fiscal functions of the Government—to budgetary economy, to control of gold, control of banking and to possible inflation. They extend as well to agriculture, to every branch of industry, to public works, to the railroads, to mortgaged homes and farms, to unemployment and to the relief of destitution.

Rather a large order, that!

Such sweeping powers for the most part were granted, only because of the acuteness of the crisis which came to a head on the very day Mr. Roosevelt took office. That day found the country in the throes of a bank depositors' panic. This panic eventually forced every banking house in the country to close the sound and the unsound alike. It forced the commodity and securities exchanges to suspend. It caused the industrial structure of the nation to totter, and it brought on partial paralysis of the normal energies of the whole American people.

Nobody now living had ever witnessed anything like that. And instinctively we, the American people, turned to Washington for salvation. We turned there for the very good reason there was nowhere else to turn. We turned, moreover, to an untried man, just as did the people when they turned to Abraham Lincoln in 1861. We turned to an Executive who had just taken the oath, to one who had only lately concluded a campaign more marked by its amiability than by thunder and lightning, and to a man, incidentally, in whose soul the amount of iron was still an unknown quantity.

We did not have to wait long for action, however. That much is easy to remember. Untroubled by any need for additional legislation, the new President at once assumed what amounted to war powers. And assuming them, he moved with swiftness and decision to meet the emergency. On the night of March 5, twenty-four hours after his inauguration, he issued two proclamations. One of them declared a bank holiday for the nation and placed an embargo upon the withdrawal and export of gold. The other summoned Congress to meet in four days.

That was action, and action with a vengeance!

These proclamations, with their martial ring, served as a curtain-raiser for a series of dramatic steps by the Federal Government, steps that followed each other with bewildering rapidity until fourteen weeks later when Congress ended its extraordinary session (extraordinary in more senses than one), and the President packed his bags for a holiday at sea. . . .

It is far too soon to put Mr. Roosevelt down as a superman, a great statesman or a man of destiny. He still has a long way to go before achieving that eminence. But it is not too much to say that he has exhibited political sagacity and administrative efficiency to an astonishing degree. The results he has to his credit—and they are breath-taking when we try to comprehend them—can not all be charged to the "super situation." There was the "hour" to be sure, but also there was the "man."

First to last in a session of Congress, the like of which none of us has ever seen, Mr. Roosevelt put through his program without one open break with the legislative branch. Such a break seemed imminent toward the end, upon the veterans compensation issue, after other issues a thousand times more important, moreover, had been disposed of. But a little compromise added to a great deal of firmness on the President's part, closed the breach and dissolved the rebellion.

The Roosevelt program with its fourteen major measures is now statutory law. That program smashed many of our cherished traditions, but none more ruthlessly than the American tradition of "rugged individualism." We are now moving along a new path of social control and planned economy, with the long arm of the Federal Government reaching out in a score of directions where before neither its strength nor its beneficence had been felt.

This central government of ours has now become the almoner to 12,000,000 unemployed and distressed people. It has become the guardian of middle-class investors, of the mortgaged-farm owner, of the mortgaged-home owner, of the bank depositor, and of the railway employee. It has become the partner of industry and of agriculture. And it has even become the friend of the beer maker and the beer drinker.

As a practical contribution to prosperity, the Government promises to expend $3,300,000,000 on public works. It has made an outright grant to the States of $500,000,000 to relieve the destitute, and it has agreed to subscribe a few hundred million more to the corporations which will undertake the refinancing of mortgages on farms and small homes. On top of that it will guarantee the interest on $2,000,000,000 of farm mortgage bonds and $2,000,000,000 home mortgage bonds. . . .

How it will all work out, we do not know. All that we do know for a moral certainty is that the old formulas, plans, policies, programs and philosophies—the old conservatism, in a word—failed us and failed wretchedly in the depressed days of the past three years. If the New Deal wins, well and good. We will kiss the past goodby without a regret. If this Deal also fails, it can scarcely leave us any worse off than we were on March 4.

DOCUMENT 5

Lorena Hickok, Report on Federal Relief Efforts (1933)

President Franklin Roosevelt appointed former social worker Harry Hopkins to administer the New Deal's federal relief program. Hopkins wasted no time, distributing $5 million in direct relief within his first two hours in office. In 1933 Hopkins hired Lorena Hickok, a journalist and a friend of Eleanor Roosevelt's, to travel throughout the country and investigate the effectiveness of New Deal relief programs. Hopkins instructed her not to gather statistics but to "talk with the unemployed, those who are on relief and those who aren't, and when you talk with them don't ever forget that but for the grace of God you, I, any of our friends might be in their shoes." In the following letter from North Dakota, Hickok reported on inadequacy in the administration of federal relief.

Minot, North Dakota, November 1, 1933

I visited today another North Dakota county—Williams county—in which the Federal Relief Administration, through the North Dakota Relief Committee, is supposed to be doing a 100 per cent relief job.

Again, as in Morton county on Monday, I found indications of inadequacy and a most urgent need for clothing.

I wish I could find words adequately to express to you the immediate need for clothing in this area. All I can say is that these people have GOT to have clothing—RIGHT AWAY. It may be Indian Summer in Washington, but it's Winter up here. They've had their first snow. Snow is forecast for tomorrow. It's COLD.

Into the relief office in Williston, county seat of Williams county, came today a little middle-aged farmer—skin like leather, heavily calloused, grimy hands—incongruously attired in a worn light flannel suit of collegiate cut, flashy blue sweater, also worn, belted tan topcoat, and cap to match. These clothes, he explained, belonged to his eldest son.

"They're all we've got now," he said. "We take turns wearing 'em."

It was the first time he had asked for relief, he said, and he thought he could pull through the winter so far as food for his family and his livestock went, even though the grasshoppers did eat up most of his crop last summer.

But they needed clothes—badly and right away. They hadn't been able to buy any for three years. Even last winter his children had been unable to go to school for lack of clothing.

There were nine in his family—he had seven children.

They needed AT ONCE a suit of underwear apiece, overshoes, and stockings all around. He wasn't even mentioning shoes. Said they could get along if they had overshoes and socks to wear inside.

The secretary of the relief committee and I figured out what it would cost, at local retail prices, to provide these articles. It came to $40.50. Nine suits of underwear at $2 each, $18; nine pairs of overshoes at $2 each, $18; nine pairs of socks at 50 cents a pair, $4.50. Total, $40.50.

And that did not include things like jackets and sweaters.

"This is just a typical case," said the secretary of the relief committee. There was certainly nothing framed about it. The secretary did not know I was in town until I showed up in his office. And the man was just one of the "customers," who happened to wander in while I was there.

"What I'd like to know," the secretary of the relief committee added, "is where we're going to get the money to buy these things.

"In September we spent $8,000 on relief in this county. In October, Bismarck cut us down to $6,000. What we're going to get in November I don't know.

"It's all federal money. All this county has got is tax warrants, and the merchants won't take them.

"We've got 450 families on relief in this county now, and the number is increasing every day at the rate of about seven. Some days we have as high as 15 new cases. Six thousand dollars a month isn't anywhere nearly enough to feed them decently and buy fuel—let alone providing clothing."

So much for inadequacy. They told me in Bismarck Monday there were five counties in the state getting 100 percent federal relief. At this rate—$6,000 each for the two counties among the five I have visited so far—they're putting out $30,000 a month. Nobody up here seems to know what we're putting into the state per month. I mean to find out when I get back to Bismarck.

I get howls all the time about the administration of our livestock relief. They all insist that the limit on the amount of livestock a farmer can own and get relief is too low. That may or may not be true, but here's one that, on the face of it, is wrong:

It seems that in order to get livestock relief a farmer must first prove that he cannot get a feed loan. That means that he must apply to the Farm Credit outfit in St. Paul for a loan, pay a $10 appraisal fee, and get turned down before he is eligible for our relief! I quote a paragraph from a letter from the county agricultural agent in Williston, to whom applications for livestock relief are made, to a prospective client:

"You will see from this letter that there is considerable red tape involved in this whole deal, and it is very likely it would be a month before anything could be arranged, and then for a very limited amount of stock."

On the face of it, there is something wrong when letters like that are going out to people who are trying to get help from us.

I don't think the trouble was with the county agent, either. He showed me his instructions—which stated that a man must be able to show that he was unable to get help from any other source....

All Summer I've been hearing, wherever I've gone, that there was going to be an urgent need for clothing this winter. As I write, I wonder, for instance, if any clothing has been distributed yet up in Northern Maine. It seems to have been a case of the relief people knowing all Summer that clothing was going to be needed this winter—but doing nothing about it. And now Winter is upon us. Up here in North Dakota, it has arrived. They must have clothing at once—NOW....

DOCUMENT 6

Huey P. Long, My First Days in the White House (1935)

Huey Pierce Long, the flamboyant senator from Louisiana, was an early supporter of Franklin Roosevelt and New Deal enthusiast. But when conditions failed to improve, Long repudiated the New Deal, blazed an independent course, and launched an extravagant campaign to redistribute the nation's wealth. Millions supported Long's Share Our Wealth movement, and the senator planned to challenge Roosevelt for the presidency but was assassinated in 1936. Long penned *My First Days in the White House* in 1935, a short novel in which he fantasized about his ascension to power and the ease with which he would solve the nation's economic crisis. In the following excerpt, Long imagines how he would convince the captains of American finance to forfeit their great fortunes and work together in devising a plan for the execution of the national Share Our Wealth program.

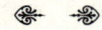

A few days later, just as dusk was falling over the city of Washington, my secretary informed me that Mr. Winthrop W. Aldrich, the New York banker, was waiting for me in the White House. He had entered the White House from the east wing, in order to avoid newspapermen. I had my secretary bring him to my office through the building. He was accompanied by his attorney, Mr. William D. Embree.

When he entered my office I recognized him, since I had met him in the Chase National Bank before I became President. We shook hands.

"Sit down, Mr. Aldrich," I said, "What can I do for you?"

"I received your letter."

"I hope you liked it."

"Perhaps I am compelled to like it," Mr. Aldrich replied. "I came here, Mr. President, in behalf of a number of gentlemen who received your recent letter concerning your Share Our Wealth program. A number of us, in response to your invitation, have assembled here in Washington, and we should like to confer with you as soon as possible. We have kept our coming from the press, as you advised us in your letter."

"How soon can you assemble here?" I inquired.

"Within the hour," replied Aldrich.

Aldrich made several telephone calls. I gave my secretary instructions to see that the visitors were escorted to the library in the White House proper. I then left the executive office with Aldrich. On our way through the building I asked him how his markets were holding up in New York.

"The markets remain about the same, Mr. President," he replied, "but there is very little buying and selling. Everybody is waiting to find out just how you intend to seize wealth."

In a very few minutes the visitors began arriving. The first to arrive were Thomas W. Lamont and George Whitney, two partners in the firm of J. P. Morgan & Co., who explained they came to represent J. Pierpont Morgan in the conference. They were accompanied by the Morgan attorney, John W. Davis, one-time Democratic nominee for the Presidency. I had met Mr. Lamont and Mr. Davis previously.

Then came Andrew W. Mellon, accompanied by

his son, Paul Mellon, and by his attorney, David A. Reed, the former United States Senator, whom I knew well by reason of his service in the Senate. Then Pierre S. du Pont and Irenée du Pont, accompanied by their attorney, William J. Donovan, the former Assistant Attorney General. Owen D. Young, Charles M. Schwab, and Eugene G. Grace came in next, followed by Bernard M. Baruch. E. T. Stotesbury, the Philadelphia banker and Morgan partner, was the last to arrive.

After all were seated, I asked:

"Is anyone representing Mr. Rockefeller, Jr.?"

Mr. Aldrich replied:

"He intends to see you later, Mr. President. He could not join us today."

I surmised that the younger Rockefeller had been badly shaken by his father's action in deeding the bulk of his fortune to the government in compliance with the Share Our Wealth program. I wondered how many more of this crowd knew of the elder Rockefeller's deed; there had been no publicity and I had not given out his letter for publication. . . .

"Well, now, gentlemen," I inquired, "what is your pleasure?"

They looked at each other, and Baruch repeated, "Pleasure? That's a good one!"

"Well, then, what are your suggestions for putting the Share Our Wealth program into effect with the least disturbance to commerce, business and industry?" I inquired.

There was no response.

"Well, let me call the roll," I next said. "What do you say, Mr. Mellon?"

I was surprised at the strength of the Pittsburgh financier's voice.

"The sooner we know your plan, I suppose, the better we will be able to discuss it."

"What do you say, Mr. Aldrich?"

"I presumed that you would explain your plan and then we would discuss it at a conference between ourselves, and later present you our views."

"Am I to understand, gentlemen, that there is no mentality in this aggregation wise enough to propose a definite plan for the seizure of great wealth and its redistribution to the masses of our people?" I demanded. "If that is true, and God forbid it, it would only go to prove that the public was being cheated when men of such inferior intelligence amassed so much wealth."

Mr. Stotesbury responded:

"Mr. President, speaking for the gentlemen to whom you sent letters in Philadelphia, I believe your limit of five million dollars is entirely too low to encourage a proper development of private commerce and private industry. I met with a number of gentlemen in Philadelphia, and we agreed that if the limit were extended to twenty-five million dollars, we could join with you in working out a program."

"Mr. President," said Aldrich, attracting my attention, "I don't agree with my good friend from Philadelphia."

I realized instantly that Aldrich knew of the elder Rockefeller's letter to me.

"I feel we must resign ourselves to the five million dollar limit, if your plan is held constitutional by the courts," Aldrich continued. "I came to hear your plan and discuss your method of procedure, if you are ready to give us the details."

"Do I understand, Mr. Aldrich, that you are reconciled to the limitation of your personal fortune to five million dollars?"

"Certainly, Mr. President, if it is constitutional," replied Mr. Aldrich.

"I believe you said you were acting in behalf of John D. Rockefeller, Jr.," I said.

Aldrich nodded.

"What is his position in this matter?" I asked.

"He believes the seizure of private capital through a capital levy is unconstitutional, and that it should be tested in the courts before it is imposed. If it is constitutional, then, of course, there can be no objection by private citizens, since it will become the law of the land. But in either event, he wishes to have the act so drawn that if it is held constitutional, its enforcement will neither disrupt nor destroy American business. For that reason he is perfectly willing to join in perfecting your program."

"How many of you gentlemen share the opinion

of Mr. Rockefeller, as expressed by Mr. Aldrich, that the banking, business and industrial leaders of our country should cooperate with me now in the drafting of a program to redistribute your fortunes, whether or not the law ultimately is held constitutional?" I inquired.

Mellon, the two du Ponts, Owen Young, Schwab, and Baruch, nodded their heads in agreement.

"What about the attitude of the Morgan firm on that?" I inquired of Lamont, who had sat silent.

"I could not say, without conferring with Mr. Morgan," replied Lamont. "My understanding with other members of my firm was that I should present our views opposing your plan, and learn its details so I could communicate them to our people."

"Do you share the same views, Mr. Stotesbury?" I asked the Philadelphia capitalist and Morgan banker.

"Mr. President, very frankly, I should like to join in any negotiations for carrying out the Share Our Wealth program in an orderly manner, but, of course, as a lifelong associate of Mr. Morgan, I feel I should be guided by his judgment."

"Well, that seems to leave the Morgan firm out of it," I said.

Turning to Aldrich, I inquired:

"Do you believe Mr. Rockefeller would accept the chairmanship of a committee of business men, bankers and industrialists to draft me a plan to carry out my Share Our Wealth program?"

"I believe so, Mr. President," replied Aldrich, "But I should like to confirm that by telephone."

I indicated the telephone on my desk.

"Call him now," I said.

In a few minutes Aldrich was relating our conversation to John D. Rockefeller, Jr., at his home in New York City. From his replies it was obvious that Mr. Rockefeller was accepting the chairmanship. When Aldrich hung up the phone, he turned around and said:

"Mr. President, Mr. Rockefeller will serve as chairman of your committee."

"That's fine," I said. "His services will allay fear throughout the business world."

I stood up, and my visitors arose in a body.

"Now, Mr. Lamont, Mr. Whitney, Mr. Davis, and Mr. Stotesbury, I believe we can excuse you," I said. "Since you feel that your firm does not care to participate in these conferences, I will abide by your decision."

John W. Davis, the Morgan lawyer, interrupted me.

"Mr. President, if you will forgive me, may I say a word?" he inquired.

I nodded.

"Mr. President, I think Mr. Lamont should be given permission to return to the conference after consulting with the other members of the firm," he said. "I feel sure that when the developments of this conference are reported to Mr. Morgan, he will desire to participate along with the other gentlemen."

"I am sorry, Mr. Davis, but your client, Mr. Morgan is refusing to accept the Share Our Wealth program," I replied. "Acting apparently upon your advice, he is going to fight it in the courts. Now, I am perfectly willing to follow the Constitution and to accept his challenge and battle it out in the courts. Recognizing him as an enemy of the Share Our Wealth Program, I don't feel it is proper to have him or any of his agents participate in any way in the drafting of the program.

"Without reflecting upon the honor or integrity of Mr. Morgan or his associates, it would be difficult to convince the American people that their active cooperation in the drafting of the plan would be for any other purpose than to weaken it or to write some loophole into it through which they might escape or defeat it in the courts. Now, I believe these other gentlemen are cooperating in good faith and will draft a plan to the best of their ability.

"In the final analysis, of course, I shall rely on them for the economic sections of the bill, but I will be forced to rely upon my own attorney general and solicitor general for the constitutional sections in the event there is any difference of opinion between this committee and the government's legal advisors."

Davis bowed. With Lamont, Whitney, and Stotesbury, he left the room.

After they departed, I said to those remaining:

"Now, gentlemen, I appoint John D. Rockefeller, Jr., chairman of a National Share Our Wealth Committee, and I appoint as additional members Andrew W. Mellon, Winthrop W. Aldrich, Pierre S. du Pont, Irenée du Pont, Owen D. Young, Charles M. Schwab, and Bernard M. Baruch. I further empower Mr. Rockefeller as chairman to name such additional members as he may desire, upon sole condition that he shall name no member from the firm of J. P. Morgan or its Philadelphia ally, Drexel and Company. You, Mr. Aldrich, will communicate that authority to Mr. Rockefeller.

"Now, gentlemen, will you join me at dinner?"

DOCUMENT 7

Charlie Storms, "Memories of the Depression" (1939)*

Beginning in 1915, when he was 14 years old, Charlie Storms migrated from oil field to oil field across Texas and Oklahoma, constructing wooden derricks at drilling sites. The discovery of the immense East Texas oil field in 1930 sparked an uncontrolled overproduction of oil. With the market soon glutted and the price of crude drastically deflated, oil companies began to reduce wages and pursue other cost-cutting measures. In the following interview, Storms describes his difficulties securing work at a decent wage during the Depression and his efforts to build a strong union movement among oil workers.

When it got really tough down here, in about '31, I had a helluva hard time. My daddy died April 21, 1931. I only had about $100 left out of my savings, and it took damned near all that to put him away. I left my wife up there in Muskogee with my mother after the burial, and I come on back. But it was '34 before I could get my family back down here. I couldn't seem to make more'n $25 on any job; they'd last about two–three days and then fold up, and there wouldn't be another one for a month.

One Christmas I was working down at Anadarko for a rig contractor. He was a tight guy; he never paid me off till he'd got his pay, and sometimes he forgot I was even working for him. He owed me about $60 that Christmas, and I got a ride up from Anadarko to come by his house to get my check. I wanted to go up to Muskogee and see the family. But his wife said he'd gone to Houston and wouldn't be back till after the first of the year. She handed me a check he'd left for me—for $25. So I had to stay in Oklahoma City that Christmas.

In '35 I was working for a contractor in the Oklahoma City field. I'd got in eight days when one noon the contractor came out and told the pusher to tell the crew that he was cutting the wages from $8 to $7 and that the cut started the first of the month, which was about two weeks before that day. When the pusher walked over and told us (we were

*From *Voices from the Oil Fields*, edited by Paul F. Lambert and Kenny A. Franks. Copyright © 1984 by the University of Oklahoma Press.

sitting around on the rig floor eating our lunch) we waited till he got through with his little spiel, and then I told him he wasn't cutting my wages a nickel.

The contractor heard us arguing and came over, and I told him the same thing. I said I'd gone to work at $8 a day, and that was what he was going to pay me if he didn't want to go to court about it. He took me off to one side and tried to argue me out of it, but it didn't do him any good. I told him I went to work at $7 a day at noon of that day, but I had eight days coming to me at $8 a day, and, by God, I was going to get it all, He said he'd pay me the $64, and did I want to work the rest of the day at $7. I said no, I'd work for $4 for the half-day, not for $3.50. He finally saw I meant it and said all right.

But that afternoon there were two men, rig builders, standing around the rig waiting for me to quit so they could try to get my job. Times was tough, but I was damned if I was going to be chiseled like that.

I got a job with another company, and then I pushed crews for a contractor for four years, in Oklahoma City, St. Louis, Ray City, Seminole, and all around the state. . . .

They tried to organize a union in '35, but didn't have much luck. In '37 the boys tried again with a CIO organizer helping them, and they had a pretty tough time getting some of the boys to join. They went on strike once; I went out, too, but we lost it. There was a big meeting down at Seminole about that strike, whether we'd go out or not.

They all thought I was a damned radical. The contractors was trying to cut us from $10 a day to $8, and I told the whole damned bunch of 'em at that meeting that I wouldn't pull on a glove for any $8 a day. Well, they finally all walked out, but we lost our strike anyway. . . .

During the strike the boys wanted me to go out to a lease and call the men off, try to get them to throw in with us. I started out there and met the contractor on the way. He stopped me and said, ". . . I know you are going out there and call my crew out on strike. If you do, I'll see you never get in another day's work in Oklahoma City!"

I told him I was sorry, but I was doing what I thought was right, and he shot his car in low gear and lit out for town. The boys seen me coming and shut down the job till I got on the lease. I hollered up at 'em and told 'em to come on out, and ever' damned one of 'em threw his gloves high as he could and picked up the tools and come on back to town.

After the strike the contractors was sore as hell, and lots of the rig builders was, too. There was only two contractors in the whole state paying $10 a day, and both of them was mad at me. I thought I was going to have to live on dirt and dew from then on, but one night the contractor who said he'd see I never got to work again called me up and said he wanted me to go to Perry, Oklahoma, for him and go to work.

I forgot about being mad at him, especially after he said he's pay me $10 a day, and went up there and worked eighteen months for him. We got along fine, too; never a cross word between us.

Then the union started again, but I stayed clear of it till I saw the boys meant business. I wasn't going to be the one that got my neck out like a Christmas turkey so somebody could take a whack at it. The ones that'd been the hardest ones to get out on strike was the first ones to try to get the new union started, and before long, about three months after they begun, a pretty strong union was up and going.

I signed up and I've tried to make a good member. Right now I'm setting here on my Royal American because there aren't any union jobs anyplace. I could go out and scab on the boys, but that'd hurt me as much or more'n it would them. Women don't quite understand that idea (I know my wife don't) but I think most men do.

We got some heels in our union, but hell, there are heels everyplace, and rig building's no better'n other jobs. We just take the good with the bad and try to line them up straight.

The union's done a helluva lot for the rig builders, I know that. Back several years ago when we didn't have one, the pusher got around $3 or $4 a day for using his car. He had to haul the crews out to the job and back, and then he had to hook on a cat-head to his car wheel and use it to pull up the steel in the rig. A cat-head's a kind of pulley; you just bolt it on your car wheel, sling a rope around it, and start up your car. It'll pull the top out of a rig if the car's anchored solid.

Now, under our union rules, the pusher gets $7 a day for the use of his car, and wages all around are better than ever before. That is, they're more regular, even if the work keeps getting slacker. A green man gets $6 a day; an intermediate man who doesn't have enough experience to be a full rig builder gets $10; and a rig builder gets $12. A pusher draws $14 a day. If a man can get in enough days a year he can get by on those wages.

Another good thing about the union is that they're getting rid of a lot of things that cause accidents and making the men realize that accident prevention's a helluva lot better than gambling on pulling through. For one thing, the union won't let anybody but the contractor—nobody else but the crew, the pusher, and the contractor—on the rig when they're running it or tearing it down. Too much danger of somebody getting hit. . . .

We've had a lot of changes like that, all of 'em for our good and the contractors, too, come in the fields, but everything isn't rosy, not by a helluva lot. The oil fields keep moving away, and all a man can do, rig builder or whatever he is, is keep following 'em. A man rents a house here like I done, buys his furniture and begins trying to live like most white folks do, and he'll have to pull up and follow the oil. Either that, or leave his family there and go by hisself and maybe not see 'em for months at a time.

We've got the wages and hours settled; now all we gotta do is get the whole damned oil industry lined up and keep it there!

DOCUMENT 8
Letters to F. D. R. (1934, 1937)

No president captured the popular imagination like Roosevelt. To some he was a satan; to many he was a saint. And Americans expressed their opinions in an unprecedented volume of mail to the White House. Roosevelt took this correspondence seriously and regularly read many of the letters himself in order to, as one aide explained, "renew his sense of contact with raw opinion." The two letters reprinted here present a sample of that "raw opinion." The first letter is an example of the millions of letters of praise that Roosevelt received. In the second, a woman from Indiana attacks the New Deal as an extravagant waste of taxpayers' money.

Cedarburg, Wis.
10^{45} A.M. Mar. 5, 1934

Mrs. F. D. Roosevelt
Washington D.C.

My dear Friend:

Just listened to the address given by your dear husband, our wonderful President. During the presidential campaign of 1932 we had in our home a darling little girl, three years old. My husband + I were great admirers of the Dem. candidate so Dolores had to listen to much talk about the great man who we hoped and prayed would be our next Pres. We are Lutherans and she is a Catholic so you'll get quite a thrill out of what I'm to tell you now. That fall Judge Karel of Mil. sent me a fine picture of our beloved President, which I placed in our Public Library. When I received this fine picture my dear mother (who has since been called Home) said to Dolores "Who is this man?" and Dolores answered without any hesitation "Why who else, but Saint Roosevelt!" The old saying goes fools and children often tell the truth and indeed we all feel if there ever was a Saint. He is one. As long as Pres. Roosevelt will be our leader under Jesus Christ we feel no fear. His speech this morning showed he feels for the "least of these" I am enclosing a snap shot of the dear little girl who acclaimed our President a Saint and rightly so.

I'm sure Pres. Roosevelt had a great day on Feb. 16, the world day of prayer, when many hearts were lifted in prayer for him all over this great land of ours.

We shall continue to ask our heavenly Father to guide and guard him in his great task as leader of the great American people.

With all good wishes for you and your fine family I am your most sincerely

Mrs. L. K. S.

Dec. 14–1937.
Columbus, Ind.

Mrs. F. D. Roosevelt,
Washington, D. C.

Mrs. Roosevelt: I suppose from your point of view the work relief, old age pensions, slum clearance and all the rest seems like a perfect remedy for all the ills of this country, but I would like for you to see the results, as the other half see them.

We have always had a shiftless, never-do-well class of people whose one and only aim in life is to live without work. I have been rubbing elbows with this class for nearly sixty years and have tried to help some of the most promising and have seen others try to help them, but it can't be done. We cannot help those who will not try to help themselves and if they do try a square deal is all they need, and by the way that is all this country needs or ever has needed: a square deal for all and then, let each one paddle their own canoe, or sink.

There has never been any necessity for any one who is able to work, being on relief in this locality, but there have been many eating the bread of charity and they have lived better than ever before. I have had taxpayers tell me that their children came from school and asked why they couldn't have nice lunches like the children on relief.

The women and children around here have had to work at the fields to help save the crops and several women fainted while at work and at the same time we couldn't go up or down the road without stumbling over some of the reliefers, moping around carrying dirt from one side of the road to the other and back again, or else asleep. I live alone on a farm and have not raised any crops for the last two years as there was no help to be had. I am feeding the stock and have been cutting the wood to keep my home fires burning. There are several reliefers around here now who have been kicked off relief, but they refuse to work unless they can get relief hours and wages, but they are so worthless no one can afford to hire them.

As for the clearance of the real slums, it can't be done as long as their inhabitants are allowed to reproduce their kind. I would like for you to see what a family of that class can do to a decent house in a short time. Such a family moved into an almost new, neat, four-room house near here last winter. They even cut down some of the shade trees for fuel, after they had burned everything they could pry loose. There were two big idle boys in the family and they could get all the fuel they wanted, just for the cutting, but the shade trees were closer and it was taking a great amount of fuel, for they had broken out several windows and they had but very little bedding. There were two women there all the time and three part of the time and there was enough good clothing tramped in the mud around the yard to have made all the bedclothes they needed. It was clothing that had been given them and they had worn it until it was too filthy to wear any longer without washing, so they threw it out and begged more. I will not try to describe their filth for you would not believe me. They paid no rent while there and left between two suns owing everyone from whom they could get a nickels worth of anything. They are just a fair sample of the class of people on whom so much of our hard earned tax-money is being squandered and on whom so much sympathy is being wasted.

As for the old people on beggars' allowances: the taxpayers have provided homes for all the old people who never liked to work, where they will be neither cold nor hungry: much better homes than most of them have ever tried to provide for themselves. They have lived many years through the most prosperous times of our country and had an opportunity to prepare for old age, but they spent their lives in idleness or worse and now they expect those who have worked like slaves, to provide a living for them and all their worthless descendants. Some of them are asking for from thirty to sixty dollars a month when I have known them to live on a dollar a week rather than go to work. There is many a little child doing without butter on its bread, so that some old sot can have his booze and tobacco: some old sot who spent his working years loafing around pool rooms and saloons, boasting that the world owed him a living.

Even the child welfare has become a racket. The parents of large families are getting divorces, so that the mothers and children can qualify for aid. The children to join the ranks of the "unemployed" as they grow up, for no child that has been raised on charity in this community has ever amounted to anything.

You people who have plenty of this worlds goods and whose money comes easy, have no idea of the heart-breaking toil and self-denial which is the lot of the working people who are trying to make an honest living, and then to have to shoulder all these unjust burdens seems like the last straw. During the worst of the depression many of the farmers had to deny their families butter, eggs, meat etc. and sell it to pay their taxes and then had to stand by and see the dead-beats carry it home to their families by the arm load, and they knew their tax money was helping pay for it. One woman saw a man carry out eight pounds of butter at one time. The crookedness, selfishness, greed and graft of the crooked politicians is making one gigantic racket out of the new deal and it is making this a nation of dead-beats and beggars and if it continues the people who will work will soon be nothing but slaves for the pampered poverty rats and I am afraid these human parasites are going to become a menace to the country unless they are disfranchised. No one should have the right to vote theirself a living at the expense of the tax payers. They learned their strength at the last election and also learned that they can get just about what they want by "voting right." They have had a taste of their coveted life of idleness, and at the rate they are increasing, they will soon control the country. The twentieth child arrived in the home of one chronic reliefer near here some time ago.

Is it any wonder the taxpayers are discouraged by all this penalizing of thrift and industry to reward shiftlessness, or that the whole country is on the brink of chaos?

    M. A. H. [female]
    Columbus, Ind.

Study Questions

1. Did Hoover and Franklin Roosevelt share assumptions about the proper role of government in society? What were their substantive disagreements?

2. How did the New Deal transform the relationship between Americans and the federal government?

3. Might Charlie Storm have found Huey Long's ideas appealing?

4. Some historians argue that the New Deal marked a watershed in American history, revolutionizing American society. Others find little revolutionary in the New Deal, stressing how it constituted little more than reformist measures designed to preserve American capitalism. Which view is more accurate?

9

World War II

After World War I, the United States retreated from an active foreign policy. Having rejected the League of Nations and the idealism of Woodrow Wilson, postwar diplomats pursued a cautious foreign policy that avoided binding commitments on behalf of international security. During the Depression, many Americans favored such policies, considering foreign affairs remote and insignificant compared to the more pressing problems of unemployment and economic stagnation.

In the mid-1930s, the rise of fascist military regimes in Germany, Italy, and Japan threatened world peace. The League of Nations utterly failed to prevent Japan's expansion in Asia, Italy's conquest of Ethiopia, and Germany's annexations of the Rhineland, Austria, and Czechoslovakia. The collapse of collective security and the impending threat of world war challenged Americans to rethink their foreign policy and role in the world.

The Berlin-Rome-Tokyo axis advance initially strengthened isolationist sentiment in the United States. The growing reality of another European war evoked haunting memories of the Great War. Fearing that Americans would once again be summoned to sacrifice their lives to resolve Europe's problems, many Americans supported a growing pacifist movement. On college campuses, students staged antiwar rallies, declaring their determination never to support American involvement in any foreign war. In Congress, legislators passed a series of neutrality acts, including an arms embargo, in an effort to ensure American noninvolvement.

The neutrality acts handcuffed President Franklin Roosevelt, who desperately wished to aid Great Britain and France without alienating pacifists in his own party. When Nazi Germany invaded Poland in September 1939, starting World War II, Roosevelt began to speak with greater authority. He urged a repeal of the neutrality acts, arguing that the Axis powers posed a formidable threat to American security and democracy, and he pledged to convert the United States into an "arsenal of democracy" (Documents 1 and 3). Citizens' groups, such as the America First Committee, continued to protest, insisting that intervention would be suicidal (Document 2). As late as September 1941, nearly 80 percent of the American public favored American neutrality in World War II, but when the Japanese attacked the American Naval Base at Pearl Harbor on December 7, 1941, popular opinion shifted.

Soldiers training at Fort Benning, Georgia. Though the United States wished to remain neutral and opposed involvement in the war, public opinion changed on December 7, 1941 when the naval base at Pearl Harbor, Hawaii was bombed by Japan. Approximately 2,400 Americans were killed and 1,300 wounded; Japanese losses were fewer than 100 casualties.

The next day, Congress, with only one dissenting vote, declared war on Japan. Within three days, Germany and Italy declared war on the United States. As Roosevelt proclaimed, "we are now in this war. We are all in it—all the way."

Critics charged that America's prosecution of the war tarnished the nation's image as defender of the free world. Even before the war, officials in the State Department were aware of Nazi atrocities against European Jews, yet they resisted relaxing immigration restrictions that would open the United States to Jewish refugees. Journalists charged that, by doing nothing, the Roosevelt administration was contributing to the tragic fate of European Jews and of undermining America's moral authority (Document 4). At home, Roosevelt capitulated to political pressure when he signed a military order authorizing the relocation of 120,000 Japanese Americans living along the West Coast to eleven interior internment camps. Although Japanese American prisoners did not experience the torture and death of Nazi concentration camps, most lost their homes and businesses, and the episode put in question the nation's commitment to democracy (Document 5).

Converting the country into an "arsenal of democracy" required a massive mobilization of American society. Manufacturing plants that had run at half-capacity during the Depression now operated overtime to assemble war matériel. Demand for labor in defense industries lured some nine million workers, who enjoyed increases in wage rates and overtime hours that doubled or tripled weekly paychecks.

The migration of people and wartime prosperity transformed other social relationships. African Americans announced a "Double-V" campaign to secure victory abroad and at home. By protesting discrimination in the defense industries and segregation in the armed forces, blacks converted race relations from a southern to a national issue, paving the way for the postwar Civil Rights Movement (Documents 6 and 7).

As men left to fight overseas, women entered the labor force in unprecedented numbers, taking jobs in defense manufacturing that once had been reserved for men (Document 8).

Within four years, the United States had been transformed from an isolationist country into the strongest power in the world. Wartime mobilization unleashed the industrial recovery and prosperity that the New Deal failed to accomplish. With the defeat of the Axis powers in 1945, Americans anticipated a postwar world in which they could enjoy freedom from want and freedom from fear. But the nation's new world role brought it into conflict with the Soviet Union, inaugurating a Cold War that threatened those freedoms both at home and abroad.

DOCUMENT 1

Franklin Delano Roosevelt, Annual Message to Congress (1941)

By June 1940, the Nazi war machine had conquered nearly all of Europe, including France, and had succeeded in driving British forces off the continent. President Roosevelt responded by announcing, over isolationist opposition, a series of measures intended to aid Great Britain. In his annual message to Congress in January 1941, Roosevelt urged legislators to repudiate the neutrality acts and enact a measure that would permit the United States to lend and lease goods and munitions to countries fighting the aggressor nations. Roosevelt concluded the speech with a list of four essential freedoms, which many Americans accepted as the basic ideals that they would fight to defend.

I address you, the Members of the Seventy-seventh Congress, at a moment unprecedented in the history of the Union. I use the word "unprecedented," because at no previous time has American security been as seriously threatened from without as it is today....

Every realist knows that the democratic way of life is at this moment being directly assailed in every part of the world—assailed either by arms or by secret spreading of poisonous propaganda by those who seek to destroy unity and promote discord in nations still at peace.

During 16 months this assault has blotted out the whole pattern of democratic life in an appalling number of independent nations, great and small. The assailants are still on the march, threatening other nations, great and small.

Therefore, as your President, performing my constitutional duty to "give to the Congress information of the state of the Union," I find it necessary to report that the future and the safety of our country and of our democracy are overwhelmingly involved in events far beyond our borders.

Armed defense of democratic existence is now being gallantly waged in four continents. If that defense fails, all the population and all the resources of Europe, Asia, Africa, and Australasia will be dominated by the conquerors. The total of those populations and their resources greatly exceeds the sum total of the population and resources of the whole of the Western Hemisphere—many times over.

In times like these it is immature—and incidentally untrue—for anybody to brag that an unprepared America, single-handed, and with one hand tied behind its back, can hold off the whole world.

No realistic American can expect from a dictator's peace international generosity, or return of true independence, or world disarmament, or freedom of expression, or freedom of religion—or even good business.

Such a peace would bring no security for us or for our neighbors. "Those who would give up essential liberty to purchase a little temporary safety deserve neither liberty nor safety."...

The need of the moment is that our actions and our policy should be devoted primarily—almost exclusively—to meeting this foreign peril. For all our domestic problems are now a part of the great emergency....

Our national policy is this:

First, by an impressive expression of the public will and without regard to partisanship, we are committed to all-inclusive national defense.

Second, by an impressive expression of the public will and without regard to partisanship, we are committed to full support of all those resolute peoples, everywhere, who are resisting aggression and are thereby keeping war away from our hemisphere. By this support, we express our determination that the democratic cause shall prevail, and we strengthen the defense and security of our own Nation.

Third, by an impressive expression of the public will and without regard to partisanship, we are committed to the proposition that principles of morality and considerations for our own security will never permit us to acquiesce in a peace dictated by aggressors and sponsored by appeasers. We know that enduring peace cannot be bought at the cost of other people's freedom....

I ... ask this Congress for authority and for funds sufficient to manufacture additional munitions and war supplies of many kinds, to be turned over to those nations which are now in actual war with aggressor nations.

Our most useful and immediate role is to act as an arsenal for them as well as for ourselves. They do not need manpower. They do need billions of dollars' worth of the weapons of defense.

The time is near when they will not be able to pay for them in ready cash. We cannot, and will not, tell them they must surrender merely because of present inability to pay for the weapons which we know they must have....

Let us say to the democracies, "We Americans are vitally concerned in your defense of freedom. We are putting forth our energies, our resources, and our organizing powers to give you the strength to regain and maintain a free world. We shall send you, in ever-increasing numbers, ships, planes, tanks, guns. This is our purpose and our pledge."

In fulfillment of this purpose we will not be intimidated by the threats of dictators that they will regard as a breach of international law and as an act of war our aid to the democracies which dare to resist their aggression. Such aid is not an act of war, even if a dictator should unilaterally proclaim it so to be.

When the dictators are ready to make war upon us, they will not wait for an act of war on our part....

As men do not live by bread alone, they do not fight by armaments alone. Those who man our defenses, and those behind them who build our defenses, must have the stamina and courage which come from an unshakable belief in the manner of life which they are defending. The mighty action which we are calling for cannot be based on a disregard of all things worth fighting for.

The Nation takes great satisfaction and much strength from the things which have been done to make its people conscious of their individual stake in the preservation of democratic life in America. Those things have toughened the fiber of our people, have renewed their faith and strengthened their devotion to the institutions we make ready to protect.

Certainly this is no time to stop thinking about the social and economic problems which are the root cause of the social revolution which is today a supreme factor in the world.

There is nothing mysterious about the foundations of a healthy and strong democracy. The basic things expected by our people of their political and economic systems are simple. They are:

Equality of opportunity for youth and for others.

Jobs for those who can work.

Security for those who need it.

The ending of special privilege for the few.

The preservation of civil liberties for all.

The enjoyment of the fruits of scientific progress in a wider and constantly rising standard of living.

These are the simple and basic things that must never be lost sight of in the turmoil and unbelievable complexity of our modern world. The inner and abiding strength of our economic and political systems is dependent upon the degree to which they fulfill these expectations....

In the future days, which we seek to make secure, we look forward to a world founded upon four essential human freedoms.

The first is freedom of speech and expression everywhere in the world.

The second is freedom of every person to worship God in his own way everywhere in the world.

The third is freedom from want, which, translated into world terms, means economic understandings which will secure to every nation a healthy peacetime life for its inhabitants everywhere in the world.

The fourth is freedom from fear—which, translated into world terms, means a world-wide reduction of armaments to such a point and in such a thorough fashion that no nation will be in a position to commit an act of physical aggression against any neighbor—anywhere in the world.

That is no vision of a distant millennium. It is a definite basis for a kind of world attainable in our own time and generation....

To that high concept there can be no end save victory.

DOCUMENT 2
Charles Lindbergh, Radio Address (1941)

In 1940 a group of isolationists organized the America First Committee to protest the United States drift toward intervention in the European war. The organization attracted individuals of all political persuasions, including aviator Charles Lindbergh, socialist organizer Norman Thomas, conservative Senator Robert Taft, of Ohio, and liberal educator Robert Hutchins. In April 1941, Lindbergh delivered the following radio address in which he outlined the major reasons why the United States should pursue a course of noninvolvement.

There are many viewpoints from which the issues of this war can be argued. Some are primarily idealistic. Some are primarily practical. One should, I believe, strive for a balance of both. But, since the subjects that can be covered in a single address are limited, tonight I shall discuss the war from a viewpoint which is primarily practical. It is not that I believe ideals are unimportant, even among the realities of war; but if a nation is to survive in a hostile world, its ideals must be backed by the hard logic of military practicability. If the outcome of war depended upon ideals alone, this would be a different world than it is today.

I know I will be severely criticized by the interventionists in America when I say we should not enter a war unless we have a reasonable chance of winning. That, they will claim, is far too materialistic a viewpoint. They will advance again the same arguments that were used to persuade France to declare war against Germany in 1939. But I do not believe that our American ideals, and our way of life, will gain through an unsuccessful war. And I know that the United States is not prepared to wage war in Europe successfully at this time. We are no better prepared today than France was when the interventionists in Europe persuaded her to attack the Siegfried line.

I have said before, and I will say again, that I believe it will be a tragedy to the entire world if the British Empire collapses. That is one of the main reasons why I opposed this war before it was declared and why I have constantly advocated a negotiated peace. I did not feel that England and France had a reasonable chance of winning. France has now been defeated; and, despite the propaganda and confusion of recent months, it is now obvious that England is losing the war. I believe this is realized even by the British Government. But they have one last desperate plan remaining. They hope that they may be able to persuade us to send another American Expeditionary Force to Europe, and to share with England militarily, as well as financially, the fiasco of this war.

I do not blame England for this hope, or for asking for our assistance. But we now know that she declared a war under circumstances which led to the defeat of every nation that sided with her from Poland to Greece. We know that in the desperation of war England promised to all those nations armed assistance that she could not send. We know that she misinformed them, as she has misinformed us, concerning her state of preparation, her military strength, and the progress of the war.

In time of war, truth is always replaced by propaganda. I do not believe we should be too quick to criticize the actions of a belligerent nation. There is always the question whether we, ourselves, would do better under similar circumstances. But we in this country have a right to think of the welfare of America first, just as the people in England thought first of their own country when they encouraged the smaller nations of Europe to fight against hopeless odds. When England asks us to enter this war, she is considering her own future and that of her Empire. In making our reply, I believe we should consider the future of the United States and that of the Western Hemisphere.

It is not only our right, but it is our obligation as American citizens, to look at this war objectively and to weigh our chances for success if we should enter it. I have attempted to do this, especially from the standpoint of aviation; and I have been forced to the conclusion that we cannot win this war for England, regardless of how much assistance we extend.

I ask you to look at the map of Europe today and see if you can suggest any way in which we could win this war if we entered it. Suppose we had a large army in America, trained and equipped. Where would we send it to fight? The campaigns of the war show only too clearly how difficult it is to force a landing, or to maintain an army, on a hostile coast.

Suppose we took our Navy from the Pacific and used it to convoy British shipping. That would not win the war for England. It would, at best, permit her to exist under the constant bombing of the German air fleet. Suppose we had an air force that we could send to Europe. Where could it operate? Some of our squadrons might be based in the British Isles, but it is physically impossible to base enough aircraft in the British Isles alone to equal in strength the aircraft that can be based on the continent of Europe.

I have asked these questions on the supposition that we had in existence an Army and an air force large enough and well enough equipped to send to Europe; and that we would dare to remove our Navy from the Pacific. Even on this basis, I do not see how we could invade the continent of Europe successfully as long as all of that continent and most of Asia is under Axis domination. But the fact is that none of these suppositions are correct. We have only a one-ocean Navy. Our Army is still untrained and inadequately equipped for foreign war. Our air force is deplorably lacking in modern fighting planes.

When these facts are cited, the interventionists shout that we are defeatists, that we are undermining the principles of democracy, and that we are giving comfort to Germany by talking about our military weakness. But everything I mention here has been published in our newspapers and in the reports of congressional hearings in Washington. Our military position is well known to the governments of Europe and Asia. Why, then, should it not be brought to the attention of our own people?

I say it is the interventionists in America as it was in England and in France, who give comfort to the enemy. I say it is they who are undermining the principles of democracy when they demand that we take a course to which more than 80 percent of our citizens are opposed. I charge them with being the real defeatists, for their policy has led to the defeat of every country that followed their advice since this war began. There is no better way to give comfort to an enemy than to divide the people of a nation over the issue of foreign war. There is no shorter road to defeat than by entering a war with inadequate preparation. Every nation that has adopted the interventionist policy of depending on someone else for its own defense has met with nothing but defeat and failure. . . .

There is a policy open to this Nation that will lead to success—a policy that leaves us free to follow our own way of life and to develop our own civilization. It is not a new and untried idea. It was advocated by Washington. It was incorporated in the Monroe Doctrine. Under its guidance the United States became the greatest Nation in the world.

It is based upon the belief that the security of a nation lies in the strength and character of its own people. It recommends the maintenance of armed forces sufficient to defend this hemisphere from attack by any combination of foreign powers. It demands faith in an independent American destiny. This is the policy of the America First Committee today. It is a policy not of isolation, but of independence; not of defeat, but of courage. It is a policy that led this Nation to success during the most trying years of our history, and it is a policy that will lead us to success again. . . .

The United States is better situated from a military standpoint than any other nation in the world. Even in our present condition of unpreparedness no foreign power is in a position to invade us today. If we concentrate on our own defenses and build the strength that this Nation should maintain, no foreign army will ever attempt to land on American shores.

War is not inevitable for this country. Such a claim is defeatism in the true sense. No one can make us fight abroad unless we ourselves are willing to do so. No one will attempt to fight us here if we arm ourselves as a great nation should be armed. Over a hundred million people in this Nation are opposed to entering the war. If the principles of democracy mean anything at all, that is reason enough for us to stay out. If we are forced into a war against the wishes of an overwhelming majority of our people, we will have proved democracy such a failure at home that there will be little use fighting for it abroad.

The time has come when those of us who believe in an independent American destiny must band together and organize for strength. We have been led toward war by a minority of our people. This minority has power. It has influence. It has a loud voice. But it does not represent the American people. During the last several years I have traveled over this country from one end to the other. I have talked to many hundreds of men and women, and I have letters from tens of thousands more, who feel the same way as you and I.

Most of these people have no influence or power. Most of them have no means of expressing their convictions, except by their vote which has always been against this war. They are the citizens who have had to work too hard at their daily jobs to organize political meetings. Hitherto, they have relied upon their vote to express their feelings; but now they find that it is hardly remembered except in the oratory of a political campaign. These people, the majority of hard-working American citizens, are with us. They are the true strength of our country. And they are beginning to realize, as you and I, that there are times when we must sacrifice our normal interests in life in order to insure the safety and the welfare of our Nation.

Such a time has come. Such a crisis is here. That is why the America First Committee has been formed—to give voice to the people who have no newspaper, or newsreel, or radio station at their command; to the people who must do the paying, and the fighting, and the dying if this country enters the war.

DOCUMENT 3

The Atlantic Charter (1941)

In August 1941, President Franklin Roosevelt met with British Prime Minister Winston Churchill off the coast of Newfoundland to discuss a series of matters relating to the world crisis. The two concluded the meeting by signing the Atlantic

Charter, which soon became the most succinct statement of Allied war aims and established a blueprint for a postwar world order. The *Chicago Tribune,* mouthpiece of midwestern isolationism, objected vehemently to Roosevelt's actions, declaring that he had committed the United States to the destruction of Nazi tyranny without the consent of the American people and that he was "determining the destiny of his country . . . in his own will, as if his subjects were without voice."

❦ ❦

The President of the United States and the Prime Minister, Mr. Churchill, representing His Majesty's Government in the United Kingdom, have met at sea.

They have been accompanied by officials of their two Governments, including high ranking officers of their military, naval, and air services.

The whole problem of the supply of munitions of war, as provided by the Lease-Lend Act, for the armed forces of the United States and for those countries actively engaged in resisting aggression has been further examined.

Lord Beaverbrook, the Minister of Supply of the British Government, has joined in these conferences. He is going to proceed to Washington to discuss further details with appropriate officials of the United States Government. These conferences will also cover the supply problems of the Soviet Union.

The President and the Prime Minister have had several conferences. They have considered the dangers to world civilization arising from the policies of military domination by conquest upon which the Hitlerite Government of Germany and other Governments associated therewith have embarked, and have made clear the steps which their countries are respectively taking for their safety in the face of these dangers.

They have agreed upon the following joint declaration:

The President of the United States of America and the Prime Minister, Mr. Churchill, representing His Majesty's Government in the United Kingdom, being met together, deem it right to make known certain common principles in the national policies of their respective countries on which they base their hope for a better future for the world.

First, their countries seek no aggrandizement, territorial or other;

Second, they desire to see no territorial changes that do not accord with the freely expressed wishes of the peoples concerned;

Third, they respect the right of all peoples to choose the form of government under which they will live; and they wish to see sovereign rights and self-government restored to those who have been forcibly deprived of them;

Fourth, they will endeavor, with due respect for their existing obligations, to further the enjoyment by all states, great or small, victor or vanquished, of access, on equal terms, to the trade and to the raw materials of the world which are needed for their economic prosperity;

Fifth, they desire to bring about the fullest collaboration between all Nations in the economic field with the object of securing, for all, improved labor standards, economic advancement, and social security;

Sixth, after the final destruction of the Nazi tyranny, they hope to see established a peace which will afford to all Nations the means of dwelling in safety within their own boundaries, and which will afford assurance that all the men in all the lands may live out their lives in freedom from fear and want;

Seventh, such a peace should enable all men to traverse the high seas and oceans without hindrance;

Eighth, they believe that all of the Nations of the world, for realistic as well as spiritual reasons, must come to the abandonment of the use of force. Since no future peace can be maintained if land, sea, or air armaments continue to be employed by Nations which threaten, or may threaten, aggression outside of their frontiers, they believe, pending the establishment of a wider and permanent system of general security, that the disarmament of such Nations is essential. They will likewise aid and encourage all other practicable measures which will lighten for peace-loving peoples the crushing burden of armaments.

DOCUMENT 4

I. F. Stone, "For the Jews—Life or Death?" (1944)

The Roosevelt administration responded slowly to reports of Nazi atrocities against European Jews. In 1944 Roosevelt announced that he would consider establishing "free ports" in the United States for the internment of Jewish refugees, but he took no definite steps. In the following article written in *The Nation*, left-wing journalist I. F. Stone, outraged at the government's indecision, urged fellow journalists to put political pressure on the Roosevelt administration to open America's borders to European Jews.

❦ ❦

[At his press conference on June 2, after this article was written, the President indicated that he was considering the conversion of an army camp in this country into a "free port" for refugees. Unfortunately, as the *New York Post* has pointed out, "his statement was conditional, indefinite. The check is still on paper and we don't even know what the amount is." In these circumstances Mr. Stone's analysis of the urgency of the situation and his plea for public pressure to secure action from the Administration are no less valid than they were before Mr. Roosevelt spoke.]

Washington, June 1

This letter, addressed specifically to fellow-newspapermen and to editors the country over, is an appeal for help. The establishment of temporary internment camps for refugees in the United States, vividly named "free ports" by Samuel Grafton of the *New York Post*, is in danger of bogging down. Every similar proposal here has bogged down until it was too late to save any lives. I have been over a mass of material, some of it confidential, dealing with the plight of the fast-disappearing Jews of Europe and with the fate of suggestions for aiding them, and it is a dreadful story.

Anything newspapermen can write about this in their own papers will help. It will help to save lives, the lives of people like ourselves. I wish I were eloquent; I wish I could put down on paper the picture that comes to me from the restrained and diplomatic language of the documents. As I write, the morning papers carry a dispatch from Lisbon reporting that the "deadline"—the idiom was never more literal—has passed for the Jews of Hungary. It is approaching for the Jews of Bulgaria, where the Nazis yesterday set up a puppet regime.

I need not dwell upon the authenticated horrors of the Nazi internment camps and death chambers for Jews. That is not tragic but a kind of insane horror. It is our part in this which is tragic. The essence of tragedy is not the doing of evil by evil men but the doing of evil by good men, out of weakness, indecision, sloth, inability to act in accordance with what they know to be right. The tragic element in the fate of the Jews of Europe lies in the failure of their friends in the West to shake loose from customary ways and bureaucratic habit, to risk inexpediency and defy prejudice, to be wholehearted, to care as deeply and fight as hard for the big words we use, for justice and for humanity, as the fanatic Nazi does for his master race or the fanatic Jap for his Emperor. A reporter in Washington cannot help seeing this weakness all about him. We are halfhearted about what little we could do to help the Jews of Europe as we are half-hearted about our economic warfare, about blacklisting those who help our enemies, about almost everything in the war except the actual fighting.

There is much we could have done to save the Jews of Europe before the war. There is much we could have done since the war began. There are still things we could do today which would give new lives to a few and hope to many. The hope that all is not black in the world for his children can be strong sustenance for a man starving in a camp or entering a gas chamber. But to feel that your friends and allies are wishy-washy folk who mean what they say but haven't got the gumption to live up to it must brew a poisonous despair. When Mr. Roosevelt established the War Refugee Board in January, he said it was "the policy of this government to take all measures within its power . . . consistent with the successful prosecution of the war . . . to rescue the victims of enemy oppression."

The facts are simple. Thanks to the International Red Cross and those good folk the Quakers, thanks to courageous non-Jewish friends in the occupied countries themselves and to intrepid Jews who run a kind of underground railway under Nazi noses, something can still be done to alleviate the suffering of the Jews in Europe and some Jews can still be got out. Even under the White Paper there are still 22,000 immigration visas available for entry into Palestine. The main problem is to get Jews over the Turkish border without a passport for transit to Palestine. "Free ports" in Turkey are needed, but the Turks, irritated by other pressures from England and the United States, are unwilling to do for Jewish refugees what we ourselves are still unwilling to do, that is, give them a temporary haven. Only an executive order by the President establishing "free ports" in this country can prove to the Turks that we are dealing with them in good faith; under present circumstances they cannot but feel contemptuous of our pleas. And the longer we delay the fewer Jews there will be left to rescue, the slimmer the chances to get them out. Between 4,000,000 and 5,000,000 European Jews have been killed since August, 1942, when the Nazi extermination campaign began.

There are people here who say the President cannot risk a move of this kind before election. I believe that an insult to the American people. I do not believe any but a few unworthy bigots would object to giving a few thousand refugees a temporary breathing spell in their flight from oppression. It is a question of Mr. Roosevelt's courage and good faith. All he is called upon to do, after all, is what Franco did months ago, yes, *Franco*. Franco established "free ports," internment camps, months ago for refugees who fled across his border, refugees, let us remember, from his own ally and patron, Hitler. Knowing the Führer's maniacal hatred for Jews, that kindness on Franco's part took considerably more courage than Mr. Roosevelt needs to face a few sneering editorials, perhaps from the *Chicago Tribune*. I say "perhaps" because I do not know that even Colonel McCormick would in fact be hostile.

Official Washington's capacity for finding excuses for inaction is endless, and many people in the State and War departments who play a part in this matter can spend months sucking their legalistic thumbs over any problem. So many things that might have been done were attempted too late. A little more than a year ago Sweden offered to take 20,000 Jewish children from occupied Europe if Britain and the United States guaranteed their feeding and after the war their repatriation. The British were fairly rapid in this case, but it took three or four months to get these assurances from the American government, and by that time the situation had worsened to a point that seems to have blocked the whole project. In another case the Bulgarian government offered visas for 1,000 Jews if arrangements could be made within a certain time for their departure. A ship was obtained at once, but it took seven weeks for British officials to get clearance for the project from London, and by that time the time limit had been passed. The records, when they can be published, will show many similar incidents.

The news that the United States had established "free ports" would bring hope to people who have now no hope. It would encourage neutrals to let in more refugees because we could take out some of those they have already admitted. Most important, it would provide the argument of example and the evidence of sincerity in the negotiations for "free ports" in Turkey, last hope of the Balkan Jews. I ask fellow-newspapermen to show the President by their expressions of opinion in their own papers that if he hesitates for fear of an unpleasant political reaction he badly misconstrues the real feelings of the American people.

DOCUMENT 5

Yoshiko Uchida, Desert Exile *(1942)*

Following the Japanese attack on Pearl Harbor, an intense wave of anti-Japanese prejudice swept the West Coast, where some 120,000 men and women of Japanese ancestry resided. White Americans questioned the loyalty of Japanese Americans, fearing that they would assist a Japanese invasion of the West Coast. Convinced of the legitimacy of such fears, President Franklin Roosevelt signed a military order authorizing the removal of Japanese Americans to interior relocation camps. The Supreme Court in 1943 upheld the constitutionality of the Japanese Internment. In the following passage, Yoshiko Uchida, then a resident of Berkeley, California, recalls the days leading up to the forced removal from her home. Uchida, born in the United States, was an American citizen. Her father had emigrated to the United States from Japan in 1917. Within days of Pearl Harbor, the FBI arrested Uchida's father and imprisoned him in a detention center in Montana.

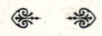

We knew it was simply a matter of time before we would be notified to evacuate Berkeley as well. A five-mile travel limit and an 8:00 P.M. curfew had already been imposed on all Japanese Americans since March, and enemy aliens were required to register and obtain identification cards. Radios with short wave, cameras, binoculars, and firearms were designated as "contraband" and had to be turned in to the police. Obediently adhering to all regulations, we even brought our box cameras to the Berkeley police station where they remained for the duration of the war.

We were told by the military that "voluntary evacuation" to areas outside the West Coast restricted zone could be made before the final notice for each sector was issued. The move was hardly "voluntary" as the Army labeled it, and most Japanese had neither the funds to leave nor a feasible destination. The three of us also considered leaving "voluntarily," but like the others, we had no one to go to outside the restricted zone.

Some of our friends warned us to consider what life would be like for three women in a "government assembly center" and urged us to go anywhere in order to remain free. On the other hand, there were those who told us of the arrests, violence, and vigilantism encountered by some who had fled "voluntarily." Either decision would have been easier had my father been with us, but without him both seemed fraught with uncertainties.

In Montana my father, too, was worried about our safety. He wrote us of an incident in Sacramento where men had gained entrance to a Japanese home by posing as FBI agents and then attacked the mother and daughter. "Please be very careful," he urged. We decided, finally, to go to the government camp where we would be with friends and presumably safe from violence. We also hoped my father's release might be facilitated if he could join us under government custody.

Each day we watched the papers for the evacuation orders covering the Berkeley area. On April 21, the headlines read: "Japs Given Evacuation Orders Here." I felt numb as I read the front page story. "Moving swiftly, without any advance notice, the Western Defense Command today ordered Berkeley's estimated 1,319 Japanese, aliens and citizens alike, evacuated to the Tanforan Assembly Center by noon, May 1." (This gave us exactly ten days' notice.) "Evacuees will report at the Civil Control Station being set up in Pilgrim Hall of the First Congregational Church . . . between the hours of 8:00 A.M. and 5:00 P.M. next Saturday and Sunday."

This was Exclusion Order Number Nineteen, which was to uproot us from our homes and send us into the Tanforan Assembly Center in San Bruno, a hastily converted racetrack.

All Japanese were required to register before the departure date, and my sister, as head of the family, went to register for us. She came home with baggage and name tags that were to bear our family number and be attached to all our belongings. From that day on we became Family Number 13453.

Although we had been preparing for the evacuation orders, still when they were actually issued, it was a sickening shock.

"Ten days! We have only ten days to get ready!" my sister said frantically. Each day she rushed about, not only taking care of our business affairs, but, as our only driver, searching for old crates and cartons for packing, and taking my mother on various errands as well.

Mama still couldn't seem to believe that we would have to leave. "How can we clear out in ten days a house we've lived in for fifteen years?" she asked sadly.

But my sister and I had no answers for her.

Mama had always been a saver, and she had a tremendous accumulation of possessions. Her frugal upbringing had caused her to save string, wrapping paper, bags, jars, boxes, even bits of silk thread left over from sewing, which were tied end to end and rolled up into a silk ball. Tucked away in the corners of her desk and bureau drawers were such things as small stuffed animals, wooden toys, *kokeshi* dolls, marbles, and even a half-finished pair of socks she was knitting for a teddy bear's paw. Many of these were "found objects" that the child in her couldn't bear to discard, but they often proved useful in providing diversion for some fidgety visiting child. These were the simple things to dispose of.

More difficult were the boxes that contained old letters from her family and friends, our old report cards from the first grade on, dozens of albums of family photographs, notebooks and sketch pads full of our childish drawings, valentines and Christmas cards we had made for our parents, innumerable guest books filled with the signatures and friendly words of those who had once been entertained. These were the things my mother couldn't bear to throw away. Because we didn't own our house, we could leave nothing behind. We had to clear the house completely, and everything in it had either to be packed for storage or thrown out.

We surveyed with desperation the vast array of dishes, lacquerware, silverware, pots and pans, books, paintings, porcelain and pottery, furniture, linens, rugs, records, curtains, garden tools, cleaning equipment, and clothing that filled our house. We put up a sign in our window reading, "Living room sofa and chair for sale." We sold things we should have kept and packed away foolish trifles we should have discarded. We sold our refrigerator, our dining room set, two sofas, an easy chair, and a brand new vacuum cleaner with attachments. Without a sensible scheme in our heads, and lacking the practical judgment of my father, the three of us packed frantically and sold recklessly. Although the young people of our church did what they could to help us, we felt desperate as the deadline approached. Our only thought was to get the house emptied in time, for we knew the Army would not wait. . . .

By now I had to leave the university, as did all the other Nisei students. We had stayed as long as we could to get credit for the spring semester, which was crucial for those of us who were seniors. My professors gave me a final grade on the basis of my midterm grades and the university granted all Nisei indefinite leaves of absence.

During the last few weeks on campus, my friends and I became sentimental and took pictures of each other at favorite campus sites. The war had jolted us into a crisis whose impact was too enormous for us to fully comprehend, and we needed these small remembrances of happier times to take with us as we went our separate ways to various government camps throughout California.

The *Daily Californian* published another letter from a Nisei student that read in part:

> We are no longer to see the campus to which many of us have been so attached for the past four years. . . . It is hoped that others who are leaving will not cherish feelings of bitterness. True, we are being uprooted from the lives that we have always lived, but if the security of the nation rests upon our leaving, then we will gladly do our part. We have come through a period of hysteria, but we cannot blame the American public for the vituperations of a small but vociferous minority of self-seeking politicians and special interest groups. We cannot condemn democracy because a few have misused the mechanism of democracy to gain their own ends. . . . In the hard days ahead, we shall try to re-create the spirit which has made us so reluctant to leave now, and our wish to those who remain is that they maintain here the democratic ideals that have operated in the past. We hope to come back and find them here.

These were brave idealistic words, but I believe they reflected the feelings of most of us at that time. . . .

The night before we left, our Swiss neighbors invited us to dinner. It was a fine feast served with our neighbors' best linens, china, and silverware. With touching concern they did their best to make our last evening in Berkeley as pleasant as possible.

I sat on the piano bench that had been in our home until a few days before and thought of the times I had sat on it when we entertained our many guests. Now, because of the alarming succession of events that even then seemed unreal, I had become a guest myself in our neighbors' home.

When we returned to our dark empty house, ur Norwegian neighbors came to say goodbye. The two girls brought gifts for each of us and hugged us goodbye.

"Come back soon," they said as they left.

But none of us knew when we would ever be back. We lay down on our mattresses and tried to sleep, knowing it was our last night in our house on Stuart Street.

DOCUMENT 6

A. Philip Randolph, "Why Should We March?" (1942)

In 1941, African American labor leader A. Philip Randolph organized the March on Washington Movement to protest discrimination in the defense industries and segregation in the armed forces. Randolph postponed the march when Roosevelt established the Fair Employment Practices Committee (FEPC), which banned racial discrimination in war industries. Understaffed and underfunded, FEPC proved only marginally successful in combatting racial discrimination in the private sector. In the following article, Randolph declares that an Allied victory over the Axis powers will be incomplete if white supremacy persists at home.

Though I have found no Negroes who want to see the United Nations lose this war, I have found many who, before the war ends, want to see the stuffing knocked out of white supremacy and of empire over subject peoples. American Negroes, involved as we are in the general issues of the conflict, are confronted not with a choice but with the challenge both to win democracy for ourselves at home and to help win the war for democracy the world over.

There is no escape from the horns of this dilemma. There ought not to be escape. For if the war for democracy is not won abroad, the fight for democracy cannot be won at home. If this war cannot be won for the white peoples, it will not be won for the darker races.

Conversely, if freedom and equality are not vouchsafed the peoples of color, the war for democracy will not be won. Unless this double-barreled thesis is accepted and applied, the darker races will never wholeheartedly fight for the victory of the United Nations. That is why those familiar with the thinking of the American Negro have sensed his lack of enthusiasm, whether among the educated or uneducated, rich or poor, professional or nonprofessional, religious or secular, rural or urban, north, south, east or west.

That is why questions are being raised by Negroes in church, labor union and fraternal society; in poolroom, barbershop, schoolroom, hospital, hair-dressing parlor; on college campus, railroad, and bus. One can hear such questions asked as these: What have Negroes to fight for? What's the difference between Hitler and that "cracker" Talmadge of Georgia? Why has a man got to be Jim Crowed to die for democracy? If you haven't got democracy yourself, how can you carry it to somebody else?

What are the reasons for this state of mind? The answer is: discrimination, segregation, Jim Crow. Witness the navy, the army, the air corps; and also government services at Washington. In many parts of the South, Negroes in Uncle Sam's uniform are being put upon, mobbed, sometimes even shot down by civilian and military police, and on occasion lynched. Vested political interests in race prejudice are so deeply entrenched that to them winning the war against Hitler is secondary to preventing Negroes from winning democracy for themselves. This is worth many divisions to Hitler and Hirohito. While labor, business, and farm are subjected to ceilings and doors and not allowed to carry on as usual, these interests trade in the dangerous business of race hate as usual.

When the defense program began and billions of the taxpayers' money were appropriated for guns, ships, tanks and bombs, Negroes presented themselves for work only to be given the cold shoulder. North as well as South, and despite their qualifications, Negroes were denied skilled employment. Not until their wrath and indignation took the form of a proposed protest march on Washington, scheduled for July 1, 1941, did things begin to move in the form of defense jobs for Negroes. The march was postponed by the timely issuance (June 25, 1941) of the famous Executive Order No. 8802 by President Roosevelt. But this order and the President's Committee on Fair Employment Practice, established thereunder, have as yet only scratched the surface by way of eliminating discriminations on account of race or color in war industry. Both management and labor unions in too many places and in too many ways are still drawing the color line.

It is to meet this situation squarely with direct action that the March on Washington Movement launched its present program of protest mass meetings. Twenty thousand were in attendance at Madison Square Garden, June 16; sixteen thousand in the Coliseum in Chicago, June 26; nine thousand in the City Auditorium of St. Louis, August 14. Meetings of such magnitude were unprecedented among Negroes. The vast throngs were drawn from all walks and levels of Negro life—businessmen, teachers, laundry workers, Pullman porters, waiters, and red caps; preachers, crapshooters, and social workers; jitterbugs and Ph.D.'s. They came and sat in silence, thinking, applauding only when they considered the truth was told, when they felt strongly that something was going to be done about it.

The March on Washington Movement is essentially a movement of the people. It is all Negro and pro-Negro, but not for that reason anti-white or anti-Semitic, or anti-Catholic, or anti-foreign, or anti-labor. Its major weapon is the non-violent demonstration of Negro mass power. Negro leadership has united back of its drive for jobs and justice. "Whether Negroes should march on Washington, and if so, when?" will be the focus of a forthcoming national conference. For the plan of a protest march has not been abandoned. Its purpose would be to demonstrate that American Negroes are in deadly earnest, and all out for their full rights. No power on earth can cause them today to abandon their fight to wipe out every vestige of second class citizenship and the dual standards that plague them.

A community is democratic only when the humblest and weakest person can enjoy the highest civil, economic, and social rights that the biggest and most powerful possess. To trample on these rights of both Negroes and poor whites is such a commonplace in the South that it takes readily to anti-social, anti-labor, anti-Semitic and anti-Catholic propaganda. It was because of laxness in enforcing the Weimar constitution in republican Germany that Nazism made headway. Oppression of the Negroes in the United States, like suppression of the Jews in Germany, may open the way for a fascist dictatorship.

By fighting for their rights now, American Negroes are helping to make America a moral and spiritual arsenal of democracy. Their fight against the poll tax, against lynch law, segregation, and Jim Crow, their fight for economic, political, and social equality, thus becomes part of the global war for freedom.

DOCUMENT 7

Sterling A. Brown, "Out of Their Mouths" (1942)

During the war, African American author Sterling Brown traveled throughout the country conducting interviews and recording conversations with black Americans. His experiences led him to conclude that "whether in army camps or juke joints or dorms or offices or commissaries or cabins or Jim Crow coaches or bus stations, I naturally found more wartime grousing than beatitudes." The following vignettes, which Brown collected, reveal the indifference many blacks expressed about defending democracy abroad while suffering prejudice and indignity at home.

Deep South—a *Soliloquy*:

"Why do you reckon white folks act like they do? I sit home studying them. A cracker is like this. He will cut his own throat just to see a Negro die along with him. Further and more, they're fussing and squabbling among theirselves so much that a man can creep up behind them unbeknownst to 'em and hit 'em on the head.

"Take Talmadge, that narrow-minded rascal. All this trouble, war, soldiers being killed by the thousands, hostages being killed, bombs falling on women and little children—and all he can do is woof about 'coeducation of the races' or 'segregation.' Somebody ought to dump him on his head in some sea or other.

"This war now. It looks like they don't want you in the navy, army, or marines. Just like before the war they didn't want you anywhere you could make a dime out of it. When those Japs first started out in the Pacific, I thought Negroes ought to thank their lucky stars that they weren't on those ships going down with the white folks. Then I got to studying and knew I was wrong. Onliest way we can get anything out of this war is to put all we can in it. That's my best judgment.

"The diffunce between the northern and the southern Negro is that the northern is a freeborn-minded Negro, but the southern is trained to say Yes-sir and No-sir all the time. That don't mean the southern Negro won't fight, but he's just more kinderhearted. The gurvenmrent is exchanging them, sending one to the north and one to the south.

"These crackers will chase a Negro like he was a jackrabbit. There ain't no right in their heart or soul.

"Do you think they will elect President Roosevelt for a fourth term? They'd better, if they know what's good for the country. I don't wish him no hard luck, but I hope he will wear out in his job. But I hope that won't be for many a long year. Yessir, I hope he dies in the White House. But I hope he lives forever. He's the best friend the Negro ever had. Bar none, Lincoln, Washington, Teddy Roosevelt. And Mrs. Roosevelt, she's the greatest woman living today.

"The party—I don't give two cents for party. My question is who's gonna do most for me, my people, all the poor people. I'm a New Dealite.

"It's remarkable how the Negro continues to keep coming on. Right out of slavery, the Negro jumped into teaching college. Course he ain't perfect. Cutting, fighting, laziness. A lot of Negroes have gone to hell and destruction fooling around with numbers and that mess. But you can't fault the Negro for that. Not much diffunce between a man robbing you in the nighttime with a gun, and robbing you in the daytime with knowledge.

"The Negroe's obstacles made a man out of him. Depression, lynching, all like that, the Negro kept coming, smiling and singing. They come on like the Japs before Singapore. You bend back the middle, the niggers (I mean Negroes) flow around the edges.

"I'm patriotic. I've got a boy in camp. Yessir, some of my blood is in the army. I love my country but I don't like the way they doing us down here in the South. . . .

Southern White Editor: "These fellows come down here and instead of doing the job with common sense, they go at it in a crusading way. They just blow open prejudices. So the died-in-the-wool traditionalist backs up, god-damning this and that to hell. The way these crusaders go about they hurt some real friends of the Negro."

Negro journalist: "Some of these southern liberals used to want to accelerate Negro progress. Now it seems that all they want to do is put on the brakes.

"A lot of white women are up in arms because they have to bring up their own children."

Dr. P. talking: . . . "The road-cop pulled up and told me I'd been exceeding the speed limit, that he'd been pacing me on the whole trip. I told him the car wouldn't go much over 40. It was a red Chrysler with wire wheels, sorta fancy. I knew he didn't like the looks of it with me behind the wheel. Both of us argued back and forth. Finally he said,'I don't know whether to shoot you or take you to jail.' "

"I said, 'Well, it won't make any difference to me. One's about as bad as the other.'

"He said, 'You don't act like you're scared at all.'

"I spoke right up. 'Why you're the last man in the world I'd be scared of. You're the *law*. You're supposed to be my protection.' "

"Man, that threw him off balance. He finally said, 'Well, Doc, you'd better watch yourself. There's a couple fellows in a pepped-up Ford (that's a Ford with a Frontenac head) on the road that are kinda mean. They'd like to pick you up in a car like this. So you take it easy now.' "

"Then he growled at me, 'But you know damn well you were doing more than 40 miles an hour.' "

White liberal: "This Negro soldier was sitting on a seat opposite to a white man. The bus was not crowded, and he wasn't sitting in front of any white. But the driver came back and told him to move. He refused. The driver shouted, 'I'm gonna move you.' The Negro took his coat off and said, 'Well I'm fixing to go off and fight for democracy. I might as well start right now.' And I want to tell you that bus driver backed down. It did me good to see it."

Harlemite (shortly after Pearl Harbor): "All these radio announcers talking about yellow this, yellow that. Don't hear them calling the Nazis white this, pink that. What in hell color do they think the Chinese are anyway! And those Filipinos on Bataan? And the British Imperial Army, I suppose they think they're all blondes?"

Folk Tales: "They're telling the story that a cracker running a lunchroom at a railroad junction got a wire ordering lunches for 500 soldiers. He got together all the bread and eggs and chickens and coffee and stuff he could. When the troop train pulled in he saw they were Negroes. He ran to the officer in charge: 'You said 500 *soldiers*. Those are just Nigra boys.' The officer told him they were soldiers in the uniform of their country. Man kept on: 'You said *soldiers*. I can't serve those boys in my place.' The captain wouldn't budge. Finally the man said to the white officers, 'Well, y'all can come in and eat but I'll have to put their food in boxes. I reckon I can stir up that many boxes.'

" 'No; these men must eat hot food.'

"But that cracker wouldn't give in. So the boys went unfed. The story goes that all the townspeople went together and put in so much money apiece to save white supremacy and the lunchroom man's money."

DOCUMENT 8

Juanita Loveless, from Rosie the Riveter Revisited (1942–1945)

Many women welcomed the opportunity to work in defense industries. Women could dutifully serve the war effort while seizing new opportunities for personal and economic freedom. Juanita Loveless, the daughter of a Texas dirt farmer, was one of those women. In 1941, at the age of seventeen she left her family in Oklahoma and moved to Hollywood, California, where she soon took a job at Vega Aircraft. In the following interview, conducted in 1986, Loveless recalls her mixed experiences as a working woman during the war. She describes the excitement of establishing economic independence but also the boredom and dangers of defense work. Although she found herself swept up by patriotic appeals to "help the boys," her testimony also alludes vividly to the decline of morale among many Americans as the war dragged on and foreshadows the disillusionment many Americans would experience in the postwar years.

❧ ❧

They were begging for workers. They didn't care whether you were black, white, young, old. They didn't really care if you could work: It got even worse in '43. I worked two jobs for a long time. I had so much work offered to me and I was not even qualified—I just had the capability of learning very fast. Within three weeks of coming to California my mind was dazzled with all the offers I had. Before the war, in Oklahoma City and in California, I'd ask people if I could get a job and they'd say: "Well, you're not old enough." But here I didn't even have to look. I was having people approach me six to ten times a day—RCA Victor wanted me to come work for them; Technicolor said they'd train me.

Actually what attracted me—it was not the money and it was not the job because I didn't even know how much money I was going to make. But the ads—they had to be bombardments: "Do Your Part," "Uncle Sam Needs You," "V for Victory." I got caught up in that patriotic "win the war," "help the boys." The patriotism that was so strong in everyone then.

Anyhow, Vega Aircraft was the first one I learned about. Someone came in two or three times to the station to get me to come to the application office. One day I said, "I'll be off tomorrow and I'll go and fill out papers." I called this girl I had met and we went together. We both went for the same job, but she was immediately hired for a more educated job because she had finished high school. I went on the assembly line....

It was very dull, very boring. The first day I thought, "Oh, this is ridiculous. I have to set here for three weeks on this bench?" What we did was we learned to buck and then we learned to rivet. I set there for three or four hours that first day and I picked up the rivet gun: "You show me once and I'll do it for you." The bucking, you have a bar. I said, "What's to learn here? Look at my hands. I've been working as a grease monkey. I could do this. I don't have to set here and train." I learned very fast.

I went into the shell the next day. First I went inside and I bucked, and then I went outside and I riveted. I was working with real seasoned workable men and it was so easy. We did strip by strip, the whole hull. We used strips of like cheesecloth and paste that had to go on the inside and across the seam. I had to do that. Then, as the riveter outside riveted, I was inside bucking. It would be like a sewing machine, you just sort of have to go along with them.

I stayed there maybe six weeks, and I worked on all parts of it, up in the wings. One by one, day by day, new faces. I would say within six months there were maybe twenty or thirty men left in Department 16 where maybe there had been fifteen hundred. One by one they disappeared. I'd have a group leader one day and two or three days later he was gone. Leadman, two or three days later he was gone. There were men in the tool crib and one by one they disappeared.

As they recruited more and more women, men with deferments were the ones that actually remained to work. Even a lot of the young women working would disappear, going into the service. I made friends with four or five girls that became WACS and WAVES and nurses. It was very more difficult to keep friends, because they came and they went so fast. . . .

I had so much work sometimes, I wouldn't even go back for my money. Sometimes they'd just mail me a check and I'd think, "Gee, now where was this?" At one period of time I had six or eight checks laying in my dresser drawer that I hadn't even cashed. I simply didn't know how to handle money. The first paycheck I got in aircraft was more money than I'd ever seen in my life. I didn't even know what to do with it. I didn't have a bank account. You couldn't buy anything much.

But we'd hang out in drive-ins or the bowling alleys. And we went to places like the Hangover, Tropics, Knickerbocker Hotel, Blackouts, Garden of Allah, Har'O Mar, the Haig on Wilshire. I was going into bars and drinking. One of my favorites was the Jade on Hollywood Boulevard. Another was the Merry-Go-Round on Vine Street. When Nat King Cole sat at the piano and sang, he wasn't even known and the piano bar went round. This was long before I ever reached twenty-one.

At first there was great resistance to women taking wartime jobs, but the need for workers soon eclipsed the stereotypical view that women could not handle what had traditionally been "men's" work. By 1945, some nineteen million women were employed, many in heavy industry, as machine tool operators, welders, and riveters.

We found places like the beach, the pier, on our day off. I think that was on Sunday, 'cause some of us were on a six-day schedule. But we hung out, we read poetry, we discussed books that were current and popular. One book was passed from one to another. It was word of honor, really; you'd pass your book on to the next person and it would eventually get back to you. And movies, mainly movies. We'd sit in the lobbies.

Young people got together in harmless, easy companion ways. Dancing was great. You got rid of your energy by dancing. You'd get a little radio and put it out on the back porch or the lawn where you were living and had everybody come over. That was it. There were no cars racing around. We had a lot of blackouts so you couldn't have outdoor picnics or beach parties.

Oh, I'll tell you where we met, workers and their relatives, brothers, sisters, boyfriends, soldiers, sailors, families. At the Biltmore Hotel. They had a tea dance in the afternoon and when my brother would come in with his friends, we'd go there. We'd bring girlfriends to dance with my brother's boyfriends or our boyfriends would bring in friends and we'd get the girls together. It really didn't make any difference, but years later I found out a lot of these friends were homosexuals. At that time I didn't even know what it meant. They were "in the closet," so to speak. I don't think many of the gays realized they were gay....

Then I began to see boys coming back. One fellow I'd gone with in 1942, I got off the bus and I'm walking home and I heard: "tap, tap, tap." I turned around and looked and I thought: "Gee, a soldier in uniform with a cane." I turned back again and I said, "My God, it's Dick." Still in uniform. He came home blind. That was my very first shock, seeing him come back blind. He could see just a little, but later became totally blind—at twenty-three years! There were two or three other fellows I had known at the bowling alley who I went with, my age. When I began to see them coming back like this, it really did something to me....

I quit because I'd look around me on the outside and I saw people not working in aircraft living an easy life. Women I had known, some that had worked and quit right away, went in and worked three or four weeks and said, "This is not for me. Forget it. To hell with it." This is touchy. I don't know how to bring this up. The morale was not that strong at the end. On our day off, we saw our friends in the neighborhood that were not working in aircraft: "I know this fellow that owns this store and I can get you anything you want"; "I can get it for you wholesale." You heard stories of people buying up the Japanese stores and of hoards of supplies in warehouses. Soap was rationed, butter, Kleenex, toilet paper, toothpaste, cigarettes, clothing, shoes. And you saw these people making a lot of money and not doing anything for the war effort, even bragging: "I kept my son out of it." You thought here are these special, privileged types of people and here I am working and sweating and eating our hearts out for the casualty lists that are coming in.

By 1944 a lot of people were questioning the war. "Why the hell are we in it?" We were attacked by the Japanese and were fighting to defend our honor. But still, this other side had the Cadillacs and the "I

The Hiroshima aftermath from the atomic bomb dropped on August 6, 1945. Years later, many view the dropping of the atomic bomb on Hiroshima and the second bomb dropped three days later on Nagasaki as the first acts of the Cold War between the United States and the Soviet Union. Japan unconditionally surrendered to the Allied Powers on August 14, 1945, bringing an end to the bloodiest war in world history.

can get it for you wholesale." They suddenly owned all the mom-and-pop stores and suddenly owned all the shoe factories. The rumblings began with that—and the discontent.

It raced through the plant, through the bowling alleys, through all the places where the young people got together. We began to break away from the older generation. We said, "Well, they brought the war on." I think when we actually began to see the boys come home in late 1943, 1944—those that had been injured had started coming back—then the rumbles grew into roars, and the young people thought maybe they were being led into this. Maybe if we would stop working so hard, they would end the war. There was also rumors that they were holding Patton back and that they were prolonging the war. That was what got us!!

I got an aversion to making anything that would hurt anybody. But I probably wouldn't have stayed in aircraft, anyway, because my skin disease got worse. It started out like a psoriasis patch and it scaled and I scratched, and I got it on my arms, my neck, my face, everyplace where I was exposed. But I had a change of heart again when I heard that my brother had been injured. I went to work for Hartman making small parts, bench work, which I hated. I stayed there about three months and I said, "This is no good. I can't do this. I've been too active and I've been a racehorse too long." I used to run up and down that plant and it must have been a mile long from one end to another.

But I felt I ought to do something to contribute. Then I reasoned with myself that I was buying war bonds, that's enough, and I'm a member of the USO. I'm doing my share! I would never have stayed as long as I did if I hadn't been motivated by the fact that in my mind war was hell. I could visualize it, but I wanted to black out some of it. I never went to see a war picture and I never wanted to read a newspaper. I never wanted to know what was going on. Maybe the older people did, but the young people didn't want to hear about what was happening in the war; they just wanted to know we were winning.

The workers in aircraft hated it. I don't care whether they worked on the assembly or the training bench, the cockpit or in the wings or the tail; whether they riveted, wired, or were the managers or group leaders; whether they were in the final assembly—I have yet to meet one who really enjoyed it. The final assembly was the best job of all because you got out of the heat and you got out of the noise. The heat and the noise, I don' know how I ever lived through it. And I've kept in touch with two or three of the women that I worked with, and most of them have tremendous hearing problems. Most of them say it came from that noise.

I would never do it again! Never, ever!!! I don't think any other woman would either. They might say they would, but no, I don't think if most women would really be truthful with you, they enjoyed working or would have stayed in it if they hadn't really been motivated by patriotism or actually having a member of the family in the war. Some used it as an excuse to break out into the world. And it was the first decent opportunity Negro women had to get away from domestic work.

Study Questions

1. Which did more to transform society, World War II or the New Deal? Why?

2. How did various Americans expand Roosevelt's Four Freedoms?

3. Are the noninterventionist arguments of people like Lindbergh convincing?

4. Many commentators have celebrated women's entry into the work force in World War II. Does Juanita Loveless's experience confirm or contradict the heroic Rosie the Riveter image?

5. World War II has often been called the "good war." What might people mean by that phrase?

10

The Culture of Prosperity

Many Americans believed that the Allied victory in World War II signaled a new world order of lasting peace abroad and perpetual prosperity at home. But within a year, hope turned to cynicism (Document 1). Soviet domination of Eastern Europe, rumors of Communist infiltration of the U.S. State Department, and fear of imminent nuclear war brought forth an era of anxiety in which Americans longed for security from threats, both foreign and domestic, real and imagined.

Postwar diplomats attempted to formulate a foreign policy ensuring American security in the emerging "cold war" with the Soviet Union. Policy analysts such as George F. Kennan initially envisioned a strategy in which the United States would check Soviet expansion, not through direct confrontation, but by assisting the development of democratic societies outside the Soviet bloc (Document 2). By the end of the 1940s, however, Communist revolution in China, news that the Soviet Union had developed an atomic bomb, and invasion of South Korea had convinced policymakers that only a massive military buildup and commitment to nuclear supremacy could guarantee security in a hostile world (Document 3). To calm popular fears of the bomb and to discredit advocates of nuclear disarmament, the government sponsored a series of civil-defense pamphlets minimizing the threat of harm from radiation and boldly proclaiming that men and women could survive a nuclear attack if they observed a set of easy-to-follow survival rules (Document 4).

Many Americans found solace through conformity to the new norms of suburban society. Beginning in the late 1940s, a massive building boom of affordable housing attracted millions of Americans who desired escape from urban congestion. During the 1950s, the number of American homeowners increased by more than nine million, the suburban population grew by 46 percent, and by decade's end nearly a third of the nation lived in suburban communities. Most who fled to the suburbs were young, white, and middle or lower middle class. Out of the cornfields surrounding the nation's central cities, suburbanites carved a new society and redefined the American dream.

Many suburbanites found security in the religious revival of the 1950s. They joined churches in record numbers, swelling nationwide membership from less than 50 percent of the population in 1940 to more than 63 percent by the late 1950s. The revival downplayed doctrine and theology, stressing instead common moral virtues and religiosity in general. President Dwight Eisenhower summed up this popular attitude toward religion when he declared, "I am the most intensely religious man I know; that does not mean I adhere to any sect." This nonsectarian religiosity found clearest articulation in Norman Vincent Peale's cult of positive thinking. Like civil defense pamphleteers, Peale assured Americans that security, happiness, and the good life were simply a matter of following a "how to" formula (Document 5).

Social critics such as David Riesman and William H. Whyte satirized the conformist character of the new suburbs. They found in communities like Park Forest, Illinois, that the values of individualism, self-discipline, and hard work had given way to a new social ethic that esteemed adjustment to group norms, an ethic ideally suited to corporate America. Suburban homes, churches, and schools, critics argued, reinforced this ethic of "belongingness" and produced a mass of uncritical conformists whose politics were as bland as their religion (Document 6).

Suburbanites established new norms for family life. The shift in population to the suburbs accompanied a postwar baby boom. Where American families in the 1930s averaged only one or two children, young couples of the 1950s had four or five. Many young suburban households subsisted on the income of both husband and wife. Once the household was established, however, most suburban women assumed the role of homemaker, often working as many as eighty-four hours of unpaid labor a week raising children and attending to household chores (Document 7). The suburban boom also stimulated the consumer-goods industries, which manufactured the cars, televisions, and appliances that homeowners demanded. Suburban teenagers comprised one of the fastest-growing groups of consumers, spending more than $10 billion a year (Document 8).

Viewed through the lens of suburbia, social commentators of the period concluded that only one class, adhering to a conservative consensus, existed in the United States. But critics objected that the flight to the suburbs had left the nation's cities gutted of resources and had led to an unprecedented separation of the affluent from the impoverished. Thus the poor, argued Michael Harrington, had "become increasingly invisible" to the middle class. He warned that unless the United States rededicated itself to the eradication of poverty, millions of Americans would continue to suffer needlessly in the richest country in the world (Document 9).

DOCUMENT 1

Kenneth MacFarland, "The Unfinished Work" (1946)

Within a year of the Allied victory, many social commentators observed that Americans feared for their country's security and doubted its ability to solve its own problems. In the following radio address delivered in September 1946, Kenneth

MacFarland, superintendent of schools in Topeka, Kansas, sounds this note of despair. Like many Americans, MacFarland believed that well-organized, well-financed Communists had infiltrated and risen to powerful positions within U.S. society and were plotting to subvert the postwar recovery. He urged Americans to rededicate themselves to the principles of democracy and demonstrate to the world that those ideals, not those of the collectivist Soviet Union, offered the best hope for peace and prosperity.

One who traveled about over the country a year ago this month, talking with taxi drivers, bell hops, policemen, business employees, and others who reflect the thinking of the man-on-the-street, found the conversation all to be along the same lines. The war was over, the boys would be coming home now, rationing would end. Truman was doing better than expected, we must resolutely work together to build one world in which war would be outlawed and the principles of the Atlantic Charter would hold sway. The keynote a year ago was one of joyous relief that the bloodiest conflict in all history had ended in complete victory over the enemy, and a feeling of faith that we had at last learned our lesson sufficiently well to outlaw war. There was confidence that an effective United Nations organization would be developed.

But today, one year after, that buoyant faith has turned to cynicism. Hope in the United Nations is largely gone. The average American has already resigned himself to a future in which there will be at least two worlds instead of one. Having given up his hope for a better world, the average man has ceased to realize how terribly important it is that we keep striving, and he has settled down to bickering over a myriad of minor issues here on the domestic scene. . . .

There is a strange fear and insecurity in America today. The people fear that in winning the war we introduced a new power into the world which may in turn engulf us. As James Reston says in a recent article,

"Among the reflective people of the country, among the leaders of the communities and those who aspire to political office, fear for the security of America and doubt about the ability of America to solve its own problems seem stronger today than ever in memory.

"It is an astonishing fact, but after an unprecedented war in which the enemies on the field of battle were entirely defeated, the people seem to feel less secure than they did before they were attacked, or even when the tide of war was running strongest against them."

In this year that has passed since the ending of the war we have found we cannot immediately shut off the hates that were generated during the struggle. Racial tensions have burst into open flame. Minority groups are being terrorized by hoodlums who seek only personal gain from such persecution. There is unprecedented confusion in our political life. Special interest groups raise slush funds to purge congressmen who failed to support their particular legislative programs. Many politicians totally forget the sacred obligation of public office holding and appeal to the basest motives to win re-election. Yes, America has retrogressed to a dangerous degree in the 387 days since General MacArthur proclaimed to the world that Japan had surrendered unconditionally. We have lost the faith that won the fight just when we needed it most to win the peace. *We have demobilized our patriotism far too soon.* . . .

Today there is a powerfully organized force that is working unceasingly to prolong the confusion. This is the first post-war period in which we have had to contend with a highly organized effort to prevent recovery. *We are fools unless we awaken to the fact that a great campaign is being carried on in America today to perpetuate chaos, and that campaign is being directed from abroad by a force that wants democracy to fail.* This highly organized and well financed power reaches into key positions in numerous organizations and publications, institutions of learning, and into the government itself. There is the new, the unprecedented, and by far the most dangerous element in the clashing cross currents which torment our times.

The identical force which is spreading the gospel of despair and dissension in America today is almost solely responsible for the black cloud that obscures the sunshine of peace on the international horizon. Out in Salt Lake City on the twelfth day of last month, America's only living Ex-President, Herbert Clark Hoover, said,

"The dominant note in the world today is not one of hope and confidence, but rather one of fear and frustration. . . . Far from freedom having been expanded in this war, it has been shrunk to far fewer nations than a quarter of a century ago . . . and it is Russia that blocks the almost universal desire for peace."

It is Russia, Hoover said, that is deliberately stalling the peace conference while it communizes Eastern Europe and exploits its economic resources. Whether we agree with Mr. Hoover or not, it can scarcely be gainsaid that behind the iron curtain which Russia has drawn across Europe lie eleven nations that were formerly independent—and that represents more countries than Hitler ever conquered. Yes, we cannot deny that the beautiful blue Danube, which turned brown when Hitler's legions marched in, has now turned to red.

No doubt the vast population of Russia yearns for peace as ardently as we do. Yet between that great people and ourselves stands the Russian government. That government consists of a group of revolutionaries who are determined that no other Russian government shall come to power the same way they did. Skilled in the school of sabotage and intrigue, that government stands today as an absolute dictatorship, wielding the power of Russia in world councils, and withholding the knowledge of the world from its own people.

So ominous is the threat of this new and unpredictable world power that the average man has all but abandoned his high hopes for permanent peace. . . .

It is in such a world and such a time that September comes again, and the miracle of the great American school system once more unfolds before eyes that have grown tired of searching for light. As millions of bright eyed youngsters put their books under their arms and trudge to school each September the world never fails to take on renewed hope. There is a dawn of a better day in the faces of the children and it simply will not be denied. Let us use this occasion and this inspiration to arouse ourselves from aimless lethargy and "to rededicate ourselves to the unfinished work." These children *must* have a future. We cannot deny them. We must build a better world. We cannot fail.

To what specific ends shall these high resolves be directed? Briefly, the goals are these:

First, *let us make democracy work.* As John Fischer so well states in his "Scared Men in the Kremlin," it is not the Red army but the communistic *idea* that we must overcome. This can be done only by demonstrating conclusively to the world that it is democracy, and not the regimented society of Russia, that can best eliminate unemployment, avoid depressions, and develop a world in which war cannot survive. We must unite behind this goal and demonstrate by actual practice the limitless power and possibilities of the democratic way of life.

Secondly, *our leadership must constantly call forth our best instead of so frequently appealing to our worst.* Our political leaders must have faith in an aroused and properly led America. Not once in our history have our people betrayed or forsaken a great leader who held out a great ideal and based his plea upon moral grounds. Our leaders must return to that great premise and be done with appeals to greed, selfishness, group interest, and class hatred.

Third, *we must rededicate ourselves to the determination that we shall not be pushed around by any dictatorship, that we shall not compromise with the immortal democratic principle of the dignity and freedom of the individual citizen everywhere.*

And finally, *we must not grow faint in our efforts to outlaw war.* The alternative is death. As the Baruch Report declares, "The choice is between the quick and the dead." Harold Fey put it well when he said that after every war the nations have put their trust in weapons which have but compounded their jeopardy. Now God has grown weary of the age old cycle. Lifting the lid on the atom, God has at last said to the world, "Choose life, or choose death, but *choose!*"

We, the living, *must* rededicate ourselves to the unfinished work.

DOCUMENT 2

George F. Kennan, "Long Telegram" (1946)

George Kennan, chargé d'affaires at the U.S. embassy in Moscow, won acclaim for his analysis of Soviet conduct. In his famous "Long Telegram" of February 1946, Kennan argued that Soviet leaders would pursue a policy of aggression in order to justify their own autocratic rule at home. Kennan insisted that the United States could contain Soviet imperialism by fostering viable democratic states outside the Communist bloc. Kennan's telegram established the framework for the U.S. strategy of containment. As President Harry Truman proclaimed in 1947, "it must be the policy of the United States to support free peoples who are resisting attempted subjugation by armed minorities or by outside pressure."

We have here a political force committed fanatically to the belief that with US there can be no permanent *modus vivendi*, that it is desirable and necessary that the internal harmony of our society be disrupted, our traditional way of life be destroyed, the international authority of our state be broken, if Soviet power is to be secure. This political force has complete power of disposition over energies of one of world's greatest peoples and resources of world's richest national territory, and is borne along by deep and powerful currents of Russian nationalism. In addition, it has an elaborate and far flung apparatus for exertion of its influence in other countries, and apparatus of amazing flexibility and versatility, managed by people whose experience and skill in underground methods are presumably without parallel in history. Finally, it is seemingly inaccessible to considerations of reality in its basic reactions. For it, the vast fund of objective fact about human society is not, as with us, the measure against which outlook is constantly being tested and re-formed, but a grab bag from which individual items are selected arbitrarily and tendentiously to bolster an outlook already preconceived. This is admittedly not a pleasant picture. Problem of how to cope with this force in [is] undoubtedly greatest task our diplomacy has ever faced and probably greatest it will ever have to face. It should be point of departure from which our political general staff work at present juncture should proceed. It should be approached with same thoroughness and care as solution of major strategic problem in war, and if necessary, with no smaller outlay in planning effort. I cannot attempt to suggest all answers here. But I would like to record my conviction that problem is within our power to solve—and that without recourse to any general military conflict. And in support of this conviction there are certain observations of a more encouraging nature I should like to make:

(1) Soviet power, unlike that of Hitlerite Germany, is neither schematic nor adventuristic. It does not work by fixed plans. It does not take unnecessary risks. Impervious to logic of reason, and it is highly sensitive to logic of force. For this reason it can easily withdraw—and usually does—when strong resistance is encountered at any point. Thus, if the adversary has sufficient force and makes clear his readiness to use it, he rarely has to do so. If situations are properly handled there need be no prestige-engaging showdowns.

(2) Gauged against Western World as a whole, Soviets are still by far the weaker force. Thus, their success will really depend on degree of cohesion, firmness and vigor which Western World can muster. And this is factor which it is within our power to influence.

(3) Success of Soviet system, as form of internal power, is not yet finally proven. It has yet to be demonstrated that it can survive supreme test of successive transfer of power from one individual or group to another. Lenin's death was first such transfer, and its effects wracked Soviet state for 15 years. After Stalin's death or retirement will be second. But even this will not be final test. Soviet internal system will now be subjected, by virtue of recent territorial expansions, to series of additional strains which once proved severe tax on Tsardom. We here are convinced that never since termination of civil war have mass of Russian people been emotionally farther removed from doctrines of Communist Party than they are today. In Russia, party has now become a great and—for the moment—highly successful apparatus of dictatorial administration, but it has ceased to be a source of emotional inspiration.

Thus, internal soundness and permanence of movement need not yet be regarded as assured.

(4) All Soviet propaganda beyond Soviet security sphere is basically negative and destructive. It should therefore be relatively easy to combat it by any intelligent and really constructive program.

For these reasons I think we may approach calmly and with good heart problem of how to deal with Russia. As to how this approach should be made, I only wish to advance, by way of conclusion, following comments:

(1) Our first step must be to apprehend, and recognize for what it is, the nature of the movement with which we are dealing. We must study it with same courage, detachment, objectivity, and same determination not to be emotionally provoked or unseated by it, with which doctor studies unruly and unreasonable individual.

(2) We must see that our public is educated to realities of Russian situation. I cannot over-emphasize importance of this. Press cannot do this alone. It must be done mainly by Government, which is necessarily more experienced and better informed on practical problems involved. In this we need not be deterred by [ugliness?] of picture. I am convinced that there would be far less hysterical anti-Sovietism in our country today if realities of this situation were better understood by our people. There is nothing as dangerous or as terrifying as the unknown. It may also be argued that to reveal more information on our difficulties with Russia would reflect unfavorably on Russian-American relations. I feel that if there is any real risk here involved, it is one which we should have courage to face, and sooner the better. But I cannot see what we would be risking. Our stake in this country, even coming on heels of tremendous demonstrations of our friendship for Russian people, is remarkably small. We have here no investments to guard, no actual trade to lose, virtually no citizens to protect, few cultural contacts to preserve. Our only stake lies in what we hope rather than what we have; and I am convinced we have better chance of realizing those

hopes if our public is enlightened and if our dealings with Russians are placed entirely on realistic and matter-of-fact basis.

(3) Much depends on health and vigor of our own society. World communism is like malignant parasite which feeds only on diseased tissue. This is point at which domestic and foreign policies meet. Every courageous and incisive measure to solve internal problems of our own society, to improve self-confidence, discipline, morale and community spirit of our own people, is a diplomatic victory over Moscow worth a thousand diplomatic notes and joint communiqués. If we cannot abandon fatalism and indifference in face of deficiencies of our own society, Moscow will profit—Moscow cannot help profiting by them in its foreign policies.

(4) We must formulate and put forward for other nations a much more positive and constructive picture of sort of world we would like to see than we have put forward in past. It is not enough to urge people to develop political processes similar to our own. Many foreign peoples, in Europe at least, are tired and frightened by experiences of past, and are less interested in abstract freedom than in security. They are seeking guidance rather than responsibilities. We should be better able than Russians to give them this. And unless we do, Russians certainly will.

(5) Finally we must have courage and self-confidence to cling to our own methods and conceptions of human society. After all, the greatest danger that can befall us in coping with this problem of Soviet communism, is that we shall allow ourselves to become like those with whom we are coping.

DOCUMENT 3

National Security Council Memorandum Number 68 (1950)

In response to a presidential directive to reassess U.S. strategic policy, a group of analysts in the State and Defense Departments issued National Security Council Memorandum Number 68 (NSC-68) in 1950. When the Soviet Union acquired atomic technology in 1949, planners in Washington began to doubt earlier assessments that the Soviet Union would never initiate a war against the United States. The authors of NSC-68 projected that by 1954 the Soviet Union would possess the capability to start a war with reasonable prospects of winning. NSC-68 recommended that the United States pursue a course of massive military expansion, including stockpiling atomic weapons. The outbreak of hostilities in Korea in 1950 seemed to confirm the validity of the analysis presented in NSC-68, and the White House approved it as official policy. By late 1950, the United States had committed itself to the largest peacetime military buildup in the country's history.

Within the past thirty-five years the world has experienced two global wars of tremendous violence. It has witnessed two revolutions—the Russian and the Chinese—of extreme scope and intensity. It has also seen the collapse of five empires—the Ottoman, the Austro-Hungarian, German, Italian and Japanese—and the drastic decline of two major imperial systems, the British and the French. During the span of one generation, the international distribution of power has been fundamentally altered. For several centuries it had proved impossible for any one nation to gain such preponderant strength that a coalition of other nations could not in time face it with greater strength. The international scene was marked by recurring periods of violence and war, but a system of sovereign and independent states was maintained, over which no state was able to achieve hegemony.

Two complex sets of factors have now basically altered this historical distribution of power. First, the defeat of Germany and Japan and the decline of the British and French Empires have interacted with the development of the United States and the Soviet Union in such a way that power has increasingly gravitated to these two centers. Second, the Soviet Union, unlike previous aspirants to hegemony, is animated by a new fanatic faith, antithetical to our own, and seeks to impose its absolute authority over the rest of the world. Conflict has, therefore, become endemic and is waged, on the part of the Soviet Union, by violent or non-violent methods in accordance with the dictates of expediency. With the development of increasingly terrifying weapons of mass destruction, every individual faces the ever-present possibility of annihilation should the conflict enter the phase of total war.

On the one hand, the people of the world yearn for relief from the anxiety arising from the risk of atomic war. On the other hand, any substantial further extension of the area under the domination of the Kremlin would raise the possibility that no coalition adequate to confront the Kremlin with greater strength could be assembled. It is in this context that this Republic and its citizens in the ascendancy of their strength stand in their deepest peril. . . .

Military Evaluation of U.S. and U.S.S.R. Atomic Capabilities

1. The United States now has an atomic capability, including both numbers and deliverability, estimated to be adequate, if effectively utilized, to deliver a serious blow against the war-making capacity of the U.S.S.R. It is doubted whether such a blow, even if it resulted in the complete destruction of the contemplated target systems, would cause the U.S.S.R. to sue for terms or present [prevent] Soviet forces from occupying Western Europe against such ground resistance as could presently be mobilized. A very serious initial blow could, however, so reduce the capabilities of the U.S.S.R. to supply and equip its military organization and its civilian population as to give the United States the prospect of developing a general military superiority in a war of long duration.

2. As the atomic capability of the U.S.S.R. increases, it will have an increased ability to hit at our atomic bases and installations and thus seriously hamper the ability of the United States to carry out an attack such as that outlined above. It is quite possible that in the near future the U.S.S.R. will have a sufficient number of atomic bombs and a sufficient deliverability to raise a question whether Britain with its present inadequate air defense could be relied upon as an advance base from which a major portion of the U.S. attack could be launched.

It is estimated that, within the next four years, the U.S.S.R. will attain the capability of seriously damaging vital centers of the United States, provided it strikes a surprise blow and provided further that the blow is opposed by no more effective opposition than we now have programmed. Such a blow could so seriously damage the United States as to greatly reduce its superiority in economic potential.

Effective opposition to this Soviet capability will require among other measures greatly increased air warning systems, air defenses, and vigorous development and implementation of a civilian defense program which has been thoroughly integrated with the military defense systems.

In time the atomic capability of the U.S.S.R. can be expected to grow to a point where, given surprise and no more effective opposition than we now have programmed, the possibility of a decisive initial attack cannot be excluded.

3. In the initial phases of an atomic war, the advantages of initiative and surprise would be very great. A police state living behind an iron curtain has an enormous advantage in maintaining the necessary security and centralization of decision required to capitalize on this advantage.

4. For the moment our atomic retaliatory capability is probably adequate to deter the Kremlin from a deliberate direct military attack against ourselves or other free peoples. However, when it calculates that it has a sufficient atomic capability to make a surprise attack on us, nullifying our atomic superiority and creating a military situation decisively in its favor, the Kremlin might be tempted to strike swiftly and with stealth. The existence of two large atomic capabilities in such a relationship might well act, therefore, not as a deterrent, but as an incitement to war.

5. A further increase in the number and power of our atomic weapons is necessary in order to assure the effectiveness of any U.S. retaliatory blow, but would not of itself seem to change the basic logic of the above points. Greatly increased general air, ground and sea strength, and increased air defense and civilian defense programs would also be necessary to provide reasonable assurance that the free world could survive an initial surprise atomic attack of the weight which it is estimated the U.S.S.R. will be capable of delivering by 1954 and still permit the free world to go on to the eventual attainment of its objectives. Furthermore, such a build-up of strength could safeguard and increase our retaliatory power, and thus might put off for some time the date when the Soviet Union could calculate that a surprise blow would be advantageous. This would provide additional time for the effects of our policies to produce a modification of the Soviet system.

6. If the U.S.S.R. develops a thermonuclear weapon ahead of the U.S., the risks of greatly increased Soviet pressure against all the free world, or an attack against the U.S., will be greatly increased.

7. If the U.S. develops a thermonuclear weapon ahead of the U.S.S.R., the U.S. should for the time being be able to bring increased pressure on the U.S.S.R. . . .

In the light of present and prospective Soviet atomic capabilities, the action which can be taken under present programs and plans, however, becomes dangerously inadequate, in both timing and scope, to accomplish the rapid progress toward the attainment of the United States political, economic, and military objectives which is now imperative.

A continuation of present trends would result in a serious decline in the strength of the free world relative to the Soviet Union and its satellites. This unfavorable trend arises from the inadequacy of current programs and plans rather than from any error in our objectives and aims. These trends lead in the direction of isolation, not by deliberate decision but by lack of the necessary basis for a vigorous initiative in the conflict with the Soviet Union.

Our position as the center of power in the free world places a heavy responsibility upon the United States for leadership. We must organize and enlist the energies and resources of the free world in a positive program for peace which will frustrate the Kremlin design for world domination by creating a situation in the free world to which the Kremlin will be compelled to adjust. Without such a cooperative effort, led by the United States, we will have to make gradual withdrawals under pressure until we discover one day that we have sacrificed positions of vital interest.

It is imperative that this trend be reversed by a much more rapid and concerted build-up of the actual strength of both the United States and the other nations of the free world. The analysis shows that this will be costly and will involve significant domestic financial and economic adjustments.

The execution of such a build-up, however, requires that the United States have an affirmative program beyond the solely defensive one of countering the threat posed by the Soviet Union. This program must light the path to peace and order among nations in a system based on freedom and justice, as contemplated in the Charter of the United Nations. Further, it must envisage the political and economic measures with which and the military shield behind which the free world can work to frustrate the Kremlin design by the strategy of the cold war; for every consideration of devotion to our fundamental values and to our national security demands that we achieve our objectives by the strategy of the cold war, building up our military strength in order that it may not have to be used. The only sure victory lies in the frustration of the Kremlin design by the steady development of the moral and material strength of the free world and its projection into the Soviet world in such a way as to bring about an internal change in the Soviet system. Such a positive program—harmonious with our fundamental national purpose and our objectives—is necessary if we are to regain and retain the initiative and to win and hold the necessary popular support and cooperation in the United States and the rest of the free world.

DOCUMENT 4

Richard Gerstell, "How You Can Survive an Atomic Bomb Blast" (1950)

NSC-68 recommended that the government expand its civil defense program. To do so it recruited Richard Gerstell, a former Navy lieutenant commander and radiologist, who had studied the effects of radiation at American atomic testing sites. Gerstell wrote the widely distributed pamphlet *How to Survive an Atomic Bomb*, as well as various articles for popular magazines such as the following excerpt from *The Saturday Evening Post*. The casual tone of this and other civil defense reports seemed directed more at reassuring an uneasy populace and at securing popular support for American nuclear expansion than at proposing a realistic plan for coping with an atomic disaster.

Basically, the only difference between the atomic bomb and the conventional explosive bomb lies in the nuclear weapon's radioactivity, which is much less of a wartime threat than most people believe.

The atomic bomb's most destructive elements are its blast and heat, which—although of far greater magnitude—are the same forces as in the ordinary bomb, and what is a defense against the blast and heat of one is a defense against the same two forces of the other.

An atomic explosion is sometimes an eccentric thing. In Nagasaki, for example, crude timber shelters covered with four feet of ordinary earth remained standing 100 yards from ground zero, the surface point directly beneath the detonation, while tile roofs were blown off buildings four miles away. The blast may bounce ineffectively off one wall and ricochet across a street to demolish another. Yet, in general the explosion follows certain predictable patterns of behavior.

It is known, for example, that relatively few direct injuries are caused by the blast or the actual "squeezing" of the bomb's pressure wave. Most injuries and fatalities are results of the blast's indirect effects—from being thrown against something or struck by a falling object. Therefore, in terms of individual protection, a person with only a few seconds' warning would lessen his chances of injury by lying flat on his stomach, face in his arms, eyes closed tightly. Instead of looking up immediately, he should remain in that position for eight or ten seconds after the detonation. This would be not only a protection against such things as flying glass but also against the temporary five minutes or so of blindness that could result from looking into the explosion's dazzling burst of light.

If one were outside at the time of a raid, this prone position should be taken in a ditch or gutter or against the base of some substantial structure—not a flimsy affair that might possibly fall on him. Inside a building, the best shelter would be the basement, and there a person should lie next to a wall, away from the windows, or against the base of some strong supporting column; definitely not in the middle of the floor, where the danger of falling beams is much greater. Although there is always a risk of being trapped in the basement, the upper floors hold the greatest hazards; for those floors—aside from being open to the radiological dangers which I will mention later—might collapse.

Except very near the point of detonation, flash burns—the second greatest cause of injury and death—can usually be avoided by the flimsiest of shielding. The ditch, gutter or wall that affords the best protection against the bomb's blast would act even as a more effective barrier against its heat. Thin cotton cloth might do the trick also. In Japan it was noted that many people suffered flower-shaped burns. It was learned that this was caused by the designs on their blouses, the lightly colored material reflecting the heat rays, the darker patterns absorbing and letting them through. In the event of an emergency, a person should always wear long trousers or slacks and loose-fitting light-colored blouses with full-length sleeves buttoned at the wrist. A hat, brim down, could help prevent many a face burn. Women should never go bare-legged. . . .

In the event of a threatened raid, there are many precautionary household measures that can and should be taken. In World War II, fire was the great destroyer, and since the heat flash of an atomic bomb could set fire to inflammable materials more than two miles from the point of detonation, it probably would be the great destroyer again. Thus it would be important to keep exposed inflammable matter to a minimum. Trash should be put in cans and covered tightly, dry leaves should be raked away from the home.

Within the house, oil burners should be shut off at the first alert, pilot lights turned off in gas stoves and water heaters, the fuel and draft doors to coal-burning furnaces and wood stoves closed. Even if an attack were to come without warning, these things should be done as quickly as possible.

Flashlights should be kept handy. Since there always is a danger that the shaking and twisting of buildings by a bomb's blast could rupture gas pipes and oil lines, it would be a foolish person who lighted a match to see his way in the darkness.

A house should be as much of an airtight compartment as it is possible to make it—doors closed, windows shut and blinds drawn. This is protection not only from fire sparks and glass splinters—in atomic explosions, unlike other kinds, windows are blown inward—but also from the nuclear weapon's radioactivity.

Survival Secrets for Atomic Attacks

ALWAYS PUT FIRST THINGS FIRST

Try to Get Shielded
If you have time, get down in a basement or subway. Should you unexpectedly be caught out-of-doors, seek shelter alongside a building, or jump in any handy ditch or gutter.

Drop Flat on Ground or Floor
To keep from being tossed about and to lessen the chances of being struck by falling and flying objects, flatten out at the base of a wall, or at the bottom of a bank.

Bury Your Face in Your Arms
When you drop flat, hide your eyes in the crook of your elbow. That will protect your face from flash burns, prevent temporary blindness and keep flying objects out of your eyes.

NEVER LOSE YOUR HEAD

With the devastating power of the atomic bomb displayed at Hiroshima and Nagasaki, and the Cold War relationship between the United States and Soviet Union in full force, the thought of a nuclear conflict between the two nations was constantly in the minds of the American people. Ads from the Federal Civil Defense Agency, such as this one, sought to reassure the public and provided somewhat unrealistic safety tips for people who may not have realized the full destructive potential of the bomb.

This radioactivity, which is the atomic bomb's only basic added hazard, is, for the layman, perhaps the most widely feared of all its forces. Many people believe that there is no defense against the bomb's invisible but penetrating ionizing rays and particles. Actually, radioactivity is the least of the nuclear bomb's threats; . . .

While protection against short-lived radiation is a matter of adequate shielding at the moment of the detonation, protection against lingering radioactivity is more than that. Although immediate shielding is important, too, it is also a matter of avoiding contaminated objects and areas after the actual explosion. . . .

All windows should be kept shut, and broken ones promptly covered with cardboard or blankets. All fireplace flues should be closed. Because wind could blow the hot ashes around or the radioactive wastes could fall out of drifting bomb clouds, householders even in areas outside the stricken one should follow these same precautions.

Also, much pollution could be brought into a house by persons, especially members of defense and rescue squads, carrying the invisible wastes on their clothes and shoes. Therefore shoes and outer garments should be removed and kept outside, later to be scrubbed in disposable tubs. The family washing machine would not be good to use here, as it might become contaminated and make other garments slightly radioactive. It would be safest for anyone connected with any defense or rescue teams to wear overalls and rubbers as well as a hat at his job. . . .

The terrible and shameful part of the whole thing is that radioactivity, which has made a great contribution to medical science, must be compared to a disease. Its discovery was heralded as a gift and a blessing to mankind. But perhaps, if understanding among nations improves sufficiently, it will be once again. Although there are defenses against the atomic bomb—and the world can go on living with it just as it has lived with poison gas and all the other former portents of mass destruction—the best defense of all is peace among men. Perhaps, in their striving for defenses against one another, the nations of the world will find and use the most obvious one.

DOCUMENT 5

Norman Vincent Peale, The Power of Positive Thinking (1952)

The Reverend Norman Vincent Peale popularized the nonsectarian, pragmatic religion of the 1950s. Through his best-selling books, radio and television appearances, and newspaper columns, Peale advised Americans not to dwell on their fears but, rather, to focus on positive, happy thoughts. According to Peale, personal problems were the result of negative thinking and unrelated to the larger social context. He assured people that they could overcome fear and anxiety through any one of his "seven simple steps" or "ten simple workable rules." In the following selection from his most famous work, Peale prescribes his formula for happiness.

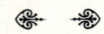

Who decides whether you shall be happy or unhappy? The answer—you do!

A television celebrity had as a guest on his program an aged man. And he was a very rare old man indeed. His remarks were entirely unpremeditated and of course absolutely unrehearsed. They simply bubbled up out of a personality that was radiant and happy. And whenever he said anything, it was so naïve, so apt, that the audience roared with laughter. They loved him. The celebrity was impressed, and enjoyed it with the others.

Finally he asked the old man why he was so happy. "You must have a wonderful secret of happiness," he suggested.

"No," replied the old man, "I haven't any great secret. It's just as plain as the nose on your face. When I get up in the morning," he explained, "I have two choices—either to be happy or to be unhappy, and what do you think I do? I just choose to be happy, and that's all there is to it."

That may seem an oversimplification, but I recall that Abraham Lincoln said that people were just about as happy as they made up their minds to be. You can be unhappy if you want to be. It is the easiest thing in the world to accomplish. Just choose unhappiness. Go around telling yourself that things aren't going well, that nothing is satisfactory, and you can be quite sure of being unhappy. But say to yourself, "Things are going nicely. Life is good. I choose happiness," and you can be quite certain of having your choice.

Children are more expert in happiness than adults. And the subtlety of Jesus Christ is remarkable, for He tells us that the way to live in this world is to have the childlike heart and mind. So don't become super-sophisticated. . . .

Many of us manufacture our own unhappiness. Of course not all unhappiness is self-created, for living conditions are responsible for not a few of our woes. Yet it is a fact that to a large extent by our thoughts and attitudes we distill out of the ingredients of life either happiness or unhappiness for ourselves.

Yet happiness is achievable and the process for obtaining it is not complicated. Anyone who desires it, who wills it, and who learns and applies the right formula may become a happy person. . . .

The happiness habit is developed by simply practicing happy thinking. Make a mental list of happy thoughts and pass them through your mind several times every day. If an unhappiness thought should enter your mind, immediately stop, consciously eject it, and substitute a happiness thought. Every morning deliberately drop happy thoughts into your conscious mind. Let a series of pictures pass across your mind of each happy experience you expect to have during the day. Savor their joy. Such thoughts will help cause events to turn out that way. Do not affirm that things will not go well that day. By merely saying that, you can actually help to make it so. You will draw to yourself every factor, large and small, that will contribute to unhappy conditions. As a result, you will find yourself asking, "Why does everything go badly for me? What is the matter with everything?"

The reason can be directly traced to the manner in which you began the day in your thoughts.

Tomorrow try this plan instead. When you get up, say out loud three times this one sentence, "This is the day which the Lord hath made; we will rejoice and be glad in it." (Psalm 118:24) Only personalize it and say, "I will rejoice and be glad in it." Repeat it in a strong, clear voice and with positive tone and emphasis. The statement, of course, is from the Bible and it is a good cure for unhappiness. If you repeat that one sentence three times before breakfast and meditate on the meaning of the words you will change the character of the day by starting off with a happiness psychology.

While dressing, say aloud a few such remarks as the following: "I believe this is going to be a wonderful day. I believe I can successfully handle all problems that will arise today. I feel good physically, mentally, emotionally. It is wonderful to be alive. I am grateful for all that I have had, for all that I now have, and for all that I shall have. Things aren't going to fall apart. God is here and He is with me and He will see me through. I thank God for every good thing." . . .

Recently, after I finished a lecture in a certain city, a big, fine-looking young man came up to me. He slapped me on the shoulder with such force that it almost bowled me over.

"Doctor," he said in a booming voice, "how about coming out with the gang? We are having a big party at the Smiths' house, and we would like you to come along. It's going to be a whale of a shindig and you ought to get in on it." So ran his racy invitation.

Well, obviously this didn't sound like a proper party for a preacher, and I was hesitant. I was afraid I might cramp everyone's style, so I began to make excuses.

"Oh, forget it," my friend told me. "Don't worry, this is your kind of party. You will be surprised. Come on along. You will get the kick of your life out of it."

So I yielded and went along with my buoyant and racy friend and he was certainly one of the most infectious personalities I had encountered in quite a while. Soon we came to a big house set back among trees with a wide, sweeping driveway up to the front door. Judging by the noise issuing from the open windows there was no question that quite a party was in progress, and I wondered what I was getting into. My host, with a great shout, dragged me into the room, and we had quite a handshaking time; he introduced me to a large group of gay and exuberant people. They were a happy, joyous lot of young folk.

I looked around for a bar, but there wasn't any. All that was being served was coffee, fruit juice, ginger ale, sandwiches, and ice cream, but there was lots of those.

"These people must have stopped somewhere before coming here," I remarked to my friend.

He was shocked, and said, "Stopped somewhere? Why, you don't understand. These people have the spirit all right, but not the kind of 'spirit' you are thinking about. I am surprised at you," he said. "Don't you realize what makes this gang so happy? They have got something. They have been set free from themselves. They have found God as a living, vital, honest-to-goodness reality. Yes," he said, "they have got spirit all right, but it isn't the kind that you get out of a bottle. They have got spirit in their hearts."

Then I saw what he meant. This wasn't a crowd of sad-faced, stodgy people. They were the leaders of the young crowd of that town, and they were having a wonderful time at this party—talking about God, and they were doing it in the most natural manner imaginable. They were telling one another about the changes that had occurred in their lives through revitalized spiritual power.

Those who have the naïve notion that you can't laugh and be gay when you are religious should have attended that party.

Well, I went away with a Bible verse running through my mind, "In him was life; and the life was the light of men." (John 1:4) That was the light I saw on the faces of those happy people. An inner light was reflected outwardly on their faces, and it came from an effervescent spiritual something that they had taken into themselves. Life means vitality, and those people obviously were getting their vitality from God. They had found the power that creates happiness.

DOCUMENT 6

David Riesman, "The National Style" (1957)

Harvard sociologist David Riesman sharply criticized America's postwar culture of prosperity. In his *The Lonely Crowd* (1950), Riesman argued that suburbia encouraged conformity to a bland consumer society. In the following paper presented at an academic conference in 1957, he relates his experiences conducting a poll of suburban voters during the 1956 presidential campaign. Riesman found that, despite their protestations against communism and their affirmations of freedom, suburban voters were complacent and lacked any passion for the ideals they professed.

During the [1956] presidential campaign Louis Harris and Stewart Alsop had come out to Chicago on one leg of their trip to take the political pulse of the country. I took Alsop's place one day and went along with Harris, polling in a suburb south of Chicago—a suburb that was being built into the wheat fields at one end while people had been living for a year or even two years in houses at the other end. It was a lower-middle-class suburb, neat, bungalow-type houses all "different," and it was a nice May day when the flowers were coming out and when the few men who weren't working were out in their incipient gardens. We asked people whom they had voted for in 1952 and they often said, "Who was running then?"—that is, who was running against Ike [President Eisenhower]. They remembered they had voted for Ike. We asked them whom they would vote for in 1956 and they said Ike. Then we raised the question as to whether the heart attack might affect the matter and they told us about their Aunt Minnie or their Uncle Bill and their diseases, as if Ike were a homey figure or a neighbor for whom they had sympathy. When we asked them what the Republicans had done that

The fifteen years that followed the end of World War II witnessed unprecedented economic growth in the United States. With postwar prosperity and the expansion of the suburbs, luxury items such as automobiles were within the reach of many people, and two-car families became common.

they especially liked, they could say nothing other than ending the war in Korea, as a few said, and then we asked them what they disliked. They said high taxes, but that was about all. The single [Adlai] Stevenson support[er] we found was an old engineer of a crusty sort who lived in the only house that had been in the area before 1955, and he came running afterward to tell us how he really felt when he saw, from our going from house to house, that we truly were taking a poll and not inquiring just about him.

Most of the people we spoke to were young housewives, often interrupted in their midday television program—as the dog used to be the hazard for the postman, so the TV has become for the inter-viewer. They were educated: they had been to high school and some to two years of college or secretarial school; they read a few magazines although hardly a book, and yet their complacency was such as to make Stewart Alsop feel that he had been unfair in lambasting people in Washington for being indolent, for he had not fully appreciated what their constituencies were like. As one looked over the flat Illinois prairie at all the signs of prosperity, it was not hard to see why these people were so bland politically and responded so to the same qualities in Ike. To be sure, some of them also liked violence with their political entertainment, and this was one of the attractions of both Kefauver and McCarthy. These people were not self-made men who remembered their struggles against hardship but, rather, a society-made generation who could not believe society would let them down, and, therefore, lacked not only the anxiety which often haunts but also the sense of accomplishment which sometimes enriches the self-made....

I have referred to the interviews done by Louis Harris as one example of the kind of blandness that I see as somehow inhuman. When I see a French or Italian movie the faces seem more alive and expressive than American faces in equivalent films. The very rich are perhaps unhappy in all countries. Their faces are often sour, fearful, and suspicious. In America millions are among the very rich in international terms, while the white-collar workers and many of the factory workers seem to me unhappy also—ill at ease in Zion.

I was also saddened by the attitude of many Stevenson supporters in the last campaign who felt that he had made a better campaign in 1952. In 1952 many of his supporters were much too starry eyed; in 1956 I felt a loss of tone among them. Stevenson's courageous attacks on H-bomb tests, which at least tried to educate people to the real problem, were dismissed by many of his supporters as poor politics or poor timing. People wanted something glamorous in Stevenson—as they thought they had found in 1952—and resented his not providing this. Stevenson made a much better campaign in 1956 in his efforts at education, at groping with some of the really serious problems of this country, but he had much less emotional support from his supporters than in 1952 when they were deluded into thinking he could win and into thinking how wonderful it was to have a semi-intellectual run for President.

Much more important than any of these experiences was my confrontation during the Polish and Hungarian uprisings in 1956 with the fact that there was a more passionate feeling for freedom in the Satellite countries (and, I gathered, among the youth of Leningrad and elsewhere in the Soviet Union itself) than one found at the time in this country. When I read the articles by young Polish writers in the emancipated Polish press, or the appeals of the short-lived Petofi Club which sparked the Hungarian revolution, I wondered how many American youth and how many American writers were as clear about freedom as these people who had been radically deprived of it. I felt almost envious of people who had so clear a goal, so clear an enemy, as compared with the problems of fighting for a kind of uncontested individuality in this country. . . .The Hungarian and Polish rebels fought, as people always do, for mixed motives, including reactionary ones; their published programs had a nineteenth century and Enlightenment flavor which at the present time, in the want of superior Utopias, remains revolutionary. It would be defeatist to conclude that one must have harsh parents in order to become strong and self-reliant children or that one must have the experience of totalitarianism in order to value freedom; nevertheless, when old oppressions have been removed, it takes a while to "discover" the new and subtle ones our better fortune presents. We have not done that in America; we have coasted on old although still pressing and dangerous problems.

DOCUMENT 7

Ladies Home Journal, "Young Mother" (1956)

In the 1956 the *Ladies Home Journal*, a popular middle-class magazine, convened a roundtable discussion to address the "plight of the young mother." To bring national attention to a system requiring women to work shockingly long hours each week with no help, the *Journal* invited four "typical" mothers—middle-class residents of single-family houses—to describe their experiences as homemakers in suburbia. In the following excerpt, Mrs. Gould and Miss Hickey are members of the *Journal*'s editorial staff, Dr. Montagu is another participant, and Mrs. Petry, Mrs. Townsend, Mrs. Erhardt, and Mrs. McKenzie are the guest mothers. Observing conventions of the day, the *Journal* did not list the mothers' first names, identifying guests only by their married names.

Mrs. Gould: As editors and parents we are extremely interested in this whole problem. The welfare of our society depends upon the type of children you young mothers and others like you are able to bring up. Anything that affects the welfare of young families is most crucial, and I do feel that the young mother, any young mother in our day, should get far more general recognition and attention than she does—not so much for her own sake as for society as a whole, or just out of sheer common sense.

Miss Hickey: And understanding. I think there is a lack of understanding, too. Since it would take all day to tell what a busy woman does all day . . . how about your high points?

Mrs. Petry: I would say in the morning—breakfast and wash time. I put the breakfast out, leave the children to eat it and run into the bathroom—that is where the washer is—and fill it up. I come back into the kitchen and shove a little in the baby's mouth and try to keep the others eating. Then I go back in the bathroom and put the clothes in the wringer and start the rinse water. That is about the end of the half-hour there. I continue then to finish the wash, and either put them out or let them see one program they like on television, and then I go out and hang the wash up.

Miss Hickey: You put that outside?

Mrs. Petry: Yes. Then I eat.

Mrs. Gould: Can you sit down and eat in peace? Are the children outdoors at that time or watching television?

Mrs. Petry: They are supposed to be outside, but they are usually running in and out. Somebody forgot something he should have eaten, or wants more milk, or a toy or something. Finally I lock the screen door. I always read something while I'm eating—two meals a day I read. When my husband isn't there, and if I am alone, or maybe just one child at the table, I read something quick. But I time it. I take no more than half an hour for eating and reading.

Miss Hickey: You work on schedule quite a bit. Why do you do that?

Mrs. Petry: Because I am very forgetful. I have an orange crayon and I write "defrost" on the refrigerator every now and then, or I forget to defrost it. If I think of something while I am washing, I write it on the mirror with an eyebrow pencil. It must sound silly, but that is the only way I can remember everything I have to do. . . .

Miss Hickey: Mrs. Ehrhardt, your quietest half-hour?

Mrs. Ehrhardt: I would say . . . that when I go out to take the wash in. There is something about getting outdoors—and I don't get out too often, except to hang out the wash and to bring it in. I really enjoy doing it. If it is a nice day, I stand outside and fold it outdoors. I think that is my quietest hour.

Miss Hickey: How often do you and your husband go out together in the evening?

Mrs. Ehrhardt: Not often. An occasional movie, which might be every couple of months or so, on an anniversary. This year is the first year we celebrated on the day we were married. We were married in June. We always celebrated it, but it might be in July or August.

It depends on our babysitter. If you cannot get anyone, you just cannot go out. I am not living near my family and I won't leave the children with teenagers. I would be afraid it might be a little hectic, and a young girl might not know what to do. So we don't get out very often. . . .

Miss Hickey: Let us hear about Mrs. Petry's recreation.

Mrs. Petry: Oh, I went to work in a department store that opened in Levittown. I begged and begged my husband to let me work, and finally he said I could go once or twice a week. I lasted for three weeks, or should I say he lasted for three weeks.

Mrs. Gould: You mean you worked in the daytime?

Mrs. Petry: Three evenings, from six until nine, and on Saturday.

Mrs. Gould: And your husband took care of the children during that time?

Mrs. Petry: Yes, but the third week, he couldn't stand it anymore, Saturday and all. In fact, I think he had to work that Saturday, so I asked if I could just come in to the store during the week. My husband was hoping they would fire me, but they didn't. But I could see that it wasn't really fair to him, because I was going out for my own pleasure.

Mrs. Gould: In other words, your working was your recreation.

Mrs. Petry: Yes, and I enjoyed it very much.

Miss Hickey: Why did you feel you wanted to do this?

Mrs. Petry: To see some people and talk to people, just to see what is going on in the world. . . .

Miss Hickey: How about your shopping experiences?

Mrs. McKenzie: Well, I don't go in the evening, because I cannot depend on Ed being home; and when he is there, he likes to have me there too. I don't know. Usually all three of the children go shopping with me. At one time I carried two and dragged the other one along behind me in the cart with the groceries. It is fun to take them all. Once a man stopped me and said, "Lady, did you know your son is eating hamburger?" He had eaten a half-pound of raw hamburger. When corn on the cob was so expensive, my oldest one begged me to buy corn on the cob, so I splurged and bought three ears for thirty-nine cents. When I got to the check-out counter, I discovered he had eaten all three, so he had to pay for the cobs.

Miss Hickey: You go once a week?

Mrs. McKenzie: Once a week or every ten days now, depending on how often I have the use of the car. That day we usually go to the park, too. . . .

Miss Hickey: Tell us about your most recent crisis.

Mrs. McKenzie: I had given a birthday party for fifteen children in my little living room, which is seven by eleven. The next morning my son, whose birthday it had been, broke out with the measles, so I had exposed fifteen children to measles, and I was the most unpopular mother in the neighborhood.

He was quite sick, and it snowed that day. Ed took Lucy sleigh riding. Both of them fell off the sled and she broke both the bones in her arm.

Mrs. Gould: Did she then get the measles?

Mrs. McKenzie: She did, and so did the baby. . . . My main problem was being in quarantine for a month. During this time that all three had measles and Lucy had broken her arm, we got a notice from the school that her tuberculin test was positive—and that meant that one of the adults living in our home had active tuberculosis. It horrified me. I kept thinking, "Here I sit killing my three children with tuberculosis." But we had to wait until they were over their contagion period before we could all go in and get x-rayed.

Miss Hickey: And the test was not correct?

Mrs. McKenzie: She had had childhood tuberculosis, but it was well healed and she was all right. About eight of ten have had childhood tuberculosis and no one knows it.

Mrs. Gould: It is quite common, but it is frightening when it occurs to you. Were your children quite sick with measles?

Mrs. McKenzie: Terribly ill.

Mrs. Gould: They had high temperatures?

Mrs. McKenzie: My children are a great deal like my father. Anything they do, they do to extreme. They are violently ill, or they are as robust as can be. There is no in-between. . . .

Dr. Montagu: There is one very large question I would like to ask. What in your lives, as they are at present, would you most like to see changed or modified?

Mrs. Ehrhardt: Well, I would like to be sure my husband's position would not require him to be transferred so often. I would like to stay in place long enough to take a few roots in the community. It would also be nice to have someone help with the housework, but I don't think I would like to have anyone live in. The houses nowadays are too small. I think you would bump into each other. Of course, I have never had any one in, so I cannot honestly give an opinion.

Mrs. Townsend: At the present time, I don't think there is anything that I would like to change in the household. We happen to be very close, and we are all very happy. I will admit that there are times when I am a little overtired, and I might be a little more than annoyed with the children, but actually it doesn't last too long. We do have a problem where we live now. There aren't any younger children for my children to play with. Therefore, they are underneath my heels just constantly, and I am not able to take the older children out the way I would like to, because of the two babies.

Miss Hickey: You have been in how many communities?

Mrs. Townsend: I have lived in Louisiana, California, New York, and for a short period in Columbia, South Carolina....

Miss Hickey: Mrs. Petry, what would you change?

Mrs. Petry: I would like more time to enjoy my children. I do take time, but if I do take as much time as I like, the work piles up. When I go back to work I feel crabby, and I don't know whether I'm mad at the children, or mad at the work or just mad at everybody sometimes.

I would also like to have a little more rest and a little more time to spend in relaxation with my husband. We never get to go out together, and the only time we have much of a conversation is just before we go to bed. And I would like to have a girl come and do my ironing.

I am happy there where we live because this is the first time we have stayed anywhere for any length of time. It will be two years in August, and it is the first home we have really had. That is why my husband left the Navy. I nearly had a nervous collapse, because it seemed I couldn't stand another minute not having him home and helping, or not helping, but just being there.

DOCUMENT 8

Life, *Essay on Teen-age Consumption* (1959)

Deprived of consumer goods as children of the Great Depression, parents in the 1950s relished the opportunity to lavish their families with countless commodities. Manufacturers soon realized the potential buying power of American teens and began devoting considerable money to advertisements promoting products for the expanding youth market. In 1959, *Life* devoted an essay to teen-age consumption and profiled Suzie Slattery, a seventeen year old from Van Nuys, California.

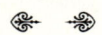

To some people the vision of a leggy adolescent happily squealing over the latest fancy present from Daddy is just another example of the way teen-agers are spoiled to death these days. But to a growing number of businessmen the picture spells out the profitable fact that the American teen-agers have emerged as a big-time consumer in the U.S. economy. They are multiplying in numbers. They spend more and have more spent on them. And they have minds of their own about what they want.

The time is past when a boy's chief possession was his bike and a girl's party wardrobe consisted of a fancy dress worn with a string of dime-store pearls. What Depression-bred parents may still think of as luxuries are looked on as necessities by their offspring. Today teen-agers surround themselves with a fantastic array of garish and often expensive baubles and amusements. They own 10 million phonographs, over a million TV sets, 13 million cameras. Nobody knows how much parents spend on them for actual necessities nor to what extent teen-agers act as hidden persuaders on their parents' other buying habits. Counting only what is spent to satisfy their special teen-age demands, the youngsters and their parents will shell out about $10 billion this year, a billion more than the total sales of GM.

Until recently businessmen have largely ignored the teen-age market. But now they are spending millions on advertising and razzle-dazzle promotional stunts. Their efforts so far seem only to have scratched the surface of a rich lode. In 1970, when the teen-age population expands from its present 18 million to 28 million, the market may be worth $20 billion. If parents have any idea of organized revolt, it is already too late. Teen-age spending is so important that such action would send quivers through the entire national economy.

At 17 Suzie Slattery of Van Nuys, Calif. fits any businessman's dream of the ideal teen-age consumer. The daughter of a reasonably well-to-do TV announcer, Suzie costs her parents close to $4,000 a year—far more than average for the country but not much more than many of the upper middle income families of her town. In an expanding economy more and more teen-agers will be moving up into Suzie's bracket or be influenced as consumers by her example.

Last year $1,500 was spent on Suzie's clothes and $550 for her entertainment. Like most teen-agers Suzie has a hearty appetite. She pays $4 every two weeks at the beauty parlor. She has her own telephone and even has her own soda fountain in the house. On summer vacation days she loves to wander with her mother through fashionable department stores, picking out frocks or furnishings for her room or silver and expensive crockery for the hope chest she has already started.

As a high school graduation present, Suzie was given a holiday cruise to Hawaii and is now in the midst of a new clothes-buying spree for college. Her parents' constant indulgence has not spoiled Suzie. She takes for granted all the luxuries that surround her because she has had them all her life. But she also has a good mind and some serious interests. A top student in her school, she is entering Occidental College this fall and will major in political science.

DOCUMENT 9

Michael Harrington, The Other America (1962)

Most early postwar social commentators focused on life in suburbia and celebrated America's long-awaited return to prosperity. A few voices protested, however, arguing that poverty persisted throughout the period. In his influential book *The Other America*, Michael Harrington contended that the poverty of the 1950s and early 1960s was a new phenomenon. As Americans fled the cities, the impoverished became increasingly separated, and hence socially isolated, from the rest of society. In the following excerpt, Harrington describes "the invisible land" of poverty that lay outside the reaches of suburbia.

The millions who are poor in the United States tend to become increasingly invisible. Here is a great mass of people, yet it takes an effort of the intellect and will even to see them.

I discovered this personally in a curious way. After I wrote my first article on poverty in America, I had all the statistics down on paper. I had proved to my satisfaction that there were around 50,000,000 poor in this country. Yet, I realized I did not believe my own figures. The poor existed in the Government reports; they were percentages and numbers in long, close columns, but they were not part of my experience. I could prove that the other America existed, but I had never been there.

My response was not accidental. It was typical of what is happening to an entire society, and it reflects profound social changes in this nation. The other America, the America of poverty, is hidden today in a way that it never was before. Its millions are socially invisible to the rest of us. . . .

There are perennial reasons that make the other America an invisible land.

Poverty is often off the beaten track. It always has been. The ordinary tourist never left the main highway, and today he rides interstate turnpikes. He does not go into the valleys of Pennsylvania where the towns look like movie sets of Wales in the thirties. He does not see the company houses in rows, the rutted roads (the poor always have bad roads whether they live in the city, in towns, or on farms), and everything is black and dirty. And even if he were to pass through such a place by accident, the tourist would not meet the unemployed men in the bar or the women coming home from a runaway sweatshop.

Then, too, beauty and myths are perennial masks of poverty. The traveler comes to the Appalachians in the lovely season. He sees the hills, the streams, the foliage—but not the poor. Or perhaps he looks at a run-down mountain house and, remembering Rousseau rather than seeing with his eyes, decides that "those people" are truly fortunate to be living the way they are and that they are lucky to be exempt from the strains and tensions of the middle class. The only problem is that "those people," the quaint inhabitants of those hills, are undereducated, underprivileged, lack medical care, and are in the process of being forced from the land into a life in the cities, where they are misfits.

These are normal and obvious causes of the invisibility of the poor. They operated a generation ago; they will be functioning a generation hence. It is more important to understand that the very development of American society is creating a new kind of blindness about poverty. The poor are increasingly slipping out of the very experience and consciousness of the nation.

If the middle class never did like ugliness and poverty, it was at least aware of them. "Across the tracks" was not a very long way to go. There were forays into the slums at Christmas time; there were charitable organizations that brought contact with the poor. Occasionally, almost everyone passed through the Negro ghetto or the blocks of tenements, if only to get downtown to work or to entertainment.

Now the American city has been transformed. The poor still inhabit the miserable housing in the central area, but they are increasingly isolated from contact with, or sight of, anybody else. Middle-class women coming in from Suburbia on a rare trip may catch the merest glimpse of the other America on the way to an evening at the theater, but their children are segregated in suburban schools. The business or professional man may drive along the fringes of slums in a car or bus, but it is not an important experience to him. The failures, the unskilled, the disabled, the aged, and the minorities are right there, across the tracks, where they have always been. But hardly anyone else is.

In short, the very development of the American city has removed poverty from the living, emotional experience of millions upon millions of middle-class Americans. Living out in the suburbs, it is easy to assume that ours is, indeed, an affluent society.

This new segregation of poverty is compounded by a well-meaning ignorance. A good many concerned and sympathetic Americans are aware that there is much discussion of urban renewal. Suddenly, driving through the city, they notice that a familiar slum has been torn down and that there are towering, modern buildings where once there had been tenements or hovels. There is a warm feeling of satisfaction, of pride in the way things are working out: the poor, it is obvious, are being taken care of.

The irony in this . . . is that the truth is nearly the exact opposite to the impression. The total impact of the various housing programs in postwar America has been to squeeze more and more people into existing slums. More often than not, the modern apartment in a towering building rents at $40 a room or more. For, during the past decade and a half, there has been more subsidization of middle- and upper-income housing than there has been of housing for the poor.

Clothes make the poor invisible too: America has the best-dressed poverty the world has ever known. For a variety of reasons, the benefits of mass production have been spread much more evenly in this area than in many others. It is much easier in the United States to be decently dressed than it is to be decently housed, fed, or doctored. Even people with terribly depressed incomes can look prosperous. . . .

And finally, the poor are politically invisible. It is one of the cruelest ironies of social life in advanced countries that the dispossessed at the bottom of society are unable to speak for themselves. The people of the other America do not, by far and large, belong to unions, to fraternal organizations, or to political parties. They are without lobbies of their own; they put forward no legislative program. As a group, they are atomized. They have no face; they have no voice.

Thus, there is not even a cynical political motive for caring about the poor, as in the old days. Because the slums are no longer centers of powerful political organizations, the politicians need not really care about their inhabitants. The slums are no longer visible to the middle class, so much of the idealistic urge to fight for those who need help is gone. Only the social agencies have a really direct involvement with the other America, and they are without any great political power. . . .

It is too early to say whether or not this phenomenon is temporary, or whether it represents a massive retrogression that will swell the numbers of the poor. To a large extent, the answer to this question will be determined by the political response of the United States in the sixties. If serious and massive action is not undertaken, it may be necessary for statisticians to add some old-fashioned, prewelfare-state poverty to the misery of the other America.

Poverty in the 1960's is invisible and it is new, and both these factors make it more tenacious. It is more isolated and politically powerless than ever before. It is laced with ironies, not the least of which is that many of the poor view progress upside-down, as a menace and a threat to their lives. And if the nation does not measure up to the challenge of automation, poverty in the 1960's might be on the increase.

Study Questions

1. In what ways were the years 1945 to 1960 an era of anxiety?
2. How did atomic weapons affect how Americans viewed the world?
3. How do you account for Norman Vincent Peale's broad appeal in the 1950s?
4. Do you agree with Riesman's assessment of suburban life as bland and conformist? How would the mothers of the *Ladies Home Journal* forum respond to Riesman?
5. Why does Harrington argue that poverty in America lies in an "invisible land?" How is the poverty of the 1950s different from that of the Depression era?

11

Demand for Civil Justice

After World War II, civil rights became a major issue on the liberal agenda. During the war, millions of African Americans left the South for northern and western cities to secure high-wage employment in the defense and other manufacturing industries. Throughout the war, blacks mobilized in support of actions such as A. Philip Randolph's March on Washington Movement to demand an end to segregation, disfranchisement, and discrimination (see Chapter 9). President Harry Truman appointed a presidential commission on civil rights in 1946, ordered the desegregation of the armed services in 1948, and proposed a ten-point legislative program aimed at guaranteeing civil rights.

At the same time, the National Association for the Advancement of Colored People (NAACP) continued its legal challenge to southern segregation. In 1954 it won a landmark decision when the Supreme Court ruled in *Brown* v. *Board of Education of Topeka* that "separate educational facilities are inherently unequal" and hence unconstitutional. The Court subsequently ordered the process of desegregation to proceed "with all deliberate speed."

Integration met with massive resistance from southern whites. Instead of relying on public officials to speed the process of desegregation, blacks took up the battle themselves. Throughout the South, blacks conducted sit-ins, bus boycotts, freedom rides, and marches to enforce court rulings and challenge southern white opposition. The Reverend Martin Luther King, Jr., founder of the Southern Christian Leadership Conference, emerged as the moral leader of southern black activism, preaching a philosophy of civil disobedience and nonviolence (Document 1). Other civil rights advocates, such as Malcolm X, challenged King's commitment to nonviolence and argued that blacks must "fight until we overcome" (Document 2).

As the Civil Rights movement gained momentum, several groups organized to advance the struggle for civil justice. In 1962 a small group of northern college students formed the Students for a Democratic Society (SDS). Within a few years, the SDS had expanded its membership to more than 100,000 and transformed itself into a vehicle for confronting poverty, racism, and violence (Document 3). In 1960 young African American activists organized the Student Nonviolent Coordinating Committee (SNCC). The SNCC emerged as one of the most effective and creative organizations of the Civil Rights movement, waging numerous civil disobedience campaigns on the frontlines of the struggle for civil justice (Document 4).

Ironically, the denunciation of the Soviet Union's human rights abuses brought our own civil rights issues to the forefront. The police use of brutality on unarmed demonstrators was witnessed on television for the first time by a horrified nation. Police tactics such as the use of firehoses, dogs, and electric cattle prods did much to undermine the southern stance on segregation and helped gain support for the Civil Rights movement.

    King's skillful leadership and televised coverage of southern law enforcement officials and vigilantes beating and brutalizing defenseless demonstrators eventually gave the Civil Rights movement a moral advantage over its opponents and won it massive public support. President Lyndon Johnson, responding to growing civil rights pressure, used his political skills to secure congressional passage of the Civil Rights Act of 1964 and the Voting Rights Act of 1965 (Document 5). Johnson also declared an "unconditional war on poverty" and championed an expansion of the welfare state through his extensive legislative program called the Great Society.

    Inspired by the activism of African Americans, women began to challenge sexism in America through their own vigorous liberation movement. Women active in the Civil Rights movement gained a greater awareness of the possibilities for fulfilling a meaningful life beyond the limitations of their roles as homemakers and mothers.

As the liberation movement gained momentum, feminist activists filed wage discrimination suits and agitated for fair divorce laws, the lifting of bans on abortion, and tougher enforcement of rape laws. Like the Civil Rights movement, the movement for women's liberation encountered stiff resistance. As Shirley Chisholm, a black member of Congress from New York, explained, sex discrimination would take far longer to eliminate than racial prejudice (Document 6).

By the late 1960s the Civil Rights movement had begun to unravel. A series of riots in impoverished inner-city ghettoes in Detroit, Newark, Los Angeles, and elsewhere forcefully revealed that economic and political equality were not assured with the passage of federal civil rights legislation. The urban rioting spurred white backlash against liberal reform. Republican presidential candidate Richard Nixon pointed to the riots as evidence of the excesses of civil rights leaders who gave sanction to the actions of hoodlums and urban terrorists. "Law and order" and "civil wrongs" became major themes of his successful 1968 campaign for the White House (Document 7). Civil rights activists quickly realized that poverty and social inequality resulted from far deeper problems than Jim Crow laws and poll taxes and despaired that the political will to solve the problems confronting the nation's African American population had evaporated (Document 8).

DOCUMENT 1

Dr. Martin Luther King, Jr., "Letter from Birmingham Jail" (1963)

In 1963 the Southern Christian Leadership Council began a series of civil rights protests in Birmingham, Alabama. During the demonstrations, Dr. Martin Luther King, Jr., was arrested and jailed for violating a state court order prohibiting public demonstrations without a permit. Eight local white clergy published an attack on King in a Birmingham newspaper, calling him a troublemaker and a Communist and criticizing his tactics as "unwise and untimely." King responded to his accusers in his famous "Letter from Birmingham Jail."

We know through painful experience that freedom is never voluntarily given by the oppressor; it must be demanded by the oppressed. Frankly, I have yet to engage in a direct-action campaign that was "well timed" in the view of those who have not suffered unduly from the disease of segregation. For years now I have heard the word "Wait!" It rings in the ear of every Negro with piercing familiarity. This "Wait" has almost always meant "Never." We must come to see, with one of our distinguished jurists, that "justice too long delayed is justice denied."

We have waited for more than 340 years for our constitutional and God-given rights. The nations of Asia and Africa are moving with jetlike speed toward gaining political independence, but we still creep at horse-and-buggy pace toward gaining a cup of coffee at a lunch counter. Perhaps it is easy for those who have never felt the stinging darts of segregation to say, "Wait." But when you have seen vicious mobs lynch your mothers and fathers at will and drown your sisters and brothers at whim; when you have seen hate-filled policemen curse, kick and even kill your black brothers and sisters; when you see the vast majority of your twenty million Negro brothers smothering in an airtight cage of poverty in the midst of an affluent society; when you suddenly find your tongue twisted and your speech stammering as you seek to explain to your six-year-old daughter why she can't go to the public amusement park that has just been advertised on television, and see tears welling up in her eyes when she is told that Funtown is closed to colored children, and see ominous clouds of inferiority beginning to form in her little mental sky, and see her beginning to distort her personality by developing an unconscious bitterness toward white people; when you have to concoct an answer for a five-year-old son who is asking: "Daddy, why do white people treat colored people so mean?"; when you take a cross-country drive and find it necessary to sleep night after night in the uncomfortable corners of your automobile because no motel will accept you; when you are humiliated day in and day out by nagging signs reading "white" and "colored"; when your first name becomes "nigger," your middle name becomes "boy" (however old you are) and your last name becomes "John," and your wife and mother are never given the respected title "Mrs."; when you are harried by day and haunted by night by the fact that you are a Negro, living constantly at tiptoe stance, never quite knowing what to expect next, and are plagued with inner fears and outer resentments; when you are forever fighting a degenerating sense of "nobodiness"—then you will understand why we find it difficult to wait. There comes a time when the cup of endurance runs over, and men are no longer willing to be plunged into the abyss of despair. I hope, sirs, you can understand our legitimate and unavoidable impatience.

You express a great deal of anxiety over our willingness to break laws. This is certainly a legitimate concern. Since we so diligently urge people to obey the Supreme Court's decision of 1954 outlawing segregation in the public schools, at first glance it may seem rather paradoxical for us consciously to break laws. One may well ask: "How can you advocate breaking some laws and obeying others?" The answer lies in the fact that there are two types of laws: just and unjust. I would be the first to advocate obeying just laws. One has not only a legal but a moral responsibility to obey just laws. Conversely, one has a moral responsibility to disobey unjust laws. I would agree with St. Augustine that "an unjust law is no law at all."

Now, what is the difference between the two? How does one determine whether a law is just or unjust? A just law is a man-made code that squares with the moral law or the law of God. An unjust law is a code that is out of harmony with the moral law. To put it in the terms of St. Thomas Aquinas: An unjust law is a human law that is not rooted in eternal law and natural law. Any law that uplifts human personality is just. Any law that degrades human personality is unjust. All segregation statutes are unjust because segregation distorts the soul and damages the personality. It gives the segregator a false sense of superiority and the segregated a false sense of inferiority. Segregation, to use the terminology of the Jewish philosopher Martin Buber, substitutes an "I–it" relationship for an "I–thou" relationship and ends up relegating persons to the status of things. Hence segregation is not only politically, economically and sociologically unsound, it is morally wrong and sinful. Paul Tillich has said that sin is separation. Is not segregation an existential expression of man's tragic separation, his awful estrangement, his terrible sinfulness? Thus it is that I can urge men to obey the 1954 decision of the Supreme Court, for it is morally right; and I can urge them to disobey segregation ordinances, for they are morally wrong.

Let us consider a more concrete example of just and unjust laws. An unjust law is a code that a numerical or power majority group compels a minority

Marchers in Montgomery, Alabama. Despite the nonviolent stance of civil rights activists, those opposed to the Civil Rights movement used violence with disregard against black and white demonstrators alike. The murders of several civil rights protesters gained national attention and culminated with James Earl Ray's assassination of Martin Luther King, Jr., the recognized leader of the Civil Rights movement, on April 4, 1968.

group to obey but does not make binding on itself. This is *difference* made legal. By the same token, a just law is a code that a majority compels a minority to follow and that it is willing to follow itself. This is *sameness* made legal.

Let me give another explanation. A law is unjust if it is inflicted on a minority that, as a result of being denied the right to vote, had no part in enacting or devising the law. Who can say that the legislature of Alabama which set up that state's segregation laws was democratically elected? Throughout Alabama all sorts of devious methods are used to prevent Negroes from becoming registered voters, and there are some counties in which, even though Negroes constitute a majority of the population, not a single Negro is registered. Can any law enacted under such circumstances be considered democratically structured?

Sometimes a law is just on its face and unjust in its application. For instance, I have been arrested on a charge of parading without a permit. Now, there is nothing wrong in having an ordinance which requires a permit for a parade. But such an ordinance becomes unjust when it is used to maintain segregation and to deny citizens the First-Amendment privilege of peaceful assembly and protest.

I hope you are able to see the distinction I am trying to point out. In no sense do I advocate evading or defying the law, as would the rabid segregationist. That would lead to anarchy. One who breaks an unjust law must do so openly, lovingly, and with a willingness to accept the penalty. I submit that an individual who breaks a law that conscience tells him is unjust, and who willingly accepts the penalty of imprisonment in order to arouse the conscience of the community over its injustice, is in reality expressing the highest respect for law.

DOCUMENT 2

Malcolm X, "The Ballot or the Bullet" (1964)

Malcolm X, a black nationalist and Muslim based in New York City's Harlem, challenged King's commitment to nonviolent civil disobedience. He spoke for many northern urban blacks frustrated with inner-city poverty and the slow, cautious pace with which white politicians pursued civil rights. On April 3, 1964, Malcolm X delivered the following address before a Congress of Racial Equality (CORE) symposium entitled "The Negro Revolt—What Comes Next?" held at the Cory Methodist Church in Cleveland, Ohio.

So, what I'm trying to impress upon you, in essence, is this: You and I in America are faced not with a segregationist conspiracy, we're faced with a government conspiracy. Everyone who's filibustering is a senator—that's the government. Everyone who's finagling in Washington, D.C., is a congressman—that's the government. You don't have anybody putting blocks in your path but people who are a part of the government. The same government that you go abroad to fight for and die for is the government that is in a conspiracy to deprive you of your voting rights, deprive you of your economic opportunities, deprive you of decent housing, deprive you of decent education. You don't need to go to the employer alone, it is the government itself, the government of America, that is responsible for the oppression and exploitation and degradation of black people in this country. And you should drop it in their lap. This government has failed the Negro. This so-called democracy has failed the Negro. And all these white liberals have definitely failed the Negro.

So, where do we go from here? First, we need some friends. We need some new allies. The entire civil-rights struggle needs a new interpretation, a broader interpretation. We need to look at this civil-rights thing from another angle—from the inside as well as from the outside. To those of us whose philosophy is black nationalism, the only way you can get involved in the civil-rights struggle is give it a new interpretation. That old interpretation excluded us. It kept us out. So, we're giving a new interpretation to the civil-rights struggle, an interpretation that will enable us to come into it, take part in it. And these handkerchief-heads who have been dillydallying and pussyfooting and compromising—we don't intend to let them pussyfoot and dillydally and compromise any longer.

How can you thank a man for giving you what's already yours? How then can you thank him for giving you only part of what's already yours? You haven't even made progress, if what's being given to you, you should have had already. That's not progress. And I love my Brother Lomax [Louis Lomax of CORE], the way he pointed out we're right back where we were in 1954. We're not even as far up as we were in 1954. We're behind where we were in 1954. There's more segregation now than there was in 1954. There's more racial animosity, more racial hatred, more racial violence today in 1964, than there was in 1954. Where is the progress?

And now you're facing a situation where the young Negro's coming up. They don't want to hear that "turn-the-other-cheek" stuff, no. In Jacksonville, those were teenagers, they were throwing Molotov cocktails. Negroes have never done that

March 26, 1964, Malcolm X and Martin Luther King, Jr., shook hands after King announced "direct action" protests if southern senators opposed the civil rights bill with a filibuster. Malcolm X predicted another march on Washington if civil rights legislation was further delayed.

before. But it shows you there's a new deal coming in. There's new thinking coming in. There's new strategy coming in. It'll be Molotov cocktails this month, hand grenades next month, and something else next month. It'll be ballots, or it'll be bullets. It'll be liberty, or it will be death. The only difference about this kind of death—it'll be reciprocal. You know what is meant by "reciprocal"? That's one of Brother Lomax's words, I stole it from him. I don't usually deal with those big words because I don't usually deal with big people. I deal with small people. I find you can get a whole lot of small people and whip hell out of a whole lot of big people. They haven't got anything to lose, and they've got everything to gain. And they'll let you know in a minute: "It takes two to tango; when I go, you go."

The black nationalists, those whose philosophy is black nationalism, in bringing about this new interpretation of the entire meaning of civil rights, look upon it as meaning, as Brother Lomax has pointed out, equality of opportunity. Well, we're justified in seeking civil rights, if it means equality of opportunity, because all we're doing there is trying to collect for our investment. Our mothers and fathers invested sweat and blood. Three hundred and ten years we worked in this country without a dime in return—I mean without a *dime* in return. You let the white man walk around here talking about how rich this country is, but you never stop to think how it got rich so quick. It got rich because you made it rich.

You take the people who are in this audience right now. They're poor, we're all poor as individuals. Our weekly salary individually amounts to hardly anything. But if you take the salary of everyone in here collectively it'll fill up a whole lot of baskets. It's a lot of wealth. If you can collect the wages of just these people right here for a year, you'll be rich—richer than rich. When you look at it like that, think how rich Uncle Sam had to become, not with this handful, but millions of black people. Your and my mother and father, who didn't work an eight-hour shift, but worked from "can't see" in the morning until "can't see" at night, and worked for nothing, making the white man rich, making Uncle Sam rich.

This is our investment. This is our contribution—our blood. Not only did we give of our free labor, we gave of our blood. Every time he had a call to arms, we were the first ones in uniform. We died on every battlefield the white man had. We have made a greater sacrifice than anybody who's standing up in America today. We have made a greater contribution and have collected less. Civil rights, for those of us whose philosophy is black nationalism, means: "Give it to us now. Don't wait for next year. Give it to us yesterday, and that's not fast enough.". . .

If you don't take this kind of stand, your little children will grow up and look at you and think "shame." If you don't take an uncompromising stand—I don't mean go out and get violent; but at the same time you should never be nonviolent unless you run into some nonviolence. I'm nonviolent with those who are nonviolent with me. But when you drop that violence on me, then you've made me go insane, and I'm not responsible for what I do. And that's the way every Negro should get. Any time you know you're within the law, within your legal rights, within your moral rights, in accord with justice, then die for what you believe in. But don't die alone. Let your dying be reciprocal. This is what is meant by equality. What's good for the goose is good for the gander. . . .

If a Negro in 1964 has to sit around and wait for some cracker senator to filibuster when it comes to the rights of black people, why, you and I should hang our heads in shame. You talk about a march on Washington in 1963, you haven't seen anything. There's some more going down in '64. And this time they're not going like they went last year. They're not going singing "We Shall Overcome."

They're not going with white friends. They're not going with placards already painted for them. They're not going with round-trip tickets. They're going with one-way tickets.

And if they don't want that nonviolent army going down there, tell them to bring the filibuster to a halt. The black nationalists aren't going to wait. Lyndon B. Johnson is the head of the Democratic Party. If he's for civil rights, let him go into the Senate next week and declare himself. Let him go in their right now and declare himself. Let him go in there and denounce the Southern branch of his party. Let him go in there right now and take a moral stand—right now, not later. Tell him, don't wait until election time. If he waits too long, brothers and sisters, he will be responsible for letting a condition develop in this country which will create a climate that will bring seeds up out of the ground with vegetation on the end of them looking like something these people never dreamed of. In 1964, it's the ballot or the bullet. Thank you.

DOCUMENT 3

Students for a Democratic Society, The Port Huron Statement (1962)

In June 1962 a small group of northern college students issued the Port Huron Statement, the manifesto of the newly organized Students for a Democratic Society (SDS). The SDS soon became the vanguard organization of a broad social movement, often called the New Left. The SDS's agenda embraced many conventional liberal reforms. Yet it also strove to reinvigorate the old left by advocating "participatory democracy" as a means of overcoming the problems of twentieth-century life such as alienation, bureaucratization, and nuclear war. In the following excerpt from the Port Huron Statement, the SDS identifies the challenges facing America and the values it hopes to promote.

We are people of this generation, bred in at least modest comfort, housed now in universities, looking uncomfortably to the world we inherit.

When we were kids the United States was the wealthiest and strongest country in the world; the only one with the atom bomb, the least scarred by modern war, an initiator of the United Nations that we thought would distribute Western influence throughout the world. Freedom and equality for each individual, government of, by, and for the people—these American values we found good, principles by which we could live as men. Many of us began maturing in complacency.

As we grew, however, our comfort was penetrated by events too troubling to dismiss. First, the permeating and victimizing fact of human degradation, symbolized by the Southern struggle against racial bigotry, compelled most of us from silence to activism. Second, the enclosing fact of the Cold War, symbolized by the presence of the Bomb, brought awareness that we ourselves, and our friends, and millions of abstract "others" we knew more directly because of our common peril, might die at any time. We might deliberately ignore, or avoid, or fail to feel all other human problems, but not these two, for these were too immediate and crushing in their impact, too challenging in the demand that we as individuals take the responsibility for encounter and resolution.

While these and other problems either directly oppressed us or rankled our consciences and became our own subjective concerns, we began to see complicated and disturbing paradoxes in our surrounding America. The declaration "all men are created equal . . ." rang hollow before the facts of Negro life in the South and the big cities of the North. The proclaimed peaceful intentions of the United States contradicted its economic and military investments in the Cold War status quo. . . .

Our work is guided by the sense that we may be the last generation in the experiment with living. But we are a minority—the vast majority of our people regard the temporary equilibriums of our society and world as eternally-functional parts. In this is perhaps the outstanding paradox: we ourselves are imbued with urgency, yet the message of our society is that there is no viable alternative to the present. Beneath the reassuring tones of the politicians, beneath the common opinion that America will "muddle through," beneath the stagnation of those who have closed their minds to the future, is the pervading feeling that there simply are no alternatives, that our times have witnessed the exhaustion not only of Utopias, but of any new departures as well. Feeling the press of complexity upon the emptiness of life, people are fearful of the thought that at any moment things might be thrust out of control. They fear change itself, since change might smash whatever invisible framework seems to hold back chaos for them now. For most Americans, all crusades are suspect, threatening. The fact that each individual sees apathy in his fellows perpetuates the common reluctance to organize for change. The dominant institutions are complex enough to blunt the minds of their potential critics, and entrenched enough to swiftly dissipate or entirely repel the energies of protest and reform, thus limiting human expectancies. Then, too, we are a materially improved society, and by our own improvements we seem to have weakened the case for further change.

Some would have us believe that Americans feel contentment amidst prosperity—but might it not be better be called a glaze above deeply-felt anxieties about their role in the new world? And if these anxieties produce a developed indifference to human affairs, do they not as well produce a yearning to believe there *is* an alternative to the present, that something *can* be done to change circumstances in the school, the workplaces, the bureaucracies, the government? It is to this latter yearning, at once the spark and engine of change, that we direct our present appeal. The search for truly democratic alternatives to the present, and a commitment to social experimentation with them, is a worthy and fulfilling human enterprise, one which moves us and, we hope, others today. . . .

A first task of any social movement is to convince people that the search for orienting theories and the creation of human values is complex but worthwhile. We are aware that to avoid platitudes we must analyze the concrete conditions of social order. But to direct such an analysis we must use the guideposts of basic principles. Our own social values involve conceptions of human beings, human relationships, and social systems.

We regard *men* as infinitely precious and possessed of unfulfilled capacities for reason, freedom, and love. In affirming these principles we are aware of countering perhaps the dominant conceptions of man in the twentieth century: that he is a thing to be manipulated, and that he is inherently incapable of directing his own affairs. We oppose the depersonalization that reduces human beings to the status of things—if anything, the brutalities of the twentieth century teach that means and ends are intimately related, that vague appeals to "posterity" cannot justify the mutilations of the present. We oppose, too, the doctrine of human incompetence because it rests essentially on the modern fact that men have been "competently" manipulated into incompetence—we see little reason why men cannot meet with increasing skill the complexities and responsibilities of their situation, if society is organized not for minority, but for majority, participation in decision-making....

Human relationships should involve fraternity and honesty. Human interdependence is contemporary fact; human brotherhood must be willed, however, as a condition of future survival and as the most appropriate form of social relations. Personal links between man and man are needed, especially to go beyond the partial and fragmentary bonds of function that bind men only as worker to worker, employer to employee, teacher to student, American to Russian....

We would replace power rooted in possession, privileged, or circumstance by power and uniqueness rooted in love, reflectiveness, reason, and creativity. As a *social system* we seek the establishment of a democracy of individual participation, governed by two central aims: that the individual share in those social decisions determining the quality and direction of his life; that society be organized to encourage independence in men and provide the media for their common participation.

In a participatory democracy, the political life would be based in several root principles:

that decision-making of basic social consequence be carried on by public groupings;

that politics be seen positively, as the art of collectively creating an acceptable pattern of social relations;

that politics has the function of bringing people out of isolation and into community, thus being a necessary, though not sufficient, means of finding meaning in personal life;

that the political order should serve to clarify problems in a way instrumental to their solution; it should provide outlets for the expression of personal grievance and aspiration; opposing views should be organized so as to illuminate choices and facilitate the attainment of goals; channels should be commonly available to relate men to knowledge and to power so that private problems—from bad recreation facilities to personal alienation—are formulated as general issues.

The economic sphere would have as its basis the principles:

that work should involve incentives worthier than money or survival. It should be educative, not stultifying; creative, not mechanical; self-directed, not manipulated, encouraging independence, a respect for others, a sense of dignity and a willingness to accept social responsibility, since it is this experience that has crucial influence on habits, perceptions and individual ethics;

that the economic experience is so personally decisive that the individual must share in its full determination;

that the economy itself is of such social importance that its major resources and means of production should be open to democratic participation and subject to democratic social regulations.

Like the political and economic ones, major social institutions—cultural, educational, rehabilitative, and others—should be generally organized with the well-being and dignity of man as the essential measure of success.

In social change or interchange, we find violence to be abhorrent because it requires generally the transformation of the target, be it a human being or a community of people, into a depersonalized object of hate. It is imperative that the means of violence be abolished and the institutions—local, national, international—that encourage nonviolence as a condition of conflict be developed.

These are our central values, in skeletal form. It remains vital to understand their denial or attainment in the context of the modern world. . . .

1. Any new left in America must be, in large measure, a left with real intellectual skills, committed to deliberativeness, honesty, reflection as working tools. The university permits the political life to be an adjunct to the academic one, and action to be informed by reason.

2. A new left must be distributed in significant social roles throughout the country. The universities are distributed in such a manner.

3. A new left must consist of younger people who matured in the post-war world, and partially be directed to the recruitment of younger people. The university is an obvious beginning point.

4. A new left must include liberals and socialists, the former for their relevance, the latter for their sense of thoroughgoing reforms in the system. The university is a more sensible place than a political party for these two traditions to begin to discuss their differences and look for political synthesis.

5. A new left must start controversy across the land, if national policies and national apathy are to be reversed. The ideal university is a community of controversy, within itself and in its effects on communities beyond.

6. A new left must transform modern complexity into issues that can be understood and felt close-up by every human being. It must give form to the feelings of helplessness and indifference, so that people may see the political, social, and economic sources of their private troubles and organize to change society. In a time of supposed prosperity, moral complacency, and political manipulation, a new left cannot rely on only aching stomachs to be the engine force of social reform. The case for change, for alternatives that will involve uncomfortable personal efforts, must be argued as never before. The university is a relevant place for all of these activities.

But we need not indulge in illusions: the university system cannot complete a movement of ordinary people making demands for a better life. From its schools and colleges across the nation, a militant left might awaken its allies, and by beginning the process towards peace, civil rights, and labor struggles, reinsert theory and idealism where too often reign confusion and political barter. The power of students and faculty united is not only potential; it has shown its actuality in the South, and in the reform movements of the North.

The bridge to political power, though, will be built through genuine cooperation, locally, nationally, and internationally, between a new left of young people, and an awakening community of allies. In each community we must look within the university and act with confidence that we can be powerful, but we must look outwards to the less exotic but more lasting struggles for justice.

To turn these possibilities into realities will involve national efforts at university reform by an alliance of students and faculty. They must wrest control of the educational process from the administrative bureaucracy. They must make fraternal and functional contact with allies in labor, civil rights, and other liberal forces outside the campus. They must import major public issues into the curriculum—research and teaching on problems of war and peace is an outstanding example. They must make debate and controversy, not dull pedantic cant, the common style for educational life. They must consciously build a base for their assault upon the loci of power.

As students for a democratic society, we are committed to stimulating this kind of social movement, this kind of vision and program in campus and community across the country. If we appear to seek the unattainable, as it has been said, then let it be known that we do so to avoid the unimaginable.

DOCUMENT 4

Charles Sherrod, Student Nonviolent Coordinating Committee Memorandum (1961)

Late in the summer of 1961 workers for the Student Nonviolent Coordinating Committee (SNCC) arrived in Albany, Georgia, to conduct a voter registration drive. Charles Sherrod, age twenty-two, and Cordell Reagon, eighteen, were two of the leading SNCC activists to come to Georgia. The two leaders, both veterans of sit-ins and freedom rides, quickly broadened the goal of their work to achieve the complete desegregation of Albany. In the following SNCC memorandum, Charles Sherrod describes his initial work in Albany and how the various members of the city's African American community united to form the Albany Movement. This episode is representative of the thousands of grass-roots efforts by southern blacks to challenge segregation and disfranchisement.

The Albany we found in October when we came down as SNCC field workers was quite different from the Albany we now know. Naturally, though, many things remain the same. The swift flowing, cool waters of the Flint River still cut off the east side of the city from the west. The paved streets remind visitors that civilization may be thought to exist in the area while the many dusty, sandy roadways in residential areas cause one to wonder where tax money goes. Beautiful homes against green backgrounds with lawns rolling up and down hills and around corners held up by the deep roots of palm and pine trees untouched by years of nature's movement, sunny days with moonlit nights—this was the Albany we had been introduced to in October. But this was not the real Albany; the real Albany was seen much later.

Albany is known by its people to be "liberal." Located in the center of such infamous counties as "Terrible Terrell," "Dogging Douglas," "Unmitigated Mitchell," "Lamentable Lee," "Unbearable Baker," and the "Unworthy Worth County." It stands out as the only metropolitan area of any prominence in Southwest Georgia. It is the crossroads of rural people in villages and towns within a radius of ninety miles. It was principally because of its location that Albany was chosen as the beachhead for Democracy in *DEEP Southwest Georgia*.

Initially, we met with every obstacle possible. We had come down with the idea of setting up office in Albany and moving on shortly to Terrell County. This idea was short-lived. We found that it would take more time than we thought to present this city of 23,000 Negroes with the idea that freedom is worth sacrifice. . . .

The first obstacle to remove . . . was the mental block in the minds of those who wanted to move but were unable for fear that we were not who we said we were. But when people began to hear us in churches, social meetings, on the streets, in the poolhalls, lunchrooms, nightclubs, and other places where people gather, they began to open up a bit. We would tell them of how it feels to be in prison, what it means to be behind bars, in jail for the cause. We explained to them that we had stopped school because we felt compelled to do so since so many of us were in chains. We explained further that there were worse chains than jail and prison. We referred to the system that imprisons men's minds and robs them of creativity. We mocked the systems that teaches men to be good Negroes instead of good men. We gave an account of the many resistances of injustice in the courts, in employment, registration, and voting. The people knew that such evils existed but when we pointed them out time and time again and emphasized the need for concerted action against them, the people began to think. At this point, we started to illustrate what had happened in Montgomery, Macon, Nashville, Charlotte, Atlanta, Savannah, Richmond, Petersburg, and many other cities where people came together and protested against an evil system. . . .

From the beginning we had, as Student Nonviolent Coordinating Committee field people, visited the NAACP Youth Chapter, introduced ourselves and outlined our project for Voter-Registration. We pointed out differences between the two organizations and advanced the hope that we could work together.

From this point we initiated meetings in the churches of the city. We had introduced ourselves to the Baptist Ministerial Alliance and the Interdenominational Alliance. We were given their support as groups and many churches opened their doors to us; others were afraid for one reason or another.

To these churches we drew the young people from the College, Trade and General High schools, and on the street. They were searching for a meaning in life. Nine committees were formed—Typists, Clubs, Writing, Telephone, Campus, communication, Sunday School communication, Ministerial communication, Boy and Girl Scouts, and a central committee of eighteen persons. Some of those were members of the NAACP Youth Chapter. They kept coming to the workshops we were holding every night at different churches. . . .

That same morning, five or six of us got together at the home of a local citizen and planned again to go to the bus terminal. At three o'clock, nine students approached the bus station, which is located only one block away from the predominantly "Negro" business area. Upon seeing the neatly dressed students walk toward the station, a large number came from the poolrooms, lunchrooms, liquor stores, and other places. . . .

The stories of faraway cities and their protests turned over in their minds. Was this a dream or was it really happening here in Albany? The students symbolized in the eyes of them who looked on, the expression of years of resentment—for police brutality, for poor housing, for dis[e]nfranchisement, for inferior education, for the whole damnable system. The fruit of years of prayer and sacrifice stood the ageless hatched-men of the South, the policeman, but the children of the new day stood tall, fearless before the legal executioners of the blacks in the DEEP south.

The bus station was full of men in blue but up through the mass of people past the men with guns and billies ready, into the terminal, they marched, quiet and quite clean. They were allowed to buy tickets to Florida but after sitting in the waiting room, they were asked to leave under the threat of arrest. They left as planned and later filed affidavits with the Interstate Commerce Commission. The idea had been delivered. In the hearts of the young and of the old, from that moment on, Segregation was dead—the funeral was to come later.

There was a meeting of minds which came about as a result of this action. It was a momentous occasion! The gathering was scheduled for one Friday evening, at a citizen's home. The proposed number of five had grown to a total of twenty interested persons who had been invited by the initial five. No one imagined the importance of this meeting. Its objective was to organize and thereby discipline a group to negotiate with the city officials. It was generally understood that the entire group would go before the officials but later three men were chosen to represent the group (THE ALBANY MOVEMENT). This committee presented to the Mayor the displeasure of the community with Segregation as connected with the following: Train station, Bus terminal, Library, Parks, Hospitals, City Buses, Juries, Jobs and other public facilities. There was no reasonable consequence of the meeting with the Mayor; it was as if there had never been communication.

But the importance of this meeting of the representatives of the Albany community at the home of a citizen lies in its structure. The real issue immediately took the floor in the form of a question: Would the organizations involved be willing to lose their identity as separate groups and cooperate under the name of "THE ALBANY MOVEMENT"? All of the organizations had to caucus—Baptist Ministerial Alliance, Interdenominational Alliance, Criterion Club, Lincoln Heights Improvement Association, Federated Women Clubs of Albany, National Association for the Advance of Colored People and its coordinate groups—Youth Council—Albany Voters League, and the Student Nonviolent Coordinating Committee. There were other interested persons who were members of such groups as the American Legion, Masons, Elks, etc., but not there as official representatives. These groups later gave their support. After a short period of deliberation the groups were ready to give their opinions. All of the groups were willing to lose their identit[ies] in the local organization except the NAACP, whose delegates requested time to receive directives from the national office.

The Albany Movement soon grew to the statue of "Spokesman" for the "Negro" community; a representative social unit with extraordinary powers of negotiations had been born. . . .

[T]he first mass meeting was called at one of the larger churches in the city—Mount Zion. A week before the meeting, enthusiasm had already been developing. There was a men's day exercise at which the Reverend Ralph Abernathy, Treasurer of the Southern Christian Leadership Conference, was the main speaker. He had been invited by the local church, but his soul-searching message touched the hearts of many, mounting enthusiastic anticipation for the mass meeting.

The night of the first Mass Meeting came! The church was packed before eight o'clock. People were everywhere, in the aisles, sitting and standing in the choir stands, hanging over the railing of the balcony upstairs, sitting in trees outside near windows, and about twenty or thirty ministers sat on the pulpit in chairs and on the floor side by side. There was no bickering. Soon a young doctor of the community took charge of the gathering, leading in the freedom songs which have grown out of the student movement during the last two years. Petitions were laid before Almighty God by one of the ministers and a challenge was directed to the assembly by the young doctor. Then arose a tall, silver-haired, outspoken veteran of the struggle. He spoke [in a] slow and determined [manner]. He referred to attempts last year to unify the community in protest against literary abuse of black men in the local paper and filled in with vivid detail the developments to the date of the Mass Meeting. Appearing also on the program was the indefatigable, only, local Negro lawyer, C. B. King. He stood flatfooted and thundered with his explosively deep voice, striking at both the inaction of the church and its hypocrisy. He also condemned local leadership in other areas for procrastination. At times he sounded like the prophet of doom but before he had finished, in his highly polished speech, he declared that our only hope was unity. This had been the real reason for the Mass Meeting—to weld the community into one bond of reason and emotion. The force to do this was generated by accounts of the released who individually described the physical situation and mental state of each, in jail.

When the last speaker among the students, Bertha Gober, had finished, there was nothing left to say. Tears filled the eyes of hard, grown men who had known personally and seen with their own eyes merciless atrocities committed by small men without conscience. As Bertha, with her small frame and baby voice told of spending Thanksgiving in jail along with other physical inconveniences, there was not a dry eye to be found. And when we rose to sing "We Shall Overcome," nobody could imagine what kept the top of the church on four corners. It was as if everyone had been lifted up on high and had been granted voices to sing with the celestial chorus in another time and in another place.

I threw my head back and closed my eyes as I sang with my whole body. I remembered walking dusty roads for weeks without food. I remembered staying up all night for two and three nights in succession writing and cutting stencils and memeographing and wondering—How Long? I remembered thinking about home, a thousand miles away and fun, games, dancing, movies, boatrides, tennis, chess, swimming,—LIFE; this was history.

But when I momentarily opened my eyes something good happened to me. I saw standing beside a dentist of the city, a man of the streets singing and smiling with joyful tears in his eyes and beside him a mailman with whom I had become acquainted along with people from all walks of life. It was then that I felt deep down within where it really counts, a warm feeling and all I could do was laugh out loud in the swelling of the singing.

DOCUMENT 5

Lyndon B. Johnson, Commencement Address at Howard University (1965)

On June 4, 1965, President Lyndon B. Johnson addressed the graduating class of Howard University, an all-black university in Washington, D.C. Johnson praised the tireless efforts of African Americans to force the nation to live up to the principles and ideals of American democracy. In a sweeping endorsement of interracial reform, Johnson, recognizing that the civil rights legislation of the 1960s marked only the "end of the beginning," pledged to dedicate the "expanding efforts" of his administration to ensuring that African Americans would achieve "not just equality as a right and a theory, but equality as a fact and a result." Johnson's speech marked the zenith of liberal reform.

Our earth is the home of revolution.

In every corner of every continent men charged with hope contend with ancient ways in pursuit of justice. They reach for the newest of weapons to realize the oldest of dreams: that each may walk in freedom and pride, stretching his talents, enjoying the fruits of the earth.

Our enemies may occasionally seize the day of change. But it is the banner of our revolution they take. And our own future is linked to this process of swift and turbulent change in many lands. But nothing, in any country, touches us more profoundly, nothing is more freighted with meaning for our own destiny, than the revolution of the Negro American.

In far too many ways American Negroes have been another nation: deprived of freedom, crippled by hatred, the doors of opportunity closed to hope.

In our time change has come to this nation too. Heroically, the American Negro—acting with impressive restraint—has peacefully protested and marched, entered the courtrooms and the seats of government, demanding a justice long denied. The voice of the Negro was the call to action. But it is a tribute to America that, once aroused, the courts and the Congress, the President and most of the people, have been the allies of progress.

Thus we have seen the high court of the country declare that discrimination based on race was repugnant to the Constitution, and therefore void. We have seen—in 1957, 1960, and again in 1964—the first civil rights legislation in almost a century....

The voting rights bill will be the latest, and among the most important, in a long series of victories. But this victory—as Winston Churchill said of another triumph for freedom—"is not the end. It is not even the beginning of the end. But it is, perhaps, the end of the beginning."

That beginning is freedom; and the barriers to that freedom are tumbling. Freedom is the right to share, fully and equally, in American society—to vote, to hold a job, to enter a public place, to go to school. It is the right to be treated, in every part of our national life, as a man equal in dignity and promise to all others.

But freedom is not enough. You do not wipe away the scars of centuries by saying: Now, you are free to go where you want, do as you desire, and choose the leaders you please.

You do not take a man who, for years, has been hobbled by chains, liberate him, bring him to the starting line of a race, saying "you are free to compete with all the others," and still justly believe you have been completely fair.

Thus it is not enough to open the gates of opportunity. All our citizens must have the ability to walk through those gates.

This is the next and the more profound stage of the battle for civil rights. We seek not just freedom but opportunity—not just legal equity but human ability—not just equality as a right and a theory, but equality as a fact and a result.

For the task is to give twenty million Negroes the same chance as every other American to learn and grow—to work and share in society—to develop their abilities—physical, mental, and spiritual, and to pursue their individual happiness.

To this end equal opportunity is essential, but not enough. Men and women of all races are born with the same range of abilities. But ability is not just the product of birth. It is stretched or stunted by the family you live with, and the neighborhood you live in—by the school you go to, and the poverty or richness of your surroundings. It is the product of a hundred unseen forces playing upon the infant, the child, and the man.

This graduating class at Howard University is witness to the indomitable determination of the Negro American to win his way in American life.

The number of Negroes in schools of high learning has almost doubled in fifteen years. The number of nonwhite professional workers has more than doubled in ten years. The median income of Negro college women now exceeds that of white college women. And these are the enormous accomplishments of distinguished individual Negroes—many of them graduates of this institution.

These are proud and impressive achievements. But they only tell the story of a growing middle class minority, steadily narrowing the gap between them and their white counterparts.

But for the great majority of Negro Americans—the poor, the unemployed, the uprooted and dispossessed—there is a grimmer story. They still are another nation. Despite the court orders and the laws, the victories and speeches, for them the walls are rising and the gulf is widening....

We are not completely sure why this is. The causes are complex and subtle. But we do know the two broad basic reasons. And we know we have to act.

First, Negroes are trapped—as many whites are trapped—in inherited, gateless poverty. They lack training and skills. They are shut in slums, without decent medical care. Private and public poverty combine to cripple their capacities.

We are attacking these evils through our poverty program, our education program, our health program and a dozen more—aimed at the root causes of poverty.

We will increase, and accelerate, and broaden this attack in years to come, until this most enduring of foes yields to our unyielding will.

But there is a *second* cause—more difficult to explain, more deeply grounded, more desperate in its force. It is the devastating heritage of long years of slavery; and a century of oppression, hatred and injustice.

For Negro poverty is not white poverty. Many of its causes and many of its cures are the same. But there are differences—deep, corrosive, obstinate differences—radiating painful roots into the community, the family, and the nature of the individual.

These differences are not racial differences. They are solely and simply the consequence of ancient brutality, past injustice, and present prejudice. They are anguishing to observe. For the Negro they are a reminder of oppression. For the white they are a reminder of guilt. But they must be faced, and dealt with, and overcome; if we are to reach the time when the only difference between Negroes and whites is the color of their skin.

Nor can we find a complete answer in the experience of other American minorities. They made a valiant, and largely successful effort to emerge from poverty and prejudice. The Negro, like these others, will have to rely mostly on his own efforts. But he cannot do it alone. For they did not have the heritage of centuries to overcome. They did not have a cultural tradition which had been twisted and battered by endless years of hatred and hopelessness. Nor were they excluded because of race or color—a feeling whose dark intensity is matched by no other prejudice in our society.

Nor can these differences be understood as isolated infirmities. They are a seamless web. They cause each other. They result from each other. They reinforce each other. Much of the Negro community is buried under a blanket of history and circumstance. It is not a lasting solution to lift just one corner. We must stand on all sides and raise the entire cover if we are to liberate our fellow citizens.

One of the differences is the increased concentration of Negroes in our cities. More than 73 per cent of all Negroes live in urban areas compared with less than 70 per cent of whites. Most of them live in slums. And most of them live together; a separated people. Men are shaped by their world. When it is a world of decay ringed by an invisible wall—when escape is arduous and uncertain, and the saving pressures of a more hopeful society are unknown—it can cripple the youth and desolate the man.

There is also the burden a dark skin can add to the search for a productive place in society. Unemployment strikes most swiftly and broadly at the Negro. This burden erodes hope. Blighted hope breeds despair. Despair brings indifference to the learning which offers a way out. And despair coupled with indifference is often the source of destructive rebellion against the fabric of society. . . .

Perhaps most important—its influence radiating to every part of life—is the breakdown of the Negro family structure. For this, most of all, white America must accept responsibility. It flows from centuries of oppression and persecution of the Negro man. It flows from the long years of degradation and discrimination which have attacked his dignity and assaulted his ability to provide for his family. . . .

Unless we work to strengthen the family—to create conditions under which most parents will stay together—all the rest: schools and playgrounds, public assistance and private concern—will not be enough to cut completely the circle of despair and deprivation.

There is no single easy answer to all these problems.

Jobs are part of the answer. They bring the income which permits a man to provide for his family.

Decent homes in decent surroundings and a chance to learn are part of the answer.

Welfare and social programs better designed to hold families together are part of the answer.

Care for the sick is part of the answer.

An understanding heart by all Americans is also part of the answer.

To all these fronts—and a dozen more—I will dedicate the expanding efforts of my administration....

It is the glorious opportunity of this generation to end the one huge wrong of the American nation—and in so doing to find America for ourselves, with the same immense thrill of discovery which gripped those who first began to realize that here, at last, was a home for freedom.

All it will take is for all of us to understand what this country is and what it must become.

The Scripture promises: "I shall light a candle of understanding in thine heart, which shall not be put out."

Together, and with millions more, we can light that candle of understanding in the heart of America.

And, once lit, it will never go out.

DOCUMENT 6

Shirley Chisholm, "I'd Rather Be Black than Female" (1970)

In 1968 Shirley Chisholm became the first black woman elected to Congress, serving as a representative from New York from 1969 to 1983. In the following article, Chisholm reflects on the obstacles she faced in pursuing her professional goals. She found that she encountered greater prejudice as a woman than as an African American. Many grievances she describes galvanized activists in the women's liberation movement of the late 1960s and 1970s.

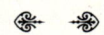

Being the first black woman elected to Congress has made me some kind of phenomenon. There are nine other blacks in Congress; there are ten other women. I was the first to overcome both handicaps at once. Of the two handicaps, being black is much less of a drawback than being female.

If I said that being black is a greater handicap than being a woman, probably no one would question me. Why? Because "we all know" there is prejudice against black people in America. That there is prejudice against women is an idea that still strikes nearly all men—and, I am afraid, most women—as bizarre.

Prejudice against blacks was invisible to most white Americans for many years. When blacks finally started to "mention" it, with sit-ins, boycotts, and freedom rides, Americans were incredulous. "Who, us?" they asked in injured tones. "We're prejudiced?" It was the start of a long, painful reeducation for white America. It will take years for whites—including those who think of themselves as liberals—to discover and eliminate the racist attitudes they all actually have.

How much harder will it be to eliminate the prejudice against women? I am sure it will be a longer struggle. Part of the problem is that women in

America are much more brainwashed and content with their roles as second-class citizens than blacks ever were.

Let me explain. I have been active in politics for more than twenty years. For all but the last six, I have done the work—all the tedious details that make the difference between victory and defeat on election day—while men reaped the rewards, which is almost invariably the lot of women in politics.

It is still women—about three million volunteers—who do most of this work in the American political world. The best any of them can hope for is the honor of being district or county vice chairman, a kind of separate-but-equal position with which a woman is rewarded for years of faithful envelope stuffing and card-party organizing. In such a job, she gets a number of free trips to state and sometimes national meetings and conventions, where her role is supposed to be to vote the way her male chairman votes.

When I tried to break out of that role in 1963 and run for the New York State Assembly seat from Brooklyn's Bedford-Stuyvesant, the resistance was bitter. From the start of that campaign, I faced undisguised hostility because of my sex.

But it was four years later, when I ran for Congress, that the question of my sex became a major issue. Among members of my own party, closed meetings were held to discuss ways of stopping me.

My opponent, the famous civil-rights leader James Farmer, tried to project a black, masculine image; he toured the neighborhood with sound trucks filled with young men wearing Afro haircuts, dashikis, and beards. While the television crews ignored me, they were not aware of a very important statistic which both I and my campaign manager, Wesley MacD. Holder knew. In my district there are 2.5 women for every man registered to vote. And those women are organized—in PTAs, church societies, card clubs, and other social and service groups. I went to them and asked their help. Mr. Farmer still doesn't quite know what hit him.

When a bright young woman graduate starts looking for a job, why is the first question always: "Can you type?" A history of prejudice lies behind that question. Why are women thought of as secretaries, not administrators? Librarians and teachers, but not doctors and lawyers? Because they are thought of as different and inferior. The happy homemaker and the contented darky are both stereotypes produced by prejudice.

Women have not even reached the level of tokenism that blacks are reaching. No women sit on the Supreme Court. Only two have held Cabinet rank and none do at present. Only two women hold ambassadorial rank. But women predominate in the lower-paying, menial, unrewarding, dead-end jobs, and when they do reach better positions, they are invariably paid less than a man gets for the same job.

If that is not prejudice, what would you call it?

A few years ago, I was talking with a political leader about a promising young woman as a candidate. "Why invest time and effort to build the girl up?" he asked me. "You know she'll only drop out of the game to have a couple of kids just about the time we're ready to run her for mayor."

Plenty of people have said similar things about me. Plenty of others have advised me, every time I tried to take another upward step, that I should go back to teaching, a woman's vocation, and leave politics to the men. I love teaching, and I am ready to go back to it as soon as I am convinced that this country no longer needs a woman's contribution.

When there are no children going to bed hungry in this rich nation, I may be ready to go back to teaching. When there is a good school for every child, I may be ready. When we do not spend our wealth on hardware to murder people, when we no longer tolerate prejudice against minorities, and when the laws against unfair housing and unfair employment practices are enforced instead of evaded, then there may be nothing more for me to do in politics.

But until that happens—and we all know it will not be this year or next—what we need is more women in politics, because we have a very special contribution to make. I hope that the example of my success will convince other women to get into politics—and not just to stuff envelopes, but to run for office.

It is women who can bring empathy, tolerance, insight, patience and persistence to government— the qualities we naturally have or have had to develop because of our suppression by men. The women of a nation mold its morals, its religion, and its politics by the lives they live. At present, our country needs women's idealism and determination, perhaps more in politics than anywhere else.

DOCUMENT 7

Richard M. Nixon, "What Has Happened to America?" (1967)*

In his 1965 Howard University commencement address, President Lyndon Johnson warned that the deplorable conditions of the nation's urban ghettoes could be "the source of destructive rebellion against the fabric of society" (see Document 5). Within two months of his speech the inhabitants of the black ghetto of Watts in Los Angeles rebelled in an explosive riot of burning and looting. In the summer of 1967 violent riots broke out in Detroit and Newark, New Jersey. The rioting fed a white backlash against liberal reform. One of the most forceful proponents of this reaction was former Vice President Richard M. Nixon. In the following article from *Reader's Digest*, Nixon blames the lawlessness on a growing permissiveness and liberal sympathy toward criminals, themes that he would emphasize in his 1968 presidential campaign.

What has happened to America?

Just three years ago this nation seemed to be completing its greatest decade of racial progress and entering one of the most hopeful periods in American history. Twenty million Negroes were at last being admitted to full membership in the society, and this social miracle was being performed with a minimum of friction and without loss of our freedom or tranquility.

With this star of racial peace and progress before us, how did it happen that last summer saw the United States blazing in an inferno of urban anarchy?...

The shocking crime and disorder in American life today flow in large measure from two fundamental changes that have occurred in the attitudes of many Americans.

First, there is the permissiveness toward violation of the law and public order by those who agree with the cause in question. Second, there is the indulgence of crime because of sympathy for the past grievances of those who have become criminals.

---

*Excerpted with permission from "What Has Happened to America?" by Richard Nixon, *Reader's Digest*, October 1967. Copyright © 1967 by the Reader's Digest Association, Inc.

Our judges have gone too far in weakening the peace forces as against the criminal forces.

Our opinion-makers have gone too far in promoting the doctrine that when a law is broken, society, not the criminal, is to blame.

Our teachers, preachers and politicians have gone too far in advocating the idea that each individual should determine what laws are good and what laws are bad, and that he then should obey the law he likes and disobey the law he dislikes.

The same permissiveness is applied to those who defy the law in pursuit of civil rights. This trend has gone so far in America that there is not only a growing tolerance of lawlessness but an increasing public acceptance of civil disobedience. Men of intellectual and moral eminence who encourage public disobedience of the law are responsible for the acts of those who inevitably follow their counsel: the poor, the ignorant and the impressionable. For example, to the professor objecting to de facto segregation, it may be crystal-clear where civil disobedience may begin and where it must end. But the boundaries have become fluid to his students and other listeners. Today in the urban slums the limits of responsible action are all but invisible. . . .

Many observers contend that the only answer to riots is to rebuild our cities and remove the basic causes of race conflict. This confuses long-range needs with short-range crises.

The problems of our great cities were decades in building; they will be decades in their solution. While attacking the problems with urgency we must await the results with patience. But we cannot have patience with urban violence. Immediate and decisive force must be the first response. For there can be no progress unless there is an end to violence and unless there is respect for the rule of law. To ensure the success of long-range programs, we must first deal with the immediate crisis—the riots.

How are riots to be prevented?

The first step is better pay and better training and higher standards for police; we must attract the highest caliber of individual to the force.

We demand many things of the man on the beat. He must protect us effectively from crime and yet be circumspect in his handling of criminals. He must handle riots with speed and firmness. He must avoid verbal as well as physical brutality. He must risk his life to protect our property. In short, we ask more of them than we ask of ourselves—and if we are going to get the kind of police protection we want, we are going to have to pay police officers what they are worth.

Second, there must be a substantial upgrading in the *number* of police. The first purpose of the added manpower is to bring the physical presence of the law into those communities where the writ of authority has ceased to run.

The responsibility of the police in these areas is not only to maintain the peace but to protect life and property. It is the Negro citizens who suffer most from racial violence. When police and firemen retreat under sniper fire from riot-torn districts to let them "burn-out," it is the Negro's district that is burned out.

America's primary effort to close its gaping racial wound should be an effort to gain the trust and the active help of the law-abiding majority of the Negro community. One thing is certain: the allegiance of Negroes to the goal of a biracial society will not be won by abandoning them and their property to scavengers and arsonists. . . .

It would be a national tragedy if last summer's orgies of looting and burning were used as an excuse to halt the Negro's economic, political and social advance toward full and equal membership in American society.

The riot statistics show that the Negro has already paid an enormous price for the violence. It was the Negro's home, often his shop, his future that were burned out by the rioters. It would be a compounded injustice now to penalize the law-abiding Negro majority for the criminal conduct of the lawless minority.

How is the country to pick up where it left off before the rioting? Some see the answer as simply more money—billions of dollars more.

Certainly money will be needed; but the extremists who threaten riots or "long hot summers in the streets" to get it are gravely mistaken to think that the threat of pillage is the way to sell Americans on social justice. Congress is responsive to the will of the people; and Congressional resistance to spending for the cities has mounted rapidly in the wake of the disorders.

Before rushing into massive new programs, Congress should find out why the programs of the past have failed. It is time to stop using the warmed-over programs of the '30's to solve the problems of the '60's.

When second- and third-generation families are living on welfare as semi-permanent wards of the state, something is drastically wrong with the program. Both the goals and the means of aiding the chronically impoverished must be restudied.

One fact that should be reflected in any new program that has not been reflected in the past is the disintegration of the Negro family. Only a minority of Negro children reaching the age of 18 have lived all their lives with both of their parents. In areas like Central Harlem more than half come from homes where one or more of the parents are permanently absent.

Of what value to the community is one of our federal programs that provides money for dependent children—only as long as the fathers stay away from the home? The discipline, guidance and example of a parent are as crucial as the quality of food and medicine in creating a productive citizen out of a slum child.

The degree of despair in the Negro community today can be accurately gauged by the number of false hopes that have been raised, and dashed on the pavement of reality. Many political figures in this country have promised too much with the passage of each new piece of social and civil-rights legislation. It is both wrong and dangerous to make promises that cannot be fulfilled, or to raise hopes that come to nothing.

No issue in our history has been so suffused with demagogy, irresponsible partisanship, vote-buying and promises of Utopia as has the century-long struggle of the American Negro from the degradation of slavery to the mainstream of American life. Normally, those are but the venial sins of American politics. But when added to the race issue, they have become explosive ingredients, and that issue cannot carry a much heavier load.

The time is now for a new candor—for straight, honest talk, and strong, effective action. Negroes have rightly and repeatedly been reminded that the divisions of centuries will not be months in passing away. But white America is dangerously deluding itself if it thinks that a handful of court decisions and civil-rights acts are going to make full competitors in our society out of children who arrive at life's starting line fresh from broken families, slum conditions, inferior schools and crime- and vice-ridden neighborhoods.

The hour is late for America. Crime and urban violence have reached the high-water mark where they either crest and recede—or we shall have to pay for their suppression and containment in the coin of freedom. . . .

To heal the wounds that have torn the nation asunder, to re-establish respect for law and the principles that have been the source of America's growth and greatness will require the example of leaders in every walk of American life. More important than that, it will require the wisdom, the patience and the personal commitment of every American.

DOCUMENT 8

Donald Wheeldin, "The Situation in Watts Today" (1967)

Few signs indicated in 1967 that any long-term solutions to urban poverty would emerge. In the following article, African American journalist Donald Wheeldin assesses the situation in Watts two years after the riots. He finds that programs that receive popular support among whites such as business investment offer little more than "finger-in-the-dike" solutions to an area devastated by unemployment, slum housing, poor health care, and disintegrating families.

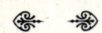

To answer the question, "what is the situation in Watts today?" is, perforce, to provide an answer to what the situation holds for every single Negro who lives in the United States.

The great though tragic Watts uprising in August, 1965, in which 36 persons (mostly Negroes) were slaughtered by police, 1,032 injured, 3,436 jailed, and $40 millions in property destroyed, is now held as responsible for the stunning defeat of Governor Edmund G. (Pat) Brown for re-election in California. Following his defeat, Brown charged that Watts and subsequent ghetto explosions brought on "the white backlash" that sent him into total political eclipse.

This is, of course, such an unsophisticated political estimate—omitting so many important factors—that, by itself, it becomes a substantial argument explaining his defeat. However, it has become popular for politicians, preachers, police officials and Negro "spokesmen" to blame everything on Watts—ranging from the Governor's defeat to the arrest of a teenager, anywhere in the state. Actually, the Governor's failure lies not in the star of Watts but, rather, in himself and his own inept coterie of underlings.

The inherent peril of Watts today, ghetto for many of Los Angeles 420,000 Negroes, is that nothing has really changed since that fateful week in August, 1965. If anything, the situation has grown alarmingly worse.

Burned-out buildings, vacant lots, boarded-up businesses still pockmark the main areas there. At the corner of 103rd Street and Compton Avenue, heart of its business section, is to be seen Mayor Sam Yorty's optimum contribution towards "an improved Watts community." It consists of a printed statement proclaiming free pony rides for the kids, over the mayor's signature. Further east on 103rd Street at Lou Dillon Avenue is to be found an old abandoned gas station that now headquarters a new organization called the Sons of Watts Improvement Association.

"Sons of Watts," ages 20–26, claim a membership of nearly 100, drawn from former neighborhood gangs.

Their stated purpose is to rebuild Watts into a prosperous community by seeking a return of job-supplying businesses and industry.

How have they been advised to do this?

They've gotten a few traffic signs posted and been urged to distribute 100 containers bearing a legend "Keep Watts Clean" in which people are asked to drop their empty bottles and trash.

Meanwhile, the Los Angeles business community boasts getting "thousands of jobs" for Watts residents which Negro spokesmen in the area contradict as being only "a few hundred." However, Aerojet General Corporation, a huge West Coast outfit with kingsized military contracts, has taken $4.5 million of government money to set up a Watts Manufacturing Company that now hires Watts Negroes to make tents for the Armed Forces. It estimates keeping "200 people busy for the next two years."

The above-mentioned are the piddling answers to a community where today 42 out of every 100 men are reported unemployed and among whom many are unemployable. Watts is the community where Los Angeles voters recently denied funds for building a hospital despite 1960 health statistics disclosing: a death rate 22.3 percent higher than the rest of Los Angeles; 65 percent of all tuberculin reactors; 46 percent of the venereal diseases; and 42 percent of all food poisoning in the city.

Stark and graphic as they are, the statistics alone do not convey the real situation in Watts. Like other black ghettos throughout the country, it is mired in a racism that threatens to suck the substance from the American Dream and turn it into a nightmare. The bald fact of Watts is that black people there are not quite considered eligible for membership in the human family....

Earlier, last May, all the tree top tall tensions that erupted in the Watts explosion threatened to break out anew after the gunning down of Leonard Deadwyler, young Negro father, rushing his pregnant wife to the hospital. After his car had pulled to the curb and stopped, Jerald Bova, a white policeman, trained his gun through the side-window and fired. He later termed it "an accident." Bova had a prior record of brutality towards Negroes.

At the massed funeral services for Deadwyler, following a fifteen block long march, Rev. W. H. Johnson, speaking on behalf of Watts ministers said: "No man's life in Watts . . . is worth more than the price of a bullet. Any innocent man may be killed in Watts. It is a jungle where inhumanity is the order of the day."

It was within this context that the late Los Angeles Police Chief William Parker poured acid into the wounds of the Negro community—as he had so often on prior occasions—by taking to the television and blistering the Negro community and its leaders as stupid and totally lacking in respect for his brand of law and order. Parker's sentiment was echoed by Mayor Yorty.

This turn of events caused great consternation, frightening some Negro leaders. Others became angered. All were worried and concerned. As a result, a hastily called meeting brought together the widest diversity of Negro groups united for the single purpose of challenging Parker and his "get tough" policy and treatment of Negroes. Sole condition for membership was being a Negro. Black spokesmen ranged from the churches to the Communists; Nationalists to the NAACP; social clubs to society matrons. They formed the Temporary Alliance of Local Organizations (TALO). During the summer, TALO financed and placed in Watts and throughout South Los Angeles a volunteer Community Alert Patrol to observe and report on police malpractices.

The CAP, equipped with 2-way radios, was an impressive step forward as it entered the ghetto areas to the cheers of the people who readily cooperate with the Negro volunteers in keeping the peace. It wasn't long before the Mexican community asked its help in setting up such a patrol in its area. Even the police who had bitterly resented CAP's presence, earlier, was forced to call on it for help in a number of cases. This volunteer action represented a first, halting step toward acquiring some "black power."

Meanwhile, others in TALO sought to press with the Los Angeles Police Commission and Chief Parker for a redress of Watts community grievances. While in the process, Parker died and some of the immediate pressures on the community receded. TALO, no longer with a single unifying object, began to dissolve....

The largest and probably most noble single thrust in an effort to retrieve and make life bearable in Watts has been undertaken by the Presbyterians through Westminster House.

With a paid staff of 100 social workers under the leadership of dedicated Morris Samuel (Father Sam) the Center is spending 66 percent of its $1,148,150 budget on a job training and employment program for Watts Negro youth.

Bluntly, this, too, is doomed to fail. Why? Because the shrinking job market, alone, will be unable to absorb the trainees. And the government doesn't have enough post offices in which to employ the rest. Beyond that what has as yet to be understood is that racism is a prop that undergirds and helps sustain this economic system. Finger-in-the-dike methods won't change it. Only a successful challenge to those who preside over it will usher in a new and different set of race relations. The power and direction of the system's present rulers are best illustrated in California by the McCone Commission Report, official document dealing with the so-called Watts Riots.

The Commission, headed by John McCone, former CIA director, spent 100 days and $250,000 in order to "... bring into clear focus ... the economic and sociological conditions in our city that underlay the gathering anger ..." It, of course, does neither.

The Report turns out to be a commingling of police public relations and anti-Negro bias. So much so that sole Negro Commission member Rev. James Edward Jones caused to be published a separate comment in which he "violently disagreed" with part of its "unjustified projection." The Report was blasted by the State Civil Rights Commission as "superficial, unoriginal and unimaginative." ...

The most compelling lesson of Watts today is that it simply is not a matter of geographic location. It kaleidoscopes the situation in which we Negroes find ourselves throughout the country. It is only a matter of degree. We're trapped in a culture pattern that has seen our parents jobless and on relief; members of our families disintegrate through poor health and slum housing; and finally, we find ourselves as inheritors of a cruel and seemingly unending cycle of economic brinkmanship in an affluent society which has brought us to the breaking point. That breaking point is demonstrated in Watts and elsewhere in the country in a thousand clashes between Negroes and police since "That Was The Week That Was" in August, 1965. ...

Nothing short of maximal government intervention on a scale equal to that now committed to the destruction of Vietnam can avert a major race holocaust in our country in our time. And there is nothing in the Johnson Administration or on the political horizon generally, that indicates any serious thought is being given the matter.

This is the reality now, leading inexorably toward a major national race crisis.

And when these present times are analyzed by future historians to unravel the whys and wherefores their starting point may well be that volatile black ghetto tucked away in South Los Angeles named Watts.

Study Questions

1. Was Martin Luther King, Jr.'s, strategy of civil disobedience and nonviolence effective? Could the strategy have been applied to address the problems in Watts that Donald Wheeldin describes?

2. What did Malcolm X mean by arguing that "The civil rights struggle needs a new interpretation"?

3. What did the authors of the Port Huron Statement mean by "participatory democracy"? How did the ideas of the New Left differ from those of earlier radical movements?

4. Do you agree with Shirley Chisholm's assessment that sexism runs deeper than racism?

5. What assumptions do Johnson, Nixon, and Wheeldin share in their assessments of the crises confronting African Americans? How do they draw different conclusions from those assumptions?

6. Did the Civil Rights movement succeed?

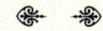

12

The Vietnam War

In 1950 the United States began to send military and economic aid in support of France's quest to regain colonial control over Indochina in Southeast Asia. With the backing of Communist China, Ho Chi Minh, a Vietnamese nationalist and founder of his nation's Communist Party, waged an intense guerrilla war to oust the French and secure independence for Vietnam. Although President Dwight D. Eisenhower subscribed to the domino theory—the notion that if Indochina fell to the Communists the rest of Asia would soon follow—he rejected U.S. military intervention (Document 1).

In 1954 Ho's forces defeated the French. Under the subsequent peace settlement, or Geneva Accords, the peninsula was divided with Ho ruling the North and the French ruling the South. The treaty provided for general elections within two years to settle the terms of reunification. Fearing that such an election would give Ho an overwhelming mandate to reunite the country, the United States helped establish a pro-American government in South Vietnam under the rule of Ngo Dinh Diem. Assured of U.S. assistance, Premier Diem refused to hold elections, thus sustaining indefinitely the division of Vietnam into two separate states.

Supporting South Vietnam became increasingly difficult for the United States. In the early 1960s a wave of popular insurgencies protesting the repressive policies of Diem threatened to topple the pro-American regime. President John F. Kennedy rejected sending combat troops, but he greatly expanded the U.S. commitment, authorizing substantial increases in economic and military aid and enlarging the number of military advisers to more than 16,000. In November 1963 a military coup that ousted Diem left a power vacuum in South Vietnam. To stabilize the government in the South and thwart attempts by North Vietnam to reunite the country under Communist rule, President Lyndon Johnson sent additional aid. He also approved U.S. support for covert military operations against the North. In August 1964 American naval vessels skirmished with North Vietnamese gunboats in the Gulf of Tonkin. To demonstrate America's determination to defend South Vietnam, Congress passed a resolution granting President Johnson authority to use unlimited military force there (Document 2). The door was now open for full-scale U.S. intervention.

The Johnson administration first hoped to defend South Vietnam through a series of aerial strikes against selected North Vietnamese targets. When these failed,

Johnson committed ground forces to the region but restricted them to defensive operations. Fearful that a withdrawal would destroy American credibility and that an invasion of North Vietnam would spark World War III, Johnson settled for a limited yet open-ended war, confining combat operations to the South. Maintaining that the Vietnam conflict was a minor engagement, Johnson neither sought a formal declaration of war nor asked the American people for support and sacrifice. U.S. forces thus found themselves locked into a protracted conflict that had no clear military objective other than to pressure Ho into a diplomatic resolution.

As U.S. involvement in the Vietnam War intensified after 1965, a vigorous antiwar movement emerged at home. Civil rights leader Martin Luther King, Jr., denounced the war as an enemy of the poor because it diverted resources from the war on poverty at home and because the burden of fighting fell disproportionately on the black and white working class (Document 3). Several groups, such as Women Strike for Peace (WSP), a coalition of middle-class housewives, organized to resist the draft. Opposition to the war also informed numerous student revolts on college campuses. From Berkeley to Columbia, college activists, many of whom participated in the civil rights movement, organized strikes and sit-ins protesting the war and demanding radical reform of the university (Documents 5 and 6).

The failure of the U.S. military to defeat decisively the North and its allies in South Vietnam fueled domestic opposition to the war. Televised news reports increasingly revealed the war to be a bloody stalemate, contradicting Johnson's repeated claims of victory at hand. Declining morale among the troops further frustrated U.S. military operations (Document 7).

Johnson's successor, Republican Richard Nixon, initiated efforts to end the U.S combat role in the war. The Nixon administration, after years of massive bombing raids on the North and a gradual withdrawal of U.S. troops, negotiated a settlement in January 1973. But veterans returned to a hostile and indifferent nation that stereotyped vets as drug-addicted criminals. Years later, many vets broke a long silence in an effort to counter such images and search for lessons from the war (Document 8).

DOCUMENT 1

Dwight D. Eisenhower, Press Conference (1954)

Early in the spring of 1954, Vietnamese forces trapped nearly 10,000 French troops at Dien Bien Phu, deep in the interior of northern Indochina. France asked the United States to help rescue its besieged army. On April 7, President Dwight Eisenhower held a press conference explaining the strategic importance of Indochina. Using the metaphor of falling dominoes, Eisenhower argued that if the Communists prevailed in Indochina, their influence would quickly spread throughout Asia, threatening Japan, Australia, and New Zealand.

Q. Robert Richards, Copley Press: Mr. President, would you mind commenting on the strategic importance of Indochina to the free world? I think there has been, across the country, some lack of understanding on just what it means to us.

THE PRESIDENT. You have, of course, both the specific and the general when you talk about such things.

First of all, you have the specific value of a locality in its production of materials that the world needs.

Then you have the possibility that many human beings pass under a dictatorship that is inimical to the free world.

Finally, you have broader considerations that might follow what you would call the "falling domino" principle. You have a row of dominoes set up, you knock over the first one, and what will happen to the last one is the certainty that it will go over very quickly. So you could have a beginning of a disintegration that would have the most profound influences.

Now, with respect to the first one, two of the items from this particular area that the world uses are tin and tungsten. They are very important. There are others, of course, the rubber plantations and so on.

Then with respect to more people passing under this domination, Asia, after all, has already lost some 450 million of its peoples to the Communist dictatorship, and we simply can't afford greater losses.

But when we come to the possible sequence of events, the loss of Indochina, of Burma, of Thailand, of the Peninsula, and Indonesia following, now you begin to talk about areas that not only multiply the disadvantages that you would suffer through loss of materials, sources of materials, but now you are talking really about millions and millions and millions of people.

Finally, the geographical position achieved thereby does many things. It turns the so-called island defensive chain of Japan, Formosa, of the Philippines and to the southward; it moves in to threaten Australia and New Zealand.

It takes away, in its economic aspects, that region that Japan must have as a trading area or Japan, in turn, will have only one place in the world to go—that is, toward the Communist areas in order to live.

So, the possible consequences of the loss are just incalculable to the free world.

DOCUMENT 2

The Gulf of Tonkin Resolution (1964)

In early August 1964, the Johnson administration announced that North Vietnamese gunboats had deliberately attacked American naval vessels in international waters. In retaliation Johnson ordered air strikes against North Vietnamese naval bases. He then asked Congress to pass a resolution granting him greater authority to deploy military force in Vietnam. Congress passed the resolution over the objections of dissenting legislators. With the resolution, Johnson hoped to send a strong message to North Vietnam and pre-empt Barry Goldwater, his Republican opponent in the upcoming presidential election, from accusing the president of being soft on communism. Johnson's request to Congress is followed here by the text of the resolution.

To the Congress of the United States:

Last night I announced to the American people that the North Vietnamese regime had conducted further deliberate attacks against U.S. naval vessels operating in international waters, and that I had therefore directed air action against gunboats and supporting facilities used in these hostile operations. This air action has now been carried out with substantial damage to the boats and facilities. Two U.S. aircraft were lost in the action.

After consultation with the leaders of both parties in the Congress, I further announced a decision to ask the Congress for a resolution expressing the unity and determination of the United States in supporting freedom and in protecting peace in southeast Asia.

These latest actions of the North Vietnamese regime have given a new and grave turn to the already serious situation in southeast Asia. Our commitments in that area are well known to the Congress. They were first made in 1954 by President Eisenhower. They were further defined in the Southeast Asia Collective Defense Treaty approved by the Senate in February 1955.

This treaty with its accompanying protocol obligates the United States and other members to act in accordance with their constitutional processes to meet Communist aggression against any of the parties or protocol states.

Our policy in southeast Asia has been consistent and unchanged since 1954. I summarized it on June 2 in four simple propositions:

1. America keeps her word. Here as elsewhere, we must and shall honor our commitments.

2. The issue is the future of southeast Asia as a whole. A threat to any nation in that region is a threat to all, and a threat to us.

3. Our purpose is peace. We have no military, political, or territorial ambitions in the area.

4. This is not just a jungle war, but a struggle for freedom on every front of human activity. Our military and economic assistance to South Vietnam and Laos in particular has the purpose of helping these countries to repel aggression and strengthen their independence.

The threat to the free nations of southeast Asia has long been clear. The North Vietnamese regime has constantly sought to take over South Vietnam and Laos. This Communist regime has violated the Geneva accords for Vietnam. It has systematically conducted a campaign of subversion, which includes the direction, training, and supply of personnel and arms for the conduct of guerrilla warfare in South Vietnamese territory. In Laos, the North Vietnamese regime has maintained military forces, used Laotian territory for infiltration into South Vietnam, and most recently carried out combat operations—all in direct violation of the Geneva agreements of 1962.

In recent months, the actions of the North Vietnamese regime have become steadily more threatening. In May, following new acts of Communist aggression in Laos, the United States undertook reconnaissance flights over Laotian territory, at the request of the Government of Laos. These flights had the essential mission of determining the situation in territory where Communist forces were preventing inspection by the International Control Commission. When the Communists attacked these aircraft, I responded by furnishing escort fighters with instructions to fire when fired upon. Thus, these latest North Vietnamese attacks on our naval vessels are not the first direct attack on Armed Forces of the United States.

As President of the United States I have concluded that I should now ask the Congress, on its pat, to join in affirming the national determination that all such attacks will be met, and that the United

States will continue in its basic policy of assisting the free nations of the area to defend their freedom.

As I have repeatedly made clear, the United States intends no rashness, and seeks no wider war. We must make it clear to all that the United States is united in its determination to bring about the end of Communist subversion and aggression in the area. We seek the full and effective restoration of the international agreements signed in Geneva in 1954, with respect to South Vietnam, and again at Geneva in 1962, with respect to Laos.

I recommend a resolution expressing the support of the Congress for all necessary action to protect our Armed Forces and to assist nations covered by the SEATO Treaty. At the same time, I assure the Congress that we shall continue readily to explore any avenues of political solution that will effectively guarantee the removal of Communist subversion and the preservation of the independence of the nations of the area.

The resolution could well be based upon similar resolutions enacted by the Congress in the past—to meet the threat to Formosa in 1955, to meet the threat to the Middle East in 1957, and to meet the threat in Cuba in 1962. It could state in the simplest terms the resolve and support of the Congress for action to deal appropriately with attacks against our Armed Forces and to defend freedom and preserve peace in southeast Asia in accordance with the obligations of the United States under the Southeast Asia Treaty. I urge the Congress to enact such a resolution promptly and thus to give convincing evidence to the aggressive Communist nations, and to the world as a whole, that our policy in southeast Asia will be carried forward—and that the peace and security of the area will be preserved.

The events of this week would in any event have made the passage of a congressional resolution essential. But there is an additional reason for doing so at a time when we are entering on 3 months of political campaigning. Hostile nations must understand that in such a period the United States will continue to protect its national interests, and that in these matters there is no division among us.

The joint resolution . . . was read, as follows: Whereas naval units of the Communist regime in Vietnam, in violation of the principles of the Charter of the United Nations and of international law, have deliberately and repeatedly attacked United States naval vessels lawfully present in international waters, and have thereby created a serious threat to international peace;

Whereas these attacks are part of a deliberate and systematic campaign of aggression that the Communist regime in North Vietnam has been waging against its neighbors and the nations joined with them in the collective defense of their freedom;

Whereas the United States is assisting the peoples of southeast Asia to protect their freedom and has no territorial, military or political ambitions in that area, but desires only that these peoples should be left in peace to work out their own destinies in their own way: Now, therefore, be it

Resolved by the Senate and House of Representatives of the United States of America in Congress assembled, That the Congress approves and supports the determination of the President, as Commander in Chief, to take all necessary measures to repel any armed attack against the forces of the United States and to prevent further aggression.

SEC. 2. The United States regards as vital to its national interest and to world peace the maintenance of international peace and security in southeast Asia. Consonant with the Constitution and the Charter of the United Nations and in accordance with its obligations under the Southeast Asia Collective Defense Treaty, the United States is, therefore, prepared, as the President determines, to take all necessary steps, including the use of armed force, to assist any member or protocol state of the Southeast Asia Collective Defense Treaty requesting assistance in defense of its freedom.

SEC. 3. This resolution shall expire when the President shall determine that the peace and security of the area is reasonably assured by international conditions created by action of the United Nations or otherwise, except that it may be terminated earlier by concurrent resolution of the Congress.

DOCUMENT 3

Dr. Martin Luther King, Jr., "A Time to Break the Silence" (1967)

Civil rights leader Martin Luther King, Jr., increasingly opposed U.S. intervention in Vietnam. On April 4, 1967, King addressed an association of clergy and laypeople opposed to the war at Riverside Church in New York City. In the following excerpt, King explains how his opposition to the war is consistent with his advocacy of civil justice at home.

I come to this magnificent house of worship tonight because my conscience leaves me no other choice. I join with you in this meeting because I am in deepest agreement with the aims and work of the organization which has brought us together: Clergy and Laymen Concerned About Vietnam. The recent statement of your executive committee are the sentiments of my own heart and I found myself in full accord when I read its opening lines: "A time comes when silence is betrayal." That time has come for us in relation to Vietnam....

Some of us who have already begun to break the silence of the night have found that the calling to speak is often a vocation of agony, but we must speak. We must speak with all the humility that is appropriate to our limited vision, but we must speak. And we must rejoice as well, for surely this is the first time in our nation's history that a significant number of its religious leaders have chosen to move beyond the prophesying of smooth patriotism to the high grounds of a firm dissent based upon the mandates of conscience and the reading of history. Perhaps a new spirit is rising among us. If it is, let us trace its movements well and pray that our own inner being may be sensitive to its guidance, for we are deeply in need of a new way beyond the darkness that seems so close around us....

Since I am a preacher by trade, I suppose it is not surprising that I have seven major reasons for bringing Vietnam into the field of my moral vision. There is at the outset a very obvious and almost facile connection between the war in Vietnam and the struggle I, and others, have been waging in America. A few years ago there was a shining moment in that struggle. It seemed as if there was a real promise of hope for the poor—both black and white—through the poverty program. There were experiments, hopes, new beginnings. Then came the buildup in Vietnam and I watched the program broken and eviscerated as if it were some idle political plaything of a society gone mad on war, and I knew that America would never invest the necessry funds or energies in rehabilitation of its poor so long as adventures like Vietnam continued to draw men and skills and money like some demonic destructive suction tube. So I was increasingly compelled to see the war as an enemy of the poor and to attack it as such.

Perhaps the more tragic recognition of reality took place when it became clear to me that the war was doing far more than devastating the hopes of the poor at home. It was sending their sons and their brothers and their husbands to fight and to die in extraordinarily high proportions relative to the rest of the population. We were taking the black young men who had been crippled by our society and sending them eight thousand miles away to guarantee liberties in Southeast Asia which they had not found in southwest Georgia and East

Harlem. So we have been repeatedly faced with the cruel irony of watching Negro and white boys on TV screens as they kill and die together for a nation that has been unable to seat them together in the same schools. So we watch them in brutal solidarity burning the huts of a poor village, but we realize that they would never live on the same block in Detroit. I could not be silent in the face of such cruel manipulation of the poor.

My third reason moves to an ever deeper level of awareness, for it grows out of my experience in the ghettos of the north over the last three years—especially the last three summers. As I have walked among the desperate, rejected and angry young men I have told them that Molotov cocktails and rifles would not solve their problems. I have tried to offer them my deepest compassion while maintaining my conviction that social change comes most meaningfully through non-violent action. But they asked—and rightly so—what about Vietnam? They asked if our own nation wasn't using massive doses of violence to solve its problems, to bring about the changes it wanted. Their questions hit home, and I knew that I could never again raise my voice against the violence of the oppressed in the ghettos without having first spoken clearly to the greatest purveyor of violence in the world today—my own government. For the sake of those boys, for the sake of this government, for the sake of the hundreds of thousands trembling under our violence, I cannot be silent.

For those who ask the question, "Aren't you a Civil Rights leader?" and thereby mean to exclude me from the movement for peace, I have this further answer. In 1957 when a group of us formed the Southern Christian Leadership Conference, we chose as our motto: "To save the soul of America." We were convinced that we could not limit our vision to certain rights for black people, but instead affirmed the conviction that America would never be free or saved from itself unless the descendants of its slaves were loosed completely from the shackle they still wear. In a way we were agreeing with Langston Hughes, that black bard of Harlem, who had written earlier:

O, yes,
I say it plain,
America was never America to me,
And yet I swear this oath—
America will be!

Now, it should be incandescently clear that no one who has any concern for the integrity and life of America today can ignore the present war. If America's soul becomes totally poisoned, part of the autopsy must read Vietnam. It can never be saved so long as it destroys the deepest hopes of men the world over. So it is that those of us who are yet determined that America *will* be are led down the path of protest and dissent, working for the health of our land.

As if the weight of such a commitment to the life and health of America were not enough, another burden of responsibility was placed upon me in 1964; and I cannot forget that the Nobel Prize for Peace was also a commission—a commission to work harder than I had ever worked before for "the brotherhood of man." This is a calling that takes me beyond national allegiances, but even if it were not present I would yet have to live with the meaning of my commitment to the ministry of Jesus Christ. To me the relationship of this ministry to the making of peace is so obvious that I sometimes marvel at those who ask me why I am speaking against the war. Could it be that they do not know that the good news was meant for all men—for communist and capitalist, for their children and ours, for black and for white, for revolutionary and conservative? Have they forgotten that my ministry is in obedience to the one who loved his enemies so fully that he died for them? What then can I say to the "Viet Cong" or to Castro or to Mao as a faithful minister of this one? Can I threaten them with death or must I not share with them my life?

Finally, as I try to delineate for you and for myself the road that leads from Montgomery to this place I would have offered all that was most valid if I simply said that I must be true to my conviction that I share with all men the calling to be a son of the living God. Beyond the calling of race or nation or creed is this vocation of sonship and brotherhood, and because I believe that the Father is deeply concerned especially for his suffering and helpless and outcast children, I come tonight to speak for them.

This I believe to be the privilege and the burden of all of us who deem ourselves bound by allegiances and loyalties which are broader and deeper than nationalism and which go beyond our nation's self-defined goals and positions. We are called to speak for the weak, for the voiceless, for victims of our nation and for those it calls enemy, for no document from human hands can make these humans any less our brothers....

Meanwhile we in the churches and synagogues have a continuing task while we urge our government to disengage itself from a disgraceful commitment. We must continue to raise our voices if our nation persists in its perverse ways in Vietnam. We must be prepared to match actions with words by seeking out every creative means of protest possible....

In 1957 a sensitive American official overseas said that it seemed to him that our nation was on the wrong side of a world revolution. During the past 10 years we have seen emerge a pattern of suppression which now has justified the presence of U.S. military "advisors" in Venezuela. This need to maintain social stability for our investments accounts for the counter-revolutionary action of American forces in Guatemala. It tells why American helicopters are being used against guerrillas in Colombia and why American napalm and green beret forces have already been active against rebels in Peru....

I am convinced that if we are to get on the right side of the world revolution, we as a nation must undergo a radical revolution of values. We must rapidly begin the shift from a "thing-oriented" society to a "person-oriented" society. When machines and computers, profit motives and property rights are considered more important than people, the giant triplets of racism, materialism, and militarism are incapable of being conquered.

A true revolution of values will soon cause us to question the fairness and justice of many of our past and present policies. On the one hand we are called to play the Good Samaritan on life's roadside; but that will be only an initial act. One day we must come to see that the whole Jericho Road must be transformed so that men and women will not be constantly beaten and robbed as they make their journey on Life's highway. True compassion is more than flinging a coin to a beggar; it is not haphazard and superficial. It comes to see that an edifice which produces beggars needs re-structuring. A true revolution of values will soon look uneasily on the glaring contrast of poverty and wealth. With righteous indignation, it will look across the seas and see individual capitalists of the West investing huge sums of money in Asia, Africa and South America, only to take the profits out with no concern for the social betterment of the countries, and say: "This is not just." It will look at our alliance with the landed gentry of Latin America and say: "This is not just." The Western arrogance of feeling that it has everything to teach others and nothing to learn from them is not just. A true revolution of values will lay hands on the world order and say of war: "This way of settling differences is not just." This business of burning human beings with napalm, of filling our nation's homes with orphans and widows, of injecting poisonous drugs of hate into the veins of peoples normally humane, of sending men home from dark and bloody battlefields physically handicapped and psychologically deranged, cannot be reconciled with wisdom, justice and love. A nation that continues year after year to spend more money on military defense than on programs of social uplift is approaching spiritual death.

DOCUMENT 4

Charlotte Keyes, "Suppose They Gave a War and No One Came" (1966)

In 1961 Dagmar Wilson and four other women founded Women Strike for Peace (WSP), a pacifist organization dedicated to ending the arms race. As the Vietnam War intensified, thousands of women joined WSP. Most activists in the organization were older women who had been active on the left in the 1930s. Many had sons who were of draft age. Unlike the youthful feminists of the 1960s, WSP activists presented themselves as traditional women, emphasizing their roles as housewives and mothers. By doing so, WSP demonstrated that the antiwar movement was not limited to the radical left and thus helped build a broad coalition against the war. In the following article from *McCall's* magazine, a woman's monthly, WSP organizer Charlotte Keyes describes why her son decided to resist the draft.

Carl Sandburg once told of a little girl who, after hearing his description of a Civil War battle, observed, "Suppose they gave a war and no one came."

Our son Gene has committed himself to that goal—to the day no one will come to war. The cost for him is high. He once told my husband and me, to our exasperation, "Jail is my destiny." And he has indeed been imprisoned four times. His last sentence was three years in a federal penitentiary for refusing induction into the armed services. At the trial, he explained why: "There is no moral validity to any part of any law whose purpose is to train people to kill one another."

What kind of oddball is our son, who decided against applying for alternative service as a conscientious objector because "that was selfish—to try to exempt just myself from military duty. It's the fact that my country, and every other country, teaches all of us that murder is right when we know it's wrong, that I must witness against?"

Who are all of these "nonviolent agitators," these "peaceniks," these draft-card burners, who are often taunted for not working daily from nine to five, but who many times put in seven days a week, from dawn to midnight, on their chosen work?

We see them on television, picketing the White House or the Pentagon or a missile base, carrying signs and solemnly marching, in silence or gaily singing. Some of them are bearded, and invariably the camera focuses on these and the long-haired ones, although the great majority have neatly trimmed hair and clean-shaven faces.

The peaceniks these days are legion—they are ninety years old and fifteen, heads of families and housewives with babies, students, young people who have gone back to tilling the soil in their search for basic realities. But a good many, as in the civil rights movement, are young and unmarried, temporarily school dropouts. The radical pacifists among them are usually living a life of voluntary poverty, in order to be free to work for the kingdom of heaven or a truly great society.

No one of them can be called typical. They are very much individualists. But the one I know best, of course, is my own son. Perhaps if we follow his career, we can get behind the bearded stereotype fed to us by newspaper, movie, cartoon and comic strip.

What is Gene like? At twenty-five, he has been in jail; has been publicly condemned in resolutions passed by veterans' organizations in his Midwestern home town, as well as by the County Board of Supervisors; has postponed indefinitely all thought of

By mid 1967, fighting in Vietnam had escalated greatly with more than 400,000 Americans involved and losses numbering as many as 300 a week. Public opposition to the war increased greatly, especially as televised broadcasts of the war prompted student protests.

any career except working for peace, because he is convinced that unless a wholly committed effort is made by him and many others, our world will soon be destroyed by nuclear catastrophe.

Is he a nut? Doesn't he think about his parents at all? How must we feel to have such a rebel for a son? Doesn't it humiliate us in our community—a university town, where my husband teaches?

To be quite honest, we have run the gamut from shock, disagreement, anger to "patient" (we always thought) explanation of why he was wrong, on to pride and finally to learning from him and changing our own lives.

Over the years, since Gene left college, we have tried to find the seeds of his present way of life and have more than once been taken aback to realize that we ourselves had planted some of them. One friend told us, "What else could you expect Gene to do the way he's been brought up?"

Well, we parents don't realize—do we?—when we inculcate our moral standards, that the children may try really to live by them. . . .

Characteristically, Gene's first letter from jail began, "Having a fine time. Wish you were here."

We were happy to be able to write him that friends and even acquaintances had been going out of their way to express their love and sympathy. One friend who wanted to visit Gene at the jail on a trip east touched us very much, and when we thanked her with all our hearts, she said, "I feel as though he's fighting our battles." Another friend phoned and bawled me out for not backing Gene up all the way. I was quite delighted to be scolded.

We had every kind of reaction to his stand. Telephone calls, of course, accusing him of being a Communist. One caller became quite interested when we pointed out that it would be impossible for a pacifist to be a Communist because he can never engage in violent revolution and because he always puts the individual's relation to God and conscience above his relation to the state, as the early Christians did. The man ended by requesting that we let him see some of our peace literature. Not all conversations ended on this friendly note, however. One man said flatly that anybody who did not obey his country's laws was a traitor.

Strangers wrote letters pro and con to the local newspapers. One man put it: "He is an admitted criminal who openly defies our laws when they interfere with his personal beliefs."

But when another answered, saying that though he did not share Gene's beliefs, he defended his right to fight for them, he received a call from the antagonistic letter writer apologizing for his own letter.

Despite our growing understanding and pride, we were never so happy as when Gene came home after seventeen days in jail. Now he is safe at last, we thought. He was safe—if beginning to plan to throw tea into Boston Harbor is safe.

Two and a half years passed before he achieved *his* tea party, years in which he engaged continually in peace activity and also in the struggle for integration (which again brought jail). But his thoughts were being drawn more and more to one profound question—the question faced by every young man of his age—what Selective Service meant to him and what it meant to his nation.

At college, on reaching his eighteenth birthday and facing the problem of registering for the draft, he had taken two solid days off from classes to struggle with his conscience in answering the questions on SSS Form No. 150, the Special Form for Conscientious Objector that he had requested.

"Do you believe in a Supreme Being?" was one of the questions, and "Describe nature of your belief which is the basis of your claim. . . . Explain how, when and from whom or what source you received the training and acquired the belief. . . . Under what circumstances, if any, do you believe in the use of force?"

Gene studied, weighed and reweighed religious and pacifist writings; advice from the Central Committee for Conscientious Objectors; the Bible. He went into a retreat and faced himself and the meaning of life. It is not a simple deed at eighteen to probe the truth, to know oneself. But at last, convinced that he could in all honesty ask for it, he requested the conscientious-objector classification.

Yet he was not easy in his mind. Such a sentence as this one in an American Friends Service Committee pamphlet stayed in his thoughts: "We are convinced that our failures are due to our own unreadiness to live boldly by the faith we hold."

Was he really living boldly by his faith, Gene asked himself, to accept this easy way of being a legal conscientious objector? Didn't the objectors get tucked away in their own little cubbyholes of alternative service, so that most people didn't even know there were those who protested the draft? Shouldn't his goal be not simply to disengage *himself* from war but to ensure that his country, by ceasing to rely on force, regain its vision of the brotherhood of all men? . . .

The clock kept ticking inexorably, and in December, Gene came home primed for action. He had now a clear and concrete plan of a way to challenge the draft law so that people would become aware it *could* be challenged. It was his belief that this law was now accepted as being as much a part of our government as the Bill of Rights. He felt most of us did not realize that whether the draft continued or was abolished lay in the hands not of some mysterious and far-off government, but in the hands of us, the people. Only we needed a shock to make us realize it, since years of legal protest by peace workers and others had wakened very few. It was as Mildred Olmsted of the Women's International League for Peace and Freedom, has said: "I have often wondered why it is that a family which would make a great protest if the government took away their automobile or even their dog, says nothing when the government takes away their sons."

In keeping with the pacifists' way of explaining all actions beforehand, Gene wrote a letter to the two local papers and told them what he planned to do: "Christmas Eve reminds us of our duty to work for peace on earth, a world without war. . . . As a prayer for peace on earth, I will be holding a vigil on Christmas Eve in front of the office of the local draft board. If I can withstand the weather, I hope to witness for twelve hours, beginning at noon. In any event, at midnight Christmas Eve, I will be using my one-A draft card to light a candle."

To burn his draft card! The idea was as new and shocking to us when he first described it as it still is to most people. At that time, though Gene was not the first to do this, there had not been many, and the whole action seemed preposterous to us.

He had talked with us and written us about this for a long time, and he listened as patiently as always to our protests. But the words of two others rang louder in his heart. There was the motto of William Lloyd Garrison's magazine, *The Liberator:* "Our country is the world—our countrymen are all mankind." And undergirding everything was Jesus' admonition: "Love your enemies, bless them that curse you, do good to them that hate you."

All I could turn to for help was the weather. I began to pray almost as hard for bad weather as Gene was praying for peace. I wanted a blizzard and temperature twenty below zero, weather even our quixotic son would admit was more than a human being could stand. But on December 24 the temperature rose. It was still cold, but had become short of unbearable. And at noon, he walked to the draft board and began his vigil.

He was dressed warmly and neatly, had on earmuffs and a dark-blue overcoat, and wore suspended from his shoulders a sign that read: "To Light This Candle with a Draft Card—A Prayer for Peace on Earth." The sign had been beautifully lettered by an artist friend. He was accompanied by his girl, who, for a large part of the day, kept vigil with him.

I was resigned and even, once again, as always seemed to happen when my worst fears were realized, proud. . . .

And so it has become. As we have watched him grow and climb his high places, we no longer argue with him, no longer call him foolish. We stand by our son, and we learn from him.

DOCUMENT 5

Columbia Strike Coordinating Committee, "Columbia Liberated" (1968)

One of the most dramatic campus uprisings of the period occurred in the spring of 1968 at Columbia University in New York City. Black and white students concerned about social justice and opposed to the war staged a massive demonstration, occupying five buildings and effectively halting university operations. For eight days, the students maintained their strike until the New York City police intervened to regain control of the campus. Violence ensued, and more than 200 students were injured and some 700 arrested. To defend their actions, the Columbia Strike Coordinating Committee issued the following manifesto.

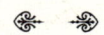

The most important fact about the Columbia strike is that Columbia exists within American society. This statement may appear to be a truism, yet it is a fact too often forgotten by observers, reporters, administrators, faculty members, and even some students. These people attempt to explain the "disturbances" as reaction to an unresponsive and archaic administrative structure, youthful outbursts of unrest much like panty raids, the product of a conspiracy by communist agents in national SDS or a handful of hard-core nihilists ("destroyers") on the campus, or just general student unrest due to the war in Vietnam.

But in reality, striking students are responding to the totality of the conditions of our society, not just one small part of it, the university. We are disgusted with the war, with racism, with being a part of a system over which we have no control, a system which demands gross inequalities of wealth and power, a

From *The Sixties Papers, Documents of a Rebellious Decade* by Judith and Stewart Albert. Reprinted with permission of Greenwood Publishing Group Inc. Westport, CT. Copyright © 1984 by Judith Albert and Stewart Albert.

National Guard troops, brought in to restore order to the campus of Kent State University, first fired tear gas on the student protesters, some of whom had been throwing stones. In the panic following the tear gas attack, the guardsmen opened fire with live ammunition, killing four students and wounding eleven. Two of the students who were killed had been uninvolved in the demonstration and were caught in the gunfire as they passed by on their way to class.

system which denies personal and social freedom and potential, a system which has to manipulate and repress us in order to exist. The university can only be seen as a cog in this machine; or, more accurately, a factory whose product is knowledge and personnel (us) useful to the functioning of the system. The specific problems of university life, its boredom and meaninglessness, help prepare us for boring and meaningless work in the "real" world. And the policies of the university—expansion into the community, exploitation of blacks and Puerto Ricans, support for imperialist wars—also serve the interests of banks, corporations, government, and military represented on the Columbia Board of Trustees and the ruling class of our society. In every way, the university is "society's child." Our attack upon the university is really an attack upon this society and its effects upon us. We have never said otherwise.

The development of the New Left at Columbia represents an organized political response to the society. We seek our task, first as identifying for ourselves and for others the nature of our society—who controls it and for what ends—and secondly, developing ways in which to transform it. We understand that only through struggle can we create a free, human society, since the present one is dominated by a small ruling class which exploits, manipulates, and distorts for its own ends—and has shown in countless ways its determination to maintain its position. The Movement at Columbia began years ago agitating and organizing students around issues such as students' power in the university (Action), support of the civil rights movement (CORE), the war in Vietnam (the Independent Committee on Vietnam). Finally, [the] Columbia chapter [of] Students for a Democratic Society initiated actions against many of the above issues as they manifest themselves on campus. Politically speaking, SDS, from its inception on campus in November, 1966, sought to unite issues, "to draw connections," to view this society as a totality. SDS united the two main themes of the movement—opposition to racial oppression and to the imperialist war in Vietnam—with our own sense of frustration, disappointment, and oppression at the quality of our lives in capitalist society.

One of the most important questions raised by the strike was who controls Columbia, and for what ends? SDS pointed to the Board of Trustees as the intersection of various corporate, financial, real-estate, and government interests outside the university which need the products of the university—personnel and knowledge—in order to exist. It is this power which we are fighting when we fight particular policies of the university such as expansion at the expense of poor people or institutional ties to the war-machine. We can hope for and possibly win certain reforms within the university, but the ultimate reforms we need—the elimination of war and exploitation—can only be gained after we overthrow the control of our country by the class of people on Columbia's Board of Trustees. In a sense,

Columbia is the place where we received our education—our revolutionary education....

But why do students, predominantly of the "middle-class," in effect, reject the university designed to integrate them into the system and instead identify with the most oppressed of this country and the world? Why did the gymnasium in Morningside Park become an issue over which Columbia was shut down for seven weeks? Why pictures of Che Guevara, Malcolm X, and red flags in the liberated buildings?

Basically, the sit-ins and strike of April and May gave us a chance to express the extreme dissatisfaction we feel at being *caught in this "system."* We rejected the gap between potential and realization in this society. We rejected our present lives in the university and our future lives in business, government or other universities like this one. In a word, we saw ourselves as oppressed, and began to understand the forces at work which make for our oppression. In turn, we saw those same forces responsible for the oppression and colonization of blacks and Puerto Ricans in ghettos, and Vietnamese and the people of the third world. By initiating a struggle in support of black and third world liberation, we create the conditions for our own freedom—by building a movement which will someday take power over our society, we will free ourselves.

As the strike and the struggle for our demands progressed, we learned more about the nature of our enemy and his unwillingness to grant any of our demands or concede any of his power. Illusions disappeared: the moral authority of the educator gave way to police violence, the faculty appeared in all its impotent glory. On the other hand, tremendous support came in from community residents, black and white alike, from university employees, from high school students, from people across the country and around the world. Inevitably, we began to reevaluate our goals and strategy. Chief among the lessons were (1) We cannot possibly win our demands alone: we must unite with other groups in the population; (2) [Our stated] demands cannot possibly be our ultimate ends: even winning all of them certainly would not go far enough toward the basic reforms we need to live as human beings in this society; (3) "Restructuring" the university, the goal of faculty groups, various "moderate" students, and even the trustees, cannot possibly create a "free" or "democratic" university out of this institution. (First, how can anyone expect any meaningful reforms when even our initial demands have not been met?) Secondly, we realize that the university is entirely synchronized with the society: how can you have a "free," human university in a society such as this? Hence the SDS slogan "A free university in a free society." The converse is equally true.

DOCUMENT 6

Richard Hofstadter, Columbia University Commencement Address (1968)

The president of Columbia University traditionally spoke at commencement, but in the wake of the student uprisings, university trustees invited Richard Hofstadter, DeWitt Clinton Professor of History, to deliver the 214th commencement address. Although Hofstadter shared student concerns about poverty, racism, and the war in Vietnam, he believed that student protesters pursued a self-destructive strategy for social change. In his address, Hofstadter defended the modern university as "a collectivity that serves as a citadel of intellectual individualism" and that maintains a commitment to academic freedom, free inquiry, and rationality. To reduce the university to a center of political action, he argued, would threaten this fragile structure and "thrust at the vitals of university life." When Hofstadter began to speak, some 300 students and a few faculty members walked out of the ceremony, not in opposition to Hofstadter, but to protest the actions of university officials throughout the tumultuous spring of 1968.

[W]hile I hope I am speaking in the interest of my university, it would be wrong to suggest that I am precisely speaking for it. It is in fact of the very essence of the conception of the modern university that I wish to put before you that no one is authorized to speak for it. A university is firmly committed to certain basic values of freedom, rationality, inquiry, discussion, and to its own internal order; but it does not have corporate views of public questions. Administrators and trustees are, of course, compelled by practical necessity to take actions that involve some assumptions about the course and meaning of public affairs; but they know that in so doing they are not expressing a corporate university judgment or committing other minds. Members of the faculties often express themselves vigorously on public issues, but they acknowledge the obligation to make it clear that they are not speaking in the name of their university. This fact of our all speaking separately is in itself a thing of great consequence, because in this age of rather overwhelming organizations and collectivities, the university is singular in being a collectivity that serves as a citadel of intellectual individualism....

A university is a community, but it is a community of a special kind—a community devoted to inquiry. It exists so that its members may inquire into truths of all sorts. Its presence marks our commitment to the idea that somewhere in society there must be an organization in which anything can be studied or questioned—not merely safe and established things but difficult and inflammatory things, the most troublesome questions of politics and war, of sex and morals, of property and national loyalty. It is governed by the ideal of academic freedom, applicable both to faculty and students. The ideal of academic freedom does indeed put extraordinary demands upon human restraint and upon our capacity for disinterested thought. Yet these demands are really of the same general order as those we regard as essential to any advanced civilization. The very possibility of civilized human discourse rests upon the willingness of people to consider that they may be mistaken. The possibility of modern democracy rests upon the willingness of governments to accept the existence of a loyal opposition, organized to reverse some of their policies and to replace them in office. Similarly, the possibility of the modern free university rests upon the willingness of society to support and sustain institutions part of whose business it is to examine, critically and without stint, the assumptions that prevail in that society. Professors are hired to teach and students are sent to learn with the quite explicit understanding that they are not required to agree with those who hire or send them.

Underlying these remarkable commitments is the belief that in the long run the university will best minister to society's needs not alone through its mundane services but through the far more important office of becoming an intellectual and spiritual balance wheel. This is a very demanding idea, an idea of tremendous sophistication, and it is hardly surprising that we have some trouble in getting it fully accepted by society or in living up to it ourselves. But just because it is demanding we should never grow tired of explaining or trying to realize it. Nor should we too quickly become impatient with those who do not immediately grasp it.

We are very much impressed now not simply by the special character of the free university but also by its fragility. The delicate thing about freedom is that while it requires restraints, it also requires that these restraints normally be self-imposed, and not forced from outside. The delicate thing about the university is that it has a mixed character, that is it is suspended between its position in the external world, with all its corruption and evils and cruelties, and the splendid world of our imagination. The university does in fact perform certain mundane services of instruction and information to society—and there are those who think it should aspire to nothing more. It does in fact constitute a kind of free forum—and there are those who want to convert it primarily into a center of political action. But above these aspects of its existence stands its essential character as a center of free inquiry and criticism—a thing not to be sacrificed for anything else. A university is not a service station. Neither is it a political society, nor a meeting place for political societies. With all its limitations and failures, and they are invariably many, it is the best and most benign side of our society insofar as that society aims to cherish the human mind. To realize its essential character, the university has to be dependent upon something less precarious than the momentary balance of forces in society. It has to pin its faith on something that is not hard-boiled or self-regarding. It has to call not merely upon critical intelligence but upon self-criticism and self-restraint. There is no group of professors or administrators, of alumni or students, there is no class or interest in our society that should consider itself exempt from exercising the self-restraint or displaying the generosity that is necessary for the university's support.

Some people argue that because the modern university, whether public or private, is supported by and is part of the larger society, it therefore shares in all the evils of society, and must be quite ruthlessly revolutionized as a necessary step in social reform, or even in social revolution. That universities do share in, and may even at some times and in some respects propagate, certain ills of our society seems to me undeniable. But to imagine that the best way to change a social order is to start by assaulting its most accessible centers of thought and study and criticism is not only to show a complete disregard for the intrinsic character of the university but also to develop a curiously self-destructive strategy for social change. If an attempt is made to politicize completely our primary centers of free argument and inquiry, they will only in the end be forced to lose their character and be reduced to centers of vocational training, nothing more. Total and pure neutrality for the university is in fact impossible, but neutrality should continue to define our aim, and we should resist the demand that the university espouse the political commitments of any of its members. This means, too, that the university should be extraordinarily chary of relationships that even suggest such a political commitment.

The university is the only great organization in modern society that considers itself obliged not just to tolerate but even to give facilities and protection to the very persons who are challenging its own rules, procedures and policies. To subvert such a fragile structure is all too easy, as we now know. That is why it requires, far more than does our political society, a scrupulous and continued dedication to the conditions of orderly and peaceable discussion. The technique of the forcible occupation and closure of a university's buildings with the intention of bringing its activities to a halt is no ordinary bargaining device—it is a thrust at the vitals of university life. It is a powerful device for control by a determined minority, and its continued use would be fatal to any university. . . .

What we need then is stability, peace, mutual confidence. The time will soon come when the first halting gestures toward conciliation can be multiplied and strengthened, when we can move more rapidly toward the reconstruction of the frame of trust.

Friends outside the university who know how serious is the damage we have suffered have asked me: How can Columbia go on after this terrible wound? I can only answer: How can it not go on? The question is not whether it will continue but in what form. Will it fall into a decline and become a third- or fourth-rate institution, will it be as distinguished as it has been for generations past, or will it somehow be made even more distinguished? Columbia is a great and—in the way Americans must reckon time—an ancient university. In this immense, rich country, we have only a limited number of institutions of comparable quality. We are living through a period in which the need for teaching and research—for the services a university performs and the things it stands for—is greater than it ever was before. What kind of a people would we be if we allowed this center of our culture and our hope to languish and fail? That is the question I must leave with you.

DOCUMENT 7

Richard Boyle, The Flower of the Dragon (1972)

Richard Boyle was a free-lance journalist who spent several years covering the Vietnam War. Boyle believed that the U.S. military and government covered up evidence of discontent, unrest, and resistance among American GIs in order to maintain the image that the war was successful. In the following selection from a book he published in 1972, Boyle describes a dramatic incident among a division of American soldiers.

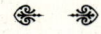

Although many of us in the Saigon press corps had heard rumors of fraggings, attacks by enlisted men on officers with a fragmentation grenade, usually slipped under the floor of the officer's hootch, it wasn't being reported to the people back home.

Then-President Lyndon Johnson, in response to the growing antiwar movement, once said, "You don't hear the boys in Vietnam protesting." Hawks consistently called for escalation "to support our boys." To be against the war, they claimed, is to stab GIs in the back. The Army brass was particularly worried about stories of GI unrest leaking out. They did everything they could to cover up, and until 1969 they were successful.

They covered up the story of the revolt in 1968 of black GIs at Long Binh Jail, the notorious Army prison outside Saigon. Fed up with abuse and beatings at the hands of the guards, black troops seized the prison, repelling successive attempts by hundreds of MPs backed up by armored cars to retake the prison. In the end, of course, the troops lost out.

The easiest way for the Army to cover up news of GI unrest was simply not to report it at the five o'clock follies. The Army's massive PR machine daily cranked out press releases about how the GIs supported the war, how high their morale was and how we were gloriously winning the hearts and minds of the Vietnamese people.

So the press simply never heard of the fraggings, of officers shot in the back by their own men, of near-revolts of whole units. Most of the newsmen, when they did go out in the field, spent their time in the officers' mess and in officers' clubs drinking with the brass. It seemed most newsmen didn't really like or understand the grunts; they felt more comfortable with the lifers.

Besides, most of the grunts didn't trust the Saigon press corps. They knew the Army's Central Intelligence Division (CID) often sent agents onto bases disguised as newsmen to get information and evidence about fraggings or possible mutinies. El Cid, as the grunts called the spies, was everywhere.

But there was another, even greater, obstacle to uncovering stories of fraggings. If a reporter wanted to go on base, he had to sign up for a military flight, giving the reason for his trip. If he told the truth and said he wanted to do a story about fraggings, the brass would try to block him every way they could—say he couldn't get to the base because of bad weather or, if they did let him go, send along a public information officer to follow him around and make sure no damaging information got out. If he lied about why he wanted to go, they would still make sure he saw and heard only what the PIO wanted.

The *Overseas Weekly* was the first paper to report on fraggings, probably because most of our stories came from the GIs themselves. On stories the Army didn't want us to know about—and there were many—we usually had to sneak on base to get the story at all.

One day in August Ann Bryan got a call from some troops at Cu Chi, headquarters of the 25th Division, who said they had a story for us. She made an arrangement for me to meet them secretly on the base.

The streets at Cu Chi had beautiful names—Maui Street and Oahu Street—but they were very drab. Behind a pizza parlor two GIs were waiting. I identified myself and we drove down the street, past the massage parlor where GIs got a five-dollar hand job.

"I think we got a safe place to meet," said one of the GIs. It was very risky for them to talk with me, because if they were caught they would probably be shipped to Firebase Jackson the next day. Jackson, they said, was a place they didn't want to be.

They took me to a small hootch. About eight GIs, half of them black and half of them white, were sitting on the floor when we entered. While they took turns watching for lifers outside, the GIs slowly began to tell me the story of two men.

"I guess I'll start by telling you about Doc—Sp4 Enoch 'Doc' Hampton," said a sandy-haired soldier, Sp4 W. C. Benn. "Doc was our friend, everybody liked Doc. He was a real good medic."

"Yeah, he never bothered nobody," said another soldier. "He treated people like you would want to be treated."

They talked about Doc for a while, then they told me about the other man, Sfc. Clarence Lowder, whom they called "Top." Things started to get bad, they said, when Top came into the unit as the new "first-shirt," or top sergeant. Top didn't think much of the new "Action Army." It was too soft. "He wished he was back in the old army," said Pfc. Rich Hanusey, a clerk in the orderly room. In the old days, Top would tell his men, he could straighten out a soldier "without going through a bunch of legal mumbo-jumbo." Top was a big, powerful man and many GIs were afraid of him. "Top would threaten to hit people or send them to Jackson," said Hanusey.

Firebase Jackson was like a death sentence. Some of the GIs doubted Top had enough power to send a man there, but nobody wanted to test him.

"He treated us like machines," said one GI. "I'm not a robot, I'm a human being." Instead of loading supplies on a truck, Top would make the men walk and carry the stuff all the way. He liked to belittle men in front of others. "He had no respect for people," Benn said.

"He was disappointed being here," said Hanusey, who had worked with Top and knew him better than most of the enlisted men. "He would have been a great first sergeant in training, the kind they use to scare trainees. But over here he was creating a fiasco." . . .

They didn't hate Top, the men in the hootch told me; they thought he was a victim of the system, just like them. He just didn't know what was going on in Vietnam, or he wouldn't have said, "Not one of them would have the guts." He hadn't been in Vietnam long enough, he didn't know that in some parts of Vietnam war existed between the grunts and the lifers.

It was just about this time that the black GIs in Top's units were beginning to think about the war, beginning to tell themselves that if they had to die they wanted to die for a cause of their own choice. To many of them the lifer sergeant was more of an enemy than the Asian peasant soldier outside the wire. There was also a different kind of white soldier in the unit.... Young white soldiers smoked grass, wore beads, and flashed the peace sign as a standard greeting. In the evenings, black and white troops would get together, blow grass, and rap. The heads and the blacks, the men in the hootch told me, were beginning to get it together. I remembered that one of the doper GIs had told me at Nha Trang: "The lifers are more afraid of what's in this camp than what's outside it."

After about two months with the unit, Top started harassing Doc Hampton about his Afro haircut, telling him to get it cut. Doc's hair was no longer than an inch and a half—within Army regulations—but Top kept pushing him to trim it.

At the mess hall one evening, Doc said that Top had "his thing," the book and the law, and that he, Doc, had *his*—an M-16 rifle. Doc said he was going to the orderly room to see the first sergeant, "Either I'll come out alone," he said, "or neither of us is coming out."

Hanusey, the clerk, was working in the orderly room when Doc came through the doorway. "His face was cold, stone cold," Hanusey said. "He looked like a man in the movies who was about to kill."

The barrel of Doc's M-16 was pointed downward, his feet planted firmly apart. Slowly he raised the barrel and fired a full clip into Top. The sergeant's back exploded as pieces of flesh and blood spattered all over the orderly room. Then Doc walked out.

Hanusey couldn't believe it, almost thinking Doc was firing blanks until he heard the empty shell casings hit the floor. It just didn't seem real. Then the captain screamed, "Stop him." Hanusey just looked down at Top, heard him groan and saw him move his head slightly, and then Top was dead.

Benn was outside when he saw Doc running for a bunker, "like a deer being chased." Suddenly there were about forty MPs and other men with shotguns and submachine guns running after Doc, shouting, "Get him, kill him."

"The chase after Doc was like a hunt, he didn't have a chance," said another GI.

The lifers cornered Doc in an empty bunker. But Doc was armed; nobody wanted to go in after him. It was a standoff. Taking up positions around the bunker, the lifers ordered him to surrender.

"I wasn't going to let it happen," said Ben Denson, a black soldier who hadn't spoken before. "If they shot Doc, there was going to be a slaughter, a bloodletting. There would have been a war." When black troops in the unit started going for their weapons, they saw that there were many whites with them.

As white and black troops started running out of their huts and bunkers towards Doc, they were blocked by armed MPs. "They wanted to gun him down and didn't want anyone to stop it," said Denson. Both sides were lining up for a confrontation and when the black and white troops trying to save Doc looked around, there were more of them than there were lifers.

Then a single shot sounded in Doc's bunker. One lifer started to make a move for the bunker, but was stopped by black troops. Two black soldiers went in. Doc Hampton was dead.

Denson had a theory about why Doc Hampton shot himself. "It was his last protest. He didn't want to be killed by his oppressors." . . .

Next morning I walked into the orderly room and asked to see the battery commander, Capt. Robert Haney. The men stopped talking and the clerks stopped typing as I walked in.

"I think your newspaper is a rag and I'm not going to write your stories for you," Haney told me over a cup of coffee at the officers' mess.

"Captain," I said. "I've got statements of thirteen men who saw what happened to Lowder and Hampton. I would like your side of the story."

Haney was startled to learn that I had sneaked on

base, interviewed his men and slept in his battery area without his knowing it. He became more cordial and agreed to answer my questions.

"It was a great surprise when I found out who had done it," he said, adding that Doc was the last man in the unit he would have expected to gun down Lowder. He admitted that the men had talked to him about Top, but added, "It never occurred to me something like this would happen. It is a trend, a part of a worldwide rebellion against authority." The Army, he said, had the same problems, generated by the rebellious attitudes of young people, as people had back home—"but we are going to take care of our problems."

"I didn't care for the way the battery had been run," Haney commented. "Individuals were not meeting Army standards in dress and in the way they looked." Doc's haircut, he said, "didn't conform." He said Doc "appeared to be intelligent," but must have had "a lapse of reasoning."

Haney thought for a moment, then asked me, "Do you think a haircut should cost a man's life?"

I tried to tell him some of the things his men had told me—that some of the GIs wanted to decide what it was they were going to die for. I told him I thought Doc Hampton had made his decision: the lifers were more his enemy than the Vietcong.

Haney recoiled at the word "lifer." "I don't like to be called a lifer," he said. "We are career soldiers; it is a patriotic calling."

DOCUMENT 8

George Swiers, " 'Demented Vets' and Other Myths" (1983)

In February 1983 a number of men and women involved in the Vietnam conflict—journalists, veterans, antiwar activists, generals, and policymakers—convened a four-day conference at the University of Southern California to discuss possible lessons from the war. One participant was George Swiers, a veteran of the war, who delivered an address on the moral obligation of veterans.

On that February afternoon in 1970 there were, unarguably, scores of curious individuals wandering around the San Francisco airport. But none could have been more outwardly curious or as purposefully driven as the young Marine. He had just turned twenty-one, though he looked and certainly felt much older. And he had just returned from the once-upon-a-time Republic of South Vietnam, a speck on the planet where reaching that age was something of a miracle.

Perched upon his bar stool like a silent sentinel, watching the sea of airport passengers, he was struck by the business as usual, etched upon face after face after face. The absurdity of it all was overwhelming.

He was, after all, the survivor of an honest-to-god magical mystery tour. A timeless, lysergic nightmare...

- where ideals and illusions could disintegrate as rapidly and violently as the human being beside you;
- where rules seemed as without boundary as the confusion and misery you existed in;
- where humiliation was so constant, so everywhere, that you stopped thinking of yourself as human.

And so, with a bravado inspired by two hours' worth of drugs and alcohol, and his uniform disheveled beyond embarrassment, he set out to speak with his Fellow Americans. To share with them his hideous secrets, to tell them what went on daily *in their names*.

Needless to say, it was impossible to find an audience, impossible even to find someone willing to hold his stare. This, he thought, is how lunatics come to speak exclusively among themselves.

The incident occurred when he happened upon the smiling middle-aged couples seated before the television. Their sin was to prefer the wisdom being offered by a program called *My Mother The Car*. The young Marine, whose very survival was owed in part to inordinate discipline, suddenly and completely lost control.

The security officers who escorted him away weren't really that rough with him; they were even tolerant of his incoherent rambling; and one of them actually said, "Listen, buddy, have a drink. You'll feel better."

This week, exactly thirteen years have passed since I was last in California. I return to a place where Vietnam is *all* that is spoken of. And there is some measure of comfort in that. But if I have learned anything in these thirteen years, it is this: *I'm not supposed to feel better*.

My friend Patrick Finnegan, a fellow activist and former grunt, often marvels at the government's willingness to permit *any* Vietnam veteran reaccess to America. For we brought with us the awful, suffocating truth of the war: that lies, though they be cleverly camouflaged, neatly packed and endorsed by presidents, are *still* lies. And that no lie clicked out in a military press release could bury deep enough the death, dishonor, and defecation that was Vietnam.

The government was quick to discredit the living proof that evil had been done; to silence those returning who hadn't already been numbed into silence. In 1971, when veterans threw their medals at the White House in protest of a war that disgusted and degraded them, the Nixon administration implied that they weren't really veterans but actors. At Miami in 1972, when we marched on the Republican Convention, broken men, reminders of a broken faith, the same administration pointed to our freshly scrubbed, non-veteran peers as a shining hope that would not "stain America."

The message sent from national leadership and embraced by the public was clear: Vietnam veterans were malcontents, liars, wackos, losers. The die was cast for a decade's indifference toward the social and economic reintegration of veterans. Hollywood, ever bizarre in its efforts to mirror life, discovered a marketable villain. *Kojack, Ironside,* and the friendly folks at *Hawaii Five-O* confronted crazed, heroin-addicted veterans with the regularity and enthusiasm Saturday morning heroes once dispensed with godless red savages. No grade-B melodrama was complete without its standard vet—a psychotic, ax-wielding rapist every bit as insulting as another one-time creature of Hollywood's imagination, the shiftless, lazy, and wide-eyed black. The demented-vet portrayal has become so casual, so commonplace, that one pictures the children of Vietnam veterans shivering beneath their blankets and wondering if Daddy will come in with a good-night kiss or a Black & Decker chain saw.

America needs its myths about the war, just as it once needed the lies. We are all of us convinced, though not all will yet admit to it, that Vietnam was a shameful abomination. *Someone* should be punished for it, indeed, deserves to be stark-raving mad because of it. The myth of 2.5 million walking time bombs tells us that someone, somewhere, in some

Without U.S. support, South Vietnam fell to the North in April 1975. Just before the surrender, employees of the U.S. embassy in Saigon hastily evacuated by helicopter.

way, is paying the price for our national sin. Absolution is lent to all others. We can live with Vietnam, without ever having to look at it.

Writing for the *Atlantic Monthly,* novelist Ward Just noted, "The Vietnam War must be scaled down to life rather than up to myth."

A detailed public autopsy on the war, and what it did to America, one in which truth is not permitted to become a casualty, should be the permanent issue of Vietnam veterans. For only through a full reckoning, a demand for examination and accountability, can the war's demons be purged.

In his January 1973, prime-time speech announcing an end to America's longest war, Richard Nixon used the phrase "peace with honor" five times. With that, the dishonorable task of sweeping the war under the rug was formally begun. Though four successive presidents have exploited the war, none of them had the moral courage to present a candid fireside chat entitled: "Vietnam Reconsidered: Lessons From a War." The legacies of Vietnam hold hostage millions of Americans who have neither seen nor heard of that faraway land: millions whose lives are ravaged by an economy still reeling from a trillion-dollar war, millions whose faith in America has so eroded that we are as gypsies—without sense of national purpose. One day, in another faraway place, other teenage Americans may fight and die for a reason as criminal as our mere reluctance to discuss Vietnam. For if we do not speak of it, others will surely rewrite the script. Each of the body bags, all of the mass graves will be reopened and their contents abracadabra-ed into a noble cause.

Vietnam veterans have their memorial now, of course. It didn't turn out to be the one-ton condolence card many of us envisioned. To the contrary, the memorial, beautiful and moving in its simplicity, provided the necessary catharsis for more than a few Vietnam veterans. November '82 also brought with it our parade. And who, this side of Pasadena at New Year's or Macy's at Thanksgiving, ever saw such a grandiose procession? There, leading it all, was none other than Gen. William Westmoreland (presumably unedited by CBS). Lovable, white-headed, reverent Westy—basking at last in the light at the end of the tunnel. Still, there were Vietnam veterans who completed the long, nightmarish path of readjustment through that process, that simple gesture of recognition.

What of readjustment for the remainder? What of those who dismiss parades and monuments as panaceas for deer hunters? What of the faceless many that Siegfried Sassoon called "The Unreturning Army"? By now it is an old and too-often told story: an inadequate GI Bill; a catalog of social problems that was staggering; employment opportunities limited or nonexistent; complicated health problems entrusted to an archaic system. In a scenario that would have pleased Kafka immensely, funds desperately needed to rebuild lives were, instead, financing an orgy of death ten thousand miles away. It is from this rubble, wrought by treachery and betrayal, that Vietnam veterans must now declare their independence. To reject forevermore the label of pitiful, helpless victim. To refuse to allow our pain to be weighed against the pain of others, or have our suffering so exaggerated as to become an indictment of the innocent.

Unemployment and underemployment are not restricted to the Vietnam veteran community. Neither do we hold the copyright on exposure to dioxin. The body count of suicide, divorce, incarceration, and substance abuse is not, all things considered, terribly discriminating. To suggest that Vietnam veterans are alone denied decent educational opportunities is ludicrous. And millions upon too-many-millions of Americans suffer from insufficient and inept health care.

A veteran who endures, and survives, the trauma of war has a moral obligation to articulate that experience to others. Not to do so is to totally abdicate one's responsibilities to the living, the once-living, and to generations yet unborn.

I remember an Edgar Lee Masters poem, "Silence," I obediently memorized as a high school junior. "Silence" in part concerned a conversation between a young boy and a very old, one-legged Civil War veteran. Asked by the boy how the leg was lost, the old soldier relives in his mind the horror of Gettysburg, but unwilling and unable to share with the boy that which his conscience demands, he answers instead, "A bear bit it off."

During 1969—a year when, for the most ambiguous of reasons, I walked the jungled mountains of someone else's country carrying a high-velocity weapon intended to terminate the lives of those who would defend it, watching those whom I loved being brutalized by the real-life spaghetti western we starred in and realizing, all of it, much too late—I often thought of the old soldier. I thought then, and know now, that his inability to share with the boy his profound grief, his unwillingness to recall the hows and whys of a leg ruined, then discarded like an insignificant chunk of meat, doomed the child to one day surrender a portion of his own anatomy and, perhaps, humanity, in the trenches of France.

There must come, through national discussion, a reckoning for Vietnam. And, very clearly, it is the war's veterans, those with insight born of deep personal tragedy, who must cry out the loudest. For it is mainly they, abandoned first on one front and then another, who have the capacity to return hope to the process.

Whether it is fair to burden the veterans with such awesome baggage is moot. We may well be asking them to step onto an emotional merry-go-round that becomes for them, and for the nation, eternal. And the result might best be described by dipping into Vietnam's macabre lexicon, where real estate, ideals, and human beings were routinely destroyed in order to save them.

But any risk is acceptable. How ironic it would be if our unwillingness to discuss Vietnam became the war's final, unpardonable sin.

This time, the hearts and minds that are there to win or lose belong to Americans.

Study Questions

1. Throughout the course of U.S. involvement in Vietnam, American policymakers insisted that Southeast Asia was a vital American interest. How did they make this argument?

2. Why did Martin Luther King, Jr., declare that the Vietnam War was the enemy of the poor?

3. In what ways did Columbia student protesters' vision of the mission of the university differ from Richard Hofstadter's?

4. In the 1980 presidential campaign, Republican Ronald Reagan asserted that the U.S. involvement in Vietnam had been a "noble cause." For whom did he speak?

13

Multicultural America

As immigrants or descendents of immigrants, many Americans tend to identify with their nation or region of origin rather than embrace a common American heritage. But in the 1960s sociologist Nathan Glazer predicted that the Civil Rights movement and the Great Society would eclipse ethnicity. As African Americans made demands for social and political integration, whites would increasingly see themselves in the same category, without ethnic distinctions. The Black Revolution and the War on Poverty, according to Glazer, posed new challenges and questions. Namely, would African Americans, as well as Asian and Mexican newcomers, follow what Glazer described as the familiar white ethnic pattern of gradual assimilation to American society (Document 1)?

Ethnic self-consciousness and assimilation dominated the debate over immigration reform. In 1965 Congress passed President Lyndon Johnson's immigration reform bill (Document 2). This legislation repealed the national origins quota system that had governed U.S. immigration policy since the 1920s. That system apportioned immigration through the implementation of quotas, so that the annual ethnic composition of all newcomers reflected that of the overall U.S. population. Consequently, immigration was restricted almost exclusively to those from northwestern Europe. Johnson's reform bill opened immigration to a "first-come, first-served" basis, regardless of country of origin. Opponents denounced the bill, objecting that it would open America's borders to hordes of impoverished, unskilled third world refugees who would take American jobs and threaten the nation's social, cultural, and Anglo-Saxon ethnic heritage (Document 3).

Since the 1880s, when Congress passed the first Chinese Exclusion Act, American lawmakers had severely restricted Asian immigration. The 1965 reform bill freed millions of Asians from Vietnam, Thailand, Taiwan, Korea, China, and Japan to come to American shores. Many settled ethnic neighborhoods in cities such as New York, Chicago, San Francisco, and Los Angeles. But in the 1980s many Asian-Americans began moving in significant numbers to suburban areas such as Monterey Park in California's San Gabriel Valley, southeast of Los Angeles. The Asian influx stimulated a cultural transformation of suburban life, but, at the same time, newcomers encountered racial hostility and watched as white residents packed up and moved out (Document 4).

Perhaps the fiercest battle over integration occurred in Boston in the 1970s. Throughout the county in the late 1960s and early 1970s, African Americans gained increasing political visibility, especially in cities such as Detroit, Cleveland, and Gary, Indiana. This, along with several court-ordered busing programs designed to achieve racial balance in public schools, fueled organized opposition and an intense racial backlash, especially among urban working-class whites. In the 1970s a federal district court ordered that pupils from all-black Roxbury be bused to Charleston, an Irish, working-class neighborhood. For three years police patrolled South Boston High School, protecting black students as they attended school. The episode generated some of the most intense confrontations of the civil rights era (Document 5).

Inspired by the activism of the Civil Rights movement, many minority groups pursued their goals through political action. Cesar Chavez, a Mexican American labor organizer, recruited Mexican migrant farm workers into the United Farm Workers Union. Through Chavez's leadership, union activists led a series of strikes, marches, and boycotts to achieve better working and living conditions for Mexican orchard workers (Document 6). The Civil Rights movement also motivated gays and lesbians to awakening Americans to discrimination against homosexuals (Document 7). Whether agitating for workers' rights, civil rights, women's rights, or gay rights, these varied activists appropriated the language of the Civil Rights movement in their struggle to redefine America not as a melting pot but as a multicultural, pluralistic society.

DOCUMENT 1

Nathan Glazer, "The Peoples of America" (1965)

Sociologist Nathan Glazer closely studied contemporary ethnicity in America. In an article written for *The Nation* in 1965, Glazer argued that ethnic self-consciousness in America moves in waves or cycles. He anticipated that the Civil Rights movement would suppress ethnic self-assertiveness among whites. In the following excerpt, Glazer discusses the relevance of the history of white immigration to African Americans.

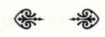

What after all is the history of the American ethnic groups but a history of group and individual adaptation to difficult circumstances? All the histories move in the same patterns. The immigrants arrive; they represent the poorest and least educated and most oppressed of their countries in Europe and Asia. They arrive ignorant of our language and customs, exploited and abused. They huddle together in the ghettos of the cities, beginning slowly to attend to their most immediate needs—organization for companionship, patterns of self-aid in crisis, churches for worship, schools to maintain the old culture. American society and government is indifferent to their needs and desires; they are allowed to do what they wish, but neither hindered nor aided. In this amorphous setting where no limits are set to group organization, they gradually form a community. Their children move through the public schools and perhaps advance themselves—if not, it may be the grandchildren who do. The children are embarrassed by the poverty and ignorance of the parents. Eventually they, or the grandchildren, learn to accept their origins as poverty and ignorance are overcome. They move into the spheres of American life in which many or all groups meet— the larger economy, politics, social life, education. Eventually many of the institutions created by the immigrants become a hindrance rather than a necessity; some are abandoned, some are changed. American society in the meantime has made a place for and even become dependent on some of these institutions, such as old-age homes and hospitals, adoption services and churches—these survive and perhaps flourish. More and more of these institutions become identified with the religious denomination, rather than the ethnic group as such. . . .

Does this history have any meaning for the American Negro? This is the question that Jews and Japanese, Irish and Italians, Poles and Czechs ask themselves. Some new immigrant groups—Puerto Ricans and Mexicans—think it does have a meaning for them. They try to model their institutions on those of earlier immigrant groups. They show the same uncertainties and confusions over what to do with the culture and language they have brought with them. The militant Negro and his white allies passionately deny the relevance or even the truth of this history. It is white history; as white history it is also the history of the exploitation of the Negro, of the creation of privilege on the basis of his unpaid and forced labor. It is not history he can accept as having any meaning for him. His fate, he insists, has been far more drastic and frightful than any other, and neither Irish famines nor Jewish pogroms make the members of these groups brothers in understanding. The hatred with which he is looked upon by whites, he believes, has nothing in common with the petty prejudices that European immigrant groups have met. And the America of today, in which he makes his great and desperate effort for full equality, he asserts, has little in common with the America of mass immigration.

A subtle intervention of government in every aspect of social life, of economy, of culture, he insists, is necessary now to create justice. Every practice must now be scrutinized anew for its impact on this totally unique and incomparable group in American life. The neighborhood school, the civil service system, the personnel procedures of our corporations, the practices of small business, the scholarship systems of our states, the composition and character of our churches, the structure of neighborhood organization, the practices of unions—all, confronted with this shibboleth, fail. The Negro has not received his due, and the essence of all of them is therefore discrimination and exclusion, and the defense of privilege. It is no wonder that ethnic self-consciousness, after its brief moment of triumph, after its legitimization in American life, now turns upon itself in confusion. After all, it is these voluntary churches, organizations, hospitals, schools, and businesses that have become the pride of ethnic groups, and the seat of whatever distinctiveness they possess. It is by way of this participation that they have become part of the very fabric of American life. But the fabric is now challenged. And looked at from another perspective, the Negro perspective, the same structure that defends some measure of uniqueness by the same token defends some measure of discrimination and exclusion.

It is impossible for the ethnic groups in America, who have already moved through so many protean forms, to be unaffected by the civil rights revolution. For this raises the question of the status of the largest of American minority groups, the one most closely bound up with American history from its very beginnings. Chinese and Japanese, perhaps Puerto Ricans and Mexican Americans can accept the patterns of development and gradual assimilation into American society that are exhibited in the history of the great European immigrant groups. For a while, some of us who studied this history and saw in its variety and flexibility some virtues for a mass, industrial society, which suppresses variety and flexibility in so many areas, hoped that the American Negro, as he entered the more open environments of Northern cities, could also move along the paths the European immigrant groups had followed.

We now wonder whether this hope was illusory. Whether it was the infection of Europeans with the virus of American racial prejudice; or the inability to confine the direct and violent conflict in the South; or the impact of slavery and Southern experience on the American Negro—it is clear, whatever the causes, that for one of the major groups in American life, the idea of pluralism, which has supported the various developments of other groups, has become a mockery. Whatever concrete definition we give to pluralism, it means a limitation of government power, a relatively free hand for private and voluntary organizations to develop their own patterns of worship, education, social life, residential concentration, and even their distinctive economic activity. All of these inevitably enhance the life of one group; from the perspective of the American Negro they are inevitably exclusive and discriminatory.

The general ideas that have justified the development of the ethnic group in America have never been too well explicated. We have tended to obscure the inevitable conflicts between individual group interest and national interest, even when they have occurred, rather than set down sharp principles to regulate the ethnic groups. If an ethnic group interest clashed with a national interest, we have been quite ruthless and even extreme in overriding the group interest. Thus two World Wars radically diminished the scale and assertiveness of German-American group life. But we have never fully developed what is permitted and what is not. Now a new national interest is becoming defined—the final liquidation of Negro separation, in all areas of our life: the economic, the social, the cultural, the residential. In every area, Negro separation, regardless of its causes, is seen as unbearable by Negroes. Inevitably this must deeply mark the future development of American ethnic groups, whose continuance contributes, in some measure, to this separation. Recently in this country there has been a positive attitude to ethnic distinctiveness. Oscar Handlin and others have argued that it does not divide the nation or weaken it in war; rather it helps integrate the immigrant groups and adds a rich strand of variety to American civilization. Now a new question arises: what is its effect on the Negro?

Perhaps, ironically, the final homogenization the American people, the creation of a common nationality replacing all other forms of national connection, will now come about because of the need to guarantee the integration of the Negro. But I believe the group character of American life is too strongly established and fits too many individual needs to be so completely suppressed. Is it not more likely that as Negro demands are in varying measure met, the Negro too will accept the virtues of our complex society, in which separation is neither forbidden nor required, but rather tolerated? Perhaps the American Negro will become another ethnic group, accepted by others and accepting himself.

DOCUMENT 2

Lyndon B. Johnson, Remarks upon Signing the Immigration Bill (1965)

In 1963 President John F. Kennedy asked Congress to revise the nation's immigration laws. The Johnson administration continued to call for immigration reform, and in 1965 Congress responded. President Johnson delivered this address upon signing the bill on Liberty Island, at the base of the Statue of Liberty.

This bill that we will sign today is not a revolutionary bill. It does not affect the lives of millions. It will not reshape the structure of our daily lives, or really add importantly to either our wealth or our power.

Yet it is still one of the most important acts of this Congress and of this administration.

For it does repair a very deep and painful flaw in the fabric of American justice. It corrects a cruel and enduring wrong in the conduct of the American Nation.

Speaker McCormack and Congressman Celler almost 40 years ago first pointed that out in their maiden speeches in the Congress. And this measure that we will sign today will really make us truer to ourselves both as a country and as a people. It will strengthen us in a hundred unseen ways.

I have come here to thank personally each Member of the Congress who labored so long and so valiantly to make this occasion come true today, and to make this bill a reality. I cannot mention all their names, for it would take much too long, but my gratitude—and that of this Nation—belongs to the 89th Congress.

We are indebted, too, to the vision of the late beloved President John Fitzgerald Kennedy, and to the support given to this measure by the then Attorney General and now Senator, Robert F. Kennedy.

In the final days of consideration, this bill had no more able champion than the present Attorney General, Nicholas Katzenbach, who, with New York's own "Manny" Celler, and Senator Ted Kennedy of Massachusetts, and Congressman Feighan of Ohio, and Senator Mansfield and Senator Dirksen constituting the leadership of the Senate, and Senator Javits, helped to guide this bill to passage, along with the help of the Members sitting in front of me today.

This bill says simply that from this day forth those wishing to immigrate to America shall be admitted on the basis of their skills and their close relationship to those already here.

This is a simple test, and it is a fair test. Those who can contribute most to this country—to its growth, to its strength, to its spirit—will be the first that are admitted to this land.

The fairness of this standard is so self-evident that we may well wonder that it has not always been applied. Yet the fact is that for over four decades the immigration policy of the United States has been twisted and has been distorted by the harsh injustice of the national origins quota system.

Under that system the ability of new immigrants to come to America depended upon the country of their birth. Only 3 countries were allowed to supply 70 percent of all the immigrants.

Families were kept apart because a husband or a wife or a child had been born in the wrong place.

Men of needed skill and talent were denied entrance because they came from southern or eastern Europe or from one of the developing continents.

This system violated the basic principle of American democracy—the principle that values and rewards each man on the basis of his merit as a man.

It has been un-American in the highest sense, because it has been untrue to the faith that brought thousands to these shores even before we were a country.

Today, with my signature, this system is abolished.

We can now believe that it will never again shadow the gate to the American Nation with the twin barriers of prejudice and privilege.

Our beautiful America was built by a nation of strangers. From a hundred different places or more they have poured forth into an empty land, joining and blending in one mighty and irresistible tide.

The land flourished because it was fed from so many sources—because it was nourished by so many cultures and traditions and peoples.

And from this experience, almost unique in the history of nations, has come America's attitude toward the rest of the world. We, because of what we are, feel safer and stronger in a world as varied as the people who make it up—a world where no country rules another and all countries can deal with the basic problems of human dignity and deal with those problems in their own way.

Now, under the monument which has welcomed so many to our shores, the American Nation returns to the finest of its traditions today.

The days of unlimited immigration are past.

But those who do come will come because of what they are, and not because of the land from which they sprung.

When the earliest settlers poured into a wild continent there was no one to ask them where they came from. The only question was: Were they sturdy enough to make the journey, were they strong enough to clear the land, were they enduring enough to make a home for freedom, and were they brave enough to die for liberty if it became necessary to do so?

And so it has been through all the great and testing moments of American history. Our history this year we see in Viet-Nam. Men there are dying—men named Fernandez and Zajac and Zelinko and Mariano and McCormick.

Neither the enemy who killed them nor the people whose independence they have fought to save ever asked them where they or their parents came from. They were all Americans. It was for free men and for America that they gave their all, they gave their lives and selves.

By eliminating that same question as a test for immigration the Congress proves ourselves worthy of those men and worthy of our own traditions as a Nation. . . .

Over my shoulders here you can see Ellis Island, whose vacant corridors echo today the joyous sound of long ago voices.

And today we can all believe that the lamp of this grand old lady is brighter today—and the golden door that she guards gleams more brilliantly in the light of an increased liberty for the people from all the countries of the globe.

DOCUMENT 3

Mrs. Robert H. V. Duncan, Testimony Before Congress on Immigration Reform (1964)

Opposition to immigration reform was intense. In 1964 Mrs. Robert H. V. Duncan, president general of the Daughters of the American Revolution (DAR), testified before a House of Representatives subcommittee holding hearings on immigration reform. Her arguments are representative of the views of the reform bill's opponents.

DAR is against H.R. 7700 and similar weakening bills because while DAR would be the first to admit the importance of immigrants to America, its membership ties linking directly with the first waves of immigrants to these shores, it would seem well, however, to point out a "then and now" difference factor currently exists attributable to time and circumstance—no uncomplimentary inference therein. A common desire shared by immigrants of all time to America has been the seeking of freedom or the escape from tyranny. But in the early days, say the first 150 years, it is noteworthy that those who came shared common Anglo-Saxon bonds and arrived with the full knowledge and intent of founders or pioneers who knew there was a wilderness to conquer and a nation to build. Their coming indicated a willingness to make a contribution and assume such a role. In the intervening years, many fine, high-caliber immigrants, and I know some at personal sacrifice, following ideals in which they believed, have likewise come to America imbued with a constructive desire to produce and add to the glory of their new homeland. They, however, have come to a Nation already established with cultural patterns set and traditions already rooted.

Further, in recent years, en masse refugee movements, though responding to the very same ideal which is America, have been motivated primarily by escape. This has had a tendency possibly to dim individual purpose and dedication and possibly project beyond other considerations, the available benefits to be secured as an American citizen.

Abandonment of the national origins system would drastically alter the source of our immigration. Any change would not take into consideration that those whose background and heritage most closely resemble our own are most readily assimilable.

Would not the abolishment of the national origin quota system work a hardship and possibly result in actual discrimination against the very nations who supplied the people who now comprise the majority of our historic population mixture? Further, such a change in our existing laws would appear to be an outright accommodation to the heaviest population explosions throughout the world—India, Asia, and Africa. Certainly these countries could naturally be expected to take full advantage of such an increased quota opportunity.

Is it, therefore, desirable or in the best interest to assign possible 10-per cent quotas to say proliferating African nations to the end that our own internal problems become manifold? America, as all other nations, is concerned over rapid population growth of this era. Staggering statistics are readily available on every hand.

Attention is called to the fact that immigration is not an alien's right; it is a privilege. With privilege comes its handmaiden responsibility. Before tampering with the present immigration law, much less destroying its basic principles, due regard must also be given to our unemployment situation.

It would seem highly incongruent if not outright incredible to find ourselves in a situation, on the one hand, waging war on poverty and unemployment at home, while on the other hand, simultaneously and indiscriminately letting down immigration bars to those abroad. Not only employment alone but mental health and retardation problems could greatly increase. Another source of concern to the heavy laden taxpayer to whom already the national debt figure is astronomical.

It is asserted that our economy will get three consumers for every worker admitted and that our economy generates jobs at a rate better than one for every three consumers. Why, then, are we presently plagued with unemployment? And how is it possible to guarantee that these new immigrants will "fill jobs that are going begging because there are not enough skilled workers in our economy who have the needed skills?" Are there enough such jobs going begging to justify destroying an immigration law which has been described as our first line of defense?

Rightly, it would seem U.S. citizens should have first claim on jobs and housing in this country. With manpower available and the recent emphasis on expanded educational facilities, why is not definite concentrated effort made to provide and accelerate vocational and special skill training for the many who either through disinclination, native inability or otherwise are not qualified potentials for schooling in the field of science, medicine, law, or other such professions?

Without the quota system it is doubtful whether or not America could indefinitely maintain its traditional heritage: Economic, cultural, social, ethnic, or even language.

Free institutions as we have known them would stand to undergo radical changes if the proposal to permit reapportionment of unused quotas is also adopted. It is felt reassignment of unused quotas would be as damaging to the basic principles of the Immigration and Nationality Act as repeal of the national origins system itself. The proviso that the President reserve a portion of the pool for allocation to qualified immigrants further extends the power of the executive branch of the Government.

No less important is the fact that it is almost impossible to adequately screen persons coming from satellite countries.

It may well be embarrassing to proponents of liberalizing amendments to find that some of the most active opposition against the McCarran-Walter Act is provided by the Communists. According to the House Committee on Un-American Activities, the Communist Party has created, and now controls, in 15 key States, 180 "front" organizations dedicated exclusively to the purpose of creating grassroots pressure in the Congress to destroy the act—which is what most of the proposed amendments would do. . . .

The well-intentioned, humanitarian plea that America's unrestricted assumption of the overpopulous, troubled, ailing people of the world within our own borders is unrealistic, impractical, and if done in excess could spell economic bankruptcy for our people from point of both employment and overladen taxes to say nothing of a collapse of morale and spiritual values if nonassimilable aliens of dissimilar ethnic background and culture by wholesale and indiscriminate transporting en masse overturn the balance of our national character.

DOCUMENT 4

Los Angeles Times, "Asian Influx Alters Life in Suburbia" (1987)

Since 1980 the Asian population of California's San Gabriel Valley has skyrocketed. Between 1983 and 1985, Monterey Park, a suburban community in the valley, was a popular destination for Asian immigrants, second only to New York City. The following selection from the *Los Angeles Times* describes how the varied Asian immigrants have recast the Valley's identity.

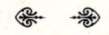

Across the entire stretch of the San Gabriel Valley, from Monterey Park in the west to Diamond Bar in the east, unprecedented numbers of Asian newcomers are dramatically changing life in the suburbs.

In one of the most sweeping demographic and social transitions ever experienced by a suburban region, the San Gabriel Valley has emerged as an improbable center of Chinese and other Asian immigration in this country.

In the last six years alone, an estimated 100,000 Chinese and other Asians have moved into a band of predominantly white bedroom communities. Fully one-half of these newcomers have resettled in eight small cities that make up the western San Gabriel Valley, an ethnic concentration unparalleled among suburban regions of the country.

Their arrival has had profound implications for nearly every institution of civic life, affecting the way schools, police, city halls, courts and post offices conduct their day-to-day business. It has meant small shifts, such as incorporating Mandarin, Cantonese and Vietnamese in the announcements that go home with schoolchildren. And it has brought more fundamental changes, transforming quiet bedroom communities into bustling cities awash in the sights, sounds and smells of distant cultures.

Business strips once moribund have been revitalized with an infusion of Asian enterprise and money. Lots that were vacant only a few years ago now support an odd meld of suburban mini-malls and pulsing Far East marketplaces. One such plaza in the city of San Gabriel features an arresting array of choices: a Filipino grocery and sandwich shop, a Vietnamese cafe, a Japanese bakery, an Indonesian deli and restaurants offering Taiwanese, Chinese, and Japanese cuisine.

"The impact is far greater than just numbers. What we are talking about is the cultural transformation of an entire region and its impact in terms of schools, ethnic relations and the resurgence of commercial life," said Charles Choy Wong, a sociologist at California State University, Los Angeles, whose doctoral thesis focused on the Chinese experience in Los Angeles and Monterey Park.

"Many companies that have come here are the overseas branch offices of companies in Taiwan and Hong Kong. The ties between the west San Gabriel Valley and the Far East are many. There is frequent travel, daily communications. We're divided by an ocean, but in reality it's just a street."

The influx mostly of ethnic Chinese from Taiwan, Vietnam, Hong Kong and China has torn at the western San Gabriel Valley's social and political framework, engendering racial backlash and a distinct form of white flight.

Since the 1950s, affluent whites have fled America's cities for the suburbs, leaving behind a concentration of poorer minorities.

But in the San Gabriel Valley today some longtime residents are attempting to keep one step ahead of a growing Asian presence by fleeing suburbs in the western valley for what they regard as more stable white suburban communities in the east valley and in Orange County.

For every one Asian newcomer who has resettled in the western San Gabriel Valley since 1980, roughly one white resident has either moved away or died, *The Times* found. The proportion of whites in the area has plummeted from 78% in 1970 to 56% in 1980 to an estimated 36% of the region's 327,000 residents today.

Over that same period, the Asian population has grown from 2% to 13% to an estimated 27%, the study of school enrollment and vital statistics shows. The region's Latino population—which experienced an increase of 10 percentage points between 1970 and 1980—has now stabilized to about 28% as Latinos are also moving from the western San Gabriel Valley to communities to the east. . . .

Although many of the newcomers share a Chinese heritage, they have come from different places and embrace vastly different dreams. They are wealthy businessmen seeking new frontiers and struggling busboys in their mid-50s. They are wives working alongside husbands in lucrative real estate firms and mothers toiling long hours in garment sweatshops for substandard wages. They are urban and westernized, rural and backward. Some speak and read four languages, while others are illiterate in their native tongues and have little hope of ever learning English. Many have come legally, fleeing political uncertainty in Taiwan and Hong Kong or the hard rural life of China. Others have come as tourists and overstayed their visas, remaining here as illegal aliens.

Many of the ethnic Chinese from Vietnam have fled war and persecution with little or no hope of returning to their homeland. But the break is not so clean for Chinese from Taiwan and Hong Kong. Couples often live apart for long periods of time with husbands traveling back and forth between family here and businesses overseas. Finally, some of the newcomers have achieved a precarious balance, reaching out and becoming a part of the American mainstream without forsaking their language and culture—one of the most ancient in the world. Still others go about their daily business tucked safely away in insular communities, secure in knowing that they seldom have to confront the larger society. Theirs is a world of Chinese-language newspapers and ethnic grocery stores and neighbors from the old country.

Together, they have recast the San Gabriel Valley's identity.

Today, the conspicuous wealth of many of the Taiwanese newcomers stands cheek by jowl with the Third World poverty of Vietnamese refugees, half of whom subsist on welfare, county statistics show.

"The area has totally changed in the last six years. When I was here, we had to drive to downtown L.A. to get Vietnamese food."

In the midst of this transition, confronted by higher rents and the sudden departure of longtime customers, a number of Anglo and Latino business owners have retired or relocated. Like Edy Wallace who for 18 years ran a flower shop on Valley Boulevard in Alhambra, many remain embittered by the experience.

Wallace said she leased her building from an Anglo landlord who had charged $515 a month in rent since renewing the lease in 1978. Three years ago, the building was sold at a big profit to a Chinese developer who raised the rent to $1,600. Wallace said the increase was beyond the prevailing market.

"We looked around for another location in the area, but property was being bought up by Asian developers and the rents were going up everywhere," said Wallace, who retired. "So much of our business had moved away and was replaced by Asians who couldn't speak English and would just as soon buy flowers from their own people." . . .

But some longtime businesses, after an initial period of cultural adjustment, have come to rely on their Chinese patrons. At Jim Marino Mercedes in Alhambra, salesmen estimate that Chinese account for 40% of their car sales.

"We get customers who arrive on Monday, buy a home on Tuesday and get a Mercedes on Wednesday," said John Rigler, a salesman. "A lot of them divide their time between Taiwan and here. They want to buy the same model here that they have back there."

"They're great customers. The only thing I've had to get used to is that some of them are very superstitious. Taiwanese, for instance, don't like the model 420 because the 4 means death in their culture. The 560 is a hot seller because 6 means prosperity."

For decades, until the repeal in 1965 of the Alien Quota Act, America represented an elusive dream for many Asians. The 41-year-old U.S. law had virtually banned immigrants from Asian countries.

Now many of the newcomers, like Morgan and Susan Wong of Arcadia, point to relatives who arrived in the years immediately after the repeal and later sponsored them and other family members in their move to this country.

"My brother told us that Arcadia was a good place to live with good schools," Susan Wong said.

Limited enrollment in Taiwan colleges consigned all but the very brightest students to a future of vocational schooling, Morgan Wong said. So he sold his small steel company in Taiwan in 1984 and moved his wife and two young daughters to Arcadia, where he opened a computer firm.

"Now my children don't live with the constant pressure of having to be the best in their class," he said.

Hoping to rekindle a flicker of the life they left behind, thousands of ethnic Chinese refugees from Vietnam have clustered in the western San Gabriel Valley over the last nine years, while their ethnic Vietnamese counterparts have concentrated in Orange County.

Local resettlement officials say as many as 30,000

Chinese Vietnamese refugees live in the 45-square-mile western San Gabriel Valley, one of the nation's largest such ethnic enclaves. By contrast, an estimated 65,000 Vietnamese refugees live in all of Orange County.

Their presence resounds in a collection of new cafes, restaurants, bakeries, supermarkets, beauty salons, dress shops and video stores that dot Valley Boulevard from Alhambra to Rosemead. It can be glimpsed in the Saigon Center pool hall where unemployed young men play a three-ball billiard game and in storefront sweatshops where refugee mothers on welfare sew garments for unreported cash wages. It can be tasted in the piquant broth of *hu tiu tom cua*, a complete soup meal of shrimp, crab, greens and thin noodles.

Stewart Kwoh, director of the Asian-Pacific American legal center of Southern California, said his organization has documented several anti-Asian racial incidents in the San Gabriel Valley. These have included aggravated assaults and vandalism against Asian families moving into all-white blocks.

In Arcadia, an Asian-style home belonging to Sho Kosugi, the star of several so-called "Ninja" movies, has served as the lightning rod for longtime residents irritated over changes in their community. His home—which stands three stories tall and features a blue tile roof, a Buddhist shrine and a red bridge—has been vandalized repeatedly since he built it two years ago.

The front windows have been broken more than 20 times with rocks or BBs, Kosugi said. Vandals have thrown nails into the swimming pool, strewn rotten fruit on the tennis court and piled garbage on the front lawn. Kosugi, who is Japanese and married to a Chinese, said passers-by yell, "Japs, go home!" almost daily. His wife his has implored him to move.

"I don't want to give up and run away. I'm not one of those types of people," Kosugi said. "My two children ask me, 'Why are they doing this to us, Dad?' I tell them that some people have biases and some people are jealous."

In Hacienda Heights, the construction of a huge Buddhist temple on a hill overlooking the community has outraged some residents and fueled resentment. The complex, which will stand 80 feet high and cost more than $10 million, will include living quarters for 30 monks and a vegetarian cafeteria open to the public.

"We moved here 10 years ago because it was kind of like country," said Alta Fuller, a Texas native who lives with her husband in a home at the foot of the hill. "I thought it was terrible to build this thing in a residential area and bring all these kinds of people here that we're not used to.

"There have been a lot of changes here. A lot of foreigners have bought homes up in the hills. There's so many of them that they've begun to call it 'Slant Hill.'"

Although acknowledging tension between the newcomers and longtime residents, elected officials and school administrators disagree that the dramatic drop in the number of white residents implies racial flight. They argue that the decline is more the reflection of an aging white community whose children have moved away and a younger white population who sold their homes at inflated prices to Chinese newcomers.

But a reporter who walked through several communities this fall had no trouble finding numerous Anglo and Latino families who were in the process of moving and bitter over the changes.

Gene and Bonnie Smith, who recently moved to Missouri after living 20 years in the same Monterey Park home, typified this group.

"To me, this will always be home," Gene Smith said. "Before the influx it was a good community. You could do a little business in town, and people were friendlier. We've become a concrete jungle with condos and town houses and unbelievable traffic. Maybe I have myself to blame for not attending more council meetings and objecting to the changes."

"I was not raised to feel the way I do today," Bonnie Smith said. "I was raised to feel that everyone is created equal. It bothers me, the dislike I have in my heart for these people. I've tried to deal with it, but I just can't. I guess I hurt too much."

DOCUMENT 5

Ione Malloy, Southie Won't Go (1975)

Ione Malloy taught English at South Boston High School from 1970 to 1977. She witnessed firsthand the often violent conflict over court-mandated busing, as white parents organized a boycott of South Boston High School to protest the desegregation order. During the confrontation over busing, Malloy kept a diary, which she later published. The following excerpts from November 1975 reveal the difficulty of teaching in this inflamed racial atmosphere and how the burden of desegregation fell on working-class high-school students, both white and black.

From my homeroom window I watched the school buses empty one by one, while an administrator, Mr. Gizzi, checked each student's class program to see whether the student belonged at the high school. As I watched, a girl's piercing screams rose from the front lobby. Troopers began running toward the building. Trooper squad cars blocked off G Street down the hill so the buses couldn't move. Mr. Gizzi stayed with the buses. Over the intercom the secretary's voice cried, "We need help here on the second floor. Please send help to the office." Isolated on the second floor in the front corner of the building, in a small room attached to two adjoining rooms, I again felt the terror of not knowing what was coming from what direction, feeling unable to protect myself or the students from an unidentified danger.

I have never had a desire to flee, just to protect the students, though I don't like the feeling of being trapped. I closed the door, turned out the lights, and told my homeroom students we would stay there and help each other. We waited—two white girls, Kathryn and Becky; James, a small, long-haired white boy; and Jeffrey, a black. In a few minutes the door opened. The gym teacher, carrying an umbrella, stood there with a trooper, their faces anxious. "Have you seen Jane?" they asked, then hurried away. What had happened? Why was the teacher carrying an umbrella? Who was Jane, and where might she have gone, we wondered, but there was no chance to ask. They had already shut the door behind them.

Then came a call for all teachers not assigned to homerooms to report to the front lobby. The call was repeated several times.

About forty minutes later, I was amazed when, from my window, I saw the last bus empty. Several minutes later the intercom announced that the school day would begin. Students should proceed to their first class. Instead, everyone just sat, afraid to move, paralyzed by the unknown.

There were only twenty minutes left in the first class, senior English. The seniors were upset. There had been fights in the South Cafeteria, in the third floor lavatory, and in room 303 on the third floor down the hall, they told me. Because the fights had broken out simultaneously, the seniors felt they had been planned. Just then the intercom requested custodians to report to the third floor lavatory and to the South Cafeteria. "To clean up the blood," the seniors explained.

Although the seniors wanted to discuss the fights, I said we would first take a quick, objective, one-word test. I was a little angry. It was better to get their minds focused on something else. In the few remaining minutes, I let them take the Luscher color preference test and talk about the correlation of color with personality. Most of them chose yellow, red, or blue in their color preference. They are a good class.

When I passed room 303 a few minutes later, the students were pushing at the door to get out. A trooper was holding them in. I told two boys at the door to go in and help their teacher. They asked, "Help *her?*" It hadn't occurred to them that she might need their help. Jack Kennedy, administrator, passed me in the corridor, his face white and drained. I stopped in the teachers' room to comb my hair. My face in the mirror looked ghastly. It must take the body time to recover its equilibrium, even after the mind has composed itself.

As I walked around the school, and felt the mood of the school, I thought, "This school is DEATH. The mood of the school is black."

The troopers were happy, however, I was surprised to see. One said, "This is more like it. It gets the old adrenalin going."

My sophomores, a mixed class of black and white students, also wanted to talk about the incidents. They explained how the fight before school had started at the front lobby door. A black girl and a white boy were going through the front lobby—the boy first. He let the door slam on her. She screamed; a black male jumped to her defense, and the fight was on. A trooper pushed a white boy back over a desk and dislocated his shoulder. A black student on the stairs started screaming insults at the white students—among them Michael Faith—and Faith lunged for him. Fights broke out everywhere in the lobby. Students rushed down from the classrooms, or out of their homerooms to aid the secretaries when they called for help on the intercom.

Anne was upset because a trooper in the cafeteria had grabbed a black girl and called her "nigger." "Nobody calls me 'nigger.'" Anne said. "My friend got her comb and got a piece of his red meat."

I played dumb and, for the benefit of white students, said, "But I hear black kids call each other 'nigger,' and they don't seem to mind." Anne said, "Nobody's called *me* 'nigger.' I don't care who he is." Louis, a black student who has come to school regularly in a taxi even when Atkins called for a boycott, sat back confidently in his fine pressed suit and said, "It's all right when another black person calls me a 'nigger,' but not a white person. Then it's an insult. If I don't know a person and he calls me 'nigger,' I don't say anything until I find out how he feels about me."

Anne said, "I hate this school. I don't never want to come back."

I concluded, "We all need more understanding.". . .

There was a faculty meeting after school. Dr. Reid took the toll of casualties and names involved in fights. Unconsciously he wiped his brow with the classic tragic sweep of his hand and said, "I don't know what we can do. We were all at our posts doing our jobs. But if a youngster will insult and another responds with his fists, there's nothing we can do—except encourage them to watch their mouths and language."

Dr. Reid announced he would like to have an honor roll assembly for sophomores. Mrs. Marie Folkart, the oldest, most respected member of the faculty, raised her hand: She hoped he wouldn't have an assembly. Usually very deferential to her, he disagreed, "I don't know about that. I think maybe we should."

The assembly, the first this year, is scheduled for Friday, a day when attendance is the lowest. . . .

The sophomore assembly convened as planned. Classes filed to assigned seats room by room without incident. Troopers lined the auditorium. The mood was ugly.

Dr. Reid entered from the rear of the hall. As he moved down the center aisle to the stage, he urged the students to stand. He stopped at my class. Martin wouldn't stand because Siegfried, behind him, wouldn't. Then James sat down—later, he told me, because the black kids—Martin and Siegfried—wouldn't stand. Dr. Reid insisted, and I insisted, but Martin refused. Dr. Reid proceeded on. Again I thought, "This school is death."

After the pledge of allegiance to the flag, Dr. Reid lectured on the courtesy of standing when a guest comes to one's home. A few students snickered. When he alluded to the troopers, the black boys in the row behind me yelled, "Get them out." Then Dr. Reid outlined the sports plan for the winter and told the assembly, "We will be together for the year. After that I don't know. But we're here, and we had better make the best of it. And let's have a little courtesy toward one another. Let's treat each other with respect and watch what we say to one another—treat each other with a little kindness. A smile goes a long way if someone accidentally bumps you, instead of pushing back." The students listened respectfully.

Then, as both black and white students crossed the stage to accept their honor roll cards from Dr. Reid, the assembly applauded.

Students left the auditorium room by room.

During the day, girl students traveled the school in roving gangs of blacks and whites, bursting out of classes at any provocation, spreading consternation among the police. "They're in holiday mood," I told the police, dismayed at the prospect of chasing pretty girls back to classrooms.

At the end of the day in homeroom, I told Martin, "Dr. Reid has put his life on the line about desegregation because it is the law. His house in South Boston is guarded. Then he asks you to stand in the assembly, and you refuse. He is your friend, the friend of all of us, and you should know that." James said to Martin, "That's right, Dr. Reid has guards."

A neighborhood crowd chanted at Dr. Reid outside the school this morning. . . .

A librarian at the Boston Public Library in Copley Square told me there are enough kids in the library all day to have school there. He doesn't know where they come from. . . .

The number of troopers in the building was increased instead of decreased, contrary to what the troopers had anticipated Friday when I talked to them.

The two black boys—Martin and Jeffrey—and one white girl, Kathryn, were present in my homeroom today. Expecting a boycott, I was surprised to see any white students in school until I learned that a walkout of white students was anticipated at 9:45 A.M., when the parents, now gathering on the sidewalk, planned to walk in to protest the presence of steel combs in the school.

Walkers (or white students) were permitted to leave by the side doors, if they preferred, so as not to be identified and, perhaps, intimidated by the now divided community. In South Boston families once friends are now enemies, since half support the antibusing boycott and the other half feel they have to educate their children.

Television cameras recorded Dr. Reid facing the protesters outside the building in the morning sunshine. He told them, "The black parents have elected no biracial council; the white students have elected none; the white parents have elected none. And frankly, the number of fights last week made me afraid."

In class Anne described the walkout. "The white kids said, 'See you Tuesday, niggers.' If the black kids had a walkout, I'd go, too. The white kids have to go, or they'll get beaten up." Gretchen, a diligent and intelligent white student, who had attended the advanced classes of the New York public schools, listened. I give her extra reading and reports because she is highly motivated. Besides Gretchen, there were five black students in the class.

I left school at the end of the day by the front lobby staircase, passing the Greek frieze laboriously painted by the art teachers in neutral dark brown last September before school began. The frieze had been nightly mutilated with spray paint and daily repaired by the art department, until finally they gave up. The frieze is now hideous: The faces are black blobs, or white blobs, or faceless with black holes for eyes. Looking at them, one teacher shuddered, "The hatred is getting to me."

DOCUMENT 6

Cesar Chavez, "God Is Beside You on the Picket Line" (1966)

In March 1966, in the midst of a prolonged and bitter strike of Mexican grape workers, Cesar Chavez organized a 250-mile Easter march from Delano, California, to Sacramento, the state capital, to dramatize the plight of migrant farm laborers. Upon reaching the capital, Chavez delivered this brief speech in which he articulated the centrality of Catholicism to the workers' cause.

❦ ❦

In the "March from Delano to Sacramento" there is a meeting of cultures and traditions; the centuries-old religious tradition of Spanish culture conjoins with the very contemporary cultural syndrome of "demonstration" springing from the spontaneity of the poor, the downtrodden, the rejected, the discriminated against bearing visibly their need and demand for equality and freedom.

In every religion-oriented culture "the pilgrimage" has had a place: a trip made with sacrifice and hardship as an expression of penance and of commitment—and often involving a petition to the patron of the pilgrimage for some sincerely sought benefit of body or soul. Pilgrimage has not passed from Mexican culture. Daily at any of the major shrines of the country and in particular at the Basilica of the Lady of Guadalupe, there arrive pilgrims from all points—some of whom may have long since walked out the pieces of rubber tire that once served them as soles, and many of whom will walk on their knees the last mile or so of the pilgrimage. Many of the "pilgrims" of Delano will have walked such pilgrimages themselves in their lives—perhaps as very small children even—and cling to the memory of the day-long marches, the camps at night, streams forded, hills climbed, the sacral aura of the sanctuary, and the "fiesta" that followed.

But throughout the Spanish-speaking world there is another tradition that touches the present march, that of the Lenten penitential processions,

Cesar Chavez helped organize poorly paid produce farmers in California into the National Farm Workers Association (NFWA). Appealing to ethnic pride, Chavez organized a national boycott that eventually resulted in a wage increase for migrant workers from $1.20 an hour in 1965 to $3.53 an hour in 1977.

where the *penitentes* would march through the streets, often in sack cloth and ashes, some even carrying crosses, as a sign of penance for their sins, and as a plea for the mercy of God. The penitential procession is also in the blood of the Mexican-American, and the Delano march will therefore be one of penance—public penance for the sins of the strikers, their own personal sins as well as their yielding perhaps to feelings of hatred and revenge in the strike itself. They hope by the march to set themselves at peace with the Lord, so that the justice of their cause will be purified of all lesser motivation.

These two great traditions of a great people meet in the Mexican-American with the belief that Delano in his "cause," his great demand for justice, freedom, and respect from a predominantly foreign cultural community in a land where he was first. The revolutions of Mexico were primarily uprisings of the poor, fighting for bread and for dignity. The Mexican-American is also a child of the revolution.

Pilgrimage, penance and revolution. The pilgrimage from Delano to Sacramento has strong religio-cultural overtones. But it is also the pilgrimage of a cultural minority which has suffered from a hostile environment, and a minority which means business.

DOCUMENT 7

The Gay Liberation Front, Come Out (1970)

In 1970, New York City police raided the Stonewall Tavern, an establishment frequented by gays, precipitating a fierce riot. The incident is generally regarded as the birth of the gay rights movement, as the riot convinced many homosexuals that only political action could prevent future acts of repression. The Gay Liberation Front (GLF) emerged as the vanguard organization of the gay rights movement, as activists participated in protest marches, published books and newspapers, and openly declared their homosexuality. In the following selection from *Come Out*, a newspaper published by the GLF in New York City, a roundtable of gay and lesbian activists discuss their personal relationship to the gay rights movement.

Pat: The first question I would like to ask you to discuss is what is your concept of the movement?

Kay: People are always asking me what the movement means, I am always asking other people what the movement means, and I don't quite know myself. For 9 or 10 years, the movement has meant to me personally the peace movement.

Bernard: Kay, the movement means something a little bit wider than you have expressed. Movements have developed all over the world, and the movement has meant to me—I've in the movement over 50 years—any attempt to change. Whether it be political change, social change, or economic change. The movement, as I understand it, means that people organize or even work privately and individually to make changes in the country. Historically there are times when you work individually, and there have been times when the movement catches up masses of people as it did in Russia before the revolution. Now the movement includes people who want to make changes whether they be Panthers who are changing the system for black people, or Woman's Liberation who are concerned with changes for women, or socialists who are concerned with changes in the system. Or whether it be an organization like the Gay Liberation Front concerned with fighting against the oppression of homosexuals, but fighting within the framework of the wider movement. These problems are not isolated, but within the context of the oppression of the system against us all.

Bob: The movement today gets me a little uptight. I find people saying I am the movement. The movement can be 5 people who refuse to pay the subway fare. During the Christmas week vigil there was a little old lady marching with me and she had on her Dove button. She was terribly non-violent and marching for what she believed was right: she wanted political prisoners freed. A cop hassled us and I was very angry. I called him a pig. She said, "Let me do it." She was sort of a hooker type—sort of a tough old broad, and she charmed him. She came back and said, "You have your way, and I have mine." That's true. This woman is as much a part of the movement as I, even though we are working in different ways.

Pat: I would like to ask you specifically—what ways have you found to get involved in the movement?

Bernard: Well, my first activity was when I was 5 years old. My parents had organized the first Student Friends of the Russian Revolution. I had a tray of little red flags and I put them on people and got money from them. When I was about 13 lots of us were arrested for picketing and handing out leaflets and demonstrating. We were helping the workers who were locked out, we were protesting the war budgets, we were protesting growing unemployment. At college, I helped organize the first NSL— The National Student League—which is the granddaddy of all student organizations. Also the John Reed Club. As time went on I got more and more involved but always from a political end because I was convinced that nothing but a change in the system could change the oppressions against blacks, against women, against children who were being unfairly employed at the time. Also against homosexuals. Now I'm working with homosexuals in the movement because I'm convinced that only in getting our rightful place in the movement and demanding an end to our own oppression can we ever really make changes for homosexuals.

Bob: I was instrumental in forming the 7 Arts chapters of CORE [Congress of Racial Equality]. Most of my past work has been with non-whites. In this chapter we demanded rights for Black people in show business. The first thing we did was break down the industrial shows. No non-caucasian had ever been hired. We threw a picket line around 8th Ave. and 57th St. where most of the Auto show rooms are. We also got off to the World's Fair—that was one of the times I was busted.

Kay: It seems that we had been arrested together. I was arrested at the World's Fair too. Politics make strange cell mates. I think I got into the movement first as a Quaker. As a Quaker I looked out my window in the West Village and noticed a lot of children smashing things. I thought in a few years they'll be big enough to push the button and, you know, somebody ought to do something now. I sort of got kidnapped by the children and started a thing called Workshop of Children which I ran for three years. During this time the civil rights thing was building up but since I was working with these children who had a great deal of trouble with the law, I felt I couldn't be arrested. I thought they couldn't distinguish between civil disobedience and crime exactly. However, as soon as that thing folded I was delighted to go to jail at the CORE demonstration you referred to, Bob.

Bob: I wasn't delighted.

Kay: I volunteered to be arrested and the Pinkerton men were so new and so non-violent it was really difficult. I finally had to dance on the bar at the Schaffer Pavillion. Then I worked with the Survivors of Nagasaki Hiroshima who were traveling around the world. I worked with the people at New England Committee for Non-violent Action. We

Members of ACT UP (AIDS Coalition to Unleash Power) marching peacefully in a gay pride parade in New York City. ACT UP has also used violent demonstration to shock the nation into taking more initiative in finding a cure for AIDS (acquired immune deficiency syndrome).

participated in the blockade at the missile base of Lamakaza, in Canada, at the white house, at prisons, and at submarine bases. And I went into the Peace Corps. I can't think of any other exciting things to brag about.

Bob: I went south after the civil rights bill was signed. We went to a public swimming pool in one demonstration. Myself, a very big black girl, and a black boy. We had a big hassle getting in; but finally we demanded in, and we got in. We joined hands and jumped into the water. There were about 50 people when we got there and in one or two seconds there were three. . . .

Bernard: In the early days of demonstrations the thing we had to fear the most were the mounted police. Most of us were under the hooves of police horses all the time. Young children, men, women—even old people. What I found was that this kind of reaction to us brought a stronger commitment from us. And also brought more and more people to the movement. I wonder if the powers that be are aware that they build the movement themselves with their actions.

Pat: It seems here as you talk about your own experiences and some of the thoughts and feelings which have come to you from those experiences we're getting a fuller meaning of the word oppression. So we might tie it up here by saying the movement is making changes in the establishment where it oppresses us. Your experiences seem to have been radicalizing. If you are in a situation where you see the extreme degrees of the establishment oppression—you see the actual physical effects on people—you become radicalized. Like you were saying, Bernard—about—

Bernard: —about the system being it's worst enemy.

Pat: I would like to ask you how you see the Gay Liberation Movement.

Bernard: I see the Gay Liberation Movement as a process which will help liberate gay people by making them fully part of the whole liberation movement. The movement for change in the system that will eventually annihilate any form of oppression. Before GLF I was active in these movements, but anonymously—nobody was conscious of the fact that I was homosexual. I think the only way we can gain respect for ourselves and any of the help that we need from everyone else in overcoming our oppression is by showing that we participate even though they don't understand why we participate. I think even among a lot of our own people we have to fight for the right to participate as homosexuals.

Bob: I've always been active as a homosexual. Openly, but never publicly. In the past six or seven months I have suddenly found myself living the life of a public homosexual. I find resentment in many parts of the movement. When I find it, I confront it. This is very healthy for me; and it's very healthy for the movement. We cant hold the movement up as being any better or any worse than the rest of us. Gay Liberation to me is seeing 35 or 40 homosexuals marching as homosexuals in a vigil to free political prisoners. We have been political prisoners, and we will be political prisoners. Homosexuals are beginning to see themselves as an oppressed minority. I don't think homosexuality is a magic tie that binds us all but in a sense there is something. It's being proud of ourselves. And I think that's what liberation will help us find—a pride that we can just stand up and be proud of ourselves as human beings.

Bernard: I want to bring up the past in one way. When I was among young people, we had no way of expressing this. I never felt sick, although the attitude then was that we were a sickness. I could only fight this when I talked to individuals. We had no public way of fighting it. And it's exciting to be able to do it now, and the fight must be a very conscious fight.

Bob: Kay, do you have anything to say. Say something, we'll have Women's Liberation after us if you don't.

Kay: I'm very new in GLF and I don't have a great deal to say to people who want to know what it is. I see half of the gay liberation as a sort of attempt to try to change other people outside of ourselves—to try to make them stop oppressing us. But the half that interests me most now, at the beginning of my gay liberation, is self liberation. I was never open or public. I always felt that I had to be a secret homosexual, and I was terrified. Indeed I am now. This article is the first time I have ever come out in a public way, and I find that a great deal of the oppression is built into myself—is built into us. So I still expect when I come out, people are going to dislike me because I am homosexual. People do dislike homosexuals. On the other hand, I myself have disliked my own homosexuality, so perhaps it's not going to be as bad as I thought.

Bernard: Although I haven't been a public homosexual, among my friends, it was always known. What interests me now is that, although I was completely loved, for me, being a homosexual, I find that now that I'm getting active in GLF there's a resentment. People wonder why I have to work as a homosexual in the movement. Why I can't take it up wherever I am in the movement. I don't think you can take it up wherever you are in the movement. It's only possible when we are working as a homosexual to take it up. I think that we should—those of us who can—be public as well as open.

Study Questions

1. Based on your study of American history, do you think Glazer's generalizations about ethnic groups are valid?

2. Why did busing as a means for achieving racial balance in historically segregated public schools generate such hostility?

3. According to the discussants in the Gay Liberation Front, can the pursuit of gay rights be separated from other liberation movements?

4. Which phrase best describes American society: a melting pot, a multicultural society, or other (specify)?

14

Republican Hegemony

In the 1970s the United States entered a period of national crisis. The Watergate scandal outraged Americans, leaving them ever more suspicious of politicians and government. Stagflation—a combination of high unemployment and double-digit inflation—and an energy crisis precipitated severe recession. Polls revealed that Americans no longer believed that they lived in an era of abundance and that many now resigned themselves to a world of permanent shortages. Defeat in Southeast Asia in 1975 and the Carter administration's failure to resolve the Iranian hostage crisis raised questions about the ability of the United States to dictate the international order.

In this climate of malaise, American politics shifted to the right in the late 1970s. Middle-class suburbanites increasingly expressed their resentment of higher taxes, expanding welfare programs, and government regulation. In the 1980 presidential campaign, Republican Ronald Reagan capitalized on this conservative reaction. Promising an era of national renewal, he pledged to restore American power abroad and revive the economy by cutting taxes and reducing government spending. Reagan defeated incumbent Jimmy Carter by a landslide, winning support from southerners, Jews, and blue-collar workers, thus cracking the Democratic coalition that had dominated American politics since the Great Depression.

Reagan blamed America's economic ills on excessive taxation, wanton social spending, and repressive federal regulation of business. As he declared in his inaugural address, "government is not the solution to our problem, government is the problem" (Document 1). To revitalize the economy, Reagan championed supply-side economics. Unlike Keynesian theory, which relied on government spending to stimulate a depressed economy, supply-siders advanced the notion that the private sector, if relieved of heavy tax burdens, would spearhead an economic boom by shifting its resources out of tax shelters and into productive investments (Document 2). Reagan initiated his economic program by cutting government spending on social programs such as food stamps, job-training, student loans, and federal aid to urban mass transit. Although critics feared that tax cuts would create unprecedented federal deficits, Reagan convinced Congress that a tax reduction would sustain high employment and generate new tax revenues.

After a deep recession in 1981–1982, Reaganomics sparked a remarkable recovery. Inflation and interest rates dropped dramatically, and the economy embarked on its second-longest expansion since World War II. Reagan's policies received the warm embrace of the nation's business leaders (Document 3). Financial wizards such as T. Boone Pickens, Ivan Boesky, and Donald Trump amassed huge fortunes masterminding corporate consolidations and leveraged buyouts. The economic boom also generated an expansion of white-collar professionals, who comprised 30 percent of the labor force. Many of these young lawyers, stockbrokers, and investment bankers moved into and renovated older, lower middle-class, inner-city neighborhoods (Document 4). Economic expansion in the 1980s also opened up professional opportunities for women, who redefined normative female roles in the workplace and family (Document 5).

In addition to conservative policies toward government and the economy, Reagan espoused the ideas of social conservatives. Alarmed by rising divorce and abortion rates, the growing social acceptance of homosexuality, and increased permissiveness and secularization in American society, fundamentalist Christian leaders such as Jerry Falwell enjoined their followers to become politically active in defense of traditional family values (Document 6).

Not everyone accepted the Reagan era as a positive good. Opponents condemned the 1980s as a new Gilded Age of greed, extravagance, selfishness, and retreat from social responsibility (Document 7). Throughout the decade the economic distance between the richest and poorest Americans widened. Profound changes in the American economy, especially the decline of the nation's productive manufacturing sector, intensified this income stratification. Throughout the Northeast and Midwest, now called the Rust Belt, steel mills and automobile plants shut down, putting millions of men and women out of work. Many plants moved their operations to Mexico, Puerto Rico, or Thailand to take advantage of lower taxes and cheap labor. Many touted the new high-tech industries of the South and Southwest, often referred to as the Sun Belt. But these firms paid the minimum wage, were aggressively antiunion, and offered few opportunities for advancement (Document 8). The search for meaningful employment in the midst of global economic change has become one of the many challenges confronting Americans at the end of the twentieth century.

DOCUMENT 1

Ronald Reagan, First Inaugural Address (1981)

As a Hollywood actor in the 1930s and 1940s, Ronald Reagan had been a liberal New Deal Democrat. In the 1950s however, while working as a corporate spokesman for General Electric, he developed conservative political views. He entered politics in the 1960s, winning two terms as governor of California. When he left office in 1974, Reagan continued to increase his political visibility, emerging as the leading spokesman of the conservative resurgence. A gifted orator, with a warm, relaxed manner, Reagan used his mastery of television and personal charm to communicate his conservative philosophy. He appealed to white middle-class voters, "a special interest group that has been too long neglected," frustrated by high taxes, social spending, and government inefficiency. In the following excerpt from his inaugural address, Reagan outlines his prescription for curing the country's economic ills.

These United States are confronted with an economic affliction of great proportions. We suffer from the longest and one of the worst sustained inflations in our national history. It distorts our economic decisions, penalizes thrift, and crushes the struggling young and the fixed-income elderly alike. It threatens to shatter the lives of millions of our people.

Idle industries have cast workers into unemployment, causing human misery and personal indignity. Those who do work are denied a fair return for their labor by a tax system which penalizes successful achievement and keeps us from maintaining full productivity.

But great as our tax burden is, it has not kept pace with public spending. For decades, we have piled deficit upon deficit, mortgaging our future and our children's future for the temporary convenience of the present. To continue this long trend is to guarantee tremendous social, cultural, political, and economic upheavals.

You and I, as individuals, can, by borrowing, live beyond our means, but for only a limited period of time. Why, then, should we think that collectively, as a nation, we are not bound by that same limitation?

We must act today in order to preserve tomorrow. And let there be no misunderstanding—we are going to begin to act, beginning today.

The economic ills we suffer have come upon us over several decades. They will not go away in days, weeks, or months, but they will go away. They will go away because we, as Americans, have the capacity now, as we have had in the past, to do whatever needs to be done to preserve this last and greatest bastion of freedom.

In this present crisis, government is not the solution to our problem.

From time to time, we have been tempted to believe that society has become too complex to be managed by self-rule, that government by an elite group is superior over government for, by, and of the people. But if no one among us is capable of governing himself, then who among us has the capacity to govern someone else? All of us together, in and out of government, must bear the burden. The solutions we seek must be equitable, with no one group singled out to pay a higher price.

We hear much of special interest groups. Our concern must be for a special interest group that has been too long neglected. It knows no sectional boundaries or ethnic and racial divisions, and it crosses political party lines. It is made up of men and women who raise our food, patrol our streets, man our mines and our factories, teach our children, keep our homes, and heal us when we are sick—professionals, industrialists, shopkeepers, clerks, cabbies, and truckdrivers. They are, in short, "We the people," this breed called Americans.

Well, this administration's objective will be a healthy, vigorous, growing economy that provides equal opportunity for all Americans, with no barriers born of bigotry or discrimination. Putting America back to work means putting all Americans back to work. Ending inflation means freeing all Americans from the terror of runaway living costs. All must share in the productive work of this "new beginning" and all must share in the bounty of a revived economy. With the idealism and fair play which are the core of our system and our strength, we can have a strong and prosperous America at peace with itself and the world.

So, as we begin, let us take inventory. We are a nation that has a government—not the other way around. And this makes us special among the nations of the Earth. Our Government has no power except that granted it by the people. It is time to check and reverse the growth of government which shows signs of having grown beyond the consent of the governed.

It is my intention to curb the size and influence of the Federal establishment and to demand recognition of the distinction between the powers granted to the Federal Government and those reserved to the States or to the people. All of us need to be reminded that the Federal Government did not create the States; the States created the Federal Government.

Now, so there will be no misunderstanding, it is not my intention to do away with government. It is, rather, to make it work—work with us, not over us; to stand by our side, not ride on our back. Government can and must provide opportunity, not smother it; foster productivity, not stifle it.

If we look to the answer as to why, for so many years, we achieved so much, prospered as no other people on Earth, it was because here, in this land, we unleashed the energy and individual genius of man to a greater extent than has ever been done before. Freedom and the dignity of the individual have been more available and assured here than in any other place on Earth. The price for this freedom at times has been high, but we have never been unwilling to pay that price.

It is no coincidence that our present troubles parallel and are proportionate to the intervention and intrusion in our lives that result from unnecessary and excessive growth of government. It is time for us to realize that we are too great a nation to limit ourselves to small dreams. We are not, as some would have us believe, doomed to an inevitable decline. I do not believe in a fate that will fall on us no matter what we do. I do believe in a fate that will fall on us if we do nothing. So, with all the creative energy at our command, let us begin an era of national renewal. Let us renew our determination, our courage, and our strength. And let us renew our faith and our hope.

DOCUMENT 2

Paul Craig Roberts, The Supply-Side Revolution (1984)

Since the New Deal, American economic policymakers had subscribed to Keynesian economic theory, which posited that government spending during a depression stimulated the economy. President Ronald Reagan's policy advisers challenged that premise, arguing that lower taxes provide better incentives to work, increase profitability, boost savings rates, and reduce inflation. In the following selection, Paul Craig Roberts explains supply-side theory and how it helped revitalize the Republican Party.

Prior to February 23, 1977, Republican economic policy focused on balancing the budget by raising taxes and cutting spending, an approach that denied the party a credible economic and political program. The Republicans were not always successful themselves at reducing spending, but if the government was going to spend, they at least wanted to pay for it with cash instead of borrowed money. This put them in conflict with Keynesian economics.

Keynesian theory explained the economy's performance in terms of the level of total spending. A budget deficit adds to total spending and helps keep employment high and the economy running at full capacity. Cutting the deficit, as the Republicans wanted to do, would reduce spending and throw people out of work, thereby lowering national income and raising the unemployment rate. The lower income would produce less tax revenue, and the higher unemployment would require larger budget expenditures for unemployment compensation, food stamps, and other support programs. The budget deficit would thus reappear from a shrunken tax base and higher income-support payments. Patient (and impatient) Democrats, economists, columnists, and editorial writers had explained many times to the obdurate Republicans that cutting the deficit would simply reduce spending on goods and services, drive the economy down, and raise the unemployment rate. Keynesians argued that the way to balance the budget was to run a deficit. Deficit spending would lift the economy, and the government's tax revenues would rise, bringing the budget into balance. Since cutting the deficit was believed to be the surest way to throw people out of work, there were not many Republican economists. When Democrat Alice Rivlin was asked why there were no Republican economists on her "nonpartisan" Congressional Budget Committee staff, she was probably telling the truth when she said she could not find any.

The focus on the deficit had left the Republicans without a competitive political program. They were perceived by the recipients of government benefits as the party always threatening to cut back on government programs such as social security, while the taxpaying part of the electorate saw Republicans as the party that was always threatening to raise taxes in order to pay for the benefits that others were receiving. The party that takes away with both hands competes badly with the party that gives away with both hands, and that simple fact explained the decline of the Republican Party, which had come to be known as the tax collector for Democratic spending programs....

Supply-side economics brought a new perspective to fiscal policy. Instead of stressing the effects on spending, supply-siders showed that tax rates directly affect the supply of goods and services. Lower tax rates mean better incentives to work, to save, to take risks, and to invest. As people respond to the higher after-tax rewards, or greater profitability, incomes rise and the tax base grows, thus feeding back some of the lost revenues to the Treasury. The saving rate also grows, providing more financing for government and private borrowing. Since Keynesian analysis left out such effects, once supply-side economics appeared on the scene the Democrats could no longer claim that government spending stimulated the economy more effectively than tax cuts. Tax cuts were now competitive, and the House Republicans began to make the most of it....

Many people also have the mistaken idea that taxes on personal income have no adverse consequences for business other than reducing the demand for products. They believe that higher tax rates on personal income help business by reducing the federal deficit and lowering interest rates. In actual fact, higher personal tax rates reduce private-sector saving and drive up both the cost of credit and the cost of labor to firms. When the Treasury examined the effects of the Kennedy tax cuts, it was found that the personal saving rate rose. This implies that the saving rate would fall if tax rates rise, and indeed the saving rate declined as bracket creep pushed savers into higher tax brackets.

Higher income tax rates raise labor costs to the firm, thereby undermining the competitiveness of its products at home and abroad. The higher the worker's marginal tax rate, the more expensive it is to the firm to protect wages from being eroded by inflation or to give real wage increases. Since additional income is taxed at the worker's highest bracket, the higher the tax rate, the larger the gross wage necessary to correspond to any net wage.

This does not meant that deficits are good for the economy. But it does mean that the argument that higher taxes are preferable to higher borrowing is at best unproved. The way this unproven argument has been used against the President's efforts to reduce tax rates and improve economic incentives is irresponsible. The key to a successful economy is incentives. Any economic policy that forgets this—even one that reduces deficits—will fail. . . .

We now have many decades of empirical evidence of the effects of disincentives on economic performance, ranging from China and the Soviet Union to the European welfare states. The effects of disincentives clearly thwart the intended results of central planning, government investment programs, and the maintenance of aggregate demand. On the other hand, there is an abundance of evidence of the positive effects of good incentives. Only free people are productive and forward-looking, but they cease to be free when their property rights are sacrificed to interest-group politics. Supply-side economics is the economics of a free society. It will prevail wherever freedom itself prevails.

DOCUMENT 3

T. Boone Pickens, "My Case for Reagan" (1984)

President Ronald Reagan received broad political support from the nation's corporate elite. One successful business leader of the era was T. Boone Pickens, chairman of Mesa Petroleum Company. Pickens, a pioneer of the new aggressive business policy of corporate takeovers and leveraged buyouts, endorsed Reagan's 1984 reelection campaign. In the following article from *Fortune* magazine, Pickens explains how Reagan's policies infused the economy with a new competitive spirit and argues that businessmen should support Reagan over Democratic challenger Walter Mondale.

When businessmen consider why they should support President Reagan's reelection, their analysis should come down to two important questions: What has allowed their companies to grow and prosper? What makes business opportunities in America different from those in any other country?

The answer is free enterprise. Our economic system is what keeps Americans employed, clothed, housed, and nourished. That system makes it possible for every American to attain his or her dream of material or spiritual wealth. It truly makes ours the land of opportunity. This year voters will have a clear choice between a President who believes in retaining the maximum amount possible of the nation's wealth in the private sector and a challenger who supports a greater role for government.

More than any other President in the last 30 years, Ronald Reagan understands the importance of free enterprise. He knows that this country's markets should be allowed to operate freely and competitively. That's the philosophy he brought to the

Ronald Reagan on horseback with his wife, Nancy Reagan. Of Reagan's primary campaign goals—balancing the budget, reducing federal spending, and increasing U. S. military strength—only the goal of increasing military strength was reached, while both government spending and the national debt soared. This led to even wider gaps among the upper, middle, and lower classes of America.

White House in 1981, and we've seen how beneficial the results are. Since President Reagan took office, inflation has dropped from nearly 14% to approximately 4%, and the prime rate has fallen from 20% to 13%.

By reducing government intervention, Reagan has injected a new competitive spirit into the marketplace. There is now an atmosphere that encourages business efficiency. For example, merger and acquisition activity, properly undertaken within the constraints of antitrust laws, has allowed companies and even entire industries to restructure and become more efficient and financially sound. Shareholders have reaped the rewards of their investments, and the government has received additional revenues as taxes are paid on those gains.

In contrast, Walter Mondale does not appear to understand what makes America work. His proposals would more heavily tax individuals and corporations, inhibit capital formation, and use government as the primary means to stimulate employment.

The cheapest, most effective way to create jobs is to encourage business growth, not to devise complicated and costly federal programs. Ronald Reagan has proved that. His policies have invigorated the market and put more Americans to work. Economic recovery is the best jobs programs this country has had. A record 107 million people are currently employed, five million more than when the Carter-Mondale Administration left office.

But Reagan has done even more for the average worker than stimulate employment. Through his tax policies, Americans are now taking home more pay. They have more money for their children's education, a new home, retirement, and investments. Some 42 million Americans have invested in shares of publicly owned companies, either directly or through mutual funds, compared with 30 million in 1980.

We've seen tangible evidence that Ronald Reagan's policies are working for America. That's important for everyone in this country. The health of U.S. business is critical to our nation's survival. We do, indeed, have a responsibility to support candidates who understand that principle—a responsibility not just to ourselves but to all citizens.

I am frequently asked by high school and college students how they can attain success from modest beginnings. My answer is simple. Like many business executives, I owe my success to the free enterprise system. I started with a good education, $2,500 in capital, and an opportunity to do something—the sky was the limit, and fortunately the same opportunity still exists.

The American free enterprise spirit is something we will be able to maintain only under a Reagan

Administration. While Walter Mondale tells us that his plan for this country is better, we've seen what better means: Mondale's recent speeches have promised increased government intervention in the market and our lives and disincentives in the form of higher taxes.

The ill effects of the Carter-Mondale Administration were far-reaching: double-digit inflation—the worst since 1946—unemployment, skyrocketing interest rates, and a crumbling economy. There is no reason to believe that a Mondale-Ferraro Administration would be any different in philosophy or outcome.

All of us realize the importance of strong leadership. It is the greatest attribute any President can have and should be a prime asset of the nation. Lack of leadership ability is one of my greatest concerns about a Mondale-Ferraro Administration. Mondale has given no indication of having such ability either as Carter's Vice President or on his own. How could a nation possibly trust the affairs of state to a person who could not make a decision as to whether Bert Lance or Charles Manatt would chair his party?

America need not take that chance when it is blessed with an incumbent President who has proven leadership qualities. Ronald Reagan has been able to instill a new sense of pride and confidence in our nation. Gone are the days of Carter-Mondale defeatism and national malaise.

In 1980 the American people realized the disastrous economic brink on which this country teetered. They wanted a change for the better, and they chose a President who accomplished that goal. On November 6, Americans will once again ask themselves if a change is in order. I think the resounding answer will be that they wish to stay the course Reagan has charted. We're no longer on the brink of disaster; both feet are planted firmly on solid ground, and the future looks bright.

I'm supporting President Reagan and Vice President Bush for those reasons, and I unabashedly ask others to support them as well. I make no apology for political participation. At stake in this election is the future of the free enterprise system. A commitment from the business community, not just a check, is required to prevent another give-away-now, pay-later disaster. And that commitment will mean for future Americans a vigorous free market, the opportunity to succeed, and an attainable American Dream.

DOCUMENT 4

Patricia Morrisroe, "The New Class" (1985)

Young urban professionals, or yuppies, were some of the most upwardly mobile people in the 1980s. *Newsweek* magazine even declared 1984 the year of the yuppie. Many of them lawyers or employed in major financial firms, yuppies favored living in urban neighborhoods such as Chicago's Lincoln Park or New York City's Upper West Side. Yuppies renovated old brownstone dwellings, converting them into expensive condominiums. Chic restaurants and expensive boutiques moved in to cater to the new residents. Gentrification, however, displaced many older residents and threatened small businesspeople, both of whom could not afford to pay skyrocketing rents. The following article from *New York* magazine profiles some of the young urban professionals who moved to New York City's Upper West Side.

❧ ❧

It's a Saturday night at 96th and Broadway. Inside the new Caramba!!! everybody's drinking frozen maragaritas and talking real estate, while outside on the traffic strip, a derelict swigs Wild Turkey and shouts obscenities. By 11 P.M., he's sound asleep on the bench, but the crowd at Caramba!!! is still going strong.

"These are the most lethal maragaritas in Manhattan," says a man in a blue pinstriped suit by Polo. He staggers out of the restaurant and into David's Cookies next door. "Get the double-chunk chocolate chip," says his girlfriend, who is window-shopping at Pildes Optical.

At the newsstand across the street, a middle-aged woman buys the Sunday *Times* and looks at the dozens of young professionals spilling out of Caramba!!! "Yuppies," she shouts. "Go home!"

But they are home. Ads in the *Times* tout the Upper West Side as "Yuppie Country," and Amsterdam is being called "Cinderella Avenue." According to a study of the years 1970 through 1980 by New York's Department of City Planning, 7,500 people between the ages of 25 and 44 flooded the area between West 70th and 86th Streets. That agegroup now makes up 47 percent of the population there. At the same time, the number of singles went up by 31 percent, while the number of families dropped 24 percent. "You want to know who's moving into the West Side?" says a woman who owns an antiques store on Amsterdam Avenue. "It's the young, the rich, and the restless."

Some older West Siders blame the newcomers for the skyrocketing rents and the uprooting of local merchants. They deplore the cuteness of Columbus Avenue and the hordes of tourists who congest the sidewalks. They worry that the neighborhood's solid middle class values will be replaced by the yuppie version of the West Side Dream: a pre-war apartment with a Food Emporium around the corner.

They can't relate to the 30-year-old on Central Park West who takes her husband's shirts to the East Side because she can't find a "quality" laundry in the neighborhood. Or to the tenants at the Sofia on West 61st Street, 50 percent of whom bought their apartments after seeing a model of the bathroom. ("They're big and very Deco," says Richard Zinn, the building's director of sales.)

The Columbia, a condominium on West 96th Street, has been called the "Yuppie Housing Project" by locals who can't believe anyone would *pay* to live on Broadway. "Didn't anyone tell these people it's a *commercial* street?" says an elderly man who is buying Rice Krispies at the Red Apple on the corner. "If I had the money for a condo, I'd move to Florida."

One third of the Columbia's units were bought by lawyers; the average income per apartment is $100,000. "It's a nice first home for couples on their way up," says developer Arthur Zeckendorf, who worked with his father, William, to build the Columbia. Once they've made it, they can move to the Park Belvedere, a condominium on West 79th Street also built by the Zeckendorfs. Sold for an average of $400 per square foot, it has attracted a better-off buyer. "I looked at the Columbia," says a 27-year-old Wall Street bond trader, "but the neighborhood was just too borderline for me." So he bought an apartment in one of the Belvedere's towers and persuaded a friend to buy one, too. "It's a great deal," he says of his $400,000 one-bedroom.

Many West Side co-ops are besieged by Wall Street financiers who use their bonuses to make down payments.

"The last five apartments in my building went to investment bankers," says a woman who owns a co-

Chapter 14 — Republican Hegemony

It merely reaffirms what you already know about yourself.

THE GOLD CARD

Economic boundaries changed greatly during the 1980s. Between 1983 and 1989 the upper middle class and the upper class saw their wealth increase by almost $3 trillion, whereas the lower middle class and the lower class saw a decline of $256 billion.

op on West End Avenue. "I want to protect my property, so it's good to have people with money move in. But I worry about the population in the next ten years. Are you going to need an MBA to get into Zabar's?" . . .

Yet for all the money being poured into the neighborhood, some of the new West Siders have a decidedly old-fashioned point of view. For every yuppie who dreams about moving from Broadway to Central Park West there are others who chose the West Side because it seemed unpretentious. "I always hated everything the East Side represented," says 33-year-old Joe Powers in between feeding mashed carrots to his five-month-old son, Mark. "The West Side always seemed to have less airs about it. To me, it's Zabar's and Fairway. Not Rúelles and Pasta & Cheese." . . .

Ten blocks uptown, 31-year-old Richard Con-way is setting up his VCR to tape Jacqueline Bisset in *Anna Karenina*. A vice-president at a Wall Street investment firm, Conway recently bought a twelfth-floor five-room co-op at 106th Street and Riverside Drive. In the past fifteen years, Conway has moved from Greenwich to Harvard to Third Avenue to Yale to Chelsea, and now to Duke Ellington Boulevard.

"This is not a yuppie neighborhood," says Conway, uncorking a bottle of white wine. "That's what I like about it. In my building, we have a wonderful mix of people. The head of the co-op board is a musical director, and we've got artists and writers and movie producers."

When Conway decided to buy a co-op, he wanted to look only north of West 96th Street. "I think a lot of the glamour is gone from the East Side," he says. "Besides, I considered it boring and staid, too much like Greenwich. I like living in a neighborhood that's ethnically diverse. Broadway has a lot of bodegas and mom-and-pop stores. To me, that's nice."

From his living room, Conway has a spectacular view of the Hudson. From the opposite end of the apartment, in the dining room, he can see a cityscape of charming turn-of-the-century brownstones. "I wonder how long they'll last," he says. "It's ironic, but everything I like about the neighborhood will probably disappear. And unfortunately, the reason is that people like me are moving into it." . . .

[Lawyer Jay] Zamansky, who grew up in Philadelphia, now makes his home in a renovated SRO next door to the Salvation Army senior citizen's home on West 95th Street. "I really wanted a place where I could establish roots," he says. Constructed around the turn of the century, the building has 30 apartments, most of which are inhabited by young professionals. "We're a real unique building," he explains. "In the summer, we have barbecues, and when our first co-op baby was born, everybody was thrilled."

Zamansky bought this apartment, a duplex with a roof garden, for a little over $100,000. "I'm real proud of it," he says. "It's the consummate bachelor pad." The ceiling is painted black, with lots of track lighting. "I met an interior designer at the Vertical Club," he explains, "and she helped me with the overall concept."

But Zamansky says he doesn't want to be the kind of person who does nothing but "work, eat at restaurants, and go to a health club. I really want to be a part of this neighborhood," he says. "I attend community-board meetings, and I registered voters in front of Zabar's. I even went into the Salvation Army's old people's home and registered senior citizens. They were just so glad to see a young face that I don't think they cared how they voted. By the way, I'm a Republican. I think it's important to put that in the article.

"I'm also very pro-development," he adds. "It makes me angry when people criticize a lot of the changes. The displacement is unfortunate, but where are we supposed to live? We have rights. We pay taxes. Whether people realize it or not, we're real assets to this community."

Twenty-nine-year-old Paula Handler, who lives with her husband in a three-bedroom apartment in the Eldorado on Central Park West between 90th and 91st Streets agrees. "These big pre-war buildings need young blood," she says. "The old people can't maintain their apartments. They resist everything, from redoing the lobby to putting in new windows. The problem is they can't switch their rental mentalities into a co-op mode."

The Handlers moved from the East Side to the Eldorado a year ago. "Frankly, I didn't know anything about Central Park West," says Paula. "I mean, I knew the Dakota, but the Eldorado? What? All I knew was that I wanted space, and I wanted old. Old is chic."

"Originally, I said no to the West Side," says Scott, a quiet man who is involved in commercial real estate.

"That's right, he did," Paula says. "He didn't like it because it was dirty and nobody we knew lived there. But I fell in love with this apartment. It was a total wreck, but it was me. We gave them an offer the minute we saw it. We even offered more than they asked because we wanted it so much."

The Handlers put in two new bathrooms and a new kitchen, and redid the plumbing and wiring. Today, the apartment, which faces the park, is completely renovated. "See what I mean about new blood?" Paula says. "It doesn't take money. It just takes creativity."

Six floors above the Handlers, Linda and Mark Reiner also had to redo their apartment completely. "It was considered the worst disaster in the building," Linda says. "The walls, which were painted magenta, royal blue, and orange, were falling down. But we really wanted to live here. We recognized how the West Side was growing, and we wanted to be a part of that."

Two years ago, they moved from a house in Hewlett Harbor, where Mark Reiner had a medical practice. "It was a risk giving up everything," he says, "but Hewlett Harbor was very sterile and uniform."

"That's why we didn't want the East Side," adds

Linda, who until recently was a practicing psychologist. "Now I sell real estate," she says. "I became addicted to it while we were looking for this apartment." The au pair brings their two-year-old son into the living room to say good night. "You wouldn't believe the children's playground in the park," Linda says. "You can barely get a place for your kid in the sandbox."

"Everybody wants to come here," says Mark. "There's nothing more exciting than living in a neighborhood in transition. It's sad, because a lot of people who live here can't afford to shop in the stores. But they're being pushed out of Manhattan, not just the West Side."

"The West Side makes you feel the difference between the haves and the have-nots," says Linda, who is dressed in a silk Chanel shirt, black pants, and pumps. "Right in our building, there's a real schism between the pre-conversion and post-conversion people. A new breed is taking over, and there's a lot of hostility. People are separated by age and economic class. The senior citizens got insider prices so low that there's a lot of resentment on all sides. At a recent meeting, one elderly person shouted, 'Well, I'm not rich like you.' But what can you do?"

"Basically, we're very optimistic," Mark says. "We feel good about the changes. The neighborhood is going to continue to improve."

Linda nods. "Definitely," she says. "For the West Side, there's no turning back."

DOCUMENT 5

Leah Rosch, "Modern-Day Mentors" (1987)

A new generation of women entered the workforce in the late 1970s and 1980s. Born in the 1950s, these women, unlike their mothers, went to college, earned graduate degrees, and sought professional careers. They took advantage of the professional opportunities that began to open up as a result of the women's movement of the late 1960s and 1970s. The following article from *Working Woman* magazine profiles two of these professional women and explains how they defined new roles for women.

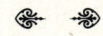

They are the generation of women who didn't grow up to be "just like Mommy," the generation of women born after World War II. Many of them unwitting pioneers, they went to college seeking legitimate degrees—not just husbands. Some went on to graduate and professional schools, then fought their way up the career ladders of the work world, putting their personal lives on hold. Some married and had children, putting their professional lives on hold. Some tried to do it all, putting their sanity on hold. But all were caught with no one to look to, save the few movie-screen models of the past—the Katharine Hepburns and Rosalind Russells—and the seductive rhetoric of the present that promised them the chance to fulfill their potential.

"Role models are necessary because they help validate your priorities," says Martha Miller, Ph.D., an organizational behaviorist and former associate dean of the Yale School of Organization and Management. "Without them, you're forced to make decisions based on little more than your instincts." And instinct was what most of these women operated on. With no contemporary work-world role models from whom to take their cues, they had no guarantees that the decisions they were making and the risks they were taking would propel them to their present state of fulfillment and success. Their choices and their worlds are all very different, but they have this in common: Each woman has defined and created for herself a rich life that fulfills her needs and her goals. It is in their willingness to follow their own instincts, to make their own rules, that they each represent the new creative process of role definition among women. . . .

Carolyn Dixon is at a loss for neither words nor passion when talking about women's health-care education or the difficulties midwives face getting licensed in the U.S. But talking about personal success is difficult for her: "It's only been in the last year or so that I've come to grips with the idea. I can now say I am successful."

To an observer, Dixon's against-all-odds story is a dictionary definition of success: Raised by her grandmother in Virginia (the family moved to Philadelphia when Dixon was 16), she earned a full academic scholarship to college (the first in her family to go). She was then accepted to medical school (which she finished in five years instead of four because she was holding down a full-time job), received honors in the obstetrics/gynecology-specialty rotation and graduated from medical school in the top 5 percent of her class.

She went on for ob/gyn training at Case Western Reserve (the only black and one of two women in her residency program). After completing her residency and passing the qualifying exams for board certification, she served for three years as a lieutenant in the National Health Service Corps, in Cleveland. In 1984 she accepted an offer to go into private practice in a walk-in clinic in Sarasota. Six months later she opened her own office; by the end of her second year she had a thriving practice, in which she sees more than 4,000 patients a year. Last year Dixon opened Sarasota's first physician-run birthing center, adjacent to her office.

As Dixon explains it, she has had difficulty accepting her accomplishments as successes because "I did what I had to do. I'm well aware of the strikes that were against me from the start, and I don't feel I can relax about things yet, because I also know I can fall just as fast as I can rise. Besides," she adds after a moment's reflection, "maybe once I can resolve some of the troubling issues in my personal life, I'll be able to feel successful."

Some of the issues she refers to are endemic to most ambitious working women—never having enough time with her children and constantly having to prove herself in a male-dominated profession. But a few of the issues are more individual. Her 12-year biracial marriage to Bernard O'Neill III, M.D., an internist and neurologist, survived a separation seven years ago, and Dixon believes that part of their ongoing problem is that they're both physicians and "the energy needed to emotionally support each other is often very limited. And I'm usually the one who's less giving," Dixon says.

Dixon admits that often family life has had to take a backseat to her professional drive. For instance, she took only three weeks off during her residency when her older child was born ("the male residents in my program were angry that I got to take any time off!") and ended up going through six baby-sitters before Sean was old enough for a day-care program. For a while she had a live-in nanny for her children, both of whom are now enrolled in private school.

This arrangement has helped to relieve a lot of the pressure but not much of the guilt, she says. "I love my children, but I have to allow myself to feel fulfilled professionally; otherwise I know I'd start resenting my family. So maybe I am successful by society's standards," Dixon finally concedes. "But don't let anyone tell you being a successful woman is easy."

Pam Kasa might have been among the original group of women astronauts if only, in 1965, she could have glimpsed the future. Even though that was the year after Congress passed the Civil Rights Act banning employment discrimination, a spate of rejections from summertime engineering jobs convinced Kasa that things would never really change, that there would always be jobs for which a woman would never be considered. Consequently, in her senior year of college she turned down a doctoral fellowship in metallurgy—sponsored by NASA—and opted for "something safe": law school.

"To this day, I still wonder if I would rather have been an engineer," Kasa says somewhat wistfully, then adds very matter-of-factly, "but I wouldn't start being an engineer *now*. What I mean is, if I had started out as an engineer then, I probably would have enjoyed it more than my early years as a lawyer."

While the NASA fellowship offer is something Kasa says she still thinks about, her decision is not something she necessarily regrets. In fact, she says she has no regrets. "The good thing about not creating a real game plan for my life is that I never have to feel particularly disappointed with where I am. And if I ever start to feel mired down, I remind myself that I have the power to change things."

Belief in her power to make changes is a constant in Kasa's life. She is a marathon runner and a triathlete ("more for the recreation than the competition"). And last year she passed the qualifying exam to become an emergency medical technician, enabling her to be a volunteer ambulance technician in Garrison, New York, where she spends weekends.

"I feel most productive when I challenge myself. There was a time a while ago when I channeled all my energies into my 9-to-5 job, which turned into a 6 A.M.-to-11 P.M. job. Now I explore things that interest me, and I find that if I'm less intensely focused on just one thing, I'm actually more productive in all my undertakings."

Kasa was working as a patent attorney when she married in 1968. The added challenge in her marriage was raising her husband's two daughters, then 5 and 7. "The responsibility of bringing them up was a real job to me, so I wasn't looking for the extra challenge in my work." In retrospect this was a good thing, she says, since patent law is "essentially a very narrow focus of expertise."

Having a built-in family preempted any decision about having children of her own. "Taking care of my stepdaughters was a big adjustment at first. Now I rarely think about wanting my own child. I'm not sorry about the way things turned out."

Kasa and her husband separated when the girls were in high school, and shortly thereafter she joined Bristol-Myers as staff counsel. In 1982 Kasa was named a vice president. "I knew I was working hard and doing a good job, but it was terrific to get the public recognition," she says, especially since she had felt that being a woman had precluded any positive recognition through her college and law-school years.

Much of Kasa's current career satisfaction comes from her capacity as mentor—being on the giving end of expertise that she wasn't fortunate enough to receive in her early career years. "I'm not bitter about it. Since I'm not unhappy with where I am now, I can't find fault with how I got here. I can, however, try to make a difference for other women, which helps make a big difference for me."

DOCUMENT 6

Jerry Falwell, Listen America! *(1981)*

Concerned that the 1960s had inaugurated an era of moral decline in the United States, conservative, fundamentalist Baptist preacher Jerry Falwell urged "God-fearing, moral Americans" to cast aside doctrinal differences and unite "to reverse the politicization of immorality in our society." Falwell opposed the Equal Rights Amendment, abortion, busing schoolchildren to achieve racial integration, and civil rights for homosexuals. To revitalize America he favored, among other things, capital punishment, school prayer, lower taxes, and a general reduction in government. President Ronald Reagan embraced Falwell's social agenda and received almost unanimous support from various grass-roots fundamentalist organizations. In the following selection from his book *Listen America!*, Falwell explains why it is imperative for Christians to become politically active.

※ ※

Bible-believing Christians and concerned moral Americans are determined to do something about the problems that we are facing as a nation....

My responsibility as a parent-pastor is more than just concern. The issue of convenience is not even up for discussion. If the moral issues are really matters of conviction that are worth living for, then they are worth fighting for. In discussing these matters further with other pastors and concerned Christian leaders, I have become convinced of the need to have a coalition of God-fearing, moral Americans to represent our convictions to our government. I realize that there would be those pastors who misunderstand our intentions. I know that some object that we are compromising in our involvement with people of different doctrinal and theological beliefs. As a fundamental, independent, separatist Baptist, I am well aware of the crucial issues of personal and ecclesiastical separation that divide fundamentalists philosophically from evangelicals and liberals. I do not believe that it is ever right to compromise the truth in order to gain an opportunity to do right. In doctrinal and spiritual matters, there is no real harmony between light and darkness.

I am convinced of two very significant factors. First, our very moral existence as a nation is at stake. There are many moral Americans who do not share our theological beliefs but who do share our moral concerns. Second, we must face the fact that it will take the greatest possible number of concerned citizens to reverse the politicization of immorality in our society. Doctrinal difference is a distinctive feature of a democracy. Our freedoms have given us the privilege and the luxury of theological disagreement. I would not for a moment encourage anyone to water down his distinctive beliefs. But we must face realistically the fact that there are Christians in the world today who have lost the luxury of disagreement. When the entire issue of Christian survival is at stake, we must be willing to band together on at least the major moral issues of the day....

Our ministry is as committed as it ever has been to the basic truths of Scripture, to essential and fundamental Christian doctrines. But we are not willing to isolate ourselves in seclusion while we sit back and watch this nation plunge headlong toward hell....

To change America we must be involved, and this includes three areas of political action:

1. Registration

A recent national poll indicated that eight million American evangelicals are not registered to vote. I am convinced that this is one of the major sins of the church today. Until concerned Christian citizens become registered voters there is very little that we can do to change the tide of political influence on the social issues in our nation. Those who object to Christians being involved in the political process are ultimately objecting to Christians being involved in the social process. The political process is really nothing more than a realization of the social process. For us to divorce ourselves from society would be to run into the kind of isolationism and monasticism that characterized the medieval hermits. Many Christians are not even aware of the importance of registering to vote. It is perfectly legal, for example, for a deputy registrar to come right to your local church at a designated time and register the entire congregation. I am convinced that those of us who are pastors have an obligation to urge our people to register to vote. I am more concerned that people exercise their freedom to vote than I am concerned for whom they vote.

2. Information

Many moral Americans are unaware of the real issues affecting them today. Many people do not know the voting record of their congressman and have no idea how he is representing them on political issues that have moral implications. This is one of the major reasons why we have established the Moral Majority organization. We want to keep the public informed on the vital moral issues. The Moral Majority, Inc., is a nonprofit organization, with headquarters in Washington, D.C. Our goal is to exert a significant influence on the spiritual and moral direction of our nation by: (a) mobilizing the grassroots of moral Americans in one clear and effective voice; (b) informing the moral majority what is going on behind their backs in Washington and in state legislatures across the country; (c) lobbying intensely in Congress to defeat left-wing, social-welfare bills that will further erode our precious freedom; (d) pushing for positive legislation such as that to establish the Family Protection Agency, which will ensure a strong, enduring America; and (e) helping the moral majority in local communities to fight pornography, homosexuality, the advocacy of immorality in school textbooks, and other issues facing each and every one of us.

Christians must keep America great by being willing to go into the halls of Congress, by getting laws passed that will protect the freedom and liberty of her citizens. The Moral Majority, Inc., was formed to acquaint Americans everywhere with the tragic decline in our nation's morals and to provide leadership in establishing an effective coalition of morally active citizens who are (a) prolife, (b) profamily, (c) promoral, and (d) pro-American. If the vast majority of Americans (84 per cent, according to George Gallup) still believe the Ten Commandments are valid today, why are we permitting a few leading amoral humanists and naturalists to take over the most influential positions in this nation? . . .

3. Mobilization

The history of the church includes the history of Christian involvement in social issues. . . .

The turning point in Christian involvement in social action seems to have been the repeal of prohibition in 1933. A wide variety of Christians and moral Americans were united in the crusade against alcohol for nearly twenty years. Led by the preaching of evangelist Billy Sunday, prohibition finally became law in 1919. Its eventual repeal caused many Christians to conclude that we have no business trying to legislate Christian morality on a non-Christian society. The Depression and World War II followed shortly thereafter, and Christian concern about social issues hit rock bottom during the fifties and sixties. We have tended to develop the attitude that our only obligation is to preach the Gospel and prepare men for heaven. We have forgotten that we are still our brother's keeper and that the same spiritual truths that prepare us to live in eternity are also essential in preparing us to live on this earth. We dare not advocate our responsibility to the society of which we are so very much a vital part. If we as moral Americans do not speak up on these essential moral issues, who then will? As Christians we need to exert our influence not only in the church but also in our business life, home life, and social and community life as well. . . .

Right living must be re-established as an American way of life. We as American citizens must recommit ourselves to the faith of our fathers and to the premises and moral foundations upon which this country was established. Now is the time to begin calling America back to God, back to the Bible, back to morality! We must be willing to live by the moral convictions that we claim to believe. There is no way that we will ever be willing to die for something for which we are not willing to live. The authority of Bible morality must once again be recognized as the legitimate guiding principle of our nation. Our love for our fellow man must ever be grounded in the truth and never be allowed to blind us from the truth that is the basis of our love for our fellow man.

DOCUMENT 7

Sidney Blumenthal, "The G.O.P. 'Me Decade'" (1984)

President Ronald Reagan acquired enormous political capital from the economic recovery of the 1980s. His style of leadership and acute ability to divert criticism preserved his extraordinary popularity and frustrated the president's liberal opponents. One of Reagan's most spirited critics was Sidney Blumenthal. In a series of articles for *The New Republic,* Blumenthal exposed the hypocrisy of Reagan's policies as well as the greed and intolerance of those who worshiped him. In the following article, Blumenthal reports on the events of the 1984 Republican National Convention, held in Dallas, which he labeled the "apotheosis of the 'Me Decade.'"

Ronald Reagan's hypocrisy works so effectively because he doesn't know he's a hypocrite. At least that's how some of his senior advisers explain it. While he rails against the breakdown of traditional values, his political operatives point to his daughter Patti, the antinuclear activist married to her yoga instructor; his son Ron, the ballet-dancer-turned-freelance-writer; and First Daughter Maureen, the divorced feminist. Reagan's handlers understand that in the eyes of voters the President's public intolerance is softened and contradicted by his private tolerance. Without his hypocrisy, they assert, the would be perceived as brittle and threatening. And because he lacks self-consciousness about his inconsistency, he can perform his political chores with convincing sincerity.

The hypocrisy that works so well for him on social issues also helps him sell his economic policies. His federal deficit encapsulates his hypocrisy here. He religiously condemns the sin, but it's what's making him happy. He has MasterCarded the recovery: reelect now, pay later.

To conservatives such as Reagan, Keynesianism has been more than an economic doctrine; the cultural consequences of Keynesianism meant the destruction of the Protestant ethnic and the self-regulating market. If Keynesianism worked, then the old gospel of success must be humbug. By deficit spending, one could get something now and never be punished. Prosperity no longer could be traced to the moral character of striving individuals as in Horatio Alger's novellas, the kind Reagan grew up on.

Thus, only by suppressing big government could America be restored. Then wealth would again be dependent on positive thinking. Reaganism is the mind cure for the bad dream of Keynesianism. When we believe, the good dreams of the past will come true. While Reagan waits for utopia, there's a free lunch.

Reagan is more a hero of consumption than production. Old-fashioned production means sacrificing oneself to an impersonal process, while modern consumption means personal transformation through appearances. Reagan represents consumption without guilt. And through his rise in the entertainment industry and the leisure class, he's been ironically able to convince us that he embodies the old ideology of a productive class. His free-market rhetoric gives a license to unfettered consumption. The clue is that pain and denial, the stock-in-trade of economic puritanism, never figure in Reagan's formula. Some of his top aides appreciate that this juncture between his words and results accounts for much of his political magic. He allows us to have whatever we want so long as we give credence to an obsolescent ideology. He's a permissive father. Ask Patti. . . .

The convention was the apotheosis of the "Me Decade." For the Republicans, the rich have the same function that the poor have for the Democrats: they are objects of compassion and even pity. Since a majority of G.O.P delegates had annual incomes in excess of $50,000, their concern was empathetic. For them, a vote for Reagan is a vote for immediate gratification. In this respect, they are true legatees of the 1960s. . . .

Dallas was an inspired choice for the convention. The town's boosters depict it as a wide open frontier, but it's tightly controlled at the top by a self-perpetuating elite. It's a city of blinding heat, freeways, and mirrored-glass buildings; it makes L.A. look like Cambridge. (One wag said, "The only reflective thing here is the glass.") Most important, Dallas is both a place and a fantasy. There's Dallas and there's *Dallas*. After the Republican platform committee finished bashing the remnants of moderate Republicanism—just as J.R. crushes Cliff Barnes every week—its members basked at an exclusive party at Southfork Ranch, the set of the mythical Ewings. Southfork, a shrine to greed, has become the most popular Dallas tourist attraction, more popular now than Dealey Plaza.

The convention opened with the bombastic presentation of Olympic gold medalists. "U.S.A.! U.S.A.!" Just as U.S.A. wasted the opposition in the Olympic games, the Republicans would waste the Democrats. Thus began a systematic effort to portray the Democratic Party as somehow illegitimate and un-American. The intent was not merely to discredit Walter Mondale. In order to build a Republican majority, the Democrats would have to be thoroughly smashed. Through almost every major speech ran a theme of the Democrats' suspect patriotism. . . .

[T]he National Conservative Political Action Committee, a New Right group that targets liberals for termination with extreme prejudice, held what amounted to a counterconvention at Nelson Bunker Hunt's Circle T Ranch, a Texas Bavaria. This was not the Dallas Museum of Art crowd. Sides of longhorn steer—the hors d'oeuvres—basted over hot coals. Indians in war bonnets danced. Cowboys performed rope tricks, a stagecoach rolled guests around a trail, and a huge brahma bull was saddled up for rides: *Yahoo!* (Honest—one woman, on the bull, yelled *"Yahoo!"*) Celebrities circulated. "I loved you in *Planet of the Apes*," a woman gushed to Charlton Heston. "Moses, Moses!" beseeched another fan.

After gorging on barbecue, the almost two thousand guests entered a gigantic air-conditioned white tent about as big as Texas Stadium for dinner. At the tent's entrance a NCPAC videotape of the history of the world, ending in its salvation by Reagan's election, was on sale. Suddenly, in slow motion, we see Reagan shot by John Hinckley: "A gunman's bullet almost did what the President's critics have not been able to do." But soon Reagan's smiling again. Jerry Falwell of Moral Majority walks by and catches Reagan's face on the screen. "Is that real?" He asked. Or is it Memorex? "Oh, he's not here yet?"

Inside the big top, plates of cold tenderloin were served, followed by NCPAC leader, Terry Dolan, with short hair, manicured moustache, tight knit shirt, stacked-heel boots, and tight jeans, a pair of aviator frame sunglasses inserted neatly into his back pocket, who pranced up to the microphone. He delivered a diatribe against the press, featuring a personal attack on *Washington Post* columnist Mary McGrory, a representative agent of demonic forces. To these conservatives, the press is the moral equivalent of communism. Pat Boone, the singer, tried to lighten things up: "How do you like this air conditioning? Who said Republicans don't care about the environment? If we don't like it, we change it." Then Chad Everett, star of "Medical Center" and a genius-level cretin, made a speech: "I want you to help me to invite you to welcome me...." Finally, Bob Hope appeared: "Four, three, two, one. I'm just testing the microphone. We bomb in five minutes. I hope I don't." Hope led the crowd on a tour through the mausoleum of popular culture: *Thanks for the memories*. And then there was a mad rush for the valet parking.

The next day, Republican women held a proper luncheon for the First Lady at the pharaonic Anatole Hotel, whose three marble atriums are sufficiently large to serve as a museum for the pyramids. The main speaker was Joan Rivers, the laughing hyena of Republicanism. No pathos about capital shortage here. When Reagan talks about a "city on a hill," she knows he's talking about Beverly Hills. "I never do housework," she said. "That's the fun of being a Republican." The ladies tittered nervously. They weren't sure whether to laugh or express shock. Rivers's heartfelt vulgarity was shattering the veneer of hypocrisy....

The next morning, August 23, Reagan addressed a prayer breakfast of more than 10,000 supporters. In his speech he offered a profoundly confused political theology. He claimed that the Founding Fathers "saw the state, in fact, as a form of moral order." But, in the 1960s, "we began to make great steps toward secularizing our nation." The secularizers are "intolerant" and "care only for the interests of the state." But wasn't the federal government "a form of moral order"? Did it lose its moral underpinnings in the 1960s? How can those who believe the American identity is not reflected in the national government also assert that that government was invested in the beginning with divine purpose? Does it follow that if there's prayer in public schools conservatives will believe that government possesses an imminent morality? Reagan then declared politics and morality, which has its foundation "in religion," to be "inseparable," contradicting Jefferson's injunction against theocracy. "Without God," Reagan said, "there is no virtue." It must follow that those who are "secularizing" are without virtue. They deprive America of virtue. They are against God. "America's party" is attempting to restore our rightful relationship with God. Reagan's fellow worshippers roared approval of the logic of holy war.

By the time of Reagan's acceptance speech, replete with more Democrat-bashing—"unconscionable.... cease its obstructionist ways"—some of his political advisers began to think that the harsh tone of the convention was not working for them. The Democratic Party, after all, is still the majority party. To succeed, Republicans must cajole the opposition to their side. By focusing the brunt of the attack on the party, the convention speakers may have reminded Democrats—and independents—why they are not Republicans. When the first post-convention polls came in, Reagan gained virtually no ground—an extraordinarily poor performance, even with his large lead. He had apparently reached his limit. Some Reagan advisers worry that his hard-edged stance on social issues might prevent some Democrats from voting for him. Reagan the laid-back, Reagan the tolerant hypocrite, Reagan the Me Decade dreamer, is the Reagan who wins biggest.

Mondale in his call for a "new realism," celebration of "hard work," and insistence on new taxes, seems to believe we must punish ourselves for our binge of self-indulgence under Reagan. Mondale's problem isn't that he overpromises, but that he underpromises. Liberals used to be the advocates of leisure, not misplaced puritanism. Even farsighted labor leaders such as Walter Reuther thought cogently about how leisure would liberate the working class. Now, through a weird alchemy, conservatives under Reagan have appropriated leisure from the liberals. While Mondale presents work as bitter medicine, Reagan says it's the road to self-fulfillment, even super-stardom. Reagan is Miller Time, Mondale is the factory whistle. Reagan promises that just possibly, if you dream hard enough, you can be rich, famous, not work hard, and live almost forever—like him. In the end, Americans want the pursuit of happiness, not blood, sweat, and tears. Almost always, the party of leisure wins elections. In recent history, that is usually the party of deficits. Reagan condemns what sustains him, and dreams on.

DOCUMENT 8

Diana Hembree, "Dead End in Silicon Valley" (1985)

Since the 1970s the American economy had begun deindustrializing as thousands of smokestack industries in the nation's Rust Belt closed. Many hailed high-tech industries as the wave of the future. In 1984, for example, 1,800 electronics firms located in California's Silicon Valley enjoyed more than $25 billion in sales. But as investigative reporter Diana Hembree of the *Santa Cruz Phoenix* discovered, the high-tech revolution did not offer rewards to the production workers who made it happen. In the following article, Hembree reports on her three-month experience working in an electronic assembly plant.

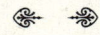

It was a cool, cloudless day when I joined the crowd of applicants at Quality Electronic Service, a small company in Santa Cruz, California. Q.E.S. had advertised for electronics assemblers—"No Experience Necessary"—and its lobby was jammed.

From the outside, the plant looked more like a real estate office than a factory. Along with hundreds of other "board shops" in the area, it makes printed circuit boards—the brains and memory banks of computers—for other high-tech firms.

Like most such shops, Q.E.S. starts its assemblers at the minimum wage. Still, with the annual unemployment rate in Santa Cruz sometimes reaching 14 per cent, the company has had little trouble attracting would-be workers.

As we filled out our application forms, I began to feel nervous. What if company officials discovered that I worked for a local biweekly, The *Santa Cruz Phoenix?* By the time Hilda Hurley, the personnel manager, called me for an interview, I was certain that I'd been rejected. I told Hilda truthfully that I was interested in electronics, and she beamed at me.

"It really *is so* interesting," she agreed. Hurley then looked at me sharply. "I trust you have health insurance?"

Startled, I lied that I did.

"Good girl!" she said. "I just like to ask, because Q.E.S. is a training shop and we don't pay benefits."

She gave me a quick rundown on the job: Pay started at $3.35 an hour and employees would receive no medical benefits or sick leave. Work began at 7:00 A.M. ("Please be prompt") and let out at 3:30 P.M., with two fifteen-minute breaks and thirty minutes for lunch.

"It may take a little getting used to," she said, "but I think you'll find this job a real challenge."

August 19, 1981

I arrived for work at 6:45 A.M. and found some workers already waiting in the back parking lot. When the warning bell rang, seventy or so employees crowded into the plant's noisy, windowless rooms. The atmosphere was casual: Most assemblers wore jeans and T-shirts, and rock music blared from a radio in the corner. At the soldering table, workers bantered with friends, and even after the final bell, some carried on muffled conversations.

"So how's our new girl?" Hilda asked cheerily when she spotted me. She is a small, buoyant, determined woman in her fifties, whose high heels clicked furiously as she rushed to trouble spots in the plant. In five minutes, I was armed with a timecard, shown the coffee room, and assigned to the clipping section.

"Everyone starts in clipping," Hilda said, adding that I would be there for only a few days. Though harried, she gave me a quick lesson on how to clip the needle-thin wires on the backs of printed circuit boards, which were bound for computers, video games, microwave equipment, and other products. The back of each board looked like a huge silver pincushion. My job was to clip the inch-long wires to between one-sixteenth and one-thirty-second of an inch—a tricky length to gauge with the naked eye. My lead, or floor supervisor, a stolid young woman named Karen, repeatedly warned me that I was clipping too high or too low. My co-workers got the same lecture, delivered methodically in a smooth, impersonal tone.

At first I was so pleased to have persuaded Q.E.S. to hire me that I clipped the tiny wires with unfeigned enthusiasm. But as the morning wore on, my neck and shoulders ached from craning over the boards, my eyes smarted, and I felt drowsy. After what seemed like interminable hours clipping boards, I stole a glance at the clock: only 9:45. I could smell a peculiar chemical odor, but had no idea what it was.

"Sleepy?" asked the older woman beside me when I tried to stifle a yawn. "It's the freon," she said confidentially, nodding at a machine a few feet away. "Go to the bathroom and splash cold water on your face and arms; that helps a little. Or, if you can't keep your eyes open a second longer, drop something on the floor and take your time picking it up. That's what I do." My partner, Gail, had taken three aspirin and offered me one. She said she always took at least three a shift. . . .

By the end of the day, my head throbbed, my neck hurt, and my eyes felt coated with sand. It was 3:27, and a few employees waited near the door. "Don't leave your seat until the bell rings!" Hilda shouted from across the room. When it did, employees left in a rush and the parking lot emptied in five minutes.

August 26

Q.E.S. was owned by an executive of Plantronics, a sleek, modern, high-tech plant down the road. The manager was Fred Freiberg, an energetic man in his late thirties. Fred strode through the plant several times a day, conferring with supervisors and occasionally joking with long-time employees. Since he spent much of his time scouring Silicon Valley for customers, he handed over the day-to-day management of the assembly room to personnel manager Hilda Hurley.

Hilda acted like a nursery school teacher, patting employees on the head with "Good girl!" and "Good boy!" praise. She alternately scolded and cajoled us to work faster, and other supervisors followed suit. Some days the assembly room rang with commands reminiscent of junior high school: "I said quiet"; "Don't slump in your chair"; "Wipe that look off your face, young lady."

"They treat us like kindergartners," said one eighteen-year-old. "It's incredible."

But in general, the supervisors were not harsh or unkind. Hilda herself was sympathetic to employees in trouble. I'd heard that when one inspector left for a week to escape a battering boyfriend, Hilda held her position open until the woman returned.

Still, her behavior was arbitrary. Once, Hilda transferred a new employe who was bothered by freon fumes to another area, confiding to the startled assembler that she had lost her own sense of taste and smell in the industry. But another employee who complained about fumes was summarily fired. "She was only here two days, and she complained in front of customers," said one veteran employee loyal to Q.E.S. . . .

September 10

Last week, I lunched near the chemical drums left over from production and memorized the labels one by one. The chemicals and heavy metals used at Q.E.S. included freon 113, tin-lead solder, acid flux, and isopropyl alcohol. Some research at the state Department of Health library yielded a list of potential effects of exposure:

- **Freon 113** (At Q.E.S., TMS Plus, or trichlorotrifloroethane.) Dissolves the skin's essential oils and can cause rashes, drying, and cracking of the skin. Acts as a depressant on the central nervous system: If inhaled at extremely high concentrations, it can cause unconsciousness and even death. Symptoms of acute over-exposure: drowsiness, nausea, giddiness, central nervous system depression, and irregular heartbeats.
- **Tin-Lead Solder** When heated, releases lead oxide fumes which can be harmful if inhaled. Airborne lead may be absorbed into the bloodstream and stored in tissues. Can cause brain damage, paralysis, colic, miscarriages, and sterility. Symptoms of lead poisoning include fatigue, irritability, headaches, tremors, "wrist drop," pain in joints, and blue line on gums.
- **Acid Flux** A corrosive liquid used to clean metal during soldering. When heated, acid flux may release fumes that can irritate the skin and respiratory tract.
- **Isopropyl Alcohol** Highly flammable. Exposure to fumes can irritate the eyes and inhalation of large quantities can cause vomiting, narcosis, and coma.

In comparison with the hazards found at semiconductor and electroplating plants, the use of toxic chemicals at Q.E.S. was moderate. But the danger was real nevertheless. The Occupational Safety and Health Administration (OSHA) had implicated freon 113 in the deaths of two young electronics workers in Santa Barbara, California. And union groups estimated that degreaser accidents in the United States cause ten to twelve deaths a year. Though OSHA recommends that workers handling freon 113 wear impervious clothing, gloves, and safety goggles, supervisors at Q.E.S. didn't even require washers to wear gloves. And I never heard a supervisor mention the hazards of freon or any other workplace chemical.

"No, we don't really use any hazardous chemicals in here," the plant secretary said in response to my question at the job orientation session. "None that could really hurt you."

September 14

This morning, Alicia Rodriguez joined the clipping section to help with a logjam of unclipped boards. Alicia had come from Mexico three years earlier and spoke no English. At forty-four, she had to help support five children and felt fortunate to have the job at Q.E.S. But she was indignant about her salary: After fourteen months at the plant, she was making $3.50 an hour.

"I call it my candy money, because that's about all you can buy with it," joked Alicia. "But I've been trying to save up for an eye exam." After months of detailed assembly work, she could no longer read the numbers on the tiny blue-black diodes in the prep room. "I'm putting some of them upside-down," she said. "It worries me."

On break, she and I lined up with other women in the bathroom to splash cold water on our hands and faces. The air in the bathroom was cool and fresh. Waiting my turn at the sink, I noticed that the trashcan near the door was really an empty Lonco chemical drum marked FLUX NEUTRALIZER: DANGER. The warning on the side read:

D-A-N-G-E-R! THIS CONTAINER CONTAINS CHEMICALS.

DO NOT PUT OTHER MATERIALS IN THIS CONTAINER.

DO NOT RE-USE CONTAINER FOR ANY PURPOSE.

DO NOT PUNCTURE, WELD, DRILL OR EXPOSE CONTAINER TO HEAT OR SOURCE OF IGNITION, INCLUDING DIRECT SUNLIGHT.

DO DISPOSE OF CONTAINER TO RECONDITIONERS OR DISPOSAL COMPANY.

The company's negligent attitude apparently rubbed off on some employees. "Big Bob," a solder machine operator, smoked near drums of flammable acids and alcohols. In the next room, workers rushed back and forth with open coffee cans of liquid freon, often narrowly avoiding collisions in their haste to refill the degreaser.

"Sure, a few of the guys like to act macho, washing their hands in freon and so on," my new floor supervisor, Ray Burks, told me during lunch. "But basically it's ignorance. And even if employees know the stuff is bad for them, what are they going to do? Worrying about chemicals is fine if you have money and options, but compared to being evicted tomorrow if you can't pay your rent, chemical fumes and skin rashes seem pretty minor."

September 15

After three-and-a-half weeks of clipping, my eyes were sensitive to sunlight, and it was hard to read for more than fifteen minutes at a stretch. Remembering that Hilda said I would be clipping for only a few days, I asked to transfer to the assembly room, but was told that all those positions were full. "We can move employees around, but it depends on their attitude," my floor supervisor said.

I decided to wait a few more days before asking again. I had noticed that Anglo men were usually transferred from the clipping section to a higher-status job within a week. Other employees told me that women and Mexican men may remain in clipping for weeks or even months. . . .

At lunch, some employees walked to a nearby sandwich shop while others met around a splintery picnic table in back of the building. Benchless and rotting, the table faced the parking lot and was only five feet away from a cluster of rusting chemical drums.

"Damn, we need longer breaks," sighed a machine operator as the warning bell rang.

"What we need is a union," said one woman unexpectedly. There was a short silence, then a solderer jumped to his feet.

"Union? Did I hear the word *union?*" He screamed in mock horror and then imitated a police siren. Another co-worker pretended to film us. "Guards, arrest them. Take them away!" she called out as employees entered the plant. . . .

This afternoon, while we assembled rows of circuit boards, Gloria Luna told me about her childhood in a peasant family in Mexico. "We were poor," she said, "and sometimes at night I'd be so hungry that I'd sneak into the kitchen and eat a handful of flour from the sack."

Suddenly she stopped talking. After loading a few more pieces, I glanced at Gloria staring owl-like into space, her eyes round and dull. She was sleeping with her eyes open. I touched her shoulder, which started her. She blinked at me and smiled.

Gloria, it turned out, was working the night shift in a local cannery. After the closing bell sounded at Q.E.S., she would collect her four-year-old girl from her husband David, who then left for his job at a local tannery. She would feed and bathe her daughter, then drop her off at a sister's house. Gloria spent the next eight or ten hours sorting brussels sprouts on a conveyor belt, arriving home at one or two in the morning. She was at the electronics plant five hours later.

"Other women at Q.E.S. are working there, too," whispered Gloria. "We don't tell nobody, 'cause maybe they'll fire you for working two jobs."

Perhaps because of working nights in an unheated cannery, Gloria, four months pregnant, had developed a rasping cough that refused to go away. At lunch, dazed with exhaustion, she stretched out in the back of her old Ford sedan and tried to catch a few minutes of sleep.

December 25

Yesterday was my last day at Q.E.S. Most employees chose to work Christmas Eve rather than forgo a day's wages. Fred Freiberg provided refreshments for the company party.

"Sometimes I don't feel like I'm twenty-four," Gloria told me at break. "Maybe because I've been doing the same thing for years and years. I'd like so bad to do something different, a job where you have big windows and do different things during the day."

As a young girl, she recalled, she was rebellious and liked to run around the hills. "But now," Gloria said. "I feel old, like an old woman. Why? I used to be so excited about everything. What happened to me?"

Epilogue, 1985

Some time after I left Q.E.S., I called my old boss, Fred Freiberg, to interview him. He seemed startled to learn that a former Q.E.S. employee wanted to write about the plant, but agreed to talk with me.

"I'd like to pay higher wages, but to do so, I'd have to raise my prices," Fred told me in his office. "And if you charge more for the boards, you don't get the job: It's that simple. The trouble is, these Silicon Valley companies want you to work at practically overseas prices."

Fred was disturbed that some of his former customers were sending their computer boards overseas or to local black-market assemblers. "Frankly, I don't see the future as bright as I used to," he said.

Then, changing his tone, Fred went on to praise Q.E.S. as an unusually clean plant with an excellent safety record. "No major accident in twelve years," he told me, "and if a supervisor isn't strict on safety, I fire 'em."

What about employees who complained of headaches and dizziness from fumes? Fred had never heard these complaints. Freon, he said, "is basically a very harmless substance." He said, however, that he didn't condone "the electronics shops in Scotts Valley that have people up to their elbows in the stuff, scrubbing boards in metal tubs. And," he added, "there are a lot of places like that, believe me."

Fred, who said he was planning on replacing the freon at Q.E.S. with an "organic" cleaner, placed much of the blame for toxic fumes on employee carelessness. "You know," he said, "we do hire a lot of 'low-end' people around here. People with bad attitudes. When employees won't follow the rules, then of course we have a problem."

He also discounted the risk of solder fumes. These are not hazardous, he said, "because the body can't absorb lead."

As he talked about other chemicals at Q.E.S., describing them as mild and harmless, a missing piece of the puzzle fell into place. Fred, it turns out, had simply learned what the chemical companies had taught him.

"Their salesmen come in here and hold training sessions," he explained. "They show how to use the chemicals and give you instructions, you know: 'Don't drink it, don't jump in it . . .'"

A while ago, I received an unexpected letter from a former Q.E.S. employee who had moved to Arizona. He had called OSHA about the fume problem at Q.E.S. and asked to see the inspection report. He received it and enclosed a copy, marked "confidential." According to the report, the OSHA inspector had conducted a wall-to-wall inspection while I was working at Q.E.S. She found no health or safety violations.

Study Questions

1. How did Americans define the American Dream in the 1980s? Who could hope to realize that dream?

2. With so much growth and prosperity, why did some Americans criticize Reagan's economic policies? Who supported them and why?

3. Many documents seem as much concerned about moral values and behavior as about economic success. How can the moral tone of politics in this period be explained?

4. Did Ronald Reagan's election mark a watershed in American history?

15

The End of the Cold War

In the early 1970s the United States began to reassess its cold war strategy. Nixon administration officials questioned the assumption that the cold war was simply an ideological struggle for survival against communism. Instead they perceived conflict with the Soviet Union as a traditional great power rivalry that could be managed and controlled rather than won. Through such measures as strategic arms limitation talks (SALT) and trade agreements, President Richard Nixon hoped to achieve détente—a relaxation of tension—with the Soviet Union. Although Presidents Gerald Ford and Jimmy Carter continued to pursue détente, cold war tensions had resumed by the end of the decade. Concerned about reports of Soviet military superiority, Carter approved a new weapons system that threatened renewal of the arms race. After the Soviet army invaded Afghanistan in 1979, Carter imposed a grain embargo, boycotted the 1980 Moscow Olympic Games, and withdrew the SALT II treaty. Détente was over.

Upon assuming office as president in 1980, Ronald Reagan completed the repudiation of détente, adopting an openly adversarial stance toward the Soviet Union. Reagan viewed the cold war in ideological terms, believing that the Soviet Union was prepared "to commit any crime, to lie, to cheat" to advance worldwide Communist revolution. He repeatedly denounced Moscow as the "focus of evil in the modern world" (Document 1). To support his rhetoric, Reagan expanded the military and sent billions of dollars in foreign aid to those fighting Soviet client states in Africa and Central America. Reagan also approved increased expenditures on research and development of the Strategic Defense Initiative (SDI), an antimissile system that would shield the United States by destroying incoming missiles in space with lasers. Although critics doubted SDI's practicality and warned that it would escalate the arms race, advocates argued that it was critical to achieving Reagan's strategy of "peace through strength" (Document 2).

In 1985 relations between the two superpowers improved as Mikhail Gorbachev assumed the leadership of the Soviet Union. Recognizing the perils afflicting the Soviet bloc, Gorbachev introduced reforms intended to open Soviet society and restructure its economy. Gorbachev also pursued arms reduction treaties with the United States. Gorbachev's policies opened the way for dramatic change as the people of the Eastern bloc demanded more meaningful reforms. Gorbachev soon found himself unable to control a popular social revolution. In 1989 the Communist regimes of Eastern Europe collapsed under pressure from mass popular protests. Nationalist movements swept through the Soviet Union as its republics declared independence from Moscow. In 1991 the Communist Party of the Soviet Union lost control of the country and Gorbachev resigned, bringing the Soviet era to a close.

Americans hailed the disintegration of the Soviet empire, proclaiming the end of the cold war. Many observers credited the Reagan administration's hard-line policy toward the Soviet Union as the decisive factor in the collapse of communism (Document 3). Others disagreed, doubting that the United States had actually won the cold war. Such critics argued that the country's cold war policies had come at a great cost as leaders repeatedly compromised principles, ideals, and the law in the forty-year crusade against communism (Document 4). Others blamed cold war policies for creating a repressive militarization of American society and culture (Document 5). With the cold war ended, defense industries curtailed their operations and military bases closed, affecting millions of American workers and military personnel and raising questions about what the promised peace dividend would look like (Document 6).

DOCUMENT 1

Ronald Reagan, Address to the National Association of Evangelicals (1983)

President Reagan's initial policy toward the Soviet Union put a low priority on arms control. Remarks by key officials in the State Department about firing nuclear "warning shots" and devising strategies for surviving a nuclear attack earned the administration a reputation for irresponsibility on arms control. By 1982 public concern over the danger of nuclear war had mounted, spawning a movement to put a "freeze" on the testing, production, and deployment of nuclear weapons. In the following address before the National Association of Evangelicals in Orlando, Florida, Reagan responded to "freeze" advocates, arguing that it would encourage the expansionist designs of the "evil empire."

During my first press conference as President, in answer to a direct question, I pointed out that, as good Marxist-Leninists, the Soviet leaders have openly and publicly declared that the only morality they recognize is that which will further their cause, which is world revolution. I think I should point out I was only quoting Lenin, their guiding spirit, who said in 1920 that they repudiate all morality that proceeds from supernatural ideas—that's their name for religion—or ideas that are outside class conceptions. Morality is entirely subordinate to the interests of class war. And everything is moral that is necessary for the annihilation of the old, exploiting social order and for uniting the proletariat.

Well, I think the refusal of many influential people to accept this elementary fact of Soviet doctrine illustrates an historical reluctance to see totalitarian powers for what they are. We saw this phenomenon in the 1930's. We see it too often today.

This doesn't mean we should isolate ourselves and refuse to seek an understanding with them. I intend to do everything I can to persuade them of our peaceful intent, to remind them that it was the West that refused to use its nuclear monopoly in the forties and fifties for territorial gain and which now proposes 50-percent cut in strategic ballistic missiles and the elimination of an entire class of land-based, intermediate-range nuclear missiles.

At the same time, however, they must be made to understand that we will never compromise our principles and standards. We will never give away our freedom. We will never abandon our belief in God. And we will never stop searching for a genuine peace. But we can assure none of these things America stands for through the so-called nuclear freeze solutions proposed by some.

The truth is that a freeze now would be a very dangerous fraud, for that is merely the illusion of peace. The reality is that we must find peace through strength.

I would agree to a freeze if only we could freeze the Soviets' global desires. A freeze at current levels of weapons would remove any incentive for the Soviets to negotiate seriously in Geneva and virtually end our chances to achieve the major arms reductions which we have proposed. Instead, they would achieve their objectives through the freeze.

A freeze would reward the Soviet Union for its enormous and unparalleled military buildup. It would prevent the essential and long overdue modernization of United States and allied defenses and would leave our aging forces increasingly vulnerable. And an honest freeze would require extensive prior negotiations on the systems and numbers to be limited and on the measures to ensure effective verification and compliance. And the kind of freeze that has been suggested would be virtually impossible to verify. Such a major effort would divert us completely from our current negotiations on achieving substantial reductions.

A number of years ago, I heard a young father, a very prominent young man in the entertainment world, addressing a tremendous gathering in California. It was during the time of the cold war, and communism and our own way of life were very much on people's minds. And he was speaking to that subject. And suddenly, though, I heard him saying, "I love my little girls more than anything———" And I said to myself, "Oh, no, don't. You can't—don't say that." But I had underestimated him. He went on: "I would rather see my little girls die now, still believing in God, than have them grow up under communism and one day die no longer believing in God."

There were thousands of young people in that audience. They came to their feet with shouts of joy. They had instantly recognized the profound truth in what he had said, with regard to the physical and the soul and what was truly important.

Yes, let us pray for the salvation of all of those who live in that totalitarian darkness—pray they will discover the joy of knowing God. But until they do, let us be aware that while they preach the supremacy of the state, declare its omnipotence over individual man, and predict its eventual domination of all peoples on the Earth, they are the focus of evil in the modern world.

It was C. S. Lewis who, in his unforgettable "Screwtape Letters," wrote: "The greatest evil is not done now in those sordid 'dens of crime' that Dickens loved to paint. It is not even done in concentration camps and labor camps. In those we see its final result. But it is conceived and ordered (moved, seconded, carried and minuted) in clear, carpeted, warmed, and well-lighted offices, by quiet men with white collars and cut fingernails and smooth-shaven cheeks who do not need to raise their voice."

Well, because these "quiet men" do not "raise their voices," because they sometimes speak in soothing tones of brotherhood and peace, because, like other dictators before them, they're always making "their final territorial demand," some would have us accept them at their word and accommodate ourselves to their aggressive impulses. But if history teaches anything, it teaches that simple-minded appeasement or wishful thinking about our adversaries is folly. It means the betrayal of our past, the squandering of our freedom.

So, I urge you to speak out against those who would place the United States in a position of military and moral inferiority. You know, I've always believed that old Screwtape reserved his best efforts for those of you in the church. So, in your discussions of the nuclear freeze proposals, I urge you to beware the temptation of pride—the temptation of blithely declaring yourselves above it all and label both sides equally at fault, to ignore the facts of history and the aggressive impulses of an evil empire, to simply call the arms race a giant misunderstanding and thereby remove yourself from the struggle between right and wrong and good and evil.

I ask you to resist the attempts of those who would have you withhold your support for our efforts, this administration's efforts, to keep America strong and free, while we negotiate real and verifiable reductions in the world's nuclear arsenals and one day, with God's help, their total elimination.

While America's military strength is important, let me add here that I've always maintained that the struggle now going on for the world will never be decided by bombs or rockets, by armies or military might. The real crisis we face today is a spiritual one; at root, it is a test of moral will and faith.

Whittaker Chambers, the man whose own religious conversion made him a witness to one of the terrible traumas of our time, the Hiss-Chambers case, wrote that the crisis of the Western World exists to the degree in which the West is indifferent to God, the degree to which it collaborates in communism's attempt to make man stand alone without God. And then he said, for Marxism-Leninism is actually the second oldest faith, first proclaimed in the Garden of Eden with the words of temptation, "Ye shall be as gods."

The Western World can answer this challenge, he wrote, "but only provided that its faith in God and the freedom He enjoins is as great as communism's faith in Man."

I believe we shall rise to the challenge. I believe that communism is another sad, bizarre chapter in human history whose last pages even now are being written. I believe this because the source of our strength in the quest for human freedom is not material, but spiritual. And because it knows no limitation, it must terrify and ultimately triumph over those who would enslave their fellow man. For in the words of Isaiah: "He giveth power to the faint; and to them that have no might He increased strength. . . . But they that wait upon the Lord shall renew their strength; they shall mount up with wings as eagles; they shall run, and not be weary. . . ."

Yes, change your world. One of our Founding Fathers, Thomas Paine, said, "We have it within our power to begin the world over again." We can do it, doing together what no one church could do by itself.

God bless you, and thank you very much.

DOCUMENT 2

Bill Chappell, Speech to the American Security Council Foundation (1985)

When President Ronald Reagan assumed the presidency, he pledged to strengthen the military and modernize the U.S. nuclear arsenal. A cornerstone of that strategy was the development of the Strategic Defense Initiative (SDI), popularly called "Star Wars." The Reagan administration touted SDI as a viable system of defense that would, in Reagan's words, render Soviet "nuclear weapons impotent and obsolete." In the following speech, Representative Bill Chappell (R-FL) defends SDI as integral to achieving peace through strength.

※ ※

You've asked me today to speak on the subject of "The Need for a Strategic Defense Initiative." That's a pretty big assignment for one so low on the totem pole as I am in matters of defense. You are going to be hearing later from General Abrahamson and several others who are really experts in the field. So I am not going to try to be so technical. Rather, I want to establish a need for SDI—not that you don't already know it. I'll probably not say anything you don't already know. But the fact that we can share together those thoughts gives us a better opportunity to carry those thoughts back to the grass roots where they are so direly needed today.

"To be prepared for war is one of the most effectual means of preserving the peace." How many of you know who said that? And isn't it an ironical statement when you really think about it. To prevent war, we must create a strong peace. Now, that quotation didn't come from President Reagan when he was trying to sell the SDI. It didn't come from some military officer over on the Hill trying to justify a particular program. It came from George Washington, nearly 200 years ago.

That sentiment has been echoed repeatedly in this century by people such as Presidents Woodrow Wilson, Franklin D. Roosevelt, John F. Kennedy and, of course, Ronald Reagan. With today's threat of nuclear welfare, it has become more incumbent upon us than ever before to ensure that peace is maintained through whatever resources we have and can develop.

It is no secret that the Soviet Union is so determined to carry out its policies—and so believes in them—that it would use force to carry out its policies. Allowing that kind of effort to go unchecked will ultimately lead to war of disastrous consequences to the whole of humanity. Its next battleground or base may be space—25 miles above your home. The United States has a vital interest in protecting its outer spaces—as well as its inner spaces—from attack. That is why the President's strategic defensive Initiative—shortened to SDI—has become so critical in our search for a system to defend against nuclear missile attack. It is why we have assembled here today as concerned policymakers and citizens to carry on this dialogue.

The Strategic Defense Initiative is our most vitally important defense program under development. Stated very simply: if we are able to devise a defensive system that negates or significantly reduces the effectiveness of Soviet ICBMs [Intercontinental Ballistic Missiles], we will have regained the lost ground that gave us strategic stability during the '50s and '60s—and into the '70s. And we will have ended our nearly forty years of dependence on an increasingly precarious policy of mutual suicidal

"QUICK—GIMME A HUNDRED TWENTY BILLION QUARTERS!"

"This political cartoon satirizes the growing public skepticism about the Strategic Defense Initiative (SDI), popularly known as Star Wars," which could be capable of destroying incoming enemy warheads in outer space where they could do limited damage. Critics argued that the initiative would force the Russians to build more capable missiles to overcome the American defense system, while costing the American taxpayers billions of dollars.

standoff—in one form or another. And if we do succeed in reducing the effectiveness of the ICBM, we will make it far easier to negotiate its reduction and eventual elimination.

Perhaps the vital importance of our SDI program can be perceived even more vividly, if we consider another possible outcome. Let us assume that the Soviet SDI effort succeeds and the U.S. is unable to generate comparable strategic defenses—what then? What then?

We, of course, acknowledge that Soviet forces already have us vastly outnumbered in manpower and conventional weaponry. And, avoiding any hair-splitting—we also realize that our nuclear forces have—at best—a rough parity with the Soviet Union at the present time. Obviously, even a partially effective Soviet strategic defense capability would establish a wide margin of Soviet superiority strategically, and thus give them dominance in all major areas of warfare. With the U.S. military in a position of pronounced inferiority, I would not want to speculate on the ultimate fate of Western civilization in general—or our nation—or society—in particular. . . .

Despite its unspecified nature, we are continually bombarded with detailed descriptions of what SDI will consist of and why it won't work.

In the words of one congressional leader, "The

Strategic Defense Initiative raises more questions than its supporters have answered so far."

Quite true, and that is a mathematically verifiable fact. But it's an unfair contest. There are many thousands devising questions of widely varying levels of worth and validity—and only a small handful of people trying to provide thoughtful—coherent—integrated—and consistent answers to the Congress—the media—and the organized opposition. Or, to paraphrase Winston Churchill's tribute to the Royal Air Force fighter pilots: "Never have so many provided detailed predictions of what a research program will ultimately determine—for so few."

Another widely quoted statement proposes a slow-down—a smaller-scale SDI research program—because—it is said—it is very unlikely that space-based anti-missile weapons can ever fully protect the U.S. population from nuclear attack.

Such statements, based on false premises, naturally lead to equally false conclusions. No responsible SDI spokesman has yet indicated an intended reliance on space-based anti-missile weapons or given such reliance that they will fully protect the U.S. population from nuclear attack. Such safely ambiguous "straw man" statements tend to raise unfounded doubts and fears, generate endless miles of hysterical newsprint, and contribute nothing to the resolution of this national debate....

With greater public support, Congress should approve the full funding level requested by the President that would allow full integration of all components of SDI. SDI is a research program, not one for the deployment of weapons—and I keep emphasizing that—you can't do piecemeal because there are so many integral parts. Certainly, General Abrahamson, when he speaks to you later, will point that out so vividly: You can't move an important part of this program or cut out one piece of it without affecting the whole. It has to be an integrated program....

Let me invite you, fellow members of the Congressional Advisory Board of the American Security Council Foundation, to learn everything you can about the Strategic Defense Initiative. Learn why it is so important to America. Acquaint yourself with all of the facts that you can. Prepare yourselves at home in the best way you can—in small groups, in study groups, in all kinds of meetings—to get the message across to our people about the importance of this program. I invite you to understand the important part you play.

Together, we can create a peace strong enough to deter war. That's what SDI is all about—a peace strong enough to deter war. But that takes a strong America; it takes initiative, technology, and all of the things we have been talking about. Let's give it our best effort.

Thank you.

DOCUMENT 3

Stephen Sestanovich, "Did the West Undo the East?" (1993)

The end of the cold war sparked a heated debate over who should take credit for winning it. In the following article in the conservative journal *National Interest*, Stephen Sestanovich, director of Russian and Eurasian Studies at the Center for Strategic and International Studies in Washington, D.C., concludes that President

Ronald Reagan's hard-line policies played a pivotal role in forcing the disintegration of Soviet communism.

❧ ☙

No one disagrees that Russian revolutions of the past were set off by international defeats—1917 by the First World War, 1905 by the loss to the Japanese; even the end of serfdom in 1861 is commonly traced to the Crimean War. "Explaining" a revolution in this way doesn't mean that defeat created social strains where none existed (abolitionist intellectuals, for example, had been promoting freedom for the serfs for decades), nor that in the war's aftermath events could only move in one direction (the Bolsheviks' victory was a matter of incredible luck). But any serious interpreter of the historical record begins by recognizing that in all three of these cases, war fundamentally altered the political balance of forces at home. If the causal links are so straightforward when we analyze the past, what (apart from churlish feelings toward Ronald Reagan) makes anyone dispute them in our own time?

Admittedly, the Soviet Union suffered no outright military defeat in the first half of the 1980s. Nevertheless, by the middle of the decade, the outlook on almost every front of Soviet foreign policy was poor and clearly deteriorating. The list of failures needs very little elaboration: INF deployments in Europe and successive large increases in the U.S. military budget; Afghanistan, Grenada, and the emergence of the "Reagan Doctrine," which put new pressure on Soviet clients in Africa, Asia, and Latin America; Moscow's exclusion from Middle East diplomacy, and the humiliation of Soviet-made weapons in the Lebanon war of 1982; the Solidarity challenge in Poland; robust Chinese economic growth against a background of continuing Sino-Soviet hostility. And all this bad news before even mentioning the Strategic Defense Initiative, which threatened a new round of military competition and highlighted Soviet technological inferiority. Eduard Shevardnadze summed up the situation as follows: Soviet foreign policy had been "out of touch with the fundamental vital interests of the country."

Merely to recite this list of Soviet setbacks is to underscore the West's role in discrediting the policy of Gorbachev's predecessors. Naturally, Georgi Arbatov, in his recent memoirs, describes as "absolute nonsense" the idea that Western toughness "helped alter Soviet policy and demonstrate the futility of its warlike course," but there is no need to take this view too seriously. After all, Soviet policy was not inherently "futile"; it was made so by the strong external opposition it produced. Had there been no such opposition, the warnings of experts like Arbatov, about how the United States would respond to this or that action, would have had no credibility. Similarly, had there been successes to balance the failures of Soviet policy—had, for example, the Afghan operation gone relatively smoothly, with the West quietly ceding Moscow a sphere of influence; or had NATO's INF policy unraveled in the face of mounting European street protests—it would have been harder for Gorbachev and his colleagues to make a comprehensive critique of past policy. Instead of proposing a completely new approach to dealing with the outside world—what they grandly called "new thinking"—they would have been much more likely to propose *ad hoc* adjustments of specific policies.

Soviet policy was particularly vulnerable because it had made a mess everywhere. This argument, if correct, implies that the unrelenting approach of the Reagan administration was probably more effective than a better balanced Western policy—beat up the Soviets here, conciliate them there—would have been. By "overdoing it," the United States gave extra credibility to individual policies that might have lacked real force on their own. This is particularly true of SDI, which raised the specter of vast increases in Soviet spending. Although its partisans sometimes talk as though SDI brought down the Soviet regime all by itself, it was always a somewhat hypothetical threat, based on military systems that had been neither developed nor tested nor deployed. What made it impossible to laugh off SDI was the Reagan record as a whole.

The Brezhnev regime had come into being in 1964 on a platform that elevated stability over Khrushchevian impulsiveness. By the early 1980s, however, this stability became outright petrification: policy was hard to change without the pressure of a crisis. Confrontational Western policies provided that pressure. There was, of course, nothing automatic about the Soviet response to crisis, and a tightening-up of the system was at the very least conceivable. Hawks on both sides of the struggle, said some commentators, had to protect their common interest in keeping the conflict going. Arbatov has gone so far as to say that U.S. policy in the early 1980s created "further obstacles on the road to reform" and almost led to a "restoration of Stalinism."

There is no doubt that the Soviet propaganda apparatus answered the policies of the Reagan administration with some of the most blood-curdling invective of the Cold War, but Stalinist rhetoric can hardly be treated as proof of Stalinist politics. Arbatov himself observes that the military-industrial complex had "escaped control" a full decade earlier, thereby refuting his own claim that U.S. policy was responsible for the "Frankenstein monster" of Soviet militarism in the first half of the 1980s. On balance, the tensions of this period seem to have *weakened* those within the Soviet leadership who argued that the best response to crisis was more of the same. It should be remembered that the notorious Marshal Ogarkov, the loudest advocate within the military of running harder to keep up with the West, was ousted even before Gorbachev came to power.

The rigidity of the Soviet system made it more likely that pressure would lead to crisis. In recalling this period for the Hoover Oral History Project, two members of the Politburo (both of them Gorbachev allies) have described the internal debate about how to respond to SDI. The commitment of resources needed to run the arms race at all was already crushing, and in the first phase of Gorbachev's tenure—when he proposed to fix the economy through resource re-allocation rather than radical reform—the idea of shifting *more* resources to the military was simply not viable. Yet the high command refused to consider "quick-fix" responses to the SDI threat. Their determination to have a full-blown strategic defense of their own dramatized the internal price of the arms race and made clear the need to shake the system up.

Gorbachev, of course, presented his program somewhat differently. In December 1984, three full months before he took over as general secretary, he assured Party conservatives that his goal was to guarantee that the Soviet Union entered the twenty-first century "in a manner worthy of a great power." For many, this statement became a kind of proof that, from the very beginning, perestroika was meant to serve geopolitical aims. There is little reason to doubt that the general staff and captains of industry saw it this way, but the picture is far less clear when it comes to Gorbachev himself. He may have spoken the language of the military establishment so as to neutralize it politically. (He had the help of in-house propagandists: as late as 1990, when reforms were already taking a severe toll on Soviet power, military billboards continued to proclaim: "The main goal of perestroika is to strengthen military readiness!") That Gorbachev could credibly claim to be serving military goals testifies again to the impact of a hostile international environment. By showing that past policies had led nowhere, Western toughness altered the internal power balance of Soviet politics in favor of fundamental change....

In the first half of the 1980s, then, Western contentiousness provided the right backdrop for Soviet re-thinking. By contrast, the congeniality of the second half of the decade created a setting in which reforms steadily expanded and eventually became uncontrollable. The impact of this détente, it should be added, did not derive from its concrete achievements, which were rather meager. Soviet-American relations had never been so warm, but in contrast to the détente of the early 1970s few agreements were reached, there was no mutual acceptance of the status quo, and the idea of resolving disputes by splitting differences never took hold. In fact, Western demands tended, if anything, to escalate, and the criteria for believing perestroika to be "serious" grew stricter. In June 1987 Reagan, never having talked much about the Berlin wall, suddenly called on Gorbachev to tear it down. The West Germans, who had long since learned to live with East Germany, began to question the division of Europe. And in 1989, acceptance of East European revolution became the test Gorbachev had to pass to preserve good relations with the West. . . .

The détente of the late 1980s—marked by more or less annual declarations that the Cold War was now really, finally, conclusively, irreversibly over (such announcements have continued into the 1990s)—had highly uneven effects in East and West. Although Soviet spokesmen announced with malicious glee that the West was being robbed of the "enemy image" on which its anti-Soviet policies had allegedly been based, Soviet decisionmaking itself was far more thoroughly transformed. Struggle against the Western world, now off its head with admiration for Gorbachev, simply could no longer be an organizing principle of society. Similarly, Gorbachev's popularity in the West may have had less impact on Western policy than on his own vanity. Did "Gorbomania" encourage him to ignore the doubts of fellow Politburo members, taking risks with the stability of the Soviet system that a less flamboyant leader, his head not turned by global celebrity, would have instantly recognized as imprudent?

The hard international environment of the early 1980s obliged the Soviet leadership to consider change, but tough Western policies alone could not finish the job. Reagan, Thatcher, Bush, and the other Western leaders who dealt with Gorbachev had only limited leverage over him. What they did, in effect, was hand him a gun and suggest that he do the honorable thing. As is often true of such situations, the victim-to-be is more likely to accept the

For nearly thirty years, the Berlin Wall effectively divided East and West Germany while symbolically dividing Communist and democratic nations. The wall was dismantled in 1989.

advice if it is offered in the gentlest possible way and if he concludes that his friends, family, and colleagues will in the end think better of him for going through with it. For Soviet communism, the international environment of the late 1980s was a relaxed setting in which, after much anguished reflection, to turn the gun on itself.

DOCUMENT 4

Wade Huntley, "The United States Was the Loser in the Cold War" (1993)

Many analysts questioned whether American hard-line tactics could be credited with ending the cold war. In the following essay, Wade Huntley, professor of politics at Whitmore College, argues that American strategy played only a limited role in crippling the Soviet system. By pursuing hawkish policies, Huntley contends, the United States compromised its own ideals, failed to measure up to its own best traditions, and left itself a spiritually weaker nation.

Who Won the Cold War?

Who won the Cold War? The answer is not as obvious as public debate would make it seem. The question itself hides a deeper one: why did the Cold War end? this latter question is best addressed by reflecting briefly on why the Cold War began.

The Cold War emerged from the smoke and ashes of World War II, which left the United States and the Soviet Union as the two superpowers. Allies but never friends, tensions between the two countries soon congealed, the Iron Curtain fell, and the basic parameters of the next era of world politics were established.

Three features distinguished the Cold War from previous Great Power structures. First, the shift from a multipolar to a bipolar world centering on the U.S. and the U.S.S.R. altered the dynamics of great power behavior by hardening alliances and intensifying the rivalry. Secondly, the introduction of nuclear weapons focused the attention of the superpowers; in retrospect, the prospect of global nuclear war induced great caution by the leadership of both countries, perhaps also preventing a large-scale conventional war between them.

Finally, the U.S. and the U.S.S.R. were set apart not only by their competition for power, but by an unprecedented degree of ideological divisiveness. The two states differed on the most basic aspirations of the human experience and the political principles necessary to pursue them. It is this feature of the Cold War that is most crucial in explicating why and how the Cold War ended.

The importance of this ideological divergence was apparent to sensitive observers from the beginning. We need look no further than George F. Kennan, the Department of State official who in 1947 originated the idea of "containment" of the Soviet Union that became a touchstone of U.S. policy throughout the Cold War. Mr. Kennan stressed the importance of Communist ideology in anticipating Soviet behavior: because its principles were "of long-term validity," the U.S.S.R. could "afford to be patient." Thus, Mr. Kennan expected Soviet leaders, unlike Napoleon or Hitler before them, to be willing to yield in particular encounters, but to be less likely to be discouraged by such passing defeats. The contest would be decided not by a key victory at some juncture, but by endurance of will over time.

If the United States could muster such will and sustain it over the long run, ultimately it would prevail. The reason was not simply U.S. military superiority over the U.S.S.R., but differences in the organizing principles of the two societies—the very differences in ideology that formed the core of the Cold War rivalry. Though World War II was but a few years past, already Mr. Kennan perceived the Soviet Union, unlike the United States, to be a nation at war with itself. Communist power and authority had been purchased only, he wrote, "at a terrible cost in human life and human hopes and energies." The Soviet people were "physically and spiritually tired," at the limits of their endurance. Thus, he concluded, "Soviet power . . . bears within it the seeds of its own decay."

It is well to remember Mr. Kennan's foresight in considering current explanations of the demise of the Soviet Union. Many scholars, seemingly more concerned with anticipating future great power configurations, take the end of the Cold War itself for granted. Perhaps more importantly, little of what scholarly attention has been paid to this question has filtered into public forums. There are (at least) four possible explanations for the end of the Cold War, only two of which have found their way into mainstream discourse in the U.S.

The first explanation is that the collapse of Soviet power is directly attributable to the confrontational policies pursued by the Reagan and Bush Administrations. In other words, the Republicans won the Cold War. According to this story, the massive increases in defense spending and uncompromising stances toward the "evil empire" inaugurated in the early 1980s pressed the Soviet Union to the wall, beyond its material capacity to respond in kind.

The second popular explanation, mostly propounded by Democrats, is best termed the "me too" explanation. It holds that Presidents Reagan and Bush were not the first to confront the Soviets, and trots out hard-line rhetoric and policies from the Truman to Kennedy to Carter Administrations. Adherents of this view want to insure that history remembers that both parties' leaders had fine moments of hard-headed intransigence.

Lost in this feeding frenzy of credit-taking have been two other possible explanations. The first is that the hard-line postures adopted by the U.S. throughout the Cold War actually did more harm than good. This view, though normally associated in the popular media with out-of-touch liberals and pacifists, has received respectable scholarly attention. According to this view, had it not been for a tendency toward wild-eyed anti-communism on the American side, the Soviet Union may have collapsed under its own weight much sooner than it did. The stridence and belligerency emanating from Washington, from the 1950 adoption of "NSC-68" onward, had little effect but to strengthen comparable hard-line views in the Kremlin.

George Kennan himself endorsed this view in a *New York Times* opinion piece last year. According to Mr. Kennan, the "greatest damage" was done not by the military policies themselves, but by the tone of those policies, which produced a "braking effect on all liberalizing tendencies in the regime." As Mr. Kennan concludes, "For this, both Democrats and Republicans have a share of the blame."

A final explanation concerning the end of the Cold War is that the policies of the United States, in substance as well as tone, were not really all that important in the course of Soviet events. This idea has rarely surfaced in public discussion, nor has it received much scholarly attention apart from Soviet specialists who have long stressed the importance of the Soviet Union's own domestic politics.

Kennan himself suggests this point, remarking, "The suggestion that any Administration had the power to influence decisively the course of a tremendous domestic political upheaval in another great country on another side of the globe is simply childish."

From this viewpoint, the only role which the United States had was indirect, in the alternative it presented to communism merely by its existence. The success of American political institutions themselves, rather than the particular policies promulgated through them, set the standard the Soviet Union could not match.

Let us push the ramifications of this final hypothesis a bit further. If Soviet-style communism truly was consumed by the poverty of its own principles, independent of U.S. policies, how should those policies be judged? Perhaps it was not only belligerent rhetoric which was extraneous to the downfall of the U.S.S.R. The U.S. may have needlessly spent billions of dollars on high-technology weapons systems, and tragically sacrificed tens of thousands of American lives in faraway jungles. Perhaps, in setting out to break the back of Soviet Communism, the U.S. simply broke its own bank instead.

The cost of the Cold War to the United States may have been even steeper spiritually than materially. In 1947 Kennan singled out one standard above military prowess or economic muscle which the Cold War would test: "To avoid destruction the United States need only measure up to its own best traditions and prove itself worthy of preservation as a great nation."

Now, with the Cold War behind us, can it truly be said that we passed this test? The paranoid red-baiting of Joseph McCarthy, the cynicism of secret CIA-sponsored coups overturning elected regimes, the breached trust of Watergate, the duplicity of the Iran-Contra affair, all add up to a weighty and depressing litany of failures. Recent revelations that secret Bush Administration policies, rooted in Cold War logic, contributed to the buildup of Iraq simply add to this sorry score. Too often both leaders and the public were willing to compromise American principles and ideals (not to mention law) in the name of fighting communism.

The United States emerged from the Cold War burdened by debt and poverty, and carrying numerous scars from self-inflicted wounds to cherished institutions—all for the sake of the superpower competition. In forging itself into a hard-line Cold War warrior, the U.S. ultimately undermined its "best traditions" more than it measured up to them. Had its leaders and citizens demonstrated greater faith in the strength of the nation's founding principles, the U.S. might have emerged from the Cold War contest economically leaner, brighter of spirit, and with its democratic institutions and values far stronger. And, to the extent that its course also diminished the potency of the alternative it posed to Soviet totalitarianism, the U.S. might have emerged from the Cold War *sooner* as well.

Who, then, really won the Cold War? Not the Republicans, nor the Democrats. Considering what might have been, the United States was a loser in the Cold War, not its winner.

If this conclusion is valid, it suggests some crucial lessons for the future. The United States now shoulders a burden of world leadership perhaps unprecedented in its history. Realists are right in suggesting that, despite the most benign intentions, this new preeminence could generate more new enemies than friends. Minimizing this tendency requires reinforcing what has always been the most important American task in the world: to hold out, chiefly by its own example, a beacon illuminating the path to freedom.

To meet the added challenges of the new era, the United States has simply to follow the sage council of Polonius: above all, to thine own self be true. Should Americans fail to learn this, perhaps the deepest lesson of the Cold War's end, the U.S. may come to lose the post–Cold War as well.

DOCUMENT 5
Cynthia Enloe, "The Morning After" (1993)

Other commentators argued that the cold war arms race militarized American society and culture. In the following article from the left-wing magazine *The Progressive*, Cynthia Enloe, professor of government at Clark University, describes how cold war militarism rested on assumptions about masculinity and feminity. She argues that these notions have become deeply entrenched and that it will be harder to uproot them than it was to dismantle the Berlin Wall.

The regimes that were essential to perpetuating the Cold War had to convince their citizenries that the world was a dangerous place. Their citizens had to behave as if surrounded by imminent danger. Having internalized an acute sense of danger, citizens would be more likely to accept the heavy taxation and the underfunding of health, housing, and education that came with high military spending. Being persuaded that danger lurked, citizens would be more willing to leave secrecy unquestioned, to leave conscription and wiretapping unchallenged.

But of course women and men do not experience danger in identical ways. In most of the societies that were drawn into the Cold War, men were thought to be manly insofar as they did not shy away from danger and perhaps even flirted with it as they protected the nation's children and women. Women, on the other hand, were considered those most vulnerable to danger. Only a foolish woman, a woman who ignored the dictates of femininity, behaved as though she was not endangered, as though a man's protection was irrelevant. If she went out alone at night, if she hitchhiked or traveled far from home without a masculine shield, she deserved what she got.

Likewise, women could be persuaded to support their governments' efforts to organize against the Cold War threat. Any man was socialized in part by the women who would look to him to provide protection, to be the brave one.

Women tried to figure out whether being a good mother meant waving a tearful though proud goodbye to a son going off to do his military service or hiding him from the army's recruiters. Men tried to suppress fears of emasculation when denied public roles in their country's political life or else took a manly pride in being allowed into the inner sanctum of their state's national-security bureaucracy. American girls dressed their Barbies in the latest doll fashion, an Air Force dress uniform.

The Cold War could not have lasted four decades without such daily acts and decisions. It is best understood as involving not simply a contest between two superpowers, each trying to absorb as many countries as possible into its own orbit, but also as a series of contests within each of those societies over the definitions of masculinity and femininity that would sustain or dilute that rivalry....

Ever since the machine gun and aerial bombing revolutionized warfare, military establishments in the most advanced industrialized societies have needed more than foot soldiers and generals. They have also needed psychologists, cartographers, factory managers, engineers, and physicists. Are the forms of prescribed masculinity identical for an aerodynamics engineer and a bomber pilot? Has our fascination with the social construction of a Rambo or a "top gun" blinded us to the sorts of gender pressures experienced by those men and women employed in the industrial and scientific establishments on which militaries now depend? . . .

William Broad has reported on another civilian subculture of the masculinized military, the Lawrence Livermore National Laboratories in California. Livermore is the site of the most esoteric research for the Strategic Defense Initiative (SDI, or "Star Wars"). Broad is not a feminist. He is barely curious about varieties of masculinity; the women whose less dramatic labors or emotional validation sustain SDI research and political lobbying are left off his canvas. Yet he does provide us with an inside look at how these male scientists talk, dream, and joke.

Few of them are married or have girlfriends. Most of them seem to live at their computer terminals, except when they take breaks to drink Cokes or consume great quantities of ice cream. They don't appear to be particularly violent; they don't wear army surplus fatigues; they don't have rifles mounted on the backs of their pickup trucks. They have a penchant for boyish pranks. And they seem to thrive on competition and to see both the scientific world and the larger world as places where rivalry is the norm.

Their cherishing of competition is the ideological trait that makes them likely candidates for militarization. The older men who recruited these young scientists in the 1980s deliberately played upon their competitiveness to attract them to SDI weapons research. Still, they appear unlikely candidates for military basic training: They are too contemptuous of collective discipline, and their notions of action seem more cerebral than physical. And yet they clearly find deep reassurances of their own manhood in the militarized science they do. And Federal decision-makers who have imagined militarization to be the bedrock of American security need those ice cream-consuming pranksters to feel those reassurances.

Women's existence in military-industrial complexes is almost invisible. In an unusual testimony,

Jean Alonso, a Raytheon employee working on the company's famed Patriot missile, described the reality of gender on the factory floor of the American military industry. As a single mother in her early forties, she was pleased to have finally landed a "real" job. When the diplomatic process in the Persian Gulf was being aborted and a military confrontation seemed inevitable to Alonso and her workmates in Andover, Massachusetts, she noticed a gender gap developing.

"A kind of pre-game excitement seemed to be stirring among some of the men," she wrote in *The Women's Review of Books*. "The only organized attempt at opposition to the war came from our informal women's group."

This was a group that had come together to press the male leadership of the electrical workers' union to take sexual harassment seriously. The union local's membership was 47 per cent women, but women's concerns were pushed far down the agenda. Sexual harassment had been as integral to missile-making as was the collusion between the Pentagon and military contractors. Yet women had found it hard to get the issue of harassment on the bargaining table, and because the New England recession was jeopardizing jobs, no one wanted to rock the corporate boat.

At this juncture in the evolving political tension between men and women at Raytheon, the Persian Gulf war broke out, and the gender gap seemed to close again. The weapons that the workers were producing made the headlines. Women as well as men around Jean Alonso became excited, forgot talk of a women's committee in the union local, and took pride instead with being "on the map" as they began to imagine that their employment future was a little more secure. Within six months, however, Raytheon began laying off workers at its missile plant.

Even at the height of Cold War paranoia, militarism couldn't have survived without constant tending, coaxing, and manipulating. Today, as yesterday, militarism cannot be perpetuated merely by drawing on raw civilian masculinity; it has always required drill sergeants. Militarism couldn't rely on men from different countries to get along in allied armies simply because they shared masculinity; it required joint maneuvers and training courses, designed to translate diverse masculinities into standardized soldiering for the sake of an alliance. Militarism couldn't get along with just men's willingness to earn their manhood credentials by soldiering; it required women to accept particular assumptions about motherhood, marriage, and unskilled work. And if women began to question either the naturalness or the wisdom of such ideas, then militarism relied on public policies to limit women's ability to act on their skepticism. . . .

The Cold War never was free of internal tensions and contradictions. Without deliberate decisions by policy-makers—some made so quietly and so far down the chain of accountability that most citizens didn't even realize they were official decisions—the peculiar relations between women and men necessary to perpetuate the Cold War might have crumbled long before 1989.

Only by digging deep into the bureaucratic archives, opening file drawers far below those holding the treaties and military budgets, can one bring these decisions—and thus the fragility of the Cold War's workings—to light. Only by looking closely at the minutiae of ordinary people's lives wherever the Cold War's brand of militarism prevailed can one explain why it began, why it didn't end earlier, and why it is so hard to terminate now. . . .

Any postwar time is fraught with questions. These post-Cold War years are no different. The first always is: What has changed? Since 1989, a lot. Any schoolchild could make a list. But a lot has not changed, and it is not at all clear what needs to be put on that list.

It remains unclear, for example, whether the end of the superpower rivalry and the collapse of communist-led regimes in Eastern Europe have so reduced the appeal of militarism that the very concept of manliness has been transformed. Have the changes witnessed in Eastern Europe, the Persian Gulf, Central America, Southeast Asia, and Southern Africa demilitarized masculinity?

If so, a principal ingredient of patriarchal culture will have been eliminated. If so, women will relate to men differently, and the state will expect new attitudes from both. If so, the state itself and international diplomacy between states won't look the same. If the Cold War is really over and the militarism it depended upon is truly on the wane, then those endings should be showing up in the politics of femininity and masculinity.

The morning after is always an ambiguous moment. What just happened? Who benefited? It is not always crystal-clear that today, the day growing out of the morning after, is a fresh, new day.

In fact, the present morning, after the formal ending of the superpower rivalry, doesn't yet look like the dawning of a brand-new day in the ongoing evolution of sexual politics. We are still living in a time when grand politics and the politics of everyday life continue to be defined in large part by the anxieties and aspirations of the Cold War. This continuity is especially evident in the reluctance of governments and of many ordinary citizens to make their militaries less central to their gendered notions of security and even identity.

We are living in a new postwar period without having resolved the questions of earlier postwar periods. It is the entire patriarchal structure of privilege and control that must be dismantled if societies are to be rid, once and for all, of militarism.

This message may be difficult for many women and men to hear in the wake of the collapse of the second superpower and the consequent reduction in tensions between nuclear-armed alliances.

Isn't the Cold War's final curtain enough to warrant a sense of relief and accomplishment?

No, unfortunately. As long as patriarchal assumptions about masculinity and femininity shape people's beliefs and identities and their relationships with one another, militarization—however temporarily stanched—lies dormant, capable of rising again, and yet again.

DOCUMENT 6

The New York Times, "The Workplace, After the Deluge" (1993)

With the end of the cold war, the Pentagon began cutting back defense expenditures and canceling production of some weapons. Companies that relied upon defense contracts for their business, such as General Electric, initiated "downsizing," closing some plants and reducing their labor force at others. The following article describes the changes at the General Electric plant in Lynn, Massachusetts, and profiles how some G.E. employees adapted to those changes.

This is the city where the General Electric Company was born a century ago. But its factories this Labor Day invite suspicions that the company might not be here much longer. Weeds grow in the fissured asphalt of the plants G.E. has closed around town, and most gates to the ones that remain open are chained shut because the gatekeepers have been dismissed. At G.E.'s main site here, the green stuff bordering the visitors' parking lot is not grass but a low-maintenance plastic coated with grit.

G.E.-Lynn has been reduced to a single business, making engines for small jet aircraft, and the work force here has been halved since the mid–1980's, to 6,200, with more cuts to come soon.

But within the somber old walls of the plants, a decade of upheaval is producing an extraordinary transformation. Here, as at much of G.E. and for that matter in much of American industry, the ways people work and the tone of the workplace have been altered by the brutally competitive environment—the recessions of the past decade, the drift of jobs abroad and social changes like the surge of working women. People are working smarter, harder, more flexibly and more cooperatively—and they're working scared.

Take working smarter. Here, as in Detroit and Buffalo, Cleveland and Scranton, Henry Ford's dumbed-down assembly line is fading fast; employees are being freed to use their heads.

Peter J. Baglioni, 53, is an example. For years an ever-more-bored operator of ever-more-automated lathes, he is the newly trained master of many machines. He can make aircraft engine parts from start to finish.

Then there's Laura A. Kozol, who has built bridges between the engineers who design the products and the machine operators who make them.

Here too, as at many "downsized" and "delayered" companies, the nonunion salaried staff has shrunk even more than the unionized blue-collar force. In some of G.E.-Lynn's plants, chains of command have collapsed to a single link between the plant manager and the worker. Operations managers like Joseph D. Reece have been routed from carpeted offices and stuffed into cubicles in cinderblock bunkers in the middle of the production floors. In the parts of G.E.-Lynn where foremen remain, they lead and coach the troops; they no longer command or discipline them.

Women, while still less than 10 percent of the work force here, are changing the culture. Catherine Lyons, 35, has broken a glass ceiling, having become a plant manager overseeing nearly 100 workers in a multiskilled shop like Mr. Baglioni's. Natalie Henry, a 23-year-old engineer a year out of the Massachusetts Institute of Technology, supervises 36 workers, most at least twice her age. Standing at her cramped booth, her knapsack on the chair because there's no time to sit, she hands out work assignments with offers of cookies. Men, her boss says, return the favor, bringing cookies to her.

The culture is changing, too. The old pinups of scantily clad women are out. Ms. Kozol, a design engineer, came across one once. "I said, 'Whose is this?'" she said. "'whoever's it is better take it down.' He did, right away."

Like the pinup, the old shield of authority, the necktie, has gone. The head of G.E.'s operations in Lynn, Timothy J. Noonan, puts his on only for trips out of town. Hourly workers can now park inside the factory gates, once the privilege of salaried workers. G.E.'s new I.D. tags carry first names in big black type and last names in agate.

Perhaps the most striking change is in labor relations. Seven years ago, workers here stormed out in a six-week "strike for respect," in part over a foreman's alleged swipe at [a] worker. Local 201 of the International Union of Electrical Workers, G.E.'s principal union, once routinely rejected the national wage agreements the parent union had negotiated with company headquarters, mostly for the fun of the fight.

Today Local 201, aroused by the continued disappearance of jobs, has mellowed. To let Mr. Baglioni take his new assignment, it agreed to set aside the rigid job classifications that restricted a worker to a single task, like running a milling machine.

"We have lowered our rhetoric," said Jeff Crosby, president of the local. "We can't afford the luxury of hot air."

Management is mellower, too. "Once it was, 'Do it my way, no arguments,'" said Randy Yetts, 54, who overhauls broken machines with three other men. This year, for the first time, they are working without a foreman and deciding for themselves how to schedule and perform their chores. "Now we have little meetings with management," he said, "and they listen to our ideas." Charles Ruiter, Local 201's business agent, said grievances have collapsed from 300 a year in the mid-1980's to 30 or so now.

There's a somber side to all these changes, however. In reducing its work force to survive and compete, G.E. must honor a seniority system that puts the youngest and newest workers on the street first. As a result, the women and minority workers who began landing unionized production jobs here in the late 1970's are losing them now. Walter J. Vick, a black benchworker, figures he will be laid off any day; the company has eliminated the training program that might have led to a better job that might have insulated him.

What remains is a blue-collar work force once again composed almost entirely of white men, most over 40. And with little probability of a significant expansion of jobs even if production of jet engines improves, women, blacks and anyone finishing high school in Lynn these days could wait a decade or more before retirements begin making room at what is still the city's biggest employer.

And while the changes seem to be improving quality and productivity at the plant, workers worry that however more skilled and efficient they become, the deck is still stacked against them.

Lynn has been looking vulnerable because of the cuts in Pentagon spending and the losses that are choking the airlines. From its headquarters in Fairfield, Conn., General Electric sells or buries ailing businesses and moves others around like ships, to wherever production is cheapest. How long will it be, wonders Wayne Starratt, a multiskilled machinist who earns about $16 an hour, before G.E. decides that Mexican workers who are paid $5 a day can learn the skills and do his work?

Hardly anyone here has not been touched by the upheaval in the workplace or had something to do with bringing it on. The experiences of the following . . . workers illustrate the changes sweeping American manufacturing.

One more step and Joseph D. Reece would have been the plant manager. Now 40, he started as a machinist at G.E. and, after earning a degree in manufacturing engineering, ascended in the hierarchy. He reached the level of operations manager of G.E.'s ill-fated factory of the future, with 11 people and more than 20 lathes reporting to him.

But Mr. Reece was swept into the "delayering"

strategy of the corporate reorganization imposed by G.E.'s chairman, John F. Welch Jr. Today, all the rungs between machinist and plant manager have been removed. Mr. Reece is called the production leader of Plant 3.

It is a senior staff job overseeing procurement, production control, shipping and supplies. He says he has kept his salary, but no one reports to him. Everyone, including the sole clerk who works with him, reports to the plant manager, Jerry Labadini.

Rather than supervise the shipping crew now, for example, he advises it. "We break the schedule down for the guys," he said. "We say, 'Here's what's on the book for next week.' From that point on, the guys manage the shipping." And if Peter Baglioni's team feels a need to bypass Mr. Reece to procure some forgings, he said, "It's fine by me. We've never been burned."

He said he has put the pecking order behind him. "You have to look at the big picture," he said. "You can drive yourself crazy if you get hung up on 'Where am I in the organization chart?' and 'Who's reporting to me?' The only reason for managers is to give directions and orders. You don't need that anymore."

Mr. Reece now works at a desk inside a crowded cinderblock structure in the middle of the production floor. In his last job, he had a corner office on the second floor of the plant and an adjacent conference room. Except for Mr. Labadini, and his secretary, Joan Lattanzio, the floor today presents an eerie gray vista of vacant offices and cubicles with unattended computer terminals.

It was harder, Mr. Reece said, to lose another emblem of authority. "I stopped wearing a necktie in January 1992," he said. "That was tough." He had been wearing neckties since his days in Roman Catholic schools. "I got real comfortable with a necktie on," he said. But shedding the tie, like the office, has helped production by bringing the staff closer to the real work of the plant. "We were just isolated from each other," he said.

G.E.-Lynn had a crusty old practice that often delayed the introduction of new products and processes: Engineers who drew the designs for engine parts did not talk to the workers who had to read the designs to make the parts. Laura A. Kozol, 27, is fixing that.

Ms. Kozol, one of the few workers here whose speech is untouched by the broad a's of eastern Massachusetts, grew up in Ohio and got her B.S. at Ohio State. After she joined G.E., the company sent her to the Massachusetts Institute of Technology for a master's in design engineering.

Ms. Kozol seems very rushed. Her walk is a run. She has a cubicle on the now partly vacant second floor of Building 69 but is rarely there. She is often downstairs, where there's a conventional production shop, a machine overhaul shop, an engine reworking shop and a cell of multiskilled workers who develop processes to pass on to other plants.

"I used to sit in a different building and have meetings with these management and manufacturing guys," Ms. Kozol said. "We would go over the introduction of a part or problems with a part, but we never talked about it with the people in the shop."

She would hear that the workers in Building 69 had difficulty adapting her designs to their machines. "I used to get mad at them," she said, "making these mistakes, requiring me to fix what were their problems."

Then she started coming over to Building 69. "Last summer, I came over full time," she said. "I can talk to the guys actually making the parts. That lets me see what they have to do to meet my requirements." Right on the spot now, she can fix a glitch in a design, rather than tie people up in meetings, paperwork and delay.

Unilaterally, said William A. Fitzgerald, the 32-year-old manager of the building, Ms. Kozol has introduced the concept of concurrent engineering to G.E.-Lynn. "She's the major driver behind concurrent engineering—the designer-in-the-shop—in all the Lynn plants," he said.

Walter J. Vick, 35, went to an agricultural high school with the thought of becoming a veterinarian. Now he is a $14.45-an-hour bench hand on Building 74's huge production floor, and he is trapped.

In Building 74, cells of multiskilled workers have yet to displace the old manufacturing systems. But here, too, much has changed. The chain of command has been truncated, and Mr. Vick says the old climate of us-versus-them has nearly evaporated.

As a bench hand, Mr. Vick sits at a small counter removing burrs form machine-cut engine parts and subassemblies. He has been doing it for five years. "I've just gotten bored," he said. "The mind goes numb some days, just deburring. But there aren't any jobs to advance yourself."

In better times, G.E. would post openings for jobs to which people like Mr. Vick could aspire. But with the work force shrinking, better jobs rarely crop up. G.E. also once ran a three-year program to train workers for better jobs. But the company has abandoned it because it could not find jobs for the graduates.

The only option now is assignment to a "multi-skilling" class and joining a cell like Peter Baglioni's. But as a bench hand, Mr. Vick lacks skill in machining, so he is ineligible. Instead, he faces the one thing he fears more than the tedium of benchwork—a layoff.

The company uses a process it calls "peer pairing" to identify salaried workers for layoff. Managers compare workers with similar jobs and shed those who compare least favorably. But under agreement with the union, the company dismisses hourly workers according to their seniority—last hired, first hired.

Mr. Vick, like all production workers a member of Local 201 of the International Union of Electrical Workers, started out at G.E.-Lynn in 1979. He is black, and the affirmative action programs of the late 1970's helped open the job market for him. But the years of layoffs at G.E. have eliminated nearly all semiskilled workers hired since 1979. "Another big cut comes through here," he said, "and I'm right on the line to go."

Study Questions

1. In what ways did the 1980s mark a return to the Cold War climate of the 1950s?

2. Is congressional oversight of foreign policy necessary? How does a democratic society best formulate a consistent foreign policy without compromising democratic principles?

3. To what extent was Reagan's strategy of seeking peace through strength responsible for the internal collapse of Soviet communism?

4. Did the United States win the Cold War?

16

Toward Postindustrial Society

Since the 1970s the United States has been undergoing a transition from an industrial to a postindustrial society, from a society based on manufacturing to one based on services. Several trends, such as the switch from producing goods to providing services, an increase in specialization and organization, a higher premium on human capital, expansion of higher education, and exponential growth in government expenditures, signal this socioeconomic transformation.

Postindustrial society has brought unprecedented benefits—greater accessibility to low-cost goods, improved health care, higher living standards, and improved communications. Despite the liberating possibilities of post-industrial development, the new economic order poses formidable challenges. At the end of the twentieth century, Americans confront a society in which the disparity in the distribution of incomes continues to widen, the restructuring of the labor force toward part-time, low-wage work is accelerating, environmental risks are increasing, and the social and cultural isolation of inner cities is intensifying.

One central feature of the postindustrial economy has been the decline of America's core corporations. The American economy of the mid-twentieth century, founded on high-volume production, has been eclipsed by one based on high-value enterprises. To remain competitive, the successful enterprise provides services rather than products. Firms offer specialized research and engineering services for solving problems, specialized marketing and consulting services needed to identify problems, and specialized financial and management services required to broker such problems. To meet these needs, corporations shift their employees from production to services. In 1990, for example, IBM classified fewer than 20,000 of its 400,000 employees as production workers engaged in traditional manufacturing. Most are involved in some sort of service such as research, engineering, sales, or customer support.

This shift to service employment does not mean that more people work in high-profile, higher-paid, glamorous professions like law, medicine, and finance. Services include low-paying, deskilled jobs such as retail, catering, and fast-food outlet work. Such employment rarely commands more than the minimum wage, is often only part-time, and does not offer benefits like medical or life insurance. According to political economist Robert Reich, who later became President Bill Clinton's Labor Secretary, this restructuring of the work force is a major cause of the widening gap between America's richest and poorest citizens (Document 1).

These trends in the labor force along with reports of the earth's environmental fragility prompted many commentators to demand that corporations become more socially and environmentally responsible. In order to achieve a sustainable future free of environmental degradation and social disintegration, forecasters advised corporations to reorient their firms away from strict profit maximizing and toward reducing consumption of natural resources and providing secure, stable, and meaningful employment (Document 2). Critics rejected such visions as impractical, arguing that business serves society best by doing its job well (Document 3).

Income disparities between rich and poor manifested themselves in spatial segregation. In the new, global, postindustrial economy geared toward communication and information, edge communities like Orange County, California, emerged as the communities of the future. Inner cities, relics of the days of high-volume industrial production, continued to decline. The concentration of poverty among their largely minority and immigrant residents intensified, and crime rates skyrocketed. Some analysts blamed the social welfare policies of the 1960s as the root cause of persistent urban poverty (Document 4). Others objected to such conclusions, insisting that impoverished ghettoes are the byproduct of a spatial restructuring of American cities brought on by deindustrialization (Document 5).

Inner-city residents were not the only people struggling at or below the poverty line. The computer revolution spawned a new class of laboring poor composed of those working as data entry clerks and telephone service representatives. Many companies reduced their labor force by firing full-time employees and rehiring them on a part-time, contract basis with no benefits. Although this arrangement saves employers millions annually in labor costs, it raises disturbing questions about the long-term consequences and social costs of such policies (Document 6).

DOCUMENT 1

Robert Reich, The Work of Nations *(1991)*

Robert Reich is an astute analyst of America's postindustrial economy. A political economist at Harvard University before becoming Labor Secretary under President Bill Clinton in 1993, Reich wrote widely on the globalization of the American economy and resulting changes in the nation's labor force. In the following excerpt, Reich attributes the growing gap in American incomes to changes in the quality of jobs available in the new global economy.

Data on the distribution of American incomes are not free from controversy. Like any data, they can be interpreted in slightly different ways, depending on the weights accorded a host of other changes that have occurred simultaneously, and also depending on which years are selected for measurement and how the measurements are done. But nearly everyone agrees that the trend, at least since the mid-1970s, has been toward inequality.

Controlling for family size, geography, and other changes, the best estimate . . . is that between 1977 and 1990 the average income of the poorest fifth of Americans declined by about 5 percent, while the richest fifth became about 9 percent wealthier. During these years, the average incomes of the poorest fifth of American *families* declined by about 7 percent, while the average income of the richest fifth of American families increased about 15 percent. That left the poorest fifth of Americans by 1990 with 3.7 percent of the nation's total income, down from 5.5 percent twenty years before—the lowest portion they have received since 1954. And it left the richest fifth with a bit over half of the nation's income—the highest portion ever recorded by the top 20 percent. The top 5 percent commanded 26 percent of the nation's total income, another record.

Picture a symmetrical wave that's highest in the middle and then gradually slopes down and out on both ends until merging with the horizon. Through the 1950s and 1960s, the distribution of income in the United States was coming to resemble just this sort of a wave. Most Americans were bunching up in the middle of the wave, enjoying medium incomes. Fewer Americans were on the sides, either very poor or very rich. Only a tiny minority were at the outermost edges, extremely poor or extremely rich. But beginning in the mid-1970s, and accelerating sharply in the 1980s, the crest of the wave began to move toward the poorer end. More Americans were poor. The middle began to sag, as the portion of middle-income Americans dropped. And the end representing the richest Americans began to elongate, as the rich became much, much richer.

The trend should not be overstated. Some researchers, selecting different years and using different measurements, have found the divergence to be somewhat less pronounced. But overall, the trend is unmistakable. There is good reason to suspect that it is not a temporary aberration, and that the gap will, if anything, grow wider. . . .

Even taken together, the conventional explanations for the widening gap between rich and poor account for only part of the answer. Interestingly, several other advanced economies—with different tax and welfare policies than the United States, and different demographic swings—have experienced a similar shift toward inequality. That the gap widened noticeably in Margaret Thatcher's Britain is perhaps no surprise, but even the benevolent social-democratic Netherlands has not been immune to the trend. A wide divergence between the incomes of a few at the top and almost everyone else has long been a seemingly immutable feature of life in many underdeveloped economies, of course, but the trend there has a new feature: Today's Third World elites are less likely to be descended from generations of wealthy landholders, more likely to have gained their wealth from the jobs they do. After the land redistribution of the 1950s, for example, Taiwan became one of the world's most egalitarian societies. But, while income is still more evenly distributed there than in most developing nations, the gap between rich and poor widened considerably during the 1980s. The streets of Taipei are now clogged with Mercedes-Benzes, Volvos, and Jaguars, as well as rickety bicycles.

One important clue: The growth in inequality within the United States (as well as in many other nations) has been dramatic even among people who already hold jobs. Recall that through most of the postwar era, at least until the mid-1970s, the wages of Americans at different income levels rose at about the same pace—roughly 2.5 to 3 percent a year. Meanwhile, the wage gap between workers at the top and those at the bottom steadily narrowed—in part, because of the benign influence of America's core corporations and labor unions in raising the bottom and constraining the top.

In those days, poverty was a consequence of not having a job. The major postwar economic challenge was to create enough jobs for all Americans able to work. Full employment was the battle cry of

American liberals, arrayed against conservatives who worried about the inflationary tendencies of a full-employment economy.

Unemployment is now less of a problem, however. In the 1970s and 1980s, over 25 million new jobs were created in the United States, 18.2 million of them in the 1980s alone. There is often a mismatch between where the jobs are and where the people are, of course. Many suburban fast-food jobs go unfilled while inner-city kids cannot easily commute to them. And the Federal Reserve Board periodically cools the economy in an effort to fight inflation, thus drafting into the inflation fight many thousands of those Americans who can least afford it. But these impediments notwithstanding, the truth is that by the last decade of the twentieth century, almost all Americans who wanted to work could find a job. And because population growth has been slowing . . . the demand for people to fill jobs is likely to be higher still in years to come. State governors and city mayors continue to worry every time a factory closes and to congratulate themselves every time they lure new jobs to their jurisdictions. Yet the more important issue over the longer term is the *quality* of jobs, not the number.

By the 1990s, many jobs failed to provide a living wage. More than half of the 32.5 million Americans whose incomes fell under the official poverty line—and nearly two-thirds of all poor children—lived in households with at least one worker. This is a much higher rate of working poor than at any other time in the postwar era. The number of impoverished working Americans climbed by nearly 2 million, or 23 percent, between 1978 and 1987 (years at similar points in the business cycle). Among full-time, year-round workers, the number who were poor climbed even more sharply—by 43 percent. In fact, two-parent families with a full-time worker fell further below the poverty line, on average, than any other type of family, including single parents on welfare.

The wage gap has been widening even within the core American corporation (or, more precisely, that portion of the global web that is formally owned and managed by Americans). By 1990, the average hourly earnings of American non-supervisory workers within American-owned corporations, adjusted for inflation, were lower than in any year since 1965. Middle-level managers fared somewhat better, although their median earnings (adjusted for inflation) were only slightly above the levels of the 1970s.

But between 1977 and 1990, top executives of American-owned corporations reaped a bonanza. Their average remuneration rose by 220 percent, or about 12 percent a year, compounded. (This is aside from the standard perquisites of company car, company plane, country club membership, estate planning, physical examinations, and so forth.) . . .

Regardless of how your job is officially classified (manufacturing, service, managerial, technical, secretarial, and so on), or the industry in which you work (automotive, steel, computer, advertising, finance, food processing), your real competitive position in the world economy is coming to depend on the function you perform in it. Herein lies the basic reason why incomes are diverging. The fortunes of routine producers are declining. In-person servers are also becoming poorer, although their fates are less clear-cut. But symbolic analysts—who solve, identify, and broker new problems—are, by and large, succeeding in the world economy.

All Americans used to be in roughly the same economic boat. Most rose or fell together, as the corporations in which they were employed, the industries comprising such corporations, and the national economy as a whole became more productive—or languished. But national borders no longer define our economic fates. We are now in different boats, one sinking rapidly, one sinking more slowly, and the third rising steadily.

The boat containing routine producers is sinking rapidly. Recall that by midcentury routine production workers in the United States were paid relatively well. The giant pyramidlike organizations at the core of each major industry coordinated their prices and investments—avoiding the harsh winds of competition and thus maintaining healthy earnings. Some of these earnings, in turn, were reinvested in new plant and equipment (yielding ever-larger-scale economies); another portion went to top managers and investors. But a large and increasing portion went to middle managers and production workers. Work stoppages posed such a threat to high-volume production that organized labor was able to exact an ever-larger premium for its cooperation. And the pattern of wages established within the core corporations influenced the pattern throughout the national economy. Thus the growth of a relatively affluent middle class, able to purchase all the wondrous things produced in high volume by the core corporations.

But, as has been observed, the core is rapidly breaking down into global webs which earn their largest profits from clever problem-solving, -identifying, and brokering. As the costs of transporting standard things and of communicating information about them continue to drop, profit margins on high-volume, standardized production are thinning, because there are few barriers to entry. Modern factories and state-of-the-art machinery can be installed almost anywhere on the globe. Routine producers in the United States, then, are in direct competition with millions of routine producers in other nations. Twelve thousand people are added to the world's population every hour, most of whom, eventually, will happily work for a small fraction of the wages of routine producers in America.

The consequence is clearest in older, heavy industries, where high-volume, standardized production continues its ineluctable move to where labor is cheapest and most accessible around the world. Thus, for example, the Maquiladora [assembly] factories cluttered along the Mexican side of the U.S. border in the sprawling shanty towns of Tijuana, Mexicali, Nogales, Agua Prieta, and Ciudad Juárez— factories owned mostly by Americans, but increasingly by Japanese—in which more than a half million routine producers assemble parts into finished goods to be shipped into the United States....

The second of the three boats, carrying in-person servers, is sinking as well, but somewhat more slowly and unevenly. Most in-person servers are paid at or just slightly above the minimum wage and many work only part-time, with the result that their take-home pay is modest, to say the least. Nor do they typically receive all the benefits (health care, life insurance, disability, and so forth) garnered by routine producers in large manufacturing corporations or by symbolic analysts affiliated with the more affluent threads of global webs. In-person servers are sheltered from the direct effects of global competition and, like everyone else, benefit from access to lower-cost products from around the world. But they are not immune to its indirect effects.

For one thing, in-person servers increasingly compete with former routine production workers, who, no longer able to find well-paying routine production jobs, have few alternatives but to seek in-person service jobs. The Bureau of Labor Statistics estimates that of the 2.8 million manufacturing workers who lost their jobs during the early 1980s, fully one-third were rehired in service jobs paying at least 20 percent less. In-person servers must also compete with high school graduates and dropouts who years before had moved easily into routine production jobs but no longer can. And if demographic predictions about the American work force in the first decades of the twenty-first century are correct (and they are likely to be, since most of the people who will comprise the work force are already identifiable), most new entrants into the job market will be black or Hispanic men, or women—groups that in years past have possessed relatively weak technical skills. This will result in an even larger number of people crowding into in-person services. Finally, in-person servers will be competing with growing numbers of immigrants, both legal and illegal, for whom in-person services will comprise the most accessible jobs. (It is estimated that between the mid-1980s and the end of the century, about a quarter of all workers entering the American labor force will be immigrants.) ...

In two respects, demographics will work in favor of in-person servers, buoying their collective boat slightly. First, as has been noted, the rate of growth of the American work force is slowing. In particular, the number of younger workers is shrinking. Between 1985 and 1995, the number of eighteen- to twenty-four-year-olds will have declined by 17.5 percent. Thus, employers will have more incentive to hire and train in-person servers whom they might previously have avoided. But this demographic relief

As the wage gap in America increases, competition for unskilled and semiskilled positions has also increased—as illustrated by this line of job applicants in Chicago.

from the competitive pressures will be only temporary. The cumulative procreative energies of the postwar baby-boomers (born between 1946 and 1964) will result in a new surge of workers by 2010 or thereabouts. And immigration—both legal and illegal—shows every sign of increasing in years to come.

Next, by the second decade of the twenty-first century, the number of Americans aged sixty-five and over will be rising precipitously, as the baby-boomers reach retirement age and live longer. Their life expectancies will lengthen not just because fewer of them will have smoked their way to their graves and more will have eaten better than their parents, but also because they will receive all sorts of expensive drugs and therapies designed to keep them alive—barely. By 2035, twice as many Americans will be elderly as in 1988, and the number of octogenarians is expected to triple. As these decaying baby-boomers ingest all the chemicals and receive all the treatments, they will need a great deal of personal attention. Millions of deteriorating bodies will require nurses, nursing-home operators, hospital administrators, orderlies, home-care providers, hospice aides, and technicians to operate and maintain all the expensive machinery that will monitor and temporarily stave off final disintegration. There might even be a booming market for euthanasia specialists. In-person servers catering to the old and ailing will be in strong demand. . . .

Unlike the boats of routine producers and in-person servers, however, the vessel containing

America's symbolic analysts is rising. Worldwide demand for their insights is growing as the ease and speed of communicating them steadily increases. Not every symbolic analyst is rising as quickly or as dramatically as every other, of course; symbolic analysts at the low end are barely holding their own in the world economy. But symbolic analysts at the top are in such great demand worldwide that they have difficulty keeping track of all their earnings. Never before in history has opulence on such a scale been gained by people who have earned it, and done so legally.

Among symbolic analysts in the middle range are American scientists and researchers who are busily selling their discoveries to global enterprise webs. They are not limited to American customers. If the strategic brokers in General Motors' headquarters refuse to pay a high price for a new means of making high-strength ceramic engines dreamed up by a team of engineers affiliated with Carnegie-Mellon University in Pittsburgh, the strategic brokers of Honda or Mercedes-Benz are likely to be more than willing.

So, too, with the insights of America's ubiquitous management consultants, which are being sold for large sums to eager entrepreneurs in Europe and Latin America. Also, the insights of America's energy consultants, sold for even larger sums to Arab sheikhs. American design engineers are providing insights to Olivetti, Mazda, Siemens, and other global webs; American marketers, techniques for learning what worldwide consumers will buy; American advertisers, ploys for ensuring that they actually do. American architects are issuing designs and blueprints for opera houses, art galleries, museums, luxury hotels, and residential complexes in the world's major cities; American commercial property developers, marketing these properties to worldwide investors and purchasers....

Almost everyone around the world is buying the skills and insights of Americans who manipulate oral and visual symbols—musicians, sound engineers, film producers, makeup artists, directors, cinematographers, actors and actresses, boxers, scriptwriters, songwriters, and set designers. Among the wealthiest of symbolic analysts are Steven Spielberg, Bill Cosby, Charles Schultz, Eddie Murphy, Sylvester Stallone, Madonna, and other star directors and performers—who are almost as well known on the streets of Dresden and Tokyo as in the Back Bay of Boston. Less well rewarded but no less renowned are the unctuous anchors on Turner Broadcasting's Cable News, who appear daily, via satellite, in places ranging from Vietnam to Nigeria. Vanna White is the world's most watched game-show hostess. Behind each of these familiar faces is a collection of American problem-solvers, -identifiers, and brokers who train, coach, advise, promote, amplify, direct, groom, represent, and otherwise add value to their talents.

DOCUMENT 2

Paul Hawken, "A Declaration of Sustainability" (1993)

Concern about the fragility of the earth's environment inspired some analysts to question the assumption that the business of business is business. One such commentator is Paul Hawken, author of several books about the relationship between commerce and the environment. In the following article, Hawken advocates a new business ethic that stresses the necessity of confronting the social and environmental problems afflicting the earth's population.

❧ ❧

I recently performed a social audit for Ben and Jerry's Homemade Inc., America's premier socially responsible company. After poking and prodding around, asking tough questions, trying to provoke debate, and generally making a nuisance of myself, I can attest that their status as the leading social pioneer in commerce is safe for at least another year. They are an outstanding company. Are there flaws? Of course. Welcome to planet Earth. But the people at Ben & Jerry's are relaxed and unflinching in their willingness to look at, discuss, and deal with problems.

In the meantime, the company continues to put ice cream shops in Harlem, pay outstanding benefits, keep a compensation ratio of seven to one from the top of the organization to the bottom, seek out vendors from disadvantaged groups, and donate generous scoops of their profits to others. And they are about toe overtake their historic rival Häagen-Dazs, the ersatz Scandinavian originator of super-premium ice cream, as the market leader in their category. At present rates of growth, Ben & Jerry's will be a $1 billion company by the end of the century. They are publicly held, nationally recognized, and rapidly growing, in part because Ben wanted to show that a socially responsible company could make it in the normal world of business.

Ben and Jerry's is just one of a growing vanguard of companies attempting to redefine their social and ethical responsibilities. These companies no longer accept the maxim that the business of business is business. Their premise is simple: Corporations, because they are the dominant institution on the planet, must squarely face the social and environmental problems that afflict humankind. Organizations such as Business for Social Responsibility and the Social Venture Network, corporate "ethics" consultants, magazines such as *In Business* and *Business Ethics*, non-profits including the Council on Economic Priorities, investment funds such as Calvert and Covenant, newsletters like *Greenmoney*, and thousands of unaffiliated companies are drawing up new codes of conduct for corporate life that integrate social, ethical, and environmental principles.

Ben and Jerry's and the roughly 2,000 other committed companies in the social responsibility movement here and abroad have combined annual sales of approximately $2 billion, or one-hundredth of 1 percent of the $20 trillion sales garnered by the estimated 80 million to 100 million enterprises worldwide. The problems they are trying to address are vast and unremittingly complex: 5.5 billion people are breeding exponentially, and fulfilling their wants and needs is stripping the earth of its biotic capacity to produce life; a climactic burst of consumption by a single species is overwhelming the skies, earth, waters, and fauna.

As the Worldwatch Institute's Lester Brown patiently explains in his annual survey, *State of the World*, every living system on earth is in decline. Making matters worse, we are having a once-in-a-billion-year blowout sale of hydrocarbons, which are being combusted into the atmosphere, effectively double glazing the planet within the next 50 years with unknown climatic results. The cornucopia of resources that are being extracted, mined, and harvested is so poorly distributed that 20 percent of the earth's people are chronically hungry or starving, while the top 20 percent of the population, largely in the north, control and consume 80 percent of the world's wealth. Since business in its myriad forms is primarily responsible for this "taking," it is appropriate that a growing number of companies ask the question, How does one honorably conduct business in the latter days of industrialism and the beginning of an ecological age? The ethical dilemma that confronts business begins with the acknowledgment that a commercial system that functions well by its own definitions unavoidably defies the greater and more profound ethic of biology. Specifically, how does business face the prospect that creating a profitable, growing company requires an intolerable abuse of the natural world?

Despite their dedicated good work, if we examine all or any of the businesses that deservedly earn high marks for social and environmental responsibility, we are faced with a sobering irony: If every company on the planet were to adopt the environmental and social practices of the best companies—of, say, the Body Shop, Patagonia, and Ben and Jerry's—the world would still be moving toward environmental degradation and collapse. In other words, if we analyze environmental effects and create an input-output model of resources and energy, the results do not even approximate a tolerable or sustainable future. If a tiny fraction of the world's most intelligent companies cannot model a sustainable world, then that tells us that being socially responsible is only one part of an overall solution, and that what we have is not a management problem but a design problem.

At present, there is a contradiction inherent in the premise of a socially responsible corporation: to wit, that a company can make the world better, can grow, and can increase profits by meeting social and environmental needs. It is a have-your-cake-and-eat-it fantasy that cannot come true if the primary cause of environmental degradation is overconsumption. Although proponents of socially responsible business are making an outstanding effort at reforming the tired old ethics of commerce, they are unintentionally creating a new rationale for companies to produce, advertise, expand, grow, capitalize, and use up resources: the rationale that they are doing good. A jet flying across the country, a car rented at an airport, an air-conditioned hotel room, a truck full of goods, a worker commuting to his or her job—all cause the same amount of environmental degradation whether they're associated with the Body Shop, the Environmental Defense Fund, or R. J. Reynolds.

In order to approximate a sustainable society, we need to describe a system of commerce and production in which each and every act is inherently sustainable and restorative. Because of the way our system of commerce is designed, businesses will not be able to fulfill their social contract with the environment or society until the system in which they operate undergoes a fundamental change, a change that brings commerce and governance into alignment with the natural world from which we receive our life. There must be an integration of economic, biologic, and human systems in order to create a sustainable and interdependent method of commerce that supports and furthers our existence. As hard as we may strive to create sustainability on a company level, we cannot fully succeed until the institutions surrounding commerce are redesigned. Just as every act of production and consumption in an industrial society leads to further environmental degradation, regardless of intention or ethos, we need to imagine—and then design—a system of commerce where the opposite is true, where doing good is like falling off a log, where the natural, everyday acts of work and life accumulate into a better world as a matter of course, not a matter of altruism. A system of sustainable commerce would involve these objectives:

1. It would reduce absolute consumption of energy and natural resources among developed nations by 80 percent within 40 to 60 years.

2. It would provide secure, stable, and meaningful employment for people everywhere.

3. It would be self-actuating as opposed to regulated, controlled, mandated, or moralistic.

4. It would honor human nature and market principles.

5. It would be perceived as more desirable than our present way of life.

6. It would exceed sustainability by restoring degraded habitats and ecosystems to their fullest biological capacity.

7. It would rely on current solar income.

8. It should be fun and engaging, and strive for an aesthetic outcome.

Business must yield to the longings of the human spirit. The most important contribution of the socially responsible business movement has little to do with recycling, nuts from the rainforest, or employing the homeless. Their gift to us is that they are leading by trying to do something, to risk, take a chance, make a change—any change. They are not waiting for "the solution," but are acting without guarantees of success or proof of purchase. This is what all of us must do. Being visionary has always been given a bad rap by commerce. But without a positive vision for humankind we can have no meaning, no work, and no purpose.

DOCUMENT 3

Doug Bandow, "Social Responsibility: A Conservative View" (1992)

Many conservative business analysts rejected the tenets of the movement for social responsiblity in business. In the following article, Doug Bandow, a senior fellow at the libertarian Cato Institute in Washington, D.C., argues that corporations, as specialized institutions, have no obligations beyond being good businesses.

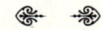

The minimalist position on the responsibility of business is expressed by Nobel laureate economist Milton Friedman and neoconservative commentator Irving Kristol, among others. In their view, a firm is solely responsible to its owners—the shareholders in the case of a corporation. Thus, for managers to engage in other endeavors, such as charitable giving, is to violate their fiduciary duty.

Although these views are dismissed as backward by today's apostles of corporate social responsibility, Friedman and Kristol are correct as far as the large picture is concerned. Corporations are specialized institutions created for a specific purpose. They are only one form of enterprise in a very diverse society with lots of different organizations. Churches exist to help people fulfill their responsibilities toward God in community with one another. Governments are instituted most basically to prevent people from violating the rights of others. Philanthropic institutions are created to do good works. Community associations are to promote one or another shared goal. And businesses are established to make a profit by meeting people's needs and wants.

Shouldn't business nevertheless "serve" society? Yes, but the way it best does so is by satisfying people's desires in an efficient manner. There are, in fact, few tasks more pressing than what Nobel laureate economist Friedrich A. von Hayek calls "maintaining a human population of this world 400 or 500 times as large as that which man could achieve in the natural hunting and gathering stage."

In short, businesses should concentrate on being good businesses. They shouldn't be charged with saving souls. Nor should they be expected to house the homeless, preserve a sense of community, or do any of many other important tasks for which other institutions have been created.

Does this mean that firms have no responsibilities other than making money? Of course not, just as individuals have obligations other than making money. But while firms have a duty to respect the rights of others, they are under no obligation to promote the interests of others. The distinction is important. Companies have responsibilities not to spew harmful pollutants into people's lungs and break contracts with their workers. They do not, however, have any obligation to underwrite a local symphony or provide their workers with popular benefits, such as family leave.

This does not mean that firms should be prohibited from promoting other goals when they desire to do so. In this regard, at least, Friedman and Kristol are wrong in opposing the idea of corporate philanthropy. E. B. Knauft may be right when he argues that charitable giving promotes a firm's bottom line. This kind of "selfishness" is a perfectly honorable reason for giving—after all, everyone benefits. Similarly, offering family leave or improved health care benefits may be a savvy step to attract top-quality workers. Going beyond the norm in pollution control may help attract environmentally conscious consumers.

Even if the firm receives no direct financial benefit from such activities, they are legitimate as long as the stockholders are aware of management's activities. When the jeans company Levi Strauss went public, for instance, it informed prospective shareholders that it intended to continue its ambitious policy of charitable giving. If shareholders are willing to funnel some of their resources through a firm to promote philanthropy or generous employee benefits, or whatever, then so be it. But this is different from philanthropic organizations browbeating companies to donate money or government mandating that they do so.

Social responsibility has become a catchword on the left, an excuse for ever-expanding government control of business. It's time that business fought back and explained that it has no more special responsibilities than anyone else. In the end, society will benefit most if business concentrates on doing its job well, rather than trying to solve the rest of the world's problems.

DOCUMENT 4

Myron Magnet, "Rebels with a Cause" (1993)

The continuing decay of urban ghettoes and the skyrocketing urban crime rate sparked a heated debate over urban poverty. In the following article Myron Magnet, an editor of Fortune magazine, attributes the decay of the inner city to a liberal permissiveness toward crime. By blaming social conditions and not individual behavior for the explosive crime rate in inner cities, liberals, according to Magnet, give sanction to criminals and contribute to the further breakdown of the social contract.

❦ ❦

It had all the makings of one of those Hollywood heartwarmers, in which the tough but loving schoolteacher charms and bullies his delinquent pupils into becoming model citizens, teenage-style. Here was George Cadwalader, a central-casting dream: a handsome ex-Marine captain with smiling, crinkly eyes and limitless courage, he had a plan irresistible in its mix of idealism, toughness, and adventure. He would gather up a crew of delinquents from the toughest neighborhoods of Massachusetts and transport them to a deserted island. There they would build their own house, cut their own firewood, and grow and cook their own food. By coming to grips with life's basic realities, they would learn responsibility and teamwork, discover inner strength and self-confidence, and be converted.

But it was Cadwalader who got converted. He woke up one morning to find all the chickens his little community was raising fluttering helplessly on the ground, dazed with pain. In a paroxysm of sadism, each chicken's two legs had been savagely wrenched out of their joints. All that could be done was to put the broken creatures out of their misery. Which boy had done such a deed, and why, Cadwalader never knew for certain.

But he knew that the certainties with which he'd started his experiment had crumbled within him. He and his associates had begun by holding "without question the assumption that bad kids were simply the products of bad environments," he recalls in *Castaways*, his striking account of the experiment. "We believed changing the environment would change the kid. . . ." Yet the vast majority of his charges didn't change, despite transplantation to the island's militantly salubrious environment.

Far from it. When he followed up his first 106 boys, he discovered that in seven years they'd been charged with 3,391 crimes, 309 of them violent. He came to feel that the boys

> appear incapable of love, driven by unfocused anger, and prone to impulsive behavior without regard to consequences. . . . [W]hen I look objectively at the trail of destruction left by our own graduates, I cannot avoid the conclusion that the world would have been a better place if most of the kids I grew to like at Penikese [Island] had never been born.

Theories of crime have to make an assumption about whether men are predisposed by nature to force and violence or whether violence gets into their hearts from some outside source. The theory Cadwalader felt his experiment had disproved is that men are intrinsically peaceful creatures, inclined, when necessary, to cooperate harmoniously with their fellows, and that the diseased social environment causes violence and crime. Crime is an artificial growth, grafted onto human life by the development of societies and governments. Central to today's ideology, this theory gives potential wrongdoers exactly the wrong message; it tends to excuse criminals from personal responsibility for crime, pinning it on social circumstances instead. . . .

These ideas became dominant at the start of the Sixties. Ramsey Clark, Lyndon Johnson's attorney general and assistant attorney general in the Kennedy Administration, luminously embodied the spirit of the age. "[C]rime among poor blacks . . . flows clearly and directly from the brutalization and dehumanization of racism, poverty, and injustice," he wrote in 1970, summing up his experience as the nation's top law-enforcement officer. For this, blame mainstream culture. "To permit conditions that breed anti-social conduct to continue is our greatest crime," he charges.

It's a sign of our present times that once George Cadwalader proved this utterly orthodox structure of thought false, he was stumped. His old theory in pieces, he lacked a new one to put in its place.

The intellectual framework he was grasping toward isn't obscure: it is the great tradition of political philosophy that includes Plato, St. Augustine, Hobbes, Burke, even Freud. Yet it is a tradition with which modern thinking has largely lost touch. It holds that as men come from the hand of nature they are instinctively aggressive, with an inbuilt inclination to violence.

The fundamental purpose of the social order is to restrain man's instinctual aggressiveness, so that human life can be something higher than a war of all against all. The great seventeenth- and eighteenth-century political theorists imagined that the restraint was accomplished by a social contract: driven to desperation by the universal warfare that made their lives "solitary, poor, nasty, brutish, and short," in Hobbes's famous phrase, men in the early ages of the world entered into an agreement, by which each man renounced his unlimited freedom of aggression in order to promote the security of all. . . .

Looked at through assumptions like these, crime takes on an entirely different appearance than the one it has in Ramsey Clark's eyes and in American orthodoxy today. Not only does the social order not *cause* crime, it is the very thing that *restrains* crime, making man's life something other than a scene of constant mutual invasion, in which all live in continual fear and danger of violence.

In this light, crime takes on the closest links to culture. For through the governmental structure of force and threat—police, judges, and prisons—is a key means by which society restrains aggression and crime, it isn't the principal means. The most powerful curb is the *internal* inhibition society builds into each man's character, the inner voice (call it reason, conscience, superego, what you will) that makes the social contract an integral part of our deepest selves.

So while to prevent crime we should worry about whether judges are too lenient or legal procedures too cumbersome, it is still more crucial to ensure that the inner barriers to violence and aggression are strongly in place. This is a cultural matter, a matter of how people bring up their children, a matter of the messages that get passed from the community to the parents and thence to the children. The object is both to transmit the necessary prohibitions against aggression to each individual and to win each individual's inner, positive assent to the social endeavor. . . .

When crime flourishes as it now does in our cities, especially crime of mindless malice, it isn't because society has so oppressed people as to bend them out of their true nature and twist them into moral deformity. It is instead because the criminals haven't been adequately socialized. Examine the contents of their minds and hearts and what you find is free-floating aggression, weak consciences, anarchic beliefs, detachment from the community and its highest values. They haven't attained the self-respect or the coherent sense of self that underlies one's ability to respect others.

This is a predictable result of unimaginably weak families, headed by immature, irresponsible girls, who are at the margin of the community, pathological in their own behavior, and too often lacking the knowledge, interest, and inner resources to be successful molders of strong characters in children. Too many underclass mothers can't enforce the necessary prohibitions for children—or for themselves. And most underclass families lack a father, a vital agent of socialization.

When the community tells such families that they are victims of social injustice, that they perhaps are not personally to blame if they commit crimes, and that it is entirely appropriate for them to nurse feelings of rage and resentment, it is asking for trouble. Worse, today's American culture holds that, in a sense, such crime isn't pathological; it is rebellion—the manly response that Americans have shown to oppression since the Boston Tea Party. . . .

Such a view of the admirably defiant criminal still holds the underclass in thrall. "They want us to settle for a little piece of nothing, like the Indians on the reservation," as one inner-city resident who grew up in a Harlem housing project recently summed up his vision of the larger society. "They got us fighting and killing each other for crumbs. In a way, the ones in jail are like political prisoners, because they refused to settle for less." . . .

Quoted in a recent newspaper article reporting that two innocent bystanders in the New York ghettoes had been killed and five more wounded in the last 48 hours, the mother of one of the wounded says: "I work ten hours a day. . . . In the morning, I have to leave before my kids do. All I can do is say a prayer, that's about it. Because you never know if you're going to come back alive, and you come home and they're going to be alive. You'll be in your house and people will be shooting through your damn window. You stick your head out your window, somebody blows your brains out."

The achievements of civilization rest upon the social order, which rests in turn upon a mutual agreement to foreswear aggression. In the ghetto, the agreement is in tatters, and the life of the civilized community is being stomped out by force and violence. In cities in which civilization should have reached its apogee, gang-ridden ghetto areas have regressed to some Dark Age when human life was organized around predatory, roving bands with continually shifting memberships....

After a 9-year-old girl in a Brooklyn ghetto had just been shot in the head by a thug's stray bullet, a neighbor—a law-abiding family man living across the street from a crack house—lamented: "Our lives have been reduced to the lowest levels of human existence." In such an anarchy, it's a wonder not when people fail to achieve all the civilized excellences but when they succeed.

DOCUMENT 5

Camilo José Vergara, "A Guide to the Ghettos" (1993)

Many social commentators took issue with the conservative interpretation of the causes of urban poverty. Writing in *The Nation*, a left-liberal weekly magazine, Camilo José Vergara argues that ghettoes are diverse places that defy easy generalization. He argues that various types of ghettoes have different causes and characteristics. He insists that public policy must not only become more sensitive to these complexities but also implement solutions that break the isolation and racial composition of ghettoes.

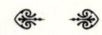

❧ ❧

If you were among the nearly 11,000 people who lived in two-story row houses in north Camden, New Jersey, in the 1960s, you could walk to work at Esterbrook Pen, at Knox Gelatin, at RCA or at J.R. Evans Leather. You could shop on Broadway, a busy three-mile commercial thoroughfare, nicknamed the Street of Lights because of its five first-run movie theaters, with their bright neon signs.

Today, hundreds of those row houses—once counted among the best ordinary urban dwellings in America—have been scooped up by bulldozers, their debris carted to a dump in Delaware. Walking along the narrow streets, one passes entire blocks without a single structure, the empty land crisscrossed by footpaths. The scattered dwellings that remain are faced with iron bars, so that they resemble cages.

With nearly half of its overwhelmingly Latino population on some form of public assistance, this once-thriving working-class neighborhood is now the poorest urban community in New Jersey. In 1986, former Mayor Alfred Pierce called Camden a reservation for the destitute. The north section of the city has become the drug center for South Jersey; it also hosts a soup kitchen and a large state prison.

North Camden is not unique. Since the riots of the 1960s, American cities have experienced profound transformations, best revealed in the spatial restructuring of their ghettoes and the emergence of new urban forms. During the past decade, however, the "underclass" and homelessness have dominated the study of urban poverty. Meanwhile, the power of the physical surroundings to shape lives, to mirror people's existence and to symbolize social relations has been ignored. When scholars from across the political spectrum discuss the factors that account for the persistence of poverty, they fail to consider its living environments. And when prescribing solutions, they overlook the very elements that define the new ghettos: the ruins and semi-ruins; the medical, warehousing and behavior-modification institutions; the various NIMBYs [Not In My Backyards], fortresses and walls; and, not least, the bitterness and anger resulting from living in these places.

Dismissing the value of information received through sight, taste, and smell, or through the emotional overtones of an informant's voice, or from the sensation of moving through the spaces studied, has led to the creation of constructs without character, individuality or a sense of place. And although the limitations of statistical data—particularly when dealing with very poor populations—are widely acknowledged, the dependence on numbers is fiercely defended. Other approaches are dismissed as impressionistic, anecdotal, as poetry or "windshield surveys."

Yet today's ghettos are diverse, rich in public and private responses to the environment, in expressions of cultural identity and in reminders of history. These communities are uncharted territory; to be understood, their forms must be identified, described, inventoried and mapped.

An examination of scores of ghettos across the nation reveals three types: "green ghettos," characterized by depopulation, vacant land overgrown by nature and ruins; "institutional ghettos," publicly financed places of confinement designed mainly for the native-born; and "new immigrant ghettos," deriving their character from an influx of immigrants, mainly Latino and West Indian. Some of these communities have continued to lose population; others have emerged where a quarter-century ago there were white ethnic blue-collar neighborhoods; and sections of older ghettos have remained stable, working neighborhoods or have been rebuilt. . . .

No single ghetto is completely green, institutional or immigrant in character. Although the overwhelming trend is toward greater waste, abandonment and depopulation, these three models are related, channeling people and land to one another. Fires and demolitions in the green ghettos provide large tracts of cleared land where poverty institutions and other facilities can be built. By default the most desperate people and neighborhoods become wards of the government in communities where, in the words of a Brooklyn organizer, "all the social disasters of the city are located."

If nothing is done to prevent it, within a decade more working-class communities are likely to belong to one of these types. Conversely, some institutional ghettos, such as the Near West Side of Chicago, are likely to be squeezed out by expanding sports and medical complexes. And the same forces of abandonment that can open the way for the modern poorhouses can at other times free land for townhouses built for working families.

These are the "reclaimed ghettos." With their horror stories of violence, public incompetence and waste, ghettos are used to provide moral justification for privately managed programs of redevelopment. Under the leadership of churches, community organizations, private developers and recent immigrants, such ghettos have kicked out most of the dependent poor and have refused to admit the institutions that serve them. Instead, they focus on attracting working families, keeping out drug dealers and building guarded enclaves.

These communities are on the verge of melding into mainstream society. But when examining the contribution of community development corporations, we need to ask ourselves whether their efforts are leading to the elimination of ghettos or toward the creation of mini-cities of exclusion within a larger wasteland.

For it is at the boundaries that the individual character of ghettos reveals itself most clearly: around embattled clusters of dwellings where ethnic groups assert themselves, in blocks where strong buildings share a wall with dilapidated crack houses, and along the perimeter of hospitals, universities and other citadels. Borders where white meets black are stark, presenting a graphic contrast between a seemingly victorious white community and what appears to be a defeated minority community. Along Mack Avenue as it crosses from Detroit's East Side into affluent Grosse Pointe, and along Chicago's East 62nd Street, the border between Woodlawn and Hyde Park (home of the University of Chicago), a history of race relations has been written into the landscape. Security measures, guards, dead-end streets, green grass on one side; vacant land, abandoned buildings, people out of work, hanging out, on the other.

Writers in the mainstream press call ghettos intractable, expressing concern with the public burden they impose. The system works for those who are motivated, many outsiders say, pointing to the presence of minorities in more affluent suburbs, to reclaimed ghettos and to the economic success of recent black, Latino and Asian immigrants.

But among many ghetto dwellers, particularly native-born African-Americans, there is growing ideological hardening and a yearning to close ranks, to re-emerge from destitution and to prosper among themselves. A journalist in Gary, Indiana, a city almost completely abandoned by whites, remarked, "I don't know why people have to have white people to succeed." A Chicago construction worker called blacks who moved to the suburbs "imitation white people." A Newark woman suggested that such people have sold out, are living a lie. "They need to take a good look in the mirror," she said.

Echoing Malcolm X, most ghetto residents I have encountered see the devastation and violence in their communities as part of a white strategy of domination. Drugs are widely perceived as part of a monstrous plot to destroy and contain poor blacks and Latinos. A Chicago minister states, "White supremacy, a system of oppression that comes out of Western society, is the real problem." A Brooklyn artist declares, "People of color have a right to be paranoid."

Within ghetto walls a new generation is growing along with new activities, ideologies, institutions and drugs. Crack sells briskly across the street from drug-treatment centers, and children walk past homeless shelters. An army of men strips cars, and hordes of scavengers push loaded shopping carts along the streets. Houses stand alone like fortresses, enclosed by fences. Dozens of cities are falling into ruin, and along their streets billboards beg people to stop killing one another.

Today, there is renewed talk of strategies to bring jobs, to improve education, to build better housing and provide adequate health care for all Americans. Such developments would certainly improve the conditions in poor communities but would not change their isolation, racial composition and fragmentation. Ghettos would continue to expand, new ones to emerge, and the anger of their residents would remain unabated.

Public policy must also address the unique characteristics of our ghettos. A crucial step is to change practices that concentrate in these communities the poor and the institutions that serve them. We need regional and national approaches to population redistribution, such as the building of low-income housing in wealthy suburbs and the elimination of the barriers that define ghettos. And as we once did in the 1960s, we need to convince ourselves that as a nation we have the power not just to improve the ghetto but to abolish it. To do this we need to go beyond the statistics and into the streets, alleys and buildings.

DOCUMENT 6

Roger Swardson, "Greetings from the Electronic Plantation" (1992)

The postindustrial economy has witnessed an expansion of service jobs, but many of these do not provide a living wage. While these semiskilled service workers benefit from access to low-cost products manufactured globally, they find themselves in severe competition with displaced routine production workers and struggling to find enough employment to make ends meet. In the following selection, Roger Swardson describes a day at work as a telephone service representative at Wireless, a direct-mail catalogue company located in Minneapolis/St. Paul. In the article he reflects on the changing meaning of work under postindustrial capitalist development.

❦ ❦

Out in the economic sector where you work all week but can't make a living, lots of us are fastened like barnacles to the bottom of the computer revolution. Soldering tiny leads on circuit boards. Plugging data into terminals. All sorts of things that tend to share one characteristic: repetition. Some of the jobs, like mine, consist of sitting in a chair while, all day long, people call you from all over the country to buy things like T-shirts that read "Compost Happens."

Just after 9 A.M., a tireless recorded voice in my headset tips me off. A catalog shopper is coming my way from across the continent. I press the appropriate key and say "Good morning, welcome to Wireless. My name is Roger. How can I help you?"

Wireless is one of five direct-mail catalogs operated by Rivertown Trading Company, a shirttail relation of Minnesota Public Radio, the spawning ground of Garrison Keillor.

This morning I walk through a new industrial park to the clusters of smokers hanging around the lone door in the block-long wall of a warehouse. Once inside, I show my picture ID to the guard behind the glass window and stick another plastic card in the time clock.

I initial the sheet that tells me when to take my morning and afternoon 15-minute breaks and half-hour lunch period. I nod good morning to two women at the group leader station that overlooks the room. They smile and nod back. Both are concentrating on computer terminals that identify scores of telephone service representatives (TSRs) like me who have logged onto the system this morning. The screens tell the group leaders exactly what all the TSRs are doing in the system and for how many seconds they have been doing it. In a seven-day period prior to Christmas 1991, despite the lousy economy, about 300 of us in two shifts wrote 87,642 mail or credit card orders, up 47 percent from the year before.

One supervisor in a headset has a distant look on her face. She's monitoring a TSR, tapping into a customer call to check on two dozen points that must be covered. The TSR will be told the results later in the day.

I fill up my coffee mug and check the printout taped to the wall next to the time card rack. The printout summarizes the results of our weekly monitorings. Ideally we should get 24 pieces of information from the customer (like home phone, work address, whether or not they want to be on our mailing list) during the course of the convesation. During the monitorings, we are graded according to how much of the data we have gotten, which is a difficult task when you've got a customer on the other end of the line who just wants to make a purchase and hang up without being asked a bunch of questions. We are expected to maintain an average above 90 percent. The names of all TSRs in the 90s have been highlighted with a blue marker. I'm at 89.6 percent. It has been suggested that I could use additional training.

I head down a double row of 20 stalls where the backsides of seated people stick out like the rumps of Guernsey cows. The room is done in tones of gray, and merchandise is pinned to white walls. The 80 stalls I can see are mostly occupied. There is a continuous yammer like audience noise before a concert. On two walls electronic scoreboards flash the number of calls completed for each of five catalogs. The total is around 2,200. A busy morning. Must have been a big catalog mailing.

I find an open stall, adjust the chair height, get my headset on, and log onto the phone and computer systems, using my password. An orange light on my console indicates that there are callers on hold.

I bring up the initial screen of the order process and tap the button on my phone to signal that I'm ready to take a customer call. A recorded voice instantly says "Wireless."

I swing right into it. "Good morning. Welcome to Wireless. My name is Roger. How can I help you?"

A woman from New Jersey is distressed.

"You have to help me."

"Sure, what's the problem?"

"I ordered a ring for my husband for our anniversary. Last night we went out and I gave it to him before dinner. Well, he's put on a little weight and it didn't fit. The poor man was so upset he couldn't eat his dinner. Today he's out there running around the neighborhood and getting red in the face."

"That's terrible. What can I do?"

"Well, I looked at the ring this morning and I ordered a size too small."

"Send it back. We'll send you another one right away."

"How long will it take?"

"If you want to pay extra I can send it overnight air. Regular delivery is 10 working days."

"Make it the 10-day. It won't kill him."

"Interface" is a word that tells millions of American workers where we fit. We are devices between you and a computer system. Various terms further identify the device: data entry, customer service, word processing, telemarketing, and others. We take reservations. We do market research. We sell people aluminum siding the minute they sit down to dinner. Every night we update computer records so that multinational corporations can begin the day on top of things. We type most of today's business communications. We do all those mundane tasks that provide computer systems with the raw data that makes them useful.

Even so, most of us are among the more than 14 million Americans who work every week but are still classified by the government as poor. The people Ross Perot talks about when he says, "I suppose when they are up to six bucks an hour in Mexico and down to six bucks here, American corporations will again begin creating jobs in this country."

Here's another way we are classified. The first sentence of my employee handbook tells me that the company "believes in the practice of employment at will, which means that employment is terminable by either the employee or the company at any time, for any reason." We are devices that accommodate the economic needs of our era. Flexible. Disposable.

Even recyclable.

Say a company is "downsizing" or "delayering" or whatever other term describes job cuts. Through a combination of early retirement, attrition, and layoffs they manage to take 200 current semi-skilled employees off the payroll over the course of a year. Say those employees were paid an average of $12 an hour with full benefits. The company then hires a temporary agency to fill openings as they occur. The agency may even have an office in the company's building. Job qualifications are determined, and the agency finds the people and trains them if necessary. The jobs will pay from $5 to $7 an hour. Even with the agency's commission, the company has just saved around $2 million annually in wages and benefits.

Improbable? A want ad placed by a temporary employment agency in my St. Paul newspaper lists four major corporations that need temporary workers. The agency is offering a $25 bonus to people with prior experience with any of the listed companies. Today, through the wonders of current economic policy, it is possible to replace yourself at a bargain rate.

Here's another way the system works. You have a data entry barn where the job routine is easy and repetitious. The problem is that your volume is changeable, with big bulges around some of the holidays. A permanent work force would be awkward, so you have a standing order with three temporary agencies.

When your temporaries show up, they are told their hours will vary as necessary with one week's advance notice. The temps will rarely get a full week's work. They can be sent home any time during the day or let go permanently for any reason. They will receive no benefits. They are subject to a probationary period and can be dropped with a call to the agency. In a relatively short time you have a high-performance, completely flexible work force. You can even offer the best of them permanent part-time jobs, again with no benefits but with a raise in pay. (This actually amounts to a savings, since you no longer have to pay the agency commission.)

Look at the costs and problems you have eliminated. Look how easy the system is to manage. All you have to do is keep weeding.

This is the employment system of the 1990s, made possible by a bankrupt economy and an increasingly desperate work force.

We are the vocational descendants of the dapper clerks in the better stores who knew your sizes and decided when your son ought to be ready for his first suit. Our voices, regardless of how we happen to look or feel that day, are fresh and animated and friendly. We just happen to be sitting here in jeans and a sweatshirt talking into a little foam ball. . . .

On this particular day I take 57 calls from 23 states. I write $4,096.59 in orders. The biggest is from a guy in California for a selection of videotapes that includes complete sets of the British television shows *Reilly, Ace of Spies* and *Rumpole of the Bailey*.

In just over eight months, working at a pace where I am either available for or taking orders more than 90 percent of the time I am logged on, I have taken 4,462 orders and booked nearly $300,000.

Even so, many jobs like mine, especially in urban America, are at risk. Workers in American cities cost more than elsewhere simply because it costs more to live here. As a result, there is a kind of ongoing economic cleansing. Software "upgrades" constantly eliminate some jobs, data barns move to cheaper rural locations, and the Caribbean and Mexico are claiming jobs.

In the meantime, take that $6-an-hour job that provides about $800 a month if you can get 40 hours a week in, and then add up rent, utilities, phone, food, and tranportation. Then try adding a family.

It doesn't add up.

"Recovery" is a wishful term. It is also a word that means something understandable. Most of us can tell whether we are recovering. Thirty-eight million people below the poverty line is not a persuasive definition of an economic "recovery."

Leading economic indicators are used by economists to describe conditions as they may be six to nine months in the future. How, if the present constantly worsens, can the future remain perpetually bright? Even schoolchildren can see that that's denial.

How else could "downsizing" be heralded for improving corporate profits and aiding the "recovery"? Fewer livelihoods mean "recovery"? For whom?

The same with "diminished expectations" or lesser livelihoods. That must mean those economic refugees from companies that let $12-an-hour people go and replaced them with $6 temporaries. These resettled workers are a non-statistical phenomenon. They are employed. But because millions of dollars have been hacked out of their paychecks, they no longer qualify for mortgages, car loans, or credit cards no matter what the interest rate. Who will spend us into the "recovery"?

Workers are getting pushed farther down the

economic ladder as laid-off skilled workers and recent college graduates secure even the menial jobs. And, on the bottom, public assistance is breaking its seams.

Surely, the term "recovery" has become a mockery of the way millions of Americans now live.

The rest of us come and go. The young. Men without jobs. People picking up some extra money. But women between 40 and 60 are always there, plugging away at countless uninspiring jobs that need doing day in and day out, year in and year out.

On break they sit together eating homemade food out of Tupperware while the rest of us use the vending machines. They show each other craft handiwork. They bring packets of photos. They take work seriously and talk about the merchandise and what kind of a day they're having. They do well at jobs many make fun of or would not do. And they succeed at life as it is.

I left a temp job at an insurance company at dusk. A woman was sitting at a terminal in word processing wearing a smock. I said something sprightly like "Working late, huh?" And that started a conversation. It happens easily with night-shift people.

Her husband put in 27 years on the production line of a company that went broke and then cheated him out of his pension. She worked for a small office-equipment firm and the same thing happened. He is now a part-time security guard. She holds down two temporary jobs. Their jobs don't provide health insurance, and they can't afford it. They put in a lifetime working, raising their kids, and they must continue working indefinitely. I was enraged but she passed it off. Gave me a brownie. Then in the lighted corner of the darkened office floor she went to work, producing letters from dictation. As I left I could hear the tape of some dayside junior exec talking through his nose about yet another intolerable situation that had come to his attention.

Study Questions

1. What are the potential social consequences of a widening income gap in the United States?

2. Do businesses have a moral obligation to act socially and environmentally responsible? In arguing for a narrow conception of corporations' social role, Doug Bandow compares businesses to churches and government. Is this comparison fair? How might Paul Hawken respond?

3. In what ways are the problems that Magnet and Vergara discuss a result of the trends in the economy that Reich describes? Do you agree with Magnet's assertion that a focus on the social causes of crime exonerates people from responsibility for their actions?

4. Should businesses be allowed to export jobs to foreign countries?

Acknowledgments

Selections not credited are in the public domain.

Chapter 7

Document 3: Excerpt from *Babbitt* by Sinclair Lewis, copyright 1922 by Harcourt Brace & Company and renewed 1950 by Sinclair Lewis, reprinted by permission of the publisher. *Document 4:* Excerpts from *Middletown in Transition* by Robert S. Lynd and Helen M. Lynd, copyright 1937 by Harcourt Brace & Company and renewed 1965 by Robert S. Lynd and Helen M. Lynd, reprinted by permission of the publisher. *Document 5:* From "Meditations of a Wage-Earning Wife" by Jane Littell. Originally published in the December 1924 issue of *The Atlantic Monthly*. Reprinted by permission. *Document 7:* "The Negro Artist" by Langston Hughes, *The Nation*, June 23, 1926. Copyright © 1926 by Langston Hughes. Reprinted by permission of Harold Ober Associates Incorporated. *Document 8:* From "Gastonia" by Mary Heaton Vorse, *Harper's Magazine*. Copyright © 1929 by Harper's Magazine. All rights reserved. Reproduced from the November issue by special permission,

Chapter 8

Document 1: From an editorial on economic conditions from *Fortune*, vol. vi, no. 3, September 1932. *Document 4:* "The New Deal for Nearly Four Months" by Frederick Essary, *The Literary Digest,* July 1, 1933, published by Funk & Wagnalls Co. *Document 5:* From "To Harry L. Hopkins" in *One Third of a Nation*, Lorena Hickok reports on the Great Depression. Edited by R. Lowitt and M. Beasley. © 1981 by the Board of Trustees of the University of Illinois. Used with permission of the editors and of the University of Illinois Press. *Document 7:* From *Voices from the Oil Fields*, edited by Paul F. Lambert and Kenny A. Franks. Copyright © 1984 by the University of Oklahoma Press. *Document 8:* Reprinted from *Down and Out in the Great Depression* edited by Robert S. McElvaine. Copyright © 1983 by The University of North Carolina Press. Used by permission of the publisher.

Chapter 9

Document 4: From "For the Jews—Life or Death?" by I. F. Stone. Reprinted from *The Nation Magazine*, June 10, 1944. Copyright © 1944 The Nation Company, L. P. *Document 5:* From *Desert Exile* by Yoshiko Uchida. Copyright © 1982 by Yoshiko Uchida. Reprinted by permission of the University of Washington Press. *Document 8:* Excerpted from permission of Simon & Schuster Macmillan from the Twayne Publishers book, *Rosie the Riveter Revisited* by Sherna Berger Gluck. Copyright © 1987 by Sherna Berger Gluck.

Chapter 10

Document 4: From "How You Can Survive An A-Bomb Blast" by Richard Gerstell. *The Saturday Evening Post,* January 7, 1950. Reprinted from *The Saturday Evening Post,* © 1950. *Document 5:* From the book: *The Power of Positive Thinking for Young People* by Norman Vincent Peale. Copyright © 1952, 1954, 1982. Used by permission of the publisher, Prentice-Hall/A Division of Simon & Schuster. *Document 6:* "The National

Style" (Abridged) by David Riesman from *The American Style: Essays in Value and Performance* by Elting E. Morison, editor. Copyright © 1958 by Massachusetts Institute of Technology. Reprinted by permission of HarperCollins Publishers, Inc. *Document 8*: "A New, $10, Billlion Power: The US Teen-Age Consumer," *Life*, 8–31–59. Life Magazine © Time Inc. Reprinted with permission. *Document 9*: Reprinted with the permission of Simon & Schuster from *The Other America: Poverty in the United States* by Michael Harrington. Copyright © 1962, 1969, 1981 by Michael Harrington.

Chapter 11

Document 1: Reprinted by arrangement with The Heirs to the Estate of Martin Luther King, Jr., c/o Joan Daves Agency as agent for the proprietor. Copyright 1963, 1964 by Martin Luther King, Jr., copyright renewed 1991, 1992 by Coretta Scott King. *Document 2*: From *Malcolm X Speaks*, edited by George Breitman. Reprinted by permission of Pathfinder Press. Copyright © 1965, 1989 by Betty Shabazz and Pathfinder Press. *Document 6*: "I'd Rather Be Black Than Female" by Shirley Chisholm, 1970. Reprinted by permission of the author. *Document 7*: Excerpted with permission from "What Has Happened to America?" by Richard Nixon, *Reader's Digest*, October 1967. Copyright © 1967 by The Reader's Digest Association, Inc.

Chapter 12

Document 3: Reprinted by arrangement with The Heirs to the Estate of Martin Luther King, Jr., c/o Joan Daves Agency as agent for the proprietor. Copyright 1967 by Martin Luther King, Jr. *Document 4:* From "Suppose They Gave a War and No One Came" by Charlotte Keyes. *McCall's Magazine,* October, 1966. *Document 5:* From *The Sixties Papers, Documents of a Rebellious Decade* by Judith and Stewart Albert. Reprinted with permission of Greenwood Publishing Group, Inc., Westport, CT. Copyright © 1984 by Judith Albert and Stewart Albert. *Document 6:* The Columbia University Commencement Address given on June 4, 1968 by Richard Hofstadter (deceased). Permission granted by Mrs. Beatrice K. Hofstadter. *Document 8:* "Demented Vets and Other Myths" by George Swiers from *Vietnam Reconsidered: Lessons from a War* by Harrison Salisbury and Larry Ceplair. Copyright © 1984 by Harrison E. Salisbury and Larry Ceplair. Reprinted by permission of HarperCollins Publishers, Inc.

Chapter 13

Document 1: From "The Peoples of America" by Nathan Glazer. Reprinted from *The Nation* magazine, September 1965. Copyright © 1965 The Nation Company, L. P. *Document 3*: From "Controversy Over U. S. Immigration" by Robert H. V. Duncan. *Pro & Con, Congressional Digest*, vol. 44, no. 5 (May 1965). Reprinted by permission. *Document 4:* "Asian Influx Alters Life in Suburbia" by Mark Arax, *Los Angeles Times,* Sunday, April 5, 1987. Copyright, 1987, Los Angeles Times. Reprinted by permission. *Document 5*: From *Southie Won't Go* by Ione Malloy. Copyright © 1986 by the Board of Trustees of the University of Illinois. Used with permission of the author and of the University of Illinois Press. *Document 6: God Is Beside You on the Picket Line* by Cesar Chavez. Reprinted by permission of the United Farm Workers.

Chapter 14

Document 5: From "Modern-Day Mentors, Five Lessons in Success" by Leah Rosch, *Working Woman*, August 1987. Reprinted by permission of the author. *Document 6*: From *Listen America* by Jerry Falwell. Copyright © 1980 by Jerry Falwell. Used by permission of Doubleday, a division of Bantam Doubleday Dell Publishing Group, Inc. *Document 7:* From *"The G.O.P. 'Me Decade,' "* by Sidney Blumenthal, *The New Republic*, September 17 and 24, 1984. Reprinted by permission. *Document 8:* From "Dead End in Silicon Valley" by Diana Hembree, *The Progressive*, October 1985. Reprinted by permission.

Chapter 15

Document 4: From "Did the West Undo the East?" by Stephen Sestanovich, *The National Interest*, Spring 1993. Reprinted by permission of the author. *Document 5:* "Who Won the Cold War?" by Wade Huntley, *Chronicle of Higher Education*, March 31, 1993. Reprinted by permission of the author. *Document 6:* From *Morning After: Sexual Politics at the End of the Cold War* by Cynthia Enloe. Copyright © 1993 The Regents of the University of California. Reprinted by permission. *Document 7:* From "The Workplace, After the Deluge" by Peter T. Kilborn, *New York Times*, September 5, 1993. Copyright © 1993 by The New York Times Company. Reprinted by permission.

Chapter 16

Document 1: From *The Work of Nations* by Robert B. Reich. Copyright © 1991 by Robert B. Reich. Reprinted by permission of Alfred A. Knopf, Inc. *Document 2:* From "A Declaration of Sustainability" by Paul Hawken, *Utne Reader*, September/October 1993. Reprinted by permission of The Spieler Agency. *Document 3:* From "Social Responsibility: A Conservative View" by Doug Bandow. *Business and Society Review*, Spring, 1992. Reprinted by permission of the author. *Document 4:* From *The Dream and the Nightmare: The Sixties' Legacy to the Underclass* by Myron Magnet. Copyright © 1993 by Myron Magnet. By permission of William Morrow & Company, Inc. *Document 5:* From "A Guide to The Ghettos" by Camilo Jose Vergara. Reprinted from *The Nation* magazine, March 15, 1993. © The Nation Company, L. P. *Document 6:* From "Greetings from the Electronic Plantation" by Roger Swardson. Reprinted by permission from *City Pages*, October 21, 1992.

Illustrations

Page 4 July 25, 1868, Harper's Weekly. *Page 8* Walter Brainerd Spencer Collection/ Special Collection Division /Tulane University. *Page 18* Library of Congress. *Page 26* Union Pacific Railroad Company. *Page 29* Denver Public Library. *Page 38* Smithsonian Institution. *Page 47* Hillman Library, University of Pennsylvania, Gaughan Collection. *Page 58* Library of Congress. *Page 61* Library of Congress. *Page 70* Brown Brothers. *Page 75* Library of Congress. *Page 83* Brown Brothers. *Page 86* Library of Congress. *Page 90* Brown Brothers. *Page 102* Library of Congress. *Page 112* American City, May, 1911. *Page 123* Library of Congress. *Page 127* Brown Brothers. *Page 143* Southern Textile Bulletin, March 14, 1927. *Page 151* The Franklin D. Roosevelt Library. *Page 153* Acme/Bettmann. *Page 168* AP/Wide World. *Page 186* The National Archives. *Page 187* AP/Wide World. *Page 215* Charles Moore/Black Star. *Page 218* Matt Heron/Black Star. *Page 220* AP/Wide World. *Page 249* UPI/Bettmann. *Page 252* John Filo. *Page 261* UPI/Bettmann. *Page 278* Bob Fitch/Black Star. *Page 281* Joel Gordon Photography. *Page 289* The White House. *Page 313* Reprinted with Special permission of King Features Syndicate. *Page 317* AP/Wide World. *Page 333* Alan Hawes/Sygma.